# TWR and Jaguar's V12 Prototype Sports Cars

## Inside TWR's World Championship Winning Team

*Other books by the same author:*

**TWR and Jaguar's XJS (2012)**

**TWR and Rover's SD1 (2014)**



First published July 2018

ISBN: 978-0-473-44255-2

Published by
ASM Publishing,
19D Jacksons Road,
Fendalton, Christchurch,
New Zealand

Typeset in Minion 9.75/13.75

# TWR and Jaguar's V12 Prototype Sports Cars

## Inside TWR's World Championship Winning Team

JAGUAR

ALLAN SCOTT

JAGUAR

## Acknowledgements

My special thanks to those who have contributed in the writing of this book.

Martin Brundle
Tony Dowe
Jan Lammers
Bill Mack
Alastair Macqueen
Alister Mitchell
Win Percy

Archive material from Autosport, Racingsportscars and Quentin Spurring.

Tim Nevinson for his assistance in edit and proof reading. Jo Dickson for book design.

Images kindly supplied by:

Ian Bamsey, Alistair Bols; Malcolm Bryan; Castrol; Paul Davis; Dave Cundy; Jaguar; Frank De Jong; Tony Dowe; Jaguar magazine.com; Bruce Jenkins; Paul Koyman; Martin Lamb; Rupert Lowes; Ian Norris; Peter Novani; Ron Russell; Sebastian Stas; Martin Straka; Wikipedia.

*All endeavours have been made to acknowledge and establish the origins of images in this publication, we regret any omissions or mistakes.*

## Contents

# Abbreviations and measurements

| | | | |
|---|---|---|---|
| Engs | Race Engine Division | in | inch |
| BSCC | British Saloon Car Championship | psi | pounds per square inch |
| ETCC | European Touring Car Championship | RON | research octane number |
| cfm | cubic feet per minute | MON | motor octane number |
| mph | miles per hour | TDC | top dead centre |
| bhp | brake horse power | ATDC | after top dead centre |
| rpm | revolutions per minute | BTDC | before top dead centre |
| BMEP | Break Mean Effective Pressure | BBDC | before bottom dead centre |
| HP | Horse Power | ABDC | after bottom dead centre |
| lb/ft | pounds/feet | | |

| | | |
|---|---|---|
| 1 inch | = | 25.4 millimetres |
| 1 mile | = | 1.61 kilometres |
| 2.24 lbs | = | 1 kilogram |
| 1.34 bhp | = | 1 kilowatt |
| 1 lb/ft | = | 1.356 Newtons metres |

## To the reader ...

The narrative in this book is set out in double columns each page.
The technical content has been boxed and subjected to a change in that format to help distinguish it from the narrative.
Personal comments/views from engineers and racing drivers have been set in three columns.

# Foreword

I have spent many hundreds of hours, and tens of thousands of miles behind or in front of Jaguar's V 12 racing engine.

The platform and backbone of my racing career has been with Jaguar. Initially sitting behind the engine in an XJS Coupe, connected only by the throttle pedal and the limitations imposed by a road going chassis. One's main method of communication is therefore sound, confirmed by the tachometer and other pressure and temperature guages.

From 1985 onwards, I drove a development of the engine mounted mid-ships in the Jaguar XJR6 for the official works return to the World Sportscar Championship. Now sitting just in front of the engine, and tightly strapped by six belts to the same carbon fibre 'tub' as the engine and gearbox. The driver could feel much more of what was going on, and after a time I could identify the sounds of individual parts of the engine. From outside the car, a spectator could hear that beautiful sound of seven litres of V12.

Once again torque, and therefore ease of driving, was a key feature. It was even possible to pull away in fifth gear when using this racing thoroughbred. The torque was ideal for the six hour and twenty-four hour races where the car has been so successful.

Despite its displacement and size, the engine was relatively easy to overrev, and like most racing engines, vulnerable on the downchange when approaching slow corners at high speed. Avoiding the over rev was a prime task.

The only downside appeared to be the overall size and weight of the engine, with its high centre of gravity. Although this may have sometimes been used incorrectly as a reason for not going faster, it is clearly a factor.

The most impressive aspect to my mind was the fuel efficiency achieved, especially in 1988. With engine management systems, and an on board leaning control, an excellent compromise between lap time and fuel consumption could be found, which was clearly a fundamental factor of Jaguar's and my World Championships.

Allan Scott and his team performed wonders with fuel consumption and reliability so that we could use all the benefits of his V12 engine to win most of the truly great long-distance sports car events around the world.

**Martin Brundle**

Jan Lammers Racing
P.O. Box 255
2040 AG Zandvoort
The Netherlands
Telephone : (31) 02507-15557
Telefax : (31) 02507-19654

My best experience must undoubted have been during our 1988 Le Mans win. When on the 5 km long straight it happened many times that the works (turbo) Porsches tried so desperately to pass us, it was a thrill to be able to pull away some five car lenghts every lap. This gave us the possibility to save the car in the corner and braking areas.

The flexibility of the engine makes it very easy to drive the car in a consistent manor, this was particularly an advantage with the 'short' 1000 or 500 kilometer races, where a little mistake could cost you a place or two in the final results.

The wide powerban and sufficient torque made us competitive off the slow corners and took us to a topspeed that was rarely matched by our opposition.

Reliability has amazed me at a number of occasions. Due to e.g. grass in the radiators or other problems, we could run the engine for ten hours with water temperatures of 110 degrees celsius and still win the race.

Also I would like to take this opportunity to thank you and your engine department for an outstanding performance achieved on this engine, which stood out so well against the other competitors with special designed race engines.

Best regards,

Jan Lammers

JAGUAR

# Introduction

It is normal today for motorsport history books to have some great photographs, some results and a quick brush over the subject to complete an artefact to display on your coffee table. In the middle of the last century motorsport books went into great detail about the technical aspects of the motor car so that the reader came away understanding much more than when he started the book, and why particular cars were competitive. This book is in the latter category, an unfashionably detailed look at Group C racing and the 1980s phenomenon that was Tom Walkinshaw, whose team orchestrated the return of Jaguar to the pinnacle of Sports Car Racing at the time when carbon fibre, sophisticated computers and underfloor aerodynamics wrested top level motorsport away from the garage floor enthusiast for ever. It's a piece of motorsport archaeology from a time when letters were sent on paper, nobody had a mobile phone, and fax was the new world.

Many will want to understand how Jaguar were persuaded into motor racing Tom's way, and the collateral damage. The truth is, and it's in here, that TWR presented Jaguar with no rational choice if they wanted to be serious players. TWR were technically right on the ball, rather than following it. From the inside, Allan explains how the outward glister hid some very steep learning curves, bruising business and heavy pedalling.

Significantly, Allan Scott was the fly on the wall when much of Tom Walkinshaw's legendary business acumen was in action. In his role as Walkinshaw's engine specialist, Allan Scott was right at the forefront of electronic engine management for racing cars, discovering a new tool to add to his significant mechanical experience in tuning production engines for racing.

For those who only have a passing interest in the technicalities but want to relive Jaguar's success or delve into the enigma that was Tom Walkinshaw, Allan has made it clear where those who find the science too arcane can just skip that detail without losing the thread. The deep technical detail and reasoning is there, but sectioned off in a different format, to give the reader a choice. Similar different format sections indicate where Allan has enlisted the help of Alastair Macqueen and Tony Dowe, co-architects of TWR Jaguar's success in Sports car racing, to present their expertise and memories to support Allan's story.

For Jaguar fans, it was a glorious time, when the hefty V12 they adored was made to bellow competitively and economically, against most cotemporary pundits' predictions. TWR eventually followed the crowd with a turbo charged V6. The how, why and wherefores behind this move from Allan's perspective makes compelling reading. TWR later leapfrogged the opposition when it became clear a Formula One engine, chassis structure and aerodynamics were the only answer to changes in sports car regulations and continued to lever Jaguars marketing success through track results at a pace no truly factory-based effort could ever sustain. That period marked the end of Allan's involvement and the rise of Ross Brawn, another story in the making.

So, Jaguar fan, technical scholar, sports racing enthusiast or student of motorsport politics, grab an armchair and hang on.

**Tim Nevinson**

X

THE GUILD OF MOTORING WRITERS
MEMBER

ANDREW J A WHYTE
Manor Cottage
16 Banbury Road
Ettington
nr. Stratford-upon-Avon
Warwickshire CV37 7TB
Telephone: (0789) 740389
VAT no: 418 5973 19

To T J Kyle, Esq.,
230 Drumnahilley Rd.,
Mullaslin,
Omagh, Co Tyrone, BT79 9JU.
cc TWR, Kidlington.

26 Jan.'87

Roger, Paul, Allan, & Co.
THE ATTACHED IS A FAIRLY TYPICAL COMMENT. PERHAPS YOU'LL THINK ABOUT MY REPLY. LONG-TERM SOMONE WILL WANT TO WRITE THE "TWR STORY" AS A BOOK!
AW

Dear Mr Kyle,

JAGUAR RACING REVIEW

Many thanks for your letter requesting more engine and other technical information on the competition cars.

I agree that this would be desirable. However, like all racing teams, TWR (outside contracters to Jaguar) reserve the right to provide only as much information as the regulations demand. As you can see from the picture, the engine is a direct injection V12 with a single ohc to each bank; however, only a very general specification is issued for the XJR-6 and this has been published in the motor magazines. Dimensions tend to alter, and the team does not always advise outsiders of such things if it doesn't have to, and if it believes there may be some advantage in keeping mum.

In the near future, my book on Jaguar racing (1954 to 1986) will be published (by Haynes Books, Sparkford, Yeovil, BA22 7JJ) and it will contain a lot of technical detail on past Jaguar competition cars. I hope that, when the present-day race programmes are complete, similarly detailed material will be made available. While a programme is still running, it is understandable (if annoying) that full specifications of racing and rally cars are kept away from the opposition where it is legitimate to do so. I've copied this letter to TWR, however, in the hope that they will keep build and test records of engines and vehicles, so that historians like myself may have access to them some day in the future.

WHY NOT START A PRIVATE TWR ARCHIVE ?? AW.

Yours sincerely,

AW.

Editor of Jaguar Racing Review for Jaguar Cars Ltd.

JAGUAR

CHAPTER ONE

# TWR – the beginning

**Six months after arriving in London from my native New Zealand in 1979 with wife Karen, I had joined Tom Walkinshaw's small team of 12 enthusiasts in November 1979, with responsibility for setting up the new Tom Walkinshaw Racing (TWR) Engine Division. Prior to this, on arrival in the UK I had briefly joined Racing Services (Engines) in Twickenham, London where I had been employed by Spike Winter and Ken Britain to build Tom Walkinshaw's Mazda RX-7 race engines. The single-entry Mazda had shown considerable promise as the year progressed and Tom had then invited me to join his team at Kidlington near the university town of Oxford. My position was to be responsible for the development and build of engines for a joint attack on the British Saloon Car Championship (BSCC) and Belgian national series – in Mazda's twin rotor Wankel engined RX-7s the following year.**

The TWR team went on to win the BSCC in 1980 with driver Win Percy in the Mazda UK and Pentax sponsored race team, winning ten out of ten races in its class. Tom Walkinshaw had also driven into second place in the Belgian series; with his Motul oil sponsored RX-7.

With these successes Tom Walkinshaw (TW) was now in expansive mode and became increasingly convinced during 1980 that the future for his growing motor racing company was to focus on representing British car manufacturers, not Japanese ones. TW's view was that any success on the race tracks of Europe would lead to raising the status and profitability of the British vehicle manufacturer involved, helped along no doubt by the partisan press that had always accompanied previous British motoring successes, in contrast to a Japanese manufacturer seen as a threat to Europe's car industry. If this could be achieved it would not only provide a solid financial base for the long-term future of TWR, but raise the public profile of TWR's ambitious leader as well.

*Kidlington workshop in 1980 showing the BSCC Pentax Mazda RX-7s for Mazda GB.*

1981 saw the beginnings of this plan take shape with the takeover of the contract for the British Leyland Motorsport supported Rover SD1 saloon car racing programme from Dave Price Racing. This Rover programme had commenced a year earlier and had shown some potential but ended with limited success in its first learning year suffering from many engine problems.

The British Saloon Car Championship was divided into engine capacity classes, and the competitor who won the most points in his class won the championship, despite not necessarily winning a race outright. TW had spotted that the conversion factor for the rotary engine capacity could give him a class advantage. The TWR Mazda was so quick it blitzed the cars in its own class and was often fighting for race victory with the Capris and Rovers in the big engine class.

TWR's Mazda RX-7 programme continued on to win the BSCC outright in 1981, with the rapidly developing two-car TWR Rover team driven by Jeff Allam and Peter Lovett eventually winning the large engine capacity division at the same time, aided by extensive development of the power units. This win by the TWR 3.5-litre V8 Rovers in 1981 had finally displace Ford's 3-litre Capri that had previously totally dominated the large capacity class. Now many of those Capri teams had what would be seen as potentially obsolete race cars by the end of 1981. They were not happy with this unexpected change of events and shift in status to TWR, leading to some discord in the series the following year.

With these results it became an increasingly important time for TW to cement his future team plans as the 1981 year closed with its most successful season to date; in the process establishing the rapidly growing TWR team as a dominant force in the British saloon car racing scene with its ability in chassis as well as engine expertise, a combination not available to other teams in the early 80s.

The controlling body for international motorsport, the FIA, chose this time to introduce new regulations for future saloon car racing, calling it 'Group A'. This change in regulations had caught TW's attention. The new Group A philosophy was based on the use of mass production vehicles with a minimum of 5000 produced over any 12-month period. They must retain their exterior profiles but many modifications to their standard production mechanical components would be allowed. The regulated changes included engines, transmissions, suspension, wheels and brake systems. These were important changes that would produce considerable increases in performance and importantly mechanical reliability over the proposed long-distance races; vital when using standard production based vehicles in the highly stressed environment of motor racing. It would also mean a considerable step required in technology with design and manufacture of special components. TW felt he was ready for that move.

The regulations were specifically aimed at allowing car manufacturer to enter high profile European motorsport without needing the special vehicles that suited the previous regulations that had led to limited manufacturer participation.

The freedoms of many key components allowed under these new Group A regulations would produce an almost level playing field and potentially closer competition between a larger range of vehicle manufacturers and vehicles. With their external appearance remaining as

*Allan Scott stands at the rear of the TWR run Rovers with their first outing at Mallory Park.*

the showroom models, winning performances on the race tracks could be used to enhance sales with a more sporting image. This was to be the marketing philosophy and promotion behind Group A.

With these new rules in mind it was time for TW to take his boldest step yet and convince a second British car manufacturer to enter not just British but European wide motor racing. His target was to be the struggling Jaguar Cars of Coventry.

Jaguar had previously built its sporting profile and resulting vehicle sales in the 1950s with many successes on British and European racing circuits; concentrating on the high profile 24 hour race at Le Mans in France. Jaguar however was now in crisis after being subjected to union labour demands and a management team missing the loyalty previously shown to its legendary founder Sir William Lyons after his retirement. Jaguar had then been subjected to economies of scale under the Leyland umbrella brand. The loss of their unique identity, pride and iconic brand became a marketing disaster for Jaguar.

New Jaguar boss John Egan had been placed into Jaguar a year before our first meetings with the brief to tell Leyland CEO Michael Edwards why loss-making Jaguar should not be closed – not what to do to keep it open. It had been a close-run thing in early 1981 with production of Jaguar's XJS Coupe temporarily ceasing as unsold vehicles became stockpiled.

Entering the European sphere of motorsport would be a massive undertaking for the small team at Kidlington, but TW was a gambler with an air of confidence few could match. I had joined him several times at Jaguar's Coventry headquarters over the remaining months of 1981 and in these meetings watched as Jaguar's management, led by John Egan (later Sir John Egan) became increasingly swayed by TW's projected and measured sincerity, not the hard man they had no doubt been earlier informed of and expected. Hanging over our heads at this time however was the previously aborted European racing venture of Broadspeed in the late 70s using Jaguar's V12 Coupes. This venture had not gone well, and had been stopped in its second year. Jaguar did have a Broadspeed racing V12 engine from that programme and it was given to me to evaluate.

We were told in these early meetings that Jaguar had come within three months of closure during the year.

*Allan Scott, with the Broadspeed V12 engine for evaluation.*

Egan was open to anything that would work for Jaguar and it was perfect timing for all concerned. There was also the problem of another potential team, led by Andy Rouse one of the drivers from the earlier aborted racing programme. They had heard of our proposals and had now contacted Jaguar, and this had to be carefully managed. Some had felt that if Jaguar was to return to motor racing it should be from the Coventry factory as had been the case with its 1950's successful ventures. Jaguar's John Egan, a marketing man sent to fix the company however admitted at the first meeting that they did not have the expertise internally to carry out such a programme, and so remained open to TWR's approaches. Alarmingly he also added that although he was attracted to the idea, Jaguar had no money for a venture such as this, however, we could buy as many cars as we liked at a substantial discount.

*Tom Walkinshaw*

JAGUAR

## Chapter Two

# Jaguar returns to motor racing

**Few would have then continued down this path after that introduction but the instincts of tenacity and ambition did not allow TW the luxury of walking away from any problem. The proposal TW finally put to Jaguar CEO John Egan towards the end of 1981 was for a semi works supported team to enter Jaguar's V12 XJS Coupe in the European Touring Car Championship (ETCC) built to the new Group A rules.**

This first year however would have to be seen primarily as a TWR venture with some factory engineering support. TW had now persuaded Jaguar to make some results-based money available for the programme. Jaguar wished to wait and see how successful the outcome would be, before making any commitment to a full return to motorsport. If the XJS was successful it would be promoted as having Jaguar's considerable engineering input and help, if unsuccessful it would have all been a private TWR venture and thus save face for Jaguar.

This joint marketing decision was heavily influenced by the experience with the earlier motor racing venture using the XJC V12 Jaguar in 1976 with the Broadspeed team. TW had astutely judged that situation and Jaguar's need to only back a winning team as the basis for his proposals. Jaguar's financial involvement with TWR was based on the first three outright placings paying £30,000, £20,000 and £10,000 respectively. As well, a year-old Japanese specification XJS that could not be sold because of poor build quality was sold to TWR for £6000 to start the venture.

Chuck Nicholson, real name Charles Nickerson, to be TW's co-driver in these 3½ hour races, had also made a considerable contribution of £70,000 per year and it was this final funding from him that had enabled TW to seal the venture. Charles should be remembered as someone who made a considerable financial contribution that helped cement the TWR/Jaguar relationship at an almost impossible time for all concerned, it may never have started without his help, and should be seen in retrospect as a timely contribution to Jaguar's eventual survival, helped by TWR's future motor racing results. This relationship continued on outside of motorsport with some early joint commercial ventures.

Alongside this European foray with Jaguar, the two-car TWR Rover programme was to continue again in the British Championship, run under a futher extension of the existing 'Group 1 plus' rules, before it too would lead to Group A in 1983.

The full story on this Rover racing programme is covered in my second book (*TWR and Rover's SD1*).

These two programmes would produce a huge workload for the new Engine Division (Engs) which in 1981 had just Barry Holland and me, increasing to three by the beginning of 1982 for the start of the Jaguar programme with 16-year-old apprentice Charlie Bamber. There were no internal machining facilities available at TWR within the young cash strapped company, and this became an

*On the Donington start line Paul Davis talks to Tom Walkinshaw with Kevin Lee and Phil Ebberson in the background.*

increasing problem for me when developing production based engines that needed many changes to produce a successful racing unit. We had to rely on outside suppliers, often unable to keep up with our timetables.

After the late start in January 1982 in preparing the first XJS for its initial race at Monza in Italy just three months later using just the one race car, a second car was then added to the team for the Spa 24 hour endurance race. Our second placing overall at the end of the 1982 European Touring Car Championship (ETCC) was a sensational result. The well-developed BMW 528 had won the early races of the season and its points advantage could not be overcome as the XJS Jaguar gained in reliability and eventually became the faster car in the series. These first year successes, culminating in first and second placings in front of the Jaguar management and an enthusiastic home crowd at Silverstone at year's end, resulted in the TWR Jaguar team finally been awarded the title of 'Full works supported effort' for 1983.

BMW became the winner of the inaugural Group A Championship, but TWR and Jaguar now had everyone's attention.

right, top: *Tom Walkinshaw, financial supporter Chuck Nicholson, and John Egan celebrate the XJS's victory at Silverstone. Without Chuck's support the XJS programme may never have started.*

bottom: *John Egan with the first of many trophies to come.*

*This busy 1982 year saw the arrival of our first daughter Martina with Karen.*

The full Jaguar XJS story is covered in my first book (*TWR and Jaguar's XJS*). It was a busy time for all as our daughter Martina's arrival at the beginning of the year had coincided with the first XJS test at Goodwood and so my wife Karen had to remain in the John Radcliff Hospital for an extra day before returning home with our new baby. With no family help or support in the UK it was a difficult time for her along with my many absences.

## 1983 Jaguar makes it official, factory backing for TWR

Two new cars were built over the winter of 82/83 and Jaguar would now raise its profile in racing as a factory team on most of Europe's iconic race circuits. The TWR Jaguar team was now a larger organisation with increased expectations and a factory supported profile. TWR Jaguar's main contacts at its Browns Lane factory in Coventry were CEO John Egan, but primarily engineering director Jim Randle. Our contacts working for Jim were technical specialist Peter Lings, Richard Akroyd who managed Jaguar's prototype procurement who then seconded Tom Seal from prototype procurement to progress these areas for us. Tom had a good understanding of Jaguar's machining capabilities and suppliers. Former Austin Rover motorsport homologation specialist Ron Elkins had also moved to Jaguar at TW's request with responsibility for vehicle homologation and team liaison. Neil Johnson, director of sales and marketing, was responsible for applying our results to their advertising and general exposure programme. Much later, as the Jaguar programme grew, TW could sense an internal unspoken division between Engineering and Marketing and would over time carefully turn this to his advantage, in the process of gaining engineering control of Jaguar's future worldwide racing programmes.

Our competition had not stood still over the winter months. BMW homologated their 635i Coupe with a larger engine and better aerodynamics than the 528i four door saloons that had won the ETCC the year before. This had then significantly changed the original analysis of the performance needed to win the ETCC with the XJS Jaguar. The goal posts had moved substantially for our team within just 12 months of the programme starting.

Despite significant race car improvements over the winter of 1982 at Kidlington, the two-car XJS team was in for a difficult time, with the multitude of lighter and more nimble 635i BMWs competing in private and factory supported teams.

TWR won the UK round at Donington in the rain to continue building the Jaguar fan club.

**WINNING AGAIN!**

You did it boy! Jaguar Chairman John Egan greets Martin Brundle after the Donington 500."He may be the youngest of Tom Walkinshaw's squad," said Egan afterwards, "but he drove like a champion today."
– *Racing Review*

Fourteen of these 635i BMWs turned out for the mid-year Spa 24 hour race against the two XJS Jaguars. Most of these suffered variously from accidents, lost wheels, clutch, gearbox, engine, differential and brake problems but the marque succeeded through safety in numbers; taking the first two places. TWR had managed to come third in this long distance race, but not with

*TWR's 1983 version of the Group A XJS had failed to win the championship. There had, however, been large steps made in the design by year's end and this would prove beneficial in 1984.*

the XJS. This had been accomplished with one of the new Group A Rovers entered by TWR as a back-up plan.

Both of these programmes had placed considerable pressure on the young growing TWR team, and it is fair to say that we were overwhelmed at times, but TW's air of confidence to all hid any deficiencies as they arose. Not one to stop looking to the future, TW had introduced the concept to me of one day taking Jaguar back to its motor racing roots – with a return to Le Mans for Jaguar.

## The Group C programme begins

A decision was made in 1983 at Coventry that Jaguar would increase its motor racing involvement and return to international sports car racing, eventually moving away from saloon cars. This plan involved a return to the prestigious Le Mans 24 hour race. That decision was driven by the successes and huge benefits gained by the Jaguar factory 30 years earlier developing the C and D-types specifically for success at Le Mans.

Initially this support would be directed towards the Group 44 team competing in the IMSA sports car series in America. Group 44 had a substantial internal profile at Jaguar head office in Coventry via Jaguar cars USA executive vice-president Mike Dale, a staunch supporter and promoter of Group 44 owner Bob Tullius. That liaison was observed with some caution by TW in early 1983, seeing his future plans and the finances available to TWR under threat within the far from profitable Jaguar Car Company as they began to formulate future plans of their own.

TWR also had future plans to enter prototype sports cars as Jaguar's factory team, and TW quietly applied his substantial thought processes to head off the growing threat and increasing support for Group 44 racing in America. One of the difficulties he faced was the fact that America was Jaguar's main car market at the time and the logical place for promotion and financial marketing support. TWR would have been viewed as a junior motorsport partner with Jaguar, providing modified touring cars. Group 44 was already racing an advanced aluminium construction Jaguar-engined sports car that was not only suitable for the American IMSA series, but with a few changes, Group C sports cars in Europe as well.

TW would have to bide his time, and hope that in the meantime the American team was not totally successful in its aims, something that was obviously at odds with what Jaguar were hoping for. In 1983 Group 44 had indicated that they were ready to compete at Le Mans in 1984 with their IMSA cars; although not focused on the new fuel economy based Group C regulations used for Le Mans, but competent enough for a toe in the water exercise. This direction was supported by a growing in confidence Jaguar management, headed via Jim Randle, the engineering director.

A way was needed to more closely monitor Jaguar's liaison with Group 44, and with these thoughts in mind TW asked me to forward a proposal for a fuel-efficient Jaguar V12 engine to suit the World Group C sports prototype series regulations, prevalent outside America.

The FIA 'Group C' regulation World Series aimed to limit high outputs from turbocharged engines by the introduction of a maximum fuel allowance in races. This series had then become totally dominated by the specialist German factory Porsche at the time, who supplied their 956 derivatives to experienced privateers alongside its own factory teams.

I was in no doubt TW's thinking in making his request to me was gaining complete control of the race engine supply to Jaguar, thereby leveraging a large element of control in the future competitive direction of both TWR and Group 44. A major part of this would be the technology exchange that Engs had in association with electronics company Zytek that had started in 1983. We were in the process of developing electronic engine management systems with this company and this was an area of new technology in motor racing; very much needed in the development of high performance fuel efficient engines of the future.

Jaguar now decided some basic performance information was needed to measure the level of competitiveness of Group 44's XJR-5 IMSA sports car. It was decided to use a known circuit where the winning Porsche 956 had just competed, and Silverstone, not far from the TWR factory, was chosen as the best venue for this test to be carried out. A deal was done with top British Porsche driver Derek Bell to drive during this test in May 1983, and give us an opinion as to its level of competitiveness.

The general consensus after this test was that the XJR-5 was perhaps up to two seconds per lap slower to the fuel than the works Porsches. As we had expected Jaguar were very positive about the outcome of this test. Britain's Derek Bell could be relied upon to give careful politically supportive comments about future competitiveness to satisfy Jaguar; as well as his German masters who were hard at work developing their IMSA-compatible 962, they would however dismiss his comments on aerodynamics.

Group 44 had backing from Jaguar USA's Mike Dale and the following correspondence between the USA and Coventry shows his thought processes on future direction.

The minutes of the meeting held at Leona, New Jersey in August 1983 indicates the technology levels involved at that time between Jaguar and Group 44. TWR did not get copies of these minutes and Bob Tullius was rightly becoming increasingly wary of TWR's involvements. He had not allowed TW to drive his XJR-5 at the Silverstone test.

These minutes were never shown to us at TWR.

*Maurice Rowe, chief photographer of* Motor, *was on the spot when the XJR-5 made its surprise appearance at Silverstone, where it was assessed by Derek Bell and Bob Tullius.*

# XJR-5 VISITS BRITAIN

ON-the-ball racing buffs were able to catch a surprise glimpse of the XJR-5 Jaguar IMSA GTP car which made its first visit to the UK recently.

An even bigger surprise was the sight of Derek Bell lapping Silverstone at high speed with it. (When one realises that Derek Bell's knowledge of the racing car development is second to none, perhaps the surprise isn't so big after all?)

Less than a year has passed since the XJR-5 made its race debut, and this season it has already scored two outright victories in the USA, as well as enough good placings to put Bob Tullius—leader of Group 44 and its G.T.P. race team—firmly into second place in the IMSA championship which still has a long way to run.

Such rapid progress is rare, but it should not make anyone jump to conclusions about the future. Bob Tullius drove the XJR-5 at Silverstone, too, in order to add his comments to those of Derek Bell. Jaguar's technicians, led by Jim Randle, have contributed a great deal to the development engineering that has gone into the XJR-5. Now that it has run on Jaguar's local circuit, its performance can be assessed that much more easily than from data compiled only in the USA, to which the car returned at the beginning of July.

*Bob Tullius with the XJR-5 at Silverstone while Jaguar's Tim Nevinson and Peter Lings to his left look on.*

With this step up in developments and commitments to a future Group C sports car programme looking increasingly likely, it had then been decided by Jaguar that TWR (Engs) would carry out the development of the Group C engine, starting late in 1983. My role then became responsible for all engine development on a new fuel efficient high performance V12 engine suitable for Group C competition.

Where this new Group C championship differed to previous sports car racing championships was that the 'engine manufacturer' would become the race team's title. These race teams more often than not made a limited number of very specialised sports cars that bore no resemblance to any manufacturers' products. Any winning results in this highly competitive series would assist in the promotion of the 'Jaguar engineering brand' and show to the world it was capable of leading edge technology in its engine designs. Porsche of Germany, considered a world leader in the automotive engineering field was dominating the series at the time with their own designed and manufactured Group C racing cars. They had been using the Group C series to add increasing credibility to an already substantive image – much as Jaguar had done in the 1950s.

This then would be the concept that motivated Jaguar to action a programme that would return it to top level motor racing at some stage in the future. While TWR as well as Group 44 would be producing and manufacturing the chassis designs, these could not be featured individually in the Group C *manufacturers'* title chase results.

Leaving behind the restrictive engine regulations in Group A and having total freedom in design with Jaguar's V12 engine would be another challenge for us at Engs. The Group C rules were based on any engine produced by the manufacturer, turbocharged or normally aspirated, with any modifications to allow an emphasis on high power outputs restricted only by the total amount of fuel available during the normal race distance of 1000kms (510 litres). This fuel would not be standard fuel available to public motorists in the host country as was the Group A ETCC rules we had previously developed engines for – but higher octane derivatives with a maximum

*to page 22 ...*

**Jaguar Cars Inc.**

**INTERNAL MEMORANDUM**

| TO: Mr. J. Randle | DATE: August 5, 1983 |
|---|---|
| COPIES: | FROM: M.H. Dale |

Thank you for the copy of the minutes of the Jaguar Car's Racing Committee meeting held on the 7th of July. If we can keep exchanging information like this it will be extremely helpful.

A few thoughts on the conditions for LeMans:

- Where would the Walkinshaw team get their experience with the XJR-5 in a 24-hour race before LeMans? Should they come to Daytona and compete alongside Group 44?
- Do we need a horsepower minimum? I fear to tread in the engineering domain but I do think it is possible to satisfy the power/fuel consumption requirements for LeMans on less than 675 horsepower.
- It might be wiser to have a broader judgment than a single lap time compared with the 956. Now that we have a 956 running in the CanAm on the same circuits as the Camel GT we can start making a comparison of average lap times compared with fuel consumption and, as you pointed out on a number of occasions, this is going to be the key to winning LeMans.

John Fitzpatrick just won a CanAm at Road America and his performance was quite revealing. Although he took on fuel twice in 160 mile race he came close to losing because he almost ran out of fuel on the last lap. His lap times were also revealing inasmuch as he qualified on the pole with a time of 2 minutes 00.622, his fastest race lap was 2 minutes 5 seconds and he spent most of the race at around 2.15 slowing down finally to 2.20. His average was approximately 2.10.

At these lap times an XJR-5 would have been running with Jim the whole of the race and made only one fuel stop without any fuel consumption difficulties whatsoever.

We appear to be making good progress in the area of pure lap speed because in the last four races we have accomplished the fastest lap in the race and, for the first time, at Sears Point we beat the March Porsche to the pole. In terms of fuel consumption we appear to be able to run competitive lap times with the March Porsche and have a 30% advantage in fuel consumption. Our major problem now is durability and I intend presenting a program to you on the 9th of August which will be aimed at changing this situation.

Taking all this into consideration I would appreciate discussion on specific conditions which the U.S. team must meet before competing at LeMans. Perhaps we could do this after the meeting on August 9th.

MHD:cld

P.S.

Also sending copy of minutes of the first U.S. Jaguar Racing Committee meeting held on August 2, 1983.

*Mike Dale of Jaguar USA is pushing the support for Group 44 to carry out the future Sports Car programme for Jaguar Cars UK.*

MINUTES OF THE U.S. JAGUAR RACING COMMITTEE

AUGUST 2, 1983 - HELD AT LEONIA, NJ

Constitution of Committee: Mr. M.H. Dale - Chairman
Mr. L. Dykstra
Mr. R.C. Tullius
Mr. L. Foushee
Mr. D.B. Scholes - Secretary

Meetings will be held bimonthly.

An agenda will be issued 7 days prior to each meeting and any matters for inclusion should be passed to the Secretary 14 days prior to the meeting.

Objective of Meeting

i) To enable report back and discussion of U.K./Gp. C racing programme.

ii) To collate U.S. Development progress for report to U.K.

iii) To enable Jaguar to monitor progress at U.S./IMSA GTP programme.

iv) To enable development programme, vehicle build, and component parts to be progressed.

v) To provide a forum for race programme discussion.

1. GTP CAR VISIT TO SILVERSTONE - D. BELL's REPORT

The report produced by Derek Bell after driving the XJR5 at Silverstone was accepted, however, there was fundamental disagreement with his comment on aerodynamics. It was considered by the committee that the aerodynamics and 'clean' front on the XJR5 was required for the proven lack of drag and low fuel consumption. Lee Dykstra was to discuss this matter with J.N. Randle. — L. Dykstra

2. 1984 GTP ENGINE REQUIREMENT PLUS IMSA RULES

Two valve engine was likely to form the basis for full 1984 season, however, four valve engine was to be progressed for early introduction into race programme as required. Latest four valve performance and fuel consumption details would be required by September 28th. — D. Scholes

Any IMSA rule change proposals would be monitored. Objections would be prepared should any change favor the turbo charged engines. It was not proposed to push for four valve homologation until the performance had been evaluated. The committee agreed that long term policy could require a turbo charged six cylinder in order to remain competitive. — R.C. Tulli

3. FUEL INJECTION

i) Initial drawing and engineering work complete for basic hardware, i.e., throttle bodies, injection holders and trumpets, etc.

Air flow test work to commence within one week.

Complete hardware available by the end of August.

ii) Two injection systems available a) VDS (Bosch) system b) Lucas Micos System. System decision required by October 1st. VDS system lead time to be ascertained. Lucas Micos progress/lead time to be ascertained. Complete system required for durability test by October 15th. — L. Dykst, D. Schol

iii) Engine controls/components for both systems to be identified and made identical where possible (injectors, pick-up modules, temperature sensors and throttle potentiometer.)

4. ENGINE COMPONENTS

i) Two Valve Cylinder Heads

Pattern work from 1st week OCT. Cstgs 2weeks after M/C 3-4 weeks.

Inlet port pattern work to be complete by end of August. Flow development and port cores to be complete by mid-September. Finalized cylinder heads required by October 1st. — R. Akroy

ii) Four Valve Cylinder Heads

Availability date to be requested. — L. Dykst

iii) Magnesium Oil Sump

Pattern work comp. Castings from 2week Sept M/C 2weeks.

Casting and machining of component required from U.K. Pattern work started. Estimated delivery by beginning of October. ✓ — R. Akroy, D. Schol

iv) Inlet and Exhaust Valves (2 valve)

Drwgs from 21/8/83. M/C 3 weeks

Nail head rather than Tulip head valves required for optimum performance.

—Drawing to be prepared for U.K. quote. — L. Foush

v) Cylinder Head Sealing

Suitable cylinder head gasket not currently available.

Engine to be prepared for 'Mosport' incorporating cylinder sealing by gas filled 'O' rings (UAP components.)

Ring Coopers 19/8/83.

Details of Cosworth 'O' ring and samples to be requested from Browns Lane Engineering. — D.B. Sch

vi) Cylinder Head Fixings

New Studs from end Aug. *

Increased strength studs EN24W and Nuts EN16T available and to be fitted for 'Mosport.' — L. Fousł

vii) Dural Main Bearing Caps

2 blocks ready 21/8/83. New main line bore size 3.1653 – 3.1658.

To be incorporated in endurance engine build. First block expected beginning September. Vandervell checking bearing size and clearances. — R. Akroy

vii) Camshaft Blanks

From 2/9/83.

Held due to Jaguar production problem.

5. GTP CHASSIS

i) Drawings for suspension fixtures, mounting points, theoretical loading data would be supplied in U.K. by late August. — L. Dyks

ii) Suspension component parts - one set front and rear would be supplied to U.K. by mid September — R.C.Tul

iii) Magnesium cast uprights would be supplied to U.K. for test when available, estimate October. — L. Dyks

iv) The torsional stiffness testing of the tub was to be discussed with J.N. Randle. The panels of every tub have been bonded together since initial build.

6. CHASSIS DESIGNATION

Chassis 001 - Now completed over 100 hours running. Expected to be retired after 1983 season. The possibility of using the vehicle as a show car was to be investigated — M.H. Da

Chassis 005 - 1983 spare to be updated to 1984 specification for 24/36 hour endurance testing at Daytona in November.

Chassis 006 - Car will be available mid-October for U.K. Group C use. Tom Walkinshaw required to provide gearbox by mid-September. — T.Walkinsh
Cost price and payment to be organized. — M.H. Dale

Chassis 007, 008, 009 - Build programme to be discussed. — D.B. Schol

7. DRIVER NEGOTIATION

The 1984 driver status for the two car GTP team was discussed. Approval and negotiations were to be undertaken. — M.H. Dale, R.C. Tulli

8. DURABILITY TEST PROCEDURE

Lee Dykstra laid down his requirement for the reliability program (appendix 1) and the various durability tests available were discussed.

i) Suspension Rig Test - to be carried out by U.K. Components to be supplied as required. — J.N. Randl

ii) Engine Durability Test - Test bed programme to be prepared. Test bed availability to be prepared. — L. Dykstra

iii) Pavée Test - Not considered valid at this time.

iv) Rolling Road Test - Full track endurance test preferred.

v) Track Endurance Test - 24/36 hour endurance test to be arranged for end of November. Test procedure to be prepared. The track test would not be carried out until the suspension units had satisfactorily passed the rig test. — R.C.Tulli, L. Dykstr

DATE OF FUTURE MEETINGS

Monday, September 26th - 2 P.M.
Monday, November 28th - Time to be notified.

CIRCULATION: COMMITTEE +

Mr. G.W. Whitehead
Mr. J.N. Randle (For Browns Lane Circulation)
R. Tarozzi (Group 44)

*... from page 20*

105 RON rating with a 5% margin of error. This rule however allowed almost any petrol formula to be used, favouring the high cylinder pressure turbocharged engines used by Porsche.

It would be a huge step up in capacity and technology for the small Engs team but for TW everything was possible and all problems fixable with his projected air of confidence that we had to just accept and go along with in his quest to dominate the engineering input to Jaguar. Group 44 saw future development problems ahead with the step up needed in engine technology, and they were now guessing we would have problems.

My relationship with ex Lucas employee Bill Gibson and his start-up company Electronic Racing Aids (ERA), had begun in early 1983 and was progressing rapidly. I had negotiated a protective contract proposal for TWR with ERA, and this had been finalised during 1983 giving us exclusivity to their current and future systems outside of Formula One, for the sum of £6000 plus hardware costs. The more cautious Bob Tullius was happy to let this important element proceed knowing that Lucas would be Jaguar's first choice of technology. Bob was focused on reliability in his IMSA programme for Jaguar, but in doing so he handed a vital part in the control of any future Group C Le Mans programme to TWR. ERA would later become a much larger company called Zytek and today is owned by the large German Continental conglomerate.

The concept and production of a Jaguar prototype racing engine had been made easier for me with the knowledge that Jaguar themselves had previously completed an exercise in designing a 4-valve per cylinder head assembly for the production V12 engine. Pattern work for casting components already existed, and would just need some refurbishment I had been told. This would make our task at Engs much easier as the hardest part for us would have already been done, or so we were led to believe. With TW limiting employment of additional staff through lack of funding at this time, we were now a total of five at Engs at the start of 1983. This programme was added to the three-car Rover (BSCC) and two-car Jaguar European (ETCC) engine programmes along with another single Rover competing in the French national championship and a limited Rover Tarmac Rally programme in the UK and Europe.

The additional tasks involved in this new V12 Group C engine programme, as well as the engineering processes needed to develop existing carburettor Rover V8 engines to electronic fuel injection with their move to Group A regulations, came with some costs. The Rover programme was needed as a back-up to the Jaguar programme for strategic and financial reasons, but something had to give, with the overstressed staff and facilities available to the TWR group. What gave was the total focus of TWR in support of the two-car Jaguar XJS team in 1983; something needed now that BMW had homologated its 635i Coupe to challenge the Jaguars.

**Jaguar Cars Inc.**

J. N. RANDLE
2 FEB 1984

**INTERNAL MEMORANDUM**

TO: Mr. J.N. Randle

DATE: February 22, 1984

COPIES: Mr. M.H. Dale

FROM: D.B. Scholes

RE: XJR-5 VEHICLE FOR FOUR VALVE DEVELOPMENT

Jim,

In order not to crowd the minutes, I agreed to contact you separately over the matter of getting you an XJR-5 for your four valve development programme.

The situation - as usual - is somewhat tricky at present, as we are not exactly falling over with spare XJR5's. However, the obvious car to send is 005, which was the Daytona Test vehicle and is fully up to date apart from the bodywork. It also has all the fuel injection harnesses fitted which you will obviously require. This vehicle is currently the spare race car and as reported in the minutes, would not be available until after Sebring regardless. Even that position may change as we are pushing Bob into more and more testing. Also, the possible logistics problems of getting to LeMans this year may leave us short of cars until after June.

The other problems that were raised at the meeting were:

1. The cost of giving or loaning you a vehicle. Either way Bob believes it will make him short by one car for the season or the period which you loan the car.
2. What would be required in the way of spares equipment?
3. What would be required in the way of mechanic/fitter training?

The best solution that we can come up with at present would be for you to arrange for a mock-up four valve engine to be sent over to Group 44 together with a couple of mechanic/fitters. Group 44 would then undertake to carry out the fitting of this engine using these mechanics, also enabling Lee to involve himself in the design and drawing of the necessary brackets, etc.

***This memo from USA's David Scholes already shows that TWR would be second best with chassis components on supply. It had to be avoided.***

After leading the 1983 series for much of the year the two XJSs had been slowly worn down by the large numbers of BMW opposition, and the TWR team was once again placed second by year's end, against BMW's more competitive 635i. This was not what was needed to carry influence and be seen as a viable partner in Group C, trailing Group 44 who were now on the move.

The supply of a Group 44 XJR-5 race car had been asked for by Jim Randle to carry out evaluation work with the proposed TWR engine in early 1984. Unknown to us a request had been made to carry out our engine testing in the USA via a memo from Mike Dale as it was already apparent that chassis supply from Group 44 was limited.

Perhaps also it suited Jaguar to have some control of this engine programme back in Group 44's hands.

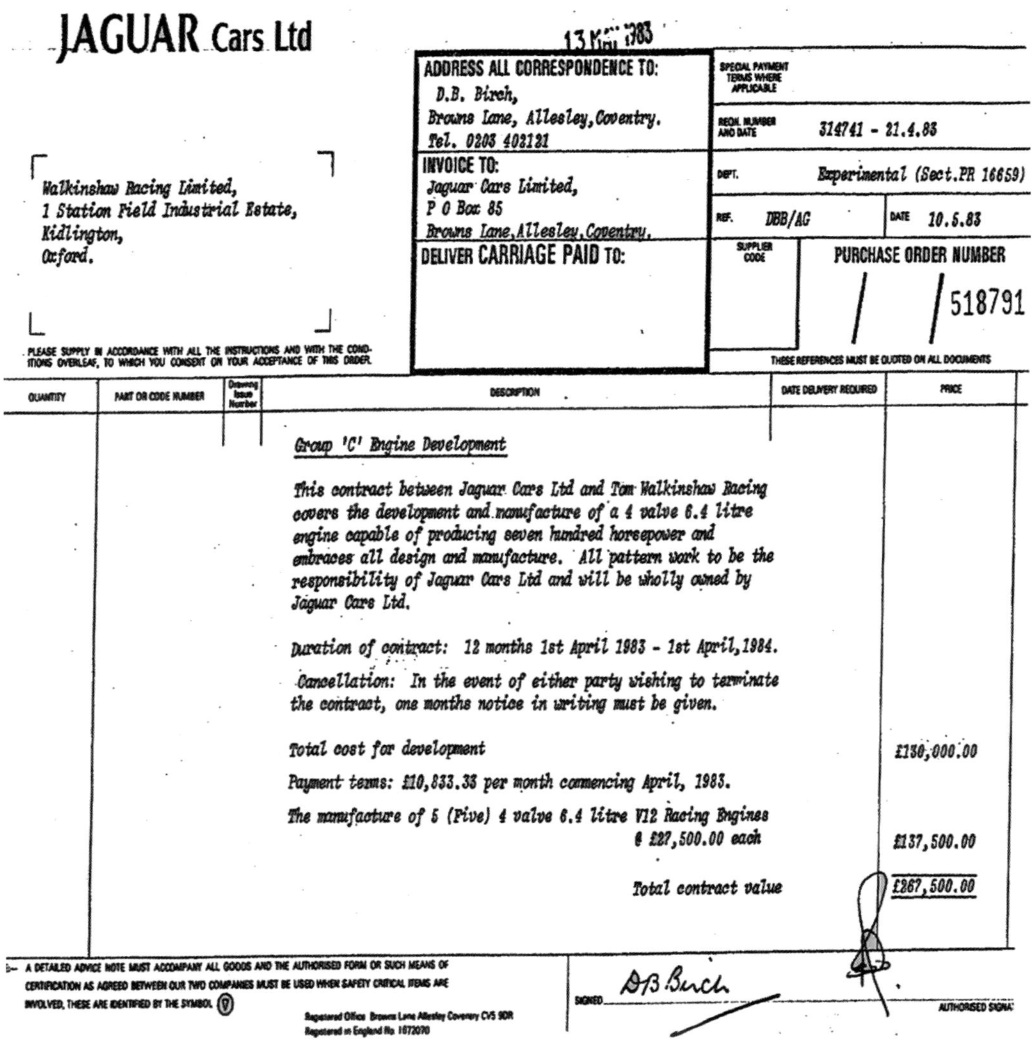

JAGUAR Cars Ltd

13 MAY 1983

ADDRESS ALL CORRESPONDENCE TO:
D.B. Birch,
Browns Lane, Allesley, Coventry.
Tel. 0203 402121

INVOICE TO:
Jaguar Cars Limited,
P O Box 85
Browns Lane, Allesley, Coventry.

DELIVER CARRIAGE PAID TO:

Walkinshaw Racing Limited,
1 Station Field Industrial Estate,
Kidlington,
Oxford.

PLEASE SUPPLY IN ACCORDANCE WITH ALL THE INSTRUCTIONS AND WITH THE CONDITIONS OVERLEAF, TO WHICH YOU CONSENT ON YOUR ACCEPTANCE OF THIS ORDER.

SPECIAL PAYMENT TERMS WHERE APPLICABLE

REQN. NUMBER AND DATE 314741 - 21.4.83

DEPT. Experimental (Sect.PR 16659)

REF. DBB/AG | DATE 10.5.83

SUPPLIER CODE | PURCHASE ORDER NUMBER / /518791

THESE REFERENCES MUST BE QUOTED ON ALL DOCUMENTS

| QUANTITY | PART OR CODE NUMBER | Drawing Issue Number | DESCRIPTION | DATE DELIVERY REQUIRED | PRICE |
|---|---|---|---|---|---|
| | | | Group 'C' Engine Development | | |
| | | | This contract between Jaguar Cars Ltd and Tom Walkinshaw Racing covers the development and manufacture of a 4 valve 6.4 litre engine capable of producing seven hundred horsepower and embraces all design and manufacture. All pattern work to be the responsibility of Jaguar Cars Ltd and will be wholly owned by Jaguar Cars Ltd. | | |
| | | | Duration of contract: 12 months 1st April 1983 - 1st April, 1984. | | |
| | | | Cancellation: In the event of either party wishing to terminate the contract, one months notice in writing must be given. | | |
| | | | Total cost for development | | £130,000.00 |
| | | | Payment terms: £10,833.33 per month commencing April, 1983. | | |
| | | | The manufacture of 5 (Five) 4 valve 6.4 litre V12 Racing Engines @ £27,500.00 each | | £137,500.00 |
| | | | Total contract value | | £267,500.00 |

A DETAILED ADVICE NOTE MUST ACCOMPANY ALL GOODS AND THE AUTHORISED FORM OR SUCH MEANS OF CERTIFICATION AS AGREED BETWEEN OUR TWO COMPANIES MUST BE USED WHEN SAFETY CRITICAL ITEMS ARE INVOLVED, THESE ARE IDENTIFIED BY THE SYMBOL

Registered Office Browns Lane Allesley Coventry CV5 9DR
Registered in England No 1672070

SIGNED D B Birch

AUTHORISED SIGNA

*The initial contract was for the manufacture of five complete engines fitted with 4-valve heads, and the price was later inflated by 15% in 1983.*

*Jaguar's first 24 hour race win with its second venture back into motorsport with TWR.*

JAGUAR

## Chapter Three

# 1984 : TWR must win Group A

**A more focused effort to win the 1984 ETCC by TWR with the XJS Coupe was desperately needed if we were to then enter the next level of competition with Jaguar, before it became too late to influence the entire future sports car outcome with Jaguar.**

A further development effort on the XJS Group A V12 engine had continued in late 1983 to be ready for the 1984 ETCC. Detailed work on a new camshaft profile, but limited to the Group A regulations of 0.413in lift from camshaft specialist Chris Walters, along with detailed reworking of the internals of the production-based exhaust and inlet manifolds, had seen the power increased by 14% to 485bhp at 7400rpm for Jaguar's 5.3-litre V12 production engine, with its rev limit now raised to 7800rpm. This along with chassis development gave the 1984 XJS a major step up against BMW's 635i that we had come second to in 1983.

TWR was by far the largest single team competing in the 1984 ETCC, with three all new XJS Jaguars competing as well as a two-car Rover team at the same time. Roger Silman had joined from the Toleman Formula One team to take an overview of the Jaguar team, managed by Paul Davis – and prepare to head up TWR's still secret prospects of entering Group C in 1985. The Rover team headed by Eddie Hinckley with support from Austin Rover's John Davenport and Andy Morrison had some successes but in a delicately handled programme involving two different manufacturers, the Jaguar XJS team had to take precedence in winning the series. This running of two separate teams in competition with each other but under the same organisation had never been contemplated before. That TW carried this cost-effective business situation for TWR off, and kept both sides happy most of the time, aptly demonstrates the negotiating and management abilities of Tom Walkinshaw.

*A confident Tom Walkinshaw with Win Percy left. Behind, author Allan Scott speaks with FIA scrutineer Marcel Servais.*

*Behind the Iron Curtain, entering the Bosonohy village at 165mph, Brno street circuit Czechoslovakia.*

The three-car TWR XJS team went on to totally dominate in 1984 with Tom Walkinshaw and Hans Heyer winning the European Touring Car Championship, including winning the blue-riband event most important to Jaguar, the long-distance Spa 24 hour race in Belgium. The timing and marketing of this result was perfect, occurring in the same week that the emerging Jaguar Company was sold by its Government owners on the UK stock market. By the end of the XJS racing programme in Europe in 1984 the benefits of motor racing in marketing for Jaguar had become evident with major increases to vehicle sales, and this boded well for TWR's future.

In the year that TWR had started negotiations with Jaguar, 1981, 1292 XJS vehicles had been produced and then production stopped because of stockpiled unsold cars. The future of Jaguar was uncertain and serious consideration was being given to closing production of the XJS Coupe for good after six years in production. The first year of the new racing programme with TWR in 1982 saw production of the XJS increase to 3455 vehicles with the introduction of the revamped HE model. 1983 saw variants of the XJS produced increasing to 4317, and that was followed by 5852 the next year when TWR won the ETCC in 1984. Winning the premier long-distance Spa 24 hour endurance race had started speculation that Jaguar may return to Le Mans, all helping the floating of Jaguar Cars on the British stock market. This move had now produced access to much needed additional funding with Jaguar Cars Ltd now masters of their own priorities and destiny.

A limited TWR XJS racing programme later continued and these included the first and third placings at Australia's prestigious Bathurst 1000km in 1985, the curtain finally coming down on the TWR XJSs with two races in New Zealand in 1987. After these many successes over 6000 XJS in various specifications would continue to be produced each year. The final outcome for a company that was under threat of ceasing to exist in 1981 became a total production run of 115,000 units over a period of 21 years. Both volumes and total length of production were a Jaguar record up to that time. Motor racing was the best cost-effective marketing tool for the XJS that Jaguar had over its entire production run, just five years of competitive racing encouraging a further 15 years of production. This programme helped save Jaguar.

The successful JaguarSport 50/50 joint venture had also begun in 1984, funded with £2½ million of cash from Jaguar, with TWR's contribution being an exchange of engine technology for Group C and Le Mans. After capitalising this new company however there was little funding left for the Group C engine programme. Many of these JaguarSport vehicles were fitted with a 6-litre version of the V12 production engine that I had initially developed alongside the racing programmes at Engs. Along with other body and suspension improvements over the following years TWR JaguarSport produced a sought after performance version that further increased the sporting image for Jaguar. The 6-litre HE version of the JaguarSport engine initially developed by me at Engs was then taken through 400-hour endurance testing by the separate TWR JaguarSport division also at Kidlington, and finally went into series production with Jaguar. All this helped extend the life of the aging XJS design. Instead of possibly ending in 1981, it finally came to the end of production in 1996.

During TW's renegotiation of TWR's Rover contract towards the end of 1984 with John Davenport of ARG Motorsport, Davenport insisted that to have the full support and focus of all divisions at TWR for his Group A European Rover programme, he needed the TWR chief to be a Rover, not a Jaguar driver. This was after his observation of support levels between the two TWR teams during the 1984 ETCC.

The Rover Competitions boss 'bought' TW out of his Jaguar XJS driving duties for 1985 and 1986 with a personal retainer of £100,000 per year to be lead driver for the Rover team in the ETCC. Much of the team funding for the now proven Group A Rover would be in the form of large bonuses on outright results, in some cases over £200,000 available per event, a larger financial prospect than anything ever offered by Jaguar for the XJS in this series. TWR's future plans in the world of motor racing with Jaguar at that time were a close secret – especially the plan to cease running the XJS in Europe for1985, as it looked like it would continue its total domination of the series. The problem we still had was that it looked as if we would have to use the Jaguar-supported Group 44 designed and built XJR-5 chassis in any future Jaguar Group C programme; not an outcome that TW wanted at all.

Now in total secret to all, including Jaguar, a top race car designer had been hired in late 1984 to produce feasibility drawings and designs for an all new TWR prototype sports car to run in 1985. But TW's driving contract with Rover for '85 and '86 meant he would not be part of the driving team in any future TWR Jaguar Group C racing programme. This would be the first time TW would not be leading the driving force in one of his teams' racing cars.

## TWR JaguarSport

TWR JaguarSport is based on a highly successful racing programme with the Jaguar XJ-S, the cars winning the 1984 European Touring Car Championship, and the 1985 Bathurst 1000kms classic in Australia.

From this foundation, we have produced a range of accessories which complement the car and lift it in appearance and performance terms, to give it extra appeal. Beyond the visible bodystyling parts and exclusive wheels, there are components for the suspension, braking and steering systems, as well as a hand built 6-litre V12 power plant. Much of the technology that is involved in this engine has come from knowledge gained while racing the Jaguar XJR-6 and 8, and TWR have employed our own, state-of-the-art fully digital engine management system to achieve outstanding levels of power and fuel efficiency.

This is the only range of performance parts that Jaguar approve for fitment through the official Jaguar Dealer network. TWR JaguarSport have a network of Appointed Distributors which spans the world, covering Europe and spreading from Norway to New Zealand.

## Progress meetings continued at Coventry and the following internal status meeting gives an idea of the ongoing agenda and support for Group 44

CONFIDENTIAL

RACING PROGRAMME - MONTHLY STATUS 9TH OCTOBER, 1984

Present: Mr J N Randle
Mr C G Edwards
Mr T N Crisp
Mr G P Lings
Mr R J Elkins
Mr D B Scholes

Mr G Johnson ) Lucas
Mr R Cattermole )

Mr A Scott TWR

Copies to: Mr T Walkinshaw ) TWR
Mr R Silman )

Mr R Tullius Group 44

cfi: Mr J L Egan

**ENGINE**

. 4 Valve Cylinder Head

Castings still not available. Latest samples scrap due to core movement. Patterns to be transferred to Sterling Metals for new samples. — R J Elkins

If these are unusable TWR will take over supply responsibility. — R J Elkins

. Rear Oil Seal

Existing rope seal has proved adequate. First mag alloy blocks will be to this condition.

Six alloy blocks are being machines at Radford to AJ6 lip seal condition. If these prove reliable later mag alloy blocks will be cast/machined to take lip seal. — R J Elkins

One alloy block with lip seal is to be supplied to Group 44 for 24 hour test. — R J Elkins

. Main Bearing Cap Failure

Oil pump capacity increased for short term. Increased bearing clearance to be tested. Bearing supply promise six weeks. — D B Scholes

Confirmation that weight saving on dural caps is in order of 24 lbs. — D B Scholes

. Timing Chain Tensioner

Samples promised 19th November, 1984. Promise to be held improved to meet 24 hour test. — R J Elkins

Production application to be reviewed. — T N Crisp

. Pistons

Cosworth type being 24 hour bench tested with aluminium liners prior ro 24 hour test. — D B Scholes

**TRANSMISSION**

. Third Gear Failure

Hewland to make gear sets with 5.933 DP and S82 material if available. EN36 will be used if S82 not available for 24 hour test. — G P Lings

Specific running-in conditions to be obtained. — R J Elkins

Additional ratios to be supplied. — G P Lings

. Crown Wheel

Larger diameter requires casing change, 12 month lead time. S82 material to be specified as interim. — G P Lings

. Input Shaft

System for incorporating greater flexibility to absorb shock loading is being investigated. — G P Lings

. Half Shafts

Larger joints now specified and fitted. Status required. — D B Scholes

. Oil Cooler

Residue found to be in Le Mans car unit. Sample to be rig tested at Browns Lane. — R J Elkins

Installation must be designed to allow unit to be replaced when a gearbox is changed. — D B Scholes

**LE MANS**

. Daytona

24 hour test at Daytona targetted 27th-30th November, 1984. — D B Scholes/ R J Elkins

. Computer Simulation

Further information gained following this years' race. Tyre growth to be included in programme. — G P Lings

. High Speed Stability

Long runway required for tests. — R J Elkins

. Tyres

Goodyear will have to improve performance. Car must be able to survive blow out. — D B Scholes

. Homologation

Full list of compliance to be available. — R J Elkins

Power controller will require repositioning for Group C. — D B Scholes

. Throttle Cable

Redesign will be rig tested but not in time for 24 hour test. — D B Scholes

. Radio

Supplier to be changed. — R J Elkins

. Parts List

Parts list to be supplied to TWR for sourcing decisions. — D B Scholes

. Petrol Specification

Le Mans Petrol Specification to be supplied to Group 44. — R J Elkins

**LUCAS MICOS**

. HT Interference

Significant improvement achieved by modified circuit. Resiting of sensor from distributor to another position, common for all engines, to be investigated. — D B Scholes/ A Scott

. Test Equipment

Package being put together for next year. — R Cattermole

. Injector Purging

Temperature switch not yet included in fuel rail. Remapped for maximum temperature. Status of testing required. — R Cattermole

. Injector Flow Rate

Testing ongoing. Effect of fuel density being investigated. — R Cattermole

. Tarozzi Heads

Expected testing in December. — R Cattermole

. M Skinner's Status Report

Still awaited. — G Johnson

. Power Boat Installation

Written quote sent, see item below. — R J Elkins

**GENERAL**

. Australia

Australian programme to be reviewed. — J N Randle/ A Scott

. Boat Programme

To be reviewed. — J N Randle

Chapter Four

# Concepts for the Group C V12 programme

**During 1984 my first attempts at producing a workable V12 prototype engine to the Group C fuel limited regulations had commenced. The actual fuel regulations were still not finalised and remained open to change. When the allowances for the Le Mans 24 hour race had proved insufficient the FIA simply decided to increase the amounts for 1985.**

It had soon become apparent that the promised Jaguar four valves per cylinder head had been done as a design exercise with little financial support when it had come to producing the intricate casting patterns. The pattern work had been produced as cheaply as possible and casting problems soon appeared. There were ongoing issues with the pattern work to cast these Jaguar designed heads and timescales were starting to slip with many rejected castings after part machining. The pressures to continue through these setbacks carried the thought that at least we would be in control of Jaguar's engine programme. When this became too hard for those involved at Jaguar, in the October 1984 meeting the problem had been simply handed over to us at Engs.

After Jaguar was floated on the stock market in mid-1984, much needed new funding became available and Jaguar's Jim Randle managed to sideline some of this for the racing programme. This new funding had been earmarked for the manufacture of up to six of the American XJR-5 race cars and it was a logical concept to have a universal chassis with both teams working together for a common goal. Tom Walkinshaw's own plans by now, however, had moved to the point of not wanting to be subjected to accepting the Group 44 XJR-5 chassis as part of the TWR racing programme.

Extensive development work with electronic engine management partner Zytek on both the XJS Jaguar and Rover race engines during this time proved vital in the next phase of development of Jaguar's V12 Group C engine. I was gaining expertise in this new area of

*First prototype four valves per cylinder engine on the dyno at Kidlington. From left Charlie Bamber, Mathew Norris and Peter Grace.*

electronic engine management programming of fuel and ignition settings, having now moved on from the earlier analogue systems to being able to programme the software in the new digital systems from Zytek – at Kidlington. This development was backed up in 1984 with extensive track testing with the XJS and Rover in the European Touring Car Series, and proved vital in the future development of the new Group C engine.

In parallel with this however was Jaguar's desire to introduce their original equipment supplier Lucas who were working on the 'in-house' Roger Cattermole designed Lucas Micos system. This was a well thought through engine management system but it was in its initial stages of prototype development, and unused in a racing situation to test electrical interference and any installation issues. Lucas was also a large company, having a slower moving committee based philosophy which I was not comfortable with and wanted to avoid.

We needed to continue with the small company re-active philosophy that had proved the best solution under racing conditions. Elements of intellectual property were also part of the mix with TWR having the rights to Zytek's future developments which would not be available with Lucas.

TW had arranged a visit to Williams Grand Prix Engineering in Didcot during the 1984 year taking a small group from Jaguar to look at their wind tunnel and make some initial investigations into the possibility of Williams producing a Group C prototype sportscar for Jaguar. This effort was mainly to destabilise the internal Jaguar support for Group 44's XJR-5 programme and bring into question the level of technologies available to Group 44 versus that available from a leading Formula One team in the UK. TW aimed the discussion at the conventional use of aluminium as the chassis material versus the new technologies of carbon fibre. It would also produce some ballpark costs for a separate chassis design and manufacture programme for Jaguar, which would not be cheap from this Formula One source. TW would also have a basis for the going rate for any future new Group C design from Williams; should TW be successful in bypassing the looming Group 44 option.

Group 44 then sent the wind tunnel model it had been using at the fixed floor University of Michigan facility to Williams. This model was then tested on the Williams rolling floor wind tunnel to give a back-to-back set of figures.

TW was at a time in his life, aged 38, where he had built a young motivated team around him. He had tasted success with winning the ETCC, greatly adding to his sense of self achievement over his former employers, BMW. The seeds for TWR and Jaguar's eventual success in Group C were being sown at this time. TW did not want to go head to head at Le Mans with Group 44 using race cars that would be more familiar to them. There would have been limited time available to become familiar with the XJR-5 that year, as well as having had no previous experience with this race car at Le Mans; something Group 44 had already experienced in 1984.

Jaguar personnel were still unaware that TWR Jaguar team manager Roger Silman had already used his former contacts in Formula One to good effect in late 1984 to contact BRM, Shadow and Arrows designer Tony Southgate to see if he would be interested in a TWR Group C programme. Tony had been subcontracting to Ford on updating their C100 Group C sports car project and was familiar with the latest concepts involved. He had penned an updated sports car for Ford but this project had not eventuated. Without any public announcements Tony Southgate had then been employed in October 1984 to produce the concept for a prototype sports car to Group C specifications for TWR.

Roger's appointment by TW involved the concept of TWR entering the top arena in motorsport one day, Formula One. Roger was focused on this future, with Group C being the stepping stone to that end, and that thought process would dominate his concepts in building the future team. The TWR race teams had now grown with firstly the XJS Jaguar team moving out of the original Unit 1 headquarters into its own building across the road, and then moving a year later into new larger premises close by at the start of 1985. Because of the uncertain futures in the motor racing world with renewable contracts, this new building was now the responsibility of Jaguar themselves, and any ongoing costs would not be a problem for TWR if future contracts with Jaguar did not materialise.

New funding however was needed by TWR for the increased costs involved, as well as the need to move from a results-based income in a first year that would be a steep learning curve, with limited prospects of any early race wins against the might of Porsche. These negotiations had started in mid-1984 and a contract was finally signed on January 16th 1985 on Jaguar Purchase Order 548406. This consisted of £1 million down and an additional 10 instalments over the year of £200,000 each. In addition, a bonus scheme was to operate to a total of £500,000 and the agreement would last for three years with inflation allowances. This contract however stipulated the use of a two-car team using the Lee Dykstra designed XJR-5 chassis with one car supplied by Jaguar and the second purchased by TWR for £90,000. The target was to finish at least fifth at Le Mans and in the World Endurance Championship to collect the bonus, using four valves per cylinder V12 engines.

With all these issues to consider there was going to have to be some delicate manoeuvring within this January 1985 contract. TW was determined to go all the way to the top in motor racing and build a business empire along the way. Ambition and success were the primary drivers, aligned with his considerable negotiating skills which would stretch Jaguar's to their limit.

In hindsight Jaguar and TWR were very lucky with their timing with all these events coming to a head by the end of 1984. Two years earlier the TWR team could not have handled the complexity of Group C, one year later with the Group 44 chassis produced and paid for by Jaguar, they would have been the race cars TWR would have had to use.

The rapidly growing Engine Division had expanded into the space the Jaguar XJS team had vacated at the end

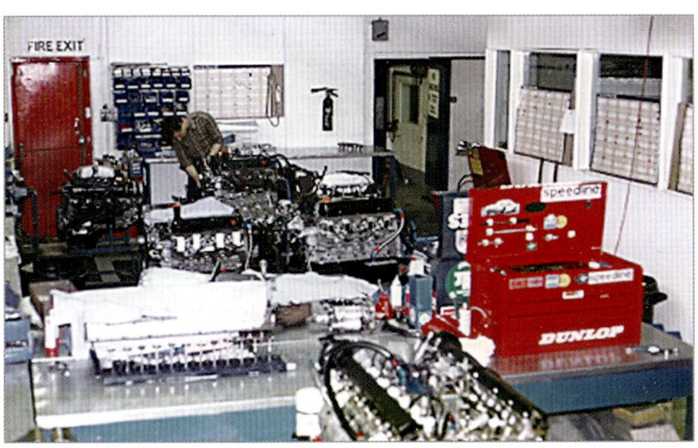


*Building up a stock of Rover and Jaguar Group A engines. Note each work bench with the year planner focusing engine builders on the delivery timetable.*

*Charlie Bamber fitting a V12 Group A engine to the Kidlington dynamometer, 1984.*

of 1983, and finally into all of the ground floor area in the original Station Fields Industrial Estate Unit 1 building at Kidlington when vacated by the Rover team, as it too moved to larger premises on the same estate. Two new dynamometer test cells were planned in the vacated areas but for now all the TWR engine programmes would have to use the single test cell that we had built ourselves in 1982, attached to the rear of the building.

The Engs work force had grown to eleven members including two in stores and procurement, and half of design draftsman Russell Sharp's time by the beginning of 1985.

My role as Manager of Engs had increasingly seen reduced 'hands on' prototype engine build work and this had finally ceased by late 1983. My responsibilities were for the design and dyno testing of both Jaguar and Rover engine programmes, working with Zytek on engine management development, as well as programming of eproms (Erasable Programmable Read-Only Memory – Engine management computers). Engine rebuild and delivery timetables, recruitment and training, as well as duties as engine trackside manager at all TWR racing events kept me well in touch with the team's needs. With the rising profile in motorsport for these two manufacturers came increased liaison needs with Jaguar at their Browns Lane headquarters, as well as progress meetings with ARG Motorsport at Cowley in Oxford.

Without any internal machining facilities at TWR my time was increasingly being taken up with procurement details and having new parts machined and supplied in a timely fashion. TW was reluctant to provide machining facilities for Engs saying that we would have a central facility one day, and this would be an ongoing problem; with that promise not eventuating during the whole time of the Jaguar Group C era. Statutory holidays and midsummer breaks taken by supplying companies never suit motorsport timetables, and this aspect would be an inherent ongoing weakness that we were forced to live with at Engs.

TW's personal expertise was a more chassis orientated one, and we suffered from his lack of personal knowledge and understanding when it came to prioritising funding. Richard Akroyd and Tom Seal were instrumental in assisting us with some of Jaguar's internal procurement facilities in support of the earlier XJS programme. By 1986 Jaguar's procurement assistance would greatly reduce with few original Jaguar components being used and we had to evolve into an 'Engs procurement team' with special technical skills to progress materials, heat treatments and price negotiation in low volume close tolerance prototype machining.

For Engs however there was some care needed in my focus on the various internal programmes. The 1985 Rover Group A programme in Europe now had Tom Walkinshaw as Rover's number one driver, and a balancing act from us at Engs was needed between these two seemingly first among equals TWR/Jaguar/Rover programmes. These teams had been set up as individual race entities with separate TWR management in separate buildings. The Jaguar Group C programme had the largest profile and importance for TWR's future, but the boss was driving a Rover and wanted to win a second European Championship by repeating his 1984 success against BMW, with increased competition from the fast-emerging turbocharged Volvo's as well.

Both TWR Rover and Jaguar teams now began pushing us at Engs for individual attention. Relationships had been well established within the teams with me attending all race meetings over the past six years and both groups worked well considering the different agendas they each had. Potential inter-divisional conflicts abound in competitive motorsport and it is normal for race teams to blame their uncompetitive race cars on the engine – and vice versa. This situation needs careful thought before responding to the many situations that may arise.

TWR was unusual in the 1980s in having an in-house Engine Division creating a greater need for unity than would perhaps normally exist when using a separate outside engine supplier. Jaguar personnel were allowed to assume my total focus was devoted to their project, which started in 1984 by me wearing just Jaguar team gear at ETCC races, and now my priority would be any Jaguar Group C races in 1985 when the Rover ETCC programme had the same dates.

This new venture in Group C and increased participation for the Group 44 IMSA team in America produced a change in focus for Jaguar's marketing department. It moved from using Group A in Europe to increase much needed vehicle sales in that part of the world against Germany's finest, to now enhancing the Jaguar 'engineering' brand worldwide. The priority for Jaguar would be a return to the proven sales formula of winning at Le Mans, the most important 24 hour race in the world, supported by Jaguar's previous successes there in the 1950s. Winning the Group C World Championship was also expected, but at this early stage was second in priority to Le Mans.

There were many on-looking doubters thinking that this next programme with TWR could never be a success. How could TWR take on the opposition in the form of the winning Porsche factory with their many years in the formula? The Italian Lancia factory with its Ferrari engine were trying and not succeeding to threaten the Porsche 956 and evolution 962C, even though Lancia's car looked to be a good one. Why would the heavy production based V12 engine be suitable in this series when governed by the new fuel efficiency restriction over periods of six hours – as well as the Le Mans 24 hour race? This fuel allowance had been reduced by 15% for the shorter six hour races from the previous year and would now give all the teams a problem when racing to this new lower limit; 51 litres per 100kms.

With these new fuel restrictions for 1985 came the need for engine technology to produce reliable high outputs, at least 650bhp with the very best fuel economy. It would also mean the best wind tunnel produced designs to generate the needed downforce; with the best compromise to fuel sapping aerodynamic drag.

Jaguar's future Group C programme would need the best drivers available, with Formula One driver Martin Brundle being top of the TWR list. British national and Porsche works driver Derek Bell was top of Jaguar's list, but TW suggested he was too expensive as his excuse for not wanting him in the TWR Jaguar team. The Group C Jaguar, which ever chassis was used, was not going to win in its first year, so why waste that money when it could be spent on the car was behind some of that thinking. Bell was also a very high-profile driver in the UK, and TW did not want independent comments concerning his TWR team in the press, as his new team found its way in this highly competitive environment. Derek Bell however also knew that the Porsche looked the better bet and was happy to stay with them.

The press was nominating various possible drivers as well at this stage with most picking Tom Walkinshaw himself as one of them. TW though had ruled himself out of this driving role from the very start to Roger and me, with his driving commitment to Rover and eventual retirement aimed just a few years away when he would turn 40 years of age. TW agreed with Roger's proposals that most former TWR Group A drivers would not be in the Group C programme as he felt that drivers with previous 'ground effects' experience in Formula One were needed. In future new drivers for the Group C Jaguar's would have to be drawn from those who had competed at that level. Team manager Roger Silman wanted to raise his and the team's status by having as many Formula One drivers as possible, and was not drawn to the prospect of having, in his view, lower class TWR saloon car drivers on his list. The immediate exceptions to this would be TWR drivers Jean-Louis Schlesser, Gianfranco Brancatelli and Hans Heyer; all on cheaper contracts.

By early 1985 Jaguar's desire to amalgamate team hardware and engineering effort heralded the arrival at TWR of a Group 44 XJR-5, to be tested with the new Engs built 4-valve V12 engine installed. The first 4-valve test engine built using the Jaguar sourced head castings had suffered from port core shift and had finally succumbed to water ingestion when a thin section of an inlet port had failed. This left the engine unusable and me with a major problem.

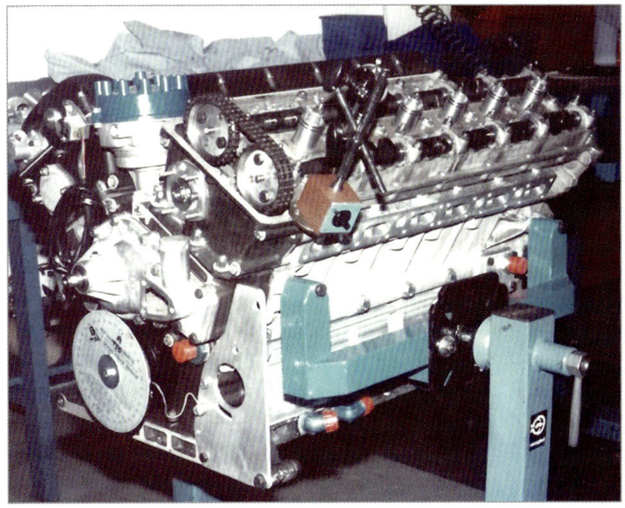

*First Group C 6232cc engine with Jaguar Coventry 4-valve head design.*

Another pair of selected castings from Jaguar's original head design were fitted to the XJR-5 to continue the test programme. By now I had grave doubts about going down this path. Production problems at Jaguar and the bulky top-heavy nature of the design didn't help my optimism for the 4-valve head.

The first outing for the TWR/Group 44 Jaguar was at Silverstone with Martin Brundle in the last week of March 1985. Martin continued the test programme with the car, now painted British Racing Green with white stripes. Testing continued at Donington and Snetterton.

*Roger Silman, Tony Southgate and Tom Walkinshaw at the Donington test.*

# Brundle tests Gp C Jaguar challenger

Martin Brundle was at Donington Park last Thursday to give the first TWR-run Jaguar Group C car its initial shakedown test. Resplendent in its British Racii Green livery the modified XJR-5 ran all day without any major problems.

The Lee Dykstra-designed chassis does not appear to have any major aerodynamic changes from its IMSA specification — as raced last year by Bob Tullius's Group 44 IMSA GTP team in America and at Le Mans. Two monocoques were sent from the USA to the TWR base at Kidlington in mid-February and they are thought to have undergone considerable internal modification to bring them into line with the Group C minimum weight limit of 850 kilos — 50 kilos under the IMSA limit.

Power output from the 6-litre V12 installation is expected to be in excess of 600bhp.

The TWR cars will be powered by the latest version of the normally-aspirated six litre V12 engines from the Coventry factory, and there is much speculation that they are using the new four-valve cylinder head that has been under development for the last year. The engine will be fitted with the Lucas Micos electronic management system raced by the IMSA team at Le Mans last year.

The modified Group 44 chassis are expected to be interim models for a limited Group C programme this year, with a new TWR design expected in 1986.

Power output this season is expected to be in excess of 600 bhp which, fuel consumption allowing, should see the cars well in contention. No official announcement of the team has yet been made, but it is expected that Martin Brundle, Stefan Johansson, Hans Heyer, David Hobbs, Jean-Louis Schlesser, Thierry Tassin and Walkinshaw himself will be driving.

The cars will run on Dunlop tyres, as opposed to the Group 44 Goodyear rubber. On the sponsorship front it is still uncertain whether the cars will carry any commercial sponsorship or whether they will race in British Racing Green. An official announcement is expected shortly.

Will the Jaguar be seen in British Racing Green — an announcement is expected shortly.

Brundle — tested without major problem.

*Press speculation continues the public relations line of a Jaguar factory supplied V12 engine.*

The 4-valve, 6.2-litre engine at this early stage in development was producing 686bhp at 7000rpm and peaking at 706bhp at 7500rpm using the Lucas Micos engine management systems that Jaguar wished to use, against my preference of using Zytek. The testing programme continued with the XJR-5 amid much conjecture from the motoring press assuming TWR would build a modified version of the XJR-5 design. This information was allowed to leak out and helped fulfil the contract signed in January while work continued in secret on TWR's own totally new Group C race car being penned at the same time by Tony Southgate.

Meanwhile former Formula One chassis manufacturer John Thompson of T.C. Prototypes had joined forces with designer Tony Southgate under the joint umbrella organisation of Auto Racing Technology (ART). They were able to oversee the manufacture by Advanced Composite Technology (ACT) of a new all-carbon fibre sports car and design for TWR. While carbon composite chassis were the norm in Formula One these slim line single seater structures had design parameters that allowed for smaller, single piece stiff structures to be built in autoclave ovens. Sports car regulations and dimensions however demanded the need for tooling and technology to produce a longer and much wider racing car structure. These first Group C chassis were to be produced at a cost of £85,000 each. Jaguar meanwhile was in the process of signing off on six new Group 44 XJR-5 race cars to be built in America at a base cost minus engine of £90,000 each, two of which were earmarked for TWR.

The soft option of accepting the USA aluminium tub and frame chassis technology and associated equipment, with one of the cars paid for by Jaguar, would have been eagerly accepted by any other team offered the kudos of a factory Jaguar contract at the time. It was a hard and very brave call by TW to decide to design and manufacture TWR's own Group C car, with the real prospect of little or no Jaguar enthusiasm or possible funding for it. This problem was amplified by having no obvious sponsor on the horizon to make up the difference in what Jaguar could afford; and what TW wanted for the full programme.

This design path at TWR outside of the TWR/Jaguar contract structure allowed all the rights to the new TWR Group C car to be held by TWR, as that design would be outside of the intellectual property rights contract between the two parties. Jaguar had ownership of all intellectual rights arising from their joint racing programmes.

This separate ownership route could make the chassis available for other manufacturers; BMW was a consideration in TW's mind as he felt they had a lighter engine as well as turbocharged technology from its Formula One programme, Roger Silman encouraging that thought path as well with Formula One in mind. TW was convinced that turbocharging was the only

*Chief mechanic Clive Parker and TWR's two in-house design draftsmen Colin Moore and Andy Scriven look on with the arrival of the first all carbon technology chassis.*

**PERFORMANCE AND FUEL CONSUMPTION ESTIMATES**

**GROUP 'C' RACING**

In order to better define the effect of engine output and vehicle weight on lap times and fuel consumption in the light of the current Group C regulations, a matrix of computer predictions has been run for two circuits, Le Mans and Silverstone, the latter being considered representative of most other WEC circuits.

Details of the methods used and full results are appended hereto, but the following major conclusions are drawn:

1. For Le Mans, a 1% improvement in lap time, i.e. about 2.0 sec, can be obtained by either a weight reduction of approximately 60 kg, or a power increase of approximately 30 bhp.
2. For Silverstone, a similar 1% improvement in lap time, representing about 0.8 secs, can be obtained by either a weight reduction of approximately 40kg or a power increase of approximately 50 bhp.
3. Hence the effect of being 50kg overweight is about 1.2% or 1.0 sec/lap at Silverstone, but for Le Mans, is not quite so critical, being about 0.8% or 1.7 sec/lap.
   Additional power, however, is more effective at Le Mans than on slower circuits, since the long straight determines that a greater proportion of work is done in overcoming aerodynamic drag.
4. For Le Mans in particular, the power useable is severely restricted by the regulation fuel allowance. Fuel consumption is of course directly related to engine output only (for a given power unit and driving pattern, a lighter car will simply go faster with a virtually unchanged fuel consumption). At our present best levels of specific fuel consumption, it appears that for Silverstone, around 680 bhp might be useful (assuming some backing off of maximum revs), whereas for Le Mans, where effectively the fuel limit is more stringent, anything over 600 bhp would only be of value for tactical useage.

**METHOD**

A matrix of results for both Le Mans and Silverstone has been produced by running the programme for 3 hypothetical engine output curves, all geometrically similar and peaking at 600, 650 and 700 bhp, all at 7500 rpm, and each for car nominal weights of 850, 900 and 950 kg, and each combination for rev limits of 7500, 7000 and 6500 rpm (+6000 rpm for Le Mans).

The 650 bhp engine curve approximates to that currently being achieved by a good 2-valve engine, and a corresponding full throttle specific fuel consumption curve is used, having a best value of approximately 0.47 pts/hp/hr (U.S. equivalent approximately 0.41 lbs/hp/hr).

For the 600 and 700 bhp engines, the geometrically similar hypothetical torque curves were obtained by approximately scaling that of the 650 bhp engine at each rpm site, and the same specific fuel consumption curve was used for each engine.

The actual car weight was assumed to be the nominal figure plus 250 lbs, the latter representing the driver and about ½ tank of fuel.

Aerodynamic factors were assumed to be for Le Mans CD= .393 CLF = -.287, CLR = -.66, while for Silverstone the 'high downforce package' was assumed with CD = .547, CLF = -.6, CLR = -1.30.

The use of more competitive tyres was simulated by using a basic tyre constant of 1.5 (rather than 1.4 as was found to be applicable to last years Le Mans Goodyears. This change alone is worth approximately 3.8 sec. at Le Mans and 2.5 sec. at Silverstone, without detriment to fuel consumption).

Gear ratios were specified for Le Mans such that for each engine, 5th was optimised to just allow the car to attain its potential ultimate maximum on the Mulsanne straight, with for all cases 2nd such that Mulsanne corner could be taken at a theoretical 3000 rpm and with the intermediate ratios spaced to give equal speed increments in between. These ratios were used so as to make the comparison between engines more valid, and they do permit the ultimate performance of the car to be estimated, but it should be pointed out that in practice, substantially higher upper ratios are recommended in the interest of economy and reduced strain, and this should be borne in mind in assessing the results obtained.

For Silverstone where there is insufficient space for the car to attain its ultimate maximum, a 5th gear giving approximately 190 mph at 7000 rpm was specified for all three engines, together with appropriate lower ratios.

It was further assumed that the lowest possible gear (other than first) in relation to the specified rev limit would be used for each corner. In comparison with what any driver would use in practice, the results are thus again optimistic in terms of lap time (by perhaps 1.5 sec. at Le Mans) and pessimistic in terms of consumption.

Furthermore, for Le Mans it was assumed that, regardless of the rev limit specified for the lower gears, speed would be built up to the maximum possible on the Mulsanne straight. The effect of applying various limits to this section of the circuit is to form the basis of a further investigation, since it is apparent that at Le Mans this year consumption is going to be critical.

**TABLE 1 – LE MANS**

| POWER BHP | LIMIT / WEIGHT KG | 7500 RPM TIME MIN SEC | 7500 RPM MPG | 7000 RPM TIME MIN SEC | 7000 RPM MPG | 6500 RPM TIME MIN SEC | 6500 RPM MPG | 6000 RPM TIME MIN SEC | 6000 RPM MPG |
|---|---|---|---|---|---|---|---|---|---|
| 600 | 850 | 3-28·4 | 5·84 | 3-29·3 | 5·98 | 3-31·0 | 6·09 | 3-33·1 | 6·14 |
| | 900 | 3-30·0 | 5·79 | 3-31·1 | 5·92 | 3-32·6 | 6·03 | 3-34·9 | 6·11 |
| | 950 | 3-31·6 | 5·75 | 3-32·6 | 5·87 | 3-34·3 | 6·02 | 3-36·6 | 6·08 |
| 650 | 850 | 3-24·8 | 5·56 | 3-25·8 | 5·69 | 3-27·5 | 5·80 | 3-29·6 | 5·85 |
| | 900 | 3-26·5 | 5·53 | 3-27·4 | 5·65 | 3-29·1 | 5·75 | 3-31·4 | 5·82 |
| | 950 | 3-28·0 | 5·49 | 3-29·1 | 5·60 | 3-30·7 | 5·72 | 3-33·0 | 5·79 |
| 700 | 850 | 3-21·7 | 5·33 | 3-22·7 | 5·45 | 3-24·4 | 5·54 | 3-26·5 | 5·59 |
| | 900 | 3-23·2 | 5·28 | 3-24·3 | 5·41 | 3-26·0 | 5·49 | 3-28·2 | 5·56 |
| | 950 | 3-24·9 | 5·25 | 3-26·0 | 5·36 | 3-27·5 | 5·46 | 3-29·9 | 5·53 |

NOTES 1) MPG FIGURES REFER TO IMPERIAL GALLONS

2) MAX. SPEEDS ON MULSANNE STRAIGHT – FOR 900KG
600 HP - 219·0 MPH
650 HP - 225·0 MPH
700 HP - 230·7 MPH
CORR^N. FOR 850KG, + 0·1 MPH; FOR 950KG, – 0·1 MPH

**TABLE 3 – SILVERSTONE**

| POWER BHP | LIMIT / WEIGHT KG | 7500 RPM TIME MIN SEC | 7500 RPM MPG | 7000 RPM TIME MIN SEC | 7000 RPM MPG | 6500 RPM TIME MIN SEC | 6500 RPM MPG |
|---|---|---|---|---|---|---|---|
| 600 | 850 | 1-17·8 | 5·57 | 1-18·2 | 5·80 | 1-18·7 | 5·95 |
| | 900 | 1-19·0 | 5·50 | 1-19·4 | 5·73 | 1-20·0 | 5·93 |
| | 950 | 1-19·8 | 5·47 | 1-20·4 | 5·71 | 1-20·8 | 5·88 |
| 650 | 850 | 1-16·9 | 5·31 | 1-17·4 | 5·52 | 1-17·9 | 5·66 |
| | 900 | 1-18·1 | 5·26 | 1-18·6 | 5·48 | 1-19·1 | 5·60 |
| | 950 | 1-18·9 | 5·23 | 1-19·5 | 5·42 | 1-19·9 | 5·58 |
| 700 | 850 | 1-16·1 | 5·07 | 1-16·6 | 5·28 | 1-17·1 | 5·37 |
| | 900 | 1-17·3 | 5·04 | 1-17·8 | 5·23 | 1-18·2 | 5·35 |
| | 950 | 1-18·1 | 5·00 | 1-18·7 | 5·23 | 1-19·1 | 5·30 |

NOTES 1) MPG FIGURES REFER TO IMPERIAL GALLONS

2) MAX. SPEEDS, APPROACHING WOODCOTE – FOR 900KG, 7500 RPM
600 HP - 179·2 MPH
650 HP - 183·5 MPH
700 HP - 189·7 MPH
AV. CORR^N. FOR 850KG, + 1·6 MPH; FOR 950KG, – 1·4 MPH
AV. CORR^N. FOR 7000 RPM, – 0·6 MPH; FOR 6500 RPM, – 1·4 MPH

*Jaguar's Peter Lings assembled the data from testing to date in a first real attempt at predicting lap times and fuel consumption relevant for an attempt at the Le Mans 24 hour race.*

way forward and had wanted me to use Jaguar's AJ6 3.2-litre straight six engines as a base, using turbocharging to increase the power. He had also asked Jaguar to do an exercise on piston cooling which they had carried out. One evening at dinner he stated that it would 'be good to just turn up the boost and blast past them (Porsche)', and this had only hardened my resolve to not go down that turbocharged route with him. Egos in a fuel based formula would be very difficult to manage.

In the very early concept stage Tony Southgate had produced the idea of a twin radiator 'lobster claw' frontal design that looked similar to the March GTP sports car. TW did not like the look of this 'copy' idea and dismissed it on looks alone, the idea discarded without any wind tunnel modelling to compare results. This design had been produced by Adrian Newey who would become the most successful car designer in Formula One history.

The work being done with the Jaguar designed 4-valve heads on our 6262cc V12 engine continued at a reduced pace, only to support the TWR XJR-5 test programme and our obligations to Jaguar with their Lucas Micos engine management system. I was coming to the conclusion that we had a real problem developing engine wise. TW, Tony Southgate and Roger Silman were not convinced on the V12 idea, but their minds were firmly focused towards the 4-valve head being needed to produce the engine efficiency for the V12 if it was going to be used. I had begun to doubt the benefits that all assumed, especially with the additional weight being added working against the handling and fuel consumption. The ability to produce a large capacity slower revving engine reduced the need for four valves per cylinder in my mind. The fact that we would struggle to get down to the 850kg weight limit, as well as the manufacturing complexities involved in supporting this engine concept without an in-house machining facility at TWR were continuing to build a case against this direction for me. We were in big trouble in early 1985. Any about turn was not going to be easy to sell. We needed an alternative supplier for head design and manufacture if we were to continue down this route. In the meantime, the first XJR-6 tub section had arrived.

```
MODIFIED CHARGE-MASS LAW CALCS PROG.
INPUT

BORE(mm)= 92.000
STROKE (mm) 78.000
NO. OF CYLINDERS=12
COMPRESSION RATIO=11.8
INLET MANIFOLD EQUIV. PULSE+BOOST PRESSURE (lbf/in^2)=17.2
INLET MANIFOLD EQUIV. PULSE PRESSURE RISE (lbf/in^2)=  2.5
INLET BOOST PRESSURE RATIO (atm abs)=  1.00
EXHAUST MANIFOLD EQUIV. PULSE+BOOST BACK PRESSURE (lbf/in^2)=15.1
EXHAUST MANIFOLD EQUIV. PULSE PRESSURE RISE (lbf/in^2)=  0.4
EXHAUST BOOST BACK PRESSURE RATIO (atm abs)=  1.00
INLET-EXHAUST PULSE PRESSURE DIFFERENCE (lbf/in^2)=   2.1
INLET MANIFOLD TEMPERATURE (deg F)= 70
BRAKE THERMAL EFFICIENCY (%)= 37
NO. OF INLET VALVES/CYLINDER= 2
INLET VALVE HEAD DIA (in)= 1.496
AV DISCHARGE COEFF ACROSS INLET VALVE= 0.38
TYPE OF FUEL USED= PETROL 99 OCTANE
SG OF FUEL AT 60 deg F= 0.702
FUEL LOWER HEATING VALUE (Qc) (Btu/lb)= 19020
ENTHALPY OF LIQUID ABOVE VAPOUR AT 60 deg F (Hlg) (Btu/lb)= -150
STOICHIOMETRIC FUEL/AIR RATIO (Fc)= 0.0670
% CO READING=  4.4
RPM= 7000

OUTPUT

SWEPT VOLUME (cm^3)=6222.2
INLET CHARGE TEMPERATURE AT BDC (deg F)=106.6
IDEAL AIR MASS FLOW (lb/min)=  58.5
ACTUAL AIR MASS FLOW (lb/min)=  63.7
ACTUAL AIR VOLUME FLOW (ft^3/s)=14.1
VOLUMETRIC EFFICIENCY (%)=109
MEAN PISTON SPEED (ft/s)= 59.7
FMEP: friction+pumping (lbf/in^2)=  43.2
FRICTION LOSS (bhp)= 147.2
PUMPING LOSS (bhp)=   -2.1
FRICTION+PUMPING LOSS (bhp)= 145.1
BMEP (lbf/in^2)= 212.5
POWER (bhp)= 713.0
TORQUE (lbf ft)= 535.0
BHP/LITRE= 114.6
GULP FACTOR= 0.40
OTTO CYCLE EFFICIENCY (%)=  62.7
RELATIVE EFFICIENCY (br.th./Otto) (%)=  59.0
BSFC (lb/bhp hr)= 0.435
AIR/FUEL RATIO= 12.3
STOICHIOMETRIC AIR/FUEL RATIO= 14.9
FUEL: % RICH=  17.4
FUEL CONSUMPTION (galls/hr)=  44.2
AT SPEED OF  180.0 mph, FUEL CONSUMPTION (mpg)=   4.1
```

***First run analysis of the 4-valve V12 engine developed at Kidlington.***

## Construction details of the first TWR XJR-6

The problems of getting the new Group C car with its V12 engine down to the weight limit of 850kgs produced the need for the best lightweight construction and carbon fibre technology; Group 44's XJR-5 was an aluminium monocoque/part space frame package that had been designed for an American series with a 50 to100kg higher weight limit.

The new carbon fibre technology that ART would use needed to be fully understood; rather than just making these lightweight materials thicker, as had been the case with the glass reinforced plastic, the load paths and weave directions had to be taken into account.

The woven elements of these new materials had to be engineered in such a way that they counteracted the forces placed on them from many different angles and so would need to be laid up and bonded in the correct directional manner to form a resistance path to compression extension and shear forces. This introduced the need to expand the analysis skills required to understand these forces, and so create the lightest and strongest construction possible. This expertise was not available at the time within TWR – hence the employment of ART to carry this out.

The basic shape of these two-seater sports cars for Group C was dictated by the rules that had a minimum windscreen size with a height of 920mm and a maximum overall car height of 1030mm, width of 2000mm, length of 4800mm and the minimum weight of 850kgs. Internally the cockpit area had to allow room for two people seated in similar fashion either side of the car's centre line, with a minimum internal dimension of 1300mm. For 1985 there was the added restriction to internal design with the driver's feet having to stay behind the centre line of the front wheels. This feature had been a discussion point in Formula One with the potential damage to driver's feet and legs in a frontal accident.

The carbon fibre manufacturing systems available in 1985 used both vacuum forming and heat treatment during the manufacturing process and this new monocoque design involving a series of separate parts would have to be made using different materials and processes over several stages, before final assembly. The rear bulkhead with its recess for the front of the long production based V12 engine was made from carbon fibre clad aluminium honeycomb section. This formed the basis of a very strong rear face to the base chassis or 'tub' structure with hard points for engine mounts inserted. The internal steel roll cage structure had two steel hoops going forward from the rear bulkhead hoop and were bonded to the inside edges of the screen pillars down to the front of the tub structure. Two steel tubular struts attached to the rear of the V12 engine's camshaft covers were angled upwards and bolted to the top of the internal roll bar structure completing a triangular feature to control vertical loading.

Sub-sections of Carbon Kevlar construction were vacuum moulded, each performing a separate structural function. There was no autoclave oven large enough to complete the whole process as one unit at the time, but when all these components were carefully assembled together in a cold bonding process, the result was an immensely strong and light sports car chassis that previous aluminium monocoque technology could never hope to achieve.

Within this first base tub structure three flexible bag tanks would be housed; with a total capacity of 100 litres of fuel as stipulated by the Group C rules. The V12 was moved as far forward as possible to close in on the desired 40/60 front to rear weight split, achieved by moulding a 100mm recess into the rear bulkhead with the front of the engine and ancillary drives housed within the recess.

On this first chassis, designated XJR-6, the front suspension's two shock absorber and coil spring assemblies were attached transversely to two large aluminium bearers fixed across the front of the tub, and these two items also helped increased the strength and driver safety in the frontal impact area. The steering was by conventional rack and pinion and unassisted. A front section was fixed to the tub to house the front mounted water radiator and attachment points for the front bodywork. On Tony Southgate's first design one additional small water radiator was positioned in the right-hand side of the rear engine bay behind the cockpit.

A removable front 'nose' made of a carbon composite material enclosed all these front structures as well as the two front wheels, allowing a single continuous aerodynamic enclosure blending with the basic chassis at points beneath the windscreen and behind the front wheels.

Understandably, being an entirely new design and process for all involved at ART it was over engineered and the final outcome was an extremely strong and safe structure surpassing all other sports car designs at the time, but still reasonably light. Getting the rest of the car down near the minimum weight limit would prove to be a harder task though. The strengths of this design would later prove their worth when Win Percy emerged unscathed from a high-speed accident on the Mulsanne straight after a tyre failure during the 1986 Le Mans 24 hour race.

Two of these initial Southgate designs were produced, numbered 185 and 285 and were completed by the middle of the 1985 year. A third chassis was constructed at year's end and benefited from refinement in the manufacturing process as well as some of Tony Southgate's revisions to the overall structure to reduce weight for 1986. This interim chassis was designated 385. The Southgate design would use Formula One derived ground effects principles where twin tapered tunnels underneath the car, increasing in size until they exited at the rear, formed part of the underbody aerodynamics to produce additional downforce allowing increased cornering speeds. The design of the under floor venturi structures was regulated by the mandatory minimum flat surface underneath the car of 1000mm wide and 800mm long and Tony Southgate extended this area to surround both front wheels with a contoured outer edge to give enough clearance for the wheels to steer. The greater the differential between this lower pressure area underneath the race car and the atmospheric pressure above it, the higher the 'downforce' created. These tunnel structures could not be sealed to the road surface with sliding skirts as had once been the practice in Formula One.

To assist this area and reduce air 'bleed' from the outside of the race car to the negative pressure areas underneath, Tony Southgate fitted small horizontal plates attached on both sides to the lower sills externally from behind the front wheel arch all the way to the rear wheels. These would act in a similar fashion to a Gurney flap preventing air flowing from the high pressure upper external side surface of the bodywork from trying to flow to the lower pressure venturi area underneath the race car. The path of this air flow would be over these 50mm wide plates thus resisting its flow, and producing some downforce in the process. These side mounted strips fitted within the mandatory 2000mm maximum width as the XJR-6 had started life 100mm narrower than the maximum allowed to reduce the frontal area and reduce drag.

The front wheels were completely contained within the bodywork and the XJR-6 was the only sports car to do this at the time. Other designs featured a tapered exit from behind the rear of the front wheels venting air in the front wheel arch area to reduce lift and counteract understeer. Louvers were later fitted to the top of the front wheel arches to assist in venting the air forced into this area from brake ducting.

All the rear mechanical components excluding the rear wheels were covered with a single piece of detachable bodywork incorporating the engine air intake. The shape of this engine cover was used to present the air flow towards the large, centrally mounted two element rear wing. It also controlled the air flow behind the rear wheels and surrounding the venturi tunnel exits. The rear wing's position relative to the engine cover was the result of wind tunnel testing of the 25% scale model and had the twin functions of producing downforce from the air flowing over it as well as ensuring a negative pressure was created directly behind where the rear tunnels exited, improving their performance.

The only disruptions to air flow in the detachable floor underbody tunnel area were the two lower suspension wishbones and driveshafts. The leading forward edges of the tunnels were later fixed shapes moulded into the floor of the rear section of the carbon tub. The rear suspension's shock absorber and spring assemblies were attached to the outer ends of an aluminium beam mounted transversely over the gearbox and formed the top mounting points for the shock absorber/spring assembly. These shock absorber/spring assemblies were mounted within the rear wheels. Figures from the wind tunnel showed an aerodynamic downforce split of 29/71 front to rear from a total of 4415lbs at 200mph [320kph] with a lift over drag figure of 3.23. These figures were scaled up from those delivered by the 25% scale model in the rolling floor wind tunnel at Imperial College.

*Rear suspension and mounting beam with underbody venturi section removed.*

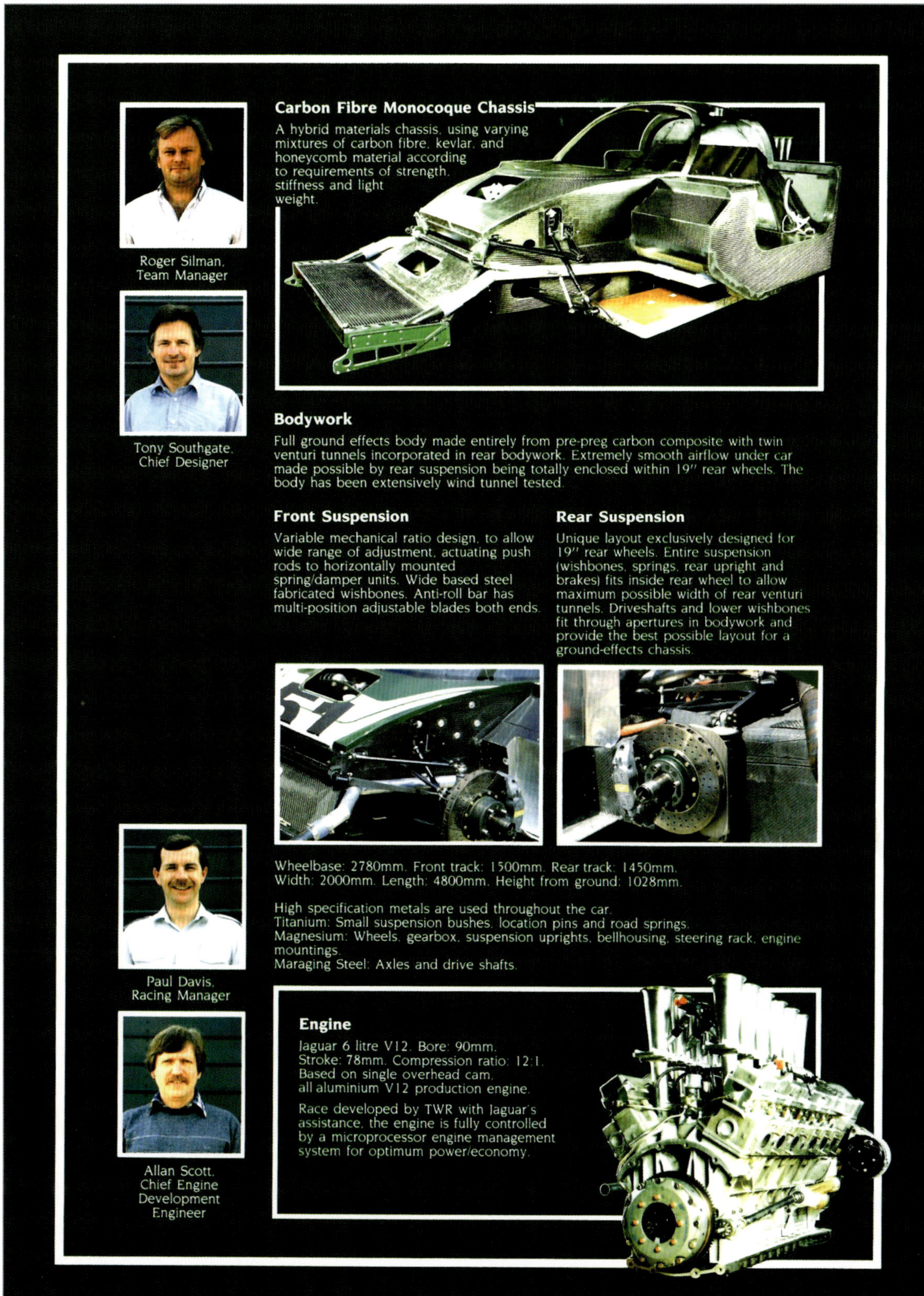

Roger Silman, Team Manager

Tony Southgate, Chief Designer

Paul Davis, Racing Manager

Allan Scott, Chief Engine Development Engineer

**Carbon Fibre Monocoque Chassis**

A hybrid materials chassis, using varying mixtures of carbon fibre, kevlar, and honeycomb material according to requirements of strength, stiffness and light weight.

**Bodywork**

Full ground effects body made entirely from pre-preg carbon composite with twin venturi tunnels incorporated in rear bodywork. Extremely smooth airflow under car made possible by rear suspension being totally enclosed within 19" rear wheels. The body has been extensively wind tunnel tested.

**Front Suspension**

Variable mechanical ratio design, to allow wide range of adjustment, actuating push rods to horizontally mounted spring/damper units. Wide based steel fabricated wishbones. Anti-roll bar has multi-position adjustable blades both ends.

**Rear Suspension**

Unique layout exclusively designed for 19" rear wheels. Entire suspension (wishbones, springs, rear upright and brakes) fits inside rear wheel to allow maximum possible width of rear venturi tunnels. Driveshafts and lower wishbones fit through apertures in bodywork and provide the best possible layout for a ground-effects chassis.

Wheelbase: 2780mm. Front track: 1500mm. Rear track: 1450mm.
Width: 2000mm. Length: 4800mm. Height from ground: 1028mm.

High specification metals are used throughout the car.
Titanium: Small suspension bushes, location pins and road springs.
Magnesium: Wheels, gearbox, suspension uprights, bellhousing, steering rack, engine mountings.
Maraging Steel: Axles and drive shafts.

**Engine**

Jaguar 6 litre V12. Bore: 90mm. Stroke: 78mm. Compression ratio: 12:1. Based on single overhead cam, all aluminium V12 production engine.

Race developed by TWR with Jaguar's assistance, the engine is fully controlled by a microprocessor engine management system for optimum power/economy.

*The Group C promotional document featuring Roger Silman, Tony Southgate, Paul Davis and author Allan Scott.*

JAGUAR

## Chapter Five

# TWR's first prototype comes together

**All detailed engine concepts had been left to us at Engs but official credence had to be given to Jaguar's input as this was part of the marketing package that supported engineering excellence as the initial XJR-5 testing proceeded. Jaguar were not involved in concept design or carried out any testing or engine development at Coventry during the entire period of using the V12 engine in Group C.**

The additional weight of the 4-valve engine of 20kgs as well as the inability to rectify casting problems with some head failures after machining was not going away in time leading to my rethink of the situation.

There was also my Lucas problem to be resolved with Jaguar and I was never sure if Engs could still count on TW's support in my quest to stay with the small Zytek electronics company; whose two owners just happened to be former top Lucas electronic engineers. Jaguar wished to use its traditional British suppliers with Dunlop and soon Castrol being involved. Jaguar wanted electronics company Lucas with their new engine management system to complete the trio of suppliers. In an ironic twist this system had grown out of an earlier conversation with Zytek owner Bill Gibson and Lucas personnel on future sequential engine management concepts. The Lucas Micos system worked well but had taken nearly two years to get from drawing board to this point and was quite bulky with separate systems for fuel and ignition. It had taken six months to rectify an HT interference problem while testing was carried out in the USA with Group 44, but the system had now been sorted and proved superior to the 48mm IDA carburettor system that was used by Group 44 in the IMSA series up 'til 1984. The two Lucas Micos units were also in the process of being amalgamated into one unit.

TW and I then attended a meeting with Lucas director David Andrews, also a racing driver and enthusiast, at Lucas after a presentation of their sequential Lucas Micos system at Kidlington. Hardware and technical support was offered at this meeting by Lucas and I had begun to make myself unpopular in my stance supporting Zytek.

I have no doubt that had Lucas offered money as well as their system and technical support that TW would have handed this area over to them. I however felt it was vital to remain totally in control of this important aspect and not become mired with a reduction in flexibility and increased communication confusion. On the other hand, I also knew TW's thought processes by now and guessed his instincts had the need for someone or something to blame if things did not work out as well as expected. Lucas could cover both aspects; need for a paid source in electronic engine management – or excuse if things did not work out fuel economy wise.

For me having to work within a large company's committee and political processes would be an outcome that would have produced frustration and friction with me wanting to lead that programme. I had watched the

Jaguar/Group 44/Lucas interaction over the development of the system and knew I did not have the patience to work within a long winded reporting structure. That was my problem, not the actual engine management hardware.

Jaguar meetings at Browns Lane were asking for increased co-operation between the two sports car teams as they were now paying for much of the engineering in 1985. They obviously felt there should be no secrets between the two teams, we should help each other was their logical conclusion. This aim was becoming increasingly difficult for me to work with, given the reporting system and progress meetings at Jaguar, especially as I was aware of the progress of TWR's own plans at the time. Strangely, TW was happy to not attend many of the Coventry meetings at that time! The synergies between IMSA and Group C engine development became less obvious over time, and the philosophy of the two teams was quite different. Bob Tullius and Group 44 were happy to do Jaguar's bidding – Tom Walkinshaw was not.

Our engine capacity was not limited in Group C, IMSA was limited to 6500cc. Group C fuel had a specified type and lower 105 RON octane rating (soon to be reduced further), and IMSA used up to 116 octane racing fuel. Group C was limited to a fuel consumption of 51 litres per 100kms; IMSA had no fuel consumption limits. Our engine in Tony Southgate's design needed to be a stressed member, meaning it was used as a support beam for the car's rear frame work to help reduce weight; the Group 44 XJR-5 was a semi-stressed member. IMSA weight limits were up to 950kgs, whereas Group C was much lighter at 850kgs.

With TWR now intending to build its own car, with its own money, both teams were going in separate directions. The move to be independent and number one for Jaguar was always going to be TWR policy; it would not be a joint racing partner with Group 44 in its relationship with Jaguar.

Four weeks after the initial XJR-5 testing started TWR announced that it would not be competing at Le Mans with the Group 44 race car, leaving Group 44 to compete for a second time in that event. Our efforts would be focused into the new Tony Southgate carbon fibre Group C race car from now on.

After continued supply and quality problems with the 4-valve heads and the XJR-5 testing just going through an evaluation situation until TWR's new car arrived it was now necessary for a complete review of the engine philosophy. I contacted Cosworth, well known for its 4-valve Formula One technology, and obtained a quote to carry out a complete design, casting and proof machining of heads for the V12 engine and put this proposal to TW. He rejected it out of hand as it was very expensive, £500,000. I was now forced to reassess the way forward and we commenced the building of a prototype two valves per cylinder engine. This decision was taken without consultation with Jaguar and included a political dimension of my own in an attempt to avoid the issue with the Lucas engine management system which was arguably tied to the 4-valve design. With TW not raising the matter of what engine management system we would use with this different engine the subject was avoided; and an interim Zytek system was then used on this non-Jaguar financed project. I however was committed to the concepts and agreements with Zytek that involved unique product support in software development, as well as gaining experience in systems programming and calculations that had started in 1984.

With Zytek we were able to introduce new ideas for control situations using the unique software written by partner Brian Mason, who was arguably the most successful engine management software engineer in the UK at that time. This would give us benefits with huge potential in the fuel restricted Group C programme.

A proven relationship already existed with this small flexible organisation that had given vital support over the previous two years to TWR's Group A racing programmes, starting with analogue and then progressing to digital systems. By 1985 they were getting their company Zytek to a position where they were fully capable of supporting the high technology requirements of modern Group C racing. This in-house technology allowed us at Engs to react to our own timescales and demands in engine digital reprogramming.

I then made the decision to develop a two-valves per cylinder engine of 6232cc, using existing components but with new pistons based on an evolution of the Group A design. This concept involved vertical valves with a flat head surface and the combustion chamber or 'bowl' in the piston with squish lands in close near contact with the flat head face. The fitting of modified Jaguar 2-valve flat face heads was to be the quickest and safest way forward. This engine would be designed initially to fit the Tony Southgate designed TWR chassis only, as a complete stressed member, in the process making it a unique mounting and load bearing solution for that particular car.

The first prototype 2-valve engine used standard Jaguar heads fitted with 46mm inlet and 38mm exhaust valves gas flowed by George Toth at Richard Longman and Co. in the Dorset town of Christchurch. The modifications were restricted by a lack of metal in the inlet port and valve seat areas, especially the short radius turn to the inlet valve throat.

Jaguar however had already been working with Group 44 on production of some thick wall castings for the IMSA regulations and this had progressed with Group 44's introduction of USA head flow specialist Robert Tarozzi. We were not party to this parallel development for use in the IMSA programme.

Internal discussions with Jaguar's development engineer Frank Philpott demonstrate how these developments take time to co-ordinate within large company structures, and Group 44 accepted these timelines. The Tarozzi head development programme started in late 1983 and then produced results in mid-1985 that they were still not happy with. TWR was not copied with the minutes of these meetings and it shows that Jaguar themselves were investigating two separate head design options; with the USA team seeing problems with the 4-valve head route.

A first set of new experimental Tarozzi 2-valve head castings had finally been produced at Jaguar and these now had my interest. While these heads were not significantly different, they included a raised exit D shaped exhaust port, and the increased amounts of material around both port areas was a vital addition with some changes to water transfer in the exhaust port area. This allowed experimental air flow without the previous concern of breaking through into water jackets as was the problem with the standard heads.

**Minutes Of The Meeting Held on 11th April 1984 To Discuss Jaguar Engineering Procurement Assistance to Group 44.**

Present:
D.B. Scholes ) Jaguar
T.D. Seal )
R.C. Tullius )
L. Foushee ) Group 44
G. Eischen )
J. Baker )

This meeting was convened in order to discuss Group 44's requirement for UK sourced racing components and Jaguar's assistance for the remainder of 1984.

Unless otherwise stated, all action on the following items is required by Jaguar Engineering Procurement Dept.

Action/ Date Req.

1. Two Valve Cylinder Heads

Three different specification cylinder heads were currently under supply consideration to Group 44.

i) Standard thin-wall casting with Philpott inlet port and AFR exhaust port. Currently the best proven cylinder head. Five pair of these heads were required urgently for Le Mans engines. — 1st May

ii) As above, but with thick wall casting. Cylinder head not yet fully proven. Some doubt remaining on coolant flow and overheating. Three pairs of these heads to be progressed with lower priority. — Mid May

iii) 'Tarozzi' designed cylinder head. Two pair to be progressed a.s.a.p. — June

2. Crankshaft

Four crankshafts to current developed condition in EN40 material being progressed — 1st May ✓

One crankshaft with further weight reduction of 4 lbs had just been delivered to Group 44. This crankshaft was to

*The minutes of April 11th 1984 show how long this head development process had been going on without a final solution.*

Mr Tarozzi was not completely happy with the outcome of the first castings and Group 44 agreed that they would wait for the better situation that Tarozzi wanted. I had been at a meeting where discussions took place about this and said nothing as it was assumed we were not interested. Afterwards I quickly discussed the situation in confidence with our Jaguar procurement person, Tom Seal, asking about the possibility of Engs having access to these six sets of casting that had been paid for out of the Group 44/Jaguar budget allowance, but no longer wanted by them. He immediately had a pair machined for us using the same valve and seat sizes from our production modified heads to save time, and fitting our 92mm bore size. These heads, when reworked by George Toth at Longman's on his flow bench worked well and provided an immediate power increase of 20bhp.

First indications on fuel consumption with this set-up looked quite good. It was commonly accepted that racing engines with 4-valve heads running at speeds of 9000/10,000rpm returned specific fuel consumptions

(SFC) of just under 0.5 pint of fuel to run 1 hp for one hour (pints/hp/hour) when using mechanical fuel injection. Our first fuel test showed that we were under this initial target.

The all up weight of these first 2-valve race engines was 255kg with all electronics and clutch, but not exhaust; a fully dressed standard Jaguar V12 engine with air conditioning pump was 300kgs. So far our race economy data had been limited to computer modelling by Jaguar's Peter Lings, the results from Group 44's Le Mans effort, and some testing at Silverstone with the Group 44 XJR-5 in Martin Brundle's hands.

The bulky V12 was a large departure from conventional Group C wisdom at the time, and I needed some rapid answers to allay increasing fears from TW with his preference for a Jaguar 3.2-litre straight six turbocharged engine. While we could measure the fuel consumption against power output, we were not sure at this stage just how long the throttle would be held wide open during each lap of the different race circuits and so indicate the amount of fuel that would be used over the race distance. We would not have a good set of figures until we were actually on the track testing the efficiency of the car as well.

The following is a first brief to try and explain where the engine programmes were by the middle of 1985 using Zytek's conventional double shot injection system. It was assumed by me, but not proven at this point; that this double shot injection system over the full four-cycle period of 720° had the potential to waste fuel by crossing it straight to the exhaust system when using long valve timing periods and high valve overlap openings. One injection period was timed with the inlet valve closed and the second with the inlet valve open over the 720° cycle. It was the fuel from the first injection period that was exposed to the still closing exhaust valve as the inlet valve was opening that was the potential problem.

TW and Roger were concerned and Tony Southgate had said from the very start, "You don't expect to win with that thing in the back, do you?". The report I then wrote to TW and Roger was an attempt to convey the results of our initial dynamometer tests after some exhaust tuning and give them some confidence in a situation they both had many concerns about; they were afraid of making a very public mistake.

It was turbocharged engines that were being used by the opposition of Porsche, and Lancia with their Ferrari

*Engs prototype two valves per cylinder 6232cc V12 engine, 1985.*

engine. They simply had the boost turned down by the driver when consumption was above the target, or turned up if they were under it. This was considered the way to go at this time allowing flexibility as situations changed during a race, and Porsche was seen by all, including TW, as the engine technology leader. I attempted to show with my report that the V12 engine could also produce some flexibility with the use of differing rpm bands.

Using modified standard Jaguar 2-valve heads, dynamometer testing had shown that a wide-open throttle would on average consume 150 litres of fuel per hour, at 5500 to 7000rpm, equating to an average of 615bhp. With an allowance of 85 litres per hour our race car could be on wide open throttle for around 57% of each lap during a 1000km six hour race; not too bad a place to start with from a first attempt.

## Memo to Tom Walkinshaw and Roger Silman on our progress at Engs in developing a fuel efficient V12 engine

### MEMO

| From | To |
|---|---|
| ALLAN SCOTT | T WALKINSHAW<br>R SILMAN |
| Our Reference: AS/DMR — Your Reference: | 17.6.85 19........ |

RESULTS FROM 2ND ENGINE TESTED

Inlet ports taper from 38mm at face to 36mm at valve guide. As opposed to straight 38mm. Cam phase angle from 100° to 102°.
New throttle slide intakes.
Modified standard heads with inlet port angle of 48° as opposed to TARROZI heads of 45°

This set-up gave slight power gains from 4500 RPM to 5000 RPM down 1% to 5750 and from then down 2%; giving 662 BHP at 7000 but still increasing.

The S.F.C. figures have become much more uniform across the range with the above specification and attention to detail on fuel and ignition. The figure of .45 S.F.C., considered to be the target of an efficient engine is exceeded by 2% to 3% up to 6500 RPM and is .447 at 7000 RPM.

On continuous running at full load, this engine consumes:

117 litres per hour at 500 BHP
136 litres per hour at 550 BHP
144 litres per hour at 600 BHP
163 litres per hour at 650 BHP

Using a rev band of 1250 RPM the following is a chart of average HP in that band and average fuel consumed with the throttle open 100% of the time.

| BAND | AV. HP. | AV.FUEL CONSUMED | INCREASE AV. H.P. | INCREASE AV. FUEL CON. |
|---|---|---|---|---|
| 4500-5750 | 524 | 126 Litres | | |
| 4750-6000 | 545 | 131 Litres | 21(4%) | 5 Ltrs (4%) |
| 5000-6250 | 565 | 137 Litres | 20(3.8%) | 6 Ltrs (4 1/4%) |
| 5250-6500 | 586 | 143 Litres | 23(3 3/4%) | 6 Ltrs (4 1/4%) |
| 5500-6750 | 604 | 148 Litres | 18(3%) | 5 Ltrs (3½%) |
| 5750-7000 | 620 | 152.6 Litres | 16 (2 3/4%) | 4 3/4 Ltrs (3%) |

The above graph shows that for an increase of 250 RPM in the rev band approximately 20 BHP increase occurs with an increase of 4% in fuel consumption.

Using the same gearing, i.e. coming out of the corners at the same RPM and pulling the same RPM down the straight, an increase in the rev limit in the gears of 500 RPM will increase the fule consumption in the region of 5%.

The engine has the flexibility to run from 525 BHP average to 625 BHP average and a fuel consumption change from one extreme to the other of 21%.

ALLAN SCOTT

As can be seen from the above figures the most efficient usage of fuel for power output occurs at 5750 R.P.M.
Maximum torque occurs at 5250-5500 but the engine consumes 1% less fuel at 5500, so the gearing should be arranged so that when changing up, the engine starts in the next gear at 5500 R.P.M. i.e. if a rev limit of 6250 R.P.M. is used the gap between the gears should be 750 R.P.M. The engine can still cope with slower exit speeds down to 4500 very well because of its flat torque curve, but the speed range of 5000-5250 has an average S.F.C. of .4735 whilst the speed range 5500 - 5750 has an average S.F.C. of .435 or, 9% MORE FUEL EFFICIENT.

Speed Range 5000 - 6000
-5½% Average H.P. 563
Average litres per hour 144.8

5250-6250
0% Average H.P. 588
Average litres per hour 150.2

5500-6250
0% (1) Average H.P. 600
Average litres per hour 151
5250-6500
Average H.P. 600
Average litres per hour 151

5500-6500
+3% (2) Average H.P. 611
Average litres per hour 156

5500-6750
+6% (3) Average H.P. 620
Average litres per hour 159.6

5500-7000
+8% (4) Average H.P. 628
Average litres per hour 163.4

The conclusion is that little can be gained by lowering the rev. limit to lower the fuel consumption and a replica specification smaller capacity engine would be needed.

ALLAN SCOTT

*Note the higher fuel consumption figures close to maximum torque. The tuned exhaust system produces its maximum resonance effect in this area, suggesting some injected fuel could be being drawn down the exhaust system rather than staying in the cylinder.*

*Normally best power is produced at close to 4 to 4.4% Co or 12.8 to 13:1 air-fuel ratios. These tests were carried out using air fuel tail pipe ratios of 13 to 13.5:1 with best power for fuel economy in mind.*

## Second generation engine specification

The second generation V12 engine began development in mid-1985, designed from the start as a 'stressed' unit forming part of the beam or bridge structure that attached the rear transaxle and suspension to the rear of the tub. The engine was mounted to the rear bulkhead at three separate points using two fixings each. The lower engine mounting was a magnesium bracket bonded into the rear of the tub with the engine's magnesium sump bolted to it, the midpoint mountings in sheer attached to the front of the cam covers, each at 30°. Two struts mounted from the top of the internal roll hoop were attached to the rear of the camshaft covers and an additional pair of tubes either side were bolted lower to outer points of the bulkhead and connected back to the gearbox bell housing, completing the vertical and horizontal triangulation of the design.

A Hewland based 5-speed gearbox that had been developed by March Engineering for the uneven firing turbocharged Buick V6 in America was chosen to work with the V12 engine.

At my insistence in late 1984, Jaguar had modified pattern work to produce and machine a V12 block casting that would take the production AJ6 six-cylinder single piece Teflon rear main seal. After casting and machining problems this vital upgrade to the V12 block finally became available to us in April of 1985, and was later put into production on all V12 engines, one instance where racing does improve the breed. Apart from the pistons all internal features of the base 6232cc V12 engine were the same for both 2- and 4-valve engines.

Although flexing with this production sand cast block was not accurately known at this time, we were reasonably happy with the inherent strength from the basic tests we carried out. Our sump closed and stiffened the 'open box' nature of the V12 blocks lower skirt and removed most of the twisting stresses from the crankshaft tunnel bore area. A total of seven, four bolt steel main caps retained the crankshaft and completed the bridging and strengthening of the crankshaft area of the block. With the possibility of twisting during high cornering loads producing some friction, the normal 0.002in to 0025in main bearing to crankshaft clearance was increased to 0.003in to 0.0035in.

The engine had been engineered to sit as low as possible and have three oil-scavenge points from the side. Even with the narrow 60° V-angle of the block assisting the exit of the exhaust primary pipes, the large chassis venturi tunnels still encroached on this space at the rear of the engine and made lowering the V12 any further impractical. The alternator was driven by its own toothed belt from the water pump pulley and was fitted on the right-hand side because the two tunnels took up all the available space around the 300mm/12in wide lower skirt of the V12 block. The tunnels tapered downward towards the front of the engine, allowing space at the front for the external oil pump on the left-hand side and the remote mounted starter motor on the right. The starter motor was attached to a shaft that travelled the length of the engine block, machined to give clearance to the tunnels, travelling rearwards to engage the ring gear.

A new EN40B crankshaft forging was produced by the standard Jaguar processes for production at Smith Clayton Forging with allowances made to cover future changes in bearing sizes and stroke. Using this process meant that a minimum of 85 forgings had to be made at one time with the new EN40 material. Peter Lings of Jaguar was tasked with producing a machining drawing for a new lightweight eight-counterbalanced crankshaft with a 78.5mm stroke to my specifications. These included the redesigned rear seal area and flywheel attaching points, standard 3in main journal diameters, but the standard 2.3in big end journals now reduced to 2.1in machined to take Chevrolet V8 big end bearings and standard Jaguar main bearings. The big end journals were hollowed out and plugged producing a finished item much lighter than the standard production 5.3-litre unit.

Both Cosworth steel and JET (USA) titanium connecting rods were used at this time based on the Chevrolet 6in V8 connecting rod.

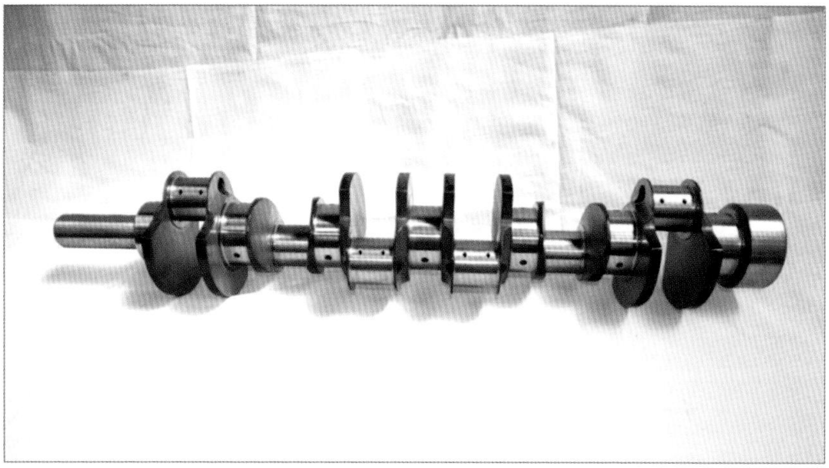

*EN40B forged crankshaft 12kgs lighter than the Standard 5.3-litre car unit.*

Cosworth produced the 92mm forged 3-ring pistons to Engs specifications with piston bowl shapes from the lessons learned with the previous Group A engines, larger and deeper valve cut outs being the main changes to the crown area. These first engines had a compression ratio of 11.8:1.

## Head gasket

One of the problems that had surfaced with the V12 engine had been the effective sealing of the head gasket area and this had been an ongoing problem with the Group 44 engines in long distance races. This had been brought under control in the Group A V12 engines with our own design of special one piece head gasket in association with Coopers Payen and able to withstand a cylinder Brake Mean Effective Pressure (BMEP) of 12 bars. (This head gasket design later became standard on all the evolution production 6-litre V12 engines fitted in Jaguar production: yet again, racing improves the breed.)

We had to rethink this area with the anticipated increased BMEP of 15 bars in Group C. The cast iron liner is a slip fit in the aluminium block, and with the different thermal expansion at operating temperatures the cast iron liner becomes a looser fit expanding at a lesser rate than the aluminium of the block. The liner movement is held in place when sitting on its mounting flange in the block by the head gasket sealing ring. Higher than production designed rpm, along with piston thrust on the compression stroke trying to push the slip fitting liner upwards, and firing loads reversing the thrust downwards leads to constant repetitive loading on the sealing ring of the head gasket from the liner.

Added to this is the difference in expansion between the iron liner and the aluminium block it sits in, reducing the clamping load slightly between liner and head gasket eyelet at operating temperatures. This could lead to combustion leakage into the cooling system and eventual loss of coolant. The attraction of staying with slip fit liners was simply one of efficient repair, with any damaged cylinders being easily replaced, eliminating the down time repair as we had no in-house machining facilities at Engs. Spare liners could be honed and placed in stock, giving better rebuild turn-around times.

Richard Weatheral of Coopers Payen had produced a very good improved one-piece head gasket for the Group A XJS V12 engine but we now needed something different again. In the interim while Richard finalised the design of the next generation of head gasket system, we used gas filled Wills O-rings as used by most engine builders at the time. The second generation head gasket consisted of 12 separate sealing rings and a one-piece outer water sealing gasket. It involved a redesign of the cylinder liner machined from a blank casting extended to protrude above the block top surface by 0.046in. This was 0.002in less than the thickness of the new perimeter water sealing gasket and it allowed the liner top face to just be in contact with the head when tightened down.

Richard Weatheral's solution consisted of a standalone triple wrap sealing ring design fitted in a 2mm deep channel machined into the new liner design's top flange face. With the sealing rings internal diameter of 98mm, and using a 92mm piston, a 3mm wide inner liner top face was produced along with engagement from the outer portion of the liner. These individual sealing rings, made from stainless steel were very robust with an internal corrugated feature that allowed the sealing ring to be compliant in compression by up to 0.004in. This liner was now positively located both at its top by the head and sealing ring and in its mid-section seated on the block mounting flange. A secondary benefit with the inner cylinder liner touching the head would be the elimination of any droplets of fuel that may accumulate in that area when using a standard head gasket configuration that could lead to end gas detonation. At this time both aluminium and cast iron liners were being trialled.

*Aluminium liner from GKN.*

*Richard Wetheral of Coopers Payen demonstrates the perimeter gasket while author Allan Scott holds the three-compound sealing rings.*

The theoretical calculations for correct sealing ring channel 'depth' in the top face of the liner was reduced in practice by 0.004in to add pre-load to the head face and allow for expansion differentials of iron and aluminium when hot. The liner also pushed into the block when the sealing rings were loaded as the heads were torqued down. An interesting feature of this system was that it had also been used on the Cooper Climax Formula One engine that had been developed by Walter Hassan, the father of the production Jaguar V12 engine, and here we were carrying on this concept with the new V12 race programme.

Later as a fine-tuning method for the complete system two different thicknesses of the perimeter water sealing gasket we made to fine tune the loading on the liner sealing rings. The heads were lightly torqued to 15lbs/ft without the outer sealing gaskets fitted, and feeler gauges used to measure the gap between the outer head surface and the block perimeter. The head was then removed and the correct thickness perimeter gasket, 0.002in greater than the measured gap fitted and the head torqued to the correct settings. This process provided the correct loading balances on the liner sealing rings and the water sealing perimeter gasket, and all loadings were to a tolerance of 0.002in.

One of the main restrictions to high power outputs with this 2-valve concept now revolved around the need of the higher valve lift with the much larger valve diameters. Both Harrison and Crane valve springs were used in these early prototypes. Valve springs for the intended high lift camshaft profile were restricted by the camshaft centreline, and having to sit inside the inverted tappet bucket. This limitation would not be as reliable as using lower lift four valves per cylinder technology with their spring specifications widely available and able to be safely housed within their inverted bucket design.

First attempts to improve this area saw the fitting of an aluminium spacer plate between the standard camshaft carrier and the head face. The timing chain had four extra links added to accommodate the raised camshaft heights and maintain its tensioner in the correct operating range. The timing chain tensioner used came from that developed for the Group A V12 engine and had a special wound spring as the standard units had a tendency to break.

Steel camshafts were machined from solid EN24 and profile ground at Reece Cams with a 74° half period and 0.610in gross lift, based on a Cosworth profile designated EA5.The camshaft design included a base circle radius increased to 0.7in (standard 0.5in) to produce a larger lobe profile with greater definition and increased nose radius. With its relatively narrow valve timing the profile needed very high valve accelerations up to 0.010 per degree, producing a valve gear design limitation in this engine of 8000rpm.

With the friction of twelve pistons and seven crankshaft main bearings, the Jaguar 2-valve engine would have to find more power and efficiency at lower rpms than a more conventional race engine of this capacity would normally use.

The first engine was fitted with a throttle butterfly system supplied by Group 44 using 48mm Webber throttle butterflies, although this was not intended to be the final specification. The dry sump oil system had a separate oil tank and initially used a bulky Weaver three scavenge and two pressure stage pump which with the pipe work involved produced a heavy unit. Later a very efficient and lightweight system supplied by Heidegger's in Liechtenstein replaced it.

A modified version of Zytek's one box engine management system from the Group A programme was initially used with larger fuel injectors that fired every 360° in the non-discretionary bank to bank manner as the Group A engines. Fuel pressure was progressively increased from 3 to 4 bars and a standard production V12 HE constant energy ignition system was used on the first prototype race engines.

On the dynamometer by April of 1985, with a compression ratio of 11.7:1, this first attempt produced a reasonably flat torque curve from 4500 to 6500rpm, as well as good basic fuel efficiency throughout the proposed rev range, although some fuel consumption problems existed at 5500 and 7000rpm areas.

Using a 50/50 mixture of 98 RON road fuel and leaded 100 octane aviation fuels we achieved a power output of 649bhp at 7000rpm and 545lbs/ft of torque at 5500rpm when mapped to an air/fuel ratio of 13:1. This fuel mix provided anti detonation features to allow high compression ratios and advanced ignition timings, but aviation fuel has little oxygen component added and this mixture was not an overall power enhancing fuel. The best ever figures produced by a modified standard Jaguar head engine by year's end was 660bhp at 7000rpm.

By the end of 1985 these engines were being tested at 13.5:1 air/fuel ratio with power dropping to 648bhp at 7000rpm.

A new throttle slide inlet system was then designed in an attempt to have an accurately machined system cylinder to cylinder, without the constant set-up needs of adjusting 12 butterflies exacerbated by heat soak that was bound to cause additional problems at the race track. TWR design draughtsman Russell Sharp completed this inlet detail design work using two different variations of trumpet lengths and taper to continue testing with.

As development progressed a new cam carrier was machined from solid to the new increased height with its front chain cover made as a separate piece. Larger 42mm cam-followers were fitted at the same time replacing the original 36mm Group A units, for two reasons. Firstly to allow additional room for large diameter valve springs needed with high lift camshaft profiles. Secondly the high-acceleration camshaft profiles needed to produce acceptable power outputs from only two valves per cylinder ran over the outer edges of the original follower and would produce rapid wear in the aluminium follower bores. These larger cam carriers were first tested on our dynamometer on June 13th, and continued the V12 development programme to what would be the definitive engine specification for the races later in the year.

## ZYTEK

### Development of the ground-breaking technology, sequential fuel injection

In parallel with Jaguar's Lucas engine management developments Bill Gibson and partner Brian Mason of Zytek had been asked by me to develop a new 'sequential' engine management system, allowing a single timed pulse within the induction cycle for each cylinder to suit the characteristics of the race engine, finding the best dynamic delivery position, leading to improved fuel consumption. The ignition would be upgraded too, with the Lucas CD system.

To accommodate this new system, in addition to the existing six slot Hall Effect crankshaft trigger, a sync trigger operating at half engine speed would be needed to indicate the beginning of each 12-cylinder firing cycle. This half speed signal could either be taken from the distributor drive, or off the camshaft. We decided to use a drive from the front of the left-hand camshaft with a circular disc and a single timing slot cut into it to provide the half engine speed signal, with one camshaft revolution covering the complete 12-cylinder cycle over 720°.

The new controlling software allowed this single injection pulse to be separately programmed to find the best injection period for power and economy, the software now knowing exactly where each cylinder was in its 720° four stroke cycle.

We noticed when developing exhaust resonance tuning the exhaust primary pipe and inlet system lengths, some fuel was being sucked from the inlet valve as it opened across to the exhaust valve before it could close. More fuel would have to be injected at that time to make up for the small amounts lost to the exhaust system. This effect could be seen in the fuel consumption figures, increasing around the maximum torque areas at 5000 and 5250rpm.

One way to reduce this problem was by grinding the exhaust and inlet cam lobes at a wider specific angle to each other. These changes produced improved fuel consumption at a slight cost to lower rpm power and torque, but the new Zytek system could eliminate these losses with selected fuel injection timing not just for best power, but best compromise *fuel consumption.*

The next major step in the engine management system was to look for improvement to fuel economy without sacrificing power, and Zytek had been tasked with that problem. With the basic mechanical specification and resonance tuning completed, the second generation 2-valve engine was in an advanced enough state to carry out a test programme on a sequential timed single injection pulse system. Both Bill and Brian of Zytek arrived at Kidlington to observe their new sequential engine management system fitted to our 2-valve Tarozzi headed 6232cc engine for the first time in late June 1985, just after my report to TW and Roger.

The results that day became the building blocks for closing the gap to Porsche and vindicated the move away from the complexities of the 4-valve engine as well. We had by now managed to reproduce the same power curve within 20 to 25bhp of the very first prototype Jaguar 4-valve head engine up to 7000rpm. Now, with the new experimental sequential system, the fuel could be timed to flow through the larger capacity injectors in a single shot resulting in the same power but using less fuel than the earlier double shot system, based on the production car Bosch 'L Jetronic' principle. The fact that these changes could be done electronically while the engine was still running under load was an impressive tool and amazing step forward for us, being the only race-team test-cell in the UK with this technology.

The fuel savings could be seen straight away and after two days of testing we had a 5% to 7% fuel saving for the same air/fuel ratio. The new Zytek software also included overrun fuel shut off where the fuel injectors were switched off every time the throttle was closed on the overrun into corners, and reactivated each time the throttle was opened. It also switched fuel back on at low rpm to allow the engine to idle. Whilst today this is normal for production car engines, these features were a huge step forward for racing engines at the time.

For those who have wondered how the TWR package using the V12 engine eventually dominated the Porsche team it has to be Porsche's failure to appreciate the real worth of this new electronic sequential injection technology. Porsche would continue to use their production based Bosch double pulse 'L Jetronic' non-sequential system in the 956B and new 962C variants for the next two years, although it was said later that this was because of budgetary constraints.

Bosch produced its excellent MP1.7 sequential system one year later in 1986 specifically designed for turbo engine applications and this system would be first used by the Sauber Mercedes team in 1987. The Porsche factory team in 1985 was looking to improve fuel economy by using their usual 2.8-litre flat-six but with increased capacity to three litres. The reduced fuel allowance forced Porsche to move from safe rich, cooler fuel settings to leaner settings requiring additional water cooling around the valves.

On the plus side, the vent slots cut into the underbody of the 956 to feed the cooling fan would not now be needed eliminating a source of interference to their under floor aerodynamics. Most of the private teams would continue with the original 2.8-litre air-cooled version from the factory for 1985.

After completion of the initial wind tunnel testing on the 25% scale model at the Imperial College London, the first all-carbon Group C car was assembled in John Thompson's premises. Final assembly was standing room only around the car with many of the small parts being hand fabricated on this first build without drawings. TW, Roger and I had then made a flying visit by helicopter to check on progress. We had landed in a car park near the building and soon after were interrupted by the irate owner of the building next door wanting to know the details of the permission given for the landing, which did not of course exist. It turned out the down draft over his building while the pilot carried out the delicate task of landing in the restricted place had blown out all the ceiling panels in his offices.

The TWR mechanics worked in shifts to complete the task of making many one-off items to fit. This car was fitted with the 6232cc fuel injected 2-valve Engs modified Tarozzi head V12 engine along with the Zytek sequential management system and the 5-speed Hewland based gearbox. This type of gearbox was considered to have a question mark over it in long distance events such as the Le Mans 24 hour race. The Porsche gearbox was a full synchromesh unit as they had felt that the dog ring type of gear selection as in the Hewland gearbox would not last these long events. Tapering of the edges of the dog rings and gears as they connected, leading to the possibility over time of jumping out of gear was behind that decision; and this was just another unknown that would have to be tested.

The short timescales for completing the new XJR-6 had put pressure on the build detail with the inevitable increases in weight as a result. The target weight of 850kgs using the 255kg V12 was only a dream at this time. On completion this first race car weighed in 100kgs over target. The XJR-6 was just 25kgs lighter than the Group 44 car that TWR had been testing, and fitted with the heavier 4-valve engine. This result was a bit embarrassing and needed to be slightly modified in reports to Jaguar after all the negative about the Group 44 XJR-5 weights earlier from us all at TWR.

**MEMO**

| From | To |
|---|---|
| ALLAN SCOTT | T WALKINSHAW<br>R SILMAN |
| Our Reference: AS/DMR — Your Reference: | 22 May 19 85 |

CONFIDENTIAL

GROUP C 2 VALVE TEST RESULTS

Jaguar V12 Engine 6222cc 92mm x 78mm.
Tarrozzi Heads, inlet 1.8", exhaust 1.450"
Steel camshafts to Cosworth EA5 profile .610/74°
Crane valve springs.
Compression Ratio 11.7 : 1
Cosworth pistons in cast iron liner.
Titanium con rods.
Coopers perimeter head gasket with Wills gas filled bore sealing ring.

The engine was tested on load for 8 hours, over a period of 4 days. The power and fuel consumption figures were taken after 7 hours.

| R.P.M. | H.P. | CO% | LITRES PER HOUR | TORQUE FT/LBS | S.F.C. PINTS/H.P./HOUR |
|---|---|---|---|---|---|
| 4500 | 459 | 2.0 | 2.0 | 522 | .463 |
| 4750 | 482 | 2.6 | 122 | 533 | .445 |
| 5000 | 513 | 3.0 | 138 | 538 | .473 |
| 5250 | 541 | 3.2 | 146 | 541 | .474 |
| 5500 | 567 | 2.8 | 143 | 541 | .443 |
| 5780 | 584 | 2.1 | 142 | 533 | .427 |
| 6000 | 612 | 3.0 | 155 | 535 | .445 |
| 6250 | 638 | 2.8 | 165 | 535 | .453 |
| 6500 | 653 | 3.2 | 174 | 528 | .467 |
| 6780 | 664 | 3.4 | 179 | 517 | .472 |
| 7000 | 675 | 3.4 | 186 | 506 | |

Correction over observed H.P. = 1.5%.

*The best figures seen with full power settings and using a modified Tarozzi 2-valve head.*

> *If the facts don't fit the theory, change the facts.*
>
> – Albert Einstein

*The TWR Group C team seen here at Silverstone – 1985.*
from left: *Frank Raferty, Lubor Schiller, Rod Benoist, Tony Bond, Andy Smart, Mr Bentley, Gary Davies and Kevin Lee.*

JAGUAR

## Chapter Six

# XJR-6 comes to life

**The first outing for the new XJR-6 was at Snetterton in early July with Martin Brundle and Mike Thackwell as test drivers. The Group 44 car with the 4-valve V12 was also at this test to set an evaluation base. Before the new car could venture out onto the track a problem with the steering rack was found as Mike Thackwell turned the steering from lock to lock in the garage before driving out. This was fixed as well as could be at the time, but would need a small redesign. Apart from this a successful limited shake down test was completed.**

Testing continued at Donington on July 30th with the XJR-6 and this test was a first serious look at running the car competitively to the fuel allowance. The car initially suffered from a badly vibrating rear wing and after changes were made by moving the wing forward, the testing continued without further problem. The car suffered from excessive understeer in this early test, a situation that was common in these types of sports cars but something that we had hoped to be overcome with Tony Southgate's technically advanced underbody design with increased forward centre of pressure compared to the Porsche. Very large rear wings made it difficult to have the aerodynamic centre of pressure forward enough under the regulations that governed the under floor area at the front of the chassis. A total of 86 laps were completed with the fuel target of 1.592 litres per lap. The average for this test was 1.64 litres, 4% over target. At this early stage gearing was not totally optimised and the understeer was producing a situation that did not help fuel consumption; so this result was very encouraging and helped to reduce some of TW and Roger's concerns.

*First installation of the 2-valve V12 engine in the XJR-6.*

Two engine problems appeared during these early tests, one being the high oil consumption with nearly four litres of oil being used, leading to the potential problems of having to replace oil in a race situation. Fortunately, the pit stops were two minutes long with the refuelling speed being limited by the meter supplied by the ruling body. Oil could be added after the tyres had been changed, but it was something Engs would have to

***First outing for the 2-valve 6232cc V12 Jaguar***
*Martin Brundle had spent time out from his Formula One duties to test and help develop the new Tony Southgate designed all carbon construction TWR XJR-6. The Group C team would soon have its first race at Mosport in Canada.*

*Martin seen here talking to Hans Heyer during the first test at Snetterton.*

fix. Oil contamination of the combustion process would raise the risk of random detonation resulting from the contaminated air/fuel mixture. We found a few years later when using Castrol's special XC27 that this special oil compound actually helped *reduce* detonation.

The second problem was discovered after the engine was dismantled for inspection. Some side loadings on the piston gudgeon pins had produced damaged circlips grooves to a point that they would have eventually failed. The gudgeon pins were shortened and a thin Teflon washer placed between the circlips and the pin ends. While this helped it did not cure the problem and a re-design was needed.

The Chevrolet V8 on which these connecting rods had been based had a different bank to bank offset to the Jaguar and this meant the modified Chevrolet connecting rod being used did not sit fully centrally in the piston with the Peter Lings designed crankshaft that had been based on his work with Group 44. This small offset caused the thrusting motion on the gudgeon pin that in turn damaged the circlip grooves.

In these early tests the understeer or front-end push persisted with the XJR-6. The first 25% scale wind tunnel model shows no radiator exit lip or front nose 'splitter'. Small wind tunnel models of this scale have some difficulty in recreating elements of detail. When I discussed the scaling of the near horizontal front radiator core density with Tony Southgate he confessed that it was impossible to do so with the timescales and wind tunnel time available to him at this early stage. This element had been completely eliminated from the first models. Fitting the water radiator at the front of the XJR-6 was to add forward weight for a better static balance. This radiator configuration would be subject to some aerodynamic lift from its horizontal position with air being ducted beneath the radiator core and then forced to flow at right angles through the core restriction and then upwards and outwards. With no power steering fitted Tony Southgate had decided to remove castor angle from the front suspension geometry to help reduce the steeering effort, and this in turn eliminated any camber change on turning, which did not help the understeer.

Testing at Silverstone continued and Mike Thackwell produced a lap time that was within half a second of the existing sports car lap record. These results were at the top end of expectations and TW and Roger began to relax a little more.

The under floor exit tunnels were the largest of any Group C car that competed, and it was the best technology available to TWR at the time. The McLaren Formula One team had earlier used the same wind tunnel to good effect for their MP4 ground effects Formula One car. It was early days and attention to detail in set-up and finding the best ride heights, springs and suspension settings to make the underbody aerodynamics work efficiently would take time and help reduce the understeer to an acceptable level.

The rear shock absorbers and springs were housed inside the 19in rear wheels and attached to the chassis via a long transverse aluminium mounting plate. This mounting plate was attached to the venturi tunnels at their outer ends with the forward end of the tunnels bolted to the rear of the tub structure, giving the tunnels an additional bracing feature to support this rear beam. It was felt that this rear mounting beam could still have some slight flexing under load and in doing so reduce rear roll stiffness when cornering. A small bracing bar was attached on each side to stabilise the beam ends and it was this modification that provided some help to the understeer problem by improving the rear roll stiffness.

The rear wheel covers being used were a first for sports cars in this series as well and indicated an improvement of 10% in downforce when fitted to the wind tunnel model. Some difficulties with their use during wheel changes were inevitable but a problem then surfaced with these covers rubbing on tyre sidewalls when out on the track. Bodywork movement or air trying to enter the low pressure area under the car produced problems with these items coming in contact with the tyre side walls, and this was just another detail to work through. It could also be a good opportunity to test the wind tunnel

*The carbon composite chassis showing the access panel to the fuel tanks.*

*The interior of the XJR-6 shows room for a passenger as stipulated by the Group C rules.*

*XJR-6 showing rear wheel covers and slots in engine cover for engine air intake.*

figures with back-to-back testing for lap time versus fuel economy with these wheel covers on and off, bearing in mind the large 10% improvements given them from the wind tunnel. Roger however was reluctant to do an extensive test and accepted all the results from the wind tunnel models.

After these first series of tests TW was quoted in *Autosport:*

> Now the first car is finished, and we have given it a run, we are still confident that we have a package capable of winning in the WEC as things stand. But it would be over-ambitious to expect to win this year, and one thing we cannot predict with any degree of accuracy is the level of competition in the future. We have a very clear idea of what we can achieve, but we are also aware that there will be a natural increase in their performance. The question is, how quickly and effectively will Porsche and Lancia be able to react? We do not know until we are actually operating within the competitive environment how easy, or how difficult it will be for us to make progress ourselves, so as to maintain our established competitive level.

After TW's refusal to use Jaguar's preferred XJR-5 option, better results were needed quickly to smooth over any negative reaction from Jaguar *engineering.* TW had developed a good rapport with Neil Johnson head of Jaguar's marketing division, and this allowed a more balanced atmosphere at Jaguar during the early stages of development of the XJR-6. The final five races of the 1985 Group C World Endurance Championship would be used as an information gathering exercise with two cars competing in races in Canada, Belgium, Japan and Malaysia. Travel arrangements and shipping logistics were now the next hurdle during this hectic development period with just the one race in the UK during the whole World Series.

## Images by Martin Lamb owner of the models

*Early examples of the wind tunnel models used to finalise the configuration of the XJR-6.*

*XJR-6 Le Mans model.*

*Note says 15 degree starting at Bulkhead with R185 indicating 15 degree tunnel ramp.*

*Wind tunnel experimental rear wing.*

JAGUAR

Chapter Seven

# The racing begins

## Mosport (Canada) – August 11th Our first race

**The introduction of Jaguar and TWR to the realities of the new Group C prototype sports car world was to be the Ontario Mosport circuit in Canada. This circuit had a considerable history of holding Grand Prix, CanAm and endurance races, and now notorious for the many bumps as a result of the harsh winter weather and reduced maintenance. The age of new generation sports cars had arrived with underbody aerodynamic features that needed stiffer suspension systems to attain stability and this track surface led to different suspension set-up needs. All of our testing and set-up conclusions had been carried out on the more modern smoother circuits used by Formula One, and this problem of an undulating and bumpy tight circuit added to the mix of first race problems with new cars. Adding even more pressure was the fact that the second car to be driven by Jean-Louis Schlesser/Hans Heyer had been sent to Canada without even turning a wheel! Schlesser had never sat in the car or indeed ever driven a Jaguar XJR-6 or any other sports car until the Friday of qualifying; he ended up setting fifth fastest time, overall!**

The factory Rothmans Porsche 962C team had the top recognised sports car drivers of the time in Derek Bell/Hans Stuck and Jacky Ickx/Jochen Mass driving race cars that were in their fourth year of development. The Kremer Barclay's Porsche team was also using the new 962C for top pairing Marc Surer/Manfred Winklehock, as well as their older 956B. Although many of the regular competitors did not make the more expensive journey to Canada, other entrants were the Chevrolet powered Sauber C9, March Porsche 83G as well as a host of smaller class C2 cars that also ran in these races. The factory Lancia had not made the trip to Canada.

The consensus at the time was that you had to be turbocharged for best engine efficiency and economy, as well as having the added benefit of the ability to turn the boost up or down to correct fuel consumption on the run. To 99% of the pundits at this time TWR/Engs had the wrong package, not only would it be a long uphill battle to close the gap to Porsche with its four-year head start, it would be an impossible one with the normally aspirated Jaguar based engine package.

Porsche competitions director Peter Falk gave the team some much needed respect at Mosport with his quotes of: "Don't they sound wonderful, just listen, that's a nice noise, reminds me of our 917s."

After qualifying he also admitted "... they have surprised us a lot. We thought that they would be fast, but the lap times are better than we expected. This circuit is hard on cars, if they can finish – well that would be particularly fine."

*Porsche boss Peter Falk*

As a debut it was a good outcome for TWR with Martin Brundle showing his many talents in securing the third fastest qualifying time behind the factory Porsches and ahead of the Kremer cars; and just 0.5 of a second behind the fastest qualifying time set by top driver Stefan Bellof the previous year.

The XJR-6s were experiencing front tyre problems with continued understeer and at this rate of consumption meant that there would be a tyre shortage before the end of the race. Late delivery to Mosport of new wider front tyres was a good effort by Dunlop's Bill Mack and these helped the understeer problem, producing a more stable race set-up. Getting tyres to last was a problem for all at this circuit and there were not enough of the new fronts for both Jaguar cars. Schlesser set a time one second slower than Brundle in the second car with the narrower front tyre. The real problem though was the hasty build process and playing safe with many items that had led to a final all up racing weight of close to 960kgs for the XJR-6 at Mosport; some 70kgs heavier than the factory Porsches which at 890kgs were themselves 35 to 40kgs over the minimum weight limit. No cars however had been able to get down to the 850kg limit up to this point.

Racing two cars to a fuel allowance was new to all the TWR team and Roger and I were still making this up on the morning of the race after all the teething problems. Having looked at the race plan it had to be done again as Roger had missed the extra warm up and slow down laps leading to the fuel allowance per race lap having to be reduced even further, not something we needed at all.

At the start Brundle who shot to the front of the 1000km race and led for the first nine laps, started the Jaguar story in fine style. This could not continue though and a degrading left front wheel bearing meant brake pad knock off problems and Martin had to pit, giving up the lead to Hans Stuck. Perhaps the wider front tyres on this car being used for the first time had produced the extra loading that caused the bearing failure. This front bearing system would need a rethink on returning to Kidlington.

The race for the second car had not been without its problems which included changing a front brake caliper, but over the six hours other race cars had some problems as well. Six hours later, with Martin Brundle and Mike Thackwell transferred to the second car with Jean-Louis Schlesser, the Jaguar claimed the lower spot on the podium having completed the last 40 minutes on 11 cylinders. One of the Crane valve springs being

*Hans Heyer, Martin Brundle, Mike Thackwell and Jean-Louis Schlesser.*

used could not keep up with the valve accelerations of the Cosworth EAS profile and a valve spring had broken allowing the head of the inlet valve to drop and be pushed through to the water jacket by the piston. But it was some fine driving and long hours by the team mechanics that had resulted in a third place for TWR/Jaguar on its debut.

The fact that this particular car had not even turned a wheel before being sent to Canada and was finished off in the pits was an outstanding result for the TWR team members involved and better than we could have hoped for. A great start for Jaguar and vindication for TW's stance on building a new technology race car for them that could only get better for the following year. The engine finished the race with no water but had survived, proving our enhanced head gasket system; and TWR had sent a message that the Jaguar was going to have to be taken seriously.

Unfortunately, this all came at a sad cost, after the Kremer Porsche driven by Manfred Winklehock crashed heavily at 130mph into a concrete wall. Motor racing had become increasingly safety conscious and driver safety was now much better than 10 years before. Sadly, on this occasion Manfred did not recover from his injuries and died in hospital the next day, it was a great loss of a well-respected driver.

An Air India 747 plane had been blown up not long before on its Trans-Atlantic flight and we had to all assemble at the airport the next day three hours early to go through special security checks. These World Series races now meant longer times away from the Kidlington workshop just when more time was needed at base to support them. Machining of new parts and delivery on time was our biggest problem without any facilities of our own at TWR, and Jaguar's Tom Seal was an invaluable help in this area in 1985.

## Spa (Belgium) – September 1st

The Group C race at Spa Francorchamps in Belgium started with the full complement of Group C competitors, 36 cars in total. It was obvious the Jaguar's would struggle with the large numbers of Porsches entered for this race; probably considered the most challenging of the circuits we were to race on. Brake cooling had been an issue with the XJR-6 but it surfaced at this track to the extent that some new air ducting to the front brakes was needed. Aston Martin was back for this race with their normally aspirated V8 but was no match for the Jaguar V12 which was estimated to have as much as a 120bhp advantage over them. The series had also stepped up to a new level since the previous year as three manufacturers were now competing with Lancia back for this race with two cars. This increased competition between turbocharged teams with high boost and special tyres for qualifying, culminated in a new record some three seconds faster than the previous year, set by Spa specialist Hans-Joachim Stuck in the Rothmans factory Porsche.

Martin Brundle though had almost equalled the previous year's top qualifying time by a Porsche; that time set on high boost by Thierry Boutsen. Martin's time showed his total commitment at this track being ten seconds faster than the next normally aspirated car, the Aston Martin.

With another set of qualifying tyres ready for his XJR-6, he had opened the car door and stepped out. On his way past to the back of the pit to change he quietly said, "there is only one of those in me". He was not prepared to chance his luck again and was 1.5 seconds quicker than our predicted best qualifying time. Martin went on to set fastest time in the pre-race warm up in the rain, and it was with some pride for all involved that TWR had a fast car on Dunlop wet tyres, sometimes a problem in the past at this challenging circuit with those tyres.

Race development of the XJR-6 was already well underway and the team brought some updates to improve front grip and tyre life. As well as the new wider front tyres a new nose had a moulded reverse lip in front of the radiator exit to add top surface downforce and improve air exit flow from the radiator. Added to an extended front splitter these modifications produced a small increase in drag to bring the centre of pressure further forward.

The drivers were again Brundle/Thackwell and Schlesser/Heyer, although this would be Hans Heyer's first race as he had not driven in the second car at Mosport. The race showed up the varying degrees of development that teams were at, with one anomaly being the most fuel efficient Porsche at Le Mans that year, the New Man Porsche, had the worst fuel consumption at Spa.

During the race both Lancia and Porsche teams swapped positions as drivers raced each other and established pecking orders. By 40% distance speeds were slowing as teams were forced to come back to the fuel allowance by running a full 22–24 lap stint to carefully recover the additional fuel used in the early stages of the race. Driving at high speeds to the fuel allowance was a new skill for the established drivers to get their heads around and this would improve with experience.

Incredibly during this race yet again a terrible accident occurred, this time between Germany's top driving talent Stefan Bellof who was the previous year's championship winner, and Porsche works driver Jacky Ickx. This happened on lap 78 of the eventual 122 lap race at the fast-uphill right-hand corner of Eau-Rouge. Both Porsches had touched and crashed into the barriers with the race having to be run under yellow flags until the track was cleared.

TWR Jaguar driver Mike Thackwell was a friend of Stefan Bellof, and seeing the accident and rescue attempts with the car on fire as well it was a particularly hard time for him to continue on in the race. I had been asked to talk to my fellow New Zealander over the radio as he could see that this was a serious accident each time he passed the scene, and was asking for updates on the driver's condition. Sadly, he had been killed instantly with the heavy impact. I was told by TW to keep him in the car and this led to Mike being given misleading updates by me. This was something Mike was very unhappy with after the race, as I was to, and at that time unaware of the full extent of their friendship.

It was a difficult time for Martin Brundle as well with Stefan being his team mate in the Formula One Tyrrell. When it was finally confirmed that Stefan had lost his battle for life in the circuit's medical centre, the teams all agreed to stop the race 23 laps from the end as a mark of respect. It was unbelievable that two such respected German drivers could lose their lives in such a short time.

The Lancia, driven by Wollek/Baldi/Patrese won their first Group C race for the year but sadly for them it was a hollow and subdued victory, second place went to the works Porsche of Stuck/Bell with Ludwig/Barilla third in a 956B. The second factory Lancia was fourth with the Brundle/Thackwell, Jaguar again finishing on 11 cylinders with a broken valve spring in fifth. The second Jaguar retired with handling problems.

*The XJR-6 at Spa 1985 with Lancia in front and Porsche behind.*

The Jaguars had been competitive and much needed data for fuel consumption versus speed had been obtained. These now indicated the XJR-6 would be competitive if we could run at the same weight as the Porsches, some 80kgs lighter.

In the aftermath of the Bellof incident, Ken Tyrrell declined to release any more of his Grand Prix drivers to other categories, meaning that TWR Jaguar would be without Martin Brundle, its key driver, for the rest of the season. Mike Thackwell also decided to concentrate on F3000 at this time, having a conflicting date in that series. The two combined was a big blow, not just for their speed but their combined experience of the XJR-6 when there wasn't much to start with in the fledgling team.

*Martin Brundle would leave TWR in 1985 because of his Formula One contract priorities.*

## Brands Hatch (Britain) – September 22nd

Jan Lammers from Holland and former Formula One champion Alan Jones were signed as replacement drivers for the Brands Hatch meeting just three weeks later and quickly settled in as if they had been driving them all year. Additional front downforce was used at the tight Kent circuit with a small front wing being added as well as an angled bib on either side of the front bodywork. New rear bodywork included changes to cooler ducting and reverse angled rear wheel arches to improve aerodynamics. Lowering the rear wing angle to reduce drag and improve fuel economy produced a similar time but made the car more difficult to drive. All these changes were aimed at increasing the front aerodynamic loading. The cars roll stiffness was mechanically changed by fitting shorter link bars for Brands Hatch in an attempt to have a more stable platform when cornering.

The driver pairing for Brands Hatch was Jones/Schlesser and Lammers/Heyer producing a fifth and sixth in qualifying in the 25-car field, almost three seconds slower than the high boost, qualifying tyre run by Patrese in the Lancia. Andrea de Cesaris set the second fastest time in the Cesare Fiorio run Lancia team's second car. The fastest qualifying Porsche time was set by Stuck, one second slower than the Lancias. Vern Schuppan and American Al Holbert in a short wheelbase 956 were here mainly to continue testing of Porsche's PDK semi-automatic gearbox in a racing situation.

Formula One driver Alan Jones had positive things to say about the Jaguar, having previously driven the Porsche he was able to give comparisons and this cheered up everyone in the team, his main problem being a lower steering ratio than he was use to in a Formula One car.

*Alan Jones at Brands Hatch.*

Jan Lammers had also driven the Porsche and like Jones enjoyed the lack of throttle lag and positive engine response to help control the car in the corners. He felt it was an advantage to have a set power output so that all

*A front wing and small bib strips to the outer edges of the front bodywork helped to control the understeer at Brands Hatch, but came at the cost of increased drag.*

positive adjustments in qualifying could be used in the race instead of being side tracked by high boost runs that would not contribute to a race set-up. In the last practice session while checking the race set-up and running to the fuel formula, less than a second covered the six fastest cars, with the two Jaguars in the middle of the group. It showed the progress the team was making in aerodynamic balance aided by the improved roll stiffness in only their third outing, still suffering from the weight disadvantage.

In the race the season-long Porsche/Lancia battle continued with the Jaguars running in their qualifying positions until Lammers pitted with a rear tyre losing pressure. On lap 15 Jones was in with similar problems caused by the rear wheel covers rubbing on the tyres and Jones now experienced a jammed throttle and engine over rev as he re-joined the race.

Different valve springs had been fitted to remedy the earlier problems and these had needed new top retaining caps. These had turned out to be marginal in design with one breaking when the throttles stuck open and Jones selected neutral to stop the car crashing. The long single throttle slide for each bank ran on roller bearings to very close clearances. We were not on top of the situation at the time, the temperature and dust causing a problem under racing conditions. The system would work perfectly on the assembly bench but moved when the engine expanded with heat and needed some adjustments to the design to overcome that problem. It was just another lesson to learn and a problem to fix. Lammers stopped on lap 35 with another rear puncture.

*XJR-6 leads the Lancia at Brands Hatch.*

Hans Heyer had moved the remaining Jaguar up to fifth as the Lancia crews slowed to recover fuel economy and both the works Rothmans/Shell Porsches retook the lead. The remaining Jaguar then suffered the same broken valve spring retainer problem having been over revved. This time the valve came in contact with the piston and eventually punched it through the head.

> The race was won by Stuck/Bell with Mass/Ickx second, followed by the Lancia's of Wollek/de Cesaris/Baldi and Patrese/Nannini, the Schuppan/ Holbert experimental PDK Porsche finished fifth.

## Fuji (Japan) – October 6th

The team had just two weeks to prepare the cars after the Brands Hatch race, ship them to Japan, clear customs and be at the Mount Fuji circuit.

This circuit with its fast approach to the long main straight was a power track with the locals being well versed in qualifying. In the home Japanese sports car races qualifying was very important with the fastest cars making TV news headlines and special Q cars often used. The advantage they had was if it rained – when it rains at Fuji it is normally very heavy. A special wet tyre for these conditions was made by Japanese tyre manufacturer Bridgestone, and they would be better than anything else in these conditions. It would be the first time in 1985 the European teams had come up against the Japanese Nissan/ Toyota, and Porsche teams who were out to prove themselves against the European 'Gaijins'.

The TWR team was extended to its limits now, being split for this weekend between the Bathurst 1000km race in Australia with three XJS Group A Jaguars, and the Group C race at Fuji in Japan. From the total of just five Group C engines including two first prototypes using modified standard Jaguar heads, and with two engines needing extensive repair after Brands Hatch, Engs were faced with a huge task to prepare for both these races.

Tom Walkinshaw was driving at Bathurst in Australia with race support from the TWR European Touring Car Rover team. Bathurst was a 1000km race that I had attended three times before while living in Australia in the early 1970s. After showing TW some tapes I had of this race it had then been decided to compete firstly with Australian John Goss in his locally built XJS in 1984.

Things had not gone well in 1984, so it was back with unfinished business for all involved with our own Group A XJS race cars. TW had liked the Australian scene with its high-profile TV before and during this event. It had become the most watched sporting feature in Australia and with viewing audiences in many other countries in excess of 100 million. TW saw the Australian scene as a possible place to expand his motor racing interests, so despite the conflicting priorities resources were spread very thinly over this weekend.

Engs foreman Peter Grace was looking after the engine side at Fuji while I was at Bathurst in Australia as it was a more important race for TW, the benefit being an A$800,000 pay day for TWR. The need to find new drivers for the Fuji event added to the difficulties at this race and we had Rover pilot Steve Soper thrown in at the deep end to partner Hans Heyer, and Mike Thackwell returned, joined by his F3000 Danish team mate John Nielsen. Soper was a saloon car driver as far as Roger was concerned and not far up his wanted list. Soper, who had never driven the Jaguar before had been sent out in the pouring rain to complete just three laps, and that was to be his total experience before the race start.

After setting impressive qualifying times on the Friday, both of the Japanese Nissan-March 85G cars driven by Hoshino and Hasemi ended up the fastest two for the day. The Rothmans Porsche team retook the honours the next day but the Nissans remained in third and fourth. Of all the circuits Fuji was the least suited to the non-turbo XJR-6 with its long straight and reduced barometric pressure at an altitude of 600 metres; leaving them in nineteenth and twentieth position out of a field of 23 turbocharged cars. This race had the largest number of engine manufacturers represented and these included: Porsche, Nissan, Toyota, Jaguar, BMW, Mazda, Ford Cosworth, Lancia and Aston Martin.

The quick turnaround time between races and major repairs needed to the heads and camshafts damaged in the preceding races meant real problems had begun to surface. The last-minute supply of new cam carriers had problems as the line boring was not perfect. Line boring the entire 700mm length of the engine in a single pass would continue to be a problem when machining components for these V12 engines. It needed the best machines in the world to eliminate cutting tip run out over this long single travel. Without our own machining facilities, the results of all this out work would never be known until the items arrived from the machinists; and they needed some late-night fettling to fit. This had resulted in camshaft seizures at Fuji with the engines needing to be rebuilt in the garages at the circuit, and the team was understandably not happy with these problems. From Japan, Roger had informed me of his dissatisfaction by telephone to Australia in a very straightforward manner. Not helping that situation was the fact that we were all happy at Bathurst after setting the two fastest qualifying times with the XJSs, and this outcome had produced some frustration between the two teams over TWR priorities. The underlying fact was TWR needed the Aussie pay day as the XJR-6 funding was not yet what was needed, resulting in the shortage of engines.

With a torrential downpour at the start of the Fuji race the European teams requested a delay to the 10.40am start and it was then agreed that the race would be shortened to 60% of the scheduled distance to allow full points and prize money, with the start further delayed till 12.20. With this delay the crowd of some 83,000 patiently waited under whatever shelter they had brought for the conditions. Various opinions from drivers after a limited practice run to check conditions had some prepared to drive if asked and some such as Hans Stuck saying it was too dangerous. Basically, if you did not have the Bridgestone 'monsoon' tyre you were in big trouble, and these were only available to their contracted teams, who all happened to be Japanese. Not surprisingly, they all wanted to run.

The race was started at 1.30pm behind the pace car to allow drivers to familiarise themselves with the conditions and by the time the pace car had let the field go all the regular Group C drivers had returned to the pits and refused to continue, and this reduced the field to 18 from 36 starters. The Bridgestone rain tyres were built for these conditions and the Japanese teams continued on until finally after two hours the officials ended the race.

Nissan had shown impressively at this Japanese home race meeting and had taken victory in the shortened race. Their car was based on the Adrian Newey March 85G chassis using the special Bridgestone tyres, with a factory supplied twin turbocharged VG30 60° V6 engine. Even on a dry track at Fuji this combination was very competitive, although a dry race over distance to the fuel allowance would have been the true test of its Group C abilities.

The race was won by Hoshino/Hagiura/Matsumoto, in a 3.0 turbo March-Nissan 85G; followed by Nakako/Morimoto/Pirro in a 2.6 turbo Nissan 05C; Sekiya/Nakajima and Akaike/Nagasaki in 2.1 turbo Dome Toyota 85Cs were third and fourth; then Hasemi/Wada in a 3.0 turbo March-Nissan 85G in fifth place.

To add to the weekends woes Japan had one of its earthquakes, a first for most of the UK contingent, and with the typhoon conditions they all just wanted to go home.

Meanwhile we were warm and dry in Australia where John Goss and Armin Hahne had just won the Bathurst 1000 in the Group A XJS with Tom Walkinshaw and Win Percy coming third. The two TWR teams were at the opposite ends of the earth as well as emotional spectrums that weekend.

## Shah Alam (Malaysia) – December 1st

Another long haul race followed in early December, the 800km Selangor race at the Shah Alam circuit would be the last race of the 1985 Group C series. TW had been reluctant to increase the limited budget until better funding was assured, so only parts to hand could be used. We both traded memos on this situation as I had expressed my frustration over his reluctance to commit to the V12's future. The Engs staff had worked tirelessly to weld cylinder heads that we could not replace, and fitted them with stronger valve spring caps. There were just 3000 spectators at Selangor, in sharp contrast to the previous season's final at Sandown Park in Melbourne, Australia, and the wet race in Japan. The difference in national interest and no doubt income was stark.

The weather conditions too were a contrast. Malaysia was hotter than anywhere experienced before with 35°C minimum temperatures. It produced huge problems for the drivers with fatigue and dehydration in the enclosed cockpit of the XJR-6.

*TWR-Jaguar team at the rained-out Fuji race. Note the blanked off radiator duct.*

Six Porsches had made the long journey along with the two Jaguars. Jan Lammers was starting to come to grips with the XJR-6 as well as the TWR team and car set-up, and this tight circuit was more suited to the Jaguar than Fuji had been. The words 'throttle response' were starting to creep into debriefing language as this feature of the normally aspirated V12 gave some benefit to car balance and drivability without the slight hesitation and sharp power build up associated with the turbo-charged engines.

It was monsoon season and at the end of qualifying a torrential downpour flooded the pit garages. While bailing out and cleaning up a very large toad appeared from nowhere and took up residence on top of our mechanic Taff's tool box.

The hoped for challenge to the Porsches in qualifying never quite eventuated when Mike Thackwell had a battery come loose on his fastest lap. The Mass/Ickx Rothmans Porsche took pole position with Stuck/Bell in the PDK automatic gearbox 956 test car second. Oscar Larrauri in the Brun Porsche was third and the XJR-6s took out fourth and fifth places. The second Jaguar had Denmark's John Nielsen returning, this time partnered with Sicilian Gianfranco Brancatelli who had been hired to drive the TWR Group A Rovers the following year. These different nationalities had to converse in English, so while they all had a good grasp of that language some care still had to be taken during debriefing to avoid confusion, not helped by my New Zealand accent.

Briton John Fitzpatrick had returned with his own Porsche team having Austrian Franz Konrad and Australian Andrew Miedecke qualifying in sixth place.

The 800km race was led from the start by both works Rothmans Porsches with Lammers third until lap 19, when the left rear tyre failed and the car left the circuit, out of the race. Thackwell in the second Jaguar was suffering from the effects of heat and was dropping back although his third place became safer as the Larrauri Porsche began to have engine problems. An exhausted Thackwell pitted early for change-over to Nielsen who rejoined in fifth, but a fine effort by lap 42 had bought his XJR-6 back up to third. This race showed up the lack of driver ventilation in the Jaguar and full stints could not be achieved by the drivers because of the temperatures in the cockpit.

It was just something else to add to the list of improvements for next year. Lammers took over from Nielsen, re-joining in fourth place and eventually regaining third, but an extra stop was now needed for the last few litres of fuel because of the out of phase driving stints. Fortunately, the fourth placed Porsche driven by Schuppan was two laps behind.

*Jan Lammers showing the physical effects of his efforts in the XJR-6 in Malaysia.*

Stuck suddenly pitted with the left-hand driveshaft broken probably the result of the PDK automatic transmission gear changes and by the time this was repaired they were out of contention. Light rain showers had helped the responsive Jaguar unlap itself to the Mass Porsche although heavier rain caused another stop for wet tyres. The Jaguar's driveability was superior in the rain and was now the quickest car on the circuit. With the slowing pace of the Porsche in the rain reducing its turbocharger speeds and increasing its turbo lag this began to show the Jaguar's advantage in these conditions.

The rain eased allowing Mass/Ickx to continue on with their win for Porsche, but the eventual second place for the XJR-6 made this long journey well worthwhile. Schuppan/Weaver were third, followed by Konrad/Miedecke in the Fitzpatrick Porsche and the Larrauri/Sigala/Jelinski Porsche was fifth.

It was as good a result as could be hoped for and a rewarding way to finish the year for the TWR Jaguar team in only their fifth Group C event.

All in all, the Group C series had been a success for Jaguar, although apart from Japan the spectator appearances were low for these long distance races. The races were long at 1000kms and frequently the fastest teams on the fuel allocation were well established by mid-distance. Driving smoothly and economically was a new skill for racers, but cars later slowing to save fuel that had been over used by its previous a driver confused spectators. Once the race had proved who could race to the fuel it then just became a matter of who had reliability, with no wheel to wheel fuel wasting racing. It wasn't the best spectacle to watch. Engs had suffered from the lack of commitment to the V12 engine from TW and Roger, but they were now coming round.

*The early attempts to counteract the understeering tendency of the XJR-6.*

*The Autosport front cover gives a thumbs up for Tom Walkinshaw and the TWR team.*

JAGUAR

CHAPTER EIGHT

# First year's evaluation

**The early season aim of getting the XJR-6 to Le Mans in 1985 was always viewed as optimistic at best but fulfilled an objective to extend the hard-working mechanics as far as possible. It did mean though that TWR had lost vital running time and experience at this event that was critical to Jaguar.**

The American Group 44 team with two XJR-5s had competed for a second time at Le Mans and early on had run close to the front of the field. High fuel consumption and eventual engine detonation using the fuel available at Le Mans, which was a much lower grade than Group 44 were experienced with had led to engine failures later in the race.

This again confirmed my thoughts concerning the Lucas/Group 44/Jaguar engine management 'committee system'. No single person being prepared to take full responsibility for changing chip settings to suit the conditions they were facing during the race. Also their engines had not been tested on Le Mans supplied fuel, a must for final ignition timing settings.

TWR had for the entire 1985 year been able to re-programme chips at will during trackside testing for our Group A cars and the Zytek engine management boxes now had external overriding quick-change dials. We were able to trim overall ignition or fuel settings during normal pit stops in around eight seconds without changing the embedded chip.

The sleek new Tony Southgate design looked a step ahead of the dominant aluminium chassis 956/962 Porsche turbos, and the paddock pundits were taken with its attractive shape and compact size. At year's end Tony Southgate could now turn his attention to the detail needed with finished drawing for components and production processes for bodywork, with just one assistant Jeff Kingston to help him with this huge task in 1985. Manufacturing processes and detail design with the benefit of race proving could also now be attended to over the winter period, with the opportunity to trim weight where the first cars had been over-engineered and hand built. Theoretically that allowed a start to 1986 with a well sorted two-car team.

With six hours being the minimum race-length, and including the Le Mans 24 hour race, the finishing rate for competitors in the 1985 series was close to 60%, and that with mainly Porsche cars in their fourth year of competition. The Jaguar in its first year had a 50% finishing rate over the six hour races if you exclude the voluntary withdrawal from Fuji. With the season finished it was time to evaluate every area and look in detail at what was needed to make the XJR-6 competitive with the 962C Porsche.

The fuel restricted formula of Group C regulations had banned alcohol and nitrous oxygen boosting elements of fuel but left everything else to be regulated by a 105 octane limit with a 5% tolerance. New fuel technology from Formula One came into the series in

1985 suiting turbocharged engines and working contrary to the aim of capping horsepower outputs. More specific regulations would make life much harder for the turbocharged engines which were using special blends within the 105 RON limits to provide anti detonation characteristics; allowing advanced ignition timings to provide good engine efficiency and help control temperatures with small capacity turbocharged engines.

TWR and Jaguar had to work on the regulators with this fuel option as the V12 was currently being disadvantaged with the open fuel rules. The instigation of lower octane road based fuels in the future as part of the concept in the fuel formula series was what was needed.

Alastair Macqueen who had been working previously in single seater formulas had now been recruited as chief engineer towards year's end 1985 and set about the task of reducing the weight of the XJR-6 by evaluation of every single detail. This was no mean task as it was not just a matter of substituting lighter materials but also included detail redesign of many small components shaving 100s of grams in many cases rather than kilograms. At least 60–70kgs would have to be reduced somehow from the complete car package to make it competitive.

For Engs it was also a matter of implementing the lessons learned and producing lighter more powerful engines with improved fuel economy for 1986. All areas, power output, fuel economy and engine weight needed substantial improvements to bring the XJR-6 up to a level that would be competitive with the new Porsche 962C. With only a limited programme for the Group A XJS cars towards the end of 1985, it had been that build team of three to four staff who had provided support for the new Group C engine development and race programme. Engines in 500km Group A races had lasted for three complete events in 1984, as opposed to the single event between rebuilds now the reality in the Group C 1000km races. The added complexity of these engines had increased over the Group A V12 build times by nearly 100% as well as an increasing proportion of more complex manufacturing to outside subcontractors.

The effort to support the engine programme had come from a small motivated workforce who put in hours above and beyond what most would tolerate; led by Peter Grace and Charlie Bamber. I took control of the electronic software programming and dynamometer testing for power output versus fuel consumption, along with liaison with Jaguar. The other half of Engs were involved with the rebuild and support of the ETCC three-car Rover programme that TW was lead driver for; I carried out the same tasks for that programme as well, attending all ETCC events.

The Jaguar engine programme however was in limbo at year's end through some indecision on the best way forward, as well as the need for increased funding. My 1986 engines specifications had been scoped and mostly drawn by Russell Sharp waiting for approval to begin manufacture of longer lead items before the last race in Malaysia. A stop had then been put on any further purchases.

The team's staff levels needed to near double, and Engs needed to be in control of its destiny with at least a two-man machine shop in-house to help remove the procurement problems with last minute deliveries of parts not machined to drawing, along with the many small engineering support items needed on a day-to-day basis. We had gone from rebuilding modified production V12s, with a handy parts supply at the end of the telephone, to *making complete* engines starting with a machined special block casting. Races were on different continents, with increased travel and freight costs; and a larger sponsor was needed, fast. Sponsorship guru Guy Edwards had been working with Jaguar during this time and was putting together proposals for them, but nothing had been finalised – or so I had been told at the time. There was perhaps however another reason in the background why the brakes had been put on the V12 build programme. TW, Roger, and Tony Southgate were not convinced that the heavy normally aspirated V12 engine was the way to go.

This was a normal reaction from any chassis minded person but every cloud has its silver lining, with the V12's engine configuration allowing the use of the much talked about large venturi tunnels to pass unobstructed to their exit points at the rear, unlike the Porsche flat-six boxer engines which obstructed this area, limiting their aerodynamic design. The V12 block was also very stiff for a production unit and could be used as a fully stressed member, unlike a straight six, saving valuable chassis weight when engineering a semi stressed engine such as Porsche's flat-six.

TW had also started some Jaguar road car development work with Max Heidegger in Liechtenstein in conjunction with the JaguarSport joint venture begun in 1984. This personal liaison was outside of my influence. TW continued to be drawn to the idea of turbocharging Jaguar's AJ6 3.2-litre straight six 2-valve at this time, mainly because Porsche was using a boxer six-cylinder engine of a similar size. Max, with his enthusiastic ideas, but few practical solutions or delivery timetables, had been lobbying this as the way to go. TW was already using valuable funding to produce a turbocharged version of the AJ6 for JaguarSport, with the aim of eventual production use in Jaguar cars.

Jaguar in America had been hit with a 'gas guzzler tax' as they had no small-engined vehicle to offset the new American car manufacturers' legislation on average fuel consumption figures across all vehicles produced in the company's range. Max and TW had both become convinced that a turbo AJ6 was the answer to reduce Jaguar Coventry's high fuel consumption figures for their production range. Heidegger had carried out successful race engine programmes and was keen to be involved with the TWR Group C effort, but using turbocharged engines. To start a turbo programme at this short notice would in my opinion have been foolhardy if not stupid, and I could only see a disadvantage at this stage. TW had begun to make fewer appearances to the staff in the engine division, an obvious difference to the many he spent in the Kidlington race shop and at Liechtenstein.

Roger was just worried about the competitiveness of the programme fullstop, not convinced after the short 1985 programme that the job could be done with what we had. In a couple of meetings with him he expressed doubts as to the viability of what we had started. He was privately promoting the idea that TWR should go single seater F3000 racing and was becoming increasingly nervous about Group C's effect on his future status in motorsport having already moved down in his mind to TWR from Formula One. Roger had been hired with the prospect of TWR one day moving to Formula One and his decision making was based on this future focus. In conversations on a few occasions he had expressed his feelings with "do you want to stand beside *that* in the pit lane", pointing at a Jaguar Group C race car that he thought would be uncompetitive – with an engine that would have no contribution in a future Formula One programme. So, there were two lobbies close to TW that were contributing to the uncertain future of the V12 race engine. BMW, a former employer of TW's services, was mentioned in passing at this time with its turbocharging expertise with small capacity engines, and could also be part of a future venture into Formula One.

I was seeing things from a different angle, having become used to preparing production engines for racing with three different manufacturers, Mazda, Rover and Jaguar. I was working on a racing programme for Jaguar, wherever that might lead, using a production based Jaguar engine being part of the rules.

The first year of any new race series at TWR had always been a struggle for everyone with a very limited development time, and straight into a race programme. Limited development budgets allowed TW to take early control and be seen to fix the inevitable problems that arose from that timing process. That had definitely been the best way in the early TWR days for TW and the team, but over time we were all getting better at our tasks and as a team knew what was needed to avoid most of these problems.

The shortest Group C races were six hours long, making reliability the main factor after fuel consumption and a huge hurdle to overcome with the inevitable new car problems. Going into its second year, Engs was better placed to put a weight reduction, power output and improved fuel efficiency design in place with Jaguar's V12 based engine.

For my hard-working team it was not encouraging to have to listen or read about how good the race car was and how much of a hindrance the V12 engine could be to its winning potential. That however is motor racing and the engine was my responsibility, and it had to be a Jaguar unit if it was going to be called a Jaguar. It was not the first time nor would it be the last that I would have to grow another layer of skin to the many already existing from my previous six years at TWR. I was convinced that an AJ6 3.2-litre straight six turbocharged engine was not the way to go before the programme started, and I still held that view after the first year, the 3.2-litre engine capacity was too small for a start.

With the moratorium on any new Group C spending, Engs turned to the Rover Group A programme implementing the new evolution upgrades to that engine pool, with a four-car Rover team in mind for 1986. There was also the prospect that 1986 would be the last year that Tom Walkinshaw would be driving the Rover and last chance he had of winning a second ETCC title, after coming second in 1985. In the meantime, we waited for TW's decision in late 1985 on the way forward for Jaguar in 1986.

It was during these months of October and November that TW's focus was not just sidetracked with the successful Bathurst XJS episode, but with another new venture. A new Porsche dealership to be called Chariots was being established and no doubt taking its place further up in the queue for TWR funding. Did TW have yet another reason in mind with the setting up of this Porsche dealership though? He already had a Mazda and BMW dealership, future racing avenues could grow from this. I did not mind widening the TWR business model; in fact, I thought it a great idea to have a broader income stream that could support motor racing in the future. Unfortunately, as time passed over the next few years this would not turn out to be the case. Money would go from the racing budget to increase the 'TWR Group' concept garages – and no dividend return to the racing teams. TW had proudly shown me the new tiled floor of Prophets BMW, and seemed oblivious to the fact that I would see my area at Kidlington with its painted over concrete surface not being as important as the new garage. It would take another three years before we had a tiled floor.

TWR

## TWR's Retail Motor Trade Background

Since acquiring a Mazda Dealership in 1979, TWR's interests in the retail motor trade have broadened to include Dealerships for Jaguar, BMW and Porsche.

This knowledge of how a Dealership works from day to day, and how specialist automotive parts can be designed, manufactured, sold and distributed gives the TWR Group a tremendous advantage when it comes to providing a thoroughly professional service in sub-contract specialist automotive parts supply.

If you couple this practical knowledge and experience with our reputation for on-track success, the TWR name carries a valuable cachet that will attract the kind of sporting motorist who is the typical customer for performance orientated parts.

## It had been a testing and successful year for Engs in 1985, with the dedicated workforce carrying out many programmes other than Group C

- Group C V12 development and a 5-race programme.
- Three-car Rover team in European Group A. (TWR placed second.)
- One-car Rover team in the French national championship (Jean-Louis Schlesser won the 1985 French National Saloon Car Championship in an evolution version of the Group A ETCC Rover.)
- One-car Rally programme in the UK with Tony Pond. (Tony Pond led the British Group A rally series till an accident on the very last event dropping him to second in the series.)
- Bathurst 1000 with three XJ-S cars at year's end. (TWR XJS Jaguars came first and third in this 1000km race in Australia.)
- JaguarSport 6-litre V12 road engines. (This development put into production at TWR JaguarSport eventually became the standard production version fitted to all Jaguar cars produced at Coventry.)

**Engs staff during 1985**

- Russell Sharp – Design draftsman
- Peter Grace – Workshop foremen and Chief engine builder
- Charlie Bamber – Chief engine builder, engine testing assistant, trackside support
- Glen Barber, Rob Benson and Dave Morris – Senior engine builders
- Mike Collett and Steve Corbett – Engine builders (two other trainee builders left during the year)
- Mathew Norris – Youth training scheme. He would show the value of this long term training scheme being the first of a group of three that would later achieve senior positions in the TWR engine division.
- Tim Pryce-Davies and Graeme Bennett – Stores and purchasing

> ***To avoid situations in which you might make mistakes maybe the biggest mistake of all.***
>
> – Peter McWilliams

*The highly modified XJR-6 for 1986 with new sponsor Silk Cut.*

JAGUAR

Chapter Nine

# Modifications to the XJR-6 for 1986

**The first full year of competition for TWR and Jaguar had commenced with extensive preparation work being carried out over the 85/86 winter period. Sealing the future of the Jaguar programme had come with the confirmation of the much-needed funding, and the former 'TWR Jaguar Team' was now designated the 'Silk Cut Jaguar Racing Team'. This was officially announced on January 14th 1986, my thirty-sixth birthday. The previous World Endurance Championship was now renamed the World Sports Prototype Championship (WSPC) for 1986. Guy Edwards had brokered the Silk Cut deal between tobacco giant Gallaher International's Chairman Peter Gilpin and Jaguar's marketing director Neil Johnson, not TWR, and it was to be for a period of three years. The subject of Guy's substantial fees for negotiating this deal and accepted by Jaguar who needed the funding assistance would be something that Tom Walkinshaw would occasionally refer to in management meetings and future negotiations.**

After this announcement came much discussion and some dissent concerning tobacco sponsorship; with the anti-smoking organisations openly criticising Jaguar for having a tobacco sponsor associated with such a high profile British engineering institution.

Jaguar, after its initial four-year low cost re-entry into motor racing with the winning XJS Coupe and the promising XJR-6, both painted in British racing green in 1985, was now facing a changing professional motor racing scene. Jaguar was being forced to change much of its historic internal perceptions, mostly based on trade sponsors with supportive news media.

Jaguar had been staffed to some extent in the early post war recovery period according to a person's rank during that conflict. A decorated spitfire pilot, Tony Rolt, had been selected as one of the drivers for its winning D-type Jaguar at the Le Mans 24 hour endurance race in France. In the 1950s and 60s the driving forces at Jaguar had been about patriotism for country and loyalty to Jaguar's charismatic founder and leader William Lyons. Very supportive and partisan British press hyped the feats and racing results via Pathe newsreels in cinemas and newspaper articles, gaining huge amounts of 'free ink' for Jaguar. It had been a time when Britain's post war revival and rebuild needed these stories. Driving the D-type on a section of the road to Le Mans justified the claim of the 'production based race car' theme promoted by Jaguar for that event, as opposed to the thought that the German and Italian opposition were outright race cars that was supported by the British press. It had been a time when Jaguar had made its mark on the world, painted British racing green, supported by Dunlop, Castrol and Lucas, three iconic Commonwealth exporting companies. Jaguar never had to pay for these public relations exercises or compete for the free media advertising. Times were different now, and whilst patriotism was still strong, media time was very costly and hard fought, and motorsport at this level to get good exposure was going to cost much more.

The carbon composite ground effects XJR-6 did not continue on with the sleek rounded lines of Jaguar's earlier racing traditions. A very small band of revered but now retired senior Jaguar personnel had expressed disappointment at the factory deal with TWR, they had felt it should be an internal factory effort – or not at all. Silk Cut was seen as a departure from a wholly automotive supported tradition, and a step too far.

Now the new race cars for 1986 had a livery with clever art work and colours designed by a studio to make them stand out and promote the *sponsor's* name; a tobacco company that had no connection to the motor industry at all. Worst of all British racing green was out; white with purple tobacco sponsorship was in.

The commercial and engineering realism was not lost on the current Jaguar directors led by John Egan however, and so the new concept of sub-contract to TWR and tobacco sponsorship producing 'bill board' paint schemes was a reality they readily accepted. The Porsche factory 962C carried very large references to their tobacco sponsor Rothman's at this time as well.

This new deal also came with the much-reduced prominence of TWR signage as well as removal from the team's title, something that TW would not have given into easily if he had been at the negotiating table. Guy Edwards had also given Jaguar a large list of possible future contacts and sponsors and these would remain his personal property, having exclusive rights to any future dealings with these companies for Jaguar. If Jaguar was to continue with Group C and possibly higher levels in the future, it needed substantial financial support. Guy Edwards was the right man at the right time; and he was able to fix Jaguar's motorsport finance problems.

With these changes to the team's title the references to TWR on the engine's cam covers now had to be deleted; the new castings would just have the 'Jaguar V12' logo with their joint engineering profile being promoted as the source for the engine, even though Jaguar was unaware of my intentions or designs for the engine concept (apart from picking up the thick wall Tarozzi heads).

1986 would be the first full year of competition for the TWR team with its Silk Cut/Jaguar XJR-6 and the series was beginning to gain popularity as the concept of manufacturers' involvement in a fuel regulated formula series grew. Also with the World Series format came the need for all teams involved to have a logical interest in sharing shipping and logistics cost. A supporting organisation had been formed and run from London by Chris Parsons called the Organisation for Sports Car Racing [OSCAR]. This company was run as a separate entity from the FIA governing body, and OSCAR had been formed to co-ordinate freight movements and logistics. Shipping and freight clearances at different ports in different parts of the world had different rules, and language barriers would be a particular problem in this new world series for individual teams. Combining teams to provide a central logistical support for race cars, supporting equipment and spares to the various race tracks around the world provided the same outcome for all of the teams when they arrived in the various host countries. This would mean that either all cars were on the grid in time for the race meeting, or all were delayed if the worst happened. This system with Chris Parsons' management worked efficiently.

## A major move forward for the XJR-6

The modifications carried out over the winter of 1985/86 had been so extensive that the Tony Southgate designed XJR-6 had become a second-generation version that deserved a new designation. The Group 44 XJR-5 had also been redesigned by Lee Dykstra in America to counter the moves by TWR, and this had been allocated XJR-7 status. There were also some thoughts from America that Group 44 had the rights to the XJR name first, and that TWR had helped themselves to it which of course was true, but if anyone did own XJR it was probably Jaguar's in the overall scheme of things.

The new driver line-up for the Silk Cut Jaguar XJR-6 for 1986 could not be settled until the Formula One teams had completed their contracts for drivers in 1986. Finally, in mid-February, two of these drivers became available and it was announced that Derek Warwick and Eddie Cheever would join the Jaguar team. Already contracted TWR drivers Jean-Louis Schlesser (France) and Gianfranco Brancatelli (Italy) would be the other two drivers for 1986. The two ex-Formula One drivers had flexible TWR contracts that allowed priority should a Formula One drive become available.

Salaries were now a point to be discussed as these Formula One drivers expected to be well rewarded for their efforts and the negotiation between TW and Eddie Cheever went down to the wire. Without being able to come to a mutual agreement TW had thanked Eddie for coming and told him to have the secretary reimburse him for his expenses in coming to Kidlington for an interview. A surprised, disappointed and concerned Cheever left the office and a disappointed and a concerned Tom Walkinshaw pondered his negotiating stance while looking out of his office window. When Cheever appeared a short time later the window was opened and he was asked what he was doing down there and that he should return back upstairs. The deal was then quickly concluded.

Derek Warwick was to have number one status in the team, something that was important to him, although TWR were very good at running multiple cars to the same specification at events; all having equal equipment and usually an equal chance.

The reports in the media on the TWR team in the lead up to the first race were still mentioning the prospect of using a 4-valve per cylinder engine, and while this rumour was never discouraged, there was now no time or capacity to continue down this path. It became obvious that reproducing the performance figures obtained from the first prototype 6232cc 4-valve engine had to be the aim for the V12 Group C 2-valve per cylinder engine to be used in 1986 and these design features had all been in place by October 1985.

It had been my policy at Engs to produce all engines to the same performance specifications. Any move forward in development would only happen when the minimum number of engines for the event had been produced for all cars. This view had come out of earlier experiences with the Rover programme that small developmental changes to engines usually had a disproportionate improvement in the minds of the driver, team manager and mechanics on the car that *did not* have the latest update. It was also the best problem solving and race management view on the day for me to have identical engines allowing two independent feedback situations; either confirming or disagreeing on a certain aspect that could be improved or focused on.

The authorisation to proceed with the V12 engine builds for 1986 had not happened after the memo from finance director John Bradley on November 8th stopped any further expenditure on the Group C programme. V12 engines were now simply not going to be manufactured in time for the 1986 season. I had considerable autonomy within the TWR team and a history of taking responsibility for all outcomes, so quickly came to the conclusion that we had to still proceed – but somehow not spend any money in doing so.

My frustrations on the lack of progress on the V12 programme continued and finally got the better of me, so I sent a note to TW on November 20th 1985.

No one should tell their boss what to do or give him an ultimatum and his reply should not be unexpected (see page 80).

Such was my frustration after TW had left for the airport without signing off the engine deal that I had gone to John Bradley's office carrying an envelope in my hand. I discussed the situation again with him and all John could do was look at the letter I was holding. He asked what was in the envelope and I replied it did not matter. It was just an envelope with nothing in it but it had John on the phone to TW and the next day I received the verbal OK to proceed. This was something I really needed as I had already proceeded with many of the procurement options on a verbal delayed payment basis, and was about to have problems in covering some of the actions I had already put in place.

I would later find out that the Guy Edwards-brokered Silk Cut deal had been signed off with Jaguar in late September 1985, but TW was still telling me it was not a done deal in mid-November. In his defence there were still lose ends to tie up, especially on who was actually going to be running the cash flow show. Jaguar may have been making some assumptions at this point with the funding distribution, and a process would have to be established to ensure an acceptable way forward for TWR existed. The revised contract with Jaguar Cars Ltd on purchase order 570197 was signed on December 16th 1985 for a total of £3.5 million.

For the two-race and one test car Group C Jaguar team I had proposed that we build a minimum of fourteen V12 engines including upgrades to the five existing 1985 units to cover the tight turn around times, especially around Le Mans. These had been budgeted out for initial build and maintenance rebuild for the 1986 year at a total of £350,000.

It was not until November 22nd that TW finally gave his go-ahead to the 1986 V12 programme and Engs could officially proceed in the three-week lead up to the Christmas/New Year break taken by the entire specialist machining sub-contract industry we worked with as well as our engine builders needing their annual break. This situation was not new in motor racing but what it meant was that specialist machine shops supporting motor racing received all their orders for the following year at the same time, January, and capacity was by then limited. Promises were of course made by them to supply on time and then the multitude of reasons would appear for the late deliveries. Whoever offered the highest prices, well-funded Formula One teams mainly, took precedence and machining costs in January through to March each year were at a premium and late delivery a normal outcome.

A reduced parts budget of £275,000 was finally approved to upgrade the five 1985 spec engines and build four new units, three less than I could live with. The total salaries for build and procurement staff for Jaguar, Rover and the special 6-litre JaguarSport engine programmes we carried out was £117,000, of which the Group C Jaguar component was about 40%. TW paid himself £300,000 per annum and along with the two ex-Formula One drivers to be hired for 1986, these three would be paid well over twice the amount of the total spend for engine rebuilds and salaries involved over the entire 1986 programme – that was soon to be raised to three race cars plus a spare/test car.

During the time the 1986 budget was put on hold in late 1985 some items had already been ordered, around £58,000 worth. The late finance approval would have the greatest impact on the casting and machining of the Tarozzi heads for the new engines, as well as the need to replace those items damaged and repaired in the two races late in 1985. With the lead times involved and the looming shut downs over the Christmas break we simply would not have the new Tarozzi heads if engines were to be built on time for the

MEMO

| From | | To |
|---|---|---|
| ALLAN SCOTT | | TOM WALKINSHAW |
| Our Reference | Your Reference | |
| AS/DMR | | 20 November 19 85 |

GROUP C 1986

I feel I should place my fears on record as to the continual slipping of the re-ordering programme of parts for Group C 1986.

Pistons, liners, valves, crankshafts, camshafts all have a 8-10 week lead time, excluding Xmas/New Year period which loses 2 weeks.

This takes delivery times to 2nd/3rd week of February if the parts were ordered today, with supply complete by late February early March.

New engines should be being built in the 1st week of February for development 3rd/4th week February before the first race on 9th March.

We are already committed to doing this first race with 1985 spec engines. I am disappointed, to put it mildly, that lessons learned this year (no development whatsoever in the six months we have been running Group C engines, while I chase parts for engines), will be wasted and with the tight schedule up to Le Mans, give no recovery time whatsoever.

I will not take responsibility for delivery times, performance or reliability of Group C engines in 1986 if the orders are not placed "BEFORE" I leave for Malaysia.

No sponsorship for 86

ALLAN SCOTT
Engine Shop Manager

cc: John Bradley
Roger Silman

| From | | To |
|---|---|---|
| TOM WALKINSHAW | | ALLAN SCOTT<br>Engine Shop Manager |
| Our Reference | Your Reference | |
| TW/DMR | | 20 November 19 85 |

GROUP C BUDGET 1986

As you are well aware we have not got any agreement regarding the Group C Budget clearance for 1986. However as the Engine Shop Manager you will take full responsibility concerning delivery times for all engine parts as and when you are given authorisation to order them.

DMRobertson.
pp TOM WALKINSHAW

above: *Memo to TW stating my concern regarding the V12 programme.*
below: *TW's reply to my November memo with engine progress placed on hold by Tom Walkinshaw.*

1986 season. Fortunately Tom Seal of Jaguar's Prototype department, who had handled the Tarozzi head pattern work and casting programme, was very keen to see it all continue, and so agreed to the ordering of new head castings along with the machining of the new castings, without our TWR order number, in October of 1985. I had a good feeling that if it all worked out well Jaguar's arm could be twisted and they would pay for this first batch at least. Our ongoing development with flow work and the larger valves fitted to these heads to suit the new larger engine capacity of 6537cc could then be available to both Jaguar teams for 1986. Group 44 needed to move on from their trusted 6-litre engines to the 6.5-litre limit that IMSA already allowed, and so both teams could have similar hardware but allowing individual tuning options to suit each programme This would I hoped remove the concept of the Lucas Micos engine management and 4-valve head programme as being the best solution for Group C, and move to a mutually beneficial outcome with common hardware for both teams; producing the shared benefits that Jaguar were looking for or at least appear to.

In late 1985 the engineering support from Jaguar seemed to have some flexibility and it was just a matter of progressing situations wherever possible with the Jaguar Prototype procurement department. I never knew that department's budget but guessed it was flexible in that it might be able to share some racing costs with various internal production prototype cost centres. I avoided bringing up any costs involved during my progress meetings with Jaguar at Browns Lane, and just pushed ideas forward. Engineering director Jim Randle was well aware of most things happening and I took my cue from him allowing things to take their course with the need to push on with engine development. Much later in 1986 there would be a reconciliation over engineering spend, but by then the XJR-6 was a winner and on track for a World Championship, making it justifiable for Jaguar to carry some of these costs under the joint engineering umbrella with Group 44.

Between my pub lunches with various machine shop managers in early October 1985, and Tom Seal from Jaguar Prototype using Jaguar's considerable influence, we managed to get a few suppliers agree to initial rough machining of various castings and other blank ferrous materials. These machine shops would then await final detail drawings from us to complete the work after TWR budget sign off, and this gave the selected machine shop managers a delaying tactic with their own accounts departments. This initial machining work was a small fraction of the overall finished cost, should the project not go ahead. The benefits gained from this would be proving the various castings and materials supplied were good for use at an early stage, allowing quick timely final machining after the late budget sign off. This was a great help at the time given the pressures and responsibilities put on us by our respective employers and finance directors. By the end of January, we had started assembling the updated 1985 engines, and were moving forward with our programme of weight reduction and increased power, with decreased fuel consumption for the 6.5-litre engine. The weight reduction programme included replacing the cast iron cylinder liners in some of the engines with nicosil coated aluminium units, producing a weight saving of almost 8kgs.

Special attention to the head casting by draftsman Russell Sharp with detailed machining produced a weight saving of 1kg per head, 2kg per engine – quite significant. The new camshaft covers with the front and rear top engine mountings points were cast in magnesium instead of the original aluminium. Lightweight drilled steel camshaft timing gears replaced the original standard cast iron gears and along with rifle drilled camshaft centres, reduced rotating mass as well as overall weight. These new timing gears were fitted with high specification duplex timing chains manufactured in France by the company that produced the special competition chains for the racing bikes in the Tour de France cycle race.

*'Jet' titanium connecting rod.*

The 1986 6.5-litre engines started life with both steel and 'Jet' titanium connecting rods because the titanium rods had yet to be tested in these engines, again having to be finally proved under racing conditions. A major weight saving came with the 'Heidegger' high performance oil pump replacing the heavy USA manufactured Weaver type pump. This compact three scavenge and one pressure unit cast in magnesium was half the size of the previous USA sourced pump and along with the reduced pipe work this one item had produced a weight reduction of another 6kgs.

Many engine nuts and bolts were changed for forged or lighter items and all these weight reductions finally added up to an overall saving of 15 to 25kgs, depending on main cap, connecting rod and liner specification. The lightest specification V12 now weighed 235kgs including flywheel, clutch, engine management control box and all wiring looms, but excluding the exhaust system. The wet sump XJS Group A engine had weighed 280kgs and a fully dressed production V12 engine 300kgs including the production compressor for air conditioning.

The winter testing of the new 6.5-litre with its many improvements had been a major step forward and with it an engine weight reduction of 15 to 20kgs. The increase in power output of almost 60bhp had been better than hoped for and the new mapping techniques enabled us to achieve it with no increase in fuel consumption. These figures all now exceeded our aim of bettering the first 4-valve 6232cc engine.

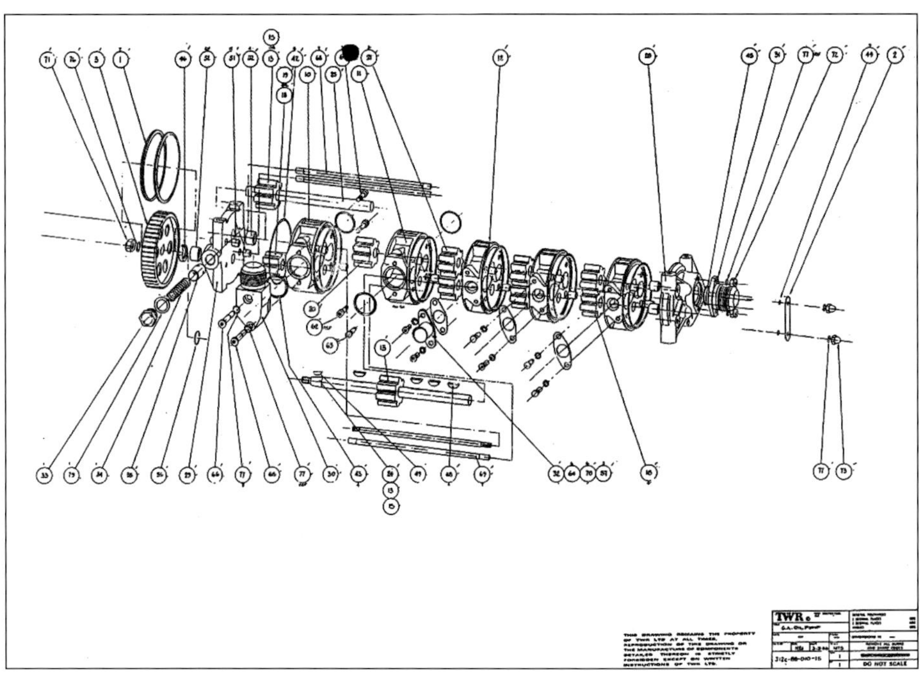

*Heidegger oil pump, one pressure and three scavenge stages as fitted to the 1986 engines.*

## 1986 6.5-litre V12 engines

The five 1985 lip seal blocks machined to be stressed members in the 1985 6.2-litre XJR-6 engines were retained, but now increased in capacity to 6537cc using a bore increase to 94mm. At the same time the trouble with the piston gudgeon pin circlips moving that we had experienced during 1985 was rectified by replacing them with an aluminium end float button and deleting the circlips. These buttons sat in the piston boss on either side of the shortened gudgeon pin and had the same outer radius as the new larger 94mm bore for 1986. These were initially set-up in a dummy liner to produce a cold gudgeon pin end float set at 0.008in minimum to allow for the expansion of the aluminium buttons.

The proposed lightening of the blocks for 1986 had revolved around substituting the four intermediate main bearing caps with aluminium ones and retaining the existing front centre and rear main caps in steel. These three steel caps would retain block rigidity and crankshaft location when under heat and stress loading from cornering conditions when racing.

The trial machining of the very long crankshaft tunnel bore for these blocks using a combination of steel and aluminium alloy main bearing caps in late 1985 proved unsuccessful; the two materials needed different cutting methods and speeds and we were not prepared to line hone this area. Under time constrains Engs was forced to drop this best compromise idea, to use engine blocks with either steel or aluminium main caps at this point. Having to utilise the various parts on hand meant new engine blocks were fitted with aluminium main bearing caps with the aim of weight saving but retaining the steel rear main bearing cap. These aluminium caps were supplied by Jaguar from base stock they had made for Group 44, but now machined to our specifications. The modified 1985 engines would retain their original all steel main bearing caps. The all steel main cap engines would be heavier, but there would be no time to test the strength in racing conditions of the new aluminium main cap engines as part of the weight reduction solution before the racing season. Group 44 had experienced a couple of aluminium main cap failures in their V12 engines by this time, and although there was a considerable weight saving, I was reluctance to totally commit to this specification, especially for the Le Mans 24 hour endurance engines.

During 1985 the Robert Tarozzi 2-valve head had been produced in Coventry by Jaguar. The pattern work had been made by Broadfield, with sand mould aluminium castings by Stirling Metals. These heads had been used on four of the original 1985 engines by year's end and it was time to look at improvements again.

One of these heads was now developed on the flow bench using a 2mm increase in valves sizes to 48mm inlet and 40mm exhaust, these larger valve sizes were now possible with the increased 94mm bore being used. Different inlet port angles were tested both on the flow bench and on engine tests between 42 and 47°. The advantage of the new Tarozzi head was that it allowed modifications in areas that the standard Jaguar heads would not allow through lack of material in the areas needed when larger valves were fitted. With the additional internal port wall material available, we eventually settled on a port angle of 45° giving good air flow and swirl characteristics. The larger 48mm inlet and 40mm exhaust valves allowed an improved port throat contour between the valve guide area and the valve seat, producing a good step forward in flow characteristics from these castings. George Toth of Richard Longman and Co. continued with experimental head flow work and substantial gas flow increases came with these modifications. Dye injected air tests showed where the majority of the air flowed through the valve throat area and how the back face shape of the inlet valve at different lifts influenced the charge turbulence.

These final test results in early 1986 were impressive and for the first time we could see that more power and better economy than had previously been anticipated could be obtained when using the less complex, cheaper and lighter 2-valve heads if limited to maximum fuel-efficient engine speeds of 6800rpm. Over those speeds the 4-valve heads became superior. This had produced the concept of running the engine to a slightly lower rpm limit for best efficiency, and led to the decision to increase the engine capacity. These modifications resulted in increased power outputs at lower rpm than had been seen with the first 4-valve test engines. Lower rpm produced lower friction losses in these complex 12-cylinder engines, and importantly increased power outputs could be produced without any increases in engine weight. From this the concept for the future of the Group C engine programme became obvious – increased capacity and lower revving V12 engines using two valves per cylinder heads. This concept produced a weight saving of 15kgs from the 4-valve concepts; critically the weight saving was high above the race car's centre of gravity.

The power output increases for 1986 would come from many directions, starting with the 4.5% engine capacity increase and raised compression ratio from the nominal 12:1 at the end of 1985, to 13.5:1 for 1986. This increased compression ratio was still possible with the basic fuel regulation of the series now being reduced to a maximum of 102 Research Octane Number (RON) fuel.The new for 1986 fuel regulations governed only by the RON method would still make special blends possible. These could include higher specific gravity fuels, and would still favour turbocharged engines over normally aspirated units. These special fuels would still allow detonation sensitive turbocharged engines to gain better efficiency. The higher cylinder pressures involved with the turbocharged engines needed higher octane fuel not only to avoid detonation but their increased cylinder temperatures were able to gain combustion improvements from high specific gravity blends. These special high-density fuels could also produce more potential energy within the regulation that restricted the fuel *volume* to 100 litres, but left the fuel density (weight) unrestricted.

One of Honda's tricks when using these high-density fuel blends in their turbocharged Formula One engine had been to pass their fuel through a tube inserted in the hot water flowing from the engine to the radiator, and raise the fuel temperature to 80°C before injecting the heated fuel into the engine. At this temperature the high specific gravities used in their Formula One fuels gave the best results in their turbocharged engine. These fuel densities were similar to diesel at 0.86 as opposed to normal petrol densities of 0.72–0.76.

After a meeting with BASF in Germany, a special batch of 102 RON with a specific gravity of 0.86 was produced for us. This turbocharged engine fuel was tested but did not deliver the results hoped for and the prospect of transporting large volumes of fuel quickly led to this avenue being dropped. A decision was then made to blend standard density 98-octane pump fuel with a controlled concentration additive we called Adron. This blend raised the octane rating to the maximum allowed under Group C rules as well as assisting with the near impossible logistics involved in transportation of large amounts of special fuels. It allowed standard pump fuel to be sourced locally at the circuits with just the transportation of concentrated additive from Kidlington (15%). The new throttle slide housings had a fuel tube cast into them to allow the return fuel to the tank to pass through the coolest part of the engine compartment directly adjacent to the induction air.

The revised 6.5-litre high compression engine running on 102 RON fuel fitted with larger valves and revised exhaust system was a major step forward.

## Lean burn mapping procedure

It was also time to review leaner burn characteristics and see what improvements could be made here. The base fuel mapping technique used on the engine dynamometer had previously been one of selecting best fuel mixture settings for maximum power, and then optimising the ignition timing. This would then be reprogrammed into the removable chip and retested.

With the modifications I had requested in 1985 from Zytek, this could now be done during engine testing without having to reprogram the engine management chip in between tests. Potentiometers to override fuel mixture and ignition timing were added to the exterior of the engine management boxes. Turning these control knobs either side of the 12 o'clock position would add or subtract from the base map, now making fine tuning on the run possible and reducing dynamometer testing time. These override controls would also now allow minor overall changes to be quickly made at pit stops during a race or when testing, without holding up progress of the race car by having to change a chip. These externally adjustable engine management units greatly reduced the time taken during the development stages of the V12 engine both on and off the track and was an example of the flexible support that we had from Zytek at minimum cost. Permanent changes to update the base map in the computer chip could then be made at a later date.

Additional power increases from the larger capacity 6.5-litre engine were no use however if they came at the cost of additional fuel consumption; the races and testing in 1985 had shown that we were right on the allowable fuel consumption limit. Our focus was now concentrated on improving this area.

In 1985 with the optimised maximum power settings of 12.8:1 air/fuel ratio being used, as the engine was leaned off, by reducing the amount of fuel injected, a corresponding loss of power with improved fuel saving occurred, at the cost of slightly reduced lap times. For the new 6.5-litre engine the mapping techniques previously used to optimise the settings were reviewed with the aim of saving fuel, but with reduced power losses.

Starting with the correct fuel/ignition base map, the engine was then leaned under full load on the dynamometer until 3% of best power was lost at around 13.6:1 air fuel ratio. But this test showed that a 3% loss in power came with the decrease in fuel being used of between 6% and 8%. The slower flame front produced by this lean state allowed a more advanced ignition timing before reaching the optimal pre-detonation point. This turned out to be an additional 2° of ignition advance. The result of this ignition advance was to recover 2% of the previously lost 3% of power. With a fuel saving of 6–8% over the accepted method of mapping at the time, this new fuel optimisation process produced best fuel economy for power output. The engine would lose just 1% of best maximum power but reduce fuel consumption by around 7% by optimising the ignition timing for this leaner 13.6 air/fuel ratio. This would form the base line for our best lean/power compromise in 1986.

Running so close to detonation led to high piston crown temperatures. A small modification to the piston second ring land with a reduced diameter of 0.003in was needed because of the increased heat build up and allowed these lean settings to be run successfully.

Boarder line oil temperatures became evident with small amounts of varnish forming around the second piston ring land area and indicated to Castrol that we were only just under control with these piston temperatures.

Again for those who would wonder how the V12 engine could compete against the perceived advantage of a turbocharged engine it should be remembered that most turbocharged engines in production run air/fuel ratios of 11.5, but in racing conditions it would be considered too lean at a 12:5 air/fuel ratio. *The lean mapping technique we developed for 1986 on the V12 engine eliminated much of the theoretical advantage a high-boost turbocharged engine had.*

The one thing I was pushing for at this time was to take the fuel consumption and car industry 'Green' formula to its logical conclusion sometime in the future by stipulating the use of road pump 98-octane fuel only; and if this could be achieved it would turn the tide in the normally aspirated V12's favour.

Work continued with fine tuning the exhaust system and inlet lengths in conjunction with the EA5 0.610in lift camshaft profile used in 1985. These improvements finally produced 736bhp at 7000rpm on the first optimised engine, up from the best dynamometer figures of 665–675bhp, that produced an average in car figure of 660bhp in 1985.

The new 6.5-litre 1986 V12 engines average maximum output of 730–736bhp was produced without air cleaners at this stage of development and 9bhp was being lost with the in-car air box and filter system being used. The in-car leaned situation was therefore further reduced to 715-720 at 7000rpm. Torque was a very impressive 580-590lbs/ft, and almost a flat line from 5000rpm to 6500rpm. Our work had increased the in-car power and torque output of the V12 by an average of 8%, but more importantly, without any increase in fuel consumption from that of 1985. Coupled with the average 15-20kg weight reduction, this engine would be a considerable improvement over that used in 1985.

| | | |
|---|---|---|
| Spark plugs: | Plug leads: | |
| Inlet valve: | Exhaust valve: | Port diameter: |
| Valve spring type: | Spring fitted length: | Trumpet length: |
| Inlet system: | | |
| Exhaust system: | | |

Correction factor: 1.016

| | RPM | LOAD | CORR. HP | TORQUE |
|---|---|---|---|---|
| ^ | 1000 | | | |
| ^ | 1500 | | | |
| ^ | 2000 | | | |
| ^ | 2500 | | | |
| ^ | 3000 | | | |
| ^ | 3500 | | | |
| ^ | 4000 | | | |
| ^ | 4250 | | | |
| ^ | 4500 | | | |
| ^ | 4750 | | | |
| ^ | 5000 | 109.5 | 556 | 584 |
| ^ | 5250 | | | |
| ^ | 5500 | 108.2 | 604 | 577 |
| ^ | 5750 | 109 | 637 | 581 |
| ^ | 6000 | 110.6 | 674 | 590 |
| ^ | 6250 | 111.1 | 705 | 593 |
| ^ | 6500 | 108.2 | 714 | 577 |
| ^ | 6750 | 106.2 | 728 | 566 |
| ^ | 7000 | 105.1 | 736 | 561 |
| ^ | 7250 | | ^C | ^C |
| ^ | 7500 | ^C | ^C | ^C |
| ^ | 7750 | ^C | ^C | ^C |
| ^ | 8000 | ^C | ^C | ^C |
| ^ | 8500 | ^C | ^C | ^C |
| ^ | 9000 | ^C | ^C | ^C |

Comments:
Corr. factor 1.03
29-4-86 Chas.
CO at 2.5% to hold load
From -3 to -4 ign. at 6500

| RPM | LOAD | CORR. HP | TORQUE |
|---|---|---|---|
| 4500 | 103.1 | 478 | 557 |
| 5000 | 104.7 | 539 | 566 |
| 5250 | 109.3 | 591 | 591 |
| 5500 | 108.6 | 615 | 587 |
| 5750 | 106.5 | 631 | 576 |
| 6000 | 108.2 | 668 | 585 |
| 6250 | 108.1 | 696 | 585 |
| 6500 | 108.8 | 728 | 588 |
| 6750 | 107 | 744 | 579 |
| 6900 | 105 | 746 | 568 |

**Note:** ***This 6.5-litre, 13.5:1 compression ratio engine tested using 102 octane fuels, can hold constant load on the dynamometer without losing power at 2.5% CO-13.5 Air/Fuel ratio. This engine was tested in April 1986 without air filters when the press was quoting the XJR-6 V12 engine as being six litres and maximum power of 660bhp.***

## Alastair Macqueen – TWR Chief Engineer ...

### Downforce split

The car was producing massive downforce very efficiently, but the centre of pressure (the point along the wheelbase where the force acts) was slightly too far back and the car lacked aero front grip at high speed. Given the cutting edge design, it was hardly surprising that the Donald Campbell wind tunnel at Imperial College in London, and real world race circuits required some correlation. It was this car that gave us that first important correlation for ground effect sportscars.

Tony's solution to the problem for 1986 was elegant, simple and very efficient. It involved starting the ground effect tunnels much further forward at the base of the driver's spine instead of at the back of the 'tub'. This required new monocoques and why the back of all the tubs from 1986 had a full width wedge shaped outer panel stretching some 600mm forward to house the start of the tunnels. This modification pulled the aerodynamic centre of pressure forward from about 30% at the front to 40% (mirroring the cars static weight distribution) with no loss of efficiency. For Le Mans a filler panel would be used to cover this area with the lower Le Mans tunnels starting behind the main chassis structure.

### Overall weight

The revision to main chassis also allowed a detailed look at any weight saving which could be applied to the tub. Amongst a host of areas which were optimised were the two front suspension bulkheads becoming carbon from aluminum. With experience of the material came confidence and many panels could be optimized and lightened. Almost 10kgs was lost from the tub and it also allowed the fuel system to be completely revised with better access to the new single tank from the original three separate ones.

### Bodywork

A complete revision of all the bodywork was undertaken to incorporate all the latest aerodynamic lessons learnt and built in a lighter glass composite.

Notable changes would be the 'stealth' panel on the radiator exit, the roof mounted engine air intake duct and larger brake cooling ducts.

### Cockpit

The controls and dashboard were all given a major revision for 1986 and then would remain largely unchanged for the next few years. The driver seating position was retained, but all the major switches and controls were brought within easy reach of the driver's right hand. A new recess was let into the tub to allow more room around the gear lever with the main switches just above.

The master switch and conventional mechanical brake balance control was just to the right of the shift lever.

Centre of the dash was a recording tachometer that would allow download of the rpm every 0.1sec flanked by the water and oil temperature gauges.

At the driver's left hand were all the auxiliary switches (lights, wipers etc.) and beneath them three more gauges for fuel pressure, oil pressure and volts.

A 'fuel used' digital readout and engine mode control were on the lower edge of this cluster.

The gauges all had red lines taped to their faces, not to show a maximum, but to shield the red needles in normal condition. In the days prior to intelligent instrumentation, the drivers had only to glance at the dash to see if there was a single line visible on each dial, if there was a divergence from normal, it would show up as two lines.

Given the size differences in the drivers, a single fixed seat shell was developed which would suit the largest of frames, and any drivers of a smaller stature would each have a specially moulded two-part foam insert to allow them to use exactly the same pedal and steering wheel position. This successfully allowed Eddie Cheever and Jan Lammers who were almost 8in different in height to drive the same car.

## XJR-6 weight reducing programme

Alastair Macqueen had been leaving no stone unturned during the winter of 85/86 in his efforts to reduce the weight of the XJR-6 with every part of the car being evaluated. In the process so many changes were introduced that it was felt that with such a step forward a new chassis identification number would be in order. The amount of water in the long transfer pipes from engine to radiator was reduced by fitting smaller diameter tubes and the engine aluminium header tank reduced in its capacity. These modifications alone would produce a reduction of 3–4kgs in the weight of the water carried. From windscreen glass to carbon body panel thickness, brakes to wheels and tyres, from hollow steering shafts to wiring looms, every item was weighed and a solution put forward for weight reduction. The cars had first raced at Mosport in 1985 at an all up race weight of 100kgs over the minimum allowed of 850kgs. Finding that much was going to be impossible.

Fuel systems and the fuel tank were looked at carefully to ensure that the vital last litres of fuel could be picked up under racing conditions, with baffles to contain and direct the last amounts of fuel under racing G-forces. The second-generation carbon chassis, designated 861 and 862 had seen some detail changes to the fuel system by moving the drivers seating area forward 25mm. The three-tank system employed in 1985 had caused some problems in picking up or transferring the last amounts of fuel. A single bag tank with pickup pumps in each corner could now be fitted behind the driver.

Tony Southgate and John Thompson also had time to look in closer detail at the chassis and they refined production methods and re-engineered components to reduce the main tub weight.

The onboard air jacks were removed and a new jacking system using quick lift air bags adopted. Four jacking holes were bonded into the structure and the pit mounted air bags lifted the race car via long pins into these points as soon as the car had stopped in the pits for tyre changes. With the refuelling during the race set by the organisers at 51 litres a minute there was plenty of time in a pit stop to change wheels as the fuel always took the longest part of the stop.

The transaxle that had begun life as a Hewland VG series was based on the March 85T unit, with magnesium casing and bell housing. Staffs Silent Gears supplied the many gear ratio choices and a modified Salisbury differential was used in all the six hour races with a spool or locked differential for the 24 hour races. These transaxle units would be later serviced by Rob Gustafson of Roni. Solid driveshafts were used with GKN universal joints.

The attention to detail by Alistair and his crew in all these areas as well as the Southgate redesigned tub resulted in finding weight savings of nearly 60kgs, and these savings, along with the engine weight reduction, had produced a car much closer to the minimum weight limit and on a par with the lightest Porsche 962 at around 885kgs in final racing conditions. Dunlop too had been working on a better tyre package with larger fronts and retaining the 4-ply nylon cross ply construction to aid the understeer problem faced in 1985. The best factory Porsche 962C with water-cooled heads weighed in at around 885kgs with other private teams up to 20kgs heavier. If TWR could match the lower weights then the XJR-6 for 1986 would be 8% lighter, with 7 to 8% more useable power to the same fuel limit. This would be a huge step forward in reducing lap time versus fuel used and a far greater gain than anything Porsche could come up with from one year to another.

This weight reduction in Group C was vital; less weight meant increased car acceleration and higher cornering speeds to produce a faster lap time with no increase in fuel consumption. Improved cornering ability through weight reduction would need a little less rear wing angle to produce the needed downforce for the same corner speeds. Lower rear wing angle meant less drag on the straight leading to higher speeds for the same power output. The 1986 cars were now beginning to look competitive and a much larger step forward than TW and Roger had envisaged.

Part of our engine update for 1986 had been to flow test every fuel injector being used over a 10,000-cycle programme at Zytek to ensure exactly the same amount of fuel was injected to each cylinder. This allowed injectors to be grouped into similar capacities and discard any injectors that flowed above or below a set output. The Bosch injectors used were very accurate but some discrepancies of up to 1.5% were found and this became a very worthwhile exercise, with these out of tolerance injectors being discarded. This process and the accuracy that Zytek could achieve with their equipment gave us the confidence to run lean engines without introducing the possibility of a weak cylinder from an out of calibration injector, leading to piston overheating and possible failure.

## Fuel versus Lap Meter

The concept of producing a fuel versus laps covered meter could be a vital step forward, for two reasons. The TWR engineers would know from the first lap and the pace all the cars in the race were running to how close their car was running to the fuel allowance while travelling at the leading cars' pace. A second benefit soon developed with the drivers using this concept's hardware as a learning tool in practice for the race, trying perhaps just one corner in a higher gear and gauge the fuel saved, versus any slowing in lap time. Drivers soon found that using the predictable 570lbs/ft of torque available in a higher gear produced measurable advantages in fuel used versus lap time lost. These benefits would be difficult to apply to the turbocharged cars which if using the same technique would result in less predictable turbo lag and boost levels mid corner.

Based on simple physics a circuit that was hard on brakes creating higher disc temperatures was going to be harder on fuel; with much of the energy created by burning fuel in the engine being disbursed as heat energy under braking. Our 'taxi meter' again could help to show the drivers the best fuel saving versus lap time lost by using some slightly earlier accelerator lifting points before braking that then resulted in slightly lighter braking needed while carrying the best speed into the corner. Not all drivers could see this as a possible advantage on some circuits, with short shifting considered a better option. Because the meter was divided into tenths of laps any changes in technique would quickly show up to be beneficial or not.

The difference between race times to the fuel allowance and racing to the capability of the car would turn out to be about half a second per kilometre, about two second per lap at the average race circuit. Not all drivers would see this as a total driving challenge as it was contrary to most racing instincts, technique as much as pure aggression being the order of the day. Drivers who were naturally quicker could become less enthusiastic when other drivers did the same lap times to the fuel allowance – but the very good ones accepted the challenge of racing to a fuel limit, and got as much out of finding new techniques to do this, confirming why they were constantly the best at their trade. The many disadvantages that had been assumed with this large V12 engine were starting to diminish rapidly in early testing in 1986 when the increased race mode flexibility became apparent. The drivers had ten separate points on each lap to check if any change in driving style had gained a few vital meters of track producing instant visual feedback for the same fuel used. These few meters repeated over six hours of racing would be the difference between winning and losing.

Porsche at this time used a fuel consumption measuring system that involved a 10 to 15 litre reserve tank and a low fuel level light in the main fuel tank. As the main tank ran out of fuel the reserve tank was switched on. This action was reported to the engineers by the driver, enabling the engineers to calculate the fuel consumption over the previous 85 litres. The engineers then had time to calculate which lap to pit on and whether they were ahead or behind the fuel target at that time. The next driver could then be briefed as to how he had to proceed in his particular phase of the 1000km race before he got into the car.

The Porsche 962C at this time ran a fixed fuel mixture and any flexibility needed was provided by adjusting the boost levels up or down to race to the fuel allowance. Overall mixture was controlled by a chip setting and this setting could be changed before qualifying or the race. Porsche drivers who looked fast in the first stint could use too much fuel, pit a lap early and make their co-driver look slower as he brought the fuel consumption back on reduced boost. Our system was superior, producing driver discipline from lap one and we were constantly aware of the lap time our drivers were running versus the fuel used to produce it.

The final piece in the 6.5-litre V12 engine electronic development was my request to have *driver* adjustable fuel and ignition override switches. These had already been fitted to the engine management boxes the year before to allow quick changes to fuelling and ignition in the pits, but had been strictly limited to changes by me only. This new in-cockpit system would allow the drivers very small changes to override the base chip programme, as they raced.

Other engine suppliers did not allow their customer teams to change any of their safe engine settings. I would continue to be in control of any adjustment to the base chip programme during the race, but they could now be carried out on the run by the driver, a first in any formula at the time.

## Telemetry system introduced

With Zytek, Engs developed a basic car to pits telemetry system for the 1986 series. Once a lap, it would relay our innovative 'taxi meter' readings from ten points on the track, and confirmed the ignition and mixture settings the driver had selected to a viewing screen in the pits. Honda in Formula One at the time had a boost profile alternative, but no driver adjustable fuel/ignition adjustment, normal practice today. Porsche would not have in-car dashboard mounted driver fuel and ignition control until 1988 when they changed to the Bosch MP1.7 sequential system. Only Porsche technicians were able to carry out changes to engine controls while the race car was stationary in the pits in 1986.

## Fuel versus laps completed meter

After the process of calibrating the fuel injectors had been carried out, I discussed the idea with Zytek that these total electronic injector pulse times could be recorded and used to produce a very accurate real-time fuel consumption reading in the race car, with the idea that it should mean something to both team and drivers. The measuring of pulse times to record fuel consumption was nothing new, it was being used in a very basic way to pass information to the fuel consumption read outs that had become fashionable on higher end passenger vehicles; but their software configuration was too vague for our use.

From this calibration exercise we already knew the amount of fuel delivered versus the injector pulse time from our calibration work. The injector 'on' time was not linear, nearly a constant one millisecond needed to open and close the injector, needing a correction factor for shorter injection periods. I discussed this basic idea with Alastair Macqueen and we both travelled to Birmingham to put the case to Bill Gibson and Brian Mason.

After a joint brain storming session, the idea of a lap counter emerged that could be programmed for each circuit with the exact amount of fuel needed for a single lap.

The programmed constant was calculated by dividing the amount of fuel allowed for the whole race by the number of laps in the race, plus the one to form up on the grid. The litres per lap constant would then be programmed in the computer to produce a calibration read out on the dash display in tenths of a lap, not litres used. The meter would be zeroed as the car left the pit garage after being topped up with fuel and sent on its warm up lap at the start of the race, and this out lap would be a chance to save fuel with special driving techniques on the way to the starting grid. Later some of the drivers would save up to a litre of fuel compared with others on this out lap, no pointless revving of the engine while waiting to exit the pit lane. This fuel saving on the out lap would give the car a small amount of fuel in hand and became a small credit on the meter, perhaps reading 1.7 laps as the car crossed the start/finish line on its first completed lap of the race (second lap in total).

If the car was running to the exact fuel allocation for that particular circuit, the car readout during the race would display exactly the same lap number when it passed the start/finish line as the laps just completed by the race car. During the race the lap readout on the meter when crossing the start/finish line would need to be within one or two tenths of the lap number indicated on the driver's pit board being shown from the pits. The driver could also be told what it should be reading by radio from his engineer each time he crossed the start/finish line.

This in-car driver control featured two dashboard mounted knobs fitted within easy reach of the driver, with settings from 0 to 5. One was for fuel mixture and the other for ignition timing change to override the base 13.6:1 air/fuel ratio and ignition settings. Again this request showed the rapid development that was possible with the working relationship available from Bill and Brian at Zytek. To my request they had simply said yes it was possible, Brian sorted the software, Bill the hardware. We had an operating system two weeks later without needing a committee decision to action, or budget discussion with our finance director – Zytek did it for nothing.

Number 3 on the 0-5 fuel control knob was the lean/power dynamometer setting with 4 and 5 adding 3% of extra fuel each, used for qualifying or after longer periods behind a pace car. This left the remaining 3-2-1 numbers as selectable leaner race settings changing the fuel mixture by 1.5% with each step down from position 3. Position 0 was set very lean and to be used when forming up on the out lap from the pits or running behind the pace car; or when we were in real trouble. The race lean positions of 3-2-1 would have the engine running at 13.5:1 to 14:1 A/F ratio on Wide Open Throttle (WOT), but produce high piston crown temperatures. At the same time the ignition timing knob had to be adjusted to the same as the fuel number with each click downwards from position 3 advancing the ignition timing half a degree and each click upwards from three retarding the ignition by one degree with the richer mixtures faster burn liable to create end gas detonation. These engines were always run on the ragged edge of detonation and to prevent pre-ignition, cold N82G Champion spark plugs were fitted. This reduced spark plug core temperatures that could instigate piston destroying pre-ignition from lean burning.

This system added greater flexibility during the race when combined with changes of up to 400rpm when short shifting from the race maximum of 7000rpm. It was also a good psychological tool with drivers feeling more in control of the situation rather than just using a few hundred rpm less, perhaps even a placebo boost control that all the pundits were saying was so necessary in this form of racing. We had in the process produced a much more flexible racing engine than most realised.

*2nd generation fuel/lap meter as fitted to 1987 Jaguars with the addition of the four tyre temperature warning lights.*

The last piece of the puzzle was the decision to have the two fuel delivery rails ducted into a single fuel pressure relief valve in the return line to the fuel tank. This Bosch mechanical unit was externally adjustable and set on the dynamometer at wide open throttle. Very small variation in fuel pressure were present from race car to race car mainly influenced by the small changes in charging voltage or fuel pump efficiencies. While these elements were so small they would have no influence on any racing outcome they did affect the complete accuracy of our electronic fuel meter using a common software program across all race cars. Any small discrepancy in a particular car could be corrected by me via the adjustable fuel regulator, normally less than half-a-pound up or down in pressure, and final error was less than one litre per racing stint using the 100 litre capacity fuel tank.

# TWR Engineering

## Engines

TWR's Engine Shop produces all the racing and road engines for the TWR Group. From the earliest days of Tom Walkinshaw's business, when Mazda RX7s with their twin rotor Wankel engines were tuned to achieve giant-killing success on the track, TWR Engineering have proven themselves more than capable of developing a powerful and reliable power unit that will live up to the rigorous and public testing it is given.

TWR Engineering have a wide experience of 4, 8 and 12-cylinder engines, from relatively mild road tuning, to full international racing specification.

There are ample facilities on site to allow building and testing of engines, with data logging of engines on test, in a new purpose-built workshop.

JAGUAR

CHAPTER TEN

# The opposition

**What was TWR up against going into the 1986 Group C series of international six hour races and the Le Mans 24 hour event, with some shorter 'Super sprint' races being tried this year?**

## Lancia

The LC2 Lancia 'Martini' livered Group C race car had competed with its Gianpaulo Dallara designed chassis and twin turbocharged Ferrari 3-litre V8 engine since 1983. The car had shown power and pace from its Ferrari engine and drivers Riccardo Patrese, Mauro Baldi, Bob Wollek and Sandro Nannini, but reliability was inconsistent and the team sadly would withdraw from competition later in 1986. The Lancia was a beautiful looking, effective and well-built package that appeared to have what was needed to be successful. The team never seemed to be totally comfortable with the new fuel regulation, and turbocharged engine builders at this time were reluctant to lean off their engines. It was also a time when more sophisticated engine management systems were needed to get the best fuel consumption from these engines, and most of these were still at the design stage.

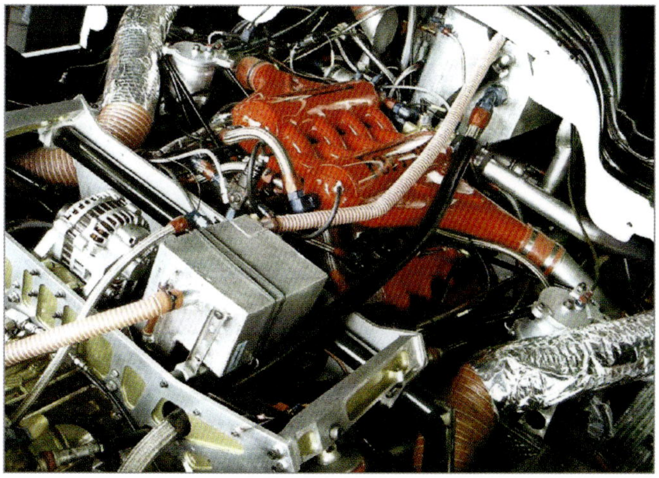

*Lancia 3-litre twin turbocharged V8 engine.*

## Porsche

The main opposition in Porsche was now in its fifth year of development, giving good factory support for private teams with upgrade packages and technical support. Porsche was the dominant force worldwide in sports car racing including America at this time. The original Porsche 956 had been produced for the start of the new sports car category, the WEC series in 1982, as a 2.65-litre, air-cooled engine fitted with mechanical fuel injection. The 962C evolution of the 956 that had been introduced in 1985 was based on changes to safety regulations for IMSA and soon to be introduced to Group C. The 962C evolution increased safety in two areas with the foot controls moved behind the centre line of the front wheels to help protect the driver's legs in a frontal impact, along with the aluminium roll cage being replaced with a steel one.

A change in wheel diameters from the 16in of the 956 to 17in front and slightly narrower 19in rear had allowed an improved venturi tunnel design to fit in that confined area at the rear. In 1985 the Porsche factory flat-six 'Boxer' engines had been up rated from air-cooled to water-cooled cylinder heads fitted to larger capacity three litre engines for qualifying and some races. The original air-cooled heads relied on rich fuel setting to assist in their cooling. Now as a result of the higher cylinder and valve temperatures being produced very safe rich mixture settings had to be discarded because of the limited fuel allowances for WSPC races, along with the increasing competitiveness of the series. Electronics had replaced mechanical injection systems with the arrival of L Jetronic non-sequential fuel injection. This Bosch system could be altered with specially programmed chips, a new technology that most Porsche teams were unable to carry out, relying on the factory dispensed units controlling their engines.

It should be remembered at this time that Porsche would have considered air/fuel ratios of 12:1 to be quite lean in their small capacity turbocharged engines because of the high cylinder pressures and temperatures produced by turbocharging – while the Jaguar V12 engine in 1986 had similar race power outputs using leaner 13.5:1 air/fuel ratios with very lean race settings up to 14:1 possible.

The engines in the Porsche programme that had started with a capacity of 2.65 litres had increased through the intervening years to 3.0 litres by 1986 as they experimented with best fuel economy or qualifying set-ups while still able to use special high-octane fuels. The downside to the new water-cooled four valves per cylinder heads and cooling system was an increase in weight, leading to the 962C with its steel roll cage and aluminium monocoque construction staying at a weight of around 885kgs even after all their detailed weight saving methods introduced for 1986. These engines were rated at 780bhp and 524lbs/ft of torque with full boost rich mixture settings that could not be used in racing conditions. The engine had to rev 1000rpm higher to achieve these power outputs than the V12, but they could not match the mid range torque of the V12's 585lbs/ft

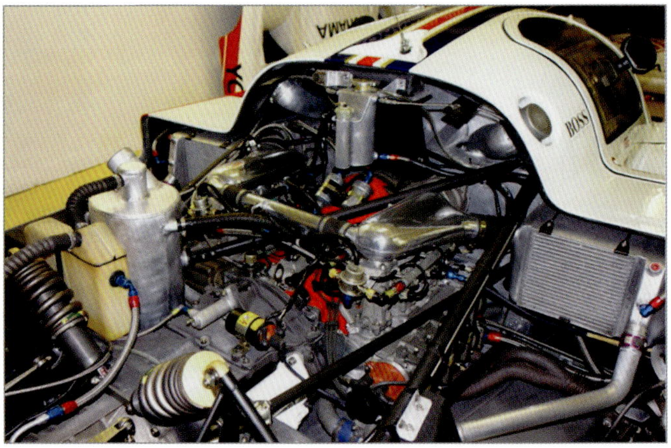

*Rothmans 956/962 Porsche engine.*

available on corner exit. Corner exit torque was important to accelerate the race car before fuel sapping drag at higher speeds was encountered.

For 1986 many of the privateer customer Porsche teams would upgrade to the new water-cooled three litre engines as well, it was also rumoured that some privateer teams were running larger engines of up to 3.4 litres. This larger capacity made sense as the 102 RON octane fuel used was possibly more susceptible to detonation using optimised advanced ignition settings. With the higher boost levels used with smaller engines, the move to larger engines needed lower boost pressures to produce the same power outputs, and would be less susceptible to high engine temperatures and detonation. More advanced ignition timings are possible when using lower boost settings and lower octane fuels. This increase in efficiency using optimised engine settings would easily overcome any slight increases in frictional losses produced with the increased engine capacity. I could never understand later in 1987 why Porsche did not use their 3.8-litre engines on lower boost when forced to use even lower octane fuel with the rule changes of 1987, there must have been some reliability issue with the use of that engine.

The factory Porsche team would have some advantage at the start of 1986 with their drivers already having competed in USA events at the beginning of the year including the Daytona 24 hour event in January. The TWR Jaguar team, with the exception of Jean-Louis Schlesser, had to start 1986 with its drivers having done testing only. They were professionals however and would soon master the situation.

## Sauber C8

Another competitor, the Sauber C8 had started life in 1985 with a twin turbocharged 90° V8 engine based on the Mercedes 4937cc M117 production engine. This race engine was rated at 700bhp and 590lbs/ft of torque for 1986, very similar to the outputs from the Jaguar V12 6.5-litre engine, and was the work of the Swiss Heini Mader tuning company. It was an interesting concept and although a little large in capacity with the high-octane fuel available favouring higher boost engines, the low boost needed with this larger engine would provide reliability and simpler tuning, and followed my line of thought on larger capacity low boost engines. Both the Sauber and the Porsche engines used the Bosch Jetronic double fuel pulse per cycle engine management systems in 1986. The Sauber team however was in the process of moving from a small privateer to larger things with its new 'Kouros' fragrances sponsor and had experience and speed in drivers Henri Pescarolo and John Nielsen. Team owner Peter Sauber from his base at Hinwil in Switzerland was another team owner determined to make his mark in the sport assisted by team manager Max Welti.

*Sauber twin turbo 5-litre V8 engine.*

# The Opposition

*LANCIA LC2*

*ROTHMANS 956/962 PORSCHE*

*SAUBER C8*

JAGUAR

CHAPTER ELEVEN

# Testing the 1986 package

**TW's bold decision to not use the Group 44 XJR-5 chassis in favour of the superior engineering and benefits of using carbon fibre technology had proved true by the start of 1986. After long hours over the winter of 85/86 the TWR team had managed a combined car and engine weight reduction of just over 80kgs.**

The TWR team was now on an equal footing with the opposition weight wise. Power and torque output had been lifted by a minimum 7% from 1985 – without any increases in fuel consumption.

All things being equal there is evidence that turbocharged engines can be up to 8% more efficient using the energy from the exhaust system, but this is totally dependent on using the best quality high octane anti-detonation fuel available to allow optimisation of ignition timing using turbocharging. This advantage is soon lost when using lower octane fuels resulting in ignition timings having to be retarded from optimum settings, and fuel mixtures still needing to be richer than those possible with normally aspirated engines. This aspect was something most pundits had not got their heads around however. Diesel technology 'direct injection petrol' engines that would help to eliminate this problem were still some twenty years in the future.

Better drivability was available with the normally aspirated V12 engine when operated on very lean engine settings or when running slower with worn tyres or in rain situations, allowing measured instant throttle adjustments. Engs had produced superior engine management technology via Zytek's one box sequential engine management system. Porsche was still using a Bosch production based programmable L Jetronic unit, and it would seem were not fully aware of the benefits of the sequential injection MP1.7 system Bosch were developing at the time. We had already proved a sequential system up to 7% more efficient when using wide period high TDC-lift racing camshaft designs with tuned exhaust systems.

The accurate fuel consumption meter fitted to the XJR-6 was also a much-needed tool in the early stages of learning the best racing solution for drivers in a competitive situation that was new to them.

These engine and chassis improvements had produced a power to weight ratio increase close to 14% with no increase in fuel consumption in full race trim; a huge step forward in less than one year. Quentin Spurring, one of the more knowledgeable commentators at the time, and a person who has kindly encouraged and supported my previous writing efforts, summed up the almost universal consensus of opinion and support for needing a turbocharged engine at the beginning of the 1986 season in *Autosport's* preview of the first race at Monza in April.

**Quentin Spurring:** The team may, indeed, have come up with a very competitive package for 1986,

> but its chances of success remain overshadowed by the use of an inflexible power plant. Even in a sprint (in fact especially in a sprint), the Jaguars will lose out badly in the event of wet-to-dry track conditions, or a substantial period under the yellow. It does look as though the musical V12 cars will be able to match the turbos in the power versus economy game this season; but whenever a race is disrupted in such a way that the drivers can later expend more fuel, the turbo men, able to screw up the boost pressure, will always be winners.

The conception here is a reasonable one but assumes greater fuel saving in the wet than would be the actual case. In the wet the turbo cars would not reduce their fuel consumption in *proportion* to their much-reduced lap times, and so not have the excess of fuel assumed available to them when conditions dried out if the race was to complete its 1000km, The XJR-6 would also be quicker in wet conditions with its better driveability, leaving the opposition turbocharged cars to use more fuel just to make up the lost ground.

However timed (six hour) race needs another thought process entirely if prolonged pace car conditions prevail and a shorter distance than the 1000kms is produced under the six hour limit, and that could move the advantage to the turbo race cars. This situation rarely occurred and when it did, caused some confusion to all competitors with the total distance (number of laps) still not really known till close to the very end. It should also be remembered that as any higher boosts were selected the air/fuel ratio mixture did not remain constant, but needed to be mapped increasingly richer as the boost pressures increased above normal race levels, along with any further retarding of ignition timings needed. *This situation would reduce fuel efficiency versus lap time gained.* It is doubtful that the time lost and fuel saved in a wet race with the Porsches could change the outcome against the Jaguars when the track had dried.

If rain was predicted we would have just run at a faster pace initially, and I believe that better performance with the total XJR-6 package in a race that ended with rain would have still produced a superior lap time to fuel used. Another factor was the TWR team philosophy with me being put under constant pressure to produce results from the engine during the race by the team. Jaguar had not given me a mandate concerning engine reliability being paramount, and I was left to make whatever settings were needed to be competitive.This was something that Porsche engineers, perhaps looking for a long career with their employer, would not easily entertain when being asked for total reliability in supporting Porsche's Engineering Brand.

Our V12 engine was actually more flexible in its ability to cover changing racing conditions than people realised.

It was obvious to us all that Porsche would have the upper hand at the start of 1986 as TWR came to grips with new drivers and race control systems. They would also feel that the Jaguar racing programme would continually suffer from being unable to get even close to their 885kgs weight limit because of its heavy V12 engine and gearbox. This no doubt lulled Porsche into a false sense of security, few believing the large step the expanding TWR team was capable of achieving over the winter of 85/86. They would not believe that TWR would arrive in 1986 with a car that could race at a weight some 70/80kgs lighter than in 1985. While Porsche produced small detailed changes to their car for 1986, the TWR XJR-6 had been given so many changes that it had now been internally designated XJR-8.

TWR was in the process of demonstrating a flexibility and reaction to change that only a smaller dynamic company can produce when up against a larger factory mentality. All the engineering inputs needed to produce this large step forward for the TWR team had come together with a common aim. They included Tony Southgate's designs and manufacturing co-operation with John Thompson, and Alastair Macqueen's dedication to detail to then turn the Silk Cut Jaguar into a successful lightweight racing car with serviceable racing application. These concepts were then all put in place by a motivated and hard working TWR team who never looked at the clock until the job was finished.

## Testing the theory

It was now time to go testing and see the result of all this hard work. We hoped that most of the advantages Porsche had in 1985 would be gone by the first race at Monza, although this was yet to be proven with considerable development work still to be done to produce the best from this new package.

After the first test of the season at Silverstone with the new XJR-6 and Eddie Cheever's very positive report compared to his earlier test in the 1985 race car, TW phoned and asked me to come to his office. He expressed some surprise at the level of engine improvement Cheever had reported and thanked Engs for their fine efforts. I was a little disappointed that he appeared so surprised because he had been kept abreast of all these new developments and improvements. It did also indicate though that both TW and Roger were still not totally convinced or understood all of the engine principles involved or indeed of the competitiveness of this V12 package.

I was able to convey these positive thoughts back to the engine division personnel. It is amazing how little praise is needed, at the right time, to promote self-esteem and dedication to get a motivated work force to continually work twelve hour days six to seven days a week for months on end.

The team moved to Paul Ricard in the south of France in mid-March of 1986 to continue a full programme of pre-season testing using the long back straight available at this circuit to simulate some early Le Mans testing. One XJR-6, with Eddie Cheever at the wheel, was dedicated to fuel consumption testing which was a considerable help for me as the team normally fitted this in along with normal race car testing. This testing would be to see how lean we could run the engine safely in a circuit situation with varying lengths of time on full throttle, and then progress to part throttle progression and driveability off corners.

In 1986 we had no on-board separate data acquisition, just some very basic information on engine over revving and throttle position information to record the amount of time on full throttle. This had a total storage capacity of just one or two laps in the engine management systems memory. The new Stack tachometers had been fitted to the 1986 cars and these could also store rpm related data for the first time.

By the time of this test in March Engs had still not built its full complement of new engines due to the late ordering of components, and we were using the updated 1985 units at this test. With the future test programmes in mind these engines needed to return to Kidlington in reusable undamaged condition after perhaps 20 hours running to indicate the engine's fuel consumption abilities under racing conditions. For Eddie Cheever though, always impatient for progress, any of my concerns were not his problem and he of course remained unaware of the late build situation and reduction in engine numbers, with all the outward indications of a well funded team.

He was intrigued with the dashboard mixture switching and the driver control that went with it and entered these tests with enthusiasm and produced sound feedback.

After agreeing to the test procedure, he duly ran laps at the 4 then the 3 (13:6 A/F ratio) setting before

*Testing continues at Silverstone.*

returning to the pits. The Champion N82G spark plugs and exhaust pipe colour were inspected with Eddie advising that everything was fine and we should go leaner. There was no on-board exhaust gas recording technology available to us at the time so things took a little longer with the removal and inspection of both front and rear spark plugs on each bank to read the porcelain and electrode colours.

I was concerned about the long straight at this circuit and longer time on wide open throttle and wanted time to work down towards the next settings. Eddie had agreed to return to the '4' position on the long straight each time he had selected one of the leaner settings. It was during one of the stops in the late morning that Eddie recalled the story to me of testing with the Alfa Romeo Formula One turbo engine programme and how he managed to blow up 16 engines, suggesting we should shortcut the procedure I had implemented. He wanted to just find the setting that the engine could not take, just one blow up was all it would take and the job would be done were his thoughts.

The testing continued working down from position 3 (race lean) to position 2 with the mixture having to be returned to position 4 at the start of the long straight. On position 2 some minor adjustments needed to be made to some hesitations appearing in throttle progression off some of the corners. Some of these part throttle transient situations would be different circuit to circuit, but could not be completely reproduced at our engine testing facility at Kidlington. These progression areas would be located and small fuelling additions made to smooth out any hesitations that would occur with the reduced overall lean settings, helping the driver with corner exit throttle control and power off the corners.

This process is referred to as dynamic fuel mapping and the remedy involved the driver sitting in the pits with the engine switched off and pressing the throttle pedal part way down to where he felt was the throttle opening area where the hesitation was. Using a voltmeter the throttle potentiometer voltage was recorded and traced on the fuel map in the computer against the rpm the driver had reported. This window area of the map would have small amounts of fuel added till the lean hesitation was corrected as we progressed from 3-2-1 with the overall fuel mixture control. With this same engine, on returning after the test we could then concentrate on these part throttle areas on the

```
Chips for PAUL RICARD 19-3-86

No 1
STD. trim box
2A fuel / ign. map [85]
Pot .45
Limiter 7200
Fuel pressure 49psi  /  Fuel meter C3  00  00
Box trim +1 FUEL  /  -1 IGN.

No 2
IN CAR control box
2A fuel / ign. based -over run lean, full load sights 6 11 12 13
changed
86 spec. 60psi fuel pressure / Fuel meter Bo  00  00
Pot .45
Limiter 7200
BOX trim  0 FUEL [rich] / -2.5 IGN
Use with air tube to air box / barometer law fitted

No 3
As No 2 WITHOUT in car control

No 4
As No 1 but IN CAR CONTROL
Use with air pipe to air box / barometer law fitted

No 5
   2/3rd.  angle  sites  +4%  approx.Lean  from  6000-8000 by 2%
approx.[result of Ricard test]

No6
  Dyno test 02  9-4-86,  +20%  at  4500  ,then  richer  down that
throttle sight.Richer 4750-5000.
  2% lean 5500-5750-6000
Ign. -3
Fuel 0  O/ALL Trim at 500 full power -
Lean to 250 OK -Very lean 100[Obove goes for all chips.]
THIS chip to be used at Monza 20-4-86.

No 7
Full load modified and accurate except below 4500rpm
This chip used at Silverstone

No 7ign
As  obove  with  part  throttle  IGN. advanced [theoretical to be
checked pre Le Mans.
```

*These are the various base chips to be tested and modified up to chip no.5, and this was carried out by Eddie Cheever over the two-day test at Paul Ricard using the Zytek system processes. Note fuel meter programme setting changes with increase fuel pressure (chip 1 and 2).*

dynamometer and optimise the ignition timing. During this time, we were monitoring fuel consumption and fuel usage versus the new 'in-car lap counter' to finally calibrate it accuracy.

After a few more tests and not long before the lunch stop I observed that the dashboard fuel switch was on ZERO when Eddie came in – the envisaged Pace Car only setting. Eddie immediately started reporting some hesitations and flat spots as he was by now well tuned into the questions he would be asked. When I pointed out the Zero mixture setting on the dash control there was a short silence and then, "Oh shit, I forgot to turn it back up to 2 before I came in" came the slightly chastened reply – he had completed 'a few' laps on the pace car setting (14.2:1) A/F ratio down the long straight.

In the end this was all very good news and proved that the larger capacity, slower revving V12 2-valve engine could take the cylinder temperatures produced at wide open throttle (WOT) and 14.0 to 14.2 to 1 air/fuel ratios, and still produce good power and reliability, the lower rpm allowing piston temperature control with lean settings. The overrun fuel cut coupled with a high idle setting was also working well for piston cooling allowing just cooling air to pass through the engine whenever the throttle was closed on gear shifts and when braking, the engine helping a little with the rear braking as well as it just compressed air without fuel.

When Cheever had completed all these tests we moved on to final correction for air intake pressure changes. The engine air intake box was connected via a small pipe to the pressure transducer in the engine management system box in a test to confirm the theoretical atmospheric pressure change map figures from Zytek were relevant in racing conditions. This final control of the engine fuel map would make small adjustments for atmospheric pressure changes on the day, altitude changes such as at the Spa or Fuji circuits as well as any unknown dynamics involved with the forward speed of the race car and its influence in varying air intake pressures.

Eddie Cheever was a very good test driver during this important early testing phase for us at Engs, and we developed a good working relationship via his enthusiasm for all things fuel saving. His pushing the envelope at these early tests took us to the limits needed earlier than we would have with a more cautious approach.

A total of fourteen hours running was carried out over the two-day test at Paul Ricard and importantly we still had an engine in good condition that when stripped down would be representative of a hard-worked race engine. The only problem encountered by the end of the test period was the clutch that had started to slip and this had limited any further testing. The 7.25in triple plate unit was returned to AP for rectification and a second diaphragm was fitted to the clutch cover to increase its clamp loading. This modification then removed any doubts about its ability to last for the Le Mans 24 hour race and proved up to the task over the entire Group C programme.

It was also found at these early test sessions in 1986 that the power delivery was not to everyone's liking, some drivers complaining of not enough part throttle progression and control producing too much power at low throttle openings. The throttle arm was then redesigned to give less initial throttle opening for the same pedal movement and then an increasing rate closer to full throttle.

Later brief full load dynamometer tests would show Wide Open Throttle 16:1 Air/Fuel ratio before unstable combustion and misfire on this racing V12 engine, but also that greater than 14.3:1 air/fuel ratios were counter-productive in a racing situation with lap time to fuel used. The 45 degree and offset inlet port angle produced good volumetric efficiency and cylinder swirl. This was aided by the bowl in piston design with its directional tapered squish lands in close contact with the head surface to enhance burn quality via squish turbulence at lean settings.

Another new system that was being tested on the XJR-6 was a front twin brake disc set-up with single caliper. This involved two separate cross drilled solid discs that were free to float on hub drive splines and the idea was to increase the normal two swept surfaces to four. A special brake caliper had been produced that used four brake pads to operate on either side of each disc. Any slight pad knock-off or taper would mean floating discs having to quickly realign themselves as the brake pads made contact and there was a danger of binding in the splines. An accident did occur while Brancatelli was testing the new system in Portugal when a disc exploded and sent the car off the track. It was decided there and

*Experimental twin front discs that were later discarded after testing accident.*

then to end any further development in that direction. My observation in using this system had been motivated by TW's need to be seen as the first team to use a potentially new idea, and advance his profile via media announcements. It was the need to show new systems to Jaguar and the public at large, rather than any sound engineering concept, or more importantly, need. The greater the braking effort you use, the less fuel efficiency for a given lap time.

With the shortest races of six hours/1000kms duration except for the Super Sprint format that varied in lengths up to 360kms, for any team trying to break into this form of motor racing the biggest hurdle would be reliability. Interestingly for the status of Group C it was probably this six hour format that dissuaded most spectators from coming to these races. From the very first Group C race visited, the main thing that was instantly obvious was the lack of spectators. For some of these races they were counted in hundreds not thousands.

Just when things were coming together at this time after a hectic assembly of engine components early in the 1986 year, some pressures had started to emerge and stress levels were being raised. During a progress meeting in TW's office with questions raised on timing of final drawings and completed engines ready for the first race at Monza, some of these pressures finally came to the surface. This particular meeting became too much for design draftsman Russell Sharp and before we could calm things down Russell stood up and said the main problem was "You Tom", with the procrastinations involved at the end of 1985. He walked out of the meeting – as well as his position at TWR.

TW just asked "What's his problem?" and did not seem to be concerned that Russell had left.

TW did not like Russell and disrespected his value to the project or to us at Engs. He seemed totally unaware of the full impact of this departure and made no effort to reconcile the problem. Russell and Engs only design drafting support were gone. We still had many drawings to finalise and he had been progressing the new throttle slide housing, with the fuel return tube inserted to help keep the fuel cool. This was vital support for Engs and was difficult to replace in the short term.

> ***We learn something every day, and lots of times it's that what we learned the day before was wrong.***
>
> **– Bill Vaughan**

JAGUAR

CHAPTER TWELVE

# 1986 Jaguar takes on Porsche

## Monza – April 20th

**The first race of 1986 was the Kouros Cup 'Supersprint' to the shorter format of 365kms with a fuel allowance of 190 litres, at Monza in Italy. We welcomed the shorter race to start the season off for the two-car XJR-6 Silk Cut Jaguar Racing Team. The TWR team now had a distinctly different look to that of the British Racing Green team of late 1985. Sadly for us Martin Brundle would not be released from his Formula One duties after the two fatal Group C accidents in 1985. Martin had been a constant help to TWR race programmes with his driving abilities over the years, and would be greatly missed. Number one status was now with Derek Warwick and team mate Eddie Cheever who had already demonstrated his engine testing abilities at Paul Ricard. Current TWR Group A Rover drivers Gianfranco Brancatelli and Jean-Louis Schlesser were in the second car.**

The Silk Cut Jaguar racing team with its large cigarette sponsor had nearly doubled in size over the winter months. I cannot recall any at management level at TWR or Jaguar that actually smoked, but this was where the money was and this money made it all happen. If these visual changes did not announce the team's arrival in a serious way, then the small piece of theatre that happened next gained the paddocks full attention. All competing cars were to be weighed before practice and both XJR-6 cars now had a lightweight engine cover fitted, too thin to last a race, and all the water drained from the engine and radiator. Engine and gearbox oil was also drained and probably a few other loose items removed as well with the cars being pushed to the weigh-in. The various Porsche team personnel standing around waiting to see the results from the weighbridge were now stunned as the two Jaguars came up 20kgs lighter than any Porsche weighed that day, both Jaguars being 855kgs. The reality was that the XJR-6 was one of the lightest cars in the field; and it was now confirmed to us it would have a true racing weight the same as the factory manual gearbox 962C at around 885kgs, other 962C teams were up to 25kgs heavier.

It was also interesting at this first race of the year that two people I did not know came up and spoke to me on the starting grid. The first a journalist saying that he could not understand why I was wasting my time with a normally aspirated package as all knew a turbo engine was more economical because of the efficiency of the exhaust charge. The second was a Porsche team engineer who had carried out some investigations into my past and enquired if I had completed my PhD degree at Imperial College London, and what the subject of my thesis had been as he would like to read it. I decided to let all that remain a mystery for him as I had not been to university. Three years of evening classes while doing an automotive apprenticeship, my engine tutor was a WWII aircraft engineer specialising in radial engines on American B17G Flying Fortresses was probably not the best subject to raise at that time.

> Qualifying had the works Porsches in tyre problems with their 962C driven by Wollek/Mass and Bell/Stuck's PDK equipped 956, Jacky Ickx having now retired from the factory team. De Cesaris in the Lancia LC2-85 pleased the small Italian crowd by taking pole position from Ludwig/Barilla in the Joest 'Taka Q' 956B with third place to the Olson/Boutsen 962C of the 'Torno' sponsored Brun team. Against the 16 turbocharged Group C cars on this fast Monza circuit the Warwick/Cheever XJR-6 qualified sixth and the Brancatelli/Schlesser sister car ninth, impressive under the circumstances against high boost opposition running at boost levels that could never be used in the race without going over the fuel allowance. The 5 or 5.6-litre Sauber/Mercedes with race sponsor Kouros had ended up twelfth just over two seconds slower than the sixth place Jaguar.

In the race the two Jaguars driven by Cheever and Schlesser were instantly on the pace and moved into third and fourth positions dicing with Stuck in the factory Porsche ahead. Ludwig lead from the start and it was not until a third of the race had passed that Cheever was able to establish himself in second position, five seconds behind the leader. Just before half distance both Jaguars began to have fluctuating fuel pressure as a problem in lifting the last amounts of fuel appeared, and so needed to pit a few laps earlier than planned.

The refuelling in each pit stop was regulated and would take almost two minutes to fill the tank with the remaining 90 litres, so there was no time pressure on the drivers during their change-over. The TWR team had spent many years racing Group A saloon cars with refuelling as well as changing tyres and drivers in less than 20 seconds; and the thought that this two-minute change would need some practise was never even considered. In this first pit stop for our Formula One drivers anything that could have possibly gone wrong with the change-over was thoroughly tried and repeated during the two minutes it took for the fuel to be taken onboard. This included the driver's seat padding being pushed in upside down and the master switch being knocked to the 'Off' position. By pitting earlier than planned the fuel tank could not take the allowable 90 litres leaving the fuel filling to continue during the last seconds of the driver change and filling the 20-litre vent bottle with the excess. This would mean either a more frugal run to the finish or a quick stop to take the unregulated fuel flow from the vent bottle towards the end of the race.

After the stops the XJRs rejoined in third and fourth places with the two Lancias increasing their pace as they had not used as much fuel as they thought. Sixteen laps from the end Warwick was out while in third place with a broken driveshaft. With one lap to go the remaining Jaguar stopped with low fuel pressure while in third. Later inspection would show eight litres of fuel still left in the tank.

> Bell/Stuck (works Porsche) won the Monza race from the Lancia of de Cesaris/Nannini, with Sigala/Brun (Porsche) third.

## Alastair Macqueen ...

The targets for weight reduction had been met, even if that was not using an on-board jacking system, but both cars were within 5kgs of the 850kgs limit.

The record books will show that neither car finished the first race of 1986, one with a driveshaft failure, and the other with a fuel system problem. However the team dinner in the Hotel de Ville after the race was one of the best TWR parties ever. It went far beyond the traditional bread roll throwing into a night of real revelry.

The cause of this was that the car was not only on the pace, as had been shown in the Monza race, but more importantly, on the fuel. The introduction of new fuel restrictions now said that cars were only allowed 510 litres for a 1000kms race. With a turbo car it was easy to turn the boost up or down to change the performance and fuel consumption. Allan Scott's latest 6.5-litre V12 engine combined with the car's diet and revised aerodynamics had hit the sweet spot.

While retirements had all been a great disappointment, it had demonstrated that the XJR-6 had actually been the fastest car racing to the fuel allowance at Monza. The few litres of fuel remaining in the tank at the end of each stint was constantly being circulated through the hot engine bay and with this increase in temperature had begun to suffer from fuel surge and vapour locks. A better method of fuel cooling would have to be designed.

Monza among other things had proven the new design of double valve springs manufactured by Schmitthelm of Germany; and although they were unable to supply an interference spring to aid harmonic damping, these springs had now successfully completed up to fourteen hours of testing. The Jaguar's competitiveness compared to 1985 had many of the Porsche opposition confused to the point that they assumed both cars had run out of fuel, and were not aware of our actual driveshaft problem. The TWR team now knew however that it could have won this race. The engines were still being quoted as 6-litre units in the press and nothing was being said to change this, few even at Jaguar were aware of the move to the larger 6.5-litre engine. Larger engines had to use more fuel was the conventional wisdom, but there was a lot more in this TWR package that would challenge this simple statement. The V12 engine's power figures were being underquoted 50bhp at the time by TW to the press, compared to the actual figures achieved on lean race settings. This was to encourage the advantage of the TWR chassis technology to the world, and suggest to Jaguar Engineering just how behind the times the Group 44 technology would have been had it been used.

After the competitive showing at Monza, the hope of winning the next round at Silverstone had become

*Three car TWR Bastos Rover team would be Tom Walkinshaw's focus for 1986.*

a genuine possibility. As had happened before with the Group A XJS programme, racing at home would once again put pressure on the team with high expectations from the UK Jaguar supporters. The media was now also talking up the probability of a maiden victory. The TWR team had just nine days to return the race cars from Italy and then prepare them for Silverstone; as well as address the broken driveshaft. These units had already been upgraded with low carbon steel material but was it just a one off or did we still have a problem?

Because of the 'no tobacco advertising' rules in the UK, the Silk Cut livery would have to be changed for Silverstone as well. This involved the substituting of wording for a series of varying block shapes producing a subliminal work that at first glance could be interpreted as the original wording. All the team clothing from Monza would be put away and a new wardrobe issued with the Silk Cut colour coding, but no mention of the sponsor's name. The BBC would refuse to televise the event if these changes were not carried out to the letter.

*Derek Warwick in conversation with motoring journalist Quentin Spurring.*

## Silverstone 1000kms – May 5th

Twenty-one C1 category cars were entered comprising Jaguar, Lancia, Porsche, Sauber Mercedes, March Porsche, Cougar Porsche and a GTP Mazda 757.

TWR were running the Rover team at Misano in Italy over this same weekend managed by Andy Morrison and Eddie Hinckley, and TW had his co-driver Win Percy covering events their while he commuted back

*Tom Walkinshaw as the Rover team driver in 1986.*

and forth between both events in the company HS125 private jet. Engs had grown in strength with Glen Barber and Dave Morris heading up the team responsible for engine rebuild and track support for this European Touring Car Rover programme. Dave would later become Ayrton Senna's race mechanic at Lotus. This allowed the Group C support team at Engs of Peter Grace, Charlie Bamber and Mathew Norris to have Group C as a priority including separate track support. I would now only attend the Rover ETCC events that did not clash with the Group C Jaguar programme.

The top qualifying time of 1:10.82 went to de Cesaris in the Lancia LC2-86 although his second attempt ended with a blown engine. A super effort by Stuck had the factory 962C Porsche second in 1:12.56 with Warwick close behind on 1:12.88. This time by the XJR-6 had been bettered in testing but it was still an amazing feat ahead of 16 turbocharged Group C1 cars; Porsche knew now they had a problem with us. The second XJR-6 of Schlesser/Brancatelli was fifth fastest, one second slower, which underlined the strength of the TWR Jaguar team.

Cheever had spent his time carrying out fuel consumption testing in the third spare car and had circulated to the fuel allowance two to three seconds slower than Warwick's best qualifying time; and it started to become clear that the Porsches would be struggling to race at that sort of pace.

After two days of dry weather practice and qualifying, race day started on the Monday morning of this bank holiday weekend. The pre-race warm up was held in wet conditions, the TWR Jaguars easily topping the timing lists, much to the enjoyment of the 26,000 British fans. By the time the 212-lap race started the weather had cleared and Nannini in the Lancia took the early lead with Jaguars taking up second and third positions after a few laps. After the first pit stops and with all of the teams' refuelling amounts on display for all to see, it was confirmed the XJR-6s were returning superior fuel consumption by pitting one lap later than the Lancia, and two laps later than the best Porsche. At just less than

*XJR-6 refuelling stop at Silverstone.*

quarter distance the Cheever/Warwick Jaguar took the lead and had lapped every Porsche as well, with just the Lancia and the second Jaguar on the same lap. The long waiting game now set in for the team. Having made its point over the first one and a half hours, it now had to continue doing the same for the next four and a half to prove it, and in these situations with a new car four and a half hours becomes a very long time indeed.

The Jaguar/Lancia lead battle continued at close quarters with Schlesser closing in and about to join them when he had to pit for a gear linkage problem. Five minutes were lost reminding us all that this race was far from over. One of the two rear wheel spats that had proved so important in helping the downforce by an additional 10% on the wind tunnel model became detached in Warwick's stint, and he pitted early to rectify that problem. His car was dispatched after fuel and tyres but without the rear wheel cover – continuing on with the battle and achieving the same lap times to the fuel.

It was then the Lancia's turn to have problems with a front brake pad change taking extra time and a fuel pressure problem over their next stint dropping the Italian car almost a lap down on the leading Jaguar.

In the end the Lancia could not recover that time with the fuel available, so the Warwick/Cheever Jaguar came home two laps ahead of the Bell/Stuck 962C and five laps ahead of Gartner/Needell in the Kremer 926C. The second XJR-6 had a battery problem late in the race and finally finished seventh.

Many were not convinced that this move forward by TWR was at all possible against Porsche, and whispers emerged while the winning XJR-6 was scrutineered. This included a careful measurement of the fuel tank capacity, as well as a long look for a secret tank or additional fuel

## The Porsche automatic gearbox

Porsche did not seem to have any large performance response available to them after this challenge to their dominance but did continue testing their semi-automatic electric shift manual gearbox in selected events during 1986. These preselected gears attached to separate shafts activated by clutches, helped eliminate turbo lag by enabling gear changes while leaving the throttle wide open. The system was called Doppelkupplung (twin clutch) although even the Germans preferred to call it the PDK system. This was the basis for the transmission system that would find its way into mass production many years later with standard fitment to Porsche and many other major manufacturers. These early prototype gearboxes fitted to the 962C came with an increase in weight of almost 30kgs. With this weight increase at the rear extremities of the 962C it was not a good racing solution as it affected the handling and rear tyre wear as well, but the Porsche factory wanted to test the system for future production use.

The pursuit of this gearbox testing programme always had me puzzled. While it would undoubtedly reduce the lap time by gear shifting with the throttle wide open and maintaining turbocharger speeds, this decrease in lap time could only come at the cost of increased fuel consumption with the throttle now being held wide open on up shifts. Also carrying the additional 30kgs was going to do nothing but increase fuel consumption. For there to be any driving and fuel consumption improvement with this system the engine electronic control system being used at that time by Porsche must have needed a more sophisticated part throttle mapping or acceleration fuel software in the throttle angle versus boost rise area, and this was possibly the case while they used the early Bosch non-sequential system. The Bosch MP1.7 sequential system with larger microprocessor capacity that was in development at this time was to become the state-of-the-art in turbo engine management systems and one of the situations it addressed was throttle angle boost mapping. The conclusion I came to is that they had to justify much of their race funding as a platform for production car development, as well as brand advertising. As the 1986 season progressed it became increasingly unloved by the regular drivers who drew the 'short straw', although it is clear now that once again, racing improved the breed.

system. After a couple of hours of careful checking Porsche heard that their worst fears were confirmed, all was OK with the winning Jaguar.

With this performance on home ground TWR's Silk Cut Jaguar team had established itself. TWR had started this Group C programme with a piece of paper 20 months earlier, along with an engine programme that few considered worthwhile. Hans Stuck had said "It's fantastic, the cars are just incredible and this result is so good for the championship. I think we are all very pleased for them" – although this probably came with the disclaimer that his thoughts did not necessarily represent those of his Porsche employers. Under the heading "A legend is reborn" the patriotic British press announced "Shout it from the rooftops; the Jaguar marque is back as a real force in World Championship Sports Car racing"

It was an enjoyable winning moment mixed with relief that it had all worked out for us with the champagne to celebrate into the early evening, and then back to our 'nearby' homes for a well earned sleep for the whole team. Tomorrow was another day, and back to reality.

The days following Silverstone were filled with final preparation for the team's first visit to the most important venue of the year, Le Mans in France. By Thursday of that same week we were testing three Jaguars at the Circuit de la Sarthe attending the Le Mans test day. There had been a small change to the corner at the end of the Mulsanne straight to avoid a new roundabout, but otherwise things were the same, with its old pit complex and fuel supplied by the circuit running through pipes the full length of the entire pit complex. Here all three cars were fitted with different bodywork, the result of wind tunnel testing to find the best compromise between a low drag for fast straight-line speed on the long Mulsanne straight versus downforce needed for good cornering speeds. The wheel bearings had also been upgraded with a larger Timken taper-roller-bearing package, removing any doubts about the marginal units previously used. The aerodynamic package for the Le Mans challenge was given the designation XJR-6LM.

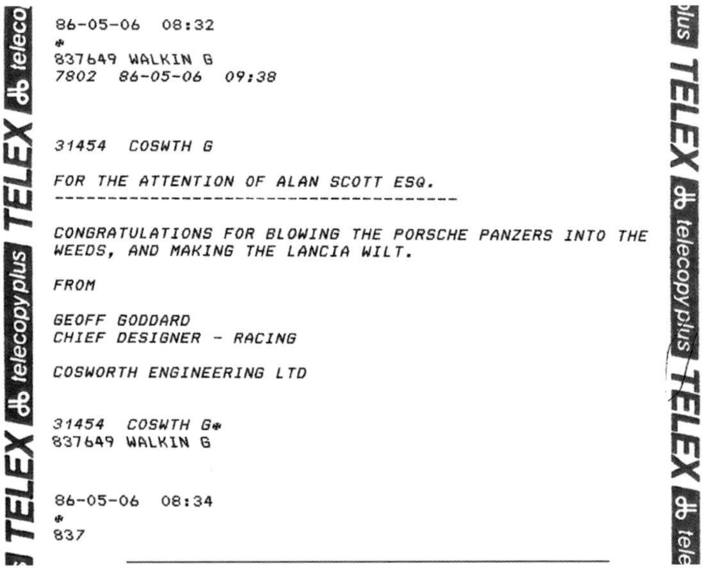
86-05-06 08:32
*
837649 WALKIN G
7802 86-05-06 09:38

31454 COSWTH G

FOR THE ATTENTION OF ALAN SCOTT ESQ.
------------------------------------

CONGRATULATIONS FOR BLOWING THE PORSCHE PANZERS INTO THE WEEDS, AND MAKING THE LANCIA WILT.

FROM

GEOFF GODDARD
CHIEF DESIGNER - RACING

COSWORTH ENGINEERING LTD

31454 COSWTH G*
837649 WALKIN G

86-05-06 08:34
*
837

*Cosworth congratulations after Silverstone win.*

## Le Mans Test

The fuel allowance for the 24 hour race in 1986 was increased to 2550 litres, a more sensible amount to allow continuous racing than the previous 2210 litres. There was a a question mark for me however with this circuit and that was the long Mulsanne straight, where the engine was running lean at wide open throttle for exactly one minute. No other circuit the XJR-6 competed at had a wide open throttle much longer than 10 seconds. On all the other circuits the shorter durations on full throttle helped the piston temperatures as the fuel injectors were switched off each time the throttle was fully closed on the overrun during braking and gear changes above a programmable rpm threshold, usually 2500–3000rpm. Below this threshold the fuel was left switched on to allow the engine to continue to run while entering the pits and idle with a closed throttle. The mechanical settings of the throttle slides were set at this Le Mans test to the relatively high engine idle speed of 1500rpm to assist cooling air to continue passing through the engine each time the throttle was closed and the injectors switched off. This allowed cool air, without fuel, to be regularly introduced to the piston crowns and exhaust valves during gear change and braking into corners when the throttle was closed. This assisted in lowering piston as well as exhaust pipe temperatures. In any turbocharged engine application at the time, this type of overrun fuel shut off programme would tend to produce lower turbine speeds and increased turbo lag.

With the long throttle opening periods on the 3.5-mile Mulsanne straight however there was still the possibility of piston failure through excessive temperatures when using any fuel setting below our normal lean fuel setting. With that in mind I had commissioned Zytek to produce a piece of software that would switch to a richer setting only on the Mulsanne straight.

The base line for this test was the same high down-force/drag aerodynamic package that had just won the race at Silverstone and this car, #51, recorded its fastest lap of 3:25.27. Two low drag Le Mans options were tested with Cheever setting a best time in car #52 of 3:21.89 and a top speed of 340km hour, and Schlesser 3:22.24 in the lowest drag bodywork option achieving a top speed of 356km hour.

This indicated some good results from the wind tunnel exercises with the two options to choose from having similar lap times. One of the problems that was emerging with the low drag Le Mans bodywork was the increased work placed on the braking system with the race cars' higher straight-line speeds and lower aerodynamic drag. What did become apparent from these first tests was that these low drag configurations at the Le Mans circuit were increasingly beneficial to fuel consumption versus lap time.

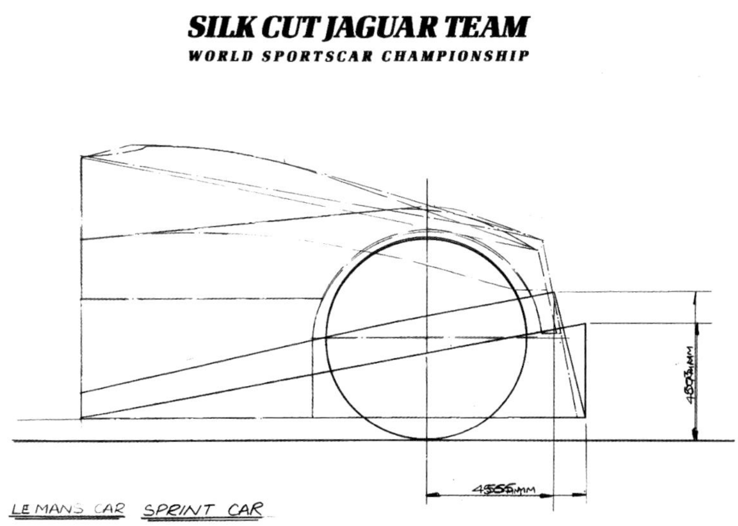


***Drawing comparing the higher sprint tunnels with the lower ones used for Le Mans to produce a lower drag and aerodynamic ballance split.***

## Alastair Macqueen ...

Car 286, the high downforce 'Silverstone' car had a little wing trimmed from it.

Car 186 had an interim downforce package with some of the Le Mans specific parts on it, but car 285 had a complete Le Mans package including rear wheel fairings, new underwing and lower mounted, single plane wing.

It was something of a surprise that the cars came away from the test with two of the fastest times, however Le Mans is not all about the lap time.

The high downforce car would produce the laptime, but was very 'slow' on the straights whilst dragging its underbody on the track due to the colossal loading. It was also using almost 25% too much fuel and anything but a 24 hour solution.

The interim car was also quick, but due to the rear wing reduction without an underbody change, was also badly balanced with far too much of the aero split to the front to be comfortable over any distance.

The chosen low drag, full Le Mans car featured many changes to the regular 'sprint' cars, but was considered the right way forward for this unique circuit and event. The obvious visual differences of nose, tail and rear wing tend to hide some much more detailed changes which included complete new underwing profile, brake discs, crown wheel and pinion ratio, lighting and a myriad of small durability upgrades. The Le Mans cars had almost halved the drag from the Silverstone car, but had also considerably reduced the Jaguar trump card of downforce.

Given the inexperience of all the team, the fact that the cars were competitive and there was still one running on Sunday morning was something of a surprise. The real prize was Le Mans experience for the whole team and and greater understanding of how the car, the structure, the suppliers and event planning could be improved for the future.

## Le Mans – May 31st to June 1st

The Silk Cut Jaguar team then returned three weeks later with three cars and set-up camp in the Le Mans pits for the big race that would start on May 31st. Already the goal posts had moved for us at Engs; The agreed two cars and a spare in testing became a three-car race team at Le Mans with just nine engines to work around the unevenly spaced testing and race schedules. The American Group 44 team was absent this year after demonstrating our ability to be competitive and also field three cars. After the speedy development of TWR's XJR-6 Bob Tullius had been disappointed with the progress of his new American based XJR-7. He had hoped with this updated design and Jaguar's backing that it would be the basis for all of Jaguar's sports car programmes. The advance in the competitiveness of the TWR Group C design had been rapid and cast a question mark over designer Lee Dykstra's efforts. Dykstra, with some help from Bob Tullius, had resigned from his position at Group 44, and his retainer from Jaguar Cars. It had become obvious with Group 44's absence at Le Mans that Jaguar's considerable support for this team, and neutral stance in dealing with both teams, had begun to turn in favour of TWR and Tom Walkinshaw after the Silverstone win. With the resignation of designer Lee Dykstra, support for the Group 44 XJR-7 had gone quiet.

In a show of solidarity and political face-saving Group 44 drivers Brian Redman and Hurley Haywood had crossed the Atlantic and would drive car #52 (186) with former TWR XJS driver Hans Heyer. No doubt this is where the third car's funding came from with TW getting his hands on Jaguar's contribution budgeted for Group 44 at this event. Car 51 (286) had Warwick/Cheever/Schlesser while the third car 53 (385) was for TWR Group A drivers Brancatelli/Percy/Hahne. Hahne had been a late replacement for Ivan Capelli who had to withdraw over conflicting sponsorship contracts.

### Mulsanne straight fuelling strategy for Le Mans

With my concern for long periods on WOT using lean settings I had commissioned a new piece of software from Zytek which monitored three parameters; *time – throttle angle – fuel correction*. Using the recording process available in the Zytek management system and monitored over a few laps we found at the Le Mans test day that except for the long Mulsanne straight, the longest period the throttle was held wide open for at any one time in any gear was seven seconds. The new piece of Zytek software was programmed using the wide open throttle *voltage* output from the throttle position sensor, and activated after that voltage setting had been held constantly for eight seconds. At that point it indicated that the race car could only be in fifth gear on the early part of the Mulsanne straight. The overall fuel mixture was then programmed to automatically switch to a richer setting, an additional 4% in this case being a level that was thought to be enough to keep piston crowns cooler on the Mulsanne straight. The management system automatically cancelled this instruction as soon as the throttle was closed at the end of the long straight. It would not be triggered on any other part of the Le Mans circuit, and only be reactivated after 8 seconds on wide open throttle had been recorded. It was a classic example of the close co-operation and relationship we had with Zytek. They would react within days of being presented with my results from the Le Mans test, with new software, and then not send a bill.

Zytec's work allowed the TWR team to have the V12 engine at best lean setting on all parts of the circuit during the 24 hour race and not have to compromise with an overall setting to suit the Mulsanne straight. A bonus was that with a larger than normal gap between the highest fourth gear available and the long fifth gear being used, there was a danger the race car would not pull strongly enough on lean fuelling after the change up into fifth gear to push the car through the air up to 340kph. The richer mixture guaranteed it.

*Brancatelli – Hahne – Percy*

*Side view of the XJR-6LM.*

*The low-drag Le Mans version of the XJR-6LM.*

SILK CUT JAGUAR

# GREAT NAMES FOR LE MANS TEAM '86

**Hurley Haywood and Brian Redman will be be flying to Le Mans from the USA to join the British team immediately after racing for the American one at Lime Rock, Connecticut, on 26 May. FOR FULL DETAILS OF JAGUAR'S LE MANS LINE-UP, SEE ACCOMPANYING SUPPLEMENT.**

**Also joining the Silk Cut Jaguar squad for Le Mans are Win Percy and Hans Heyer: Tom Walkinshaw has not forgotten the work they put in to ensure that he won the 1984 Francorchamps 24-hour race in the TWR XJ-S—*and* that year's Touring Car Championship, too.**

*Haywood and Redman were seconded from the Group 44 team to drive a TWR XJR-6, with Group 44 not returning to Le Mans.*

## Le Mans race

Tuesday May 27th was scrutineering and then the two practice sessions each day on Wednesday and Thursday. These sessions were divided into two categories; day light from 6.30pm to 8.30pm and then night time 9.30–11.30pm. All drivers had to have three timed laps in qualifying under both daylight and night time conditions. The change to the corner off the Mulsanne straight had resulted in a faster exit with the circuit length reduced by 94 metres to 13.582kms (8.406 miles).

The first practice saw Jaguar falter with all three cars returning to the pits when the aluminium sheet under the radiator as part of the air ducting was dislodged by high air pressure on the long high speed Mulsanne straight. This was just typical new car gremlins and they were all soon fixed and back out with the aim of getting all drivers qualified, a process that would take most of both sessions on this first day of practice. During practice Derek Warwick had been asked over the public address system what he thought of Group C racing and Le Mans, and had given the reply, "Well it's not Formula One is it."

After the effort put in by all the team we did not need to be reminded this was second best in our number one driver's mind. We had all made sacrifices to get this far, I had just taken a call from my wife Karen that evening informing me she had suffered a miscarriage with our second child, she was having to cope without the support of any family in the UK and telling me to stay at Le Mans. The team had worked long dedicated hours to produce a race car that could take on the Porsche factory team after its first single car test little more than 12 months earlier.

After Wednesday and Thursday's practice sessions in changing weather conditions over both days, the final qualifying times were: Wollek/Mass/Schuppan, Porsche 962C (Rothmans Porsche), 3:15.99; Stuck/Bell/Holbert, Porsche 962C (Rothmans Porsche), 3:16.60; Barilla/Ludwig/'Winter', Porsche 956B (Joest Racing), 3:17.11; Bousten/Theys/Ferté, Porsche 956 (Brun Motorsport), 3:20.10; Warwick/Schlesser/Cheever, Jaguar XJR-6 (Silk Cut Jaguar), 3:21.60; Larrauri/Pareja/Gouhier, Porsche 962C (Brun Motorsport), 3:23.47; Heyer/Haywood/Redman, Jaguar XJR-6 LM (Silk Cut Jaguar), 3:24.95; Schuppan/Olson, Porsche 962C (Rothmans Porsche), 3:25.34; Quester/Pescarolo/Danner, Sauber C8 Mercedes (Kouros Racing Team), 3:26.69; Raphanel/De Cadenet/Courage, Cougar C12 Porsche (Primagaz Team Cougar), 3:26.98; Follmer/Morton/Miller/Barilla, Porsche 956 (Joest Racing), 3:27.37; Sigala/Brun/Jelinski Porsche 962C (Brun Motorsport), 3:28.05; Nielsen/Thackwell, Sauber C8 Mercedes (Kouros Racing Team), 3:29.22; Brancatelli/Percy/Hahn, Jaguar XJR-6 LM (Silk Cut Jaguar), 3:29.24.

Friday is a free day at Le Mans and the three cars were pulled apart and rebuilt ready for the start on Saturday afternoon. Most in the team were very hopeful of a good result but it was the first 24 hour race with this extended three-car team with only one of the three cars having drivers familiar with it. A large amount of organisation was needed over an extended period of time to get to this first Le Mans race from TWR for Jaguar, and now it would be the real test of all car systems over the length of this long race.

## Driver check list should the car stop out on the circuit

LE MANS 1986 ENGINE CUTOUT CHECK LIST

CHECK
Fuel pressure
Volt meter and dash gauges [Try master switch]
Connections to engine management system.

ENGINE COMPARTEMENT CHECK
Swap over to spare trigger lead
CHECK
H.T. Lead, spark box to distributer
2 multi plugs to side of spark box
Wire to RED throttle pot on side of injection system
Flick injecter switch up and down twice, listen for injecters cracking on and off.

If engine does not start immediately at any time, stop cranking flick injecter switch to prime engine, then start.

IF VOLTAGE LOW, two termanals at rear of alternater; battery leads, earth wire alternater to block, belt.

Sir John Egan had been selected as honorary starter with Jaguar's official return to Le Mans and to the cheers of the estimated 10,000 British supporters, waved the flag to begin the race at 4pm on Saturday afternoon.

The 24 hour race started with the three Jaguars running at race pace and Warwick moving into second position during his first stint. The Porsche brigade had its first real competition at Le Mans for many years. Car 52 (Redman/Haywood/Heyer in XJR-6/186) was the first casualty after 54 laps with fuel pickup problems and was unable to make it back to the pits. Car 53 (Brancatelli/Percy/Hahne in XJR-6/385) had maintained a good pace and was in sixth position when a driveshaft broke at the 10-hour mark. There had been some concerns prior to the race with the drive angles of the universal joints on the Le Mans specification cars and a backup plan had been thought through. The cars were carrying a special tool to lock the broken shaft so that it could return to the pits with some drive from the limited slip differential. This meant the driver had to crawl into the venturi tunnel and carry out the task but it was next to impossible for someone other than an experienced mechanic to carry out the procedure successfully. The process was attempted many times by driver Win Percy but the procedure kept failing leading to the cars eventual withdrawal after covering 155 laps.

Meanwhile the Warwick/Cheever/Schlesser Car 51 had established itself in a challenging second place behind the Bell/Stuck/Holbert Porsche 962C throughout the night and into the daylight of Sunday morning. Schlesser then had a huge moment when at around 8.30am on lap 239 a rear tyre blew and by the time the car had been bought to a halt, the parts of the flailing carcase had ripped bodywork and suspension to the extent that it was not able to be repaired. Sadly, the last car was retired. Although the engine had just over five hours of practice and stayed in for the race and then completed sixteen and a half hours, the total 22 hours on Car 51was still not the full test Engs needed.

The now familiar postscript to the many disappointed British and Jaguar fans was sprayed in large letters "We will be back" with another saying "Thanks for coming".

This race was marred by the death of Joe Gartner, when a failed transmission locked the rear wheels of his Porsche and the resulting accident impact taking the life of a man who was in the process of fast establishing himself as one of the top drivers in Group C.

The final results for the 1986 Le Mans 24 hour race were: Bell/Stuck/Holbert Porsche 962C; Larrauri/Pareja/Gouhier Porsche 962C; Follmer/Morton/Miller Porsche 956; Fouche/Villotta/Velez Porsche 956B; Lassig/Ballabio/Wood Porsche 956.

*Jaguar fans are promised a return.*

The team returned to Kidlington and a debrief on the following Wednesday. There were some lessons to be learned but TWR had put on a very professional challenge first time out, and it would just be more of the same for 1987 with detail changes along the way.

After the removal of the engine from Car 51 a sample of oil was sent to Motul for analysis and this demonstrates the existing partnership between Engs and oil supplier Motul. TWR were also the UK distributors of this French oil company's fully synthetic product and Castrol was not being used at this time. Motul was the world's first fully synthetic oil and I had used it from the very start in all TWR engine programmes with a high level of confidence. Motul would soon be phased out and Castrol product used as confidence grew with their equally as good product. The oil analysis shows how the internal elements of the V12 engine are working with their product, giving them confirmation that the oil is working in a suitable environment and informing us of any degradation of internal materials. Engine integrity had come out well, the fuel dilution indicated by the high PB level was a common problem in long distance races. I had hoped that this problem would be reduced with the overrun fuel shut off system we had introduced, but more work would be needed in that area although PB (lead) is a lubricant as well and does not degrade the oil, just viscosity.

TELEX

ATTN. MR. TIPPET
RE: 300V/LE MANS JAGUAR N.51

THERE IS AN IMPORTANT DILUTION OF OILBY PETROL. THIS OFTEN HAPPENS WITH THIS KIND OF ENGINE. WE FOUND, WITH YOUR SAMPLE:

- PETROL : 2,5 POURCENT ON THE OIL
- VISCOSTIY AT 100 DEGRES C: 13,66 CST
  (THE NORMAL VALVE IS 17 CST)

THE VISCOSITY DECREASES DURING THE RACE BECAUSE OF PETORL DILUTION.
THIS CAUSES OIL PRESSURE TO DECREASE.

HOWEVER, NOTE THAT A 13,66 VISCOSITY IS STILL ENOUGH TO ENSURE CORRECT LUBRICATION.

REGARDS

A. ROUS

TELEX NO 86-2693

17.7.86

ATT MR TIPPET

RE; 300V/LE MANS JAGUAR N.51

HERE IS THE ANALYSIS OF THE WEAR METALS IN THE OIL.

AMOUNTS ARE GIVEN IN PARTS PER MILLION [PPM];

FE; 46
CR; LESS THAN 1
AL; 71
CU; 11
SN; 5
PB; 703
MO; 37
SI; 12
NA; 8

THE AMOUNT OF FE [CYLINDERS AND CAMSHAFT] AND AL AND SI [PISTONS] ARE LOW COMPARED TO RACING CONDITIONS.

THE AMOUNT OF LEAD IS DUE TO PETROL DILUTION [CF OUR TLX 86/2889]

***Motul synthetic oil had served our engines well in the past and we were using it for the Le Mans race in 1986. It shows some fuel dilution.***

## Norisring – June 29th

Three weeks later and it was the first direct assault on Porsche home ground at the short 1.43-mile street circuit of the Norisring. This was in the Bavarian area of Nuremberg/Nurnberg where the military might of the Third Reich had once been assembled on vast areas of concrete before proceeding with their military displays. The concrete paving still existed under shallow ground cover making awning pegs almost impossible to drive in. The TWR team set up camp in park-like surroundings for a weekend that would have a completely different feel from that of the normal dedicated circuit racing structure, allowing much more interaction with spectators.

It was the first time TWR had seen this circuit and because it was a short distance 'sprint' format, the three cars entered would have just a single driver in each. These were Warwick and Cheever, with Schlesser driving a new XJR-6 that had just been completed at Kidlington. For Dunlop though this event was more of a geography lesson with the German Nurnberg name being known to most as Nuremberg. Dunlop had sent its entire shipment of Jaguar tyres to the Nurburgring racing circuit, 400kms away. On arrival an apologetic Bill Mack had informed us that there were no tyres, just the ones on the race cars, but a truck was hopefully on its way from the Nurburgring.

The circuit layout was designed such that the large run off area on the left-hand corner before the pit straight start/finish line offered the ability to rejoin the circuit at speed if you had 'overrun' the corner into that run off area. Starting from the off-track position the driver could enter the pit straight at a higher speed than taking the corner in the normal fashion and that was a choice for the qualifying lap, something the TWR drivers had soon thought through.

This race was part of the German Supercup Series as well as Group C, and had Hans Stuck in his special PDK gearbox 962C based Supercup chassis with reportedly an electronically improved 3-litre engine, to uphold German/Porsche honours; he duly took the fastest time. Ludwig in the Joest/Blaupunkt 956B and then Bob Wollek in the increasingly competitive UK built Richard Lloyd 956 GTi were second and third respectively in their earlier specification shorter wheel base 956 versions. Cheever was the fastest Jaguar here in fourth, Warwick sixth and Schlesser 0.3s slower in eighth.

The track was tough on cars with the XJR-6 leaving the road surface on the many bumps. The brakes had been fitted with water cooling and the engine temperatures were high, especially the oil.

The fuel allowance for this 79 lap 180km race was one tank full and although theoretically an increased allowance at 54 litres per 100kms the constant accelerating and hard braking on this street circuit did not allow for any real rhythm; but with this additional fuel allowance the Jaguars were slightly disadvantaged. Cheever had calculated at least 1200 gearshifts in the 67-minute race. With its inner-city location this would be the best supported race of the series with an estimated 75,000 spectators turning out in the hot summer conditions, producing some very revealing distractions for the TWR crew in between preparing cars for the race.

*Cheever taking second place at Norisring.*

The early pace had Ludwig ahead of Stuck, with Cheever in fourth and Warwick being shuffled back a few places. Stuck then retook the lead and Cheever established his Jaguar in third place close behind. Suddenly at one third of the race distance Stuck was in the pits with a reported broken gearbox switch and this promoted the Jaguars to second and fifth. Schlesser was having problems with a jamming accelerator pedal and was effectively out of the running finishing on seventeenth.

> Cheever maintained his second place with a broken gear knob producing a bloodied hand by the race's end. Warwick on flat spotted tyres finishing five seconds behind in third. Ludwig was uncatchable though and won by eight seconds, his car running out of fuel across the finishing line and the Jaguars with just two litres of fuel left at the end of the race, these three having lapped every other car in the race.

The customer Porsche engines had moved from 2.65 to 2.8-litres for 1986 and the up rated 3-litre units in the Stuck and Ludwig cars showed that economy was coming to them with lower boost engines optimised on special high-density fuel. It also showed that it needed something special from Porsche to be on equal terms with the Jaguars, efficiency wise. Running the privateers on updated 1985 specifications no doubt suited Porsche's engine inventory, logistics and income, but the large privateer support programme could now offer little in the way of support if something was to go wrong with the factory cars. The single driver format was always going to produce an interesting result for the Drivers Championship with the Cheever/Warwick pairing now on different points at 35 and 32.5 respectively, half points issued because of the shorter race format.

## Brands Hatch – July 20th

Three weeks later the second UK race for 1986 was at the Kent circuit of Brands Hatch, the second part of a double promotion the circuit ran in conjunction with the British Grand Prix the week before. Stuck and Bell had produced a deal with the Joest team as the Porsche factory was not attending this race due we were told to financial constraints; or were they concerned about competing on a track familiar to TWR after the Silverstone domination and embarrassment back at Stuttgart.

> Stuck set the fastest time in qualifying in the Joest Porsche 956B on Goodyear tyres. Interestingly, both Stuck and Bell felt that this car had a better set-up than their own Dunlop shod factory car. Cheever and Warwick put in yet another great effort in qualifying with second and third fastest times ahead of Boutsen/Jelinski in the Brun 956, de Cesaris/Giacomelli in the Lancia LC2-85 and the unique Richard Lloyd Racing GTi 956 Porsche driven by Wollek/Baldi; with a further ten turbocharged cars following.

TWR team manager Roger Silman had been presented with a problem after the race in Germany with the points difference between the two Jaguar drivers from that race resulting in Cheever's favour. Derek Warwick would not be able to win the series if they stayed together in the same race car, and so it had been decided to split these two drivers. This change would produce two contending cars in the TWR team; instead of one favoured stronger team supported by the Schlesser/Brancatelli number two combination. Warwick/Schlesser would be considered the stronger pairing while Cheever would pair up with his 'Sicilian friend' Brancatelli, moving the support pendulum back towards Derek.

Splitting the Warwick/Cheever pairing up had the twin benefits of producing two cars able to win a race as well as giving Warwick the chance to regain the points lead by being partnered with Jean-Louis Schlesser. Derek expected some favouritism and status within the team from his personal links with Roger, and there's little doubt promises had been made to that effect by Roger to sign him up.

TWR had raced three-car teams for many years and few special demands had been put on me from TW during the time he had been a Mazda/XJS Jaguar/Rover TWR team driver – I had expected a reasonable continuation of the same situation. Engs was working through systems and engine building processes to produce as equal equipment as possible for all involved to help keep all race eventualities alive; this thought process supported the best outcome from a *team's* point of view for TWR/Jaguar/Silk Cut, with drivers hopefully supporting that concept.

The pre-race warm up had Warwick setting the fastest time ahead of de Cesaris and Stuck, from Brancatelli in the second XJR-6 and James Weaver in the March-Porsche 85G.

Derek was unhappy with his race car, due possibly to an ill fitting underbody, and he changed to the spare car #53.

The start of the 236-lap 992.6km race was watched by 40,000 British fans and the initial order was Stuck, Warwick, Cheever and Wollek. Cheever pitted early with a loosening wheel hub and after refuelling was a lap down on the leaders. The race was then marred with full course yellow flags and miss-timed pace cars. The pace cars did not pick up the leaders as the rules at that time did not insist that they did, and cars that had pitted were allowed to rejoin immediately causing advantages and disadvantages to many competitors. The race controls systems for long distance races needed some serious attention, including using the standard American pace car protocol where competitors were waved by the pace car until the race leader joined in behind. Those cars that had not pitted under these conditions were given a reprieve two laps later when another accident caused another pace car deployment, but Cheever came out the looser in both of these situations.

At quarter distance and after another pace car lasting eight laps the race settled down with Schlesser's Jaguar in first place and Mauro Baldi in the Liqui Moly 956 GTi began to make his move from fifth up to second place. Nearing mid-distance and after two fuel stops the order was Warwick/Schlesser, Wollek/Baldi and de Cesaris/Giacomelli in the Lancia, but with a one lap penalty. The leading Jaguar was suffering with fluctuating fuel pressure in the hot conditions and pitted to have its fuel pumps and filters changed.

Problems with the fuel system here were mainly on left hand corners with fuel pickup problems at low fuel levels. New car problems and constant checks of the fuel tank for adjustments to ensure it never exceeded the 100 litre limit had earlier seen debris from the foam fibres used inside the bag tank causing pumps to jam and I had insisted that because of this the fuel filters should be placed downstream of the fuel pumps to protect them. The fuel pump's close impellor tolerances meant that the slightest grit contamination would jam the fuel pump and this had happened in the early development of the XJR-6. The cars now had a quick-change system to cover that eventuality. Fuel recirculation through the injection system back to the fuel tank became hotter as the fuel reduced to the last 10 litres and its temperature climbed over 55°C, causing partial vapour locks. We had fitted a fuel cooler by the engine air intake after the German sprint race to both XJR-6s and this had helped but not totally excluded the hot fuel problem.

This was exacerbated by the fact that we used a base 97 octane standard pump fuel with an additive to bring the rating up to 102, not special high density high Reid vapour pressure fuels used by the opposition turbocharged engines and aviation fuels. From a pure logistics point-of-view we only needed to carry the concentrated additive on board the trucks. The fact that the engine misfire only happened on the left-hand

*The UK built Richard Lloyd Racing Porsche GTi*

corner though meant that there was a secondary problem with the in-car system as well. Both Jaguars were three laps down by now with Brancatelli needing replacement bodywork having collided with a slower C2.

After 150 laps the Baldi/Wollek GTi Porsche was well established in the lead followed by Stuck/Bell with the Jaguars fifth and sixth. After yet another pace car the race finally finished with the RLR Porsche of Wollek/Baldi winning by four laps ahead of Stuck/Bell with Boutsen/Jelinski just holding off a fast finishing Warwick/Schlesser in fourth and Cheever/Brancatelli finishing in sixth.

It was a race that could certainly have been won but the combination of fuel problems, traffic accidents and pace car irregularities conspired against that. This result moved Warwick into second place in the championship, half a point ahead of Cheever.

An interesting situation had developed during this race with Bell in the Joest Porsche running some developments of their electronic engine management system and that situation can be compared to where we were with the Zytek managed 6.5-litre V12 engines. In this race adjustments had been made to the fuel settings on the Joest Porsche when it had first pitted as it was running too lean and misfiring at higher rpm. This richer fuel setting resulted in Stuck exceeding the fuel allowance in the next stint. To repair this problem the engine now had to be reverted to its original lean setting and with Bell now in the car on the race track he was contacted via the radio and told to turn his engine and master switch off, and then restart the engine. By switching the power to the electronic management system off, it would default to the original lean map, saving fuel but still producing the high rpm miss fire.

This situation led me to believe that Porsche had a simple overall electronic override system but it had not been tailored to track use as we had done with the extensive pre-season engine testing with Cheever. Decision making at the race circuits to fine tune any hesitations with lean settings was now normal for me with well educated drivers giving good feedback. This would not be the case at Porsche with more emphasis on their dynamometer development and it was impossible to simulate all the race conditions using just that development programme. Eddie Cheever was particularly tuned into the reporting of the changing dynamic situations from circuit to circuit, as was Schlesser with electronic systems we had worked on together during development of the Rover V8 engine, leading to his winning of the French National Saloon Car Championship in 1985.

Engs had the concept of giving the drivers in-car adjustment for instant fuel mixture and ignition timing change, with the ability to reverse any decisions instantly. Along with the fuel meter readout at 10 separate points each lap, all this information placed added control of any changing situation in the hands of the TWR drivers during the race.

## Jerez – August 3rd

This race weekend just two weeks after Brands Hatch and run under very hot 38°C conditions, was TWR's for the taking. There would be no factory or Joest Porsches and three XJR-6s were taken to this Spanish track. The driver line-up was considerably strengthened with the addition of Jan Lammers, and Martin Brundle was temporarily released from his Formula One contract.

The pairing of Martin Brundle with Eddie Cheever and Jan Lammers with Derek Warwick was to add strength at this race and take as many points as possible from the opposition to give Derek the best chance at the title. Schlesser/Brancatelli would rejoin in the third car.

Eddie Cheever was getting a little tired of my frequent references to team work and co-operation with each other to pool knowledge, and this finally got the better of him in the hot conditions at Jerez in Spain. I was invited to walk with him to the rear of the pit garage where he pointedly asked who his biggest enemy was. Knowing it would be a trick question I decided to remain silent. "My team mates" was his answer. "I have to be fastest to the fuel, not them." After this explanation we were all singing off the same hymn sheet, well apparently anyway. Derek Warwick was not so keen on the fuel consumption concept, wishing he could just get on and race and did not have the same enthusiasm and attention to detail in this area as Eddie Cheever, and I had been relaying some of Eddie's feedback to the Warwick/Lammers set-up, and Eddie was not happy with that.

Something that would have future consequences at the end of the season started here at Jerez. TW was absent having a conflicting race weekend with the Rover team in the ETCC and tension was starting to build beneath the surface with Roger's opaque leanings towards friend Warwick, hence Cheever's earlier discussions with me. Some car handling problems at Jerez had centred on bumps in the braking areas causing instability at the rear. Schlesser decided to disconnect the rear anti roll bar on his car, something that was considered not the thing to do with the inherent understeer bias with the XJR-6, and proceeded to set a time faster than Warwick. Schlesser was a thinker, with a good engineering mind, and former Formula 3 driver coming second to Alain Prost in that French Series. Derek then asked for the cars to be swapped as he felt something was wrong with his car. He was not only unhappy with his car set-up but wanted an engine change as well. Sensing this would possibly set the scene for a future that Engs simply would not be able to keep up with – I had to decline his request, an action that neither of us was happy with.

There had been a limited number of new engines allowed to be built for 1986 and while Engs could just keep up with servicing these units, we could not afford extra rebuilds of engines with no obvious problems. The number of engines allowed to be built at the beginning of the year, nine in total, were for a two-car Silk Cut team and it had now grown to three cars here at Jerez, and extra testing programmes were constantly being introduced with a fourth car, altering the rebuild schedules and creating some all-night work for Engs. These facts of course could not be relayed to Derek and obviously he did not understand the position I was in when declining his request, in what looked to him a very well funded and focused team.

After the car swap both drivers had something to prove and it was Schlesser setting the fastest time of all three Jaguars and second fastest qualifying time behind the Brun/Jelinski Fortuna Porsche. Cheever was half a second slower in third and Warwick in fourth. After changing a rear shock-absorber the car was more to Warwick's liking and ready for race day, which had attracted 4500 spectators.

A debacle then ensued after the race start at the first corner, the two Jaguar team mates touched and with Cheever following close behind and not able to take avoiding action had all three cars off the track. With

*Three XJRs off on the first corner of Jarama would prove costly with the Championship lost at the end of the year.*

**Photos:** *Autosport*

cars needing repair, and Warwick stuck in the sand trap for two laps, the game plan was gone at the first corner. Brancatelli was able to continue but by now had a damaged under tray while Cheever lost two and a half minutes in the pits having a new nose cone fitted, and after five minutes of digging in the gravel trap Warwick was finally away.

Brancatelli's race was over on lap 12 of the 86-lap 'Sprint' race with a broken driveshaft. Cheever showed the competitiveness of the XJR-6 by regaining his lap lost in the pits but was still a long way behind the leader, Argentinean Oscar Larrauri in the Brun Porsche. The Jaguar's were on a one stop strategy in this shortened race with one mid-distance pit stop, when Warwick, unannounced, pitted on lap 36. Changing over to Lammers at this earlier stage in the race meant that all the fuel could not be put in the race car and Jan would have to pit again before the end to take on the remaining fuel. Derek did the only thing possible under these circumstances and left for home soon after his apology to the team, when he realised what he had done. For me his mind was in Formula One, not Group C racing. Cheever was now absent and reported a broken driveshaft leaving Brundle without a race drive for his weekend's efforts. After all this Lammers had made his way up to third and retained the position at the end after pitting again for the last amounts of fuel.

As events would later pan out this was where TWR lost the 1986 World Championship, the easiest race of the series should have ended in a 1-2-3 and produce a points-gap too large for Bell/Stuck to overtake with that team missing some rounds of the championship. Had the cars not been under pressure to make a comeback at Jerez and racing to their own safer pace off the circuit's many curbs, it is possible that the driveshaft problems would not have appeared, maybe.

The broken driveshafts had been replaced with different maraging steel units with machined splines. Maraging steels are a special class of low-carbon ultra-high-strength steels that are known for possessing superior strength and toughness without losing malleability. These units would later be replaced with Uni-Carden manufactured units using more flexible hollow steel shafts with rolled splines, allowing some twisting of the shaft to absorb shock, and these later proved to be the best solution.

## Nurburgring – August 24th

Another three-week gap and then back to Germany on the 'new' Nurburgring track situated beside the famous original track. Changeable weather in this mountainous region, similar to Spa in Belgium, is the order of the day and this continued for the race weekend. The TWR team had arrived earlier in the week to carry out testing as it would be the first time the Jaguars had run on this track, but Warwick had an accident during the test resulting in his car being badly damaged and not able to be repaired before the race.

The resulting two-car team for the race weekend had three drivers each with Warwick joining Lammers and Heyer. Wet then dry qualifying and practice periods resulted in the fastest top five positions going to Boutsen/Brun, Stuck/Bell, Cheever/Schlesser/Heyer, Baldi/Niedzwiedz, Mass/Wollek with Warwick ninth.

Showing continued improvement was the Kouros Sauber Mercedes with our original TWR Group C driver, ex-pat New Zealander and F3000 competitor Mike Thackwell on board for this race; a very respectable sixth place in qualifying had been achieved. The time between the last race for the Sauber, at Le Mans almost three months before, had been put to good use in the full size fixed floor Mercedes wind tunnel, and some good advances had been achieved with its aerodynamics and new three tier rear wing.

The Sunday 1000km race had miserable rain and fog conditions for the thirty-one competitors to contend with and the opening laps were carried out in near blind conditions as the drivers tried to find gaps in the spray. Cheever had started well but was out with a broken gearbox on lap seven. The early running had Thackwell's Mercedes working its way to the front and eventually passing Stuck to take the lead, with Warwick coming through in third place although some distance from the leaders.

With increasing fog conditions and decreasing visibility the inevitable collision between race cars started, and the pace car was deployed. Once again, the system did not pick up the leaders; Thackwell in the Sauber Mercedes and Stuck in the factory Porsche. This handed them both almost a full lap as they proceeded at racing speed while the pace car proceeded very slowly around the track stacking up the remaining cars behind it. Incredibly the pace car slowed even more when it came upon the debris in the track from the previous accidents and this started cars behind having to take avoiding action in the bad visibility. An already difficult situation was then joined by the race leaders and other cars that had been ahead of the pace car and were unaware that the race had been slowed so much; still travelling at high speeds in the near zero visibility.

The ensuing accidents on the start finish line area with the field all but stopped when Stuck, Weaver, Baldi and Boutsen arrived at 140mph were frightening as it all happened in front of our pit area. A marshal had been hit but thankfully survived and Warwick had been advised of the approaching accident with just enough time to move out of line to the left while the four Porsches desperately tried to find a way down the right-hand side of the track testing the pits Armco barrier in the process. Stuck's Porsche was virtually cut in half taking out the entire left side off the car and others were too damaged to continue. On lap 22 the race was red flagged.

The restart had Warwick immediately behind Thackwell and as the track dried the XJR-6's Dunlops came into the zone and the Jaguar took the lead 20 laps after the restart. At the pit stop hand over from Warwick to Lammers a problem with the air jacks meant that Lammers rejoined the race on the same tyres, but still in the lead. With a healthy lead after another 64 laps Lammers engine developed a severe oil leak and pitted. The only remaining original part in the V12 engine, the rear camshaft oil feed pipe had fractured after being damaged in transit and any thought of replacing it was out of the question as the lower banjo bolt was inaccessible within the large venturi tunnels. In a futile attempt the pipe was closed off and the car sent out again, it lasted four laps before the camshaft seized. Another bitter blow in a race we should have won.

The race finished after 121 laps, just over half the scheduled distance with the Sauber Mercedes of Thackwell/Pescarolo taking a maiden victory for the team and Mercedes engine. Baldi/Niedzwiedz in the RLR Porsche finished second and John Fitzpatrick's Danone 956 Porsche third.

## Spa – September 15th

The TWR team had arrived early for this event and carried out pre-race testing on the Thursday. Engs had been given the OK to build a tenth engine and this was a prototype, 6829cc V12, with increased stroke of 82mm; this unit introduced as part of the future development for 1987. By this time, I had learned some fundamental facts when applying the normally aspirated V12 engine programme to this Group C formula.

No matter what we did the fuel efficiency of the V12 engine began to decrease above 6800rpm. This result was produced by two conditions existing with the engine configuration being used.

Increased frictional losses above 6800rpm in the large engine were then beginning to play their part, combined with the bowl in piston flat head combustion design reaching its maximum effective range around that rpm as well. We were at the stage of some important decision making for the future and this was behind the

*5-litre single overhead camshaft turbocharged Mercedes based engine in the Sauber C8, took its first victory at the Nurburgring with Thackwell and Pescarolo.*

Spa 6.8-litre V12 engine test. At this time Engs had to re-evaluate a commitment to produce at Kidlington an all-new 4-valves per cylinder head, as a development for the 1987 championship.

After finally having to admit that the Jaguar based 4-valve head was not suitable, and the potential problems for me involved with that decision, I had contacted former TWR design draftsman Russell Sharp. He had left some months before this and he now had some regrets over his actions in the meeting mentioned earlier with TW. We had a discussion about doing some sub-contract work for me, as a suitable qualified replacement for us had not yet been sourced in the common TWR drawing office. A 4-valve head programme needed a single concentrated effort outside of the normal day-to-day pressures of keeping up with the race programme.

I had completed my own investigation of the important valve and port angle principles involved and produced a scope for an all new head design. I had then agreed verbally with Russell that we could work together on this programme. Russell was capable of the design details as well as liaising with casting and machining facilities. That would reduce my involvement during the current racing season, and be the best solution cost wise as well. Unfortunately, when I had put this idea forward to TW he had immediately rejected it – for purely personal reasons on his part the matter would not be considered.

With the lower valve lifts used with the 4-valve concept, the current valve spring technology would easily produce a bullet proof system over the much longer 24 hour races. Because of the high lifts and rapid acceleration needed to produce the high horse power outputs from our current 2-valve V12 engines we were over stressing the valve springs. Their ultimate design specifications were compromised by having to fit within the inverted bucket design (cam follower) of the 2-valve heads; we did not have a bullet proof system in 24 hour races.

But by now the 2-valve V12 and engine management concepts being used had proved to be much more competitive than TW, Roger and Tony Southgate had ever envisaged and so the pressure to change had reduced. We could further increase power with the current 2-valve V12 engine via an increase in engine capacity with the benefit of no added weight penalty, and at the same time retain the fuel economy with a marginal improvement in lap time. If we could get this series to adopt normal road 98-octane fuel for 1987 then the turbo engines would have most of their advantages reduced and the pendulum would swing back to help neutralise any differential between the two engine concepts.

I was however a little sceptical that Porsche would accept our proposal, even though the concept of Group C was a nod to the perception that the industry needed to accept that one day there would be an oil crisis. Developing economical engines that used the fuel available to the everyday motorist would surely be a logical move within this Group C concept; and based on that reasoning this idea had already begun to be put forward by us. This would stipulate the use of low lead 98 RON road based fuels.

Not until recently with the advent of direct injection turbocharged petrol engines have they been able to produce superior efficiency and flexibility when using standard road based fuels.

The new prototype 6829cc engine was fitted to Eddie Cheever's car at the Spa test for him to evaluate and report back, as I felt he had the best feel for these things. He reported that this engine had that little bit extra out of Eau Rouge to help produce a few extra km/h at the beginning of the long uphill straight at Spa. He also reported the increased flexibility allowed slightly lower rpm in some areas for the same lap time, and seemed easier to keep to the fuel allowance than the 6.5-litre engine. It was definitely a slightly better, not slightly worse, lap time to fuel used being the conclusion from this test. The idea of *increasing* the engine capacity to improve fuel efficiency under *racing* conditions was a philosophy that had few believers, including my boss. With all the extensive information Alastair Macqueen and the team were amassing in our second season, we were in the process of fine tuning a best outcome under racing conditions. The only advantage therefore in progressing 4-valve heads for this engine was for increased reliability with the valve train in the endurance events of Le Mans and a future Daytona. Valve spring supplier Schmitthelm of Germany did not have a complete answer for our current engine.

In the dry Thursday testing conditions Cheever had set a very competitive time of 2:07.3, a similar time to that set by the fastest Porsche and three seconds faster than Brundle's brave attempts in 1985. Without a second engine available for Warwick to the same specification I was never going to get away with leaving that engine in for the race and so it was removed and replaced with the normal 1986 specification 6.5-litre engine.

A cat and mouse game with the changing weather conditions and decisions on when to use the soft qualifying tyres over the two sessions had left team manager Roger Silman with few good options, but the outcome of Cheever fourth and fastest Jaguar, and Warwick fifth on this track that favoured the turbo cars was a very good result indeed. Cheever's time was 0.5s slower than that set with the 5% larger engine capacity on the Thursday, and just 0.9s from the fastest qualifying time set by Boutsen/Jelinski, an increasingly competitive combination in the Brun Jaegermeister 962C; with Stuck/Bell and Mass/Wollek following in the two factory Rothmans 962C's.

It was also becoming an increasingly confident time for TW and Roger with the XJR-6's aerodynamic downforce being compared to Formula One technology. With this in mind the XJR-6 had titanium plates fitted to points on the underbody for this race. These were just thick enough to rub on various sections of the track and produce some spectacular sparks just as the current group of Formula One cars were doing. This feature was to demonstrate that the TWR XJR-6 was now well ahead of the Porsche 962C in the ground effects stakes and up with Formula One technology; and this would continue the TWR franchise image of leading edge development in whatever category it raced in.

The daunting high-speed left/right uphill Eau Rouge corner could be taken in fifth gear by the brave in the Jaguar camp on this circuit and demonstrated the Jaguar's superiority here. Here the torque of the V12 exiting that corner onto the uphill straight at lower rpm in fifth gear also came into play allowing a long fifth gear period to accelerate the race cars all the way to the end of the straight saving fuel.

It had rained once again for the pre-race warm up and the two Jaguars set the fastest times in these wet conditions; but it soon dried out and with changeable weather promised, the 145 lap 1006km race started with clearer skies and a dry track. The early laps saw close racing with Baldi in the RLR Porsche taking the lead from Boutsen and the two Jaguar's close behind Bell in his Porsche. Warwick pitted early with a vibration from an out of balance wheel handing over to Lammers. Then Schlesser, after replacing Cheever, had to have his windscreen cleaned when a broken oil line on the factory Porsche had sprayed oil over it; leaving the Jaguar's third and fifth.

By half distance five cars were still on the same lap, three Porsches and two Jaguars. With thirty odd laps to go the hard work that Cheever and Schlesser had put in to carry their Jaguar back up to the leading bunch was over with Schlesser having a rear puncture and losing too much time to remain in contention. The last pit stops were short ones to take on the remaining fuel allocation and the closest race of the year was down to four cars over the last twenty laps. This was soon reduced to three cars as the Blaupunkt Porsche of Ludwig slowed having gone over its fuel allowance and would have to slow to reach the finishing line, leaving Warwick in third place still eighteen seconds behind the Rothmans Porsche driven by Bell. With five laps to go it was only Warwick in the XJR-6 that could continue at racing speed after Bell had been told over the radio to back off and the Jaguar moved into second place with two laps to go and 5.5s from the leader. The next to last lap the gap was 2.8s and as Boutsen approached the second last corner before the finish line his car hesitated with low fuel pressure as the pumps searched for the last drops of fuel, allowing Warwick to close right behind him. It was now the Jaguar's turn to lose fuel pressure on the run to the finish line and the race was lost by 0.8s after 1006kms. The post-race check over found the leading Jaguar's fuel tank had six litres of fuel left, the car still struggling to pickup the last elements of fuel under racing G-forces and cost Warwick and the team a well driven win.

Bell/Stuck was third and Ludwig/Barilla a lap down in fourth with Cheever/Schlesser fifth.

***Accomplishing the almost impossible means only that the boss will add it to your regular duties.***

**– Doug Larson**

## Nurburgring No.2 – September 21st

The Nurburgring 'Supercup' round, one week after the Spa race was the fourth and last of the German series consisting of 39 laps of the 'new' circuit totalling 177kms. It was Cheever who would drive the single TWR Jaguar against the large field of local Porsche teams and the privately entered Lancia for Bruno Giacomelli. For this race the 6829cc V12 engine would be fitted to continue the testing programme for the following year and would be a good test of its competitiveness against the Porsches on their home ground, as well as allowing the Spa engines to be rebuilt.

All year drivers had been complaining about the speed differentials between the smaller C2 category cars in qualifying and the race, a problem that had especially been seen at the earlier Brands Hatch meeting, and by now little compassion was being shown to their position on the race track by the larger C1 race cars. The electronic fuel meter, reading out in a tenth of a lap had shown just how much fuel could be lost when lapping these slower cars with early braking leading to slower entry and exit from the corners and losing their momentum behind the slower C2 race cars. Cheever had then gone out in the later part of practice in 'education' mode as he rounded up some of these cars and demonstrated a no holds barred approach to overtaking and cutting back across making sure in the process they remembered to keep out of his Jaguar's way during the race. One of these manoeuvres had ended with the Gebhardt C2 having its nose chopped off and being punted into the barriers causing reasonable damage to the car. Cheever's return to the pits later was greeted by the offended driver raining blows to his helmet before he could exit the car. It continued out of the car although was never going to amount to much as both had their helmets on. This 'educational' process on Cheever's part just demonstrated the attention to detail he would put in to have the best chance of winning.

*Typical pit working conditions at the time.*

Stuck had to use his backup car after a practice accident, this car being fitted with a racing version of the ABS braking system to continue Porsche's testing of technology via racing.

The final fastest practice times for the 14 entrants were Stuck, Ludwig, Cheever, Giacomelli and Wollek, three Porsches, one Jaguar and Lancia.

Saturday started the TV presentation of this well marketed race with two seven lap heats with the finishing order reversed for the second heat. Stuck was penalise one minute in the first heat for a driving infringement leaving Ludwig as winner followed by Cheever and the Brun Porsches of Jelinski and Larrauri. With his one-minute penalty Stuck was now on the front row for the second heat which he proceeded to win with Larrauri second followed by Wollek and Cheever very close.

This new format then decided the starting positions for the main race on Sunday and after amalgamating both heat results Cheever ended up on the front row with Larrauri, Wollek and Jelinski next with Giacomelli and Stuck back on the third row, giving Cheever a head start over his biggest rival in this race, Stuck. Cheever lost some ground at the start and circulated in third place behind Stuck and Wollek for the early part of the race, moving into second when the boost control on Wollek's RLR Porsche became faulty. Ludwig now joined the top three briefly before spinning off leaving Stuck and Cheever with a comfortable 30 second lead over the rest of the field. The gap between the two leading cars remained at three seconds for the rest of the race reducing by one second at the start of the last lap. Exiting the last corner Stuck's Porsche ran low on fuel pressure and Cheever was through to take the win by 0.54s. Ludwig was third and Giacomelli fourth, with all the remaining cars a lap down.

It was here after a straightforward race between the two manufacturers that the tide looked to be turning against the Porsche teams as it was only Stuck and Ludwig with the best factory supported engines that were now a threat to TWR Jaguar. The once dominant privateer teams of Joest and Brun were beginning to struggle as larger capacity flat-six engines and electronic controls continued to be developed throughout the year; the days of Porsche customer engines being able to produce a winning combination were looking increasingly remote. Much needed income for the Porsche works team from supplying the older already existing hardware was about to be challenged with these customer engines unable to produce a supporting role against the Jaguars should the works team have a problem in the race. This race at the Nurburgring was a great story for Jaguar to capitalise on, with the Porsches being beaten on their home ground. It continued the marketing plan of presenting resurgence in British automotive technology to rival that of the best in Germany, via the Jaguar brand. It was also the best test Engs could have in deciding the final specification V12 engine for 1987.

## Fuji – October 6th

It was less than two weeks after the Nurburgring race that the Silk Cut Jaguar XJR-6s would have to be at the Mt Fuji Circuit in Japan. The championship leaders going into this last race were Stuck/Bell in the Rothmans Porsche with Warwick in second place just 13 points behind. Travelling to this event was still in the days when airlines could not fly over the Soviet Union and the team undertook the long flight via the North Pole to Alaska. After a brief refuelling stop the second leg of the journey to Tokyo completed the 24 hour total flight. It was then a £78 taxi ride to the Tokyo Jaguar dealer to collect the courtesy car and local driver for the journey to our accommodation at Lake Yamanakako, a short drive from the Fuji circuit. Our driver then insisted on travelling at less than the legal speed limit and had to be constantly cajoled into speeding up and eventually after another six hours, we arrived at the holiday lodge that would be home for the next four days. The caterers had also disbursed bacon and sausages to team members at Heathrow to hand carry through Japanese customs to enable the mechanics to have a decent 'British' breakfast and feel a little more at home.

The final race of the year in Japan was at least dryer than 1985 and the Jaguars were very competitive on this fast track which was ideally suited to the high boost turbocharged cars in qualifying. The factory Porsche team had the PDK transmissions as well as the new ABS braking system and Derek Bell was unhappy with both these items being tested when the championship was at stake. The PDK preselect transmission used during the series had also proved to be hard on its driveshafts, and Bell/Stuck did not need the added weight or possible driveshaft problem in their quest for the championship title. The compromise was the removal of the ABS braking system.

This was to be the most interesting race of the season with both Japanese manufacturers Nissan and Toyota being pitched against the Group C regulars at their home

*Japanese circuit named after the majestic Mount Fuji close by.*

circuit in cars that were very fast, but yet to prove they were able to run to the fuel allocation. Local drivers were out to make a name for themselves against the famous foreign 'Gaijins' and qualifying was just as important as the race for many of these teams. Whoever was the fastest in qualifying made the evening news, especially if the visitors had been beaten. TV time given to the race winners the following night, especially if they were foreigners, would be less.

Lotus Formula One driver Satoru Nakajima duly took fastest time but this was in the team's test car that he would not use in the race, and the time was disallowed.

The Brun Porsches of Jelinski/Stanley Dickens and Larrauri/Pareja were then elevated to fastest qualifiers to take front row honours. Stuck/Bell were third with the first Japanese team of Hoshino/Nakako in the Newey designed 85 March-Nissan fourth.

Fuji would be the most difficult qualifying race of the year for the Jaguars with over 30 mostly turbocharged C1 class cars competing, producing the largest field of the series. To add to the problem all the TWR Jaguar drivers had never driven there before. Cheever once again was fastest with 13th position and Warwick close behind in 17th on a higher altitude circuit suiting turbocharged engines. Further practice sessions were used to produce a good race set-up with no point trying to find a starting position slightly higher up the field.

The European Porsches settled into the lead with the Jaguars continually moving up over the first 10 laps to be in sixth and ninth position as the local Japanese drivers began to run a pace that reflected their fuel consumption. The first real change to the situation came with Stuck having to pit with a wheel problem after trying to lap one of the slower cars. Soon after this the pace car was out onto the track, coinciding with the leaders beginning to make their scheduled pit stops. While trying to pick up the leader, who was by now in the pits, most of the field was waved passed the pace car and completed an extra lap while others were held at the pit exit waiting for the pace car to come by. Both works Porsches came out of the situation best with Stuck moving from sixteenth to second and the Jaguars losing ground, held at the pit exit. Warwick's chances of the title began to look in trouble with Lammers having to pit with a hub failure and nearly twelve minutes were lost replacing it. That meant Warwick transferred to the fourth placed Cheever XJR-6 on lap 76 of the 226-lap race. By half distance the Warwick/Cheever Jaguar had caught and passed championship rival Bell and moved into third place. Soon after this the Porsche was delayed with a broken driveshaft and rejoined well down the placings. This move to Warwick's favour was neutralised as soon after, he left the track up the chicane escape road, and was charged with ignoring the marshal's instruction when rejoining the track. A compulsory pit stop as punishment now put this car out of its fuelling sequence and the battle continued.

The second Jaguar had been further delayed with gear selection problems losing more time to repair broken linkage. In a cruel twist of fate Cheever running in second place and closing fast on the leader Ghinzani came to a halt at the end of the straight after hitting some large pieces of rubber breaking a headlight. He thought this had caused the engine to cut out and was out of the car to check it over. It turned out the master switch had somehow been knocked off and a vital lap was lost. After the next change back to Warwick the XJR-6 was soon running in the second place it needed to take the title when he had to pit with 12 laps to go with a misfiring engine. It took a couple of minutes to find the faulty chassis wiring loom connection and rejoin in third place. At this point the race positions were in confusion with the organisers and many other teams having the Jaguar still in second place.

TWR Silk Cut Jaguar and Derek Warwick were given second place and the Drivers Championship. This was disputed and the race organisers used the works Porsche computer to reassess the final placings, making the Jaguar third and loosing the championship. There had been constant technicalities raised with pace cars and pit exit control that had received no response when questions were asked by the TWR team during the race. When Derek Warwick had used the escape road he had been called back to the pits for a time delaying penalty, yet the winning car had passed another under yellow flags with no penalty.

The final outcome was a third place, which was the position the TWR timing crew had as well, which meant that Warwick had missed the 1986 Drivers Championship by just one point.

*A pensive Derek Bell*
*initially assuming they have lost the championship.*

Derek appeared to be quite happy with his year stating after the Fuji race. "You know, at the beginning of the year I thought that there was no way that we'd be able to challenge for the championship. I thought we'd have a few sparkling moments, but on average I thought that Porsche would be much stronger."

This no doubt reflected the feelings that abounded in late January when team manager Roger Silman had signed him up for the programme. Many were happy with the results, exceeding their expectations for 1986, but not for me. This was one that got away, TWR lost a championship that was there for the taking.

The year however was not over with discussions continuing over changes to the formula and a further reduction in fuel allowance and some controls on aerodynamic profiles. The move from 105 RON to 102 had meant very little change in reality, and it was in TWR/Engs interests to have this fuel rating lowered. My proposal to Tom Walkinshaw was to use standard 98 RON octane fuel only, as this would penalise the turbo engines more than our high compression normally aspirated V12. It was also a proposal that I never thought would be accepted by Porsche as their engines relied on specialised fuel.

## Trade off for 1987

The TWR team also began a testing programme with the lower drag Le Mans race set-ups. As the 1986 year came to a close different underbody venturi profiles and fuel consumption reduction tests were carried out as some proposals on rule changes were being put forward and options being left open. The aspects considered were a 10% reduction in fuel, reduced underbody venturi height, and the use of commercial 98-octane petrol.

The conclusions were a further reduction in fuel allowance would cause some disruption to the series and is not recommended. The losses for the XJR V12 6.5-litre engine tested on 98-octane pump fuel with the ignition retarded 3° for this test to simulate the reduction in compression ration from 13.5 to 12.5 were minimal. We expected a much larger problem for turbocharged engines. Underbody venturi height reductions were more in line with Le Mans thinking and so for that race at least would not cause a problem for TWR. This reduction was seen to help the Porsche camp and would therefore be used as a trade off to get the quantity of fuel to remain the same, but be replaced not just with a reduction to 98-octane, but standard road fuel specifications.

The last race at Fuji in Japan had seen the TWR Jaguar team come so close to winning the World Group C Series. This had been a major wake up call for Porsche and the XJR-6 was now on equal terms, with more updates planned for 1987.

Various problems during the year had masked the competitiveness of the XJR-6 in the final results. Eliminate any one of the problems, broken driveshafts, the 3-car off at Jerez or the pace car situation and TWR Jaguar would have won the 1986 championship with ease.

At this time TW had also been working with Max Heidegger in Liechtenstein on turbocharging of Jaguar's production AJ6 engine as a JaguarSport programme, an engine he had considered as an alternative in the XJR-6 for 1986. Although it was never said at the time it later began to appear to me that TW's evolving plans were to have most future development work carried out in Liechtenstein, at least Jaguar production and JaguarSport engines – and racing programmes that involved turbocharged engines. TW was able to have some of his ideas come to fruition with Max Heidegger, something he had on previous occasion had difficulty in convincing me of their merit. He enjoyed his relationship with Max Heidegger and the Liechtenstein organisation, and alternative ideas were coming from that direction also, both still convinced of turbocharging's future. This could eventually mean having mainly a rebuild facility at Kidlington sometime in the future, something he probably knew I would not be happy with. This growing situation with Max Heidegger would allow TW a greater level of involvement in engines than he had with me on the V12 programme; now that he was officially retiring at the end of 1986 from driving, with the end of the Rover programme. There was also another plan growing in the background that had not yet fully seen the light though.

Since 1983 I had spent some time convincing TW to venture 'down under' to the Bathurst race in Australia. After the win there with the XJS Jaguars in 1985, and TW's high profile with the extensive media coverage, discussions with Holden to develop their Special Vehicles division as well as the possibility of running the Holden Racing Team had begun.

One year later TW was in the process of forming a joint venture with Holden to produce limited edition performance vehicles in a similar manner to the association TWR had with Jaguar. This would also entail taking control of the Peter Brock run Holden Racing Team sometime in the future. TW had then negotiated a development programme for the V8 engine and a special aerodynamics package for their VL Commodore to compete in Group A. This new engine programme was added to my list in November for development over the winter, alongside the new XJR-8 V12 programme. The TWR Rover Group A programme had now ceased.

I had stayed over in Japan with some members of the Jaguar XJS Group A team who had arrived early to prepare two cars for what was to be one of the last races for the TWR XJS Jaguars, two weeks later at the Mount Fuji circuit. My task after this Fuji race was a quick trip to Australia to organise the purchase of four Holden V8 Group A engines from the Roadways Racing team and have them sent back to TWR in Kidlington for analysis and further development over the winter of 1986/87.

**T W R S I L K C U T J A G U A R**

**ILLUSTRATION OF PERFORMANCE LIMITATION**

**SET BY LOW VENTURI EXIT HEIGHT**

1. Side elevation of Silk Cut Jaguar XJR-6 in normal Sprint car specification with venturi exit details.
2. Side elevation of Silk Cut Jaguar XJR-6 in Le Mans car specification with venturi exit details.
3. Lap times achieved by Sprint car in the most recent Silverstone G.P. test day.
4. Lap times achieved by Le Mans car just two days previously.
5. TABLE 1 : Illustrates an increase in lap time at Silverstone of 4 seconds but with an increase in top speed of 10 kph for the low venturi specification car.

   The comparison at Le Mans provides an identical lap time but with an increase of 40 kph for the low venturi specification car.

TABLE 1 : TUNNEL SPECS

| | SILVERSTONE | | LE MANS | |
|---|---|---|---|---|
| CAR SPEC | LAP TIME | TOP SPEED KPH | LAP TIME | TOP SPEED KPH |
| 1986 HIGH VENTURI SPEC | 1 - 13.0 | 292 | 3.30.0 | 320 |
| 1986 LOW VENTURI SPEC (LE MANS SPEC) | 1 - 17.0 | 302 | 3.30.0 | 360 |

**T W R S I L K C U T J A G U A R**

**ILLUSTRATION OF PERFORMANCE LIMITATION**

**SET UP BY COMMERCIAL FUEL AND A 10% REDUCTION**

TABLE 2 : Illustrates an overall increase in lap time of 3.7 seconds at Silverstone with a reduction of 7 kph on top speed.

At Le Mans the lap time is increased by 8 seconds and the top speed reduced by 4 kph.

TABLE 2 : FUEL SPECS

| | SILVERSTONE | | LE MANS | |
|---|---|---|---|---|
| FUEL SPEC | LAP TIME | TOP SPEED KPH | LAP TIME | TOP SPEED KPH |
| 1986 SPEC | 1 - 13.0 | 292 | 3.30.0 | 360 |
| COMMERCIAL FUEL ONLY | 1 - 13.8 | 290 | 3.31.0 | 356 |
| 10% REDUCTION IN FUEL | 1 - 17.5 | 285 | 3.38.0 | 356 |

*The tests illustrated here show the results for the various proposals that were being put forward to changes in the regulations for 1987.*

As I had lived in Sydney Australia for three years in the early 70s and being a native of nearby New Zealand, TW felt I fitted in well with that situation.

Some pressures had also started to build in the USA, where the XJR-7 of Group 44 was not performing as well as hoped. The 6-litre engine they had been using was increased to 6.5 litres using my larger 94mm liner and piston details. In the space of 18 months we had gone from using some Group 44 engine parts to cobble together the first Group C V12 engine, to now being seen by Jaguar at Browns Lane as the leader in V12 race engine design; supplying technology to the American team.

TWR Jaguar team manager Roger Silman had put together a formidable team in less than 18 months and was now justly very proud to stand beside the XJR-6 in the pit lane. His personal need to have high profile Formula One drivers in the team led to the departure of Brancatelli back to his first love, touring cars, and the sacking of Jean-Louis Schlesser, surprising after he had put in a solid and competitive year. I was disappointed with this move as Jean-Louis was a thinking engineering driver totally suited to the demands of the Group C fuel based formula. Schlesser would then accept a position to drive for the up and coming Sauber Mercedes team later in 1987, taking with him the trackside electronic engine management testing methods that we had worked together on over three years. This had included the Rover saloon days in France and European Touring Car as well as the two-year testing evolution with the XJR-6. Roger dismissed this as being of no consequence when I raised my concerns. Unfortunately for Roger this situation would later return to haunt him when Schlesser would go on to be double World Sports Car Champion with Sauber Mercedes in 1989 and 1990, defeating TWR/Jaguar.

16 September 1986

ENGINE DEPARTMENT BUDGET 1986

| | Actual Expenditure | Budgeted Expenditure | Surplus / (Deficit) |
|---|---|---|---|
| | £ | £ | £ |
| GENERAL | | | |
| Fixed Overhead | 94 000 | 94 000 | - |
| Freight | 6 400 | 4 000 | ( 2 400) |
| Travel & Subsistence | 1 800 | 3 000 | 1 200 |
| Motor expenses & Fuel | 6 800 | 12 000 | 5 200 |
| Equipment repairs & Upkeep | 9 200 | 5 600 | ( 3 600) |
| General Consumables | 26 500 | 15 200 | (11 300) |
| Sundries | 1 900 | 1 000 | ( 900) |
| Consultancy | 32 000 | 24 000 | ( 8 000) |
| | 178 600 | 158 800 | (19 800) |
| JAGUAR GROUP C | | | |
| Development | 48 000 | 40 000 | ( 8 000) |
| Parts | 322 000 | 280 000 | (42 000) |
| Salaries | 129 900 | 117 600 | (12 300) |
| | 499 900 | 437 600 | (62 300) |
| ROVER | | | |
| Parts | 140 000 | 125 000 | (15 000) |
| Salaries | 67 300 | 66 500 | ( 800) |
| | 207 300 | 191 500 | (15 800) |
| TOTAL | 885 800 | 787 900 | (97 900) |

*Total expenditure in 1986 for both engine programmes at TWR.*
*Meetings were held to approve over-budget expenditure. TW and two drivers' salaries were just over twice the allocation to Jaguar Group C engine development and maintenance.*

JAGUAR

CHAPTER THIRTEEN

# Development of the XJR-8 and 7-litre engine

**In addition to what we felt was a good set of results for our first full year of World Series Sports Prototype Racing, 1986 ended with British industry's approval for the TWR Jaguar with a Design Council Award for Tony Southgate and the XJR-6.**

The many lessons learned with the XJR-6 would be put to good use over the winter in preparation for the 1987 season. TWR Jaguar's opposition, an improved Porsche 962C and the growing competitiveness of the Sauber Mercedes would lift the WSPC series to a new level of competitiveness – as well as introduce some rule changes.

The major change for Engs and the Jaguar team had come with the acceptance of our proposal that the fuel specification should be that of the standard 98-octane fuel used by the entrant's customers. Pressure had been applied to the Group C turbo teams associated with high profile automotive companies to embrace the use of standard EU road fuels and the timing was now right to have this put into effect. Testing to further reduce fuel allowances at the end of 1986 had proved unworkable. Group C with its fuel restrictions was promoted as a responsible form of motor racing and could now be seen also a proving ground for road car derived engines as opposed to exotic fuel brews that could never be used in everyday motor cars. The revised regulations gave more justification for Group C teams to access their manufacturers' research budgets to help fund their motor racing – this being the mindset behind our proposal aimed at Porsche and Mercedes.

The change to road-car petrol was a major help to us and it was a surprise to me that the turbo teams had gone along with our proposals on this one. All engines would suffer some loss of performance with this lower specification fuel, but small capacity high boost turbocharged engines would suffer the most, while the normally aspirated engines, such as the Jaguar V12, would suffer least. Mercedes' 5-litre V8, running only 1.65 bar of boost, would not be as handicapped as Porsche with their 3-litre engines. Overall, this was a positive move for TWR and Engs going into 1987, with Tony Southgate and Alastair Macqueen fine tuning the aerodynamic package.

It is worth looking at how the differences in approach between the entrants in Group C, their company structures and outlook might affect the upcoming 1987 season, as well as the 'turbocharged versus normally aspirated' battle we were by now familiar with.

Could differences in approach influence the scales of victory at year's end?

Just what were the strengths and weaknesses of each team at this time?

Racing was a business for the Porsche factory with its immense engineering and design resources, and with a proven winning car concept – it would support what it knew worked best for them. Porsche manufactured many Group C and IMSA racing cars for private customer teams and had to service these teams with parts and upgrades as they were developed. Against this world leading factory sports car racing team TWR would have perhaps the one asset needed to penetrate the dominance of Porsche in Group C and later IMSA. That asset would be small team flexibility – focused solely on itself.

TWR, with no private race teams to support, could make its car and engine changes without the concern of having to resupply a large group of customer cars; and then having expensive existing parts inventories become obsolete if a new concept to keep up with increased competition was developed. We also had less time consuming internal procedures or design sign off meetings, not having to follow an accepted larger company philosophy that would have slowed rapid change at Porsche. These freedoms included the established relationship between Tony Southgate and John Thompson in race car design and manufacture, Alastair Macqueen as chief engineer producing the detailed chassis solutions in the racing environment, and myself at Engs providing the power unit development having attended all the races and seen the issues at first hand. We were all allowed a relatively free hand at this time in producing our individual solutions. Decision making was a relatively individual process within our respective departments. We simply reported these conclusions to TW and Roger, usually in separate divisional meetings.

In this competitive situation it would have been perfectly normal to have some tension develop between the three areas, but both Tony Southgate and Alastair Macqueen were non verbally-aggressive, and were well controlled professional characters. This helped the cohesive outlook between us all. We also had a supportive race team working for us, which was a large part of the fast-growing success story of Jaguar and TWR. They added 100% support to the tasks asked of them without looking at the clock.

Whenever Engs had been put under pressure to help with a particular circuit or situation that needed reduced fuel usage, we just made a decision at the time and ran the engine on the ragged edge of lean misfire and pre-detonation, without having predetermined safety limitations set by a higher authority. The TWR philosophy that I was well familiar with from the earlier saloon car days had always been winning and taking chances along the way to achieve this, rarely just driving to finish.

Porsche racing was very aligned with their road car philosophy of engineering reliability, their engineers needing to promote the image of engineering excellence as a major part of the motor racing partnership with the parent company. This racing image assisted in selling large volumes of high performance vehicles, and its engineering durability was a high priority. While Jaguar wished the same philosophy, they had never called us to meetings to discuss or influence race track outcomes. Jaguar had come to trust TWR's judgement over the years and to their credit had stepped back from demanding engineering overview on decision making.They left it to TWR personnel to ask for Jaguar's help as and when it was needed.

Tony Southgate had maintained his independence, operating from his studio at home assisted by Jeff Kingston, and along with Alastair Macqueen, Tony reported to Roger Silman in the first instance. Paul Davis continued to assist Roger with team management when his JaguarSport duties allowed. In the TWR drawing office supporting all internal programmes were Colin Moore and Andy Scriven reporting to Roger Silman. As Engs manager I continued to report to Tom Walkinshaw.

TW had taken an overall view chairing meetings and approving directions taken by the various areas of the Group C team, as well as leading the Rover Group A team and being its lead driver in the ETC Championship in 1986. He had always enjoyed the day-to-day challenges of improving the Group A saloon car's engineering performance, and this had fulfilled that ambition for him during the first two years of the XJR-6 programme. TW had now finished his driving contract with Austin Rover which left Andy Morrison and Eddie Hinckley to switch to the new venture with Holden Australia, producing and testing their new Group A Commodore race car. This joint venture with Holden Special Vehicles (HSV) and the Holden Racing Team (HRT) based in Melbourne would be finalised later in 1987. TW would have more time to concentrate on the TWR Group business expansion into vehicle dealerships outside of motor racing – as well as being seen to influence some of the engineering involved in what by the end of 1986 was potentially a winning Jaguar WSPC programme. By mid-year 1987 Roger Silman would be made a main board director to join finance director John Bradley and chairman Tom Walkinshaw, and I was given the title of general manager on my business card; TW was good at giving titles. There would be a reason for this as I would find out later.

The update on XJR-6 would be known as XJR-8 for 1987 and with over 60 detailed modifications – the chassis had developed into an excellent package. Our race strategies had been polished and equipment levels built up. Engs was beginning to see the benefit of 18 months of intensive development of the V12 engine and had been able to lay down the 1987 specifications after the successful testing of the 6.8-litre engine at Spa and the Nurburgring. This gave us the basis for some confidence for TWR and Jaguar's challenge to the five-year dominance of the all-conquering Porsche.

The one-off test during practice at Spa in 1986 and the race win at the Nurburgring with the larger 6828cc engine had shown that an even larger capacity engine could be contemplated and still remain fuel efficient in the Jaguar XJR-8. Engs did by now have a stock of ten engines including the single 6.8-litre by the last race of 1986, but any new designs would have to be included within these existing units. We still did not have our own in-house machining facilities despite requests for basic machinery, and this inevitably affected some processes and decisions that had to be made. Even if just one corner on a race circuit could be taken in a higher gear, this had added up to a few litres of fuel over six hours. This showed the need for an engine producing large amounts of mid range torque at lower less friction rpm and produced the concept for 1987.

After my visit to Australia to negotiate the purchase and delivery of four Holden V8 engines, TW had asked me to concentrate dyno development time on this project starting in early 1987 motivated by the need to impress his new Holden partners before signing a joint venture programme. They had no doubt been given very encouraging prospects by TW to close these deals and this programme now seemed to be more important to TW than the Jaguar V12 engine work.

## V12 engine upgrades for 1987

There were two ways to go about the V12 engine upgrade. Increase the stroke, or increase the bore and stroke. A larger capacity engine would not achieve its ultimate power output potential with the current head specifications including valve sizes. Increasing the bore size to 96mm would allow the fitting of 3mm larger valves, but using these larger sizes would come with the need to move the valve centres in the heads further apart. This change would have a major knock on effect with the need to completely rework machining of new heads, camshaft carriers and new camshafts with different lobe spacings, as well as new cylinder liners and remachining of the block. A 96mm bore when utilized with the existing 78.5 (6818cc) or new 82mm (7122cc) stroke crankshaft would improve performance throughout the rpm range and allow improved top end breathing to help in qualifying and general engine efficiency. My first choice was the larger valve 96mm bore and 82mm stroke 7122cc engine.

Unfortunately, the time and costs involved in this best V12 engine choice became the overriding factor in the decision not to proceed with the larger valve 96mm bore option. Increasingly the engine continued to give excellent fuel mileage up to 6500rpm but by 7000rpm was 4% less efficient, for a given power output, increasing to 6% at 7500rpm. Increased friction, from increased engine speeds, as well as reducing combustion efficiency in our two valves per cylinder engine design were both coming into play by 6800rpm. The second choice would be to retain the existing 94mm bore and fit an even longer 84mm stroke crankshaft, this would produce an engine size of 6995cc and was a simpler option; just needing a new longer stroke crankshaft available from the initial stockpile of 85 forgings that Jaguar had produced in 1985.

With the longer 84mm stroke came the need to devise a way to retain the existing internal hardware. The piston gudgeon pin however could not be raised anymore to lower the compression height as it was touching the oil ring already. The solution was to machine a 3mm deep chamber into each of the six combustion faces of the flat head face. The existing valve seats were already slightly recessed and needed only small amounts of material to be machined during this process. Heads were flow tested and valve inserts cut for best gas flow results using valve back face angles between 30° and 37°. This design produced a piston crown that protruded 2mm above the liner into the machined recess in the head, leaving a 0.040in squish clearance. New 84mm crankshafts from existing forgings would replace the ones that had already done one and a half season's racing, and complete this new 7-litre engine. All other parts from the 1986 engines transferred over. This was the best financial solution and made the best utilisation of stock in hand, and meant we could retain most existing components for yet another full season because of the lower rpm involved.

For 98 RON 89 MON (USA94) fuel the compression ratio of the 7-litre engines was reduced from 13.5 to 12.25:1, by machining a larger bowl in the existing piston stock. The change in compression ratio and lower octane fuel would produce a small loss of efficiency and top end power output, becoming more noticeable over 6750rpm. The increase in power and torque throughout the fuel-efficient range would allow more low rpm flexibility during the race, with less time loss when cornering with a higher gear to keep to the fuel allowance.

The V12 engines cost TWR £28,000–£30,000 in parts for a complete new engine including electronics, and took around 200 hours to build, test, and check over before delivery. A normal rebuild involved a parts cost of around £6000, plus 100 to 150 hours labour. The cost effectiveness of the 'long stroke' approach began to show dividends with overall programme expenditure actually reducing in 1987, keeping TW happy.

Design draftsmen Andy Scriven and Colin Moore drew the updated and new parts for the 6995cc engine, a considerable task with constant fine tuning or changes to a manufacturing process and heat treatment processes all needing amendments to existing drawings.

The new 84mm crankshaft design would mean that the pin overlap would be less, effectively reducing its strength. An example of how the tests were carried out on the crankshaft to determine its failure mode with different stroke lengths is shown on page 135.

The off-season gave us time to look at finer details and one of these was to reduce engine rebuild times. The 2.1in big end bearing shells came in two different sizes with a tolerance of 0.001in, and after careful measuring of the crankshaft, these items were hand selected and then fitted, a time-consuming job and possible source of small differences producing small changes in hot oil pressures being reported by drivers. We had earlier been told that Vandervell, the engine bearing suppliers, had a production tooling wear allowance which created this problem. I was able to use the supplier relationship between Jaguar Cars and Vandervell, the original equipment supplier to Jaguar, to good effect with this problem. The 84mm crankshafts made at Farndon Engineering had a new inspection process and limited tolerances for 1987, and these were to a maximum tolerance of 0.0003in finished size in both taper and ovality. If we could reduce the bearing shell tolerances to zero, then with the crankshaft and bearing inspection processes we had in place, bearings could be fitted and be correct first time.

Vandervell's John Nash informed us that his factory tooling was about to be renewed as it had come to the end of its useful life and he offered to do a one-time production run with the commencement of the new tooling, producing bearings with a tolerance of 0.0001in, ten times less than what could occur in production.

In fact it transpired that the actual size variations were not produced by Vandervell's production methods, but with the steel backing material they were supplied with over different times. Our one-time production run would be made from a single batch of selected steel sheet certified to produce a consistent bearing shell thickness. The overlay copper/lead material that Vandervell applied was consistent and so the end product was totally controlled. These bearings were put through Vandervell's inspection system and came with a signed off inspection report. After the exact dimensions of the one-time free of charge bearing supply from Vandervell were accurately measured to produce 0.0022in big end and 0.003in main bearing clearances, final journal dimensions were nominated, then Farndon Engineering's signed off crankshafts were double checked by the newly created one-man inspection department at Engs, ensuring less than half of one thousandths of an inch tolerance across all engines for the rest of the V12 programme, bringing conformity to oil pressure and reducing build times by eliminating selected bearing shells.

Another upgrade was to reduce oil consumption to an absolute minimum. Integrity over all 12 cylinders was needed to reduce the effect of oil that may come past the piston rings reducing the fuel specification. High oil consumption was evident right from the start of the V12 programme in 1985, and various measures had been taken to reduce it.

A deal had been done with Castrol to part-sponsor the Jaguar team after Castrol had been awarded the original equipment oil supply contract for all new Jaguar production cars built at Coventry. All the profit for Castrol from this deal at the same price as Jaguar's previous oil supplier was given as the sponsorship from Castrol, a win/win for all concerned. Castrol were our oil supplier with their 15/50 and lighter 10/60 grade oils, but we used the 15/50 version to help the oil consumption problem.

Lighter oil viscosities have a considerable positive effect on short run cold temperature conditions in a customer's normal daily drive. The improvements with production cars from these lightweight oils comes from the fact that most vehicle journeys are made with the oils only briefly reaching operating temperature, and the lighter grades in these situations do give considerable improvements in loss of friction from cold oil. Back-to-back tests using a minimum100°C engine oil gallery temperature in our test cells at Kidlington could not produce any results that suggested one would be better than the other with the oil at this temperature.

The synthetic oil supplied from Castrol at this time was later given the code name XC27 and this was a special derivative of their commercial synthetic racing oil. I told Castrol's John Bristow that our main issue was with steel running on steel components, such as our camshafts and cam followers, so John added almost 5% of manganese to our unique supply. Later testing with this oil and manganese additive in our Turbo V6 engine showed that it actually slightly delayed the onset of detonation.

The main culprit in oil consumption however was found to be cylinder liner distortion with the free standing slip fit cylinder liner supported halfway down the liner. This distortion was investigated with the aim of reducing blow-by and oil consumption. The test involved the partial assembly of an engine with liners, heads and main bearing caps bolted in place. This allowed the measurements to take place from the bottom of the liner where it protruded into the crankcase area of the block. Measurements of the liner bore diameters were taken with the liners under compression from the cylinder head via the sealing ring down to the mid liner seat area. A distinct bowing in the centre of the liner between the liner seat and the liner head face was discovered. These measurements were then compared to the liner without any compression loadings.

This problem was eventually fixed by final honing the liners pre-loaded in a slave block, and removing up to 0.003in distortion, allowing the rings to travel in a round and parallel bore when the engine was fully assembled.

With all of these modifications oil consumption was reduced to an acceptable level. This process would take most of the year to fully implement and update all engines and was a laborious process the engine builders did not enjoy. Various cylinder honing techniques and hones were tried with some reduction in oil consumption coming with the use of the multi-fingered 'Bobble' honing technique. Because of the amount of material needing to be removed with this process the Mahle aluminium liners with their thin Nicosil coating could no longer be used and all engines reverted to the cast iron liner material.

## Fatigue test of the 7-litre crankshafts

26 FEB 1987

MIRA,
Watling Street,
Nuneaton,
Warwickshire, CV10 0TU.

The Automotive Technology Centre

Our Ref: JN/JC/216164

24th February, 1987

Mr. T. Seal,
Tom Walkinshaw Racing Ltd.,
Engine Division ,
Unit 1,
Station Field Industrial Estate,
Kidlington,
Oxford.
OX5 1JD.

Dear Mr. Seal,

We have now completed the bending fatigue tests on the 82 mm-stroke and 84 mm-stroke versions of the V-12 crankshafts, with the following results :

(1) 82 mm stroke , tested on Web No 2

| Bending Moment , lbf.in | Cycles , millions |
|---|---|
| ±10,000 | Unbroken after 2.03 |
| ±12,000 | Unbroken after 2.04 |
| ±14,000 | Broken after 0.28 |

(2) 84 mm stroke , tested on Web No 2

| Bending Moment , lbf.in | Cycles , millions |
|---|---|
| ±10,000 | Unbroken after 2.01 |
| ±12,000 | Unbroken after 2.00 |
| ±14,000 | Broken after 2.05 |

In each case, failure commenced from the crankpin fillet and progressed through the test web to the main-journal fillet.

When comparing these results with that obtained previously on the 78.5 mm-stroke version, the present specimens, both of which,it is understood, were not subjected to cold-straightening, and both of which failed at a bending moment of ± 14,000 lbf.in, were somewhat weaker than the shortest-stroke version. Since this failed at ±18,000 lbf.in, they (ie, the 82 and 84 mm versions) are approximately 25 per cent lower in strength under these particular test conditions. This reduction in strength, of course, is what would be anticipated from the reduced overlap of the crankpin and main-journals which arises from the increase in stroke. It might further be expected that, although the 82 mm and 84 mm versions failed at the same bending moment, the 82 mm would have lasted the longer of the two; however, there will inevitably be some degree of scatter in this type of testing, both between the processing of the specimens and in the setting-up of the test machine, and this is probably the explanation for the difference in life between these two crankshafts. A point I feel worth emphasising is the significant loss in strength which can be introduced by a cold-straightening operation after nitriding, as shown by the results obtained previously on the 87 mm-stroke version (see our letter dated 13th January, 1987).

.............../

The Motor Industry Research Association
A Company Limited by Guarantee. Registered in England No. 402570
Director: C. Ashley, C.B.E., B.Sc., Ph.D., C.Eng., F.I.Mech.E. Secretary: V. J. Thomas, M.A., F.C.A.
Telephone: Nuneaton (0203) 348541 Telex: 311277 Fax: (0203) 343772

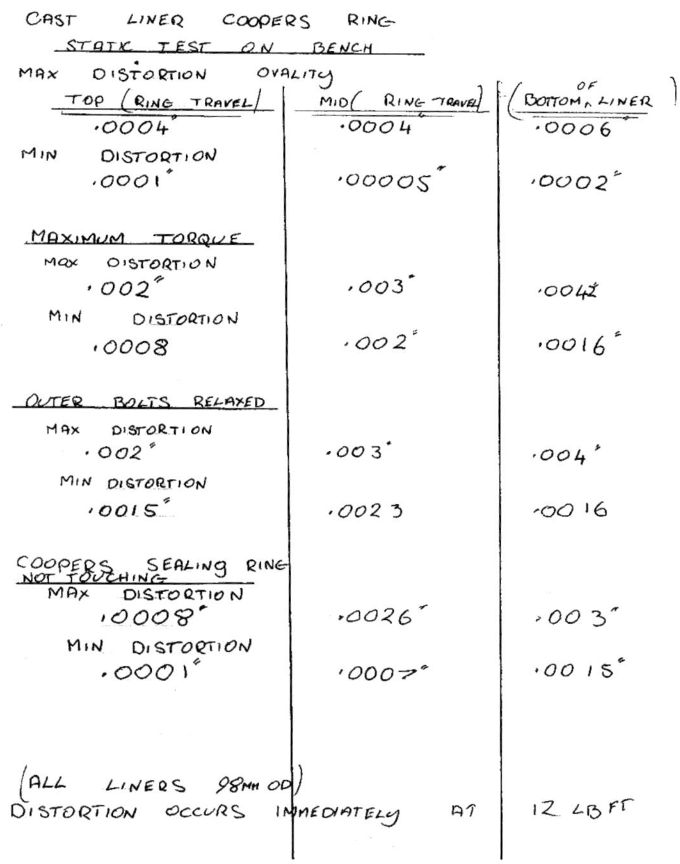

CAST LINER COOPERS RING

STATIC TEST ON BENCH

MAX DISTORTION OVALITY

| | TOP (RING TRAVEL) | MID (RING TRAVEL) | (BOTTOM OF LINER) |
|---|---|---|---|
| MAX DISTORTION | .0004" | .0004 | .0006 |
| MIN DISTORTION | .0001" | .00005" | .0002" |
| **MAXIMUM TORQUE** | | | |
| MAX DISTORTION | .002" | .003" | .004 |
| MIN DISTORTION | .0008 | .002" | .0016" |
| **OUTER BOLTS RELAXED** | | | |
| MAX DISTORTION | .002" | .003" | .004" |
| MIN DISTORTION | .0015" | .0023 | .0016 |
| **COOPERS SEALING RING NOT TOUCHING** | | | |
| MAX DISTORTION | .0008" | .0026" | .003" |
| MIN DISTORTION | .0001" | .0007" | .0015" |

(ALL LINERS 98MM OD)

DISTORTION OCCURS IMMEDIATELY AT 12 LB FT

***This distortion test showed out of round and taper of 0.002in with distortion commencing after just 12lbs of load on the liner top face.***

Piston rings were assembled on a slave piston and passed up and down a slave liner using a light abrasive solution and the contact face areas inspected. Any ring found to have a slight defect after this process was not used and this process enabled reduced run in time on the dynamometer, with full load being applied 15 minutes after start up. This pre lapping process was needed as high quality synthetic oils resist the ring bedding in process, so valuable time was saved when using these high wear resistant oils on the test bed.

Part of our engine test sign off was recording the amount of blow-by or combustion leakages past the cylinder sealing rings, as well as the crankcase internal pressures. The large capacity oil scavenge pump gears on the engine could suck air back through an open engine breather if we had used that system, and produce aerated oil. This V12 engine had always been run with a sealed engine breather system from the very start to remove the need for a de-aeration system in the oil tanks. Any engine blow-by was removed from the scavenged oil delivery to the dry sump tank and was vented from the oil tank to the atmosphere.

During 1986 dynamometer testing when measuring the crankcase pressure and blow-by we had some small variations in power outputs that did not coincide with the increased or decreased cylinder blow-by figures recorded. The main culprits turned out to be the spring-loaded front and rear main seals, the powerful dry sump scavenge system sucked air past them back into the engine. We fitted these seals back to front, so air trying to enter actually pressed the seal back onto the crankshaft sealing surfaces.

Workshop foreman Peter Grace continued with these tests to completely seal the engine and found the last air leak source was from the distributor shaft, solving that finally sealed the complete engine. This work generated many benefits, not only preventing aeration of the oil, but allowing the crankshaft and con rods to move in a partial vacuum, increasing power output by close to 10bhp with no economy penalty, the Holy Grail.

Some fine tuning of the air temperature correction system and software laws were carried out during the 1987 racing season. While our system had been running a theoretical Lucas correction law, small anomalies were turning up, with the engine fuel mixture running slightly richer than we wanted, especially in cooler weather. The front mounted radiator with its hot air exit over the windscreen, allowed some heated air to enter the engine air scoop directly behind the roof line. The air exiting the front mounted radiator produced engine air intake temperatures averaging around 40°C, and these warmer air flows from the radiator resulted in a small loss of power. It was not a problem as long as these varying temperatures could send exactly the corrected amount of fuel at the right time to maintain best fuel efficiency. To carry these small adjustments out a very fast reacting air temperature thermistor was needed, and I did not think that we were getting the best results using the one we had. This had only a minute effect on the overall race but was the next thing on a diminishing list to attend to.

The air temperature sensor had not only to contend with normal day or night temperature changes, sudden clouding over or rain, but also short stop/start situations where the engine remained hot after being switched off while refuelling. This action increased the engine air box temperatures with heat rising from exhaust systems, but being quickly cooled when restarted and air was flowing once again. The brass body of the small Lucas air thermistor was obviously subject to heat soak and this affected the internal thermistor elements response time; the actual software was not the problem.

To prove this situation a test was carried out where an air thermistor was wired to a 12-volt battery and placed in a cup of boiling water and the voltage output noted. After recording the maximum temperature, the thermistor was plunged into a bucket of 20° water and the reaction time noted. It took 12 seconds to return to the lower temperature when fully immersed in the cold water, indicating that a 6° or 7° change would take up to one second to respond, and this was too slow to react to dynamic changes going on in the engine compartment. In our racing situation the thermistor was reflecting its mechanical makeup and surroundings as much as the air temperature entering the engine. I developed a correction slope with small deviations to the theoretical map with a flat section to suit the average dynamics of the XJR-8 engine compartment but still having some correction values to assist cold start up and hotter than normal conditions.

The cold end at minus 24° to 40°C is outside anything that we would be racing in and so it was reset to the mid range figures as for the plus 19° to 46°C, as was the very hot 86° to 132°C area. When a temperature thermistor malfunctions, it will read either end of the scale and the engine will perform badly. With my programming strategy the engine would revert to average settings and avert a serious malfunction during a race should the thermistor have an electrical failure. The 19° to 40°C area was left with no correction value purely because we could not rely on effective quick changes from our production Lucas thermistor. A hot reading around 70°C produced by heat rise during a pit stop did not reflect the true correction value needed as the temperature sensed in that situation was mechanical heat rise, and not the actual air intake temperature when the engine was restarted. If left with the correct theoretical adjustment for a temperature of up to 70°C the engine would be leaned excessively leading to a harder hot pit restart, and then take too long to revert to reading the correct air temperature after rejoining the track.

The initial 1987 spec 6995cc engines, running on lean race settings, with the compression ratio reduced from 13.5:1 to 12.25:1 and using the 1986 EA5 camshaft produced very similar maximum power output on 98 RON low lead fuel to the 6.5-litre, but at a lower 6750rpm, continuing with a small drop in output by 7250rpm. Maximum lean mixture torque however increased 4% to 605lbs/ft at 5000/5500rpm with both power and torque maximum outputs occurring 300rpm lower than the 6537cc engine of 1986.

It was now obvious that the engine was not breathing as well with the larger cylinder capacity using the original valve sizes and so a revisit of all the tuning points was undertaken. What the engine really needed at this time was larger valve sizes but this option was not pursued because of the cost and time implications discussed earlier in the chapter.

Winter dynamometer development of the 6995cc (7-litre) engine involved retesting of the exhaust system lengths, some detail changes to the camshaft were now needed. Geoff Goddard of Cosworth offered to produce a new profile at no cost and with the constant pressure to save money this was welcomed. Using a wider 76° half period inlet profile (304° total duration) and slightly reduced lift of .580in, and a profile with a 74° half period

(296° total duration) and .560in lift were the configurations I asked him to work with. This combination was settled on for the best torque/fuel but reduced slightly top end power, with the code numbers EA15 and EA16 respectively. Unfortunately this choice of free assistance would later produce a weakness in the V12 programme that took too long to rectify after proceeding down this route, not using our proven but expensive camshaft designer from the Group A days, Chris Walters. Detail work continued with the inlet system and ports being increased by 2mm to assist the top end air flow. All of these tuning inputs, camshaft profiles, timing and phase angles, inlet and exhaust lengths, were constantly revised as each item was individually changed to find the best solution to gain power that used the least amount of fuel.

With some power being lost with the 1986 specification air box and impregnated cotton air filter, Piper Cross, a company specialising in air filter technology were asked to provide a solution for us to test. A triple layer foam filter was supplied, each layer with increasing foam densities, supported by a wire frame and now completely surrounding the inlet system. This system not only cleaned the air flow from the air intake situated behind the roof line of the XJR-8, but then removed any turbulence and directed the air path straight down towards the inlet trumpets. When the design was finalised not only were the small losses with the previous system eliminated but output actually increased by 2–3bhp.

After the development phase on the 98-octane fuel, power outputs were raised to 735bhp at 6750rpm with maximum torque increased to 600-610lbs/ft. between 5000/6250rpm with the Piper Cross air filters fitted.

The torque curve was now very flat and stayed within 5% of its maximum between 4250rpm and 6500rpm. Throughout that rpm range the 7-litre engine produced 40 to 45bhp more than the 1986 6.5-litre engine.

This produced BMEP figures of 215lbs [14.65 bar] at 5000/5500rpm and 211lbs [14.40 bar] at 6000rpm. Depending on circuit fuel consumption, the engine was normally short shifted (next gear selected), between 6500rpm and 6800rpm.

This 6995cc engine continued testing with decreasing amounts of fuel at wide open throttle. The ignition timing variations with these fuel mixture changes were carefully tested and ignition correction plots made as the engine was progressively leaned. We continued with the three-dimensional ignition mapping of advance versus rpm and throttle angle with the additional ignition timing correction for selected Air/Fuel ratios. None of the race engine management systems available at this time had exhaust gas mixture feedback (closed loop air/fuel or Lambda control) to automatically produce ignition timing correction with fuel mixture change.

To eliminate any possible confusion with the twin fuel/ignition dashboard adjusting system used in 1986 these two switches were amalgamated in 1987 into a single 0-5 adjusting switch. New software from Zytek automatically changed the ignition timing in step with the selected fuel changes.

*Piper Cross foam air filter, 1.875in diameter exhaust primary pipe system and the Zytek developed heat sensor in front of the rear tyre.*

# ENGINE TEST CARD

| TNO | — | TEST NO. | |
|---|---|---|---|
| ENG. TYPE | GDC V12 | ENG. NO. | 87 C 03 |
| DATE | 8/2/87 | | |
| OIL PRESS. | 80 psi | OIL TEMP. | 80°–100° |
| WATER TEMP. | 90°c | | |
| FUEL PRESS. | 60 PSI | BARO. PRESS. | 1017 |
| HYDROM. | –1 | | |
| CELL TEMP. | 13.3 55 | CORR. FIGURE | ·417 29·6147. 1·008 |

| RPM | LOAD | | CORR. BHP | TORQUE | CO FIG. (Fuel Ign CO) |
|---|---|---|---|---|---|
| 4500 | 110 | +31 | 499 | 582·12 | +3 –1 |
| 4750 | 111.3 | +40 | 533 | 589 | +3½ –1 |
| 5000 | 115.1 | +41 | 580 | 609 | +3½ 0 |
| 5250 | 114.8 | +45 | 607·5 | 607·5 | +2 0 X |
| 5500 | 111.9 | +37 | 620·3 | 592 | +1½ –1 |
| 5750 | 112.3 | +38 | 651 | 594 | +2 0 |
| 6000 | 114 | +40 | 689·4 | 603 | +3 0 |
| 6250 | 113.4 | +43 | 714·4 | 600 | +3 –½ |
| 6500 | 111.9 | +52 | 733 | 592 | +3 –½ |
| 6750 | 108.1 | +50 | 735·5 | 572 | +2½ 0 |
| 7000 | 103.8 | +37 | 732·4 | 549 | +2 0 |

COMMENTS

TRIM 350
4* FUEL

**TWR JAGUAR – TESTING SCHEDULE UPTO LE MANS**

| | | |
|---|---|---|
| 6 FEBRUARY | DONINGTON | 187 – 186 Shake Down |
| 10 – 13 FEBRUARY | PAUL RICARD | 187 – 186 – 386 |
| 2 MARCH | SILVERSTONE | 187 – 186 |
| 12 MARCH | SILVERSTONE | 187 – 186 – 287 Shake Down |
| 19 MARCH | JARAMA | 287 – 187 – (386) |
| (26 MARCH | JEREZ | 287 – 187 – (386) ) |
| 9 APRIL | MONZA | 287 – 187 – (386) |
| 16 APRIL | DONINGTON | 186 – 286 Shake Down (187/287) |
| 23 APRIL | SILVERSTONE – With F1 Teams | 187/287 – 286 |
| 5 MAY | SILVERSTONE – To be Confirmed (TEST & PRESS DAY) | 287 – 187 – 386 – 186 – 286 |
| 17 MAY | LE MANS TEST | 186 – 286 – (386/387) |
| 4 JUNE | DONINGTON | 186 – 286 – (386/387) |

27 January 1987

*The 7-litre engine produces almost 100bhp per litre at 6000rpm, and a 2% variation in torque between 4750 and 6500rpm.*

## Le Mans

Perhaps the biggest improvement with this 7-litre upgrade would be seen at the Le Mans 24 hour endurance race.

The lower drag bodywork and rear wing used at Le Mans produced better fuel consumption than the normal high downforce set-up, but the main problem for us with Le Mans was the huge speed differentials on this circuit. The slowest corner was taken in second gear at 2750rpm and 60kms, with up to 360kms being reached at the end of the long 3.5-mile Mulsanne straight. The 5-speed gearbox, having to cope with bridging a 300km gap, needed wider gear ratios than normal. The 7-litre engine now produced 530lbs/ft of torque at *2500rpm* helping to accelerate from this low speed second gear exit. The wider gear ratios had resulted in large rpm gaps between the gears, becoming more evident with the fourth to fifth change on the Mulsanne straight; at a speed when the race car was approaching its maximum aerodynamic drag. When changing from fourth to fifth on the Mulsanne straight, the engine needed to be taken up to 7000rpm to compensate for the large gap between these two gears. If this gear shift was made earlier at a lower rpm, the engine was barely producing enough horse power to continue accelerating the race car in fifth gear when in full lean mode. This limited the ultimate terminal speed in fifth gear. With the 7-litre's increased mid-range power the larger capacity engine improved this situation. A 6-speed gearbox, not needed at all the other circuits used, was now really the best solution for Le Mans to close the gaps, but this never seemed to be on TW and Roger's radars.

## Castrol and Le Mans

One positive side effect with the lean burn V12 engine, with its throttle actuated fuel shut off whenever the throttle was closed on gear changing or braking, was the low fuel dilution of the engine's oil these actions produced. We had worked on this aspect with our ring pack and engine fueling to greatly reduce this problem. Too lean and poor fuel burn would result in reversing the dilution problem. Carburettors flood under some racing conditions and this degrades oil over long distances to a much greater degree than fuel injection does. Long distance racing produces a slow degradation of the engine oil as small amounts of unburned fuel make their way passed the ring pack and into the sump. Engines suffering bearing failure towards the end of a 24 hour race generally do so because of the dilution of their engine oil with unburned petrol. This dilution degrades the lubrication ability and consistently reduces the viscosity of the oil. Gone are the days of motoring around in a 24 hour race with some time up your sleeve for a quick oil change, 24 hour races now were 24 hours of racing.

Motul oil that TWR had previously used in all its racing engines was now finally sidelined. The advantages of having a close technical relationship with major manufacturers such as Castrol are well demonstrated in many situations and the Le Mans race was one of them. The problem of degrading oil pressure over time as oil becomes diluted and reduced in viscosity is exacerbated with changes in temperature. The saying that it is always darkest before dawn is partially true, it is also the coldest. Hours of running behind cars that are leaking small amounts of oil along with the dust and tyre rubber, slowly find their way into water and oil radiator surfaces with the compounds forming to partially block the cooling air through the radiator cores. With the cold temperatures before dawn the potential problem is not seen, but as the sun rises, so do the temperatures. Fuel diluted oil temperatures begin to rise, water temperatures in aluminium engine blocks rise also and expand main bearing clearances; oil pressure then starts to drop with reports coming over the radio. Maintaining a minimum hot oil temperature of 100°C after the oil coolers produced an after bearings temperature of 120°C into the sump and at these temperatures helped remove most of the elements of fuel from the oil by turning them into a fuel vapour. This vapour could then be scavenged by the three pump scavenge stages and vented to the atmosphere via the oil tank breather.

The dropping oil pressure problem was a situation that John Bristow of Castrol was able to control with their expertise in specialised lubricants. Four litres of a rare blue coloured substance used by them for oil viscosity control were given to me for the next Le Mans races. Between 14 and 16 hours into the 24 hour race, half a litre of the fluid was added to the oil tanks of the race cars during their brief pit stop. Oil viscosity and pressure would then be maintained as the oil temperature increased with the new day. Later testing of oil from Le Mans was found to have a slightly higher viscosity than the original oil using this additive; helping to increase its lubricating integrity for the later stages of the race with partially blocked oil coolers raising oil temperatures.

One problem seen in 1986 had been difficulty with starter motors after switching off in pit stops. The regulations stated that engines must be switched off for refuelling and that the car must be restarted with its onboard starting system. With the starter motors getting very hot in their isolated and inaccessible positions by the rear bulkhead underneath the exhaust system, repairs were almost impossible. Even after ducting cooling air to the insulated starter motor the problem could still occur and was especially a concern at Le Mans. The final fix was a $CO^2$ fire extinguisher, aimed down the air duct tube, its very cold gas instantly cooling enough for the starter motor to work again.

Three new chassis were manufactured for 1987 with the number 187/287/387 and now officially designated XJR-8. These new tubs continued the sculptured under floor area starting immediately behind the mandated 800mm flat underbody surface and angled upwards at 11°. The lower Le Mans tunnels would still start in the same place as before at the rear of the tub, with filler plates used to allow all tubs to convert to Le Mans specifications if needed. The engine cover had a lead in area sculptured into the rear of the roof to help air entry to the engine and allow a reduction of the air intake hump in the tail section. An air duct for the drivers was incorporated in the nose section above the radiator inlet and connected to a tube into the cockpit to help keep the drivers cool.

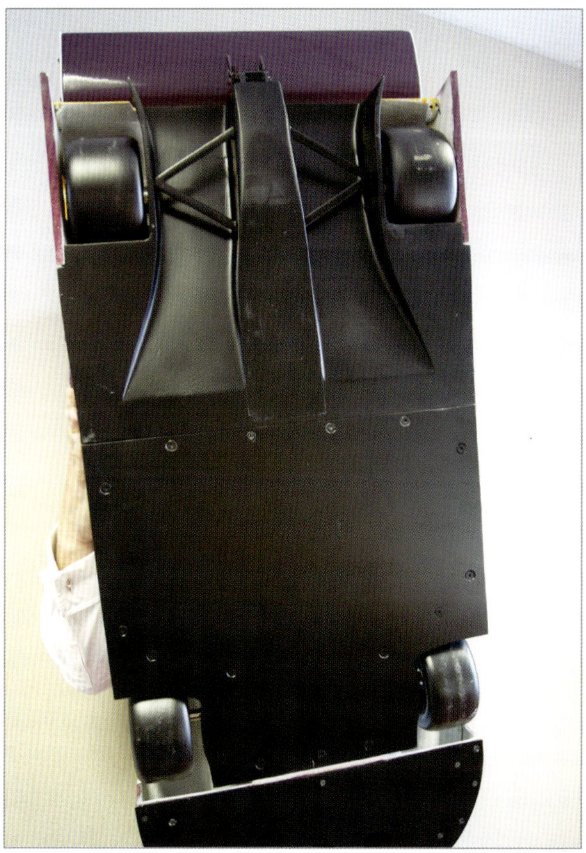

above – left: *The tunnel configuration used at Le Mans from 1986 to 1989 showing the venturi entry starting behind the main tub structure as first designed in 1985. The sprint design for 1986 had the venturi entrance further forward sculptured into the tub floor;* right: *Modifications for 1987 to the front include a driver fresh air duct through the radiator exit.*

(Images by Martin Lamb, model owner)

Doors had the hinge mechanism revised to include a leading-edge hinge, to hold the forward edge more securely in place at high speed and produce an up and forward position for better driver access as opposed to the earlier gull-wing style. Under floor rubbing strips were added in vulnerable areas to eliminate repairs from contact with the track surface and with improved manufacturing processes and attention to detail, these new tubs were state-of-the-art and formed the basis of the new Jaguar Group C race car designated XJR-8. Detail changes to the interior included hatches to allow better access to the fuel tank with its constant need for capacity checks and attention to fuel pump pickup systems. The fuel pump assemblies were now housed in a frame with quick change fuel lines and mounting points as well as the battery, all now being serviced through specific hatches accessed internally through each side pod. These features separated servicing areas and allowed two teams simultaneously to investigate any in car engine or electrical related problem very quickly should they appear during a race. Changes to front and rear roll bar systems included new mounts and an all carbon front anti roll bar replaced the heavy steel bar, producing increased roll stiffness ability as well as a 50% weight reduction. The front full carbon bar had three times the stiffness of the previous steel bar.

I had put forward the suggestion that the cars should lift off slightly earlier in the braking areas, then using hard braking, to aid fuel consumption versus time lost, but this seemed a driving concept that was unacceptable. Silverstone was having annual competitions using small light handmade vehicles, with tiny engines, and were being used to see who could produce the best fuel

*The front suspension showing the carbon anti roll bar.*

## Alastair Macqueen – 1987...

The air jacks returned to being car mounted to make pit stops swifter in 1987. Wheels changed to die cast Dymags from sand cast Speedline, again in the search for weight reduction and durability.

One major step forward was a small blue electronics box on top of the dash board. This was a joint development between TWR and Zytek who looked after the engine management system. This box had two functions, both displaying vital information to the driver. Firstly it showed the surface temperature of each tyre from the information supplied by infrared temperature senders looking at the inside of the tread area on each tyre. Alarm lights would flash if a tyre exceeded a preset level, and then could be investigated by the driver to see if that tyre was temporarily overloaded in a corner or was continuing to rise in temperature. That could indicate a puncture. The real world data was very useful to Dunlop.

The second fuel used function was to show the drivers 'laps worth of fuel used' so they could see every lap how close they were to the target.

It took the more intelligent drivers no time at all to work out that the car used a little more fuel when it was 'fat' with fuel at the beginning of a stint and that they could bring it back during the second part. It also gave them instant notification of how their driving style was working as they set points on the track to check the reading (in tenths of a lap) on every passing.

As Eddie Cheever would say "It's like spending on a credit card, you know you've got to pay it back!"

consumption figures over a set course of the race track. I had taken an interest in what they were doing to achieve the best results and there seemed to be a universal way that these vehicles were driven; accelerate out of the corner and coast into the next corner, maintaining as much corner exit speed as possible. While this was not the answer in our racing situation it did point to a fundamental efficiency model. Circuits that produce high brake temperatures are less fuel efficient, and only the drivers can help that situation. Short shifting and increased leaning of the engine would continue to be the two main tools used by the TWR team. Any additional brake ducting air fed into the enclosed front wheel arch was also not going to help, as some of this air would be vented into the low pressure flat area underneath the race car.

AP 4 pot brake calipers that were used had different piston diameters top and bottom, typically 0.25in, to apply differing pressure to each end of the brake pad to allow for increases in disc temperature as it passed through the brake pads. This eliminated the pad 'wedging' and eventual long pedal associated with uneven pad wear.

A failure with a rear driveshaft universal joint had been experienced at Le Mans the year before and Castrol had been tasked with producing improved grease for these items. The hollow rolled spline driveshaft with the ability to twist under load and remove some transmission shocks were supplied by Uni-Carden of Germany as well as larger universal joints. These driveshafts and universal joints were extensively rig tested at the transmission testing facility at Jaguar, and proved to be very good items.

## Dunlop Kevlar cross ply tyre development

Although we had been supplied with Kevlar construction tyres in Group A from 1984, the larger size of the Group C tyres had taken Dunlop sometime to develop a suitable Kevlar construction for the Jaguar programme. Nylon 4-ply cross ply construction tyres had been used up till now on 17in front and 19in rear diameters. Stronger material Kevlar 2-ply cross ply tyres maintained a more consistent growth in diameter with their stronger construction, producing better cornering with a lower slip angle. The 2-ply construction had lower rolling resistance and improved fuel consumption. These tyres were available to the factory Porsche team as well and were needed to counter what had been seen as an advantage the Brun team had with its Michelins; they were 3kgs lighter over the set of four tyres.

*Bill Mack*
*Dunlop Tyre technician for TWR.*

With all these changes it was time to continue the testing programme and the XJR-8 had set some very fast testing times with the press being party to the many chassis updates on the revised XJR-8. The 7-litre engines also had revised camshafts, exhaust system diameters and upgraded software. The engine upgrades and the improved Dunlop Kevlar tyres in back-to-back testing alone produced a one and a half second improvement in lap time to the same fuel on the Silverstone GP track.

For 1987 I had lost my two best test drivers, Jean-Louis Schlesser had been dropped from the team at the end of 1986, and Eddie Cheever was not available as Formula One was his priority. The 7-litre engine's initial test was down to the new driver signed for 1987, Raul Boesel. Boesel had tested initially with the 6.5-litre engine, and then carried out the first 7-litre test at Silverstone. He had reported he was able to exit the tight chicane in third gear, instead of having to use second gear with the 6.5-litre engine. This not only saved one down change for the chicane, more importantly it also eliminated one up change after the chicane, saving the time lost during a gearshift with the manual five speed March 85T based gearbox. This use of a higher gear allowed the engine to remain in its lower rpm fuel and friction efficient range for longer periods. The increased in car torque, of 600-610bs/ft on lean base settings of 13.6:1 A/F ratio between 5000/6000rpm, was producing improved results from its greater flexibility. Boesel set a time of 1:09.6, in lightweight qualifying trim, three seconds faster than Cheever's qualifying time the year before.

The XJR-8 had always shown very good speed at its home track of Silverstone and this would extend further with the 6995cc engine. Some of the fast corners, this was still the old circuit in 1987, could now be taken in fifth gear instead of fourth gear if the fuel consumption needed some fine tuning. This action, which left little room for error on the driver's part, would bring the fuel meter back on target, with just a few tenths of a second lost in lap time from the fuel savings being produced; and proved to be more effective fuel/time wise at this circuit than short shifting. An addition for 1987 would be a refrigerated unit in the pits to chill the fuel to increase its density.

At the Silverstone test shared with the Williams Formula One team, part-owner and engineering director Patrick Head came over to have a look at the carbon bar, although in this configuration it was not a system that could be used by them. These bars had limited deflection, the softest being 2000kgs per 25mm (2 tons per inch). This extremely stiff front roll bar was to counteract the weight of the heavy engine and gearbox in the rear but challenged the cars understeering tendency. With the large number of curbs that had been introduced to racing circuits the XJR-8 with this configuration would have to be careful and avoid most of them. The front roll bar redesign of mountings and direct attachment to the upright had a second purpose serving to give some additional freedom to new brake ducting as this had been marginal in the XJR-6 Jaguar.

Warwick and Cheever were keeping their options open for 1987 and this was a distraction TWR did not need. The team had produced better results than anyone had expected, but both were working on Formula One drives for 1987. Cheever had competed in an American CART race at the end of 1986 and all these issues no doubt included elements of playing hard to get for monetary reasons, with Formula One being their first love.

The driver situation was a TW and Roger decision and with Schlesser's sacking for no good reason that I could see performance wise, I had to keep any thoughts to myself. I however did need some consistency and continuity for the many reasons involving development of the electronic engine management applications mentioned in previous chapters, some drivers worked well with this situation and some did not. During this uncertain time Jan Lammers of the Netherlands was signed for the 1987 season and he would prove to be a driver that could help us in applying himself to give good feedback to specific engine programmes. Former McLaren and Silverstone GP winner John Watson also joined the team bringing a wealth of racing experience and an interesting personality, happy to discuss a broad range of topics and lighten the atmosphere a little. With pre-season testing again at the Paul Ricard circuit in the winterless south of France in March it was an opportunity for new drivers to acquaint themselves with the XJR-8 Jaguar. Both XJR-6 and XJR-8 were tested together to understand the progression and benefits and allow dynamic mapping and lean settings to be perfected in the new 7-litre V12 engine. It was at this test that 29-year-old Raul Boesel from Brazil impressed with his driving abilities and was signed to the TWR Silk Cut Jaguar team. Group A saloon car drivers Percy, Heyer and Hahne tested at Paul Ricard as the backup team for the Le Mans assault.

Both Warwick and Cheever signed to drive for the Arrows team with Cheever being available for the Jaguar programme in selected non-clashing events. Warwick had almost signed with TWR but at the very last minute was offered the drive with the Arrows team and Formula One was where his heart was. Warwick, Schlesser and Brancatelli would not drive for TWR in 1987.

No machine shop or staff additions, although at the time of writing the memo (see opposite page) TW was already in discussions to enter the IMSA series.

MACHINE SHOP:
TWO MAJOR MACHINING OPERATIONS WE HAVE FACED THIS YEAR ARE:
V12 CYLINDER BLOCKS.
4 VALVE HEADS.

ALL ENGINES HAVE BEEN REBLOCKED THIS YEAR (20) AT A COST OF £30,000 IN MACHINING.

BEST DELIVERY FROM R.C. SMITH OUR SUPPLIER IS 3 BLOCKS PER MONTH AFTER A TOOL UP TIME OF 4 WEEKS.

WE HAVE USED FIVE OTHER SUPPLIERS OVER THE LAST YEAR AND HAVE FAITH IN ONLY ONE OF THESE. (R.C. SMITH)

NEW L99 STRENGTHEN BLOCK ON STREAM IN JUNE 88. OVER THE NEXT 9 MONTHS WE WILL NEED TO MACHINE UP ANOTHER 20 OF THESE NEW BLOCKS FOR 88 AND 89 REQUIREMENTS.

THIS TOTALS £60,000 OVER A TWO YEAR PERIOD (NOTE 20 BLOCKS TO MACHINE WILL TAKE 6 - 7 MONTHS)

A GOOD HORIZONTAL BORER WHICH IS CAPABLE OF MACHINING THESE BLOCKS COSTS £25,000. SALARY FOR GOOD MACHINIST £16 - 17,000 P.A.

PROTOTYPE WORK ON 4 VALVE HEADS AT COSWORTH PRICES WOULD BE £35 - 40,000, IN THE FIRST YEAR AND £25,000 PER YEAR IN REPLACEMENTS. GOOD SECOND HAND MACHINE TO DO THIS JOB IS £25,000, UP TO £65,000 FOR NEW UNIT.

IT WOULD TAKE 6 MONTHS TO SET UP AND RUN RELIABLY BUT WITH AN OUTLAY OF APPROX £50,000 - £75,000 AND A SALARY ALLOWANCE OF £35,000 FOR THE DEPARTMENT, THE SAVINGS ON THE BLOCK AND HEAD WORK ALONE WOULD BE APPROX £50,000 - £60,000 P.A., PROBABLY BEING 7 MONTHS CAPACITY.

THE AIM OF THIS TWO MAN AND A Y.T.S. PERSON DEPARTMENT WOULD BE TO SAVE APPROX £80,000 P.A. IN MACHINING COSTS AND HELP CONSIDERABLY IN OUR ABILITY TO KNOW EXACTLY WHEN PARTS ARE READY FOR DELIVERY AND ALSO GIVE CONSIDERABLE FLEXABILITY IN ANY PROTOTYPE DEVELOPMENT WORK.

## MEMO

| From | To |
|---|---|
| ALLAN SCOTT | TOM WALKINSHAW<br>JOHN BRADLEY<br>6 April, 19 87 |

**ENGINE DIVISION - HOURS WORKED IN THE LAST SIX WEEKS.**

I would draw your attention to the hours currently being worked in the Jaguar Division of the Engine Shop which simply cannot continue.

| | Hrs/day | Days off in last 6 weeks |
|---|---|---|
| P. Grace | 12 hrs | 0 |
| C. Bamber | 10 hrs | 2 weeks off sick, + 2 days |
| M. Norris | 12 hrs + | 1 day |
| N. Peters | 12 hrs + | 1 day |
| S. Gray | 12 hrs + | 0 |
| D. Delaney | 10 hrs | 6 |
| A. Penny | 10 hrs | 1day/week at college, 6 days |

May we discuss, this week, bringing numbers up to previous years before good people make mistakes or look elsewhere for employment!

ALLAN SCOTT.

M E M O

To : Allan Scott From : Tom Walkinshaw
cc : John Bradley

Monday, 6 April 1987

Re : Work Schedule in the Engine Division

I have read with interest your memo concerning hours worked by some of your staff in recent times.

The number of staff allocated to the Engine Division is as your plan for the 1987 racing season. In fact, there should now be a surplus of staff owing to the lack of Group A Racing this year.

It is one of your duties, in your role as Manager of the Engine Division, to organize your workforce effectively so that your staff are able to work reasonable hours.

I look forward to hearing that this has been achieved.

Tom.

*Appeals to TW for an in-house Machine Shop to aid our work flow, and the need to hire more people are ignored. This all indicates his inability to come to the workshop to talk things through with the engine builders and me to see for himself.*
*He is now working with Heideggers in Liechtenstein on various engine projects and is rarely seen in the Engs workshop.*

JAGUAR

Chapter Fourteen

# The 1987 season

## Jarama – March 22nd

**As we headed to Jarama in Spain the UK press confidently picked the XJR-8 as the car to beat. The move to using 98-octane fuel and its application to the V12 was not fully recognised by the general public, but I had many times envisaged the worried looks on the faces at Weissach with this change. A larger engine running on lower boost to allow optimised ignition timing was the best option in this situation, and Porsche had obvious difficulty in adapting to that concept; but Sauber Mercedes did not.**

For the few who were not convinced of the 1987 TWR Jaguar package, almost as big a step against the opposition as had turned up at Monza the year before, Eddie Cheever took pole position at Jarama with Jan Lammers 0.15 seconds behind. Stuck in the Rothmans Porsche was close behind on the same Dunlop tyres and the UK entered Britten-Lloyd 962 Porsche in fourth but 1.5 seconds slower. A normally aspirated pole position in any formula would make people sit up and take notice.

Jarama was a 'sprint' race of 109 laps totalling 361kms (225 miles) with just the one scheduled stop. After the two Jaguars had settled into the lead with Stuck being the only car able to cover the pace sitting in third, Cheever had to pit early on lap 45 to top up the oil. The loss of oil had been a problem during practice and after some investigation was later traced to the oil tank being incorrectly manufactured. The baffles had not been made correctly allowing oil to flow up the rear of the tank under acceleration G-forces and out of the breather hose at the top. The TWR drawing office carried out some small detail changes to my specifications, and attention to detail in manufacture was all that was needed for this problem to be fixed for the next race. The Jaguar could not take all of its fuel allocation because of stopping 10 laps earlier than scheduled and with Boesel now at the wheel would have to pit just before the end of the race for the last amounts of fuel. Lammers stopped on schedule with just a four seconds lead over Stuck but an unusual slow pit stop for the TWR team had Watson out just behind Bell after the Porsche's pit stop. Watson calmly waited his chances and they came nine laps later when he took the lead. Boesel's hurried and frustrated additional pit stop had him departing with the fuel hose still attached and snapping the connector, allowing fuel to pure out. With team members running in separate directions it was Engs' Charlie Bamber, having experienced a similar situation in the Rover European series when a fuel valve jammed, who grabbed the fuel hose and held it as high above his head as he could. This action just matched the height of the remaining fuel in the overhead tank and stopped the flow, although he was covered in fuel. With most team members standing back I had both physically and morally supported Charlie in a situation we had both thought through with our previous experience in the

Rover team. Tom commenting later to me that although this was an admirable act, he did not need both of his Jaguar engine people to go up in flames, which shows where his sympathies lay as well as his thinking process with the absence of any possible effects on our families. Perhaps he could have asked one of the mechanics to take over. Neither of us was wearing any flame proof overalls, just the normal team gear.

Boesel later caught the second placed Porsche driven by Bell but had difficulty passing as well as being blocked by other cars not happy with the thought that they were being lapped once again, going a lap down in a race that was just one third of the usual distance! While Watson continued in the lead the second Jaguar started to have fuel pickup problems in the Spanish heat and its challenge halted, eventually finishing third. Watson slowed towards the end and cruised over the finish line ahead of Bell with Boesel 0.5 sec behind, the only cars on the same lap. The Watson/Lammers winner had eight litres of fuel left while the Porsche had just three litres remaining in its tank.

The winter development by both TWR and the factory Porsche team, aided by the new Dunlop Kevlar tyres, had shaken the existing privateer Porsches' confidence with the Kremer and Brun teams next up, but three laps down. A new era had begun and the TWR team had now reached a point where both of its cars and drivers were capable of winning races. The shorter race had been a good exercise to start the season and iron out some small bugs and sharpen up the systems for the rest of the season.

A celebration for the team was held at the Restaurante Don Fernando on the Sunday night before the team moved south to Jerez for the first 1000km race of the season the following weekend; preparation for this race being done far from home, in the back of the transporter. One thing that was helping was the fuel chilling we had introduced, not only helping in these hot conditions but also altering the density of the fuel by around 1.5% from the ambient temperatures. This had also produced a need to have a software package for fuel temperature.

This fuel temperature law shows a reduction of 3% to the normal map setting when the chilled fuel was put in the race car (minus 10° to 30°C). With fuel injected cars, the fuel constantly circulates, as the pressure regulator bypasses fuel not consumed back to the tank. This unused fuel has been heated up by proximity to the engine. When there is little fuel left in the tank it has been passed close to the engine many times, holding considerable residual heat.

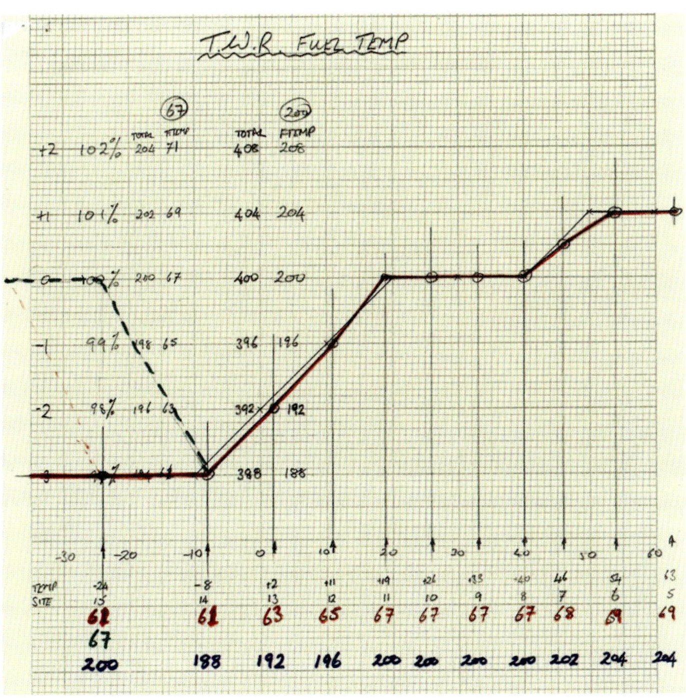


The fuel correction then returns to normal map setting at 20°C during the first part of the race stint as the chilled fuel warms up and stays that way until the fuel temperature reached 40°C. As the last few litres of the fuel were circulated before the next fuel stop the temperatures began to quickly exceed the first stages of the fuel's initial vapourisation point, so for the last few laps an extra 1% of fuel was added to the normal map setting as it reached 55°C.

This fuel temperature correction system was unique to Engs development at the time and controlled chilled road fuels over the wide temperatures involved in this form of racing.

## Jerez – March 29th

The Spanish races always seemed to struggle with race administration in one way or another and at Jerez the circuit fuel supply of 98 was a strange colour. Strange for pump fuel, but not for aviation fuel that is. After the Friday and Saturday practice the fuel was replaced with the regulation standard road fuel and competitors told to discard their stocks of the high-octane version. No checks were carried out. Meanwhile Stuck had pole position, four seconds faster than Jelinski's time the previous year, followed by Lammers/Watson 0.7sec slower with Mass/Wollek in the second factory Porsche third and Cheever/Boesel fourth, a time set by Boesel on race tyres. Lammer's time was 4.5 seconds faster than that set by the XJR-6 the year before with help from the Kevlar qualifying tyres.

Cheever was not having a good weekend having crashed the spare car in testing, and then not signing on at drivers' briefing had him penalised with the removal of his qualifying time which would have had him in second place. Some concerns were being expressed with the high-speed bumps at Jerez and Lammers had a broken gearbox in the pre-race warm up.

In the race the pattern settled down with Stuck leading and a Jaguar/Porsche/Jaguar train behind. Lap 17 produced the first change with Lammers suffering a collapsed front wheel bearing needing a nine-minute pit stop to rectify. Around the two-hour mark with Watson now driving, that XJR-8 suffered a broken driveshaft and could not return to the pits. The slow nature of this circuit caused a potential problem with the rules where races were 1000kms long, but also subject to a maximum time limit. The TWR team had set a fuel strategy for a 1000km race but if it was run to a maximum time instead it would be possible that the race would finish before the 1000kms were up. This would mean the fuel allowance over 'time' distance would be too conservative.

The two Rothmans Porsches and lone Jaguar circulated closely over the next couple of hours with Cheever losing the lead and precious time having to avoid a backmarker in an off-circuit manoeuvre. At his next pit stop the front nose section was replaced and grass removed from the radiators. Six hours is a long time for something to go wrong and it continued to do so, Boesel having to pit to have the nose strapped on as some of the fixing points for the nose were broken.

The Bell/Stuck Porsche had then broken fourth gear and slipped from contention with the Jaguar in second and Mass/Wollek ahead by a lap until the four-and a half-hour mark. It then suffered terminal transmission problems brought on by the constant high-speed bumps on the circuit producing freewheeling and sudden grip. It was now a matter of driving till six hours were up.

Cheever/Boesel XJR-8 finished in the lead three laps ahead of the second placed Kremer Porsche on Yokohama tyres from the Stuck/Bell Rothmans Porsche a further three laps down in third.

Cheever/Boesel led the series on 32 points from Stuck/Bell 27.5 and Lammers/Watson fourth on 20 points.

*Porsche–Jaguar train at Jerez.*

## Monza – April 12th

After the two weeks away in Spain, the team returned to prepare the cars at Kidlington, and then back to Monza in Italy, all in the following 10 days. This was also a hectic time for Engs with just enough of the latest new engines to be built available for Monza. F3000 driver John Nielsen of Denmark had joined the team to substitute for Cheever who was in Rio with the Arrows Formula One team. The fast Monza circuit became a challenge for the Porsches who were out to regain some honour by taking the first four fastest times in qualifying. The high downforce XJR-8s needed some compromise settings for speed and drag at Monza with only moderate improvement on the previous year's XJR-6's time, three seconds slower than Stuck's pole here. This was a surprise when compared to the performances at the two slower speed circuits at the start of the season indicating some difficulty with the sprint car configuration on fast circuits with longer straights. The factory Rothmans 962C though was three seconds faster than its best time the year before. These cars were running the unloved PDK semi-automatic gearboxes, but fitted with the new 3-litre engines using water cooling for the heads, not yet available to the privateer teams. Some problems in practice would see both factory cars revert to the conventional manual gearboxes preferred by the drivers. The privateer teams were having engine problems; no doubt caused by the lower octane fuel and the longer wide open throttle times on this fast circuit, coupled with the need to lean the engines for economy, producing excessive heat. A total of eight engines were lost to Porsche entrants before race day arrived.

The race started with indifferent weather which would be something to keep an eye on over the 1000km 173 lap race. Boesel had tucked in behind Stuck after the first lap and with the factory Porsche now reset to race fuel boost, the Jaguar overtook it on the run down to the chicane at the end of the straight. Lammers next tried the same approach but lost the battle for the chicane entry and spun, rejoining in sixth. Motivated by this mistake he had moved up to second position by the time of the first fuel stops after Stuck had to pit with a puncture.

The driver changes to Nielsen and Watson had these two taking the lead during their stint with Mass in the second Rothmans 962 staying with them, while the remaining Porsche brigade fought amongst themselves causing small delays. The two Jaguars and lone factory Porsche continued in close order till lap 82 when Mass had a turbo problem that would take a long time to fix when he pitted. From half distance the race was TWRs to lose as the Lammers/Watson car slowly edged away from Boesel/Nielsen who were reporting that their engine seemed a bit flat on their lean setting. The last scheduled stops 20 laps before the races end were carried out just before the threatening weather finally broke and Lammers pitted once again for wet weather tyres a few laps from the end. Boesel's run suddenly came to an end, he had stayed out for one more lap and the increasing rain made the slick tyres useless; within sight of the pit entrance he left the circuit to be stranded in the gravel run off area. TWR's first 1-2 finish had been lost but Lammers/Watson had won the Monza race with a fine showing of total domination two laps ahead of the Stuck/Bell Porsche who could hardly believe their luck after all their problems. The evidence of the XJR-8's dominance at Monza was shown with the privateer Fortuna/Brun 962, the Porsche team to beat in 1986, finishing five laps down in third place.

This was a great lift for the team and we were all grateful that Jaguar boss John Egan had selected the right race to come to; he was convinced he brought bad luck as the cars seemed to have problems whenever he came to view a race. Unseen by most, these last three TWR results became a final positive turning point in TWR and Jaguar's racing relationship, along with the beginnings of the eventual demise of factory backing for Group 44/Jaguar America.

## Silverstone – May 4th

The TWR Jaguar team had time to carry out an extensive rebuild of the race cars with the four-week gap before the home race at Silverstone. Some of the Porsche contenders had not arrived, one complaining about the quality of fuel that would be supplied! For the Autoglass Silverstone race TWR had entered three cars, two regular XJR-8s and one XJR8-LM, the low drag version to be raced at Le Mans and engineered by Ken Page. Martin Brundle/John Nielsen would race this car as a test of the many new systems employed since the previous year and to complete a comparison test between the two specification cars in lap time versus fuel used.

The lower venturi tunnels and single element rear wing along with shorter front splitter and reduced turn up on the front radiator exit produced a lower downforce/low drag combination. The drivers reported a more difficult car to drive in this configuration but even with the slower corner exit speeds it was still 10kms faster on all the straights. John Nielsen's feedback was "You have to turn into the corners, wait for it to breakaway, and then catch it". When asked if this was every corner he replied "Yes, two or three times."

To help with the driveshaft angle problem with universal joints at Le Mans in 1986, the engine/gearbox assembly had been tilted 2.5° to raise the gearbox and produce better driveshaft alignment. It now appeared that the tilting of the engine and raising of the 75kg gearbox by 50mm at the rear had a more destabilising effect than was first envisaged. A nose flip-up and small return was fitted for the race to assist the front aerodynamic grip for Silverstone, but nothing could be done for the raised centre of gravity at the rear of the XJR8-LM. The net result was a car nearly three seconds slower than the high downforce XJR-8 but being able to run flat out on a 13.2:1 A/F ratio and still not use all the fuel allowance.

The second newcomer to Silverstone was the appearance of the all new Sauber C9 Mercedes from Peter Sauber's team in Switzerland with backing from fragrance manufacturer 'Kouros'. Ex-pat New Zealander Mike Thackwell put on an impressive display in qualifying to just miss the pole position by less than a 0.01sec. This new design had many similarities to the Jaguar XJR-6 concept but was fitted with the Mercedes M117 all alloy 5.0-litre twin turbocharged 90° V8 engine. Sauber's large engine low boost configuration joined TWR Jaguar as the second team to challenge Porsche's small engine high boost concept when using low octane fuel. The huge amount of corner exit torque produced from the Sauber was well controlled via its Michelin radial tyres. With the factory 962s being split by the Sauber C9, a returning Cheever and Lammers followed fourth and fifth fastest in qualifying, one second slower than the front row turbo cars.

The success of the XJR-8s in the previous three races had produced a good turnout of supporters, over 23,000, for the Sunday race start in cold conditions over 210 laps. We had first spectated at the 1984 event with just a few thousand attending.

Thackwell in the Sauber Mercedes took an early lead followed by the two XJR-8s but Mass in the second factory Porsche was already in fuel pressure problems and out of contention. By lap 33, Jaguars were in first and second positions with the Le Mans specification car in fifth. Both Jaguars continued in the lead and Pescarolo, now in the Sauber was slowing, in trouble with the lean mixture settings as the C9 was tuned to save fuel. The C9 was the first Group C car to use the new Bosch MP1.7 sequential engine management system. With all refuelling amounts on public display in the pits it was known by the TWR team that the C9 was 4% over allocation and no real threat if this continued. Later in the race a rear suspension failure stopped what had been a very impressive debut for this new car.

*XJR8-LM minus rear wheel covers.*

By lap 50, Nielsen in the XJR8-LM had moved past Bell's Porsche and a Jaguar 1-2-3 at Silverstone was almost too good to be true. By one third distance the leading Jaguars had lapped all but the Stuck/Bell Porsche and soon after pit stops and fuel consumption calculations were put into race strategies this Porsche too went one lap down. Suddenly on lap 129 Boesel was into the pits with a puncture and after returning to the race track immediately came back in to have the suspension checked out. Nothing could be found and he continued on having lost a lap with Watson now leading and Stuck in second place. Nielsen running in fourth had collided with Sigala's Torno Porsche and both cars then spun off the track, Nielsen returning for a new nose cone. The pace car was dispatched while the Porsche was removed from the track; once again the officials had problems with procedures. The agreed procedure was that one lap before the race was to recommence, the roof flashing lights would be turned off; and with the TWR team thinking the race was continuing under pace car conditions, Watson had been asked to pit. Unfortunately, this procedure had not happened and the pace car then left the track and proceeded into the pit entry lane at slow speed keeping the Jaguar behind while the race continued at high speed; there was no pit lane speed limit in those days. Stuck had one lap earlier been allowed to exit the pits during the pace car period without waiting for the pace car to pass, this had allowed him to unlap himself and so all the hard work by the three Jaguars came back to nothing, with 80 laps of the race to go. Unfortunately for the Brundle/Nielsen XJR8-LM during its earlier spin the car had run backwards at high speed before the driver could engage the clutch and the sudden reversal of the engine had caused the timing chain to jump a tooth and advance the valve timing. This meant that the inlet valve was coming in contact with the piston crown and after some time eventually one of the valves failed and the car was withdrawn, but not with a broken valve spring as many have reported.

With just 25 laps to go a large accident occurred on the pit straight and once again the field was bunched up behind the pace car; but bringing to a head the problem that the TWR team had been working with all year. Cheever was not able to compete in all rounds of the championship because of his Formula One commitments and Lammers/Watson were both showing the sort of consistency that would give them the championship. Telling drivers to run to team orders was a demoralising process and was a situation that TW had always been reluctant to issue, especially at this early stage in the championship. After the restart a motivated Cheever with fuel left over after the pace car laps moved slowly away from Lammers, he was not in the mood to move over for the sake of helping the points situation. It was also a face-saving exercise for his Formula One compatriots and understandable, and with both drivers circulating at maximum speed causing some concern to TWR race control they soon after were told to 'Hold' and ensure the magical 1-2 finish for TWR Silk Cut Jaguar in front of its home crowd at Silverstone. Cheever went on to set a new lap record and finish six second ahead of Lammers, justifying his position in not moving over to allow Lammers additional points, as far as he was concerned. Stuck/Bell finished a lap down in third.

The press duly reported that a valve spring had broken in the XJR-LM and TW did not correct this reporting; I had decided long before to not challenge anything said in the press, hoping the results would speak for themselves. The handling of the XJR8-LM was a problem though with its 75kg gearbox sitting 50mm higher not helping at all.

After these first four races a definite pattern had emerged. The works Porsches had progressed into a league of their own compared to being more evenly matched against some of the top customer cars in previous years. This was partly due to the Dunlop Kevlar

*Tom Walkinshaw and Eddie Cheever share a lighter moment.*

tyre now being able to match the previously superior Michelin that the Brun team had used in 1986, and the factory's larger capacity engines with their water-cooled heads, being able to withstand the higher temperatures produced when running leaner mixtures, along with improvements in engine management systems. Some of the top teams such as Brun/Kremer/Joest developed their own engine versions and were now struggling with the need for advanced electronic technology. It was also interesting that Joest had not come to Silverstone because they did not trust the fuel quality which of course was standard EU pump fuel. This team in previous years had excellent fuel consumption, sometimes almost unbelievably so in the early parts of races in the days of fuel quality restricted by (RON) only. With the reduction to 102-octane in 1986 and now 98 pump-fuel these earlier advantages were gone. Germany always had and continued to have very good fuel technology through companies such as chemical giant BASF dating back to the synthetic fuels used in aircraft engines during WWII.

The TWR team was riding on a high and now team manager Roger Silman had a very confident manner compared to the insecure one just 15 months previously. The XJR-8 had been fine tuned to accept the attributes and disadvantages of the 7-litre V12 engine, and now with the switch to standard road fuel the final pieces had fallen into place in producing a superior fuel-efficient package.

Roger was able to motivate and manage the many differing characters that had been assembled in the 1987 driver line up. Cheever was high spirited and competitive, Boesel, fitting into a new team and learning his new craft was more withdrawn. John Nielsen was a solid dependable fast driver who did his job without any fuss, and although he had good English we had to be careful that he fully understood the debriefing meetings. John Watson was a Formula One driver now in the twilight of his competitive driving career with a professional attitude, and was not so overwhelmed by the increasingly confident attitude of TW and Roger. Martin Brundle was a long-time friend of the company and held in high regard after helping to make up the deficit in some

**Tom Walkinshaw Racing Ltd**

**1, Station Field Industrial Estate. Kidlington. Oxford.**

13 May 1987

AWS/CDG

Jim Randle
Jaguar Cars Ltd
Browns Lane
Allesley
Coventry

Dear Jim

RE : ENGINE FAILURE AT SILVERSTONE IN CAR NO 6 10 MAY 1987

On strip down after the Race, it was found that the inlet valves had all touched the pistons, by jumping a tooth forward in the valve timing.

This had placed the cam followers under stress and eventually one broke. Parts were then pushed through the side of the cam carrier by the cam lobe, causing the oil smoke on entry to the pit lane.

The crankshaft gear's lower half is surrounded by a special cover to resist chain jumping, and this was found to be partially broken.

Conclusion :

Car No 6 was involved in a collision with a Porsche, and spun backwards off the circuit, the driver being unable to depress the clutch quickly enough, and allowing the engine to be accellerated backwards. Immediately on his return to the track, he complained of a loss of performance, followed soon after with a report of a metalic noise in the engine. Some 23 laps later, the car retired.

Yours sincerely

ALLAN SCOTT
TWR Engine Division

**Telephone: Kidlington (STD - 08675) 71565 2 lines**
**Company registered in England No: 1290423**
**Telex: 837649**

***Silverstone engine damage report to Jim Randle on the Le Mans specification car.***

of the earlier TWR race cars. He never had an 'off day', he always produced the goods when they were needed, sandwiching this programme with his Formula One career. TW had helped finance part of his earlier driving days in the Eddie Jordan Formula 3 team allowing continued close racing against future world champion Ayrton Senna. He had been grateful for this help at a critical time in his driving career, and because of that felt obliged whenever TW called.

This depth of driving talent meant any combination in either of the two race cars could win the race or produce the best outcome for the TWR Silk Cut Jaguar team. The last thing Roger needed with this mix in 1987 was a driver with a number one status and team focus to support that strategy. The team was free to make the best of each situation with all being given an equal chance and it would be decided later in the season if a particular driver needed support to win the championship. Any of the drivers could be champion and all the drivers had to accept this situation, reducing any possible tension or game playing. It was a formula that had been carried more or less throughout the previous TWR saloon car programmes and something I felt more comfortable with.

## TWR wins all Jaguars' future racing programmes

These latest results had finally brought the future of Jaguar's racing programmes to a head, and TW's constant careful manipulation and raising of doubt in any given situation concerning Group 44 results in the USA had led to Jaguar finally being swayed in TWR's direction. Engs had started behind the V12 development curve in 1985 but were now seen to be leading Group 44 in this area by some margin. It was announced that TWR was now to carry out Jaguar's entire race programme and this included their most important market, America. This was a situation that needed careful handling as Bob Tullius and Group 44 were held in high regard by the American press, racing public, Jaguar supporters as well as Jaguar America's British management.

Immediately following Silverstone and the fourth victory in a row for the XJR-8, TW, Roger and I flew from Heathrow to America with the aim of setting up a headquarters there to take control of Jaguar's IMSA programme. TW had a surprise for us with tickets on Concorde as a thank you for the first four winning results. We arrived at lunch time and were driven for 90 minutes through the beautiful Virginia countryside with its horse ranches and painted wooded rail fences to the Group 44 factory. I was asked to make a mental inventory and machinery valuation without making it obvious as to any intentions to the workforce as we walked around, and then it was back to the airport.

The main problem with the Group 44 factory was its position in a very affluent area with its high housing costs. Some Group 44 members were driving 50 miles each way to work from lower priced housing areas. There was also Bob Tullius's valuation which at first glance looked twice the property and contents value; something you would have expected under the circumstances. It was then first class back on BA overnight for Roger and I to make us think this was the way it was going to be with the increased workload in the future; and then home for breakfast.

From door to door it had taken 23 hours and I could still get to work on time that morning, proving that we could handle the new American programme without any problem, we would just be sleeping on an aeroplane seat occasionally rather than a bed. As TW had always shown with his typical confidence, it would not be any problem just bolting-on the American IMSA programme.

While it would have its own team based in America, the additional engine rebuilds and trackside support would be out of Engs at Kidlington, with all race engines being flown back and forth over the Atlantic. There were some anomalies and unknowns in the different IMSA regulations but TW brushed these aside as inconsequential.

My family had also grown with the birth of our second daughter Courtney, four weeks previously. Thirty years later she has her own accommodation/bar/restaurant 'Karma Traders' in Kampot, Cambodia.

The main benefit to TWR would be financial with the handing on of used or now obsolete XJR-6 race cars and other items, especially expensive lightweight bodywork that could now have damage repaired using fillers and used in a programme that had a heavier weight limit than Group C. American motor racing, in TW and Rogers view, was behind the UK technology wise and would be a push over, using hand me down items that had already been used and paid for in Group C. This written off inventory could now be billed once again and charged to the American budget. It was to be a cash cow with winning relatively easy in Roger's mind against the Porsche opposition, and the Nissan team that had proved fast but very fragile.

To make life even easier for Engs the engine capacity limit of 6.5 litres was to be increased to 7 litres, according to TW that is, enabling our Group C based units to be used with little additional work, just piston changes for higher compression to allow for the higher-octane racing fuel that was allowed. This would mean that I simply could up the inventory of a proven engine and have no problems. We had though just spent two years proving that turbocharged engines had an advantage when using the much higher-octane fuels such as those used in IMSA, and they had been hard to beat with our normally aspirated V12. IMSA had no turbocharger boost or fuel consumption limitations, using an air restrictor to control turbocharged engines, meanwhile our 7-litre based engines were limited in their breathing ability and needed to be totally redeveloped to produce higher power outputs in the unrestricted fuel formula that was IMSA.

TW was happy that nothing would be a problem but I could not see why they would raise the engine capacity just to suit us. The much-touted superiority of the Tony Southgate ground effects design compared to that of the Group 44 Lee Dykstra XJR-7 would not go unnoticed by the locals either. Were American teams and politics going to absorb the aspirations of Tom Walkinshaw after beating the factory Porsches in Europe, and let the British in to steamroller their own event with the majority of teams running Porsches? I had my doubts.

## Le Mans testing

After the Group 44 location appraisal and subsequent decision that their headquarters were in the wrong area in America, it was back to Kidlington and Jaguar's main focus for the year – the Le Mans 24 hour race in France. In the build up to this event the first revised XJR8-LM, chassis 186 had been tested at Snetterton, Donington and Silverstone producing some detail changes to increase the durability of bodywork and refit the original steel rear roll bar linkage. The low drag bodywork also produced a race car that started to suffer brake overheating problems at these tighter circuits, especially Donington, but this was not expected to be a problem at Le Mans. Chassis 186 and 286 had been converted to 1987 Le Mans specification with the new chassis 387 being completed in time for the test. The Le Mans test day was one week after the Silverstone race with all three XJR8-LM cars running different aerodynamic packages as Tony Southgate fine tuned his results from the Imperial College wind tunnel.

This work had produced a car for Le Mans with increased downforce, drag reduced by 13%, and new nose profiles. All cars continued as the Silverstone Le Mans test car including tilting the engine by 2.5° from its forward mounting position. This raised the centre of gravity further for the heavy gearbox assembly section at the rear, and contributed to the problems Nielsen had first reported at Silverstone. The Silverstone race had shown that the LM specification was fast in a straight line but now less stable through corners with the higher transmission position.

This particular area of the car with its heavy and high centre of gravity had always been portrayed as the Achilles heel of the Group C programme. With this aspect in mind I had during the year carried out a paper exercise revising the whole engine installation with removing the lower skirt of the engine block and incorporating the main bearing caps in a one-piece sump package. This would accommodate a lower original engine position by 50mm and need a completely new gearbox design to raise the output shaft heights and incorporate the six forward gears now needed at Le Mans. The alternative option was to use the existing gearbox and use stepped gears from the crankshaft to the original gearbox input shaft but leaving the gearbox at the same height.

This upgrade would have given good overall gains especially for the 24 hour events, now about to include the Daytona 24 hour event in Florida next January. It would also extend the life of the V12 engine in Group C with considerable development opportunities and weight reduction still possible for 1988 and certainly 1989. As it turned out the development of the 7-litre engine would effectively cease after the first quarter of 1987 as TW's thoughts on turbocharging a small capacity six-cylinder engine began to grow.

The Le Mans engines were as sprint specification but with slightly reduced compression ratio of 12:1, a larger capacity Lucas alternator to feed the additional lighting need at night time, and heavier throttle return springs. Over time dirt was being ingested into the roller bearing tracks of the throttle slides and towards the end of the 24 hour race the throttles would become sticky.

*Le Mans venturi tunnels with the realigned driveshaft angle from the raised gearbox.*

The revised specifications had the driveshafts running above the venturi tunnels, and a new lower mounted single plane rear wing formed an extension of the rear bodywork; this feature producing a negative pressure area beneath it, directly behind the tunnel exits and encouraging increased flow through both tunnels. The effect was lower drag, improved downforce with the lower centre of pressure moved rearwards compared to the sprint specification. Changes had also been carried out to the rear bodywork to assist flow through the engine compartment and reduce heat build up of mechanical components such as the starter motor. The rear wheel covers, unloved by the mechanics with their difficulty in refitting after pit stop wheel changes when different rear bodywork components were replaced or damaged, were now removed. Another front wheel bearing solution had been designed and fitted as well for 1987.

With the addition of strengthened bodywork, headlights, driveshaft joints and backup systems the Le Mans cars were nearly 20kgs heavier than the sprint car specification. The Le Mans test day would produce an outright fastest time for Boesel and speeds in excess of 360kmh. With the revised Dunlop chicane, times were not comparable with the previous year. The various combinations used on the three cars had their top speeds, lap times and fuel consumption analysed to compare with the wind tunnel findings of the XJR8-LM specification, allowing final detail decisions to be made.

In the lead up to this year's Le Mans most things had gone well for Engs except for the fact that we had now upset our near neighbours with the continuous exhaust noise from our two new dynamometer cells replacing the single cell at the rear of our building. The official opening of the cells had been at the 10-year anniversary celebration and was a much-needed addition to our Engine division. With an ever-expanding industrial site such as the one where TWR were based in at Kidlington, new industrial units had been built on the back boundary of unit 1 where Engs was based as well as across the canal opposite. The unpatriotic owner of a timber yard across the canal became unhappy with the long hours of engine testing and resultant exhaust fumes entering their buildings now that their windows had been opened with the arrival of summer, and Le Mans. Notes were being passed and olive branches offered, some might think

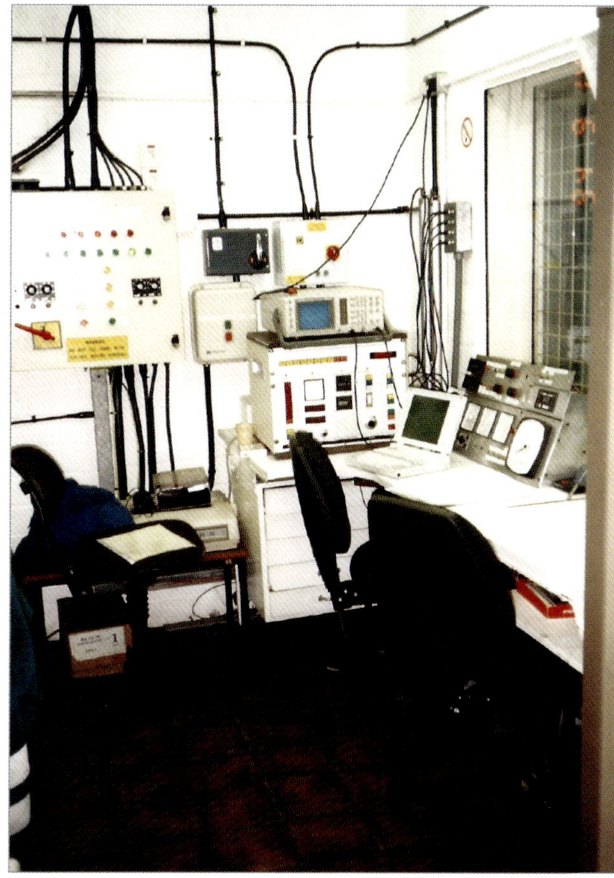

*The central command area servicing the two new dynamometer cells opened in 1987.*

including economical elements of the truth from me at crucial times as well, to allow the testing to continue. It all did however come to a head later and we had to then fit the exhaust stacks with additional blown fresh air to dilute the emissions.

The TWR team left Kidlington on the Monday and set up the pit area with team photograph on the Tuesday. Practice and qualifying would be held Wednesday and Thursday nights, with drivers having to complete three laps in both daylight and darkness to qualify. Wednesday practice would continue to focus on qualifying all drivers in these conditions before any attempts at a fast time, and depending on weather predictions this would be left to the Thursday practice. Friday was used to completely examine every aspect of the cars in preparation for the race start at 4pm the following day. The three TWR XJR8-LM cars were entered with drivers Cheever/Boesel in car 4 (387); Lammers/Watson in car 5 (286) and

Brundle/Nielsen in car 6 (186). Percy and Hahne were reserve drivers as it was unusual to expect just two drivers in each car to do all the driving, but it was possible. Strong driver pairings familiar with the race car were often reluctant to have a third reserve driver in their car if they were unsure of how that driver would look after it.

During practice American Price Cobb had a huge accident in the third Rothmans factory Porsche and vaulted the barriers ripping parts of the fuel tank in the process. This unrestrained accident finally came to a halt on the wrong side of the barriers completely wrecked and on fire. Cobb was unhurt and transferred to the Liqui Moly version of the 962 with Palmer/Weaver, but left the factory with just two cars to start the long event. The talk amongst the drivers at Le Mans was now all about safety, with the main concern being the low height of the Armco barriers and their inability to contain racing cars at high speeds; the organisers needed to pay more attention to safety with a race that had begun many years before when none was needed.

Final fastest qualifying times for the 1987 Le Mans event were taken by the factory Porsches of Wollek in 3:21.09; Stuck 3:24.12; the Jaguars were next up and all evenly matched with Cheever/Boesel 3:24.36; Brundle/Nielsen 3:24.68; Lammers/Watson 3:24.98 and the next Porsche two seconds slower in sixth.

The British fans, all 30,000 of them we were told, had arrived to see a Jaguar victory and had assembled opposite the Jaguar pits in a carnival and patriotic flag waving mood. The drizzle during the Saturday continued until the start and produced some uncertainty on the initial lap behind the pace car as to when the field would be released. After an additional lap the 24 hour race was underway in light rain conditions with the factory Porsches leading the Jaguars driven by Brundle, Lammers and Cheever. Incredibly, some of the Porsches were in engine trouble already with lean settings on the long Mulsanne straight overheating pistons and by the seventh lap both Joest and one Kremer Porsche were out with damaged pistons. Soon after this, the factory Porsche of Mass/Wollek/Schuppan was stopped in the pits, engine failure again being the problem. The V12s of course had the automatic enrichment mode for the Mulsanne straight that we had developed with Zytek the year before.

TWR's XJR-8s had put pressure on the entire Porsche programme and they were now out of their comfort zone in an attempt to be competitive. Reprogrammed chips from the Stuttgart factory were being blamed, a situation that was out of the hands of the private teams. The very early phase of the race had cars pitting to change to dry tyres, and Porsches for chip changes, before it finally settled down to five cars on the lead lap; Stuck–Nielsen–Palmer–Cheever–Lammers and Johnny Dumfries in the first of the two Sauber Mercedes.

*TWR team at Le Mans – 1987*

## John Watson describes a lap of Le Mans ...

Some changes had been made to the circuit for 1987 and John Watson's description of a 1987 lap follows.

Leaving the pits, I accelerate up the hill to Dunlop Curve, which used to be a 170mph sweep. Now the new complex demands you have to drop down below 100mph in third gear on entry. The corner is a right then left S-bend which serves no purpose for sports cars – Dunlop has always been quick, but never a dangerous corner, but now its going to be particularly hazardous at night as you can't see the apexes. Exit in third and up into fourth under the Dunlop Bridge. Prior to the new chicane I would have been approaching the Esses at 170mph – now i'ts a much gentler approach with later braking, finding third gear and powering through the left–right at around 130mph.

Tertre Rouge follows immediately with its high outside walls and here I have the Jaguar briefly into fourth before back to third. I would reckon to exit here at 130mph, making sure I have a tidy and fast exit line, as once you go onto the Mulsanne it's all down to straight line power. The Jaguar can reach the magic 230mph a quarter of the way down the straight, and then you just sit there at 6500rpm (note telemetry shows just 100rpm increase during this last period of the straight).

There is time to check instruments, flex your arms – but all the time you have to be wary of cars you are passing. The speed differential between our C1 class and the slower C2 cars can be as much as 50mph. The Mulsanne is bumpy, but the Jaguar is more stable than other cars I have raced at Le Mans previously –you have to stay one side or the other if you want to avoid the centre line hump which everyday traffic has created over the years.

Through the infamous 'kink', over the hill and then braking hard for Mulsanne corner, where a new supermarket demanded a roundabout last year removing the sharp right-hand Mulsanne exit corner. This new corner has two apexes joined by a short straight – you cannot see the second apex from the straight which is the crucial one so all your braking down to 75mph has to be done before the first part.

As you burst out of it in second gear you just have time to look to your signalling pit on your right. Up through third, fourth and fifth and you are travelling almost as fast as you were on the Mulsanne straight as you head for Indianapolis. There are two slight kinks on the way, and at 200mph this to me is the danger area – I'm overtaking cars which are considerably slower and may not have seen me in their mirrors.

Indianapolis is a classic second gear left and right, cambered in our favour, but again slower cars are committed to the racing line and can be a worry. I leave this part at 80mph and head off for Arnarge, just a few hundred metres down the road, staying in third then onto the brakes and right down to first for the slowest corner on the La Sarthe circuit. At 55mph I just point and squirt the car and get back up to speed as quickly as possible. On to the Porsche Curves the road is wide and fast and you accelerate briefly in fifth at 190mph before changing down to third. Porsche Curves present a fast but tricky series of left and rights in third but fourth is OK in the race if you need to look after the fuel. Third here gives more driveability, the first corner is fairly easy but the last one is all wrong with an adverse camber. If there is to be an accident or oil down on the circuit it will be here and I always approach it cautiously. Then out of the Curves at 130mph and hard acceleration up to fifth on the run to the final Ford Chicane just before the pit straight. Hard braking and being careful to avoid the high kerb in the second gear 80mph left and 60mph right. There is no way you can rush through them – just be neat and tidy, and then I am powering passed the pits in fourth gear touching 170mph on the way to Dunlop....

The first problem for TWR came two and a half hours into the race with Cheever into the pits with a puncture but managing to return to the circuit without damaging his bodywork. The first pace car period happened soon after with the Fortuna Porsche driven by Schafer crashing over the Armco barriers. By the fourth hour both the Saubers were out and this was not unexpected as the new cars had started racing just a few weeks before. Pescarolo in his Sauber had been stopped out on the track for so long, about two hours, that when he had finally made repairs and returned to the pits, his team had packed up and left, his pit was deserted! They did then return though and the car carried on, finally retiring at midnight.

Conditions around this time in the dark were difficult, with slight rain but not enough to use intermediate tyres, producing the need to keep the slicks hot in the colder conditions. Jaguar #4 pitted and lost two laps having a throttle cable replaced leaving two Porsches and two Jaguars on the lead lap. James Weaver survived a potentially dangerous moment when a fuel line leaked and fire destroyed the BRL Liqui Moly Porsche. This led to a long 30-minute period under the pace car; a situation that suited the Porsches to help conserve their fuel. Jaguar car #5 had the engine cover come loose, and the stop to repair that enabled the factory Porsche to establish a definite lead, thanks mainly to brilliant driving by Stuck in the difficult semi wet conditions.

Just before half distance the rhythm of the race was shattered in the TWR pits as news came through that an overdue Win Percy had suffered a huge accident on the Mulsanne straight soon after he had started his stint at the wheel. A rear tyre had failed at high speed sending the XJR8-LM into the Armco barriers and broken the car in half at its weakest point; the gearbox bell housing. Describing to me later the sequence of events Win had said that he was amazed after the initial impact that he had suffered such little trauma in the accident; he said that he had then just reached around to open the door to try and get out. During this process there was an almighty crash and he was thrown about and after what seemed a long time it all went quiet again. Win had been upside down flying through the air for so long after the first impact he had though the accident was over.

With all the damage to clear and Armco barriers to repair the racing was delayed for two hours as the field circulated behind the pace car and the gamble that the leading Porsche had taken in pushing hard and not

*to page 160 ...*

## Win Percy describes his accident ...

Tom suggested I fly out with him and it was on that flight over he broke the news to me that he wanted me to qualify only, and then be on standby, but to not take part in the race. I started to protest but when you know Tom and he has decided something then it is very difficult to argue about anything. He confirmed I would be paid but that Jan Lammers and John Watson would do the race together. Qualifying went well and my times were equal to theirs so I was relaxed. Our car #5 was to be used as the hare and stretch the Porsches on fuel consumption and all seemed to be going well as planned. I was asleep around midnight when Tom woke me up to ask if I would after all be prepared to drive, of course the answer was yes. I asked what had changed and he told me that John Watson did not want to drive again in the dark. I was sent to the doctor to make sure I was fully awake and suitably prepared, then told there was no rush as Jan was staying in for another 50 minutes. Our car was in second when Jan pitted and all going well, I jumped in but it is possible I touched the brake pedal while they were changing the brake pads, and a caliper piston had popped out. This then led to a slow pit stop.

I joined the race feeling great and ready for the challenge, sadly on my first lap out at the back of the circuit near Arnarge there had been a big accident with wreckage strewn around. I slowed and attempted to go around all the debris I could see, then back around passed the pits and off on my first flying lap. (I was later told that the marshals at the quarter distance post down the Mulsanne straight witnessed sparks coming from under my car.) Unaware of any trouble I carried on flat out until the car started to

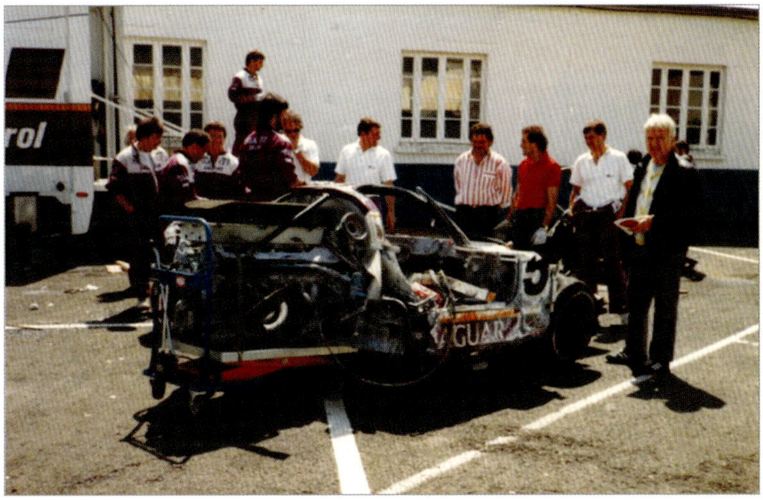

*The TWR team inspect the badly damaged XJR-8 after Win Percy's accident.*

vibrate more than I had experienced before and just as I was thinking about lifting the accelerator there was an almighty explosion, the only way I can explain it. The car took off upwards into the night sky, rear end first. Instinctively I let go of the steering wheel and brought my legs up from the pedals.

I guess thinking that at that speed around 230mph plus it was going to be more like an aircraft crash, I even closed my eyes. It was suddenly silent but I sensed I was still moving very quickly and when I opened my eyes I was gently turning over and over above the trees becoming aware that things were about to get very painful. The first impact hurt; there were short spells until the next impact, but each getting less violent. At one point I was aware of my helmet dragging along the ground and I was trying to lift my head up, then what was left of this amazing car came to stop on its bottom. I quietly thanked God, undid my belts, carefully unplugged my radio aerial as they cost £1 each and Tom had told us to be careful with them. Not so much for the value of course but the fact that it was important they continued to work at all times.

It turned out I had picked up a puncture and the tyre had let go in a big way about 300 metres before the Mulsanne 'kink' and the car had eventually come to a stop about 600 metres further down the track from where the crash had started, even finding its way around the kink. The tyre when it blew had taken off the rear wing so with that missing and the car turning around was the reason the rear took off first.

I walked away from the wreck without a scratch and climbed over the Armco barrier fence to be greeted by a group who offered to take me back to the pits, to find Tom as white as a sheet and asking if I had any idea of what happened. I explained I did not and went through the few details I could remember. He insisted I go and get some sleep and then told me that he had had a dream about one of the cars crashing and I had been the driver. That was why he had not wanted me to drive the car in the first place.

*Kevlar fused ends show overheating failure with heat generated from puncture causing Win Percy's crash.*

*... from page 158*
worrying about the fuel consumption now paid off. With this length of time behind the pace car it was becoming increasingly harder for TWR to win the race with its superior fuel consumption package now not the deciding factor; although Porsche had a boost limit for this 24 hour race. Also there was the tyre failure to evaluate and decisions to be made on whether it was a puncture or an actual tyre failure (blowout). As the sun rose on Sunday the racing once again continued at full speed. The Jaguars were running the original nylon 4-ply tyre construction until Dunlop could come up with a reasonable answer to the possible cause of the failure and validate the use of the Kevlar construction tyres once again.

The Jaguars were now run flat out and just when it seemed that they could close the gap to the leading Porsche, Boesel misjudged a section of track, sliding off and damaging the nose section. Replacement would cost four laps. With a possible tyre problem hanging over the team it was Nielsen who pitted next with a vibration and then with this still worrying him, another stop to change tyres, dropping a lap to the leaders. Cheever then had a problem with his gearbox resulting in a broken reverse gear punching a hole through the side of the casing. The hole was repaired as well as possible and the car continued on but both Jaguars had dropped off the lead lap. With just over two-thirds of the race completed the Brundle/Nielsen XJR8-LM retired with a lack of water and damaged engine.

The temporary fix to the gearbox of the Cheever/Boesel Jaguar then failed allowing oil onto the exhaust system and starting a fire. The rear of the gearbox was removed and the gear set replaced and holed casing repaired, this procedure completed in twenty minutes. The start of the last quarter of the race began once again behind the pace car with just 18 cars running out of the 48 that had started 18 hours before. The last surviving XJR-8 then lost fuel pressure and Boesel's investigations entailed the removal of the engine cover. With nothing found but fuel pressure restored, the tail section had not been properly attached and this was ripped off needing more repairs in the pits. The fuel pressure would occasionally continue to be a problem, but with two hours from the end it was a suspension upright that then needed replacing and any hope of a minor place was gone. The Cheever/Boesel/Lammers TWR Silk Cut Jaguar XJR8-LM finished in fifth after completing 324 laps and earning some handy points for Cheever and Boesel as well as the minimum fifth placing bonus from Jaguar.

Stuck/Bell in the Rothmans Porsche 962LM completed a dominant win after 354 laps, 20 laps clear of the second place Obermaier/Primagaz Porsche 962 of Laessig/de Driver/Yver. Third place after completing 331 laps was the Courage-Porsche of Courage/Raphanel/Regout. After the valiant efforts on the Cheever/Boesel car the team of Clive Parker/Jeff Wilson/Alva Claxton and Tim Strudwick were awarded the 'Prix ESCRA' trophy for best support crew.

The XJR8-LM with the raised gearbox had been a difficult combination to master with all the drivers feeling the car was very nervous and difficult to drive.

Porsche's Derek Bell said afterwards, "The Jaguars were quicker than us on the straight but we caught up with them without any problem on the corners. This did wonders for our morale when we were battling it out with them in the late evening. We knew that anything was possible and that we could win the race. You might say it was us who put the pressure on Jaguar rather than the other way around."

Martin Brundle concurred with this sentiment, "We had a road holding problem. I was worn out because the car was so difficult to drive and we were flat out."

When the Brundle/Nielsen engine was later stripped down it was found to have a broken inlet valve spring leading to contact with the piston and destroying that cylinder. With the pressure continuing to build on TWR to win this important race TW and Roger had felt that the Brundle/Nielsen car had a good chance of winning, and that the engine failure had let this opportunity slip from our grasp. The press had this down as a blown head gasket and it had to be left at that.

This particular race was always going to be hard to win with over three hours run behind the pace car. The relative fuel economy of the XJR8-LM could not be a deciding factor, letting the remaining Porsche off the hook of marginal settings in fuel mixture and ignition timing that had caused the early Porsche engine failures. It had been a good chance lost though, as only one factory Porsche survived out of the main contingent from the first hour of the 24 hour race.

The championship placings now were Stuck/Bell 74; Cheever/Boesel 60; Lammers/Watson 55.

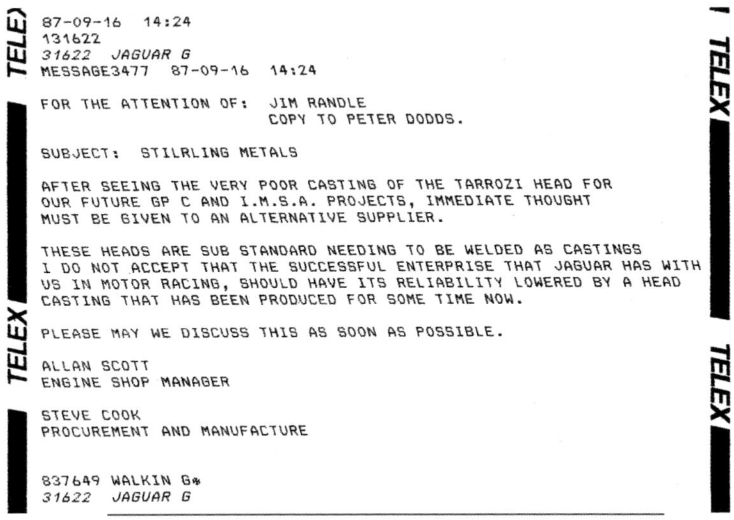

TELEX

87-09-16 14:24
131622
31622 JAGUAR G
MESSAGE3477 87-09-16 14:24

FOR THE ATTENTION OF: JIM RANDLE
COPY TO PETER DODDS.

SUBJECT: STILRLING METALS

AFTER SEEING THE VERY POOR CASTING OF THE TARROZI HEAD FOR OUR FUTURE GP C AND I.M.S.A. PROJECTS, IMMEDIATE THOUGHT MUST BE GIVEN TO AN ALTERNATIVE SUPPLIER.

THESE HEADS ARE SUB STANDARD NEEDING TO BE WELDED AS CASTINGS I DO NOT ACCEPT THAT THE SUCCESSFUL ENTERPRISE THAT JAGUAR HAS WITH US IN MOTOR RACING, SHOULD HAVE ITS RELIABILITY LOWERED BY A HEAD CASTING THAT HAS BEEN PRODUCED FOR SOME TIME NOW.

PLEASE MAY WE DISCUSS THIS AS SOON AS POSSIBLE.

ALLAN SCOTT
ENGINE SHOP MANAGER

STEVE COOK
PROCUREMENT AND MANUFACTURE

837649 WALKIN G*
31622 JAGUAR G

***Some issues still existed with the supply of head castings from Jaguar.***

## Norisring – June 28th

Two weeks after Le Mans it was back to the Norisring in early July. This race would follow the similar 'short race' format as 1986 on the converted street circuit, but divided into two races. Each would be of 77 laps of the 1.4-mile circuit and the total 360km distance would include the pace and slow down laps to comply with the mandatory 190 litre fuel allowance. Again, German honour was at stake with the two Jaguars against the twelve Porsches and two Sauber C9 Mercedes. Lancia had also made a one-off appearance in the Mussato supported entry for Konrad/Giacomelli.

Qualifying had Stuck/Bell on pole in the Shell Fuels factory Porsche followed by the Joest entry of Ludwig/Wollek and Thackwell/Reuter in the Sauber, 0.4sec separating these three; Cheever/Boesel were fourth and Lammers/Watson seventh. The UK BLR Liqui Moly team had built a new car after the disastrous Le Mans fire and managed ninth a fine effort. 75,000 people turned up for race day.

From the start Thackwell took an early lead, easily the fastest car in a straight line. The race settled down until Stuck was hit from behind and rejoined in tenth while Baldi in the BLR Porsche moved past Lammers and Cheever for third. Cheever pitted on lap 23 to have the fuel pumps changed and then the fuel regulator. Constant measuring of the fuel tank capacity to have it as close to 100 litres, but not over, had allowed small amounts of the internal fibres fitted to these bag tanks to enter the fuel circuit. One of these had jammed the regulator valve. Lammers had settled into fourth place behind Wollek while Thackwell and Baldi diced for the lead until lap 30 when the new Liqui Moly car took the lead and at the same time Lammers moved in behind the Sauber for third. Thackwell then slowed with heat exhaustion, something he had suffered while driving in the heat of Malaysia in the XJR-6 in 1985, and Lammers was through to second. Lammers took the lead at mid-distance but this was short lived as the car was retired having broken its transmission on the bumpy surface on lap 42. This was to be the loss of a fast combination with team mate Watson having posted fastest time in the pre-race warm up. The race finished in some confusion over the results. The 45-minute break between races became an hour and a half while final positions and starting order for the second race was sorted. Baldi's win in the BLR Porsche was not in dispute, but after Wollek had stopped 50 metres from the finishing line out of fuel, it was Stuck's second place after two pit stops and a spin which was doubted by many, with Jelinski in the Joest Porsche third. The much-delayed Cheever was awarded thirteenth.

The second race was then run and Boesel in the Jaguar with its fuel pressure problem fixed displayed a fine drive from his seventh place on the starting grid, moving up to second by lap 23; while the race between Palmer in the BRL Porsche and Bell for third place ended with Bell in fuel pressure problems. The second race was won by Ludwig in the Joest Porsche, but in an example of how careful you have to be with fuel tank capacity this car was later excluded when the tank capacity was found to be 1.5 litres over the allowable 100. The final results for the second race were a win for the TWR Jaguar and Raul Boesel, followed by Palmer and Mass. The BRL Liqui Moly Porsche of Baldi/Palmer became the winners of the event on aggregate.

The other aggregate placings over the two-race event were Mass/Larrauri – Brun/Jaegermeister 962; John Winter/Stanley Dickens – Joest/Sachs 962; and Cheever/Boesel – TWR Silk Cut Jaguar XJR-8 in fourth overall.

After this event Porsche formally announced they were withdrawing the Factory Team cars for the remainder of the year. The latest 3-litre water-cooled engines and electronics would be made available to the top private teams; they had won Le Mans and there would be little benefit from the probability of coming second to Jaguar in the remaining races of 1987.

## Hockenheim – July 5th

This non-championship round had just the one Jaguar for Boesel on German home ground. Hans Stuck won here with Boesel third amongst nine Porches filling all the other top ten placings.

## Brands Hatch – July 26th

Back on home ground at Brands Hatch during the last week of July, the tables were turned in qualifying. TWR was always the away team in Europe where most circuits were never visited from one year to the next and it was one of the team's strengths to produce the best set-up possible at a foreign circuit in the few practice sessions available before a race. The European teams would now have to face the same challenges and many of them had decided to miss this race, including Sauber, leaving just eight cars to contest the top class. Stuck/Bell had found themselves a drive with Joest-Porsche, and Mass with a Brun Porsche for this race in the factory's absence.

The Lammers/Watson Jaguar took the fastest qualifying time with Boesel/Nielsen second, Baldi/Dumfries BLR Porsche third and Stuck fourth.

The BLR Liqui Moly 962 had never been a great favourite of the Porsche factory with its British (John Thompson) tub and changed aerodynamics but this package was now proving to be very competitive and they could not ignore it. Although a factory 3-litre engine was available to them the team continued with its customer 2.8-litre, setting the fastest Porsche time and proving a point to many.

Lammers set a new Group C qualifying record, two seconds faster than the year before, with the BLR Porsche 1.2 seconds quicker than Stuck's pole time of 1986. Fourth placed Stuck in Joest's 962 improved by 0.1 sec over his previous year's time. Weights at this race were 870 and 876kgs for the Jaguars, 859kgs for the UK team's BLR Porsche with the other European based Porsches ranging from 887kgs to 911kgs. The Jaguars were having some problems with the bumps at Brands Hatch, so a compromise set-up on the spare T car was tested and proved to be the direction to take. The top three qualifiers set the same scene in the pre-race warm up raising the expectation levels of a home win for the 35,000 in attendance.

Lammers took an early lead in the 238-lap race with Boesel held up behind Baldi, building up frustration that soon led to him coming off second best in a passing manoeuvre. Hasty body repairs had him out again but one lap down on the leaders and out of sync with following fuel stops. Lammers however was in a race of his own increasing his lead over the BLR Porsche by one second a lap and Boesel delivered a face-saving drive to bring his XJR-8 back up to third by quarter distance. By the end of the second fuel stops the Jaguars had shown that they could run at this pace to the fuel while the opposition were in trouble. Boesel and Nielsen were now the stars of the comeback race with Boesel finally on Baldi's tail by mid-distance and a repeat of the earlier dog fight continued. The first pace car period happened soon after and this time the TWR team would be the beneficiaries with Lammers pitting without having to circulate behind the pace car. With Boesel coming in to refuel at the same time, the second Jaguar was back on the same refuelling schedule as the others, not now requiring an additional short fill near the end to take the last of the fuel allowance. The driver-change to Watson in the leading XJR-8 led to the end of the dream run for this crew as a rear wheel bearing failed and 12 minutes were spent on its return to the pits to replace the complete upright assembly. The 26 minutes under the pace car worked against the superior fuel consumption of the Jaguars, and Dumfries now in the BLR Porsche had fuel to spare and increased boost to use to stay just ahead of Nielsen. At the second last stop both cars were together but the BLR Porsche needed front brake pads from this hectic race pace, but with a better brake set-up and higher downforce/drag combination, the XJR-8 did not. The quicker pit stop let Boesel out in front, free to run at its own pace. Boesel took his remaining fuel on lap 211 and remained in the car at the last stop, with the challenge starting to wilt from Dumfries as his fuel began to run low.

Boesel/Nielsen won the race by 1:13 from the Baldi/Dumfries BLR Porsche, with Lammers/Watson putting on a great drive that took them past the Stuck/Bell Porsche into third place.

If all the C1 cars competing had been able to run a perfect race, both XJR-8s would have been two laps ahead of the BRL Porsche and another two ahead of Stuck/Bell in the Joest Porsche, indicating the competitiveness of the Jaguar package on home soil.

Boesel now led the championship on 90 points, from Bell/Stuck on 84, Cheever on 70 and Lammers/Watson on 67 points.

This was also the race where a new face appeared observing the team and race proceedings with more than normal interest – it was Tony Dowe, a UK national but resident in the USA. He had just been recruited as head of the as yet to be assembled TWR America Division, to take TWR Jaguar into IMSA in America.

*The two Jaguars lead at the start of the Brands Hatch race.*

## Nurburgring – August 30th

Four weeks later it was back to Germany and the new Nurburgring for round eight of the Group C championship. The two-car Sauber team, looking to improve on its obvious potential was reduced to a single entry after Friday's practice. Dumfries had now moved to Sauber and he had collided with a slower C2 car resulting in damaged suspension pickup points on the chassis, making it impossible to repair in time.

The BLR Porsche of Baldi/Palmer once again showed its speed with the fastest time in qualifying. Cheever showed his considerable talent to be just 0.4sec slower for second place on the grid, and the Thackwell/Pescarolo Sauber joined now by Dumfries took third 0.25sec ahead of Lammers in the second XJR-8.

First of the 'normal' Porsches was the Joest/Blaupunkt 956 of Ludwig/Wollek a full second slower than the BRL modified 962. Stuck/Bell had Rothmans backing for the second ex-works 962C run by Joest and were sixth fastest. The XJR-8's qualifying times were very impressive on a circuit that historically had never been kind to any of TWR's endeavours here. It had also produced, with some relief, the possibility that this race could lead to TWR tying up the Manufacturers Championship for Jaguar, with two races still remaining.

From the very beginning of the 221 lap 1000km race pole man Baldi had a boost response problem from an engine that had been replaced just prior to the start. Cheever, alongside, had surged ahead then backed off to let the pole position car set the pace as they crossed the start line. He was immediately engulfed by the cars behind and ended up fourth on the first lap. This was only a minor setback until the local stewards decided he had jumped the start and imposed a 60 second penalty. Baldi was effectively out of the race needing two pit stops to rectify the engine installation problems that had resulted from the time pressure placed on the team before the start of the race. Ludwig was the clear leader followed by Thackwell in the Sauber with Lammers and Cheever close behind.

Jan Lammers was soon out of the race however with a broken cam follower, an engine item that had not previously given any trouble, the result of a manufacturing fault. Ludwig pitted early on lap 30 to short fill with 71 litres of fuel and our maths showed he was on the fuel target although it seemed an interesting strategy to take. The shorter time stopped then increased Ludwig's lead over the cars on normally scheduled stops after 38 laps taking a full complement of fuel. Boesel's progress after the first pit stop was hampered by brake problems but he managed to drive around this problem and allow some normality to return to the system and finally move into second place by the end of his stint.

With half the race completed the leading Joest Porsche of Ludwig/Wollek retired with a broken gearbox allowing the Cheever/Boesel XJR-8 to take the lead. Behind them were the Sauber Mercedes and then Mass a lap down in the Brun 962, both these teams using Michelin tyres. Stuck/Bell in the second Joest run Rothmans 962 had moved up to fourth, and as with all the other Porsche runners, they were running on Goodyear rubber instead of the Dunlop's the works had used. Lap 136 had Thackwell in the Sauber in trouble with fuel pressure problems and then soon after the loss of third gear led to the C9 being retired. This left the leading Jaguar XJR-8 an amazing three laps clear of the Brun team's Porsche driven by Mass/Larrauri, and Stuck/Bell in third. Stuck/Bell though managed to move into second place over the last few laps as all the remaining race cars struggled, virtually out of fuel, putting Mass/Larrauri into third, both of these Porsches equipped with the factory water-cooled 3-litre engines. Cheever drove the TWR Jaguar to the finish, and this was a great way to win the Manufacturers Championship for Jaguar – by three laps on German soil.

Cheever/Boesel, XJR-8 (Silk Cut Jaguar); Stuck/Bell, Porsche 962C (Joest Racing); Mass/Larrauri, Porsche 962C (Brun Motorsport); Jelinski/'Winter'/Dickens, Porsche 962C (Joest Racing)

The luxury of winning a title before the last race of the year is one that is not experienced very often and this release of pressure added to what was becoming a very memorable year.

T-shirts had been printed and carried to the race in anticipation of a win and carried the message 'TWR World Champions '87' in large letters on the front, with a barely visible Jaguar and jumping cat logo sandwiched in between. Jaguar missed an opportunity by not producing their own versions, but TW was certainly not going to miss this one! Stuck/Bell had gained valuable points with their second placing, although the tide was turning in Boesel's favour for the Drivers Championship. Boesel would now be given priority in team race strategy to assist in winning the title over the last two races.

*T-shirt worn by the TWR team to celebrate winning the Manufacturers Championship.*

## Spa Francorchamps

The Spa event had become the most important race of the later part of the year for TWR for two reasons. After winning the Manufacturers Championship for Jaguar it was time to concentrate on winning the Drivers Championship and the chance to finish this at Spa, before the last race at Fuji in Japan with its unpredictable weather a reality. Secondly it had just been announced publicly that TWR would be taking over the Jaguar IMSA programme in the USA, and Spa was to be the venue where the American motoring media would be brought over to be introduced to the TWR team.

Tony Dowe, who had been working for the USA Newman/Haas Champ car team now headed up the new TWR IMSA programme to start in 1988 and had begun assembling his USA team. He had immediately recruited an associate of his, Ian Reed, formerly of the Penske Champ car team, as chief engineer. These two were then brought to Spa to manage one of the race cars in a test of their abilities, and to observe how the TWR team operated.

The mathematical chance for TWR's highest scoring driver Raul Boesel's to win the championship was to be greatly enhanced with an entry of three Jaguars here. More drivers were needed and the strategy was to have no less than seven for this race. This allowed two drivers per car with the seventh driver, Raul Boesel, to be cross entered in all three. Boesel would not start in any of the cars but wait till the last fuelling stops to decide which car had the best chance of winning, before driving the last portion of the race, to be registered as a finisher in that selected car. Tony Dowe and Ian Reed were given the task of managing Boesel and the strategy needed to produce the best result, with Boesel having to complete 30% of the race distance to be classified. The driver pairings for the three XJR-8s were Cheever/Nielsen; Lammers/Watson and a returning Martin Brundle with the only driver that had never driven the XJR-8 before, Johnny Dumfries, an heir to Scottish nobility as the Marquess of Bute. The three cars were engineered by Alastair Macqueen; Eddie Hinckley and Paul Davis.

Friday had got off to a bad start with Brundle putting his car into the barriers and needing repairs to both ends of the car that included a radiator and rear suspension.

Saturday saw the 3-litre engined BLR Liqui Moly Porsche driven by Jonathan Palmer average just over 200kph to set the fastest time of 2:04.11 with Lammers in second. 1986 TWR driver Jean-Louis Schlesser had joined the Kouros sponsored Sauber C9 at Spa and proceeded to set third fastest time, making me to continue wondering why he had been let go by Roger. Mike Thackwell then

*Tony Dowe standing, talks to TWR USA Engineer Ian Reed. On his right is new recruit Johnny Dumfries and assistant team manager/car engineer Paul Davis.*

took over the C9 to set second fastest time with Lammers and Cheever up next. After Brundle's accident repair on Friday night, Dumfries had managed to get the tight bus stop all wrong, resulting in an even larger rebuild before the race start for car #6. Even with all these problems, Brundle had managed to set sixth fastest time.

The USA motoring press, along with its many Jaguar dealers, were devoted Jaguar followers in the USA and had become very aligned with Group 44 and their racing programme over the years. They were very disappointed with the switch to a UK team and loss of Group 44 to IMSA. Media were flown from the USA to the Spa event to watch the TWR team in action, and then treated to a fine dinner afterwards at one of the best restaurants in Belgium. Along with the American media it was a full turnout for the Jaguar management for this important event; TWR trying to win the Drivers Championship as well as the hearts and respect of the American media. David Boole, for Jaguar UK media was assisted by Ian Norris who was to become the USA Jaguar Inc. media and liaison contact. Sir John Egan (knighted in 1986), Ron Elkins Jaguar's TWR UK liaison, and marketing director Roger Putnam who had replaced Neil Johnson when he left to head up the UK Territorial Army. On hand to help with the transition to the 1988 IMSA programme was USA Jaguar Inc. senior vice-president sales and marketing Mike Dale. It was not an easy time for Mike Dale as he had been a staunch supporter of Bob Tullius in the days when Group 44 had been the only American competitor supporting the troubled British Leyland amalgamation concept. Tullius had successfully raced Triumph TR7 and XJS Jaguars before the Jaguar America backed entry into IMSA. Both had common interests in owning and flying vintage aeroplanes and that had produced a mutual respect beyond the business relationship of marketing Jaguar's vehicles via Group 44's on track exploits. It was Mike Dale who had to break the news of TWR taking over the IMSA roll and we all realised how difficult that would have been.

The race started with the usual Spa weather lottery and the C9 Sauber briefly leading before minor mechanical problems needed attention leaving Palmer's BLR Porsche in the lead with the three Jaguars behind. Light rain and cooling temperatures seemed to have an effect on the fuel consumption in Cheever's car as

*Author Allan Scott and Jaguar USA's Mike Dale seem happy about the outcome at Spa.*

well as poor handling, and it took two laps to come up with a fix with the engine management system in cooler weather. With the changeable light rain conditions, tyre choices became crucial as it was not enough for full wets and too much for slicks from time to time, so patience was needed by all the drivers. Additional rear wing angle was added to the Lammers/Watson car to help the handling in these conditions and by mid-distance the BLR Porsche was unable to keep up with its limited choice of Goodyear tyres.

Amazingly, the twice rebuilt Brundle/Dumfries car ran strongly at the front and was chosen as the car to hand over to Boesel for just over one and a half hours, the minimum needed to collect maximum points for the driver's title. At the car's last stop, Brundle, who was handling the difficult conditions best, rejoined the #6 XJR-8 and drove it to the finish.

> The race was stopped after the maximum allowed six hours, three laps short of 1000kms, with the Boesel/Brundle/Dumfries XJR-8 taking first place. Watson had driven into second place and a hard charging Cheever had to settle for fourth, just missing out on the podium because of the shortened race.

Boesel was now World Sports Car Champion, Tony Dowe and Ian Reed could not believe their luck with their first race for TWR producing a world champion; and confirmation for the Jaguar management that they had made the right choice for their IMSA racing programme. It was also a very timely introduction for the American media to TWR – they were all impressed with the professionalism of Tom Walkinshaw, at his verbal best in these situations, as well as how the whole team operated. They seemed happy to write positive comments giving TWR a healthy introduction to the American scene on their return. It had been an instant and successful transition in their sympathies and TWR now seen to be a force to take Jaguar to the winners' circle. Winning the WSPC title with Raoul Boesel at Spa that weekend was a considerable lift to TWR's engineering profile. Porsche dominance had been broken for the first time in five years of the modern Group C, and few would have believed that possible 18 months before.

*Raul Boesel is the Drivers World Champion for 1987.*

## Japan – September 27th

The final race of the year and the long haul to Japan via Alaska in the last weekend of September had removed any real pressure on the team, with both championships won. The main interest would be to see how competitive the local Japanese manufacturers of Nissan, Toyota and Mazda would be under racing conditions to the fuel allowance. The race was to be reduced to the 'sprint' format and fuel allowance, but this time moving to the northern Sendai circuit, a first for all the foreign teams. On arrival there was some confusion when it was found that the circuit had not passed its safety inspection, and with this late notification a major logistics change was needed to revert to the Fuji circuit. Some sponsorship contracts had been compromised as they had been based around the Sendai location, and many were not happy. The format would revert to 1000kms and the dubious weather at the Fuji circuit.

In qualifying the turbocharged locals of Wada – 3-litre Nissan; Lees – 2-litre Minolta Toyota and Ross Cheever in the Dome Toyota were ahead of Baldi in the BLR Porsche. Lammers was the first Jaguar in sixth and Boesel tenth. With little to gain Stuck had stayed at home and Derek Bell partnered Geoff Brabham in the Vern Schuppan Porsche. One person missing from this last race was our boss who was soon to become a father for the first time, ensuring a more relaxed end of year without results pressure.

The weather remained dry and the usual 'over fuel allowance' sprinting at the start settled down with Lees' Toyota leading the early part of the race. Lammers stayed with the leaders and changed over to Watson, while Lees changed to former Australian Formula One Champion Alan Jones. Positions stayed much the same as a pace car event closed the field. By half distance however all three Toyotas were out with engine troubles. The turbocharged cars had to respect their fuel allowances by this time and only the BLR Porsche could maintain the pace.

Lammers/Watson and Boesel/Dumfries held the two front positions to the end to cap off a great year for TWR Silk Cut Jaguar. Third and three laps down were Baldi/Thackwell/Matsuda in the BRL Porsche followed three further laps behind by Mass/Larrauri Brun's Takefuji Porsche, Dickens/Jelinski/Winter's Taka-Q Joest Porsche and Bell/Brabham's Rothmans Schuppan Porsche; all these six laps down on the Jaguar.

The end of TWR's most successful year in motor racing had Jaguar winning the Manufacturers' title as well as the Drivers Championship with Raul Boesel on 127 points. Jan Lammers and John Watson had been placed joint second in the Drivers Championship on 102 points, a fitting end for this very competitive and reliable pairing, who could have just as easily been outright Drivers Champions. Eddie Cheever who had not competed in all the events because of his Formula One priorities was

*TWR and Jaguar members celebrate the 1-2-3 driver and manufacturer positions at the last race in Japan.*

next up in the Drivers Championship, 100 points ahead of the first Porsche drivers, Stuck and Bell on 99 points. Could it get any better than this for TWR?

It was time to relax and return home for a well earned rest. For Engs however it was just the start in preparing for the new IMSA programme in America. TW had promised an easy entry for us using mildly changed 7-litre Group C engines; but I had heard just before leaving for Japan that this had all changed with a review of the IMSA rules.

*Team manager Roger Silman reporting back to Tom Walkinshaw with from left Lynden Swainston, John Nielsen, Jaguar liaison Alan Hodge, Alastair Macqueen and Johnny Dumfries.*

*Jan Lammers*

above: *Eddie Hinckley;*
right: *Paul Davis in party mood on the flight home.*

It had also been a milestone year in TWR's development with the tenth anniversary of Tom Walkinshaw Racing after moving from London to Number 1 Station Fields Industrial Estate in Kidlington, Oxford, with first employees Eddie Hinckley and Campbell Ritchie. Now with 120 staff at Kidlington and many other industrial and garage businesses forming the TWR Group, a special celebration had been held at year's end. Awards were given to long standing members and the large number of TWR Group employees felt a sense of belonging to a special company. TWR Group events were being recorded in a monthly magazine.

With all this success however there were winds of change blowing as more dealerships were added and a major deal completed with the General Motors Australian Holden manufacturer on the other side of the world. This situation had gathered momentum in 1987 and led to TW asking me to go to Australia to head up the new Holden venture there. I had surprised TW and Roger by declining the move to manage this position without giving TW any of my real reasons, but my instincts told me it would involve phone calls in the middle of the night because of the time difference, and many short notice long aeroplane journeys back to the UK. TW was taking an increasing interest in the engine side of things; just when I felt we were getting this under control. The success of the V12 engine however had now confused some, if not all of his plans. This would be a more strategic time in our relationship than I at first recognised, with TW convinced I would jump at the chance to run the Australian business; leaving him to progress engine development via Max Heidegger, with Engs just being a rebuild facility. I had lived in Sydney for three years in the early 70s and instigated TWR's interests there by showing TW Bathurst videos that had been sent to me. This had led to winning the Bathurst 1000 with the XJS in 1985 and my subsequent visit to close the deal to purchase four Holden V8 engines for testing and development in support of the Group A Holden progamme.

GROUP C ENGINES

SUMMARY OF PROPOSED 1987 BUDGET

| | £ | £ | Original Cost |
|---|---|---|---|
| Rebuilds | 39,537.00 | | |
| Additional Maintenance & Lifeing | 22,044.00 | 61,581.00 | 71,550.00 |
| Cost of Updating 1986 Engines | | 37,354.00 | 56,000.00 |
| Le Mans | | 22,300.00 | |
| Back-Up Spares | | 20,600.00 | |
| Proposed Development | | 59,750.00 | |
| * 9 Engines Carried Forward | | --- | |
| | TOTAL | £201,585.00 | £230,200.00 |
| Credit In Stores - | | £50,700.00 | |

* Used Engine value to be agreed

*With amortised support costs and salaries the engine costs to win the World Championship were just less than £500,000.*

*Caithness commissioned decanter and glasses given to me after winning the 1987 World Sportscar Championship.*

> ***Reality is merely an illusion, albeit a very persistent one.***
>
> – Albert Einstein

JAGUAR

## Chapter Fifteen

# Preparing for 1988

**1988 would be a year of exponential growth and change for the TWR Group. A large undertaking had commenced with Holden in Australia that included establishing the Holden two-car racing team and Holden Special Vehicle (HSV) after-market performance vehicle manufacturing and sales, mirroring the successful model of Jaguar racing teams and the JaguarSport production car performance business. By now the TWR Group also had a growing collection of automotive sales franchises later to be called Silverstone Motor Group, including Jaguar, Mazda, BMW, Porsche and Nissan. TWR was exemplifying the mantra 'Win on Sunday sell on Monday'.**

You could be forgiven for thinking that it was business as usual for the Jaguar racing arm, but fresh from their success at the highest level they had raced so far, they were taking on a whole new series at that level in a different continent, in addition to defending their WSPC crown. America was Jaguar's largest single market and Jaguar wanted to promote vehicle sales via race wins. A two-car IMSA series programme would begin in America, with yet another offshore base with its first event a 24 hour marathon at Daytona in the first month of the new year. If we didn't already think we knew what busy meant, we soon would.

After the successful championship winning year of 1987 the Jaguar Group C cars would need only minor detail changes, but now the XJR-8's success began to work against TWR; new amendments to the Group C rules in the interests of parity were to be introduced for 1988. These changes could potentially harm the Jaguar XJR-8 more than the other competitors, but some parity was needed if all competitors were to stay in the series and continue the public interest formed over the preceding two years. TWR was not likely to agree with that sentiment, not wanting to compromise a winning formula, but it was now our turn to lose some of the advantage the opposition felt TWR had. The narrow V12 block's lower skirt width of 300mm (12in) had allowed steep tunnel profiles on either side of the engine, exiting through the suspension and driveshafts between the rear wheels and the gearbox to the rear. The Porsche 962C, in common with earlier derivatives, had a low mounted flat-six engine configuration that encroached in this important area. For 1988 the rules were amended to produce a much lower tunnel rear exit height. These lower heights would suit other competitors but give the TWR team a new set of parameters to have to set up, with the potential of lower downforce needing a review of strategy.

With the arrival of the IMSA programme for 1988, important decisions on commonality for best efficiency had to be addressed, with some differences in rules needing to be adopted to suit the basic car designs. A decision was made to adopt 17in wheel diameters across both Group C and IMSA, with the IMSA rules stipulating common diameters front and rear as opposed to the

17in front and 19in rear wheels used up to this point in Group C. It also made good sense financially, as well as having a common tyre inventory for Dunlop, along with the greater volume of important feedback produced from two separate teams using the same tyres.

With the adoption of the new 17in rear wheels and lower profile tyres came the opportunity to further enhance the engineering of the Group C cars in areas that would retain much of the performance and improve reliability. The introduction of smaller diameter rear wheels and tyres allowed some aerodynamic changes to the rear bodywork of the cars to try and compensate for the changes to tunnel exit heights. These changes included a lower profile engine cover and reduced bodywork height over the rear wheel arch area. Changes in this area produced better air flow to the rear wing and that allowed a revised mounting position lower down, better able to create a low pressure area behind the new lower venturi exits. A major result of these changes with the new Dunlop smaller diameter Kevlar tyre meant raising of the rear ride height to regain original ground clearance. This in turn raised the gearbox output drives to a higher position and removed most of the driveshaft angle that had produced problems previously, as well as allowing the drive shafts to travel above the lower tunnels, not through them as in 1987. All this meant that the proven 1987 package became obsolete, and produced a new aero and tyre programme for Group C. IMSA did not follow the Group C regulations and so the high venturi 1987 system and bodywork would be tested and carried over for those cars with the changes to 17in wheels housed within the 1987 Group C bodywork.

Speed and load testing became necessary with the new tyres which would be subject to the high speeds of Le Mans as well as the additional G-forces of the Daytona 31 degree banking over 24 hours. These tyre tests, carried out in late 1987 at the Daytona and Talladega banked circuits had proved Dunlop's Kevlar materials could safely operate when running at higher speeds and tyre loadings than previously seen. With the smaller diameter wheels and tyres, the Group C cars would have a lower volume of rear rubber available, and any effect this would have on endurance would have to be dealt with at the time. The March based 5-speed gearboxes now had their own bespoke TWR designed and manufactured magnesium bell housing and a casing with bespoke suspension and rear beam fixing points to make this unit part of the upgrade to produce the 1988 XJR-9 package, rather than being adapted for use as before.

After winning eight of the ten races in 1987 WSPC, only minor upgrades were made to the successful 7-litre engine package to be used in 1988 as the concept was working well, and TW was reluctant to fund any major changes as they did not fit his longer term plans that were already in place. My proposals for 1988 however were a considerable reworking of the engine to allow it to be lowered 50mm in the chassis by using a new sump system combining the engine main bearing caps, lightweight magnesium heads, second generation aluminium liners and titanium connecting rods, which along with other smaller details including titanium valves and side directed carbon induction system to allow a lower engine cover would have reduced the engine weight by 25 to 30kgs and improved air flow to the rear wing. This would be of

## Alastair Macqueen commented ...

The Group C tunnels required a much more inventive solution to retain the downforce and efficiency that was at the core of the cars' success. A number of different solutions were tried on the 25% wind tunnel model and the solution that gave the best results was probably not one anyone would have guessed at.

The forward 'collection area' under the car remained unaltered, as did the ramp angle up to the new permitted maximum height (about the same level as the driveshafts). From that point (about the leading edge of the rear wheel) the roof of the tunnels ran horizontal to the rear of the car at a whisker under the new regulation height. What was not controlled was the width of the tunnels and by carefully shrink-wrapping the gearbox area of the car, the air was allowed to continue its expansion in the horizontal plane. With the careful reduction in rear deck height and the optimisation of the rear wing position the XJR-9 retained virtually all the downforce of the '87 car and actually became slightly more efficient whilst maintaining the all important front split.

limited use if the 75kg gearbox could not be totally reinvented to be lowered by a similar amount as well which was where I felt an advantage lay. Roger had suggested if I wanted to go down that route I would have to design and manufacture the step gear arrangement needed to marry the lower engine installation with the original gearbox height, and that was not going to produce the complete change I felt was needed. For me we needed a bespoke TWR designed 6-speed gearbox with higher output drive centres, and this was deemed too hard by Roger.

To add pressure to the engine situation in September 1987 the IMSA organisers came out with totally new engine regulation proposals; resulting in the need for us to quickly develop and build a much smaller capacity 6-litre version of the Group C V12 engine for America.

The first race for this new smaller concept engine would be less than 10 weeks after the first prototype development engine had been built – and this race would be at the 24 hours of Daytona. With this new IMSA programme the final step in my development of the V12 engine was not going to happen, and retaining as much commonality between the two programmes was always a necessity driven by cost and the time available. Welcome to America.

## 1988 V12 engine updates

The engines for Le Mans continued to have a 12:1 compression ratio while others were converted with a new piston giving 12.5:1 compression and detailed changes to the squish lands. These new pistons were fitted with a revised ring pack consisting of a 1.5mm tapered face 'Napier' second compression scraper ring to reduce oil consumption, and ball bearing steel 1mm top compression rings. Another of the detail changes was to the twin throttle slides that had been attached to a common actuating lever, and had a single Lucas rotating throttle potentiometer delivering the throttle angle signal to the engine management system. This could allow small variations in converting the linear throttle slide movement to a circular potentiometer movement and this system was replaced for 1988. With the twin throttles set-up to move together, a new linear potentiometer was fixed to operate in parallel with the slides, giving

ENG TEST AND DATA SHEET.

| ENG. GRP C 2 VALVE V12 | ENG NO. 88C OS | DATE. 16/8/88 |
|---|---|---|
| OIL PRESS. 60 PSI | 45psi | CELL TEMP. 26.5°C |
| OIL TEMP. 80° | 100°C | HYDROM. 1025 -7 |
| WATER TEMP. 85° | 90°C | CORR. 1.034 |

| SPD. | LOAD. | HP. | IN" HG. | FUEL. | IGN. | CO% |
|---|---|---|---|---|---|---|
| 4000 | | | | | | |
| 4250 | | | | | | |
| 4500 | 107.6 | 500 | -8 | +2.5 | -2.5 | 2.5 |
| 4750 | 108.8 | 534 | -8 | +2.5 | -2.75 | 2.75 |
| 5000 | 112.7 | 582 | -7 | +2.5 | -2.5 | 2.5 |
| 5250 | 112.1 | 608 | -7 | +2.5 | -2.5 | 2.2 |
| 5500 | 111.8 | 635 | -6 | +2.5 | -2 | 2.6 |
| 5750 | 111.8 | 664 | -5.5 | +2.5 | -2.5 | 2.7 |
| 6000 | 112 | 694 | -4 | +2.5 | -2.75 | 3 |
| 6250 | 111.2 | 718 | -3.5 | +2.5 | -2.75 | 3 |
| 6500 | 108.8 | 731 | -1 | +2.5 | -2.75 | |
| 6750 | 105.8 | 738 | -3 | +3.5 | -3 | 3 |
| 7000 | 102.5 | 741 | 0 | +3.5 | -2.75 | 3 |
| 7250 | 100.5 | 753 | 0 | +2.5 | -2.5 | 3 |
| 7500 | | | | | | |
| 7750 | | | | | | |

| BORE / STROKE. 94 × 84. | COMP RATIO. 12.5:1 | |
|---|---|---|
| EXH LENGTH. | PRI. 22" 1⅞ | SEC. 23" 2¼ |
| PLUGS. N82G | CAMS. EA 15/15 100° | |
| PORT Ø. 40mm | DATA SET. NURBURG 2A | |
| FUEL. 4* | | |
| HIGH SPD DYNO. | | |

***There is now less than 1% change in torque between 5000 and 6000rpm. With the engine tested at 13.4 to 13.6 air/fuel ratio and a cell temperature of 26.5°. These are SAE corrected figures, using Barometric, Hydrometer and temperature correction tables to produce an industry SAE rating for this engine. Note 'IN HG' column indicating the crankcase vacuum produced with the help of the fourth scavenge section added for 1988. This was the most powerful 7-litre engine we ever produced using the wider period exhaust timing giving 100bhp per litre from a 2-valve 583cc cylinder at 6000rpm.***

a more consistent reading to the engine management, especially with lean part throttle settings. These high quality linear potentiometers had been designed for music recording studios and used as controls on their mixing tables during recording sessions. The engines were then fitted with an additional fourth pump segment to scavenge the right hand rear section of the sump as well as produce a greater crankcase depression. This addition had come from the results of oil retention tests on the Daytona banking in late 1987. The exhaust camshaft duration was increased by 8° with the specification called 15/15 and used to carry out a review of the exhaust system diameters and lengths.

While using a smaller diameter exhaust system in testing with the IMSA 6000cc engine, it was decided to retest the 6995cc Group C engine in this area and reassess the small torque hollow at 5500rpm. The end result was primary exhaust pipe lengths being reduced in diameter to 1.75in from 1.875in, joining a 3-piece collector into a secondary pipe with a diameter of 2.25ins reduced from 2.5. These two secondary pipes on each bank then entered a single 3in tail pipe over the gearbox and exiting either side of the rear wing mount. The final tail pipe length was not particularly critical, but was set at the length that needed to exit the car and the primary and secondary pipes tested with that length. The primary and secondary lengths were tested with 3in extension pieces initially and when a best result from these tests eventuated the final tests were carried out 1in at a time. These refinements now resulted in a torque curve that was within 2% of a flat line between 4750rpm and 6250rpm and produced 700bhp at 6000rpm on the 12.5:1 compression engines running 98 RON fuel (94 USA). The detailed exhaust and camshaft work had been concentrated on the 5250 to 6000rpm area and the V12 now produced its maximum torque at 5000 and 6000rpm, although as has been stated, this was as close to a flat line as you will get in any engine. The Group C 2-valve V12 engine was now producing 100bhp per litre at 6000rpm using a single cylinder capacity of 583cc.

The final development of the 2-valve 7-litre V12 for the 1988 season was now finished. Most of the changes coming from a refined exhaust system and an increase of 8° total duration on the exhaust camshaft profile to increase the power output above 6250rpm. Contributing to the improved top end power was the detailed work with the oil scavenging system both in the windage skinning tray and the fitting of a fourth oil scavenge system to the right-hand rear of the block.

Manufacturing processes that had been proven in previous years can change without notice and the heat treatment of some of our steel items, camshafts in particular, became one of these casualties. Health and Safety was catching up with the heat treatment industry and its use of cyanide, a deadly poison, in some of the processes used. Engs began having problems with the steel camshafts pitting after short running in 1987 and it was traced to a new heat treatment process trying to eliminate or use a process with greatly reduced cyanide. We had not been alerted to this by G Homer our heat treatment company and my visit to the company to see why things had changed also turned up another anomaly. Their chemical bath was changed once a week with its main use by vehicle manufacturers to heat treat cast iron components, and it was these components which were fouling the chemical bath by week's end, adding to the problem for non-cast iron materials. The fix

Note the radius on the edges of both sides of the camshaft lobe. Tilting of the cam follower or the slightest misalignment in the parallelism of the two components can lead to the very edge of the lobe initially striking the cam follower and breaking through the oil film before the cam follower can run in full contact with the lobe. This leads to radial scratch marks on the follower surface and while not causing any problems in a normal sprint specification life cycle, it meant that followers needed replacing each time. These hollow drilled camshafts were pressurised with oil to lubricate their main bearings and also the cam follower face, using a 1mm (0.040in) spark eroded hole on the heel of the lobe. This image shows the pitting of the surface when using the new heat treatment process dictated by Health & Safety changes in the heat treatment industry.

*camshaft lobe*

was all Engs consignments would now be treated on only one day in the week, immediately after the bath had been cleaned and new solution added each Monday morning. While this fixed most problems the camshaft results were still not good enough for a 24 hour engine and we had new cast iron items manufactured at Lidmet. Cast iron has better natural lubricating abilities with its carbon content and surface ability to retain lubricant compared to steel, and eventually all camshafts were converted over to cast iron material. The cast camshafts had a reduced central drilling for lightness to maintain strength and 1kg was added to the engine's rotating mass.

The best options for V12 engine development remained as stated earlier, redesign and replacement of cam carriers, camshafts and port detail which would make a substantial amount of current equipment obsolete, an expense that could not be justified by TW. This design, developed for ultimate power at 7400rpm with increased bore size allowing larger valve sizes creating an engine capacity of 7.2 litres using 13:5 compression ratio was capable of achieving 800bhp on 98 RON fuel; and could have been the specification for the next three years using the revised lower position lightweight engine that had been proposed to TW and Roger.

COSWORTH — COSWORTH ENGINEERING LTD.

Piston mass 1988

ST. JAMES MILL ROAD • NORTHAMPTON • NN5 5JJ • U.K.
Tel: (0604) 52444 Telex: 31454 Fax: (0604) 586380

Our Ref: JR/PG

6th June 1988

Mr Allan Scott
Tom Walkinshaw Racing Ltd
Engine Division
Unit 1
Station Field Industrial Estate
Kidlington
Oxford
OX5 1JD

Dear Allan

**C1 PISTON PA0856**

The current length given to us to reduce pins to coincides with our length for DFX and DFZ pins.

Externally, DFX and DFZ pins are the same but the DFZ pin has larger parallel and taper bores making it 18 gms lighter.

In an effort to reduce the weight of PA0856 we have modified the drawing to show the 18 gms lighter pin PA0987. The piston crown has been thinned off by .65mm and the 89mm radium at the botton of the piston has been deepened by .70mm.

The above features should show a reasonable weight reduction and will take effect on your batch of 100 pistons due mid-June.

Yours sincerely

J Roper
Manager Piston & Forge Depts

Registered in England No. 612057 Registered Office: St. James Mill Road, Northampton NN5 5JJ.

*Detailed changes to lighten the pistons were carried out and introduced during the year.*

## Version two of the 4-valve V12 engine

Engs had continued working on a prototype 7-litre V12 fitted with a new design of 4-valve heads after the original concept using Jaguar derived experimental heads had proved unsuccessful; and this work had taken up considerable effort and time during 1987. Al Melling, an independent designer, but not known to me, approached TW with his own design for the V12 at a fraction of the costs involved after another round of negotiations with Cosworth for design, pattern work, their unique low pressure up-draught casting technique and final machining. A meeting was organised at Kidlington and we were presented with some very basic drawing with the obvious needs for some redesign, especially the very large port diameters indicating a lack of understanding. I was not impressed with the basic square shapes and size of the concept; or Melling's partner producing large Group C Jaguar images for TW to sign, something that would soon hang on an office wall. She was a good communicator and presenter of Melling's work at the Kidlington meeting, and a programme was instigated by TW to build four prototype engines to this design. This would satisfy our contract with Jaguar and the exchange of technology involved with the initial JaguarSport funding contract. I had my doubts about the whole design process but TW felt the only way forward for the V12 was 4-valve heads, and he liked the very low initial costs, 10% of Cosworth's price.

Because of my workload the sub contract of tooling and manufacture was left to Melling and it soon became apparent that the results were not up to our standards or needs. Much later the first prototype was tested but our improvements to the 7-litre engine for 1988 meant that this experimental 4-valve did not produce large increases in power outputs at lower rpm compared to the well-developed 2-valve engine. Figures for fuel consumption at these lower rpms in its early stage of development could not justify any move to this being a must have for the 1000km races, hampered by its higher centre of gravity and increased weight of around 15kgs with steel valves and extra camshafts. It could, after considerable refinement be a better outcome for the 24 hour races with the lower lift camshafts producing a more reliable valve train, but the raised centre of gravity that had been experienced at Le Mans in 1987 producing a more unpredictable package when using a low downforce specification would negate much of any advantage.

After many disappointments I terminated the contract with Al Melling's company and refused a final payment of £20,000 which started court proceedings that resulted in no final payment being paid. Later claims of supplying technology for the winning Le Mans V12 engine and other technology that 'confidentiality' did not allow him to fully expand on continued to surface. This though was a constant theme for the programmes and not reserved for just TWR. Melling produced a successful single overhead camshaft two valves per cylinder V8 engine some time later for a sports car application, and it looked amazingly like a V8 version of our 2-valve V12 engine.

The use of this 4-valve engine at Brands Hatch covered some of the earlier contract liabilities with Jaguar and gave TW and Roger the ability to evaluate the situation for themselves to realise it was not the major step forward they had both always envisaged. The programme was then put on hold and final development left for another day. One of these engines would go on to be used in the prototype XJ220 sports car project produced by Jaguar and on show later at the NEC Exhibition Centre automotive show in Birmingham. I had to make decisions, and that would entail just covering the contract with Jaguar, the step forward that was envisaged at the very start had now passed. The IMSA rules suited 2-valve engines because of increased weight restrictions associated with 4-valve engines; and that was the final element that decided the V12's future configuration; to remain as currently used.

ENG TEST AND DATA SHEET.

| ENG. GRP C 4 VALVE V12 | ENG NO. 88 C 10 | DATE. 16/7/88 |
|---|---|---|
| OIL PRESS. 75 psi | | CELL TEMP. 20°c |
| OIL TEMP. 70°c | 100°c | HYDROM. 1022 −2 |
| WATER TEMP. 85°c | 90°c | CORR. 1.0235 |

| SPD. | LOAD. | HP. | IN" HG. | FUEL. | IGN. | CO% |
|---|---|---|---|---|---|---|
| 4000 | | | | | | |
| 4250 | | BHP/Litre | | | | |
| 4500 589 | 109.6 | 504 72 | 2 | −2.5 | −3 | 3.5% |
| 4750 602 | 112 | 544 77.7 | 2 | −3 | −2.5 | 3.3% |
| 5000 629 | 117 | 598 85.4 | 1 | −1 | −3.5 | 3.5 |
| 5250 631 | 117.5 | 631 90.1 | 1 | −.5 | −2.5 | 3.0 |
| 5500 606 | 112.8 | 634 90.6 | 0 | −2.5 | −2 | 2.8 |
| 5750 602 | 112 | 659 94.1 | 0 | −4.5 | −2.5 | 3.0 |
| 6000 624 | 116.2 | 713 101.8 | 0 | −1 | −3 | 3.8 |
| 6250 627 | 116.6 | 745 106.4 | 0 | −1 | −2 | 3.0 |
| 6500 616 | 114.3 | 760 108.5 | 0 | −1 | −1.5 | 3.0 |
| 6750 599 | 111.4 | 769.6 110 | 0 | 0 | −.5 | 3.0 |
| 7000 580 | 108 | 773 110.4 | 0 | 0 | −.5 | 3.5 |
| 7250 569 | 105.9 | 785 112.1 | 0 | −1.5 | −1.5 | 3.0 |
| 7500 | | | | | | |
| 7750 | | | | | | |

BORE / STROKE. 94 x 84 — COMP RATIO. 12.25:1

EXH LENGTH. — PRI. 29" 2" DIA — SEC. 20" 2½" DIA

PLUGS. C9E .028" GAP — CAMS. EA 17 100° TIMED.

PORT Ø. — DATA SET. 4V2 (E.M.2)

FUEL. 4*

NO AIR FILTER.

Gearchange Average 5500 – 7000 R.P.M. = 729.875 B.H.P.

***4-valve V12 engine driven at Brands Hatch by John Watson***

The power test for the initial 4-valve 7-litre V12 that later ran just the once at Brands Hatch in the hands of John Watson during 1988 can be seen above. The exhaust system had not been finalised, and was the early version used with the Jaguar factory heads in 1985, and this compromised the power output by at least 25bhp.

The joint venture with Holden Special Vehicles had also developed to the point where Engs had been tasked with the development of the production 307cu in Holden V8 engine to the Group A rules for saloon car racing in Australia, and possibly Europe as well. Pressure of work had made this programme last priority for me and TW was getting a little impatient with my lack of dedication to it. Holden was a major focus for him in 1988 with the takeover of the Holden Special Vehicles operation in Melbourne, and this would produce a long term profitable relationship with General Motors Holden and focus for the TWR Group. TW had all but stopped driving racing cars, and had now taken a keener interest in engines.

I had also finalised the development work to produce a 6-litre production 'HE' V12 engine for JaguarSport to replace Jaguar's current 5.3-litre engine in production, during the 1987 championship winning year. The production specification and emission control work was then handed over to the JaguarSport engineering department, based at Kidlington. While this was a separate department under Ian Brown, I had to relocate two fully trained V12 engine builders to JaguarSport to support the JaguarSport work. I was still required to review progress on that project via Anthony Moss, another former Engs employee, now project development engineer at JaguarSport. This 6-litre engine would later replace the original 5.3-litre V12 and become original equipment for all V12 powered Jaguars, with a considerable payday for TW.

Despite my own personal misgivings, TW was now more than ever focused on turbocharging as the future. At the end of 1986 a 12-month notice of termination for the TWR Rover programme had not been actioned by Austin Rover Motorsport, with changes in that manufacturer's top-level management seemingly unaware of the clause, and this lack of action carried a £100,000 penalty payable to TWR. There had been a disputed £100,000 fine earlier in the Rover programme with the British motorsport's governing body in 1984, with TWR eventually having to pay. Somehow Austin Rover Motorsport had forgotten to inform its superiors of the contract cessation penalty clause – for the same amount. This situation had led to a possible future dispute and it would be easier to take in kind rather than expensive court proceedings. The design rights and tooling of the engine for Austin Rover's Metro 6R4 rally car, a normally aspirated 90° uneven firing V6 engine, were now a written off asset within Austin Rover Motorsport. This engine had started to look very attractive to TW in mitigation; also, it could be transferable in a deal with Motorsport rather than troubling the upper echelons of the Austin Rover Group board. By mid-1987 this became a done deal, and TWR were owners of this engine, based on a cutdown Rover V8 block.

For me this was an action that you 'had to be careful that you get what you wished for'. At a time that seemed to be the height of success for us at Engs, TW and I had begun to see things differently. He was convinced both sports car programmes should go turbocharged with Max Heidegger in Liechtenstein producing most of the technological needs, with my help. His proposal was to be a 3.2-litre capacity because that was what Porsche used, and we now had the rights and tooling to the existing design of a normally aspirated engine that suited that philosophy – but had never actually been designed for the increased cylinder pressures involved with turbocharging!

My counter proposal, if we were to not carry out the ultimate 7.2-litre V12 development with lighter and lower engine and gearbox, was to use the heavy duty cross bolted Rover block as a basis to produce a 4.2-litre conventional even-firing V8 engine, fitted with a new 4-valve head design. Both 6R4 V6 and V8 engines retained the same bore centre and main head stud locations, because the V6 had grown out of the basic Rover block design. New head pattern work designs would simply carry an addition to the existing three cylinder per head design which we had access to. This 4.2-litre V8 format would be a lower-boost engine more suitable for all the anti-detonation reasons covered earlier. I also felt it may have a future as a production-based engine for Range Rover or Jaguar. TW's reasoning against that idea was that Jaguar would never use a V8, and it would look wrong in a Jaguar racing programme relying heavily on its point of difference, the V12 engine, in the American market. Yet somehow a V6 would.

After Ford's late takeover of Jaguar, the first thing they instigated was phasing out the V12 and replacing it with the V8 Jaguar was already developing. This therefore was a reason to follow the more compact V6 configuration was TW's thinking more likely to reflect a future Jaguar production engine. The focus for me during 1988 would be Group C with existing 7-litre and IMSA 6-litre engines, as well as the development of all new turbocharged engines for IMSA and Group C. The Group C unit would be low octane fuel consumption based unlimited size format, while the IMSA engine would be restricted to three litres, with air inlet restrictors but no fuel restrictions in quality and quantity. Each of these programmes would need a very different approach with little in common hardware or concept wise; but TW saw them as basically the same engine. Heidegger would develop and produce a Group C only version in parallel with Engs.

As TWR entered its second year of being the team to beat in Group C, the Sauber C9 with its 4970cc Mercedes Benz V8 engine, fitted with production 2-valve heads and twin KKK turbochargers was replacing the Porsche 962C as the key opposition. Much of the on-track development for the C9 was now in the hands of former TWR driver Jean-Louis Schlesser. The MP1.7 Bosch sequential engine management system had been fitted to these Mader tuned engines the previous year, but now the engine project had been taken in-house at Mercedes Benz. With their full weight behind this programme, Mercedes produced 30 race engines by the start of the season, almost three times the number of Group C V12 engines allowed in the TWR programme budget. This configuration was following a similar thought process, with the use of maximum torque off the corners and fast acceleration up to the area, around 250kph (155mph) where the sprint downforce bodywork began to suffer with excessive drag, and the time versus fuel consumed equation became a little less efficient. During the year Schlesser confirmed this V8 turbo engine was giving good fuel consumption using 1.65 bar (9.5psi) boost and 6500rpm with their production 2-valve heads. That low boost level was compatible with best ignition timing using 98 RON fuel; as we would confirm with the V6 turbo project during development in 1988,.

The works Porsche 962C was also to be fitted with the Bosch MP1.7 sequential engine management system in 1988, two and a half years after we had developed a sequential system for the V12, and this would extend its competitive life and continue to make it the car to beat at Le Mans. The new Bosch engine management system also had onboard driver controls as we had pioneered, controlling alternative fuel and boost strategies, and with its sequential injection timing the MP1.7 was now the state-of-the-art system. The downside for this smaller turbocharged Porsche engine was that it had to use 2.2 bar of boost, which was a cylinder pressure that 98-octane was not suited to.

### *TWR and Jaguar's IMSA contract*

| | |
|---|---|
| Date: | 5 June 1987 |
| Parties: | Jaguar Cars Limited<br>Tom Walkinshaw Racing Limited |
| Price: | Fee for 1988 = £4,289,000. Fee for next 2 years to be agreed in August and Sept of preceding year or else increased by US RPI in default of agreement. TWR or team personnel keep all prize and starting monies. [Note development services during 1987 of £654,000 to build IMSA versions of Group C cars] |
| Annual Fee: | Payable 1/3 on Oct 1 of year preceding and balance in 4 equal instalments on Jan 1, April 1, June 1 and Aug 1. |
| Championship: | IMSA CAMEL GT Championship for prototypes – 15 races |
| Team: | [Sponsor] Jaguar Team – [sponsor was subsequently Castrol] |
| Number of Cars: | 2 Cars |
| Drivers: | Chosen by TWR with Jaguar's approval. Each driver to be available to Jaguar by mutual agreement. |
| Extra Races: | plus or minus up to 3 at £108k each. Additional races by negotiation |
| Sponsorship: | Jaguar decides the complete livery of the racecars and team. |
| Term: | 1988, 1989 and 1990 and if not extended to terminate on 31 Dec 1990 |
| Termination: | Usual right for termination upon breach etc. Jaguar could also terminate for convenience depending upon timing by paying for a termination before 1988 of 90% of the 1988 fee, for a termination in 1989 upon payment of 45% of the outstanding balance plus 45% of the 1988 fee and for an early termination in 1990 upon payment of 45% of any unpaid balance for 1990. |
| Renewal Notice: | Jaguar to advise not less than 6 months before end of contract (Dec 1990) whether it wants to extend and if so on what terms. |
| Obligations: | Enter not less than 2 cars at each of the Championship races; act as the official Jaguar works team; Tom to attend each race wherever possible. |

**Tom Walkinshaw Racing Ltd**

1988 IMSA CALENDAR.

| Date | Venue | Duration |
|---|---|---|
| 30/31 January | DAYTONA<br>Florida | 24 Hours |
| 28 February | MIAMI<br>Florida | 3 Hours |
| 19 March | SEBRING<br>Florida | 12 Hours |
| 10 April | ROAD ATLANTA<br>Gainesville, Georgia | 3 Hours/500 Kms |
| 24 April | WEST PALM BEACH<br>Florida | 3 Hours |
| 30 May | LIME ROCK<br>Conneticut | 150 Laps/3 Hours |
| 5 June | MID-OHIO<br>Lexington, Ohio | 3 Hours/500 Kms |
| 3 July | WATKINS GLEN<br>New York | 3 Hours/500 Kms |
| 17 July | ROAD AMERICA<br>Elkhart Lake, Wisconsin | 3 Hours/500 Kms |
| July 31 | PORTLAND<br>Oregon | 3 Hours/500 Kms |
| 7 August | SEARS POINT<br>Sonoma, California | 2 Hours/300 Kms |
| 4 September | SAN ANTONIO<br>Texas | 3 Hours |
| 12 October | COLUMBUS<br>Ohio | 300 Kms/2½ Hours |
| (9 October TENTATIVE | NORFOLK<br>Virginia | 3 Hours) |
| ~~23 October~~ 6 Nov | DEL MAR<br>California | 2 Hours |

*The 1988 American IMSA race schedule.*

JAGUAR

## Chapter Sixteen

# IMSA 1988

**As the successful 1987 Group C Championship had wound down the focus had turned to Jaguar's new programme in America – IMSA. Various locations had been analysed for logistical and workforce recruitment reasons and then the final choices left to the local knowledge of the new management team. After looking at Indianapolis, home of the Indy 500, TW agreed with Tony Dowe to base the new team further north in Indiana in a small University town called Valparaiso, situated a short drive east across the state border from Chicago with its global communication airport hub. The settling in period for the new team would be very short indeed, given that its first challenge was in January of the new year – the Daytona 24 hour race in Florida.**

While the Group C and IMSA USA series were very similar in basic rules, there were differences that would need special attention. Detail changes between the Group C and IMSA cars were the increased fuel tank size from 100 litres to 120 litres. The IMSA wheel regulation would mean a logistical decision had to be made based on costs, as well as tyre sizes available from Dunlop for both programmes. The solution we chose was 17in diameter wheels. The IMSA race cars used the original 1987 Group C bodywork and venturi tunnels. Both Group C and IMSA cars shared a common central tub allowing flexibility between any of the three configurations needed; low drag Le Mans, high downforce IMSA and medium downforce Group C. The IMSA minimum car weights were on a sliding scale depending on the type of engine being used and this was set by the IMSA regulators to give some parity to the series. Both Jaguar car types were designated XJR-9 for 1988 with three cars available to the American team. Chassis 188 and 388 were former 1987 Group C cars while chassis 288 was a completely new car. These were all fitted with the larger 1987 Group C specification ground effect tunnels and bodywork, known among the American team as 'Watfords' as opposed to the lower 1988 specification Group C tunnels known as 'Dartfords', named after car tunnels in the London area for those not familiar with these origins.

The main differences in the engine rules for IMSA were freedom of high octane fuels, but without special additives such as oxygen bearing nitrous agents. The second was an engine limit of 6.5 litres which we could live with from our previous experiences with the Group C engine in 1986. A case had then been put forward by TW for the normally aspirated engine capacity in IMSA to be increased to seven litres, and this had appeared to be eventually ratified by the IMSA governing body later in 1987. This made a lot of sense for TW as Engs had only to design a new high compression piston to go with the high octane fuel available. To improve top end power a wider camshaft period would be used and this along with remapping the management system and small changes to the exhaust to enhance top end power would be a relatively straightforward solution for this 100% increase in Engs workload; along with its Trans Atlantic logistics of supply. Engs would have a standardised 7-litre engine, with base units being transferable within both race series, with the simple change of pistons and camshafts and associated engine management details. For TW this was all going to be a walk in the park and I need not have any concerns, it would all be relatively easy. It needs to be remembered that unlike Group C, the fuels allowed for the turbocharged engines in IMSA were to a very high specification, and allowed much higher boost levels at lower engine rpm when used with their mandatory pre-compressor 57mm air restrictor. The IMSA air restrictor specification allowed similar maximum bhp outputs but also high boost levels at lower rpm and this produced an engine with high corner exit torque, something we also had with the 7-litre V12, but not with a smaller capacity V12 engine.

The conservative IMSA officials had then issued a bulletin later in 1987 saying they wanted to increase the emphasis on 'ground effects' downforce aerodynamics and move forward with current world thinking. This bulletin though did have a certain uneasy feeling of potential politics to it. It was also all probably too good to be true, the 7-litre V12 engined ground effects XJR-8 had soundly beaten Porsche in 1987 using these two combinations, and the locals were most unlikely to roll over. After little discussion a second bulletin had then been issued and the earlier thought process had completely reversed. It declared that all race cars were to maintain a minimum 'ride height' or ground clearance of 2in (51mm). This gap between the underside of the car's bodywork and the road was unrestricted in Group C, and played an important part in producing the downforce generated by being close to the ground; the underbody venturi shape needed close proximity to the road surface for best effect.

There had then been a second regulation change in September; the ruling allowing an engine capacity of seven litres had again been challenged by team owners, resulting in a new class for 2-valve single overhead camshaft engines to be introduced for 1988 – with *reduced* engine capacity. This was directly aimed at our Jaguar V12 engine as all of the other large capacity engines competing in IMSA were based on American push rod V8s and they would be exempt from reduced capacity. This ruling resulted in a reduced engine capacity limit to six litres (366cu in), which just happened to affect us only. TW's engine philosophy of having a common base engine was about to be turned on its head. This process had been presented to us as the IMSA regulators being prepared to help us, but then being overruled by all the competitors – welcome to American politics. It can also be safely assumed that had the American Group 44 team continued with Jaguar's race programme in 1988, these rules would not have eventuated.

With Jaguar now having won the WSPC title, and soundly beating the Porsche 962C in the process, the mainstay of the IMSA series, single turbo Porsche 956 and 962 derivatives had looked under threat. I could have lived with the status quo of 6.5 litres (396cu in) as it had always shown to be a good compromise for this V12 engine. Logistically we also still had a few parts, crankshafts and pistons from the 1986 programme to get us started. Now the reduction to six litres would need the manufacture of new long lead items, as well as reduce our competitiveness to a dangerous point. The single turbocharged cars with their air restrictor of 57mm for their 3-litre engines in 1988 were capable of producing an easy 750bhp with high boost corner exit torque from the current range of turbocharged engines Porsche and Nissan were using.

We had therefore suffered a backlash from our competitiveness and world success, with IMSA now making up rules to support its turbocharged local teams. The 6.5-litre V12 engine was very effective, the extra half litre with longer stroke crankshaft adding that all important flexibility on the tighter road circuits. Perhaps the 1987 IMSA engine options should not have been challenged by TW in the first place. TW and Roger though were of the opinion that IMSA would be easy coming from their feelings that the UK technology was superior and the fact they had just won a world championship. Being new to the American scene they also did not have the same influence or relationships with the sport's administrators as they had in Group C, but that thought seemed irrelevant. As far as I was concerned from an engine point of view I believed we were screwed by these biased engine capacity rules from the very start. The USA Nissan team had been through a troubled couple of years and had suffered from reliability problems and most had advised us that they would not be a threat, so all of Kidlington's evaluations of the opposition were based on our knowledge of the Porsche 962.

Tom Walkinshaw however never put up any real fight over the engine capacity change, convinced his future lay with a turbo derivative six-cylinder engine soon in the future. This was a thought process that was being influenced by his association with Max Heidegger in Liechtenstein where TW had placed experimental work for JaguarSport – turbocharging a road going version of Jaguar's AJ6 engine, and now Group C with turbo.

While TWR Group C and TWR America had their separate teams in separate countries, Engs would now service both teams from the UK. Brian Sheridan was recruited in the USA to be the Engs representative based in Valparaiso. His responsibilities were engine movements and rebuild co-ordination with increasing trackside support as his experience grew allowing him to service any minor engine repairs. The first race of the year for Engs was to be in January, the Daytona 24 hour, not four months later in April as it would be with the Kidlington Group C programme. This timetable now put Engs into a situation where all of the year was full-on supporting races. The normal pre-Christmas through New Year time was where annual holidays would be taken, these people were now needed to lend considerable support to the USA series. We were in trouble with the late change to the reduced engine capacity ruling; not forgetting that this new unproven 6-litre engine design was to have its first outing at a 24 hour race.

I produced a proposal showing the IMSA restrictor size was too large given the proposed 6000cc limit for our normally aspirated V12 engine based on known facts from the Formula 3 air restricted formula, and these were sent to Ian Reed at Valparaiso and subsequently submitted to the IMSA governing body for their comment (see page 182).

With this presentation and limited discussion afterwards, the rules remained the same. TWR at this time had mainly been up against a three-car Porsche factory team, in a series where the advanced engine management systems and fuel consumption technologies were out of the reach of most private teams, putting them at a disadvantage to us in Group C. In IMSA there were many highly competitive private Porsche teams as well as the emergence of Nissan after a couple of consolidation years, in this unrestricted fuel formula series. TW's recalcitrance in pushing for a normally aspirated capacity equivalent indicated to me that he was already committed in his mind to phasing out the V12.

With the limited end of season testing behind the new TWR IMSA team it was a case of working through the festive season to get the three cars ready for the long haul from Valparaiso in the north of the USA all the way down south to Daytona in Florida. Guy Edwards who had delivered the Silk Cut sponsorship to the Jaguar Group C team had produced a deal with Castrol to provide some of the sponsorship for the USA based IMSA team.

Having the 24 hour race at Daytona added to the TWR racing calendar five months before the Le Mans race was a good move for the TWR racing group as a whole; with time available between these two long distance races to act on any lessons learned. The new IMSA team under Tony Dowe would also add a second dimension to TWR's third attempt at Le Mans, a second self-contained team with 24 hour experience to add support to the UK Group C team. It was with this in mind that IMSA and Group C cars would share interchangeable parts wherever possible, to make logistical and financial sense. With the adoption of 17in wheel diameters for both series, this move would double the feedback on the different compounds and constructions available from Dunlop, and test these over a wide range of conditions that included track temperatures and varying road surfaces.

All race engines would be air freighted from the UK via Chicago airport to the USA base at Valparaiso, and Charlie Bamber and I would provide backup support on race days as well as supporting the Group C world programme. Used 6-litre engines from the IMSA series would be air freighted back to Kidlington in the UK for rebuild and dyno testing before being rotated back to Valparaiso.

The idea behind the addition of the American IMSA team was mainly a financial one, being able to leverage utilisation of team infrastructure systems in the UK. TWR America could be supplied with previously

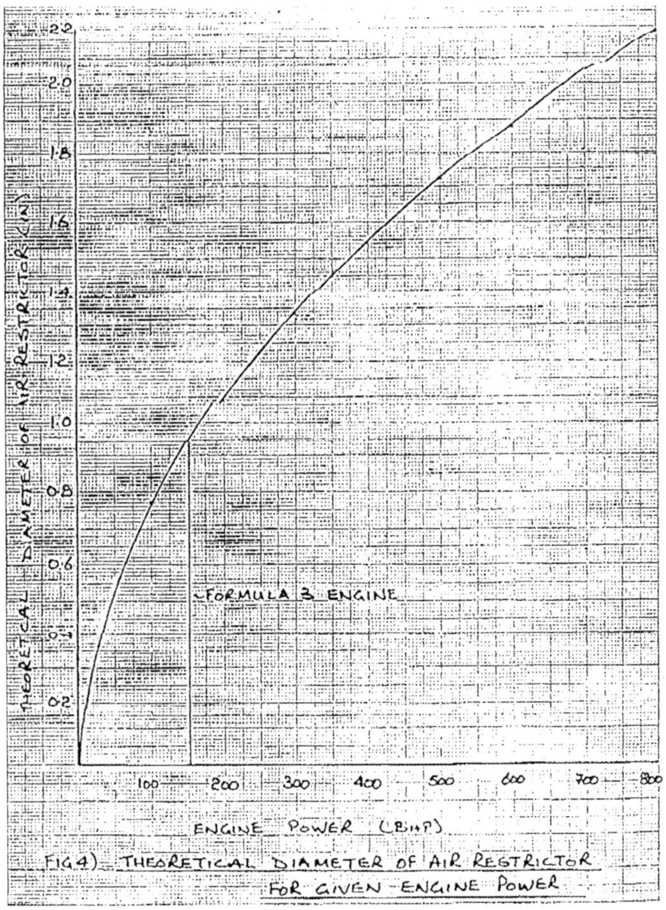


*Estimated power outputs for normally aspirated engines using various sizes of air restrictor.*

**Tom Walkinshaw Racing Inc.**

1001 Sturdy Rd., Valparaiso, IN 46382

December 3, 1987

Mr. Mark E. Raffauf
Vice President, Operations
I.M.S.A.
P.O. Box 3465
Bridgeport, Conn. 06605

Dear Mark,

T.W.R. recently commissioned an engineering study to determine how the new I.M.S.A. 1988 rules will affect us, from both an engine and chassis standpoint. There is one aspect of the study that I think you should be made aware of.

I attached the results of this study relating to air restrictors and engine horse power.

If you read through the attached sheets you will see that the size of air restrictor required to give a maximum horsepower of 600 H.P. is about 48 mm. A 1988 spec restrictor of 57 mm should give considerably more than that. Looking at the attached graph, I estimate that a 57 mm restrictor should allow around 800 H.P. A 54 mm restrictor should give around 725 H.P.

While I appreciate that I.M.S.A. must have conducted an exhaustive study in order to have specified 57 mm for the size of an inlet restrictor, I would like to alert you to the fact that a 57 mm restrictor will allow significantly more than the 600 H.P. that I.M.S.A. have announced as their intended maximum H.P.

Needless to say, a 6 liter, normally aspirated, 2 valve per cylinder engine will not produce more than 620-630 H.P.

I appreciate that the 1988 rules have already been announced and that there is good reason to "wait and see" before revising the rules. However, I believe that an air restrictor revision will become necessary. At this time, could you please consider a revision to 50 or 48 mm in order to bring all engine power outputs down to around 600 H.P.

I would appreciate your comments on this matter.

Sincerely,

T.W.R., INC.

Ian Reed
Chief Engineer

Enclosure

CC: Tom Walkinshaw
Roger Silman
Alan Scott
Tony Dowe
File

*My proposal for equality within the new engine regulations.*

used Group C recycled, obsolete, or repaired carbon bodywork because of its 50kg higher minimum weight limit. This to some extent made the IMSA team's job initially harder as some of the hand me downs needed considerable re-work to produce the effective car that Tony Dowe and Ian Reed were determined to produce.

## Testing programme in the USA

Two IMSA specification cars were sent to the USA and run at the Big Spring, Texas, airfield track for the first shakedown test supported by Kidlington personnel, some of whom made the move to Valparaiso in late 1987. The cars were then taken to Daytona in Florida for an extended test, fitted with Group C engines as the new 6-litre units needed with the last-minute rules change were still in manufacture. This test was mainly to prove the new Dunlop tyres on the smaller 17in diameter rear wheels, previously 19in.

The track used at Daytona for the 24 hour race is a mixture of the NASCAR east banking and main straight, then turning left down onto the slower infield section, more like a conventional race circuit, then rejoining the banked track at the end of the NASCAR back straight. It did not need lots of drag inducing downforce on the NASCAR banking part of the circuit, but then needed all it could get on the slower infield section. The tyre test was to see how the tyres stood up to the additional loading produced by the 31° banking on this circuit, as we had no previous experience in that area. TW could not resist the opportunity to announce TWR to the American media with some fast times from this test while using the 7-litre engines, making the efforts Ian and myself had been making to challenge the oppositions air restrictor sizes redundant overnight.

For us at Engs this Daytona test also showed up a small problem with our oil scavenge system. The Daytona race is run in an anti clockwise direction, while all the Group C races were run in a clockwise direction, with the oil scavenge system more suitable for the clockwise direction. A test was carried out with John Nielsen running the car flat out around the banking and then switching the engine off at its exit onto the straight at around 190mph (305kms), then turning down the track and onto the fortunately wide pit lane entrance, freewheeling at high speed in neutral into the pit area. The engine cover was then quickly removed and oil tank level checked. This test revealed that two and a half litres (three-quarters of a US gallon) were not being returned from the engine, and that was the amount remaining in the right-hand corner of the engine with the higher G-forces produced on the banking. This oil was then coming in contact with high speed internal engine components and had produced higher than normal oil temperatures, and an unknown small amount of lost power through oil drag. This problem had been anticipated which was why we had carried out the test, and a basic fix designed before the test had been added to the build specification of the IMSA engines.

A new scavenge source was needed in the right-hand rear area of the engine and we came up with a retro fit internal pickup tube in that area and accessed by drilling through the block's lower skirt. This connected the internal gallery tube drilled with small holes to an additional scavenge line ducted around the front of the engine to the external oil pump. A redesign of the lightweight Heidegger oil pump added a fourth scavenge housing and pump gears, the best solution in the time available. This addition then became standard on all V12 engines by the start of 1988, helping to reduce oil temperatures and drag through crankshaft and oil contact. This area needed the complete redesign of the sump I had proposed with my V12 engine upgrade, but that had been dismissed on cost grounds with the future heading towards development of the V6 engine.

Just to show that nothing can be taken for granted, the race cars showed a problem with the water system and radiator that had never been experienced before, when inspected back at the new base in Valparaiso. The hard water of Florida had reacted in the hot engines and produces a white chalky substance that could potentially partially block a a radiator, or cause internal problems. In the future all water would come from the same source in Valparaiso and be carried to all the circuits in the transporter.

## Redesign of the V12 engine for IMSA

The change in regulations to reduce the engine capacity from seven to six litres was notified four months before the start of the Daytona 24 hour race, to be held in January 1988. This late notification forced an engine design concept that was dictated by time and my experience to date, and in the end left just the one solution. A new lightweight crankshaft design with a stroke reduced from the 7-litre engine's 84mm to 72mm was drawn up in the first instance as this was the longest lead time, and was machined by Farndon Engineering from Jaguar's stock of EN40B forgings. This concept allowed the use of the current Group C engines 94mm bore dimensions, cylinder liners; connecting rods, camshafts and valve gear being also retained. A new piston with a lower gudgeon pin position to produce a higher compression height to accommodate the shorter stroke, as well as a revised bowl shape to allow a 13.5:1 compression ratio was manufactured by Cosworth. The new head castings had 2mm smaller diameter inlet tracts machined to improve mid range torque, and were flat faced without the 3mm chamber as used on the 7-litre engines. The block, sump, and oil systems and ancillaries remained interchangeable on all engines. Detail changes to the intake system were developed later, but the throttle slide system and inlet trumpets remained as the Group C unit. The first engine returned 680bhp at 7250rpm using the Group C exhaust dimensions as time to test final exhaust dimensions and have them produced in time for the Daytona race was now out of the question.

The first engine was available by the end of November and shipped to Valparaiso in December to join the preparation for the Daytona 24 hour race the following January. The only change at this time to the Engs specification for the new 6-litre IMSA engine was the switch from Champion to Bosch spark plugs. This was purely for commercial reasons with Tony Dowe having secured their sponsorship support and they proved to be a good and reliable product. It was hoped that Brian Sheridan along with Don Beadle would move towards some post race services and minor repairs between engine rebuilds at Valparaiso, helping out with the inevitable transport problems between countries. With this in mind a store of engine supporting spares was assembled to be based with the team to use in servicing the 6-litre units.

Lastly, unlike Group C, the IMSA series had a noise limit at the trackside, and we were now just over this limit after testing, and a silencing system was needed. Further investigation showed that just one decibel measuring unit was used at each event and normally on the outside of the circuit. Before the Daytona race the two tail pipes that exited at the rear of the gearbox and faced downwards were modified. This modification consisted of the bent tailpipes being cut and having small butting flanges welded on and held together using a V band clamping system. When it was ascertained which side of the track the decibel meter was set up on, the 45 degree downward angled tailpipes were simply swivelled in the opposite direction and reclamped, pointing the noise away from the meter. This was just enough to lower the noise levels to the legal levels without the use of silencers.

And so it was that the TWR IMSA Jaguar team arrived at Daytona for its first race, and a 24 hour one at that. It would be a combined effort for this first race with TWR Castrol Jaguar USA being assisted by selected members from Kidlington in the UK.

***Statistics –***
***The only science that enables different experts using the same figures to draw different conclusions.***

*Testing at Daytona late 1987.*

*Chief Engineer Ian Reed, in correspondence dated November 4th and 10th, shows the detail he produced to get this new team on track and unify resources between the two countries. This was the first time a different engineer and team had been able to take a general view of the situation outside of Kidlington.*

From:- IAN REED November 4 1987

TECHNICAL SUMMARY OF DAYTONA TEST

1). TIRES

i). Tire Pressures were set much higher than normal.

Optimum COLD pressures were:-

22 psi L.H Front 32 psi R.H Front

30 psi L.H Rear 36 psi R.H Rear

ii). Tire Compounds

Front
Settled at 222 Right Front, 254 Left Front.

Rear
278 rears were best on both sides. Mixing constructions or compounds in the rear was not as stable or as quick.

Soft race tires (254 all round) did not improve lap times.

iii). Cambers
Optimized at -0.5 R.H Front, +0.5 R.H Rear.
LHS as standard.

iv). Tires need curing before extensive runs.

v). Constructions.

Non-V construction seemed slightly quicker but showed more heat build up in the tire carcass.
V construction showed less heat build up and would probably be the best race tire.

2). HANDLING

i). Standard geometry was fine.
ii). Disconnecting R.A.R.B improved traction off slow corners.
iii). No R.A.R.B loads outside front tire on banking.
iv). 1250 springs F. + R. seemed worse than 1500 F. + R.
v). STD F.A.R.B seems O.K
vi). Removing front packers really helped braking and corner entry.
vii). No rear packers either.
viii) 1 deg Front Castor for Daytona.
ix). 220 lbs of cross weight gives unsettled braking and uncertain entry into turns.

3). AERO

Reducing downforce helped lap time.
Final setting was Nose profile + 1 inch Front Splitter.
Rear wing Flap set at 16.5 degrees.
No other "Add Ons".

4). BRAKES

i). Bedded DS-11 pads best. Jap pads were too hard and seeme to coat the disks.
Temps look good with DS 11. Temps stabilized at

| | |
|---|---|
| 350 degC L.H Front | 350 degC R.H Front |
| 380 degC L.H Rear | 350 degC R.H Rear |

Higher L.H rear temp probably due to "Body Mods" ahead o the Brake duct.

ii). New thin wall, non-drilled disks look good. 24 Hour Spe Wear rates seem better with these disks.

iii). Car 188 suffered severe disk unbalance after approx. 250 miles.
This was probably due to warping.
All disks need to be carefully balanced.

5). ENGINES

| | | | |
|---|---|---|---|
| Engine # 10. | Car 188. | 181 Laps. | 644 Miles |
| Engine # 11 | Car 288. | 76 Laps. | 270 Miles |
| Engine # 5 | Car 288. | 233 Laps. | 829 Miles |

6). OIL SYSTEM

No real difference seen between the two oil pipe routes.
4 stage scavenge pump required.

7). FUEL SYSTEM

i). Fuel pickup seems OK.
ii). Filling seems OK.
iii). Heat appears to cause vapor locking after about 20/27 laps on a long run. Fuel temperature was seen at 52 deg.C, much higher than ever encountered before.

8). FUEL MILEAGE

Fuel mileages were :-

| | | |
|---|---|---|
| Car 188. | 3.95 Miles/U.S Gall | (3.41 liters/lap) |
| Car 288 | 4.03 Miles/U.S Gall | (3.34 liters/lap) |
| | 4.03 Miles/U.S Gall | (3.34 liters/lap) |
| | 4.19 Miles/U.S Gall | (3.21 liters/lap) |
| | 3.97 Miles/U.S Gall | (3.39 liters/lap) |

All of above were at #5 on the fuel knob with the main box set 3% (?) rich.

9). TRANSMISSION

Spool found to be slightly better than a diff.
Use Spool for 24 hour spec.

Final Ratios were :- 15/40
19/35
23/32
26/29
29/27

10). DAMPERS

No changes. As set up sheet.

11). WHEEL BEARINGS

A good set of standard bearings will last perhaps 18 hours.
Car 188 suffered a cage failure on the L.H Front.
Long Distance Set-up required.

12). ITEMS NOT TESTED.

i). Weight distribution changes.
ii). Lights and night driving.

PROBLEMS

(NOT IN ORDER OF IMPORTANCE)

A). HIGH UNDER ENGINE COVER TEMPERATURES.

HIGH OIL TEMPERATURE

i). Low air pressure drop across cooler.
ii). Poor air flow path to rear extraction point.
iii). Holes in tail only small improvement.
iv). Exhaust radiating heat to top of tail and back of airbox.
v). Air exit gap much smaller than Group C car.

PROPOSED SOLUTIONS

i). Machine series of holes in rear beam to allow better airflow. T.S to fax details to VALPO.
ii). Ceramic coat exhaust pipes.
iii). Water/ Oil Intercooler.
iv). Design small additional water cooler for tough cooling circuits.
This extra cooler to reside where current oil cooler is located.
v). Tail Mods.
Le-Mans type entry ducts in tail.
Louvres on top surface in rear.
Narrow up rear brake ducts for more louvre area.
vi) Design taller, narrower rear brake ducts.
vii). Heat insulate around front of engine with ceramic tile or equivalent thermal insulation.

B). MINOR ODD PROBLEMS.

i). Driver vents hit knees of J.N
ii). 2 Zytek boxes failed on Car 288.
iii). Problems with fit of output flanges and hubs.
iv). Rear Wheel covers are sucked in and rub against the rear tires
v). Wipers do not clear far enough on LHS of windscreen for driving on banking.
vi). Front Brake duct hosing needs better fixing on chassis end.
vii). Rear wheel arch plastic pads are sucked down and need fixing up in the center of each pad.
viii) Quick release steering does not release on car 288.
ix). Tacho red light comes on at 5000 rpm and then glows at increasing intensity up to 7000 rpm.
x). Air jack venting. New system is 3.44 secs to drop car.
Old system is 2.34 secs to drop car.
xi). Water Hose came off. Thick wall hose vs. jubilee clip clamping force.
AVIMO's ?
xii). Rear wing flap end rib delaminated. Old Flap ?

C). DAYTONA RACE PROBLEMS

i). Signallers are based away from pits. How are we going to do communications ?

D). IMSA TEAM PROBLEMS

i). Pocket Steel and Ali wheel nuts for wheel gun sockets.
ii). Sort wheel air gun problem.
iii). Finalize air lift design.
iv). Calibrate all springs on spring tester.
v). Put Bilsteins on shock dyno.
vi). Get Flat plate.
vii). Check all rear wing calibrations are the same.
viii) Need passenger seat for 288.
ix). Proper printed job lists.
x). Proper box for Pit Signal signs.
xi). Standardize rear axles ?
xii). Proper tire dia tape.
xiii) Organize some oil and water drip trays.
xiv). Gate hinges for rear wheel covers for quick pit stops.
xv). Need an "OK" sign for pit signals.
xvi). Brake pyrometer for each car.
xvii) Throttle cable shield by throttle pedal for all cars.
xviii) Get Spring color coding chart.
xix). Secure water temperature on 288.

From:- IAN REED | ISSUE 3 | November 10 1987

POST DAYTONA TEST PROBLEMS

PROBLEMS THAT REQUIRE U.K ATTENTION

HIGH UNDER ENGINE COVER AND OIL TEMPERATURES

| ACTION | | SOLUTIONS |
|---|---|---|
| TS | 1). | Machine series of holes in rear beam to allow better airflow. T.S to fax details to USA. |
| TS | 2). | Water/ Oil Intercooler. |
| TS | 3). | Design small additional water cooler for tough cooling circuits. This extra cooler to reside where current oil cooler is located. |
| AM/TS | 4). | Do we need a bigger water cooler if we use the heat exchanger ? |
| TS | 5). | Tail Mods. Le-Mans type entry ducts in tail. Louvres on top surface in rear. Narrow up rear brake ducts for more louvre area. |
| TS | 6). | Design taller, narrower rear brake ducts. |

OTHER CAR PROBLEMS.

| | | |
|---|---|---|
| AM | 1). | Driver vents hit knees of J.N. Has there been a design mod ? |
| AM | 2). | 2 Zytek boxes failed on Car 200. |
| AM | 3). | Problems with fit of output flanges and hubs. |
| AM | 4). | Rear wing flap end rib delaminated. Old Flap ? |
| WB | | Solution:- UK to investigate. WB to send back part. |
| AM | 5). | Rear Axle/Drive Flange coned washer is too tight on I.D. and was a problem in the upright changes. |
| AM | 6). | Winston and Billy think that with the current disk mounting arrangement, it is possible for a brake disk to be assembled slightly eccentric to the axle center line. There is then no way for the disk to return to concentricity. |

ENGINE RELATED PROBLEMS

| | | |
|---|---|---|
| AS | 1). | Engine oil leak in car 288 ? What was the real cause ? |
| AS | 2). | Engine Oil Breathers. What is correct latest spec. ? |

OTHER ITEMS REQUIRING UK ACTION.

1). Long Distance axle assys on 1 car (Car 188) at Big Spring.
2). High Downforce tail on 388 at Big Spring.
3). 6 Liter Engines and ancillaries for 188 and 288. Exhaust systems for 188 and 288 ?
4). Unglued, changeable windscreens for all 3 cars at Daytona.
5). Bodywork stock levels. IMSA is a "Contact Sport". We need to discuss stock levels and supply lead times of noses and tails ?
6). No Center tail support for 188. 2 spares please.

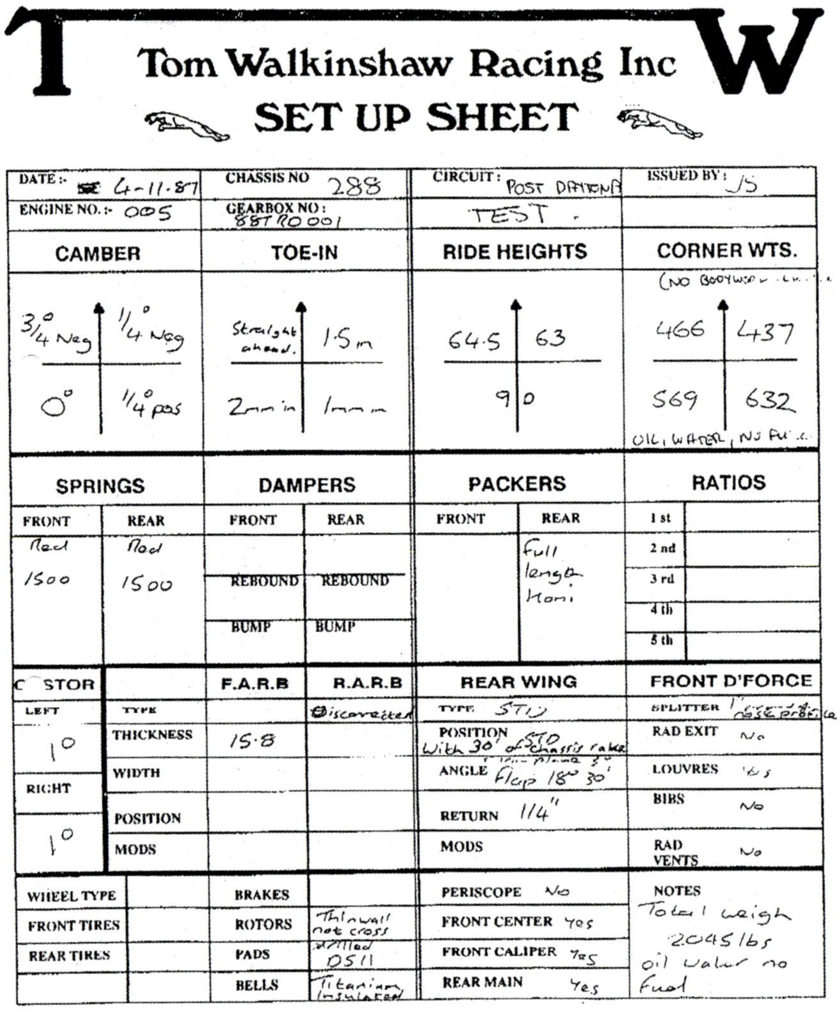

Tom Walkinshaw Racing Inc

SET UP SHEET

| DATE :- 4-11-87 | CHASSIS NO 288 | CIRCUIT : POST DAYTONA | ISSUED BY : JS |
|---|---|---|---|
| ENGINE NO. :- 005 | GEARBOX NO : 88TR0001 | TEST . | |

| CAMBER | TOE-IN | RIDE HEIGHTS | CORNER WTS. |
|---|---|---|---|
| 3/4° Neg / 1/4° Neg | Straight ahead. / 1.5m | 64.5 / 63 | (NO BODYWORK [illegible]) 466 / 437 |
| 0° / 1/4° pos | 2mm in / 1mm [illegible] | 9 / 0 | 569 / 632 OIL, WATER, NO FUEL |

| SPRINGS FRONT | SPRINGS REAR | DAMPERS FRONT | DAMPERS REAR | PACKERS FRONT | PACKERS REAR | RATIOS | |
|---|---|---|---|---|---|---|---|
| Red | Red | | | | Full length Honi | 1st | |
| 1500 | 1500 | REBOUND | REBOUND | | | 2nd | |
| | | BUMP | BUMP | | | 3rd | |
| | | | | | | 4th | |
| | | | | | | 5th | |

| CASTOR | | F.A.R.B | R.A.R.B | REAR WING | FRONT D'FORCE |
|---|---|---|---|---|---|
| LEFT | TYPE | | Disconnected | TYPE STD | SPLITTER [illegible] nose profile |
| 1° | THICKNESS | 15.8 | | POSITION STD With 30' of chassis rake | RAD EXIT No |
| RIGHT | WIDTH | | | ANGLE [illegible] plane 3° Flap 18° 30' | LOUVRES Yes |
| 1° | POSITION | | | RETURN 1/4" | BIBS No |
| | MODS | | | MODS | RAD VENTS No |

| WHEEL TYPE | | BRAKES | | PERISCOPE No | NOTES |
|---|---|---|---|---|---|
| FRONT TIRES | | ROTORS | Thin wall not cross | FRONT CENTER Yes | Total weigh 2045 lbs |
| REAR TIRES | | PADS | drilled DS11 | FRONT CALIPER Yes | oil water no |
| | | BELLS | Titanium Insulated | REAR MAIN Yes | Fuel |

*Different suspension set up was needed for Daytona's banked circuit.*

*Zytek engine management box showing external programme over-ride controls.*

Chapter Seventeen

# TWR enters the American scene

**The Kidlington team flew from Heathrow via Atlanta along with some delays, the linking flight to Daytona stopped off in Jacksonville just to add to the late 1am in the morning arrival after 14 hours and little sleep; before the 8.30am start the next day. Some of the first nights leading up to this major race at Daytona have a late working restriction with a curfew of 6pm in place, mechanics need to finish work early. This ensured that cars would need to be well prepared before they arrived at Daytona, and eliminated poorly prepared last-minute entries from doing 'all nighters' and the team being tired before the race even started.**

This was a rule that those from the UK were not used to and a job list that would take till 9pm had been assembled for Engs support technicians for the first day, with the mechanics needing to work late as well. As always, these things can be negotiated and when the official announced that we had 15 minutes before leaving it was time for me to brush off the New Zealand diplomatic skills, after all working with our USA friends would have to be easier than my previous experience in the1980s with the Czechoslovakian police. Negotiations were fairly one sided but we all kept calm and worked on. At five minutes to six the sheriff turned up, he had been summoned by radio and announced that anyone still inside the building at 6pm would be taken downtown. Tools began to be put away and overalls removed when precisely at 6pm the sheriff started pushing the buttons on the roller doors. The last ones out rolled under the doors with inches to spare. So it was an interesting welcome to the USA, any negotiating skills are trumped by those with guns, which I should have realised from the start.

We were also entering a new area with our V12 engines, using higher rpm and racing hard with no fuel limits to worry about, with more than a chance of missed gear shifts or early down-changes breaking the 8000rpm safe limit of the valve gear. After the first day of practice we set good times so I was summoned by the scrutineer and told that an engine capacity check was needed. Group 44 had entered with their XJR-7, now called an Eagle, and we had earlier overtaken their car during practice on the front straight and set considerably faster lap times with the TWR/Castrol/Jaguars. I had good connections with Cosworth and Farndon Engineering in the UK and had monitored work schedules out of America with both of these suppliers; and found that no new parts that would be needed for a 6000cc V12 had been produced for Group 44.

The engine from car 61, #88I06, was selected by the scrutineer and removed from the car and taken to a secure building where with one head removed the capacity check began. Engine removal was not a problem for us as some engines were down to be changed because we had not had enough time to fit the fourth oil scavenge system to all the engines. Because this process included drilling a hole in the side of the block, the fourth scavenge system could not be retro fitted without dismantling back at Kidlington. The difference between USA cubic inches and the European metric capacity was my concern and I asked how many decimal places the metric conversion rate would be taken so that we could agree on the conversion calculations. I was given a no comment look as the scrutineer proceeded to produce a 6in imperial [inches] steel rule from his top pocket to measure the bore diameter, and then the stroke. I asked again what conversion factor he was going to use to convert cubic inches to metric litres as we were right on the 6-litre capacity limit but the IMSA rules were in cubic inches. "Do not worry sir, I am just checking to see that it is not *seven litres*" was the disarming reply from the IMSA scrutineer. This was an amazing statement to make and left me wondering what other competitors might be doing; if it had been 6005cc with a UK scrutineer it would have been out of the race, with qualifying times disallowed and a large fine. It was obvious that something had been said after the Jaguar's qualifying times were very close to the earlier testing times set with our 7-litre engines. He then agreed that our engine was 6-litres, although it seemed to me at the time if we had been the previous limit of 6500cc,that he would have given the OK, as it would not have been the seven litres he had been asked to check for.

Just before the Saturday race start at 3.30pm team manager Tony Dowe was asked by the media how he thought things would go for the new team and in his usual confident way replied, "Well we are going to win it aren't we.""No point in being superstitious then," were my thoughts on hearing that.

Jaguar America boss Mike Dale had discussed the differences between European and American thinking with me before this race started, and emphasised that it was more of a 'show' in America. He had been asked by a couple of long-time Jaguar supporters who were guests at this event if I could put some Castrol R oil in the fuel to give that special aroma in the pit lane that they used to get from the D-type Jaguar's at Le Mans in the 1950s. America was a bit different and I doubt the expression on my face completely hid my thoughts about that request.

Qualifying for the Sunbank Daytona 24 hours race was TWR's first real introduction and test for the American scene, up against the turbocharged engines of Porsche and Nissan, both capable of producing at least an additional 50bhp more than our engine. Qualifying was a single-car format held on the Thursday in colder conditions than normal. Jaguar #60 were off to a bad start with an 11-cylinder engine that had to be changed, finding out later that an incorrectly fitted wiring loom had stopped one of the injectors from functioning.

> The Wollek/Baldi/Redman 962 Busby/BF Goodrich Porsche took pole position with 1:38.917.

This was followed by a brave lap from Lammers whose Jaguar understeered onto the banked section after a desperate attack of the last infield chicane with his race car sliding all the way up the four-lane wide 31° banking to clip the perimeter guard rail with the rear wing end plate and scratch some paint work as well.

> Lammers/Sullivan/Jones in #61 Jaguar stopped the clock at 1:39.362, followed by Cobb/Dyson/Weaver/Schuppan in the Dyson/Blaupunkt Porsche 962 on 1:40.176, and Cheever/Dumfries/Watson in the #66 Jaguar 1:40.179, with Sigala/Brancatelli/Larrauri (962 Brun/Torno Porsche) 1:40.611. Brundle/Nielsen/Boesel's #60 Jaguar clocked 1:40.716 with their race engine fitted and set to the 7200rpm race limit while the other two had 7800rpm available.

The Group 44 Eagle with Tullius/Ganz/Haywood driving had qualified fourteenth with a 1:44.86 and this had vindicated Jaguar America's decision to back TWR. This close qualifying had elevated the competition at Daytona to a new degree and TWR/Castrol/Jaguar had announced their arrival, in the process finishing any chance of reverting to the previous engine limit of 6500cc. Al Holbert's team had won the two previous 24 hour races and was the favourite to win again; Porsche had won the last 11 races held on this banked oval and infield race track, and TWR Jaguar were the first to seriously challenge this dominance in a very long time.

## 1988 Daytona Race Personnel

### AMERICAN TEAM

**Accommodation – January 26**

PIRATES COVE BEACH LODGE:
3501 South Atlantic Avenue
Daytona Beach Shores, FL 32019

TEL: (904) 767-8740 - Jodi

Winston Bush/John Simmonds
Carl Azevedo/Mike Hughes
John Jackson/Butch Winkle
Phil Denny/Mark Pivec
John McLellan/Jim Faulconer
Frank Rafferty/Frank Varela
Ira Chez/Dave Girton
Howard Minckler/Larry Zelesnik

Alan Turner
Larry Randlett
Graeme Fuller/Brian Sheridan
Gloria Blaha/Louis Blaha
Steve Ave/Rose Ave

Derek Clarson
John Williams

Ken Kirkpatrick
Scott Martin
John Clifford
John Ward
A. Nichols
J. Murphy
Mick Canning
Vick Fincher

Mr. Neilsen Sr. Arrival 29th

Craig McCann

### KIDLINGTON TEAM

**Depart London Gatwick – January 27**

Roger Silman
Tony Southgate
Alastair Macqueen
Kevin Lee
Allan Scott
Clive Parker
Jeff Wilson
Alva Claxton
Jerry Pyman
Mark Owen
Keith Partridge
Chris Partridge
Glen Barber
Steve Gray
David Vinson (to confirm)
Tom Ryan
Charlie Bamber

## The Sunbank Daytona (24 hours) – January 30–31st

A total of 75 race cars had taken the starting flag and early on the Jaguars found it hard to keep up the hectic pace, and by the time of the first pit stops all three Jaguars were struggling to stay on the same lap as the leaders. Half a dozen Porsches moved ahead of us with Weaver eventually passing the Jaguar trio on lap 43 to put them a lap down. It was obvious that their plan was to go all out early on, and try to go a lap up on the Jaguars because of the expected pace car involvement during the race; this feature of American racing was used much more often than we were used to in Group C. One hour and twenty minutes into the race the Dyson Porsche pitted with a broken fifth gear that was repaired but put them out of contention. The next phase had the Al Holbert team in the lead with positions changing during the second fuel stops and then full course yellow flags allowed two of the Jaguars to stay on the lead lap. The first problem for Jaguar was a fuel pump failure for #60 needing a five minute stop to rectify and losing four laps in the process. The Tullius Eagle was out after three and a half hours with a blown head gasket and the race settled into the night. With a number of full course yellows and the race cars held behind the pace car as accident damage and cars were retrieved, it was Ian Reed's experience of these conditions that came to the fore as over time he manipulated the #60 Jaguar to retrieve three of the lost laps and bring this car into contention once again.

As the early evening progressed, Stuck in the Bayside/Havoline Porsche came in contact with slower cars and suffered some body and suspension damage, and although repaired, this competitive trio were out of a winning place. Midnight saw the three Jaguars lined up immediately behind the three leading BFG, Holbert and Brun Porsches making a spectacular site as they turned off the front banked straight down onto the infield section of the track. The pace and push from TWR was on, with the race entering a new phase for seasoned Porsche competitors. In previous races at Daytona the Porsche teams had settled into a holding pattern after 10 hours, reducing pressure on car and driver

### 1988 Daytona Pit Stop Crews

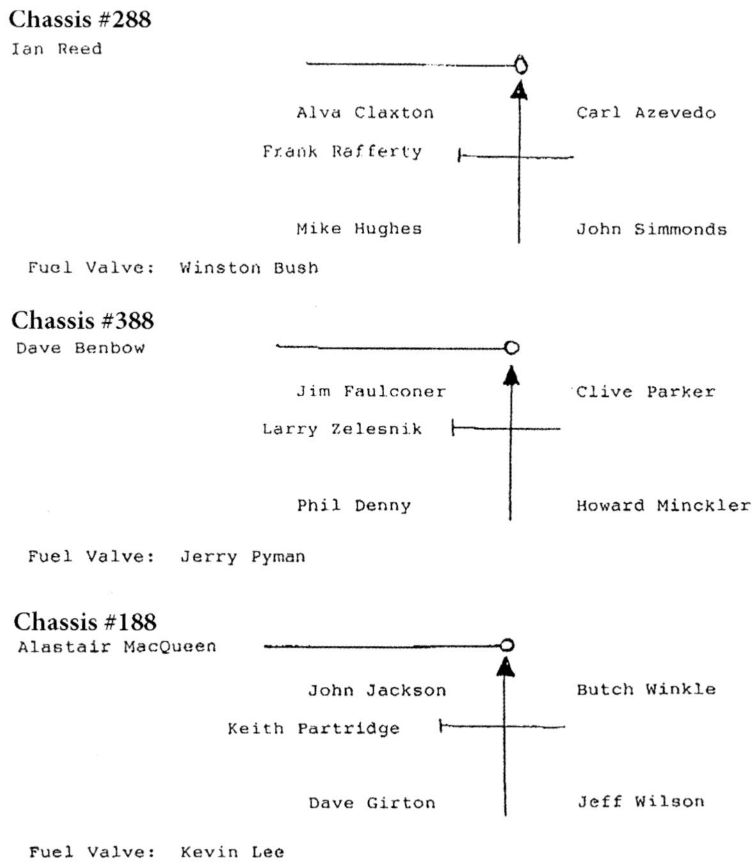


and waiting to see which Porsche would survive. This time it was three Porsches versus three Jaguars, and the Porsches had to step up to maintain a full racing pace.

The first to break under this pressure was the Brun Porsche with a blown engine. 3am saw more pit stops for fuel and slick tyres being changed for wets as showers turned to rain and drivers earned their retainers as skill in the changing conditions became a feature. It was the BFG Porsche that was caught out in these pressure conditions with an accident that damaged bodywork and punctured tyres, but this car's talented crew would remain in contention. The Foyt/Al Unser Jr/Forbes-Robinson Porsche was the next to slow with a broken fifth gear, the second for a Porsche here, costing them an hour to fix. With the dawn of a new Sunday the two Holbert/Miller and Busby/BF Goodrich Porsches led the three Jaguars and with around eight hours to go it looked a more even situation for the TWR/Castrol/Jaguar team. This was not to last with the #61 Jaguar suffering from noisy valve gear and low oil pressure after a jammed oil pump relief valve had caused bearing failure, and the car was out. The leading Holbert Porsche had been setting the pace in both wet and dry conditions with Derek Bell and Chip Robinson making it the car to beat when suddenly it slowed with a broken exhaust. It appeared that the pipe to the wastegate had broken leading to malfunction of the boost control, and along with a throttle problem this took some time to fix.

Over the last six hours it was down to the single BFG Porsche followed by the two Jaguars with the #60 car of Brundle/Nielsen/Boesel gaining on the leader. Things began to heat up now with no quarter being asked or given and it was Redman in the BFG Porsche who entered this phase in determined fashion with a questionable manoeuvre on John Nielsen putting the Jaguar a lap down; but in the contact his Porsche cut a tyre and headed for the pits for a hasty nose repair and fuel top up. This all happened close to the pit entrance and so little time was lost for them. Around this time the #66 Jaguar had begun to sound increasingly rough but still keeping up a reasonable pace in the hands of John Watson but unable to mount any challenge, and so it now came down to a single Porsche and Jaguar battle. Soon after the Porsche North America factory supported car of Al Holbert stopped out on track with a blown engine, probably caused by over boosting with the wastegate problem. The battle continued with Wollek in the BFG car being chased hard by John Nielsen in the #60 Jaguar.

Another full course yellow had cars pitting and pressure began to tell here. The pit exit road has a sharp left hand turn to take the cars away from the normal exit from the banking to merge with the infield track, and this turn had seen quite a few make mistakes on cold tyres, with no pit lane speed restriction in those days. Judging a full course yellow and the pace car was a technique that Ian Reed had earlier used to bring the #60 Jaguar back into contention. If the race car can exit to the infield ahead of the pace car that is taking a longer way around the track, this enables a high-speed lap rejoining the line behind the pace car again, and in doing so gains a lap but is at the back of the field. It was Baldi in the leading Porsche that fell into this trap as he tried to exit the pit corner at speed to be ahead of the pace car as it came by, but on cold tyres left the exit road and damaged the nose of his car. By this time all the spare noses of the Busby/BF Goodrich Porsche had been used up and word was sent out to other teams for a spare. The Porsche continued to circulate while a replacement was found and then pitted to have the nose replaced. This all came at a cost to the Porsche and when the race settled back into the last hour the #60 Jaguar was one and a half laps in the lead. To dampen any comeback chances from the second placed Porsche soon after this the driver's door flew off and with this being part of the air ducting for the engines intercooler, a finishing mode had to be selected by that team. The pressure was then released from the Jaguar,

*#60 pressing on over the final hours of the Daytona race.*

although it did not feel like that for us all at the time. As the last hour of any 24 hour race commences it feels as if time has been deliberately slowed. Vowing not to look at your watch as often, and when you finally relent, perhaps only five minutes have passed.

> The race finished with the winning Jaguar #60 of Brundle/Nielsen/Boesel on 728 laps; Wollek/Baldi/Redman-Porsche 727 laps; Cheever/Watson/Dumfries #61 Jaguar 713 laps; Stuck/Ludwig/van der Merwe-Porsche 694 laps; Rothbarth/Bernardo/Jourdain/Stevens-Porsche 680 laps; Foyt/Al Unser jr/Forbes-Robinson Porsche 675 laps and Holbert/Bell/Robinson-Porsche 660 laps.

It was a special win for the new TWR America team headed by Tony Dowe and engineered by Ian Reed. The pressure had been on throughout this race until the very last hour, evidenced by the number of accidents with bodywork damage, as well as gearbox and engine failures suffered by the many experienced and normally reliable Porsche teams. With the extensive media hype associated with this major sporting event came the rewards for Castrol and Jaguar. Castrol's John Gardella indicated that their three-year agreement was paid for by the winning of this single event.

Jaguar were relying heavily on new race results to help revive and promote Jaguar's existing motorsport heritage, its point of difference being the luxury image associated with large V12 engined road cars. This could be seen as contrary to the growing need to reduce fuel consumption in vehicles, as emissions and the prospect of 'peak oil' and higher fuel prices loomed in the future. Jaguar's road cars had been subjected to the new American 'gas guzzler tax' and Jaguar America was subtlety promoting the fact that this was perhaps not a bad thing for its demographic. Perhaps owning a V12 Jaguar was a badge of affluence, after all it was a special imported European vehicle with its unique V12 engine, setting it apart from the run of the mill American V8s. This victory implied on the V12 engine a status and kudos in the American market having just beaten what was seen as the best engine engineering company in the world; Porsche of Germany. We had been given three years to win this prestigious race and most of the Jaguar directors and senior management were on hand to witness the result they could not have dared dream of so early in the change-over of the American race programme to TWR.

That night a hasty venue had been arranged at a local hotel with dinner for all the team, with tired people drinking too much. Sir John Egan stood up and gave a magnificent speech that needed a little assistance from the back of his chair and the euphoric mood was only tempered by exhaustion. Tony Southgate and I finally took a taxi back to our hotel at 10.30pm after working for 38 hours straight and halfway through a sentence Tony stopped talking and was asleep. I soon joined him.

*Brundle, Boesel and Nielsen, winners of the 1988 Sunbank Daytona 24 hour event.*

*Daytona winners circle with author Allan Scott, Tony Dowe and Wolfgang Huestedt of Bosch spark plugs.*

ENG TEST AND DATA SHEET.

| G. TYPE | IMSA V12 6000cc | ENG. NO | 88107 | DATE | 16/2/88 |
|---|---|---|---|---|---|
| L PRESS. | 60 | OIL TEMP. | 90 | WATER TEMP. | 85 |
| EL PRESS. | 60 | BARO. PRESS. | 30.268 1025 | HYDROM. | -2 |
| LL TEMP. | 6°C | CORR. FIGURE | .237 30.031 = .975 | | |

| RPM | LOAD | CORR. BHP | | TORQUE | | CO% |
|---|---|---|---|---|---|---|
| 4000 | | | | | | |
| 4250 | | | | | | |
| 4500 | 93.1 | 419 | 13.5 | 409 | | 3.1% |
| 4750 | 94.9 | 451 | 14 | 440 | | 3.8% |
| 5000 | 98.7 | 494 | 15 | 481 | -2 | 3.4% |
| 5250 | 99.3 | 521 | 14 | 506 | | 3.8 |
| 5500 | 98.2 | 540 | 14 | 527 | | |
| 5750 | 99.8 | 574 | 13 | 560 | | 4 |
| 6000 | 101.3 | 606 | 11 | 593 | | |
| 6250 | 102.8 | 643 | | 627 | | |
| 6500 | 102.4 | 666 | 11 | 649 | | 4.2% |
| 6750 | 99.8 | 674 | 10 | 657 | | |
| 7000 | 98.0 | 686 | 9 | 669 | | |
| 7250 | 96.8 | 702 | 8 | 684 | | |
| 7500 | 94.0 | 705 | 7 | 687 | | |

COMMENTS

IMSA 8 Program
100° Split EA 15/16
13-1.

| G. TYPE | IMSA V12 | ENG. NO | 88109. | DATE | 9-6-88 |
|---|---|---|---|---|---|
| PRESS. | | OIL TEMP. | | WATER TEMP. | |
| EL PRESS. | | BARO. PRESS. | 1021 | HYDROM. | +2 |
| LL TEMP. | 18°C | CORR. FIGURE | 1.015 | | |

| RPM | LOAD | CORR. BHP | VACUUM | OIL PRESSURE |
|---|---|---|---|---|
| 4500 | 92.3 (91.2) | 421 | -12 | 55 |
| 4750 | 93.5 | 450 | -12 | 60 |
| 5000 | 95.9 (95.1) | 486 | -12 | 60 |
| 5250 | 97.8 | 521 | -12 | 55 |
| 5500 | 97.0 (96.3) | 541 | -12 | 55 |
| 5750 | 97.0 | 566 | -11 | 60 |
| 6000 | 98.7 (98.0) | 601 | -11 | 60 |
| 6250 | 99.4 | 630 | -10.5 | 60 |
| 6500 | 99.7 (99.2) | 657 | -9.5 | 60 |
| 6750 | 96.9 | 663 | -9.5 | 60 |
| 7000 | 94.0 | 667 | -9 | 65 |
| 7250 | 93.7 | 689 | -8.5 | 65 |
| 7500 | 92.5 | 704 | -8 | 70 |
| 7680 (MAX) | 92.0 | 717 | -8 | 70 |

COMMENTS

Large torque honed liners (.007 clearance)
13.5-1 comp.
Old type interference springs
TPO B 15°/10
38 MM Intakes - not coated internally.
Ign -2 Fuel +2
no air filter fitted for complete test.
air filter fitted (bracketed figures)
Max RPM obtainable on Dyno 7680 - rev limit set @ 7900 soft cut, + 7950 hard cut.
continued

The third placed XJR-9D had its engine removed for examination at Kidlington. Tappet clearances had closed up and an exhaust valve had partially burnt out. It turned out our procurement manager had succumbed to hype from a parts supplier and their rep had convinced him that they could supply superior valve seat material to the one we used, and had offered a special deal to be involved. He had made this change without consulting me. We ran a system that had a specific sign off procedure and I was not impressed with the naivety involved

top right: ***Eng Test Cards – the first attempt at optimising exhaust lengths and diameters are seen with this test producing 700bhp from 6 litres. It was estimated we were 50bhp down on the fully developed turbocharged 3-litre engines.***
bottom right: ***Optimisation for improved top end using 7900rpm on the race track.***

by all concerned. Motor racing is a tough world and situations arise that need hard decisions, as well as send signals to those who remain when compromising basic management procedures. He was not fired but given help to find alternative employment over a reasonable timeframe, with his replacement fully understanding procedures from day one. This showed the worth of doing two 24 hour races a year; all the heads were replaced over time with original specification valve seat inserts, in time for the Le Mans race.

*Miami*

## Miami (3 hours) – February 28th

After a complete rebuild the three Jaguars returned to Florida once again and the street circuit of Miami. These street circuits have concrete barriers and little room for mistakes. They are hard on brakes, engine temperatures and accidents, with difficulty of overtaking.

Qualifying times were: Brabham/Morton, Nissan ZX-T88, 1:9.802 Ludwig/Stuck, Porsche, 1:11.846; Brundle/Nielsen, XJR-9, 1:12.109; Robinson/Bell, Porsche, 1:12.726; Foyt/Dyson. Porsche, 1:12.822; Lammers/Jones, XJR-9, 1:13.236.

In the race this became a closely fought battle from the start, with five cars eventually finishing on the same lap after an intensive 124 laps. Brundle had this race under control but was deemed to have overtaken a slower car under the caution flag and was forced to return to the pits for a stop-go penalty. Cheever/Boesel retired their XJR-9 with low oil pressure and the Lammers/Jones XJR-9 had spun out of contention losing a lap in the process. Brundle returned in 'all-out' mode and closed down on the Cobb/Weaver Porsche in the final laps but could not pass, to end up second by 0.69 of a second.

Final placings for the race were: Cobb/Weaver, Porsche 962, 373.740kms, 124.246; Brundle/Nielsen, Jaguar XJR-9, 124; Larrauri, Porsche 962, 124; Robinson/Bell, Porsche 962, 124; Ludwig/Stuck, Porsche 962, 124 and Lammers/Jones, Jaguar XJR-9, 123.

## 12 Hours of Sebring Grand Prix of Endurance – March 19th

Three XJR-9Ds were brought out for this event with just two cars to enter the race. Crews were Brundle/Nielsen/Boesel and Lammers/Jones/Sullivan. Porsche were here in force determined to avenge Daytona, and their cars seemed much happier on this circuit with its many bumps than the XJR-9D Jaguars were.

Porsche were focused on the long distance races and the strongest teams had Robinson in the Al Holbert 962 on pole with 1:55.846 and Cobb/Weaver Dyson Racing 1:55.864. Brundle/Nielsen/Boesel XJR-9D 1:55.985; Ludwig/Stuck Bayside Porsche 1:56.116, then Lammers/Jones/Sullivan XJR-9D 1:56.402.

The third Jaguar would be used for testing suspension changes and would not be used in the race while Nielsen would be cross entered in both cars to give him the best chance of scoring points. The Nissans were not entered.

Lammers had his XJR-9D running in third place when overtaking a slower car had body contact and a return to the pits for repair. Brundle took up the chase in third

*XJR-9 – Sebring*

until slowed with a puncture that dropped him back. This car was later out with the first and only failure of a Cosworth piston in the entire V12 programme, showing the integrity of that supplier. Any chance of a podium finished with a broken gearbox and although this was rebuilt in just under 45 minutes the result was seventh for this Jaguar and with 'Big John' Nielsen transferred to it he earned vital points to remain the points leader in the series.

Final placings for the Sebring Grand Prix were as follows: Stuck/Ludwig, Porsche 962, 2103.380kms; 'Winter'/Jelinski/Barilla, Porsche 962; Cobb/Weaver, Porsche 962; Foyt/Haywood, Porsche 962; Adams/Hotchkis/Hotchkis Jr, Porsche 962; Dallenbach Jr/Jones, Chevrolet Corvette; Lammers/Jones/Sullivan/Nielsen, Jaguar XJR-9D.

## Road Atlanta (500kms) – April 10th

It was at this race that the tide would turn for Nissan and against TWR, setting the scene for years to come. Air restricted turbocharged engines are able to use high boost levels at lower engine rpm, but need constantly reducing boost management as the engine increases in rpm. This means that when using a fixed boost level with a mechanical wastegate it had to be set at what the air restrictor would allow at *maximum* engine rpm. Nissan now introduced its Electromotive electronic wastegate boost control system and this was a game changer. With the lower volumes of air flowing through the air restrictor at lower engine rpm being well below the restrictor's maximum flow rates, boost levels could be raised to increase the air delivery and allow maximum air flow at all engine situations. As the engine rpm increased this boost level would have to diminish and this boost profile could only be produced via electronic controls, not the flat profile that a mechanical wastegate produced. By this time Bosch had also produced its MP1.7 system with electronic boost control and this added new life to the 962 as engines became adapted over the year.

Geoff Brabham had set the fastest time but after testing of the new version of the ZX-T with the new engine control system he had opted to start the race with the new car, having to then start from the back of the field.

This produced a starting grid of: Watson/Nielsen XJR-9D 1:11.763; Robinson/Bell Holbert 962 1:12.523; Wallace/Jones XJR-9D 1:12.854; Forbes-Robinson/Theys Chevrolet Corvette 1:13.405.

Both Jaguars ran at the front and seemed to have the pace covered but it was Brabham in the Nissan who was quickly working his way through the field and by mid-race became the leader. Nielsen regained the lead, with Jones and the Robinson/Bell 962 behind, but it was Brabham who took out the close win from Nielsen with Jones spinning in the later stages to allow the 962 to take third place.

Final placings were Brabham/Morton, Nissan GTP ZX-T, 2:38.11; Watson/Nielsen, Jaguar XJR-9, 2:38.15; Robinson/Bell, Porsche 962; Wallace/Jones, Jaguar XJR-9; Cobb/Weaver, Porsche 962.

*Heavy braking needed on the USA circuits shows glowing front brake discs.*

## West Palm Beach (3 hour) – April 24th

Qualifying times for this race were:

Brabham/Morton, Nissan GTP ZX-T, 58.762; Brundle/Nielsen, Jaguar XJR-9; Lammers/Jones, Jaguar XJR-9; Earl/Kline, Spice SE88P Pontiac Firebird GTP, 1:00.293; Nielsen/Brundle, Jaguar XJR-9, 1:00.609; Robinson/Bell, Porsche 962, 1:00.902.

Note: Second fastest Jaguar #66 did not start.

The two other Jaguars were competitive here and pushed the Nissan until the Brundle/Nielsen car was slowed with fuel pressure problems and later stopped completely with a broken gearbox. Lammers/Jones took the chase all the way to the last pit stop where a problem with a wheel cover slowed the tyre change and this allowed Brabham's Nissan to take the win by seven seconds.

Final placings were Brabham/Morton, Nissan GTP ZX-T, 3:00:46.524, 388.431kms, 128.933; Lammers/Jones, Jaguar XJR-9, 3:00:54.087; Cobb/Weaver, Porsche 962 GTi; Earl/Kline, Spice SE88P Pontiac Firebird GTP; Mead/McAdam, Fabcar GTP Chevrolet.

## Lime Rock (150 laps) – May 30th

The XJR-9s had some updates to the wing end plates before this race.

Brundle/Nielsen #60 came out the fastest qualifier on 0:44.885 ahead of Brabham/Morton (Nissan) 0:45.067; Robinson 0:45.431 in the Holbert 962; Weaver 0:45.570 Dyson 962 with the Lammers/Jones #61 XJR-9 0:46.549. All cars were under the series' previous record.

It was another close race at the short Lime Rock track with Brabham moving into the lead initially, but Brundle/Nielsen fought back to take the lead halfway through. Nielsen's lead was removed when Brabham forced him wide a few laps from the end and this win was lost by 0.12 of a second. The #61 Jaguar backed this up in third place.

Final results were Geoff Brabham, Nissan GTP ZX-T, 2:13:55.828, 369.345kms; Brundle/Nielsen, Jaguar XJR-9, 2:13:55.949; Lammers/Jones, Jaguar XJR-9; Chip Robinson, Porsche 962; Earl/Kline, Spice SE88P Pontiac Firebird GTP.

## Mid Ohio (150 laps) – June 5th

The #83 Nissan produced the fastest qualifying time (1:19.955) with a change to the driver line up in this car, Tom Gloy replacing Morton. The followers were Cobb/Weaver in the Dyson RLR 962; Wollek/Baldi, Busby 962; Lammers/Jones XJR-9; Robinson/Bell/Holbert 962 and Brundle/Nielsen XJR-9.

It was a repeat result for the Valparaiso team with Brundle closing down on Brabham in the later laps of the race but finishing eight seconds behind the winner.

Brabham/Gloy, Nissan GTP ZX-T, 3:05:06.566, 498.253kms; Brundle/Nielsen, Jaguar XJR-9, 3:05:20.040; Lammers/Jones, Jaguar XJR-9; Cobb/Weaver, Porsche 962 GTi; Wollek/Baldi, Porsche 962; Robinson/Bell, Porsche 962.

## Watkins Glen (500kms) – July 3rd

The XJR-9s were off the pace here, on their first visit to a circuit where it was thought they should do well.

Qualifying times were: Brabham/Morton, Nissan GTP ZX-T, 1:34.737; Robinson/Bell, Porsche 962, 1:36.822; Cobb/Weaver, Porsche 962 GTi, 1:36.978; Wollek/Baldi, Porsche 962, 1:36.996; Brundle/Nielsen, Jaguar XJR-9, 1:37.034; Lammers/Jones, Jaguar XJR-9, 1:37.895.

The race was a disappointment for the team as Brundle was out on lap 11 with electrical problems that could not be repaired in time and this meant that points leader John Nielsen would not be adding to his total. The #61 XJR-9 fared little better with Lammers having a rear tyre blowout and after handing over to Jones the car was in an accident while overtaking a slower competitor and did not finish for the team.

Final placings were: Brabham/Morton, Nissan GTP ZX-T, 2:43:33.773, 499.997kms; Robinson/Bell, Porsche 962, 2:43:55.406; van der Merwe/Forbes-Robinson, Chevrolet Corvette GTP; Wollek/Baldi, Porsche 962; Leven/Dyson, Porsche 962.

## Road America (500kms) – July 17th

The qualifying times for Road America were Larrauri/Brun, Porsche 962, 2:19.487; Brundle/Nielsen, Jaguar XJR-9; van der Merwe/Forbes-Robinson, Chevrolet Corvette GTP, 2:30.506; Lammers/Jones, Jaguar XJR-9; Brabham/Morton, Nissan GTP ZX-T.

Tensions were beginning to rise in this contest with a timing dispute for Brabham leaving him to start behind the two Jaguars. Lammers and Brabham set the scene on the warm-up lap as they clashed for starting position with Lammers losing a rear wheel cover in the process. They continued to trade blows and it was the Nissan that had to have some hasty repairs at its next pit stop. Brundle on the front row managed to lead up to 25 laps before fuel pressure problems slowed his progress allowing the Nissan and two Porsches to pass. It would be a salvaged fourth and fifth place for the XJR-9s.

Final placings for the race were: Brabham/Morton, Nissan GTP ZX-T; Robinson/Bell, Porsche 962; Cobb/Weaver, Porsche 962 GTi; Brundle/Nielsen, Jaguar XJR-9; Lammers/Jones, Jaguar XJR-9.

## Portland (300kms) – July 31st

This shorter race allowed a single driver for the complete distance and Nissan entered two ZX-Ts for Brabham and Morton.

Qualifying times were: Geoff Brabham, Nissan GTP ZX-T, 57.970; John Morton, Nissan GTP ZX-T, 59.435; Bob Wollek, Porsche 962, 59.460; Cobb/Weaver, Porsche 962 GTi, 1:00.123; Lammers/Jones, Jaguar XJR-9, 1:00.592; Brundle/Nielsen, Jaguar XJR-9, 1:00.852.

The XJR's qualifying times showed the Nissan's were continuing their domination of this series and that would be confirmed in the race. Brabham led Morton and the Jaguars followed all on the same lap; but the best that could come was a third for Brundle/Nielsen and fourth for Lammers/Jones.

The final results were: Geoff Brabham, Nissan GTP ZX-T, 1:41:26.550, 298.944kms; John Morton, Nissan GTP ZX-T, 1:51:45.840; Brundle/Nielsen, Jaguar XJR-9; and Lammers/Jones, Jaguar XJR-9; Cobb/Weaver, Porsche 962 GTi

## Sears Point (300kms) August 14th

Qualifying times were:

Brabham Nissan ZX-T, 1:23.139; Brundle/Nielsen, XJR-9, 1:24.033; Lammers/Jones XJR-9, 1:25.572; Earl/Kline, Spice Pontiac 1:24.587; Cobb/Weaver, Dyson GTi 962, 1:25.003; Morton/Gloy, 1:25.408.

A great battle commenced between Brabham and Brundle with Brundle eventually taking the lead. Nielsen driving the last stint tried hard to defend this position but again Brabham managed to pass and go on to win. A good effort from Lammers/Jones after having to pit for a tyre took them back to third place.

Final placings were: Geoff Brabham, Nissan GTP ZX-T, 1:50:37.945, 304.528kms; Brundle/Nielsen, Jaguar XJR-9, 1:50:40.775; Lammers/Jones, Jaguar XJR-9; Cobb/Weaver, Porsche 962 GTi; Bob Wollek, Porsche 962; Robinson/Bell, Porsche 962.

## San Antonio (3 hours) September 4th

Qualifying times were: Brabham/Morton, Nissan GTP ZX-T, 1:04.944; Cobb/Weaver, Porsche 962 GTi, 1:05.906; Nielsen/Wallace Jaguar XJR-9, 1:05.934; van der Merwe/Forbes-Robinson, Chevrolet Corvette GTP, 1:05.966; Earl/Kline, Spice SE88P Pontiac Firebird GTP, 1:06.615; and Watson/Jones, Jaguar XJR-9, 1:07.86.

Jones crashed heavily in practice to the extent that his car would need major repairs, removing the TWR America team's use of a test car. Jones teamed up with Watson, and Nielsen with Wallace. Brabham's run of victories would end here with a driveshaft CV joint failure, but Wallace had brake failure leading to a crash, with the car too badly damaged to continue. Jones/Watson were troubled by a Jaguar that was not handling perfectly and although running in second place as the race drew to a close they could not challenge the Dyson RLR Porsche of Cobb/Weaver.

Final placings for this race were: Cobb/Weaver, Porsche 962 GTi, 381.640kms; Watson/Jones, Jaguar XJR-9; Earl/Kline, Spice SE88P Pontiac Firebird GTP; Durst/Brockman, Spice SE88P Buick; and Bundy/Graham, Porsche 962.

## Columbus (300km) – October 2nd

The qualifying times for the Columbus 300km were:

Derek Daly, Nissan GTP ZX-T, 1:30.500; Brabham, Nissan GTP ZX-T, 1:31.113; Bobby Rahal, Chevrolet Corvette GTP, 1:31.826; Lammers/Jones/Nielsen, Jaguar XJR-9, 1:32.275; Brundle/Nielsen, XJR-9; Wollek/Bald, Porsche 962, 1:32.342.

Derek Daly had joined the Nissan two-car driver line up and Daly and Brabham would drive the entire distance of this shorter race. Top Indy Car driver Bobby Rahal was entered in the Chevrolet Corvette and soon made this combination a contender qualifying ahead of the XJR-9s of Lammers/Jones and Brundle/Nielsen. Brundle was taken out of the race by a slower car that turned in front of him leaving Nielsen to replace Jones in the second Jaguar. This XJR-9 had been delayed with repairs to bodywork after coming in contact with Daly's Nissan. The best that these two drivers could do was to salvage a final tenth position. This result meant that Nielsen could not remain in contention and the championship was won by Brabham with one race still to come.

Final results were: Brabham, Nissan GTP ZX-T, 2:18:18.564, 299.821kms; Klaus Ludwig, Porsche 962, 2:18:21.884; Wollek/Baldi, Porsche 962; Baldwin/Hobbs, Chevrolet Corvette GTP; van der Merwe/Forbes-Robinson, Chevrolet Corvette GTP; Durst/Brockman, Spice SE88P Buick.

## Del Mar (2 Hours) – October 23rd

And so to the last race of the 1988 series at Del Mar in its parkland settings in southern California. The Jaguar team, now down to just the two cars, had another fraught start here with Nielsen in contact with another car and hitting a concrete wall; the car was too badly damaged to continue.

Lammers and Brundle were the selected drivers for the single XJR-9 and this car was on pole with 1:06.529; Wollek in the Busby 962 achieved 1:06.929; Sarel van de Merwe in the Lola Corvette 1:07.692; The Nissan ZX-Ts of Brabham (1:08.219) and Daly (1:08.807) qualified ahead of Ludwig's Bayside 962 on 1:09.810.

Lammers led the start and pulled out a gap over the Wollek 962 only to have the field close up under a full caution period allowing Brabham to close up and eventually take the lead. After a mid-race pit stop Brundle fought back in great style, retaking Brabham who in trying to keep up with Brundle had an uncharacteristic crash and was out of the race. Running the soft tyre compounds here had produced fast times but another stop was needed for Brundle to take on a new set of tyres. This gamble paid off as the leading cars continued on their worn tyres and Brundle managed to eliminate his 40 second deficit to the two leading Porsches and retake the lead a few minutes from the end. It was a great way to finish the year along with the US$140,000 prize and bonus money from this event.

Final placings for the this final race of this series was Lammers/Brundle, Jaguar XJR-9, 2:00:57.944, 226.596kms; Klaus Ludwig, Porsche 962, 2:01:06.428; Bob Wollek, Porsche 962; Derek Daly, Nissan GTP ZX-T; Bobby Rahal, Chevrolet Corvette GTP; Cobb/Weaver, Porsche 962 GTi.

Geoff Brabham had an outstanding year, the clear winner of the Drivers Championship with 186 points, ahead of Jaguar's John Nielsen with 140, Price Cobb 137, James Weaver 131, and Jaguar drivers Martin Brundle 127, Davy Jones 118, and Jan Lammers 112.

Whilst Brabham was consistently fast, it was the electromotive electronic waste gate on the Nissan which gave him the tools to do the job within the prescribed regulations.

*The big money winners of 1988 collecting $140,000 from Camel Cigarettes at Del Mar. From left: Jan Lammers, Jack Manning (Sports Marketing Enterprises), Jean Liles (Miss Camel GT), and Martin Brundle.*

And so ended the first year of TWR's venture in the American IMSA series. There were two or three fundamental issues relating to the XJR-9s performance during the year, the first being the reduced torque off the corners with the rule change to a maximum six litres for the Jaguar V12 engine; the Brits threat to the establishment had been neutered and it became Nissan's year. Kidlington had seen the American series as just an extension of what had gone before in Group C, but there was a substantial difference between fuel restricted Group C racing and the free fuel consumption of IMSA. IMSA meant flat out racing all the time and having to overtake the car in front the hard way; not having the luxury of being able to bide your time keeping up the rhythm while waiting for the car ahead to struggle with its fuel consumption as was the case in Group C. This meant safer overtaking manoeuvres in Group C eliminating fuel consuming blocking tactics or over aggressive driving resulting in

right: ***Technical Summary of the Grattan Test carried out on September 21st*** – *continued on next page*

TECHNICAL SUMMARY; GRATTAN TEST 21/09/88

OBJECTIVES

1) To evaluate the relative merits of various nose louver configurations, identified as follows:
   a) Double louver,our current standard spec.
   b) Triple louver.
   c) Datsun.
   d) 1.5 Datsun.
2) The effect of mechanical droop restriction on the front suspension.
3) Increased rebound settings on rear dampers.
4) The effect of increased front static camber settings.
5) To bed in brake pads for the forthcoming race at Columbus.
6) To check out the telemetry system and verify the accuracy of the functions used, and to evaluate the possible benefits of such a system under race conditions.

   The results of this test will be the subject of a sererate report to be furnished by Ian Reed.

INITIAL SET UP

The car was configured in our usual high downforce set up for slow speed circuits. Sprint tail, high tunnels, long splitter nose plus 1" bibs. SB2 and M2B dampers fitted with 900lb front and 800lb rear springs. Rear wing set at 27.5. Standard small rear wing end plates had to be used due to the unavailability of the large end plates following San Antonio race. Standard F.A.R.B and 6mm R.A.R.B. were fitted. Tyres 254 LF 160 RF
194 LR 254 RR

The telemetry system had been fitted and operated in the workshop. It was fitted to the car throughout the days activities and was monitored continuously.

CONDITIONS

The day was overcast with very occasional drizzle. Maximum temperatures only reached 60 F, but were generally below this mark. The circuit was dry with the odd puddle or two which finally disappeared by mid afternoon.

TEST RESULTS

The first three runs were used to bed in discs and pads, as well as to get Davy Jones familiar with the circuit.

1) NOSES

Double louver; Little turn in US especially over rises in slow corners
US on exit to high speed corners
Best lap 71.87
Ave lap 72.24

Reducing the rad opening from 42" to 32" and reducing the rad blank from 18" down to 15" maintained the same water temp but INCREASED US in slow and medium speed corners.
Best lap 71.35
Ave lap 71.79

### *Technical Summary of the Grattan Test* – *continued*

Triple louver; As above fitted with reduced rad opening. No change in handling, but the car felt more consistant.
Best lap 71.31
Ave lap 71.52
Reopening rad inlet to 42" made the front to pointy, not so well balanced.
Best lap 71.48
Ave lap 71.67

Double louver; Repeat test #1. Car feels more consistent than last run but definitely has less front grip.
Best lap 70.78
Ave lap 71.09

Datsun louver; Much more front grip, OS almost everywhere, nose scraping down the straight.
Best lap 70.99
Ave lap 71.29 ( 2 timed laps only )

1.5 Datsun; More front grip again. Steering is heavier and less lock is needed in all turns. Lost rear grip.
Best lap 70.61
Ave lap 70.97

At this point the rear wing was increased to max in an effort to balance the car. Throughout the morning it became apparent the car was too soft. At this time lunch was taken and the settings changed as follows;
Front springs up to 1100lbs
Rear springs up to 1000lbs
R.A.R.B up to 8mm
1.5 Datsun nose
29.5 ( max ) rear wing setting

The initial run after lunch was over 10 laps to set a base line for the afternoon session. Front of the car like it is on railroad tracks. If pushed really hard snaps into OS then breaks traction.
Best lap 70.54
Ave lap 70.75

M2E rear dampers; Lost a little front grip over the rises, but the rear is more progressive. DJ " Really nice balance "
Best lap 70.27
Ave lap 70.39

Zero front droop; Lost rear traction. Steering lighter and less sensitive over the rises. Less confidence than the last run.
Best lap 70.35
Ave lap 70.59

.25" front droop; Helped the front little more grip. Tail still lose not as much as last run. Good change of direction.
Best lap 70.45
Ave lap 70.66

M2F rear dampers; Improved traction, but the rear slides out over the rises. Good balance although not the confidence of earlier runs.
Best lap 70.09
Ave lap 70.96

M2E rear dampers, .5" front droop; "Really really nice – good balance " Gooc over rises. Possible to break traction on off camber corners.
Best lap 70.13
Ave lap 70.47

Front camber to 2 deg neg; No change in handling, but steering lighter and car weaving and hopping over bumps under braking.
Best lap 70.56
Ave lap 70.73

Fit new tyres; Nervous under braking, using more road than prior to camber adjustment on the exit to all corners. Not so easy or comfortable to drive as earlier.
Best lap 70.06
Ave lap 70.17

Remove P.F's from tail; No detectable change in handling but lost 100 – 150 revs at the end of the front straight.
Best lap 70.30
Ave lap 70.45

<u>NOTE :</u> Ave lap is average of the four fastest laps in each configuration.

*This test was to find a solution to the XJR-9's understeering character and test alternative shock absorbers.*

much less contact between the competing cars than with IMSA. The only real problem in Group C was passing much slower cars, this could be done instantly to not lose momentum and break the fuel saving rhythms. In IMSA, if the Jaguars could match the Nissan's torque off the corners the XJR-9 would have been in a much better track position between corners to then challenge under braking, instead it was just catch up in the braking areas. This had led to extensive bodywork and chassis damage repairs which added weight, non replacement of these parts did not help our competitiveness as the series went on. Group C racing was on most of the tracks upgraded for ground effect Formula One races, and one of the weaknesses with the XJR-9 was its dislike of bumpy circuits.

The need for engine servicing support at Valparaiso for me had not proceeded as planned with some reluctance to take responsibility for that outcome increasing during the year. Brian was a technical person who wanted to sit in an office and come up with some ideas that needed long lead times and money that did not exist. He was not privy to the 'big picture' at Kidlington and so he had departed by year's end. Don Beadle had taken over this position and we flew him back to Kidlington at the end of the year to update him on some procedures and determine what levels of servicing could be achieved at Valparaiso. The intention was to do this each year and so build the skill level and support at the American base, but fate would intervene to stop that progress. Don had returned home to family for Christmas and being a busy time two Pan Am flights had left Heathrow for Chicago at similar times. One was the flight blown up over Lockerby, and very fortunately Don was on the later flight. Distraught scenes at Chicago O'Hare as family waited to confirm who was on which flight meant that Don's family would not allow him to fly to the UK again, which was totally understandable. It just meant that Engs had to carry out 99% of all engine work with limited support at Valparaiso in the future.

HANDLING

a). The ride heights were 54 mm front and 80 mm rear.

b). Car 188 raced with 900 front and 1000 rear springs, a STD FARB and 6 mm RARB.
The shocks were Monroe SB2 Fronts (-3R, #6B) and M2B Rears ( -0R, #1B).

Both cars arrived with 900 Front and 800 Rear springs, STD FARB's and 8 mm RARB's. The drivers complained initially about poor grip and a U.S through the fast corners.
Changing to 1000 rear springs reduced the U.S without sacrificing the traction.

c). Dampers.
The front dampers were not changed all weekend.
Car 288 tested M2E rear dampers with stiffer rebound after comments of a fast roll breakaway. The rear dampers were changed back to M2B after the M2E dampers did not give a predictable breakaway.

d). Anti Roll Bars
Both cars tested a 25% FARB. This did not help with front grip, was worse in the braking areas and as the grip level dropped, gave a less predictable breakaway.

e). AERO

The cars raced High IMSA tails and 88 spec High underwings.
The noses were fitted with 1 inch Bibs and Long splitters.
The noses were fitted with rad exit returns.
The rear wing settings were 30.0 degs with a 0.5 inch R Flap.
The rear wings were fitted with large sideplates.

The noses were fitted with 1.5 Datsun nose louvers.

BRAKES

Car 288 ran with 13.5 front and 13.0 inch rear carbon disks and pads with A.P calipers in practice.
Using the full kit with auxiliary brake caliper cooling, the temperatures and wear rates were very good. The car would have raced with these brakes.
Car 188 raced with 2459 pads, Brembo calipers and 13.5 inch disks.

| | | |
|---|---|---|
| Car 188 | 2459 Pads. | Race: Front 0.00184 "/Lap. Rear 0.00155 "/Lap |
| Car 288 | C/C Disks/Pads. | Practice: Front 0.0000164 (!) "/Lap.<br>Rear 0.0000113"/Lap |

COOLING
Water and Oil cooling were no problem.
The water temperature was 80 deg C. in the race with no blank.
With both LHS and RHS oil coolers, the oil temp was 95 deg C.

Fuel cooling was a problem on Car 288. In practice, Car 288 was reaching temperatures of 43 deg F. A gauge check confirmed this.

Car 188 was only reaching 32 deg C with a sealed tail.

GEARS
Engine revs were limited to 7650 rpm.

Race ratios were :- 15/40
17/39
19/35
21/34
24/32

First Gear could be used 4 times per lap, but in the race it was possible to use 2nd instead.

FUEL MILEAGE

Car 188 used 3.46 m.p.g

*Technical Summary of the Del Mar race dated October 31st.*

1989 V12 PARTS REVISION LIST

1988 PARTS WHICH ARE O.K

Front and Rear Axles
Front and Rear Wheel bearing Assemblies.
Front Bellcrank
Steering Rack
Front Air Jacks
Mk 2 Floating Brake mounting system for Steel disks.
F.A.R.B
Bellhousing
Clutch operating mechanism
Rear Beams...NO LIGHTENING HOLES PLEASE
Gearshift mechanism
R.A.R.B
Rear Upright Castings
Driveshafts
Output Flanges
RTWB Inner Bolts
RTWB Outer Bolts
Water Radiator
Water Radiator Mounting system.
Non Quick release steering column.
Wiper and associated mechanism.
Tub Fuel system and fuel tank.

Noses.................must be lightweight spec. We will add louvers here.
High Downforce Tail...must be lightweight spec.
Low downforce tail....must be lightweight spec.
Nose splitters
Exhausts

1988 PARTS WHICH NEED MAY NEED REVISING

Front Upright Castings...Geometry Change ?
Front Top Wishbone.......Radials ?
Front Lower Wishbone.....Radials ?
Front Push Rod...........Radials ?
Track Rods...............Radials ?
Front Brake Ducting...18" Wheels, 14.5" Disks, Carbon/Carbon Brakes, etc. etc.
Front and Rear Disk Bells...18" Wheels, 14.5" Disks, Carbon/Carbon Brakes, etc.

Rear Top Wishbone........Radials ?
Rear Lower Wishbones.....Radials ?

Rear Wing................We are starting to need more rear downforce.
Rear Wing Mounting Plates...If Wing is changed.

1988 PARTS WHICH NEED REVISING

Front Lower Wishbone..Increased Stiffness
Wheel Nut.............To IMSA Steel Spec.
FLWB Inboard Inserts..3/8 Bolts used now.
Brake Calipers........Bigger Disks.
Carbon/Carbon Brake ducting.
Dash Board............Add Digital Brake Bal. Meter.
Damper Inserts.......Monroe
Rear Beam Stays and inserts...Beefed up for Daytona.
Gearbox oil outlet union
Front Air Jack Tops...Quick vent tops.
Rear Air Jack Tops....Quick vent tops.
Fuel Pump Packs...    Need to be redesigned, relocated, Metal Check valves.
RHS Body Sidepanels...IMSA Oil Coolers.
Throttle Cable........USA Cables ?
Electric Mirrors......These are too easily removed by walls on street circuits.
Tub Sideskirts........Need to be Carbon/Kevlar.

*A list of the updates needed for 1989 sent to Kidlington at the end of the 1988 season.*

JAGUAR

Chapter Eighteen

# The 1988 Group C season

## Jerez – March 6th

**The first Group C events of the 1988 season were back-to-back race weekends at the Jerez and Jarama circuits in the heat of the early Spanish summer. The team had arrived early to Jerez to carry out testing. The final results from the 1988 rule changes to the underbody aerodynamics that had led to total revision of the venturi tunnels were uppermost in engineer Alastair Macqueen's mind at this time. The format was 800kms with a proportional fuel allocation for the three uprated Jaguar race cars now designated XJR-9. The new Sauber C9 which resembled the Jaguar profile much more than the Porsche 962C had the benefit of increased support from the Mercedes factory with engine development as well as extensive aerodynamic work in their full size non-rolling floor wind tunnel. Sponsor Kouros had been replaced by AEG Olympia and the Sauber team was now a better funded and supported operation than before. Quoted as having 720bhp when running to race fuel, what our drivers were now reporting at the start of the 1988 season was the Merc's initial torque out of the slower corners, pulling away from our Jaguar's with their 620 to 630lbs/ft of torque, by one and up to two car lengths sometimes. Former TWR driver, Jean-Louis Schlesser, with a point to prove, took pole position with a time of 1:28.67 ahead of Brundle/Cheever in a new XJR-9 chassis 588 on 1:30.66, and Lammers/Dumfries in 488 on 1:31.73. Nielsen/Watson with new signing Andy Wallace took fourth place in chassis 187 with 1:32.26. Martin Brundle had returned to us for a full season this year.**

While Porsche were no longer contenders for outright placings, Mercedes now were, and the sole C9 battled with the Jaguars from the start, and it was not until after the first round of fuel stops that all three Jaguars managed to get ahead of the Schlesser/Baldi C9. This all began to unravel as the two leading XJR-9s eventually retired with transmission problems leaving the Watson/Nielsen/Wallace XJR-9 to finish 24.5 seconds behind the winning C9. In third place and two laps down was the Joest/Blaupunkt 962C of Wollek/Ludwig and the BLR UK Porsche with Weaver being joined by Derek Bell in fourth, but seven laps behind the leaders. The C9's pace was a wake-up call for us all; the only apparent weakness in this combination was its rear tyres' ability to keep up with the increased power.

## Jarama – March 13th

The team travelled on to Jarama where the TWR Silk Cut Jaguars were prepared for the next race the following weekend, a sprint format 300km event. There had been some handling problems with the cars at Jerez and these were investigated and changes made to produce an improved set-up. This was centred on the aerodynamic package and new parts were brought out from Kidlington during the week. In qualifying the turbocharged C9 again took the pole position with 1:14.35, Lammers/Dumfries were second fastest this time and much closer on 1:14.98 with Brundle/Cheever in third 1:15.33. Nielsen ran into one of the slower C2 class cars, damaging his nose cone, and after this was hastily replaced by the mechanics, it left little time to complete a fast lap to salvage fourth with 1:15.6. He then had a huge spin that ended in hitting a marshal's parked car, with damage to both. The BLR Porsche would not start the race after an accident on the warm up lap, and it was the Schlesser C9 that initially led, but then dropping behind Brundle and Dumfries. Constant pressure from Schlesser forced Dumfries into a spin just 13 laps from the end, putting that Jaguar out of the race. It was left to Brundle to finish 19 seconds ahead of the Schlesser/Baldi Mercedes. Nielsen/Watson in the XJR-9 were third and the Brun 962 of Reuter/Schafer fourth, both cars two laps down on the leaders. The team returned to base after being away for two weeks for a well-earned rest, before a complete rebuild of the cars and travel on to Italy three weeks later.

## Monza – April 10

Monza, with its long straight is a power circuit and the turbo cars all had a point to prove. Lancia had turned up for their home race and Riccardo Patrese had set the qualifying pace with a 1:31.0, but a few fast laps seemed to be all this car was capable of as it later failed to feature in the race. Schlesser and Baldi were joined by third driver Jochen Mass who had been testing here earlier in the week with what was hoped to be an improvement to the Michelin rear tyres. Unfortunately, this had all turned out badly for them, with the experimental tyres failing at high speed, and they had to be discarded for this race. They were still close behind though, with a best time of 1:31.7. The Joest 962C using Goodyear tyres and driven by Ludwig was the first of the privateer teams to attempt to close the gap to the top teams with a special engine, rumoured to be of larger capacity, along with upgraded turbos and intercooler, and were third on 1:32.05. The Dunlop-tyred XJR-9s were next up with identical times of 1:33.62, one and a half seconds faster than the previous year, a good showing considering the new aero package that had to be used. Schlesser, gaining in confidence, had ventured tongue in cheek to TWR team manager Roger that the C9 must now be a better car than the XJR-9 to produce these results, seeing as how he had been dismissed by Roger as not being fast enough to be a Jaguar driver just over one year before.

This year's first full length 1000km race at Monza was shaping up to be different, and from the very start Larrauri/Sigala in the Brun Torno Porsche and Ludwig/Wollek in the Joest Porsches started a fast pace, along with the Schlesser/Mass C9. Brundle was in fourth and a frantic Lammers was trying to make up time having to start from the back of the grid after a low battery had prevented his car from starting when the field had moved off on its rolling start lap. By lap 25 the leaders Ludwig–Schlesser–Larrauri had pulled away from Brundle followed by Lammers in the second Jaguar, we were running to the fuel allowance and doubted that those ahead were. The C9 stopped for the first time on lap 27, Brundle on lap 30; it was going to be a long and interesting race with Cheever and Dumfries now in the Jaguars. Sigala, now in the Brun Porsche began to lose touch with the front runners and was being caught by both Jaguars. An unscheduled stop by Cheever to change a blistered front tyre had our cars out of sequence, his Jaguar up to second, and Lammers being lapped just before half distance.

On lap 88 of 173, Baldi in the C9 encountered brake problems and spun with Lammers Jaguar so close behind that he hit the spinning Sauber Mercedes and both cars returned to the pits. The C9 was easily repairable but not so the Lammers Jaguar, which needed a new radiator. Meanwhile, Brundle took the lead. The Brundle/Cheever pairing had driven a fast race to the fuel allowance and this car began to pull away in the lead by around one second each lap from Wollek's Joest Porsche. Lap 112 had Cheever back in the leading Jaguar while a few laps later Dumfries in the accident repaired XJR-9, with no fuel to worry about was trying to make up for lost time but got bogged in the gravel run off after a spin. This had also happened in earlier practice and one of the mechanics had taped a child's plastic bucket and spade inside the car after all the work created for them of cleaning out the gravel afterwards. After the final fuel stops Brundle had a lead of almost one lap over Baldi in the C9 and Wollek's 962C, while Larrauri had been delayed with some repairs needed after coming in contact with another car in his Porsche. Brundle then caught Baldi and Wollek and with these cars over their fuel allowance they eventually decided the better strategy was to let him pass and go a lap down as they may not have enough fuel to finish the race. Wollek then pitted for about eight laps with a 'brake' problem but with no fuel left in the tower it was obvious to us that the Porsche privateers had decided to break the status quo of looking off the pace by not running to the fuel allowance. They were obviously low on fuel, maybe in the forlorn hope of a long pace car period or perhaps this tactic of covering the race pace showed the needed improvements to the Porsche factory. The Porsche factory team was only competing at Le Mans this year and had found much improvement with the sequential MP1.7 Bosch engine management system, but would not release this specification to the private teams until after Le Mans. This race also showed the value of the fuel metering system in the XJR-9s and of being aware from the start the best pace and fuel settings to run over the 1000kms. This was now the fourth year of use of Zytek's sequential engine management system which was critical to our success, and the latest limited engine updates were working well.

> The final results were: Brundle/Cheever, Jaguar XJR-9 173 laps; Schlesser/Baldi/Mass, Mercedes-Benz C9, 172 laps; Larrauri/Sigala, Brun/Porsche, 171 laps; Jelinski/Winter, Joest Porsche, 168 laps and Ludwig/Wollek, Joest Porsche 164 laps.

After the increased interest from the events at Monza and the battle growing between Sauber and TWR, the home race at Silverstone was attracting increased press coverage and spectator support. By fielding just one C9 Schlesser/Baldi had taken the lead in the Drivers Championship on 85 points to the shared results of the Jaguar two-car team leaving Brundle/Cheever on 60 and Watson/Nielsen on 42. The manufacturer teams' standings were reversed with the Silk Cut Jaguar team on 90, Sauber Mercedes 85, Joest Porsche 47, Brun Porsche 46 and the Britten Lloyd Racing and Kremer Porsches 20.

The main talking point now was Sauber Mercedes who were coming to this race with two cars, along with a backup test car. TWR would field just two cars with a third test/spare car with driver combinations of Brundle/Cheever and Lammers/Dumfries. This decision showed that there was total team focus for the Brundle/Cheever pairing for the Drivers Championship, and little for the now sidelined Nielsen/Watson combination that were third in the drivers points, as a backup for that championship. With the problems to date for Lammers/Dumfries leaving that pairing pointless, even at this early stage their main focus would be supporting the Teams Championship.

The increased profile of the Group C teams and raised status of the whole event had by now attracted the attentions of the FIA ruling body, and they had decided that the OSCAR organisation run by Chris Parsons to co-ordinate the series and all logistics was in breach of the FIA rules. Meetings were now being held to discuss how this would all be handled in the future, and proposals for new engine rules to differentiate between engine types, 2-valve, 4-valve and turbocharged being raised by the FIA, and they would be the final arbiter on regulations. These proposals were being reviewed by the teams with their inevitable vested interest conclusions being presented, and it now brought some uncertainty into the series. With Mercedes, Porsche and Jaguar factories involved and the prospect of increased amounts of money being available from those sources, Formula One's Bernie Ecclestone was paying more than a passing interest in the series, with his thoughts that this attractive funding would be better represented in his series.

## Silverstone – May 8th

The growth of the series was demonstrated with the arrival of 35,000 spectators on race day, even though it was raining. The rain managed to ease, and the serious business of qualifying began. Stepping up to running two cars with one of them having never raced before was stretching the Sauber team as it was plagued with various electronic and boost control problems and they had lost both engines on Friday when pushing the limits on engine settings to breaking point. Schlesser/Mass were in the new 13kg lighter C9 with Baldi/Weaver in the updated 1987 car.

> Schlesser finally took pole position with 1:15.02 followed by Cheever/Brundle 1:16.67, Baldi/Weaver 1:16.74, and Wollek/Streiff/Hobbs 1:16.86.

Lammers had complained of a difficult car to drive and wound up sixth 1:17.38. With no obvious fix for the problem, chassis 488 would be a non-starter and he switched to the T (spare) car for the next day's race.

Having their usual pre-Le Mans outing were Mazda with their new GTP specification 767C fitted with a four rotor engine, and run by the Alan Docking team, qualifying ninth of the twelve entrants in the C1 class on 1:20.23.

Race day started with rain and the old concern with Dunlop wet tyres versus the probably superior Michelins of the C9 continued until the rain stopped long enough to allow the race start on slick tyres. The two C9s and Cheever started the race as if in a sprint and all three cars swapped position from third to first during this early stage with both the Sauber C9s battling each other as well. Lammers ran in fourth with the fuel computer not working and at the first fuel stop it was found he had been running on the conservative side. These four cars were soon in a class of their own with the Nigel Stroud designed BLR Porsche consistently fastest of the Porsche brigade, falling back and soon lapped.

Brundle took over the lead Jaguar and set a pace that Mass and Weaver in the C9s could not match, extending his lead during this session to 30 seconds by the next refuelling stop. Dumfries had managed to close the gap during this time but damaged the rear body work while passing Weaver in the second C9 and repairs to this, added to set up niggles on the spare car hindered his fuel efficient charge back. The Saubers had been using extra boost on the straights to stay with the Jaguar up front and they were now slightly over their fuel allowances. The final run to the flag stayed in the same order with Brundle/Cheever having a margin of 35 seconds and 1.5 litres of fuel left in the tank from Schlesser/Mass, and Baldi/Weaver the last car on the lead lap in third. The BLR Porsche of Bell/Needell finished five laps down in fourth and the ill-handling XJR-9 of Lammers/Dumfries with faulty fuel meter was never in contention running out of fuel six laps from the end to finish in fifth. A marginally oversize fuel tank by 1.5 litres was later found at scrutineering on the BLR Porsche, and this promoted the Lammers/Dumfries XJR-9 to fourth. The Joest Porsches were out of contention in this race, finishing up in fifth and sixth but nine and twelve laps behind the leaders. It was a close race for us over 210 laps and 1000kms with Brundle's driving ability making the vital difference on this occasion.

FACSIMILE MESSAGE

HOLDEN SPECIAL VEHICLES

224 Ferntree Gully Road
Notting Hill 3168
Victoria Australia
Telephone (03) 543 4500
Fax 543 7746

TWR Fax 8675 79352

TO: MR. ALAN SCOTT
COMPANY: TWR GROUP
FAX NO:

FROM: TOM WALKINSHAW
DATE: MAY 16, 1988
DATE !

ALAN, AFTER SEEING THE EXTENT OF THE DAMAGE TO THE HOLDEN TEST ENGINE, I FEEL WE NEED A MODEST SPEC. TEST PLODDER TO ENABLE US TO GET SOME CHASSIS DEVELOPMENT DONE, AS UP UNTIL NOW WE HAVE ACHIEVED LITTE OR NOTHING IN THIS AREA. WOULD IT BE POSSIBLE TO BUILD A TEST ENGINE AND THEN CONTINUE YOUR RACE ENGINE DEVELOPMENT ON ANOTHER SEPARATE ENGINE.

TOM

C.C. R. SILMAN
K. PAGE

***TW asking for a new design of Holden V8 engine while he is in Australia two weeks before Le Mans, with me in the USA the next weekend.***

Schlesser afterwards expressed his surprise at the straight-line speed of the XJR9 while running to the fuel. The updates to the 7-litre engine with my main efforts clustered around the 6000rpm area that was producing 700bhp were proving very effective in race pace to fuel used. I was left wondering how things would have looked using the 'lower position lightweight 7.2 litre engine and gearbox' proposal.

We were by now only working on the V6 turbo development programme for Group C with no further V12 engine development. The first running of the prototype V6 engine had promptly snapped two of its lightweight aluminium main bearing caps and literally dropped them in the sump when taken up to race boost. This engine designed for a normally aspirated power application that in its original form had produced half the power needed in Group C, was going to be a difficult one to master.

There was little time to relax after this race as preparation had already been well underway in the lead up to the biggest race of the year, Le Mans. TW had said it was a three-year programme and with 1988 being the third year there was maximum pressure being applied to produce a five-car assault on this race. TWR were quite capable of running three cars in the 1000km races and probably four at the home Silverstone race to reduce Saubers chances in the Championship, but preparations to send five cars to Le Mans had reduced this effort to just two cars for the Silverstone race; and this had been a compromise with the Championship in mind.

During this time Engs were supporting TWR's other programmes with the new Holden venture in Australia as well as the first year of the American IMSA series. I was covering the additional race support programme needed to optimise the suitability of the 6-litre engine at the various USA race tracks with their shorter sprint format. In the month between Silverstone and Le Mans I had covered the Lime Rock and Mid Ohio races in America and arrived back at base after the Silk Cut team had left for Le Mans. My job at base was to take the call on Tuesday night for anything that may have been forgotten and then leave at 5am Wednesday and drive to Le Mans to be ready for the first Wednesday night practice. Hopes were high for this race as we had earlier started the American IMSA programme off in the best way possible in January taking the new TWR America team to a win and third place in their first event at Daytona, equipped with our smaller 6-litre V12 engine.

## Le Mans

There would be no pre-Le Mans test at the French circuit to ensure the handling problems of the previous year had been fully removed by lowering the gearbox to the original position, because the circuit was being up graded with triple layer ARMCO barriers and resurfacing of the Mulsanne straight to remove the bumps. Minor changes to the circuit still need close attention and being presented with these new situations at 8pm on the Wednesday night before the race start on Saturday was not what the team needed. With the planned five cars entered it would mean many new drivers in attendance unfamiliar with the XJR-9 and the team. Wallace, Jones, Daly, Cogan and Sullivan had not raced there before, and six of the drivers, all very talented, had never raced to a fuel consumption formula before. Most of the testing would have to be done as and when time allowed in the UK. The five USA based drivers had been recruited by TWR America boss Tony Dowe to add a different feel and perspective to the team. This was by far the biggest thing TWR had ever done and it was also about TW showing he could do something that all the other teams could not do.

The Porsche factory team had not attended races in 1988 and put all its efforts into updating its reliable 962C. This had entailed a new underbody profile and rear engine cover and wing for Le Mans. Extensive development of the 3-litre water-cooled engine include the Bosch MP1.7 sequential engine management system, complete with in car electronic boost control and map selections covering qualifying, racing and pace car applications. As well an over boost button was fitted on the steering wheel which raised the normal 2.1 bars absolute boost to 2.4 bars for ten seconds. Hans Stuck had ventured that the car probably had an extra 50bhp in qualifying trim and considerable improvement in fuel economy.

My main concern on arrival was seeing the three-car works team with the large SHELL signage on all their cars; although TW and Roger were ambivalent about my concerns when they were raised. We were unable to test any of this Le Mans fuel on the dynamometer at Kidlington to check its detonation sensitivity, and make any fine changes to the ignition timing. Porsche had been very embarrassed with the many engine failures the year before due to detonation from the changes to fuel specification for 1987, and did not want a repeat involving unknown fuel. The Le Mans organisers had a long tradition of doing things their way; one of them was to supply all competitors with fuel. I had noticed during 1988 when the fuel specifications were published at each race venue that exactly the same

*Porsche's updated 1988 Le Mans challenger with technical partner Shell Oils at pre-event inspection.*

specifications, in the same typeface, were being presented by some of the circuits including Le Mans which I thought unusual, bearing in mind the different countries and suppliers involved.

The usual two-night practice over Wednesday and Thursday with drivers having to complete a minimum of three timed laps in the day light and three in the dark kept the TWR team busy just ensuring this happened, with just Brundle and Lammers going for a time. The cars all reported some understeer and slower speeds than expected on the Mulsanne straight after this first session and some adjustments were needed to find a better balance the next day in time for final Thursday practice. The onboard tyre temperature monitors had shown high temperatures and some blistering had occurred with the smaller diameter rear tyres and pressures were changed to try and overcome this. The slower Mulsanne speeds were put down to the resealing of the surface there; this had been the reason for the cancellation of pre-race testing while the resurfacing was carried out. The Mulsanne had previously been a very bumpy ride with its poor surface and these bumps had constantly bled off the Jaguar's underbody downforce. Now with the smooth surface the race cars were being pushed harder into the road; resulting in increased drag and tyre temperatures was the best conclusion put forward.

By Thursday evening all the other drivers were more familiar with the situation and car set-up, with final qualifying times being set on race rubber to help with the race set-up and tyre temperatures. Boesel had set his time in total darkness after being delayed with an engine change caused by overheating engine oil after the cooler duct had been damaged. The Porsche factory times were set with special qualifying tyres on high boost settings and these tyres could only last for one lap. Both Porsche and Jaguar were on Dunlop tyres and this at least was one equaliser for the race.

> Stuck/Bell 3.15.64; Wollek/Schuppan/Van der Merwe 3.18.62; Mario–Michael–John Andretti 3:21.77 all three works Porsche 962LM. Brundle/Nielsen 3:21.78 Jaguar (car #1); Dickens/Winter/Jelinski 3:23.3 Joest Porsche; Lammers/Dumfries/Wallace 3:23.74 Jaguar (car #2).
>
> The remaining Jaguars were the American crew of Sullivan/Jones/Cobb 3.25.42 (Jaguar #21) ninth; the team who had not raced the XJR-9 before Daly/Perkins/Cogan 3.26.78 (Jaguar #22) eleventh and Watson/Boesel/Pescarolo 3.26.82 (Jaguar #3) twelfth.

One part of the challenge to Jaguar had already disappeared before the start of the race, with Sauber pulling out of the event on safety grounds. There had been some issues previously with tyres and Jean-Louis Schlesser had opted for his own reasons about tyres to stay at home for this race. Klaus Niedzwiedz who had replaced Schlesser then had a tyre explode at high speed and extensively damaged his race car. After much discussion new UK team manager Dave Price was faced with the hard decision to withdraw.

Friday saw the Jaguars completely stripped down and carefully reassembled, engines would only be changed if they had reported problems and this would always be the case at Le Mans as we simply did not have a stock of engines to replace them all and continue with the next race programme.

*The TWR team line up behind the five XJR-9LM Jaguars.*

*The American team ran car 21.*
from left: *Danny Sullivan, Tony Dowe, Ian Reed, Davy Jones with Price Cobb seated.*

**CAR MANAGERS**

| Cars | | Engine Man |
|---|---|---|
| 186 | No 22 | Matthew |
| 188 | No 21 | Brian |
| 287 | No 3 | Greg |
| 488 | No 2 | Glen |
| 588 | No 1 | Grant/Chas |

Repairs to cars by CHAS & GLEN + Engine Man on that car.

Vests to be exchanged with mechanics and mechanic to cover if needed on fuel handle.

CHAS / GLEN back up GREG / BRIAN

| Number to work on car | Job | Time |
|---|---|---|
| 2 men | Air Box | 9 mins |
| 1 man | Alternator | 9 mins |
| 1 man | Belts - water pump | 5 mins? |
| 2 men | Distributor Caps | 12 mins |
| 2 men | Engine loom | 3 mins |
| | with oil pressure & temp working | 5 mins. |
| 2 men | Fuel rail | 9 mins |
| | Exchange airbox complete | |
| 2 men | Fuel regulator | 4 mins |
| 3 men | Intake system | 12 mins |
| 2 men | Injector | |
| | Change air box | 9 mins |
| 2 men | Oil feed pipe (cams.) | 2 mins |
| | under tray off | |
| 2 men | Scavenge pipes | |
| 1 man | Sender block (temps) | 4 mins |
| 2 - 4 men | Spark Plug - complete | 8 - 10 mins |
| 1 man | Starter motor | 7 mins |
| 2 men | Sticking throttle | 12 mins |
| 2 men | Water pump (not possible) | |
| 2 men | Wiring looms in air box | |
| | Air box change | 9 mins |

Oil pipes off engine.
Chassis loom.
Battery.
Throttle cable.
To be changed by chassis crew.

NOTE : Quick change air box will have no fuel cooling ability.

Extra 4 minutes to have fuel cooling.

As night falls / temperatures drop - remember cooler blanking.

above: *I supplied the car managers with a list of potential problems during the race and how long it would take for Engs personnel to make repairs.*

**DRIVERS AND CAR MANAGERS - LE MANS 1988**

**Engine lacks power** :

CHECK : Fuel pressure (constant or drops around corners).
Oil pressure and 'temperature'.
Water temperature.
Battery voltage.

**Low oil pressure / oil light coming on** :

CHECK : Oil temperature.
Pressure drop on corners?
Light on at lower R.P.M.?

**Engine misfire** :

CHECK : Fuel pressure.
Battery voltage.
Misfire at part or full throttles.
Intermittent or constant (cylinder out).
Mechanical noises.
Master switch.

**Engine stops** :

CHECK : Fuel pressure.
Dash board lights.
Does engine turn on starter motor.
Engine noises before it stopped.
Battery voltage.
Master switch
Main loom multi plug to side of E.C.U.

**Remove engine cover** :

NOTE : Replace stay pins after refitting.

H.T. lead to Lucas spark box.
Multi plugs to side of spark box.

Swop over spare trigger lead; 3 multi plugs on side of air box; connect bottom multi plug to centre and centre to bottom.

If stopped with low voltage or electrical short, check wires on rear of alternator, shorting on heat shield, or main lead to starter off and shorting on body.

Allan Scott
02 June 1988

*Driver problem solving list.*
*Drivers and car managers were briefed on what to look for if certain problems arose and check these first before reporting any problem to me – e.g.: 'Oil light comes on' – see checks to make to show why this may be the problem – low oil level, hot oil temperature.*

*The Sauber Mercedes team that later withdrew.*

# Le Mans Race Personnel

T. Walkinshaw. R Silman. T Southgate. A Scott.

Group C team.

| | |
|---|---|
| K Lee. | |
| A Macqueen. | Engineer car. |
| E Hinckley | Engineer car. |
| K Page. | Engineer car. |
| A Beckett. | Controls parts during race. |

Four mechanics per car.

588) J Wilson. A Claxton. T Strudwick. M Bellars.
488). R Benoist. J Pyman. C Tuckey. N Weeks.
287). C Parker. C Morgan. G Davies. M Shurety.

| Fabricators. | Job during race. | Job prior to race. |
|---|---|---|
| M Owen. | Fueling. | In charge of fabricating/bodywork. |
| M Blackwell. | Fireman. | Fabricating/bodywork. |
| R Harding. | Fireman. | Fabricating/bodywork. |
| M Buskell. | Bodywork. | Bodywork. |

Truckies.

| | | |
|---|---|---|
| K Partridge. | Fueling. | In charge of truck crew. |
| P Roberts. | Fueling. | Pit equipment. |
| B Wright. | Tyre moving. | Air bottles fueling etc. |
| R Steur. | Fueling. | Air bottles fueling etc. |
| | plus all 4 keep awning truck clean and tidy. | |
| V Cowley. | Tyre moving. | Wheel moving/cleaning. |
| D Warren. | Tyre moving wheel weight tape. | |

Extras.

| | | |
|---|---|---|
| S Gardener. | Fireman. | Storeman in small truck |
| C Gibson. | Drivers, Pit to Paddock. | |
| B Furn. | Fueling. | Group C spares. |
| B Robertson. | Fueling. | Look after IMSA truck. |

Engine men.

| | |
|---|---|
| C Bamber. | Floating engine man. |
| G Hunt | Operate fuel deadman 287. |
| M Norris. | Operate fuel deadman 186. |
| G Barber. | Operate fuel deadman 488. |
| G Rushton. | Operate fuel deadman 588. |

TOTAL OF 41 BRITISH PERSONNEL.

Extra extra's.

| | |
|---|---|
| J Percy. Radio Link to Mulsanne. | |
| C Moore. Radio link to Mulsanne. | Stickers on bodywork. |
| E Cowcill. D MacGill. J English | Timekeepers. |
| T Daff. D Bettinson. C Haywood. N Payne | .. .. |
| D Vinson. T Ryan. M Tarratt | Trainers. |
| Dr I Robertson | Doctor. |
| B Gibson. B Mason | Zytek. |
| R Gustafson. D Payne. | Roni. |
| J Thompson. E Clarricoats. | ART. |
| B Liddell. M Coventry. | Flatbed Drivers. |
| G Kingston. | Motorbike for circuit. |
| A Longland. D Longland. K Quatermass. | Signallers. |
| P Quatermass. C Watts. P Morley. | |
| C Foskett. M Crowley. G Britten. | |
| I Schuler. M Bates. R Bates. | |
| G Britten. G Jinks. | |

TOTAL OF 35 BRITISH EXTRAS.
ROOMS REQUIRED FOR 21 EXTRAS ONLY.

Drivers.

M Brundle.
J Nielsen.
J Lammers.
J Dumfries.
A Wallace.
J Watson.
R Boesel.
H Pescarolo.

TOTAL OF 8 BRITISH TEAM DRIVERS.
TOTAL OF 84 IN BRITISH TEAM.

IMSA Team.

T Dowe.
P Davis. (from England).

| | |
|---|---|
| I Reed. | Engineer car. |
| D Benbow. | Engineer car. |
| W Bush. | Controls parts during race. |

Four mechanics per car.

188). J Jackson. C McCann. P Denny. H Minckler.
186). J Simmonds. M Hughes. C Azevedo. B Winkle.
(M Hughes fueling on 186).

| | Job during race. | Job prior to race. |
|---|---|---|
| Fabricator. | | |
| F Rafferty. | Fueling | Fabricating/bodywork. |
| Engine men. | | |
| B Sheriden. | Operate fuel deadman 188. | |
| Truckies. | | |
| K Siwieck. | Tyre moving. | Air bottles fueling etc. |
| K Wilson. | Tyre moving. | Tyre moving/wheel wieght tape |
| Bodywork. | | |
| J Mclellen. | Fueling. | Bodywork. |
| Extras. | | |
| L Zelesnik. | Fueling. (188) | Tyre moving. |
| J Faulconer. | RR wheel 186. | Pit equipment. |
| D Girton. | Fireman. | IMSA spares. |

TOTAL OF 21 IMSA TEAM PERSONNEL.
AIR TICKETS FOR 19 ONLY. (PLUS DRIVERS).

IMSA Drivers.

D Sullivan.
D Jones.
P Cobb.
D Daly.
K Cogan.
L Perkins.

TOTAL OF 6 IMSA TEAM DRIVERS.
TOTAL OF 27 IN IMSA TEAM.
GRAND TOTAL OF 111 PEOPLE.

---

TWR SILK CUT JAGUAR TEAM
LE MANS MOVEMENT SCHEDULE
11/12 JUNE 1988

TUESDAY 24 MAY
Car 188 arrives London Heathrow
John Jackson to Kidlington

WEDNESDAY 1 JUNE
SHAKEDOWN TESTING AT SILVERSTONE.

Car 1 - 588 - John Watson
Car 2 - 488 - Johnny Dumfries
Car 3 - 287 - Henri Pescarolo
Car 21 - 188 - Andy Wallace
Car 22 - 186 - Larry Perkins

| | | |
|---|---|---|
| Race Truck | PR/BW | OFR 925X |
| Race Truck | BR | A659 OUD |
| Spares Truck | KP | C200 FWL |
| | RS/TS/AM | OT |
| | EH/KP/PD/KL | OT |
| | AWS/CB/GB/MN | OT |
| 588 - J Wilson/A Claxton/T Strudwick | | E660 AHR |
| 488 - R Benoist/J Pyman/C Tuckey | | E660 AHR |
| 287 - C Parker/C Morgan/N Weeks | | E660 AHR |
| 188 - J Jackson/B Furn | | E159 VKJ |
| 186 - G Davies/M Shurety/M Bellars | | E160 VKJ |
| Depart KIDLINGTON | 1100 | |
| TESTING TIMES : | 1400 - 1700 | |

*The UK test programme for the five XJR-9LM cars and drivers.*

## Le Mans Pre Race Checklist

**FRONT SUSPENSION AND STEERING**

1. CHECK FRONT HUB NUT TORQUE
2. CHECK RACK FOR FREE MOVEMENT
3. CHECK UNIBALLS FOR EXCESSIVE PLAY
4. CLEAN AND INSPECT WISHBONES
5. INSPECT F.A.R.B. ENDS
6. SPANNER CHECK

**REAR SUSPENSION**

1. CHECK HUB NUT TORQUE
2. CLEAN AND INSPECT UPRIGHTS
3. CLEAN AND INSPECT WISHBONES
4. CHECK UNIBALLS AND JOINTS
5. CHECK REAR BEAM AND SUPPORTS
6. SPANNER CHECK

**BRAKES**

1. MEASURE PAD WEAR
2. CHECK DISCS FOR CRACKING
3. CHECK DISC TO BELL BOLTS
4. CHECK CALIPER PISTONS FOR FREE RETURN
5. CHECK BALANCE BAR ASSEMBLY AND CABLE
6. BLEED BRAKES AND CHECK FOR LEAKS
7. CLEAN AIR INTAKE GRILLS
8. CHECK PEDALS AND MOUNTINGS
9. CHECK DUCTING
10. INSPECT FLUID LINES

**TRANSMISSION**

1. CHECK DRIVESHAFT FLANGE BOLTS
2. CHECK CV RUBBER BOOTS AND VENT TUBES
3. CHECK GEAR BOX INTERNAL SUPPORT SIDE BOLTS
4. CHECK GEAR LINKAGE AND MOUNTINGS AND LUBE, LINKAGE
5. CHECK GEAR BOX FOR LEAKS
6. CLEAN AIR INTAKE TO OIL COOLER
7. SPANNER CHECK

**FUEL SYSTEM**

1. CHECK BOTH HIGH PRESSURE PUMPS AND FLOW CHECK
2. CHANGE FUEL FILTER
3. CHECK LOW PRESSURE PUMPS
4. CHECK FOR LEAKS
5. CHECK FILLER NECK MOUNTINGS
6. CHECK OPERATION OF BREATHER VALVES
7. CHECK LOCATION OF HIGH PRESSURE PUMP ASSY

**COOLING SYSTEM**

1. CHECK RADIATOR FOR DAMAGE AND CLEAN AIR INTAKE
2. CHECK ALL CLIPS AND PRESSURE TEST SYSTEM
3. CHECK FLUID LEVEL

**ELECTRICAL**

1. CHECK ALL LIGHTING COMPONENTS - INCLUDING INDICATORS AND STOP LAMPS
2. CHECK ALL WIRING FOR DAMAGE AND SECURITY
3. CHECK ALTERNATOR MOUNTINGS AND CONNECTIONS
4. CHECK STARTER MOUNTINGS AND CONNECTIONS
5. CHECK BATTERY MOUNTINGS AND CONNECTIONS
6. CHARGE BATTERY

**GENERAL**

1. CHECK NOSE BOX FOR DAMAGE
2. CHECK UNDERSIDE FOR DAMAGE
3. CHECK FLUSH FITTING OF RAD UNDERPANEL AND REAR UNDERTRAY
4. CHECK WING AND MOUNTINGS
5. CHECK SIDE SKIRTS FOR DAMAGE
6. CHECK OVERALL WIDTH TO 2M
7. CHECK DOORS, HINGES, CATCHES AND FLUSH FITTINGS
8. CHECK NOSE AND TAIL FOR DAMAGE
9. CHECK FIRE EXTINGUISHER LOCATION
10. CLEAN AIR INTAKE TO ENGINE OIL COOLER AND COOLER
11. CHARGE RADIO BATTERY
12. CHECK SCREEN FOR CRACKS AND SECURITY
13. CHECK COMPLETE EXHAUST FOR CRACKS OR DAMAGE
14. CHECK STARTER MOTOR SHROUD

*The Friday comprehensive checklist for the XJR-9LMs.*

*France's well known Le Mans and Formula One driver Henri Pescarolo.*

*The Hawaiian Tropic girls were always a feature on the starting grid at Le Mans.*

## Le Mans Pit Stop Plan

### Car 1, 2, 3

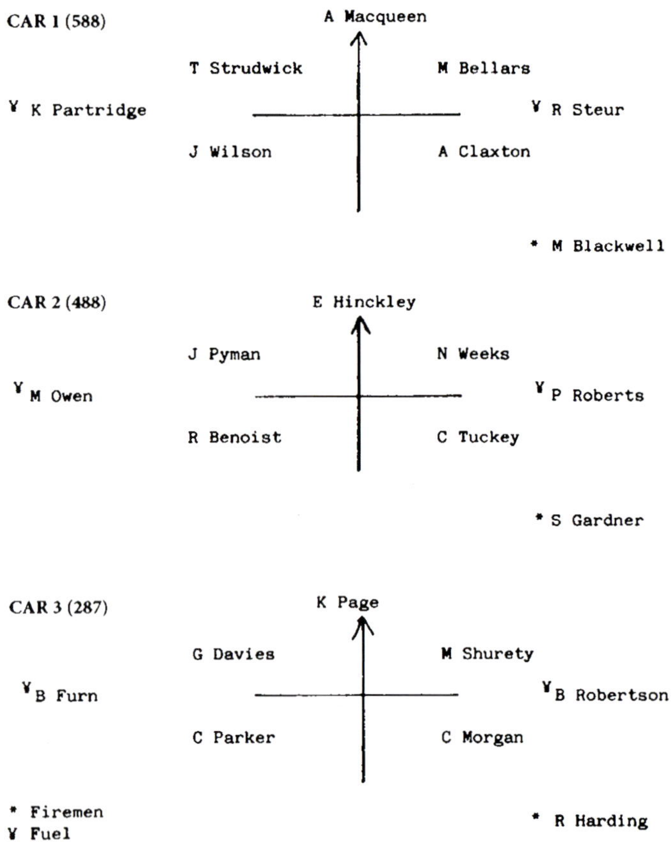


### Car 22 and 23

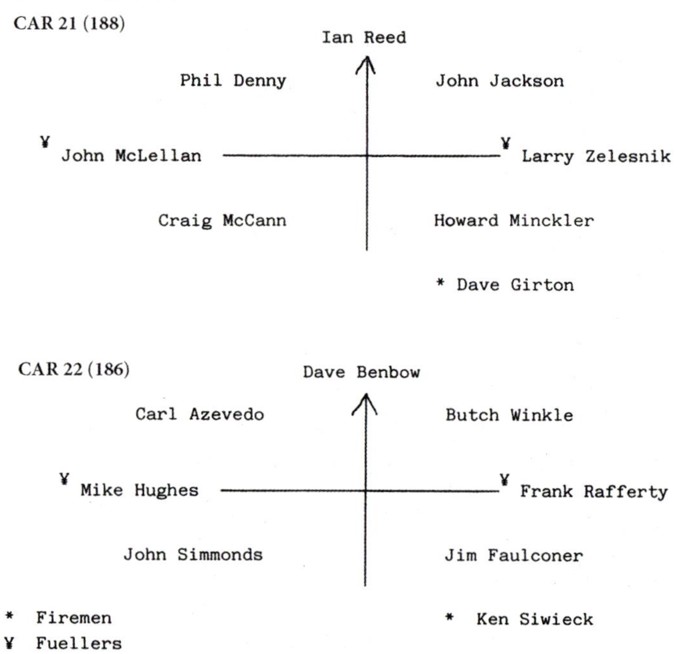


## *The race*

The 24 hours would start at 3pm on Saturday after the spectacular flying display by the French air force, and it became official that in excess of 215,000 enthusiasts had come to see the 56th running of this historical event, many of them Brits located opposite the Jaguar pits to cheer on the Jaguars. Stuck lead from the start with Lammers pleasing the crowd with his second place and on lap six taking the lead, with the five Jaguars all in the top 10 placings. Lammers at this early stage seemed to have a faster car than Brundle. One of the problems that had surfaced in practice was snap oversteer into slow corners for the Jaguars and solutions had been tried for the race. Brundle circulating in fifth had disconnected the rear anti roll bar, and it seemed that was not working as well in the race as the drivers had expected. The #2 Jaguar engineered by Eddie Hinckley was almost 10kph faster than all the other Jaguars, and able to overtake the Porsches on the Mulsanne straight. This was a welcome outcome but also seemed a mystery to some in the team. Post race it was found the front ride or splitter height had been raised 10mm, reducing front downforce on the straight where it was not needed, and had the happy consequence of reducing nose down car rake producing reduced drag, increasing the maximum speed.

*Lammers leads the factory Porches early in the race.*

Porsche pitted all three of their cars on lap 13 causing some administration problems with that strategy, and when all driver and fuel changes had been made Dumfries' Jaguar now led the three Porsches with Jaguars fourth, fifth, seventh and eighth. Nielsen had a spin just two hours into the race as he came to grips with the imperfect set-up with this car; it cost them one lap by the time he was mobile again. The #2 Jaguar seemed to

*Eddie Hinckley*

be the only one that could match the works Porsche pace and by now it had become obvious that this was because it was almost 10kph faster on the Mulsanne than the other Jaguars.

The lead was lost after Lammers made contact with the Brun Porsche losing a minute to repair the Jaguar's rear bodywork. The Brun Porsche then ran into the tyre barrier around 9pm and was out of the race, while new boy Andy Wallace double stinted the leading Jaguar regaining half the time that had been lost in the pits. The teams had all settled down to their various tasks by now when suddenly Michel Ferté's Cougar was engulfed in a large fire in the crowded lane pit area; always a problem at Le Mans, but good response by the team soon had it out.

The first Jaguar retirement came at just after 11pm and Boesel was out with a broken gearbox shaft, but Porsche were also in trouble with the Andretti family car, needing a pit stop to repair water leakage, costing them three laps. A slow pit stop by the leaders Stuck and Schuppan over a radio miscommunication allowed the Jaguar in second place to edge closer and take the lead with Dumfries at the wheel. The lead of the race as it progressed towards half distance swapped back and forth as pit stops for fuel and tyres were made, but overall the three leading cars were still on the same lap and close together. The fourth place #1 Jaguar drivers were not happy with the handling of their car and in trying to keep up with the pace Nielsen left the road losing two laps in the process, before being able to rejoin and continue on.

By half distance Jaguar #2 led from Stuck/Ludwig/Bell, a hard working Brundle/Nielsen, the Andretti family Porsche, Dickens/Winter/Jelinski in the Joest Porsche, Wollek/Schuppan/Van der Merwe works Porsche, and Hobbs/Theys/Konrad in the second Joest Porsche, with the third Jaguar of Le Mans newcomers Daly/Perkins/Cogan moving into eighth.

In the early hours of the morning the leading Porsche suddenly slowed and its problem was that it had run low on fuel, now stopping and starting its way around the track losing valuable time on its way back to the pits. It was this reversal of their fortunes that put the Lammers/Dumfries/Wallace Jaguar firmly in the lead. The TWR USA team's move up the placings had at one stage reached third, but their car would spend a long time in the pits with gearbox problems centred on the differential pinion bearings and although valiant efforts were made to fix the situation this car continued to drop from contention as the problem then reappeared for a second time. Porsche had also just suffered their first engine failure due to water loss, something that had shown up earlier with the Andretti family car, and the #18 factory Porsche of Wollek/Schuppan/Van der Merwe was out of the race. Porsche were down to the two factory cars with Joest's two cars in support while TWR/Jaguar had three cars remaining after the other two had succumbed to transmission problems.

During the night the leading Jaguar continued without mishap but Stuck/Ludwig in the #17 Porsche were the

*John, Michel and Mario, the famous Andretti family from America, in one of the three works Porches.*

stars of this period closing down on the Jaguar without too much regard to fuel usage. They proceeded to regain the lost lap and get to within 25 seconds of the leading Jaguar. There had up to this point been no fuel saving pace car interventions and it looked like Porsche were maybe counting on one or two periods later in the race to rectify their fuel consumption problem.

The #1 Jaguar had been driven hard by Brundle/Nielsen and by 1am was in third, one lap down on the leaders, and three laps ahead of the Joest Porsche of Jelinski/Winter/Dickens, with the Andretti family Porsche and the third Jaguar of Daly/Perkins/Cogan a further three laps behind them. Positions remained for the two front runners with little more than a minute separating them until the early morning light showed Lammers the state of the windscreen crack that the team had been living with during the night. On the high speed Mulsanne straight the screen was flexing inwards to such a degree that Lammers radioed in that it would have to be replaced at the fuel stop with the danger of it imploding. This problem had been anticipated and the screen was held in by a quick release fastening system and was changed in less than four minutes during the normal two minute flow regulated fuel stop, but it left the Jaguar in second place. The problems with the Porsche factory cars losing an engine and the repairs needed to the Andretti car to prevent a similar fate had the team concerned, and with their obvious pace and the probability of a future pace car to close up the field, they had decided to change the water pump and pipe work at the next stop on their leading car. This task was carried out in seven minutes and provided the first healthy leaders gap for the Jaguar team, and promoted the Brundle/Nielsen Jaguar to second.

This situation was to be short lived however, and engine problems were to continue but this time it would be the Brundle/Nielsen Jaguar that would have to retire five hours from the end with a loss of water, but not from a head gasket as some reported. (A faulty head casting was the culprit here, report later in this chapter.) Six hours from the end the rain clouds gathered and light rain developed at different parts of the circuit, but where we were it seemed too dry for wet tyres. Lammers stayed in the car at this next stop with new slicks, but the rain then increased and he returned for Dunlop intermediates, losing precious time to the Porsche, but confirming to them that intermediates were needed. Porsche too then changed to intermediates and Stuck set about reducing the time to the leading Jaguar in spectacular fashion with the thought that less laps would be completed in the twenty-four hours if these conditions continued. They had nothing to lose with a five lap lead over third place and by now were over their fuel limit with this strategy. Conditions continued with lighter rain not totally suiting both tyre choices and this began to wear Stuck's intermediates more than the Jaguars, and once again the distance was stabilised.

From the twenty-one hour mark to the finish the British crowd were on their feet, roaring with delight each time one of the three Jaguars came passed the pits as they sensed a Jaguar victory. Bell had then driven a short stint as well as Stuck with an apparent fuel pickup problem the reason for their shorter stints. With two hours to go and one and a half minutes separating the Porsche from the leading Jaguar, the #17 Porsche had a longer stop than normal with a hasty fuel pump change. Ludwig was now in for the final run to the flag and unlapped the Porsche in a determined effort to be in a position to challenge for the lead.

During the later stages of the race something that had been kept from most of the team, all the commentators and most importantly the Porsche teams was that Lammers had a gearbox problem. He had discussed the situation after Boesel's failure earlier in the race and had been told by him that the car had just the once been hard to get into fourth gear and then had nothing when he had changed up to fifth. Jan Lammers had felt exactly the same situation over one hour before the end of the

*Allan Scott discusses progress with Tom Walkinshaw.*

*Chief engineer Alastair Macqueen*

race and had wisely made the decision to leave his race car in fourth gear. The last pit stop was a short one with just 23 litres left to fill the tank and go, the Porsche on its last stop however would need to take on its remaining 57 litres, and that would mean an additional 41 seconds stationary in the pit with the regulated refuelling flows. Jan Lammers then had the #2 car leaving the last pit stop in a very measured way so as to not indicate it was a fourth gear departure, and all the careful low speed mapping and seven litres of the V12 allowed a calm departure in fourth gear, and this was the way it would continue for the remaining hour, stuck in fourth gear.

Over the last two hours TW had handed me the headphones to talk through any engine problem Jan Lammers might have had, and I concentrated on adjusting the gap to the following Porsche; showing he had little to worry about. He would try harder when the gap closed too much and I would then encourage the situation by holding the gap constant for a couple of laps.

By the end of the race Ludwig was flying in the #17 Porsche as they sensed that something was amiss with the Jaguar and closed to within one and a half minutes once again. The Daly/Perkins/Cogan Jaguar was securely in fourth place after doing all they had been asked to do as a supporting crew. As the race came to a close the other remaining Jaguars were asked to form up behind, with TW saying they could push the car #2 car over the last lap if the gearbox had failed. It was then a nail biting finish with the commencement of the last lap and the flag marshal posts waving all their flags, including the yellow caution one; meaning the race was already won with no overtaking allowed under waved yellow caution flags. The three remaining Jaguars (car #21 had rejoined after the transmission repair), lined up for a formation finish. As they came into view the British crowd climbed over the barriers engulfing the three finishers, and and stopped Lammer's Jaguar before he could cross the finish line. Such was my paranoia and relief at getting the result that I was convinced the cars had to pass the finishing line and began searching the FIA yellow book while all the others crowded onto the circuit. Jan Lammers emerged to stand on the roof of his Jaguar draped in the Union Jack with the crowd roaring their approval.

I am sure I saw a tear in TW's eyes and there certainly were many in the Jaguar directors' eyes as well. It was a huge moment, not just for TWR and Jaguar, but for Britain as well, returning to take on the European car industry, just as the C and D-types had done before to establish the Jaguar Brand in the 1950s. There was just one thing missing, the BBC had decided we did not stand a chance of winning against Porsche and they were not there to cover the finish live. The winning car when later checked had one lap of fuel, seven litres left in the tank from the allocated 2550 litres allowed. It had been a close-run thing with three broken transmissions and one broken engine out of the five cars that started, and this vindicated Tom Walkinshaw's decision to field the five cars in what seemed an impossible task at the time.

*The British crowd come over the barriers and stop Lammers Jaguar on the track before he could cross the finishing line.*

Most TWR employees involved in racing at Kidlington had attended in one form or another to show the magnitude of the TWR organisation, and this amounted to a total of almost 100 people in supporting this five-car adventure. Jaguar had a 50% finishing record as did Porsche with three of the eight cars suffering engine failures and one from accident damage.

While all concerned had played their part in this success, it was Jan Lammers who made the right decisions under pressure at the right time to bring this result to fruition. His decision, when he felt that the gear change into fourth was not normal, to then leave the car in that gear for the last hour and a half of the race, was one that even the best would probably not have taken. He had tutored new boy Andy Wallace before the event in a road car showing where higher gears could be used as well as care on the downshifts, especially the long gap from fifth to fourth, to eliminate over revving the engine and causing additional stress on the valve springs. The car set-up also contributed in two ways, making the winning car less wearing to drive and 10kph faster on the straight – without compromising the rest of the circuit.

CAR 22 ENG 88 C 08.

| STOP TIME | OIL | FUEL | THROUGH FLOW METER. |
|---|---|---|---|
| SAT | | | |
| 1. 1545 | NONE | 92L | |
| 2. 1630 | 2 LITRES | 175L | |
| 3. 1718 | NONE | 265L | |
| 4. 1806 | 1.8 LITRE | 354L | |
| 5. CAR SPUN | NONE | 393L | * TOTAL OIL USED* |
| 6. 1919 | NONE | 483L | |
| 7. 1949SHT STP | NONE | 542L | 25.8 LITRES |
| 8. 2030 | 2 LITRES | 627L | |
| 9. 2125 | NONE | 714L | |
| 10.2213 | 2 LITRES | 808L | |
| 11.2231 | NONE | 821L | |
| 12.2316 | NONE | 905L | |
| 13.000£ SUN | 2 LITRES | 990L | |
| 14.0055 | NONE | 1086L | |
| 15.0145 | 2 LITRES | 1167L | |
| 16.0235 | NONE | 1248L | |
| 17.0323 | 2 LITRES | 1336L | |
| 18.0411 | NONE | 1420L | |
| 19.0500 | 2 LITRES | 1509L | |
| 20.0548 | NONE | 1606L | |
| 21.0636 | 2 LITRES | 1700L | |
| 22.0725 | NONE | 1767L | |
| 23.0811 | 2 LITRES | 1852L | |
| 24.0903 | NONE | 1942L | |
| 25.0955 | 2 LITRES | 2031L | |
| 26.1045 | NONE | 2131L | * SOME FUEL IN VENT |
| 27.1120 | NONE | 2171L | BOTTLE WET TYRE STOP. |
| 28.1216 | 2 LITRES | 2262L | |
| 29.1305 | NONE | 2349L | |
| 30.1354 | 2 LITRES | 2419L | |
| 31.LAST STOP | NONE | 2449 LITRES. | |

*Sir John Egan, Andy Wallace, Johnny Dumfries, Jan Lammers and Tom Walkinshaw*

### Car #2

| | FUEL | & TIME | OIL | TOTAL |
|---|---|---|---|---|
| 1 | 84 | [illegible] | — | |
| 2 | 89 | [illegible] | 2 | 173 |
| 3 | 87 | [illegible] | ¾ | 260 |
| 4 | 87 | 18·00 | 1 | 347 |
| 5 | 87 | 18·48 | ¾ | 434 |
| 6 | 94 | 19·35 | ¾ | 528 |
| 7 | 84 | 20·22 | 1 | 612 |
| 8 | 87 | 21·09 | 1¾ | 699 |
| 9 | 84 | 21·56 | 1 | 783 |
| 10 | 80 | 22·45 | ¾ | 863 |
| 11 | 85 | 23·31 | 1 | 948 |
| 12 | 90 | 24·22 | 1 | 1038 |
| 13 | 89 | 1·13 | 1 | 1127 |
| 14 | 88 | 2·05 | 1 | 1215 |
| 15 | 90 | 2·55 | 1 | 1305 |
| 16 | 92 | 3·46 | 1 | 1397 |
| 17 | 87 | 4·38 | 2 | 1484 |
| 18 | 88 | 5·29 | — | 1572 |
| 19 | 88 | 6·20 | 2 | 1660 |
| 20 | 43 | 6·36 | — | 1703 |
| 21 | 65 | 7·25 | 1¾ | 1768 |
| 22 | 89 | 8·15 | 1 | 1857 |
| 23 | 92 | 9·05 | 1½ | 1949 |
| 24 | 42 | 9·33 | — | 1991 |
| 25 | 92 | 10·22 | — | 2083 |
| 26 | 89 | 11·15 | 1½ | 2172 |
| 27 | 6 | 11·20 | | 2178 |
| 28 | 73 | 12·15 | 1 | 2251 |
| 29 | 90 | 13·05 | 1 | 2341 |
| 30 | 87 | 13·57 | 2 | 2428 |
| 31 | 20 | 14·40 | — | 2448 |

above right: ***Fuel/oil consumption records for the fourth placed car #22.***

right: ***Fuel/oil consumption records for the winning car #2.***

Everyone was happy and felt part of the result as TW appeared on the podium and took the accolades from the crowd, with his winning crew of Lammers, Dumfries and Wallace. This result was a major step up in profile for TWR and kudos for Tom Walkinshaw, but would present some unseen effects as well. Roger was bitterly disappointed that he had not been able to be on the podium in recognition of his position, and loudly voiced his disappointment at the way he had been treated to TW on his return to Kidlington.

Unfortunately for the Drivers Championship, the leading points scoring Jaguar crew had not taken this win, but an opportunity for the non-starting Sauber Mercedes team had also been lost, with the overall points position staying the same. In all the 'after Le Mans' interviews and driver comments the broken transmission on the winning Jaguar was never mentioned, and when I unwittingly recalled this aspect at the Jaguar victory dinner later when sitting with engineering director Jim Randle, he expressed surprise as he had not been told about it. At the same time, I had to add another layer of skin as two VIP Jaguar guests on our table congratulated Jim on the fantastic sounding V12 engines that he had produced to win Le Mans for Jaguar and Britain. I also had to tap my wife on her foot to stop her reaction to this dismissal of our efforts.

Senior managers had assembled in the new board room at Broadstone on the Wednesday after Le Mans and I was looking forward to TW telling us what his plans were now that we had achieved all that he had ever set out to do. It had been a rapid rise from one RX7 Mazda and twelve staff just over eight years before when I had joined, to achieve the dream of working with a British car manufacturer and return Jaguar to its former glory, with 120 people now employed at the Kidlington Industrial Estate. Everyone was in good spirits as the door opened but it was TW's secretary who had come in to say that we should talk amongst ourselves, as Tom would not be attending the meeting. The rumour was that he was at the Covent Garden Flower Show and would be meeting the Queen Mother; so that was more important than us were my thoughts. My fellow managers just accepted this as normal and did not seem to share my disappointment. It felt a strategic time for me as we had all followed an obvious path over the years; one car becoming two, British series becoming European, and then World, and America. Most could second guess the future decisions and saw a constantly upward direction. All this had been focused on the eventual winning of the World Championship and Le Mans – that had now been achieved. What was the next step, so we could all fully understand the big picture?

LETTER

Tom Walkinshaw Racing Ltd.
Att; Mr Alan Scott
1, Stationfield Industrial Estate
Kidlington,
Oxford,

ENGLAND

June 26, 1988

Dear Alan,

We allready spoke on the phone, but with this letter I would like to give some substance to my thanks for what you have done for us during the Le Mans weekend.

I was most pleased about the little changes you made as the weekend progressed, and I thought about the "engine departement" a lot specially when I was outrunning the Porsches on the long straight!

It was just a 24 hour long treat, and I was very greatful for it.

A nice memory!!

I hope to see you soon,

Best regards,

Jan Lammers

**LE MANS CELEBRATION DINNER**

*The Directors of Jaguar Cars invite*

MR + MRS A. SCOTT

*to*

*Dinner on Wednesday 13th July 1988*

*at*

*Packington Hall*

7.30 for 8.00pm — Black Tie

TW came to my office later in the week and said, "I have put out for a long time, now it is time to take back." He had taken huge financial risks up to this point and the Le Mans win was to now be used to raise the value of future contracts for the TWR Group. At what onlookers would see as the height of success and a huge future in motor racing, already some of the ideals up to this point that had been the mainstay of arriving at this success were about to be challenged – with money and the growing 'TWR Group' concept now being the primary motivation for Tom Walkinshaw. Engs had also become fully involved in the new direction for Group C that TW had finally insisted on, using a turbocharged uneven firing V6 engine. For the first time in the nine year history of the Engine Division TW had not taken my advice on the vital concepts involved when setting a path for the way forward in the future, preferring to listen to advice from Liechtenstein.

The failure on the Brundle/Nielsen XJR-9 engine was a flaw in the casting process. A review of the methods and materials used was carried out with Jaguar, and this problem was resolved.

23.6.88

ENGINE 05 CAR NO.1.

LOSS OF WATER A FAILURE AFTER 2850 MILES.

ENGINE WAS STRIPPED AND ALL LINERS CRACK TESTED. THESE WERE FOUND TO BE OK.

LARGE CRACKS WERE VISABLE ON 'A' BANK RUNNING ACROSS THE HEAD FROM THE CENTRE OF THE INLET PORT THROUGH THE VALVE GUIDE BOSS TOWARDS THE WATER JACKET.

'B' BANK WAS PRESSURE TESTED IN HOT WATER TO 60 PSI AND HELD PRESSURE.

INSPECTION OF THE BORE SEALING RINGS SHOWED SLIGHT BLOW BY ON NO.4 'B' BANK AND EXTENSIVE FRETTING OF THE SEALING RINGS INTO THE HEAD, ON ALL CYLINDERS. A HARDNESS TEST ONLY JUST REGISTERED ON 'B' BANK AND 'A' BANK SHOWED 65B ROCKWELL. THE INLET VALVE SEAT INSERT HAD FALLEN OUT OF NO.1. CYLINDER 'B' BANK THIS BEING THE NOISE THAT WAS HEARD AT THE LAST PIT STOP, WHEN THE ENGINE WAS FINALLY SHUT DOWN. THESE SIGNS INDICATED THAT 'B' BANK HEAD RUN MUCH HOTTER THAN 'A' BANK.

THE SINGLE WATER PUMP ON THE V12 ENGINE HAS EXITS TO THE BLOCK AT TWO DIFFERENT HEIGHTS, 'A' BANK BEING SOME 1 1/2 - 2" LOWER THAT 'B' BANK. AS THE WATER LEVEL DROPPED IN THE ENGINE, THE HIGHER EXIT HEIGHT OF 'B' BANK ALLOWED ALL THE WATER TO FLOW THROUGH THE 'A' SIDE AND SO CAUSE 'B' BANK TO SEVERLEY OVER HEAT.

CONCLUSION:

'A' HEAD (ALWAYS HAVING THE BEST COOLING) CRACKED BETWEEN STUD CENTRES THROUGH THE INLET PORT TO THE WATER JACKET AND OVER A PERIOD OF 2-3 HOURS WATER WAS LOST THROUGH THE ENGINE.
THE RADIATOR WAS COLD TO TOUCH ON THE 2ND TO LAST PIT TOP, INDICATING TOTAL LOSS OF WATER. THE SLIGHT GASKET BLOW BY AN 'B' BANK WAS THEN THE RESULT OF MAJOR OVERHEATING AND NOT THE CAUSE OF THE WATER LOSS.
THIS HEAD WAS NEW FOR THE RACE AND WILL BE ANALISED TO SEE WHY IT CRACKED.
ALL OTHER COMPONENTS WERE FOUND TO BE IN GOOD CONDITION ON COMPLETE DISASSEMBLY.
THE STEEL CAMS HAVE SLIGHT SCUFF MARKS BUT WOULD NOT HAVE STARTED ANY PROBLEMS FOR AT LEAST ANOTHER 2000 MILES.

*Brundle/Nielsen head casting failure report.*

## Before and after testing of the Le Mans winning engine

TYPE: GRP C 2 VALVE V12 | ENG. NO.: 88C08 | DATE: 16/5/88
PRESS.: 60 PSI | OIL TEMP.: 80°C | WATER TEMP.: 85°C
L PRESS.: 60 PSI | BARO. PRESS.: 1017 | HYDROM.: -5
L TEMP.: 23°C | CORR. FIGURE: 1.037

| RPM | LOAD | CORR. BHP | IN" HG | CO FIG. |
|---|---|---|---|---|
| 4500 | 104.3 | 486 | -3" | 2.8% |
| 4750 | 105.7 | 520 | -2" | 2.5% |
| 5000 | 108.9 | 564 | 0 | 3.0% |
| 5250 | 106.4 | 579 | 0 | 3.0% |
| 5500 | 106 | 604 | 0 | 4.0% |
| 5750 | 107 | 638 | 0 | 3.2% |
| 6000 | 110.2 | 685 | 0 | 3.2% |
| 6250 | 108.9 | 705 | 0 | 3.5% |
| 6500 | 105.6 | 711 | 0 | 3.0% |
| 6750 | 102.4 | 716 | 0 | 2.8% |
| 7000 | 98.3 | 713 | 0 | 2.8% |
| 7250 | 94 | 706 | 0 | 3.5% |

12:1 COMP — COMMENTS — 84mm X 94mm
MK 2 INTERFERENCE SPRINGS
EA 15/15 CAMS 100°
TORQUE HONED LINERS. BRG STEEL TOP RINGS (LAPPED)
AIR FILTER FITTED.
CRANK DAMPER/80 AMP ALT
4 STAGE SCAVENGE
TESTED ON (TWR C3) EMR FUEL +2: IGN -1.5

*The winning engine from Le Mans when tested from new at 13.4:1 air/fuel ratio with the lower compression ratio of 12:1 and ignition retarded 1.5° from optimum.*

TYPE: GRP C 2 VALVE V12 | ENG. NO.: 88 C 08 | DATE: 22/6/88
PRESS.: 55 PSI | OIL TEMP.: 80°C | WATER TEMP.: 85°C
L PRESS.: 60 PSI | BARO. PRESS.: 1029 | HYDROM.: -7
L TEMP.: 23°C | CORR. FIGURE: 1.012

| RPM | LOAD | CORR. BHP | IN" HG | CO FIG. |
|---|---|---|---|---|
| 4500 | 106.4 | 484 | -1 | 2.6 |
| 4750 | 106.9 | 513 | 0 | 2.4 |
| 5000 | 110 | 556 | 0 | 2.6 |
| 5250 | 109.2 | 580 | 0 | 2.8 |
| 5500 | 108.3 | 602 | 0 | 3.3 |
| 5750 | 109.6 | 637 | 0 | 4.0 |
| 6000 | 111 | 673 | 0 | 4.0 |
| 6250 | 109 | 695 | 0 | 4.1 |
| 6500 | 108.2 | 711 | 0 | 4.0 |
| 6750 | 105 | 717 | 0 | 3.6 |
| 7000 | 100 | 708 | 0 | 4.0 |
| 7250 | | | | |

COMMENTS
AS TEST DATED 16/5/88 EXCEPT POST LE MANS RACE 4095 MILES (UNSERVICED)
TESTED ON LE MANS 3 DATA SET IGN -1.5 FUEL +3

*Winning engine tested on the lean setting as used throughout the Le Mans race and after completing 4095 miles. Note at these Le Mans settings the air/fuel ratio is around 14 to 1 up to 5750rpm and 13.0 at 7000rpm after the 4% additional fuel has been added on the Mulsanne straight. The result is virtually unchanged in performance after completing over 4000 miles.*

***The City of Coventry turned out to congratulate Jaguar and the TWR team on its Le Mans victory with an open coach tour through the streets to a mayoral reception at City Hall.***

*Parade through the streets of Coventry.*

*Outside City Hall with the Mayor and team reception inside.*

*Le Mans winners Johnnie Dumfries, Jan Lammers and Andy Wallace aboard their Coventry victory parade XJS.*

*Mayoral reception at City Hall, Coventry.*

## Brno, Czechoslovakia – July 10th

The old street circuit of Brno in Czechoslovakia that TWR had visited numerous time before with the XJS Jaguar and Rover SD1 was now gone and it had been replaced with a well thought out new circuit of 5.425kms (3.37 miles) with good viewing areas for spectators. This one-year old facility was very good and surprisingly so when you consider that it was still within the Russian influenced zone, and we were still a year away from the downfall of the Berlin Wall. Many teams had decided to miss this one with a total of seventeen cars for the Supersprint format 360kms (223.7 miles) race to be watched by a huge turnout of enthusiastic event starved locals; 80,000 turning up on race day.

Qualifying had Brundle with experimental carbon brakes and both Jaguars fitted with deeper wing endplates to help isolate the tunnel exit points from atmospheric pressures. Lammers/Dumfries were not happy with their set-up and tested the spare car as well, but stayed with their race car for qualifying. Brundle had set the fastest time and it took the Mercedes till near the end of the session to better it, Brundle eventually ending up third fastest.

> Baldi in the Mercedes C9 1:46.44; Schlesser 1:46.70; Brundle 1:47.03; Wollek, Joest Porsche 1:47.18 and Lammers 1:48.29.

This race start was hectic with the longer than usual distance from the departing pace car and the first corner with all five qualifiers thinking they had a chance to lead the race. It was Brundle who missed out the most

*Brno winning Sauber C9*

as the initial pattern settled into Baldi–Mass–Lammers–Brundle–Wollek. The Jaguars could not cover this early pace with Brundle suffering from more understeer from his car than he would have liked, but this all changed with the leading Mercedes into the pits with a puncture on lap 10. Schlesser had been cross entered in both cars just to cover this eventuality and would join the best option at the next pit stop. Lammers had moved into second with Wollek behind and Brundle struggling with the handling problems in his car. Lammers too was soon in trouble with a puncture on lap 15 and returned to the race in fifth. None of this disadvantage was going to be regained later as might have been the case in a full distance race. During Brundle's pit stop to hand over to Nielsen, the front tyres were changed and this had an immediate positive effect on this car as it rejoined and Nielsen ran second to Schlesser. Dumfries in the second Jaguar moved past the Joest Porsche, with Weaver in the second Mercedes behind in fourth. Nielsen slowly reduced the gap to Schlesser but was never in a position to challenge him and eventually drove for second place finishing 20 seconds behind the winning C9 Mercedes, with Dumfries third, and Weaver in the Mercedes fourth. The Jaguars and Mercedes were equal here and the early tyre problem for Brundle that caused the use of more fuel versus lap time removed what would have been a very close-run thing, along with the reasonable possibility of a race win had the Jaguar been ahead after the mid race pit stop. By now the writing was well and truly on the wall for Jaguar and TWR who had lost their advantage to the Mercedes team; and Schlesser/Mass increased their lead in the Drivers Championship, closing on Jaguar in the Manufacturers Championship.

## 1000kms Brands Hatch – July 24th

Back to a full-length race at Brands Hatch two weeks after the shorter one at Brno and having to meet the expectations of the large Jaguar home crowd, although reduced a little to 30,000 because of the cold rainy conditions. Interest had been raised with one of the Jaguars being fitted with a 4-valves per cylinder engine. After many false dawns involving production processes, a workable version of Al Melling's drawings was finally able to be produced by us at Eng to be tested at this race. From Friday's practice the Mercedes team were showing their constant improvement and although it was their first time at this circuit with the C9, they led Friday's times and found the best weather window on the Saturday as well to take out the front row.

The pole position was gained by Schlesser/Baldi with 1:14.17 and Mass 1:15.06; Ludwig/Wollek in Joest's 962 1:16.36, then the first of the XJR-9 Silk Cut Jaguars on 1:17.68. Jelinski/Winter were fifth in Joest's second car on 1:17.95 followed by the Nielsen/Wallace/Brundle Jaguar with 1:18.49. The 7-litre 4-valve engine fitted to chassis 187 ended up eighth in the hands of Watson/Jones on 1:19.58.

*4-valve engine used just the single time at Brands Hatch.*

The race start was dry but with threats of later rain, and the pole position C9 having a poor start dropped back to fourth behind the leading Joest Porsche, Mass Mercedes and Lammers Jaguar. Lammers was in handling problems from the start and drifted back to allow Nielsen to carry the challenge, but suddenly the second placed Mercedes was out after contact with a slower car spinning ahead of it. Watson in the 4-valve engined Jaguar then passed Lammers and finally ended up in second place briefly as Nielsen pitted with a slow puncture. Soon after this car had pitted for its scheduled stop, Jones in the 4-valve engine Jaguar returned to the pits with an off-tune engine, traced to a broken rotor arm. The ignition system was different on this configuration of engine with the normal distributor not fitting in the central V section through lack of room. The rotor was driven off the back of one of the camshafts and with some torsional vibrations produced there had broken the small drive lug on the rotor. It would be a simple problem to fix in the future, but for now the car would be withdrawn. For me this engine was never a serious alternative to what we were using, but this race ensured that we had covered our very early obligations to Jaguar in their funding of the 4-valve development; although most of that money had been sidelined for other projects including JaguarSport.

With 20% of the race distance covered Nielsen led from both Joest Porsches and Dumfries in a better handling Jaguar after changes to the front bodywork. Schlesser was trying to make up for lost time but in doing so his rear tyres were giving up under the strain and his times soon slowed again. Good stints by Nielsen and Dumfries moved both up to challenge Wollek's Porsche. Lammers had Schlesser trying to pass but he came off second best and spent some time regaining the track after an off onto the slippery grass.

Just before half time the light rain started and became too much for hot slick tyres and after a lucky recovery Wallace in the leading Jaguar pitted for intermediate tyres. With the race pattern settling in, Brundle with the best championship position, joined this car and set off in the damp conditions. These conditions were not to last, options had been covered by Lammers and Ludwig staying out on their slick tyres, and with the track beginning to dry they now had the better tyre combination. The next stops for those on intermediates would be back to slicks. At mid-distance Ludwig in the Joest Porsche led from the two Jaguars, but soon succumbed to a failed engine, this car going over its fuel allowance in the expectation of the need for pace cars. Brundle and Dumfries led the race and the Wollek Porsche began to drop back going one lap down.

This was the way the race continued on with Brundle easing out a one minute lead over the second Jaguar and the third placed Porsche not able to challenge. 28 laps from the finish however things changed and the Lammers/Dumfries Jaguar was into the pits with a short circuit in the dashboard causing a fire, and final retirement. Brundle/Wallace/Nielsen finished with 240 laps, Wollek/Ludwig second on 239 laps with Schlesser/Baldi five laps behind the winning Jaguar after all the Mercedes' rear tyre problems, probably a legacy of their lack of testing at this circuit. The demise of the second Jaguar was an added disappointment for the team as it allowed Schlesser in his Mercedes to gain a third place and vital extra points to just stay in the lead of the championship from Brundle; otherwise they would have been tied at this point.

Drivers – Schlesser 159; Brundle 155; Baldi 143; Ludwig 115; Cheever 100; 'Winter' 99; Wollek 98; Jelinski 91; Mass 82; Lammers and Dumfries 72.

## Visit by the Duke of Kent

At this time, we had the honour of a visit from the Duke of Kent and his allocated fifteen minutes turned into thirty-five as he showed interest in what we were doing. The engine builders who were a little nervous about speaking to him had elected to work at the back of the shop while others had been primed to display and discuss the particular operation they were carrying out in a selected area. It became obvious he had seen this type of presentation before and quickly made his way to the back to talk with the people there. A group of us later adjourned to the Bear at Woodstock for lunch and it was a proud TW who had now met a second member of the Royal family.

*The Duke of Kent speaks with Allan Scott while chief of parts cleaning processes Bob Goldsbury looks on.*

HOW TO ADDRESS HIS ROYAL HIGHNESS THE DUKE OF KENT

Directors/Senior Managers:

should bow from the neck as they shake hands and say Good Morning/Afternoon Your Royal Highness. From then on Sir should be used.

Employees at work:

should act normally, addressing HRH as "Sir" throughout
anyone sitting should remain seated

Tea Party guests:

should address HRH as "Sir"
do not curtsy or bow
Ladies don't wear hats - or trousers - but e.g. skirt and blouse
Don't wear any badges
HRH will move to each group so don't follow him round!
HRH will always lead the conversation - do not make any controversial or political comments
Do not allow one person to "hog" the conversation - or HRH will simply move to the next group
HRH may or may not shake hands with each individual - but be prepared to hold your cup steady in your left hand!

*The Duke of Kent showed a keen interest in the V12 engine being displayed by Steve Gray.*

*Karen Scott, Allan Scott, Duke of Kent and Tom Walkinshaw.*

## Nurburgring, Germany – September 3rd-4th

A new format was tried at this event with races over two days of the weekend. From the outset the weather was going to play a part with rain forecast, not uncommon in this hilly area of Germany. To add to the new idea was that Saturday would be an evening race starting at 7pm and soon this format would show up the circuit management's weakness when the cars started practise on the Thursday. No lighting at the circuit had drivers missing the start finish line flag, and as well they could not see the corner marshals' posts. Over Friday and Saturday the situation was slowly rectified with identifying reflectors and high visibility vests for the marshals. Added to these problems was the technical scrutineering after first qualifying with the Mercedes deemed to have a moveable aerodynamic structure. This involved flexible tape sealing the entry points of the suspension wishbones into the cars tunnels, a complete farce. Jaguar were not exempt with Brundle's tunnels deemed 2mm to high; the outcome being those times were disallowed and both cars had therefore not qualified; and would have to do so in the evening session with its forecast of rain. Lammers had his qualifying session reduced with a broken fourth gear and so it would be a tense night time session in the rain for a few teams.

Technical advancement had also arrived for this race in Germany along with a larger than normal Porsche entry. The Bosch MP1.7 sequential engine management system had now been fitted to both of Joest's and Brun's cars, as well as the single teams of a returning BLR with Porsche UK support, Kremer and Dauer in their respective 962 Porsches. The C9 Mercedes had been the first to use this system and were now using the latest electronic boost control as well to help tailor their power curve for best tyre wear, which had been a weakness earlier on. Previously all boost control for Porsche had been via a mechanical system.

On the last lap of qualifying Brundle had been unable to see the session finishing flag and was greeted by marshals standing in the road as he continued on to get the best out of his qualifying tyres after being constantly held up earlier on, nearly collecting one of them in the process. Final qualifying had Baldi with new partner Johansson fastest with 1:24.92; Schlesser on 1:25.72; Wollek/Barilla 1:26.25; Lammers/Dumfries 1:26.71 and a delayed Brundle partnered with Cheever for this race on 1:27.5.

The race was started an hour early at 6pm in appalling wet conditions under the pace car. Confusion reigned as well deciding which laps to count as the race finally went green and Lammers, his car set up for the wet, took the lead and began pulling away from the cars behind. Cheever moved past cars ahead of him in these difficult conditions before a race stoppage behind the pace car on lap 16 and then a full course yellow for the next eleven laps bunched the field up. Schlesser then set about Cheever on the restart and there were bumps and off-circuit manoeuvres testing drivers and bodywork; with Schlesser the only Mercedes on Michelin's latest rain tyres now after Lammers. Lammers pitted on lap 40 with a 42 second lead and both Jaguars would need another refuelling stop before the end. Schlesser stayed out trying to complete the race on one refuelling stop and hoping for another pace car, finally coming in on lap 52. The Jaguars led until their next and last stops allowing Mass in the Mercedes to take the lead, followed by the Jaguars of Dumfries and Brundle 40 seconds respectively behind.

The Porsches were out of contention by now with Jelinski in the Joest and Reuter in the Brun the best of the rest with conditions worsening as fog rolled in and teams expecting the race to be stopped. Dumfries chances then came to an end with a hard punt in the rear from the Brun Porsche puncturing its oil cooler, and although the Porsche carried on he was losing large amounts of time. Dumfries held onto second with Brundle immediately behind him, but some confusion at the finish over when the race had actually started continued with the finish flag being shown to the Jaguars and not Mass in the winning Mercedes. TWR this time had been out manoeuvred by Mercedes when deciding on the safe option of two-stopping but having the fastest cars in the race. Reuter was fourth and Wollek/Barilla fifth both two laps down. Jelinski/Winter and the ill-handling second Mercedes of Baldi/Johansson finished three laps behind the leaders. Along with this new format the cars were sealed and placed in their respective garages to start the second half of the 1000km race the next day. Cars would be released from this impound situation 90 minutes before the start of the second race.

### *Race two*

The rain was clearing before the start and tyre choices for the semi-wet conditions had many different solutions lining up for the restart. At the rolling start Baldi lost control on his Mercedes team's second best choice (Schlesser getting the last of the best option), hitting the barriers and was out with broken suspension. Dumfries started alongside Schlesser and was determined to take the lead but was also out on the first lap crashing in the process. A broken rear wing mount mean a long 22 minute stop in the pits for his repairs. Schlesser's wet tyres were better in the very early laps before Brundle's intermediate tyres come into their own on the drying track making Schlesser pit for slicks on lap 11, and rejoined in fifth but then drove up to second place less than ten laps later. Brundle continued with tyres not perfect for the drier conditions and pitted on schedule. Cheever then continued to set a fast pace and the Mercedes and Jaguars swapped the leading positions as refuelling stops emerged. Cheever had a handy lead towards the end by 40 seconds but this race was not over with his engine starting to sound rough and had to back off to take second place behind Schlesser. Wollek/Barilla; Jelinski/Winter and Huysman/Brun followed.

> On aggregate the final results were Schlesser/Mass (Mercedes); Brundle/Cheever (Jaguar), Wollek/Barilla; Jelinski/Winter; Reuter/Pareja; Brun/Huysman; Hobbs/Donnelly in Porsches.

*Engs new small parts inspection area with granite table and digital measuring equipment.*

Lammers/Dumfries were placed eighth after Dumfries had rejoined this race but had a second coming together with a slower car needing a new nose before returning to finish in twelfth.

The Manufacturers and Drivers Championships were becoming a closely fought battle as the team returned to Belgium for the race at Spa with similar weather patterns encountered at the Nurburgring two weeks before.

## Spa – September 18th

"It's raining so we must be at Spa" was on most lips as Friday saw very heavy rain in Friday's unofficial practice, with Lammers seeming to enjoy the challenge and both Jaguars setting fastest times. This was an added boost to TWR's confidence as the Mercedes team had Michelin's latest wet weather tyres considered the best tyre in these conditions. Saturday was drying and the qualifying battle between Jaguar and Mercedes continued and would finish with the last half hour having the slower C2 cars removed to allow a clearer track. The last part of qualifying had a totally dry track and both Mercedes and Jaguar teams were separated by less than half a second. After fitting the very soft qualifying tyres it was Lammers fastest, Baldi second, Cheever third followed by Schlesser.

> The final positions were Baldi 2:02.25, Lammers 2:03.11, Schlesser 2:03.65, and Cheever who had been delayed on both his runs 2:03.84.

Wollek in a new chassis for Joest Porsche was the first for that marque with 2:31.62 followed by Jelinski's FAT Brun Porsche on 2:09.25. Dunlop's new radial tyres were being tested here by Cheever to see if they may be an improvement over the Kevlar cross ply construction used up to this point. Brundle had used the spare XJR-9 and would wait to see the best outcome before choosing which car to join.

Sunday light rain returned and the midday start had some difficult tyre choices to make with conditions not suited to full wet weather tyres. Lammers was on a mission and held position through the famed Eau Rouge complex to take the lead and pull away from the C9, but after creating a 13 second lead over the next few laps had a puncture and rejoined in seventh. Both C9s led third-placed Cheever and he was eventually joined by Lammers in fourth. Cheever's car and tyre set-up were not the best for the semi-wet conditions and this produced a fuel consumption problem for him. TWR fitted intermediate tyres at the fuel stop but these were not a better solution in the conditions. Lap 40 of the eventual 142 lap race had the Sauber Mercedes in control and Johansson asked to let Schlesser through because of his points situation, Lammers and Cheever half a minute and one minute behind. Cheever was about to come in for fuel on lap 50, but the last few litres did not pickup and he stopped out on the track. Brundle took over the remaining Jaguar with some small changes to the fuel counter and mixture and continued his battle with the Dunlop intermediate tyres, looking unable to make any headway to his main rival Schlesser in the championship stakes. Visibility problems seemed to affect the second place Mercedes more than others and his lead over Brundle began to diminish. By two-thirds distance the Schlesser/Mass C9 was in a race of its own, going a lap ahead of the following cars and this situation would greatly reduce Brundle's championship chances.

Less than 30 laps from the end the leading Schlesser/Mass C9 pulled in with a broken right rear suspension arm and the following 13 minute repair ended their chances of a win. Although Brundle now inherited the lead and needed a final stop for fuel, the Baldi/Johansson Mercedes were fuelled to the end. After Brundle's final fuel stop he returned in second place and quickly closed on the leading C9 but then the rain became a little heavier putting his intermediate tyres once again in a situation they were not suited to. The race finished after six hours with Baldi/Johansson 24 seconds ahead of Brundle/Lammers/Dumfries; Schlesser/Mass third three laps down; Brun's Larrauri/Reuter Porsche four laps behind the winners. Five Porsches had retired, three with blown engines.

*The starting grid at Spa.*

**POINTS POSITION AFTER SPA**

**TEAMS**

| | Je | Ja | Mo | Si | LM | Br | BH | Nu | Sp | Fu | Sa | Total |
|---|---|---|---|---|---|---|---|---|---|---|---|---|
| Jaguar | 30 | 20 | 40 | 40 | 60 | 15 | 40 | 30 | 30 | | | 305 |
| Mercedes | 40 | 15 | 30 | 30 | - | 20 | 24 | 40 | 40 | | | 239 |
| | | | | | | | | | | (40) | (20) | (299 max) |

**DRIVERS**

| | Je | Ja | Mo | Si | LM | Br | BH | Nu | Sp | Fu | Sa | Total |
|---|---|---|---|---|---|---|---|---|---|---|---|---|
| Schlesser | 1st | 2nd | 2nd | 2nd | - | 1st | 3rd | 1st | 3rd | | | |
| | 40 | 15 | 30 | 30 | - | 20 | 24 | 40 | 24 | | | = 223 (-15) |
| | | | | | | | | | | +(1st) | +(1st) | = (208) |
| | | | | | | | | | | (40) | (20) | = 283 |
| worst points | | 15 | | | 0 | 20 | | | | | 20 | = 55 |
| | | | | | | | | | | | | 228 |
| worst positions | | 15 | | | 0 | | 24 | | 24 | | | = 63 |
| | | | | | | | | | | | | 220 |
| Brundle | - | 1st | 1st | 1st | - | 2nd | 1st | 2nd | 2nd | | | |
| | - | 20 | 40 | 40 | - | 15 | 40 | 30 | 30 | | | = 215 |
| | | | | | | | | | | +(2nd) | - | |
| | | | | | | | | | | (30) | - | = 245 |
| worst points | 0 | | | | 0 | 15 | | | | | 0 | = 15 |
| | | | | | | | | | | | | 230 |
| worst positions | 0 | | | | 0 | 15 | | | | | 0 | = 15 |
| | | | | | | | | | | | | 230 |

**IF :-**
MB wins in Fuji he wins Drivers Championship.
JLS/Baldi wins in Fuji and Sandown with MB 2nd in Fuji, MB wins.
JLS is 2nd in Fuji and 1st in Sandown = 218
with MB 3rd in Fuji and 2nd in Sandown = 224
JLS is 3rd in Fuji and 1st in Sandown = 208 (263 - 0 - 15 - 20 - 20)

If MB does not score again = 215.

Therefore, JLS has to finish 1st or 2nd in Fuji or MB wins.
Baldi has to finish 1st in Fuji or MB wins.

Roger Silman
Monday, 19 September 1988

***The Manufacturers Championship was Jaguar 305 and Mercedes 239; and Jaguar had now won this championship for the second time. Mercedes could win both of the remaining races but still not win the championship. The Drivers Championship however hung in the balance over the two remaining races.***

## Fuji – October 9th

The penultimate round of the 1988 series in Japan would be crucial with a chance for Martin Brundle to take the Drivers Championship. A first or second placing at this event for Brundle had the title in his favour but a win for Schlesser and a poor result from the Brundle/Cheever combination would end the current advantage. It was a full turnout for manufacturers here in Japan with Jaguar, Mercedes, Porsche, Toyota, Nissan and Mazda. Qualifying had Fuji's changeable weather patterns once again, and within a short time the rain had returned and finished any hopes of setting faster times. Fastest time was set by the From A 3.2-litre 962 of Okada/Dickens 1:18.21 followed by Hasemi/Suzuki 962 1:18.285, both cars on Bridgestone tyres. Baldi/Streiff were the quickest C9 1:18.39 with the Porsche factory having a change from its normal livery with support from Japanese company Omron as well as its driver line up with American Price Cobb joining Ludwig in fourth 1:18.59. The two XJR-9s were split by less than a tenth of a second with Lammers/Dumfries 1:19.756 and Brundle/Cheever 1:19.815 in sixth and seventh a good showing on this fast circuit with average speeds well over 200kph. Main rival Schlesser/Mass/Acheson faced a few problems to post eighth fastest time 1:20.002.

Race day was dry which meant a hard, straightforward race with no wet weather to interrupt the normal flow and throw unknowns into the strategies. The race settled into its first pattern with Baldi C9, Ludwig 962, Lammers XJR-9, Mass C9 and Wollek 962. Japanese resident Lees was the best of the locals for Toyota and a slow starting Cheever, before the first real changes began. Baldi suffered brake troubles with the effort needed to slow the car at the end of the straight from its 320kph terminal speeds and pitted for repairs that became too hard to rectify; to be soon followed by Lammers with a blown tyre and body damage from contact with the barriers and he was out of the race.

The next stage had Acheson's C9 leading, swapping to Schlesser, and Cheever moving into second spot. Brundle joined the race and soon took the lead as Schlesser had a mysterious engine cut and returned to the pits for rectification thinking it was a fuel pressure problem. That area seemed OK and things returned to normal by turning the master switch off and on again. More bad luck was to come for Schlesser with a wastegate failure needing a pit stop to rectify and dropping down the order. After that repair he was unable to make up the time lost and with the two Porsches ahead of him putting up a fast race pace the chances of regaining a podium placing to keep his championship hopes alive left him out of the equation. Brundle's consistently fast pace to the fuel slowly moved the XJR-9 one lap ahead of the rest of the field. The XJR-9 driver and car combination here was superior to the C9 with their marginal brakes and was subsequently never challenged on its way to an emphatic victory, one lap ahead of the second placed factory Porsche of Cobb/Ludwig and the third place 962 of Jelinski/'Winter' (Louis Krages) three laps behind the winners. Schlesser eventually finished fifth, four laps down. Brundle was now Drivers Champion for 1988.

The writing was on the wall for TWR, the Mercedes and Jaguar were evenly matched and only two more years remained in this series before a change of rules in 1991 would make all these cars obsolete. Schlesser was very disappointed, driven no doubt by his need to show TWR team manager Roger Silman that he had made a mistake in sacking him at the end of 1986; his satisfaction would have to wait for another day. The Japanese race cars had no answer over the 1000kms of this fuel limited race and it was a poor showing from all of them, struggling to get into the top ten finishers. Rumours began to surface that Mercedes were serious about 1989, and Martin Brundle was on the top of their driver wanted list.

## Sandown Park, Australia 360kms – November 20th

By now the championship positions were finalised and the long haul to Australia for the European and Japanese teams meant that most did not make this journey for financial reasons; the event was poorly supported. Two cars from Jaguar and Mercedes were supported by two privateer Porsches and a locally built Chevrolet powered sports car; just seven cars in C1 with this race having eleven C2s making up the numbers. There were two other promoted races on at the time, Joest had four cars at Kyalami in South Africa, and Brun, Kremer and BLR Porsches at Tampa Florida, all been tempted away to these events with the support of the various promoter's financial inducements. TWR had been experimenting with carbon discs and with nothing to lose it was decided to use this race as a test bed for the new technology as the team took a more relaxed view of the proceedings.

Qualifying had Schlesser 1:28.62, Baldi 1:29.98, Lammers 1:30.2 and Brundle 1:30.95.

From the race start both C9s took the lead and began to quickly move away from the two Jaguars. This continued until rain started around lap 14 but the gap remained until the first and only pit stops in this shorter race. Schlesser pitted just ahead of Baldi's sister C9 with both Jaguars almost a minute down on the leaders. Perhaps the TWR tyre choice had been too conservative, leading Brundle to run a softer compound for the second stint and this proved to be a better choice. The end result was a dominant win for Schlesser and Baldi with Brundle almost a lap down and Dumfries just being lapped at the finish. This re-awakened the doubt in the TWR team that the V12 was now obsolete, but the difference here was out of the ordinary. Some could be put down to the feeling that Dunlop had not developed a suitable radial ply tyre as others had, as well as a team without any pressure going through the end of season motions, but there was another factor involved. A fuel sample taken from the C9s after the race turned out to be the main reason for the performance, it was not the correct commercial grade fuel, but something that had all the hallmarks of high octane aviation fuel. With nothing to be proved it was all allowed to quietly disappear.

Drivers Champion results were: Martin Brundle, Jean-Louis Schlesser, Mauro Baldi, Eddie Cheever.

So, another year had come to an end for Group C, but work continued back at Kidlington in support of an extensive revision list that had already been circulated to attend to each detail that could be improved. The decision had been made to run an all new car with a V6 turbo engine in 1989.

## Extracts from official journal of the TWR Group

### ROYAL VISIT TO TWR BY HRH THE DUKE OF KENT

On Monday, September 12th, the whole of TWR's Kidlington estate was bristling with tension, awaiting the arrival of His Royal Highness, the Duke of Kent. The visit was a private one, at the Duke's request, and he had come to see the base from where the Le Mans-winning Jaguars had been built.

After being greeted by Tom Walkinshaw, and refreshed with coffee in the boardroom, His Royal Highness toured the Engine Shop, Herbie Clips and the Group C Shop. Here he not only met the crew who worked on the Le Mans-winning car – Rod Benoist, Jeremy Pyman, Nigel Weeks and Chris Tuckey – but also Jan Lammers, Johnnie Dumfries and Andy Wallace were there too. After touring the workshop, Jan Lammers invited the Duke to get into the race winning car, an invitation which he was unable to resist. Tom then took pleasure in closing the door down on the Duke, to get the full impression of claustrophia that the car can create.

After lunch the tour resumed and the Duke visited TWR Special Vehicle Operations' workshop and warehouse, and Jaguar Sport Limited.

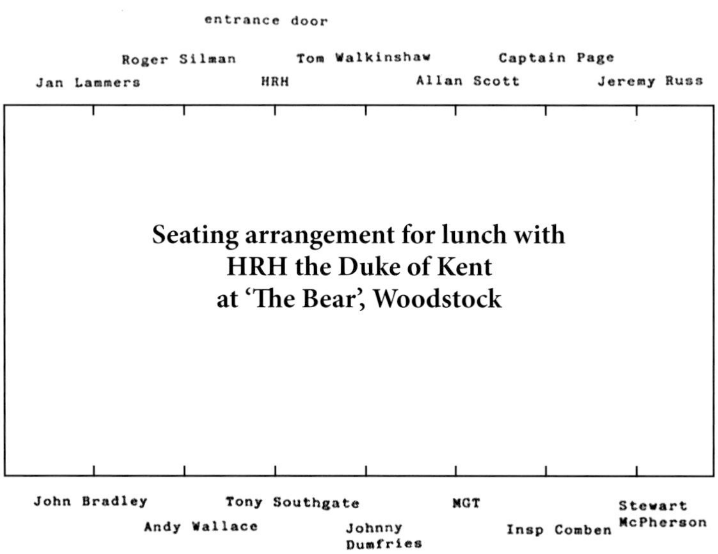


Seating arrangement for lunch with HRH the Duke of Kent at 'The Bear', Woodstock

PIT BOARD No10
OFFICIAL JOURNAL OF THE TWR GROUP

### *THE* DOUBLE FOR TWR SILK CUT JAGUAR TEAM

What a fabulous year, with Le Mans as an appetiser and the Teams Championship as an entree, Martin Brundle's Drivers Championship is a sweet finale to the year. We still have one round to go, in Australia, but the year belongs to TWR Jaguar.

Martin Brundle's World Championship is a just reward for a year taken away from Formula One where he was fed up with mid-field performance in mid-field cars, he may find a single-seater drive as a result of success with us.

Unlike last year, when we were up against the factory and leading privateer Porches, this year has been all about TWR vs Sauber Mercedes. Only twice have the works Porsche team competed – at Le Mans and Fuji, and next year it looks as if they will be away altogether, concentrating their efforts on CART (Indianapolis) racing.

In has been a sustained battle all year long. Sauber Mercedes won the first race at Jerez, and although we fought back and scored more victories during the year, Jean-Louis Schlesser remained in the lead of the Drivers Championship until Spa, when he finished third to Martin Brundle's second. Despite our team victory at Le Mans, neither Martin Brundle nor Jean-Louis Schlesser scored, so the result, where double points were available, did not affect the Drivers standings.

What made the difference was TWR's consistency. Whenever the TWR team did not win, we were second. More importantly as far as the Drivers' title is concerned, Martin Brundle only failed to finish outside the top two places on two occasions – at Jerez and Le Mans – when he retired.

## Castrol Technical Support

At year's end we carried out a progress meeting with Castrol led by John Bristow. John was a helpful person to us at Engs and his expertise along with his technical analysis and report of the wear conditions with our winning V12 engine show the level at which the TWR team worked with its Castrol sponsor.

**John Bristow and Alan Moir carried out a detailed inspection of the Le Mans and Daytona winning engines at Kidlington and the following is their peer review of the internal components of the Daytona and Le Mans engines.**

Daytona Engine:

After 2600 miles the engine was very clean.

Head - Good
Valves - Good
Followers - Good

Slight scuffing of the main bearings was attributed to dirt ingress - the Jaguar engine uses a 2-stage (course/fine) dry foam filter. It was suggested that Castrol's foam air filter oil could be used, to good effect, in preventing fine particles entering the engine. One badly worn cam lobe was noted (ca. 10 hours from total failure) however this was not thought to be lubricant related. A move to chilled cast cams should solve this problem.

Le Mans Engine:

The Le Mans engine was found to be in very good condition. The cam, as in the Daytona engine, was tuftrided steel and showed no signs of scuffing or pitting. The head is shimmed so that the piston touches the head on the overrun, this prevents any build up of deposits!

Crank - Good
Bearings - Good
Head - Very Good
Valves - Very Good

Oil consumption - ca 1 litre/hour

Used Oil Analysis:

In both the Daytona and Le Mans engines, the level of wear metals during practice was fairly high - expected as the engine was running-in. Wear metal levels at the end of each race were very low, and the oil was in generally good condition.

New Engine Oil - XC 27

This oil, a derivative of Formula RS, was designed to give an extra 10°C of protection.

Jaguar reported that the new oil had been successfully bench tested with good results. A slight power loss at high rpm was noted (ca 2 hp in over 600 hp). A power loss in the Jaguar engine at high temperature is due to changes in the volumetric efficiency of the piston.

# Castrol's Detailed Inspection Report of the Le Mans winning engine

L E M A N S 1 9 8 8

24 HOURS 3600 MILES

PISTON DEPOSITS

| Cyl. No | Description |
|---|---|
| 1L | Brown, black varnish in top groove. Brown varnish in 2nd groove. Light brown varnish on 1st ring land. Trace straw varnish on 2nd ring land. Undercrown 70% Brown 30% Black. |
| 1R | Brown, black varnish in top groove. Brown varnish in 2nd groove. Light straw varnish on 1st ring land. Undercrown 100% dark brown. |
| 2L | Brown, black varnish in top groove. Brown varnish in 2nd groove. Light brown varnish on 1st ring land. Trace straw varnish on 2nd ring land. Undercrown 100% dark brown. |
| 2R | Brown, black varnish in top groove. Brown varnish in 2nd groove. Light straw varnish on 1st ring land. Undercrown 100% dark brown. |
| 3L | Brown, black varnish in top groove. Brown varnish in 2nd groove. Light brown varnish on 1st ring land. Trace straw varnish on 2nd ring land. Undercrown 100% dark brown. |
| 3R | Brown, black varnish in top groove. Brown varnish in 2nd groove. Light straw varnish on 1st ring land. Undercrown 100% dark brown. |
| 4L | Brown, black varnish in top groove. Brown varnish in 2nd groove. Light brown varnish on 1st ring land. Trace straw varnish on 2nd ring land. Undercrown 100% dark brown. |
| 4R | Brown, black varnish in top groove. Brown varnish in 2nd groove. Light straw varnish on 1st ring land. Undercrown 100% dark brown. |
| 5L | Brown, black varnish in top groove. Brown varnish in 2nd groove. Light straw varnish on 1st ring land. 2nd ring land was clean. Undercrown 100% dark brown. |
| 5R | Brown, black varnish in top groove. Brown varnish in 2nd groove. Light straw varnish on 1st ring land. Undercrown 100% dark brown. |
| 6L | Brown, black varnish in top groove. Brown varnish in 2nd groove. Light brown varnish on 1st ring land. Trace straw varnish on 2nd ring land. Undercrown 100% dark brown. |
| 6R | Brown, black varnish in top groove. Brown varnish in 2nd groove. Light straw varnish on 1st ring land. Undercrown 100% dark brown. |

KEY: L - Left Bank (B) R - Right Bank (A)

L E M A N S 1 9 8 8

24 HOURS 3600 MILES

CAMSHAFT

Cam No: Comments

| Cam No | Left Bank Camshaft | Cam No | Right Bank Camshaft |
|---|---|---|---|
| 1. | No scuffing or pitting | 1. | No scuffing or pitting |
| 2. | No scuffing or pitting | 2. | No scuffing or pitting |
| 3. | No scuffing or pitting | 3. | No scuffing or pitting |
| 4. | No scuffing or pitting | 4. | No scuffing or pitting |
| 5. | No scuffing or pitting | 5. | No scuffing or pitting |
| 6. | No scuffing or pitting | 6. | No scuffing or pitting |
| 7. | No scuffing or pitting | 7. | No scuffing or pitting |
| 8. | No scuffing or pitting | 8. | No scuffing or pitting |
| 9. | No scuffing or pitting | 9. | No scuffing or pitting |
| 10. | No scuffing or pitting | 10. | No scuffing or pitting |
| 11. | No scuffing or pitting | 11. | No scuffing or pitting |
| 12. | No scuffing or pitting | 12. | No scuffing or pitting |

L E M A N S 1 9 8 8

24 HOURS 3600 MILES

ENGINE INSPECTION OBSERVATIONS

**Cylinders and Pistons**

There was no evidence of unusual or significant deposits or wear on the cylinder liners. All pistons were in satisfactory condition there being no evidence of unusual deposit formation or excessive wear. There were signs showing that some of the piston crowns had made light contact with the cylinder head. However, the contact had not appeared to have caused any serious problems. The piston rings were in good condition with no evidence of scuffing or excessive wear.

**Crankshaft and Associated Bearings**

All crankshaft main and connecting rod bearing journals were in a satisfactory condition. There were signs of hard rubbing/burnishing contact on the crankcase halves of No's 1 and 2 main bearing shells. A trace of scoring was evident on No. 5 main bearing shells predominately on the cap half. Otherwise the main bearing shells were in satisfactory condition. The connecting rod bearing shell rod halves showed traces of medium rubbing/burnishing. The cap halves were satisfactory from the left hand bank (B). However the right hand bank (A) cap halves showed traces of overlay fatigue/erosion on No's 2, 3, 4 & 5. Traces of debris/dirt particles were embedded in the surface of all the bearing shells to a lesser or greater extent.

**Camshaft and Cam Followers**

All cams on both camshafts were in good condition with no evidence of scuffing or pitting. All cam followers were in satisfactory condition showing good rotation and no evidence of scuffing or pitting.

**Combustion Chamber Deposits**

Combustion chamber deposits were generally even and had not given rise to any preignition or detonation damage.

*Castrol is interested in the varnish deposits as this is the residuals formed when oil becomes over heated and breaks down when running lean engine settings produces high piston temperatures.*

£5550.00 / ;
Bonus –

100%
Charlie Bamber ~~419.55~~ £370.00
Rob Benson ~~419.55~~
Jim Brown ~~419.55~~
Steve Gray ~~419.55~~
Steve Harding ~~419.55~~
Greg Hunt ~~419.55~~
Steven Mooney ~~419.55~~
Robin Moore ~~419.55~~
Matthew Norris ~~419.55~~
Neil Peters ~~419.55~~
Grant Rushton ~~419.55~~
Pete Tyrrell ~~419.55~~
Nigel Webb ~~419.55~~

50% Andrew Penny £185.00
Huw Jenkins
Ian Bickerton
Glen Barber

OK [signature]

*Workshop staff responsible for the 1988 racing successes in Group C and IMSA and bonus paid at year end.*

## Castrol's Inspection of the Le Mans winning engine

*left* *right*

*pistons*

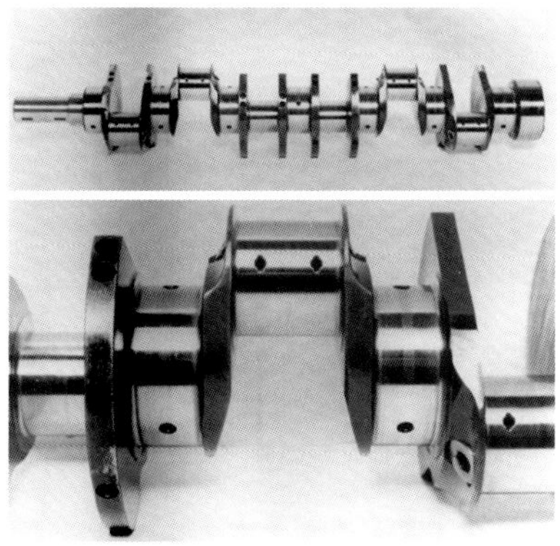

*crankshaft*

*cam followers*

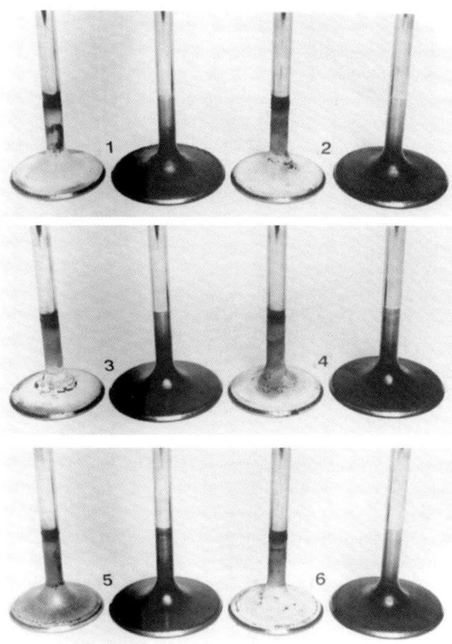


*inlet and exhaust valves*

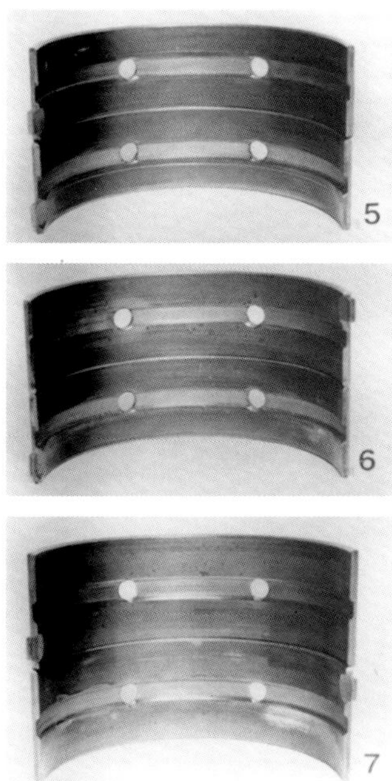


*main bearings*

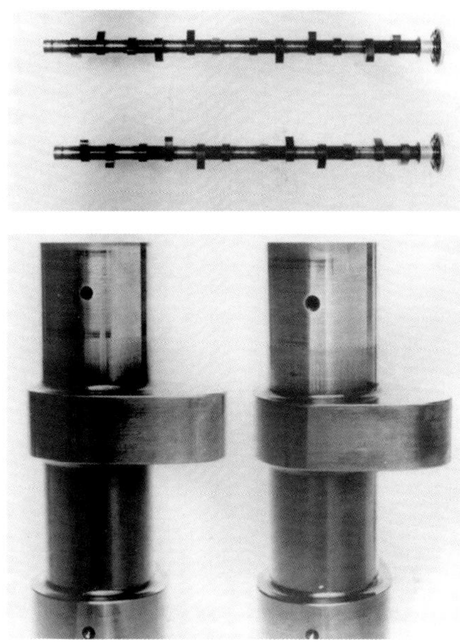

*steel camshafts*

## Castrol meeting to discuss transmission oil, grease and brake fluids

**XD 71 Transmission Oil**

The TWR/Jaguar transmission requires a thin lubricant whereas the final drive requires a thicker lubricant, therefore a wide range multigrade is required.

A range of oils were tested in a special track session at Silverstone. One product lowered the average running temperature by 10 - 15°C. This was subsequently tested in a number of practice sessions, no evidence of wear or pitting was reported, after 973 miles of use.

Alistair MacQueen indicated that he would like to see either rig comparisons between the oils, or a successful trial at Daytona, before final approval is granted. "In car" comparisons give problems with accurate control of relative conditions. It was decided that the possibility of rig evaluations at SWRI or GKN would be investigated.

**ACTION: N D Ainscough**

TWR-Jaguar indicated the following changes to be made to the gearbox for the 1989 season.

1. Strap size to be increased.
2. Fourth gear to be made wider.
3. Pinion increased in length, with no holes drilled, and composition to be changed.

**EA 41 Wheel-Bearing Grease**

TWR/Jaguar reported that the wheel bearing grease had been satisfactorily tested in race conditions. Wheel-bearing problems had been eliminated by redesign, however the grease was thought to be as good, if not better, than their current product.

Castrol indicated that modifications to EA 41 (EA 64/65) have given lower running temperatures in rig tests, and that these greases have now been supplied to race teams.

Alistair MacQueen requested 6 x 3 kg tins of grease for the 1989 seasons, and commented that despite high effective wheel loadings and car speeds plus heat-sock from the brakes, the Castrol grease gave no problems. The TWR Inc team will also move to using this grease.

**EA 44 Driveshaft Grease**

TWR/Jaguar reported that the driveshafts are run in by Jaguar before being supplied to TWR. It has been found that each driveshaft offers a different "temperature signature", with 10°C difference possible between shafts. Driveshaft assembles were to be changed every 4000 km (two practice and race sessions) for reasons of mechanical fatigue A programme of work based on back to back comparison between the present Kluber Grease and the Castrol candidate was agreed as the best course of action. Mr Elkins agreed to assist with obtaining test space at Coventy. The Kluber Grease for thi: ɜst would be supplied from Kidlington.

**ACTION: A MacQueen/ R Elkins**

**Brake Fluid**

Mrs E.A. Brookes gave a presentation on SRF, then showed an analysis of the Brake fluid taken from the Le Mans car. This fluid still had a vapour lock point of over 270°C.

TWR/Jaguar reported a number of field problems:-

1. Dry ice was packed into the sill or the car to cool the fuel - whilst stopped in the pits the adjacent brake line froze!
2. The standard ventilated disc and calipar had been running at ~ 600°C (not a fluid problem). Modifications have reduced this temperature to 400°C.
3. Carbon discs/titanium caliper - introduced to save weight (in the order of 15 kg), however the extremely high running temperatures (ca 450 - 800°C) has resulted in heat transfer to the brake fluid with the car stationary having just pulled into the pits, leading to vapour lock.

   Carbon brakes gave a number of other problems:-

   a) Cost (ca £4000)
   b) A car covered in Carbon black!
   c) Temperature control (no friction outside 350 - 800°C operating temperature)

Due to 1989's weight limit changes there is no particular advantage to using Carbon discs, so conventional discs/calipers would be used. However, TWR/Jaguar commented that a higher boiling brake fluid would be useful, and that they were not overly concerned about very low temperature performance.

N G Pound.

N G Pound
DEVELOPMENT CHEMIST
\OTHERS\NP06\BZ
11 January 1989

## Jaguar's report on the head casting failure on the Brundle/Nielsen XJR-9 at Le Mans

JAGUAR | DEVELOPMENT / TEST REPORT | REPORT

1. INTRODUCTION:-

A piece of the failed cylinder head from the XJR-9 Le Mans car driven by Martin Brundle was submitted to the Laboratory for metallurgical examination. The head had cracked during the race, causing a substantial water leak which forced the car to retire.

2. RESULTS:-

2.1 Visual Investigation:-

Examination of the broken section of the 'A' bank cylinder head revealed that cracking had occurred in the region of the exhaust valve guide on number 5 cylinder. The cracking , clearly identifiable by the blackened fracture surface compared with the clean fracture faces produced when the head was manually broken during removal, ran from the valve seat through to the upper horizontal head face. More, similar, cracking was said to be present on the remainder of the head which is to be submitted to the Laboratory in the near future.

2.2 CHEMICAL COMPOSITION:-

| | Specification (BS 1490 LM25TF) | Result |
|---|---|---|
| Copper | 0.1% max | 0.00% |
| Magnesium | 0.20-0.45% | 0.39% |
| Silicon | 6.5 -7.5% | 6.48% |
| Iron | 0.5% Max | 0.29% |
| Manganese | 0.3% Max | 0.017% |
| Nickel | 0.1% Max | 0.026% |
| Zinc | 0.1% Max | 0.030% |
| Lead | 0.1% Max | 0.010% |
| Tin | 0.05% Max | 0.032% |
| Titanium | 0.2% Max | 0.207% |

2.3 HARDNESS MEASUREMENTS:-

Specification (LM25TF) 90-110HB

Ten hardness measurements were taken, on both horizontal faces of the cylinder head, to ascertain whether any softening of the material had taken place due to over-heating.

In all instances the hardness reading was 100-104HB, no softening would appear to have taken place.

2.4 MICROSTRUCTURAL INVESTIGATION:-

The cast aluminium exhibited a satisfactory microstructure consisting of rounded silicon particles in an aluminium rich matrix. A significant amount of porosity was seen to be present throughout the section, whilst this level of porosity is typical on production engines it is not desirable.

Porosity will weaken the casting, this is particularly problematical in thin sections such as those present in the cylinder head.

No other metallurgical defects were apparent that could have contributed to the failure.

There had been many internal changes to the TWR Group with its constant expansion coming to a head in 1988, with the addition of the IMSA and Holden programmes joining the UK based racing businesses. At the beginning of 1988 the Engs workshop had grown to utilise most of the original TWR building plus a new addition at 1 Kidlington Industrial Estate, with the upstairs offices being used by the finance and accounts department. TW's original office in this building would be left locked and only occasionally used by the end of 1988. He had relocated with support staff during the year to sumptuous offices at Broadstone, a large 800 acre country estate in the Oxfordshire countryside that he had purchased, about 35 minutes drive from Kidlington.

The TWR Group concept was now well established with a high profile in motor racing and new vehicle franchises. The vehicle dealership business included TWR Jaguar Coventry and Leamington, Prophets BMW Solihull and Gerrards Cross, Chariots Porsche St Albans and Oxford, Mazda Swindon and Alfa Romeo Dorchester. TW's oversight of the expanding group had managers of the various divisions reporting directly in the same style as he had used when the group was a smaller motor racing business. There was a three-man board of directors that included finance, but no single forum for senior management to have a contributory overview for best sharing of all resources and expertise. It was the normal 'divide and rule' concept used by most single-minded entrepreneurs and so accepted by most managers. The staff levels at the Kidlington base now exceeded 200 personnel within eight separate divisions. Jaguar Racing; Race Engine Division; Drawing Office; JaguarSport; Special Vehicle Operations (SVO); Herbie Clips Manufacturing; Finance, Accounts and Legal. Press and Public Relations were in the process of relocating to Broadstone. Just one business, Dunlop race tyre retailing had been closed at the Kidlington site, through it not being profitable.

A helicopter at Broadstone and the company jet based at the nearby Kidlington airfield bridged the communication and transportation gaps. The first company jet had been the Hawker Sidley 125 whose only problem had been its inability to climb

## Extracts from PIT BOARD official journal of the TWR Group

# GROWTH OF THE ENGINE SHOP

In order to satisfy the needs of the IMSA racing programme, an extension of the Engine Shop has been built, taking it right up to the canal. Half of the space has been given over to an improved Parts Department, and the remainder is now occupied by the IMSA Engine Building crew who now have room to swing a throttle slide, and the Road Engine Building Department, transferred from Unit 15A.

Eric Crawley heads up IMSA Engine Department with Nigel Webb as a recent newcomer, Ian Bickerton, Jim Brown and Andrew Penny build Group C engines, Nigel Eames is Procurement Manager, and Barry Pudwell is Engine Shop Buyer.

It case anyone gets the wrong idea, Andrew Penny is not a new member of staff, he is just acutely camera shy.

*Eric Crawley*

*Nigel Eames*

*Barry Pudwell*

*Andrew Penny*

*Jim Brown*

*Ian Bickerton*

*Nigel Webb*

out of the Kidlington airport at a sufficient rate to gain the high altitude needed to stay out of the Heathrow flight control system when on our way to Europe. This had meant that the plane could be sent in a holding departure direction that suited the international flight control system, not Tom Walkinshaw. With the new Lear 35 the flight plan was now straight up to an altitude above domestic flight paths. At low altitude we were still subject to American Air Force control from their huge base at Upper Heyford. F1-11 fighter jets had right of way around the Kidlington area in the first few minutes of the Lear's near vertical climb to its cruising altitude above the incoming flight paths of the Heathrow bound 747s.

In any rapidly expanding business, and the TWR Group was certainly rapidly expanding at this time, financial controls need rapid expansion as well. John Bradley, nicknamed 'digger' by Andy Morrison because of his initials 'JCB', as finance director was very approachable and had a sympathetic listening manner with managers who wanted more money for their respective divisions, as we all did. Long term managers who had been with the company from the time of its earlier beginnings were used to presenting TW with these requests and getting his OK. As these demands grew with the business expansion, JCB had increasing difficulty in keeping track of these side deals and negotiations; and no doubt TW's rapid and spontaneous non-motorsport deal making as well.

Michael Boon was appointed financial controller of Tom Walkinshaw Racing by John Bradley at this time and systems were introduced that now demanded divisional managers to communicate requests via a paperwork system to financial control for approval. Personal requests and meetings had diminished with less of TW's time being available, in a business that now had outlets from the UK and Europe, to America and Australia. Michael filled this roll well although there would always continue to be the inevitable problems that arose from discussions and decisions made with TW at the race track or in the aeroplane that

**MEMO** A. Scott

| From | To |
|---|---|
| John Bradley | All General Managers<br>Accounts, Jeremy Russ,<br>Dave Shuck, Peter Cannan |
| Our Reference / Your Reference | June 8 19 88 |

**Re: New Staff**

1. **Michael Boon has been appointed Financial Controller of Tom Walkinshaw Racing Ltd. Michael, who commences work at Kidlington on Monday 13th June, will eventually be responsible for all accounting functions connected with the TWR Kidlington operations excluding JaguarSport.**

2. **Alan Gibson has been appointed Financial Controller of JaguarSport Ltd. Alan commences employment on Monday 20th June and will be based in Unit 17 at Kidlington.**

3. **As a result of the expansion of TWR's chain of motor dealerships, John Withers has been appointed Financial Controller of TWR Garages Ltd to concentrate solely on that division.**

pp. **John Bradley**

*Michael Boon*

*New financial controllers at TWR Group.*

contradicted earlier agreements. After these were added into the budgeted plan at Kidlington they could now be questioned by finance, and sometimes reversed by them without further discussion. This meant TW could agree that a request was reasonable, and then leave it to finance to refuse the request, so that he did not have to say no and give a reason. There was increasing demand on the cash flow *produced by the racing teams* as inevitably the latest business add-on outside of Motorsport needed some unforeseen additional expenditure from time to time before it was able to meet its business plan. This produced a need for increasing financial control as assets were made to perform at their very best within the bank's lending system, normal practice for a rapidly expanding business with TWR's very ambitious leader.

Requests by Engs for the capital expenditure needed to take us onto the next level of data acquisition and control systems for the two dynamometers as well as workshop equipment were hard to come by with only limited expenditure available. The real need at this time was for Engs to have a two-man prototype machine shop to increase flexibility and reduce reliance on commercial machine shops and their constantly moving timetables in Coventry, an hour and a half drive away. These machine shops usually produced good products but they were subject to their own staff problems and public holidays holding up promised deliveries. TW and Roger were thinking of a universal TWR machine shop one day, and until then, Engs requests continued to be ignored. Throughout all of the engine programmes this would be a major let down for me, producing the need to train people over time in the highly skilled technical procurement field, with price and delivery negotiation skills to match those of the machine shop owners' verbal skills and financial ambitions. TWR was changing from a focused motor racing team to a much larger business based on motor racing.

There was little time to relax by the beginning of December 1988 as we transferred effort to Tony Dowe's Valparaiso American based team in its quest to win the Daytona 24 hour race in seven weeks time.

## V12 engines used in Group C 1988

TO: MICHAEL BOON

FROM: CHARLES BAMBER

DATE: 8.5.89

RE: ENGINE MOVEMENTS TO JAGUAR RACING 1988–1989

| ENGINE NO. | CHASSIS NO. | TEST/RACE DATE |
|---|---|---|
| 88C05 | 488 | 11.2.88 |
| 88C04 | 588 | 11.2.88 |
| 88C02 | 186 | 16.2.88 |
| 88C05 | 488 | 16.2.88 |
| 88C04 | 588 | 16.2.88 |
| 88C04 | 187 | 6.3.88 |
| 88C01 | 187 | 6.3.88 |
| 88C03 | 488 | 6.3.88 |
| 88C07 | 588 | 6.3.88 |
| 88C04 | 187 | 13.3.88 |
| 88C01 | 187 | 13.3.88 |
| 88C05 | 588 | 13.3.88 |
| 88C02 | 488 | 13.3.88 |
| 88C06 | 588 | 13.3.88 |
| 88C01 | 186 | 28.3.88 |
| 88C02 | 287 | 28.3.88 |
| 88C03 | 187 | 28.3.88 |
| 88C03 | 187 | 10.4.88 |
| 88C07 | 488 | 10.4.88 |
| 88C08 | 588 | 10.4.88 |
| 88C03 | 187 | 13.4.88 |
| 88C06 | 186 | 20.4.88 |
| 88C05 | 287 | 20.4.88 |
| 88C03 | 187 | 20.4.88 |
| 88C06 | 187 | 28.4.88 |
| 88C05 | 287 | 28.4.88 |
| 88C04 | 588 | 8.5.88 |
| 88C03 | 488 | 8.5.88 |
| 88C06 | 187 | 8.5.88 |

| ENGINE NO. | CHASSIS NO. | TEST/RACE DATE |
|---|---|---|
| 88C01 | 588 | 12.6.88 |
| 88C04 | 488 | 12.6.88 |
| 88C05 | 588 | 12.6.88 |
| 88C06 | 488 | 12.6.88 |
| 88C08 | 186 | 12.6.88 |
| 88C02 | 188 | 12.6.88 |
| 88C07 | 287 | 12.6.88 |
| 88C03 | 287 | 12.6.88 |
| 88C01 | 688 | 10.7.88 |
| 88C04 | 187 | 10.7.88 |
| 88C07 | 588 | |
| 88C02 | 588 | 10.7.88 |
| 88C01 | 688 | 14.7.88 |
| 88C05 | 588 | 24.7.88 |
| 88C08 | 688 | 24.7.88 |
| 88C10 | 187 | 24.7.88 |
| 88C02 | 588 | 27.7.88 |
| 88C11 | 688 | 8.8.88 |
| 88C01 | 588 | 8.8.88 |
| 88C03 | 187 | ?.8.88 |
| 88C03 | 287 | ?.8.88 |
| 88C02 | 588 | 4.9.88 |
| 88C08 | 688 | 4.9.88 |
| 88C03 | 287 | 4.9.88 |
| 88C04 | 688 | 18.9.88 |
| 88C05 | 588 | 18.9.88 |
| 88C07 | 587 | 18.9.88 |
| 88C02 | 588 | 9.10.88 |
| 88C08 | 688 | 9.10.88 |
| 88C04 | 588 | 9.10.88 |
| 88C07 | ? | JaguarSport |
| 88C06 | 488 | JaguarSport |
| 88C05 | 588 | 20.11.88 |
| 88C08 | 688 | 20.11.88 |
| 88C03 | 688 | 20.11.88 |

# The TWR magazine kept everyone in touch with the expanded Group businesses

PIT BOARD

*Holden Special Vehicles staff, gathered around the first HSV 88, reading from left to right: John Golding, Tony Davies, Rachael Gill, Matt Schofield, Peter Robbins, Ian Park, Danny Chettle, Howard Penrose, Martyn Watt, Marc Curtis, Bob Lockett, Adam Kenner, Mark Hubbard, Lindsay Harrison, Shawn Hockey, Mick Henry, John Volarich, John Crennan, Russel Spokes, Ian Hodsson, David Elliot, Andrew Murphy, Ron Janke, David Gray, Debbie Karmel, Russel McGoldrick, Rex Nesbitt, Peter Cannan, Sam Vaysman, John Vassilou, Ian 'Blue' Dorward, Mick Finn, John Vercese, John McInerney, Bruce Scott and John Harvey, Absentees and new starters not shown include Barbara Wallace, Steve Noonan, Lyall Roberts and Greg Johnstone.*

## Greetings from Notting Hill

Holden Special Vehicles have made great progress in establishing a network of HSV Team Dealers. A total of 82 Holden dealers have signed up for this prestige franchise and supplies of the much-awaited Commodore are now flowing from the factory.

The car has been well-received in the Press and by the public. On a performance/value for money index, the HSV Commodore Group A scores very highly in Australia, where competitive cars are usually European imports and cost considerably more. To underline the performance potential of the Commodore Group A, John Crennan's Marketing Guide compares the Group with some illustrious competitors.

As well as the Commodore, Holden Special Vehicles are producing the SV88, a high speed, sporting Holden Calais, and have just launched the Holden Astra in 3-door hatch and 4-door saloon formats.

During June, John Crennan, Managing Director of HSV, came over to the UK for a series of meetings at TWR Group companies. He also managed to fit in his first visit to the Le Mans, and watched an historic and memorable victory by the TWR Silk Cut Jaguar Team.

Photo: David Sparrow

## Elegant launch for 5 series at Brocket Hall

Martin Wilcock and his close-knit team at Prophets of Gerrards Cross launched the new 5 Series BMW in elegant style at Brocket Hall. An impressive mansion, Brocket Hall was built by James Paine in 1760, but dates back to 1239, when the original building was named Watershypps. Brocket Hall is not open to the public, but can be booked for conferences and company events, when the whole building is made available to the guests of the day. A rather alarming concept to begin with, in fact the Chippendale furniture and beautiful paintings were all respected and emerged safe when the day was over.

The day's schedule was simple. Ride and drive from 10.00 through till 4.00 pm. A break for guests to change, a visit to Lord Brocket's collection of Ferraris, followed by a formal dinner and then dancing to Lord Colwyns Jazz Quartet.

On the day, everything went extremely smoothly. There were no mechanical gremlins to disturb the plans. The visit to the Ferrari collection was so popular that a second group had to be arranged, but the delay was hardly noticeable. Lord Brocket gave an extremely entertaining after-dinner speech, outlining his family history, which includes some saucy highlights concerning two of his ancestors. The wives of the first and second Lord Melbourne both had affairs, the first with the Prince of Wales (later George IV) and the second with Lord Byron.

The point of the exercise was to show off the new car in an attractive setting, and give the invited guests a day they would remember. In that it was a complete success, and Martin Wilcock is more than happy with the rate of sales.

## Tom's Awards

On July 20th the Worshipful Company of Carmen's Award of Merit was awarded jointly to Jaguar Cars plc and Tom Walkinshaw Racing, to mark the three year collaboration which culminated in victory for the TWR Jaguar XJR-9LM in the 1988 24 hour race at Le Mans. This award was their spontaneous reaction to the Jaguar victory after the BBC had so clearly failed to give the event the recognition and exposure it deserves.

The award took place in the presence of the immediate past Master of the Worshipful Company, the Princess Royal. Sir John Egan and Tom Walkinshaw received the medals, which were presented by the Assistant Master.

Later in the same day, Tom was presented with a framed print of Porsche's post-Le Mans press advertisement, by Peter Bulbeck, Managing Director of Porsche Cars (Great Britain) Limited, and Hans Halbach, Director of Marketing and Operations at Porsche AG.

JAGUAR

## Chapter Nineteen

# A change in engine concept for 1989

**It had been planned that 1988 would be the last year of using the V12 engine in all races entered by TWR other than the Sebring 12 hours and both 24 hour endurance events at Le Mans and Daytona in the future. TW had gone with his wish to move to a turbocharged engine concept, a move I had many doubts about concerning the engine to be used, but this development programme had become the focus for us at Engs during 1988. TW and Roger had felt in the early days of Group C that the aluminium monocoque Porsche 962C was an inferior design compared to the Tony Southgate proposals, and that its 3-litre twin turbocharged engine was what made the difference. The first full Group C year in 1986 with the XJR-6 had seen a considerable improvement in the engineering base for both the XJR-6 and the V12 engines, producing greater than expected success in that year. This had delayed TW's option to use the small capacity turbocharged engine that he had championed from the outset, to be based on Jaguar's AJ6 3.2-litre 2-valve engine. The Group C programme for 1987 had produced a renewed focus on using the V12, but TW had only delayed his mindset, not changed it.**

A switch to an alternative option on which engine to use came about from an unexpected direction and produced a deal to receive the rights and tooling attached to ARG Motorsports 3-litre 90° *uneven* firing V6 engine they had designed for their 6R4 rally programme. This deal was in lieu of the penalty fee payable to TWR by Austin Rover for contract non-compliance when ending the Group A Rover contract, and had been put in place by TW in late 1987. This normally aspirated engine design had been selected as the base unit for the next step up in competition for Jaguar's racing programme, a change to small capacity turbocharged engines. This former ARG Motorsport engine programme had started life as a 90 degree Rover V8 block, with two cylinders cut off, and then fitted with their own design of belt driven four valves per cylinder heads.

The configuration produced an uneven firing sequence because of the V8's 90° block angle when adapted to a six-cylinder configuration using a firing interval of 120° instead of the 90° of the block design. This problem can only be rectified by offsetting each big end journal in the crankshaft by 15° from the common centre line. An inherent problem with that design when used with a highly stressed turbocharging application produces weakness through the area adjoining the pair of big end journals; leading to the need for increased journal diameters to compensate, producing a heavy crankshaft and connecting rod. This design feature was *not* part of ARG's original design concept using a common big end pin for pairs of cylinders, and this design was inherited by TWR because it came with a large number of spare parts which included steel crankshafts that just happened to be suitable for the 3-litre capacity limit in IMSA. It was estimated that this overall turbocharged package with extra intercoolers and turbochargers would be up to 50kgs lighter than the current V12 engine. TW was also saying at this time we should be looking at using this engine in a F3000 programme with its 3-litre engine capacity limit, with the assumption that series would be a pathway to an eventual Formula One team for TWR.

I could understand TW's thought processes with this engine being suitable for the many applications he had in mind, as well as the zero cost attraction, but there was simply too many assumptions on his part concerning the suitability of this base unit. It was also difficult to understand TW's commitment to this path after we had managed to introduce the standard fuel specification which had effectively nullified the assumed efficiency from the *indirect* injection turbocharged engines that were used at that time. We had seen first hand the problems Porsche had at Le Mans in 1987 after many years to refine the mechanical development of the flat-six engine when having to simply retune the settings for lower grade fuel. This new 3-litre V6 engine would be limited to a maximum capacity of around 3.7 litres for Group C – and this was still too small an engine size in my opinion when needing a low boost anti detonation concept for best fuel efficiently. My counter proposals have been summarised in earlier chapters.

Those alternative V12 proposals would have given an option that was very cost effective but also may not have been able to constantly match the Sauber/Mercedes with their expected competitiveness in 1989, but importantly for Jaguar, improve the prospects of winning the endurance races at Le Mans, Daytona and Sebring for a few more years to come. Jaguar had always stated their focus was winning 24 hour endurance events especially Le Mans first, and the Championship second. This was

### *TWR and Jaguar's Group C contract*

| | |
|---|---|
| Date: | 28 October 1988 |
| Parties: | Jaguar Cars Limited<br>Tom Walkinshaw Racing Limited |
| Price: | Fee for 1989 = £5,179,000 plus 6 × 1986-1988 chassis purchased by TWR from Jaguar for £750,000 for resale but not to race teams. Fee for next years to be agreed in August and Sept of preceding year or else increased by RPI in default of agreement. TWR or team personnel keep all prize and starting monies. [Note fee for 1990 season subsequently agreed at £8,319,000.] |
| Annual Fee: | Payable 1/3 on Oct 1 of year preceding and balance in 4 equal instalments on Jan 1, April 1, June 1 and Aug 1. |
| Championship: | FIA Group C World Sportscar Championship |
| Team: | Silk Cut Jaguar Team |
| Number of Cars: | 3 Cars |
| Drivers: | Chosen by TWR with Jaguar's approval. Each driver to be available to Jaguar foc for up to 5 days per annum. |
| Extra Races: | up to 2 at £150k each. Additional by negotiation |
| Chassis Ownership: | TWR to own all chassis built for 1989 – 1991 agreement. |
| Sponsorship: | Jaguar decides the complete livery of the racecars and team. |
| Term: | 1989, 1990 and 1991 |
| Termination: | Usual right for termination upon breach etc. Jaguar could also terminate for convenience depending upon timing upon payment of 35% of the year's fee in 1989 or 25% of the year's fee for 1990 or 20% of the year's fee for 1991 if after 1st October the year before. |
| Renewal Notice: | Jaguar to advise not less than 6 months before end of contract (Sep 1991) whether it want to extend and if so on what terms. |
| Obligations: | Enter not less than 3 cars at Le Mans and 2 cars at each of the other Championship races; act as the official Jaguar works team; Tom to attend each race wherever possible. |

to continue their heritage associated with the earlier successes in the 50s at Le Mans, and back endurance race wins into a marketing concept of sporting reliability for Jaguar road cars. The only update for the V12 engine for 1989 had been the fitting of larger capacity 468 fuel injectors to shorten the fuel injection period and test for best timing positions and this proved to give a marginal 1% improvement in fuel consumption. The turbo engine package including intercoolers and wastegates would have only a small improvement in the centre of gravity when attached to the same gearbox centreline as the V12.

At this time the regulations for Group C were also reviewed and the minimum car weights for 1989 were raised to 900kgs from the existing 850kgs, nullifying some of this weight saving thought process using the V6 engine. This additional weight could be added via a thin flat plate under the car and also reduce the centre of gravity and so regain some advantage. The V12 powered cars had always been up to 35kgs over the minimum weight limit, but the Porsche and Mercedes were that much over to. There was no turning back from the V6 turbo decision resulting from the Austin Rover contract penalty, it was a done deal during the championship winning 1987 year.

There was by 1989 many TWR business proposals becoming reality with JaguarSport and other large production projects that would need emissions control systems in place; in fact this business was fast becoming larger than the racing business. Zytek had been moving on from just race car engine management systems and expanding into this new larger scale area with cost effective support for TWR. TW however was not a fan of Zytek joint owner Bill Gibson for his own reasons, and it was during 1988 that major decisions engine management wise were being made based on this personality clash rather than big picture reasoning. This thought process was encouraged by Max Heidegger to move away from Zytek to his preferred option, Bosch.

I had put a deal together during 1988 to have TWR buy a 50% share of Zytek for £500,000,

**NOTE TO ALLAN SCOTT**
**FROM CHRIS BOWERMAN** **15.2.89**

**ENGINE SHOP - LABOUR COSTS**

It is proposed to introduce an hours analysis system into the workshop to assist all Management to obtain a better understanding of the workshop performance. The numerous advantages are detailed below:

1. Analyse productive and non productive hours.
2. Develop trends for budgets and forecasts on build, re-builds, dyno time and support activities.
3. Monitor actual hours taken for accurate Inter Company charge out and external invoicing.
4. Provide statistical information to support headcount requirements.
5. Total integrated system with parts operation for engine costing.
6. Establish the efficiency of individual engine builders and whole department if required.
7. Provide some basis for calculating an individuals merit increase and bonuses.
8. Assist in recording holiday and sickness time.
9. Determine split of standard and overtime hours worked to monitor and control overtime trends.
10. Identify the value of Work in Progress.

Michael Boon and I would welcome the opportunity to discuss this proposal in the near future. Kindly advise suitable time.

Chris

Chris Bowerman

Report each wk.
Analise monthly

*Control systems being introduced to TWR's racing divisions.*

feeling that they were a very talented electronics company and that Engs and TWR should cement this relationship for the future, especially with some of the TWR road car projects now being developed. All had gone ahead as planned until Bill Gibson and Brian Mason, at final signing of the contract, had asked that I become a director of the joint venture company. TW had not been totally comfortable with Bill Gibson all along and took exception to being told who should be the directors; perhaps TW feeling I was too biased towards Zytek when making future engine decisions, something he now wanted more control of. Bill and Brian left the meeting and came down to my office to tell me in some amazement that the deal was off. I had spent some time with Zytek in an extensive upgrade of their engine management system with many additional features and this was now dropped. Over the years since then parts of Zytek have been bought by Motorola and finally a buyout by Continental of Germany at huge multiples of the original half share price.

This loss of the Zytek joint venture was then the catalyst in the decision to use the new Bosch MP1.7 sequential engine management system and data acquisition for future turbocharged engines, but not replace the V12 system. The new Bosch MP1.7 was superior as a turbocharged engine control system, with four separate throttle angle map features and better electronic wastegate control software. Now with the proposed Zytek partnership off, their previously unfunded software development available to me ceased. The Bosch system had a very good and equally expensive data acquisition system so necessary for a turbo programme and this was the direction funding would take.

The problem in IMSA by now was fairly obvious, our 6-litre V12 engine was not going to match the well developed 3-litre turbocharged installations the Porsche and Nissan teams were using after years of development with virtually free fuel specification and consumption. Staying with the V12 option needed a reversal of the original regulations to allow us the use of a 6.5-litre engine while using the existing car weight limits, needed to match the torque off the corners of the turbo cars. Added to the capacity increase and using the same applications in engine weight reduction and lower engine installation as my Group C car proposals would have produced a very competitive IMSA race car in both sprint and long distance races. However, any threats or bluffs of reviewing our continuation in IMSA if we were not allowed to return to the original regulations of a 6.5-litre engine to have an even playing field was never pursued by TW. Without the prospect of returning to IMSA's original engine capacity rules for us, TWR's IMSA engine programme needed to change to the format used by the two opposition competitors who were using turbocharged engines; but to a completely different specification and format to that proposed for Group C.

Just two years were left in the current Group C series before rule changes to an entirely different concept using 3.5-litre Formula One based engines in new 750kg lightweight race car designs. That situation had added to my reluctance to move to a turbocharged programme on top of the reasons already stated, leaving no time for its ultimate development. TW had now turned from his own internal race engine division's advice after ten years to seek influence and direction from Max Heidegger over future turbocharged engine programmes. Max was a very straight and genuine enthusiast, running a small five-man team at his R&D facility in Liechtenstein. He had the luxury of developing his ideas without any of the time constraints and pressures that are involved when supplying a team's racing and testing programme. TW loved talking about new possibilities and patents with Max and had already spent a large amount of money over the last two years on a turbocharged programme for JaguarSport, leading, it was assumed by them both to full production in future Jaguar road cars.

HEIDEGGER
HEIDEGGER ENGINE DEVELOPMENT LTD.
Landstrasse 89
9495 Triesen
Fürstentum Liechtenstein
Telefon (075) 23177
Telex 889469
Fax Nr. (075) 29231

Liechtensteinische Landesbank, Vaduz
Bank in Liechtenstein AG, Vaduz

TELEFAX-MESSAGE

To Tom Walkinshaw Racing Ltd. Fax-No. 0044 - 8675 79352
Station Field
Industrial Estate
GB- Kidlington/Oxford
Attn Tim Cunningham Pages (incl. cover page) 1
Subject
Comments

Dear Tim

Refering to your Telex we are sorry to tell you that we are not in a position to pass on the manual of the Bosch 1.7 System.

As told to Mr Walkinshaw, we have had to sign an agreement of secrecy with Bosch, not to give any information, concerning their system, to persons who are not employed in our company.

I hope that you will unterstand our situation.

Best regards,
HEIDEGGER ENGINE DEV. LTD.
Rudi Mayer

*After TW had decided to leave Zytek and go with Bosch for engine management our request for DATA Systems to work the programme was declined*

Engine Development - Heidegger

This includes invoices to the end of April. The budget of £20,000 per month was a general provision, not based on HEDL budget, and the total budget of £240,000 is to be now split between V6 and other projects.

*Memo dated 30.5.89 showing the constant flow of cash to Heidegger's in Liechtenstein over a period of four years.*

## Notes from Engine Meeting dated August 22nd 1988

AWS Removable liners in the future - first fixed.

AWS 98mm bore for Group C even 100mm.

AWS 'C' 3.8 litres x 1 bar of boost.

MH. AWS Crank oil drillings wrong - std engine.

MH Crank oil drillings redesigned.

AWS Max rpm 8,000.

MH 84/85 mm strok OK for 8,000 - 8,500 rpm.

AWS Pistons with skirts.

[illegible] Stiffer piston - MH open mind.

AWS Not long stroke engine.

MH Big pistons wrong - RM agrees.

AWS Needs pin overlap - MH not necessary. CRANK.

AWS/MH Agree on bore and stroke for F.3000 !

MH 3.4 litre enough.

AWS High compression = winning engine.

MH Agrees.

MH 92 v 98 bore and prove which is best.

AWS Can cool large piston with spiral.

MH Cannot cool sides.

TW Honda do not burn pistons because they spend 10% of turn-over.

AWS To investigate ceramic coating on pistons in America - to prove with gas torch !

TW Has a paper - copy to TS. ?

AWS Connecting rods.

MH Has a rod 148 mm - CL straight through.

MH 78 mm stroke should be OK.

AWS. MH Does not like gudgeon pin going up.

MH Gudgeon Pin going up is no problem.<br>77 mm stroke common between engines.<br>Common crank and rods.<br>F.3000 - 2 rings 'C' - 3 rings. GpC 78mm F3000 75mm.

AWS Jet titanium rods as Honda.

AWS Jet titanium rod cheaper $200

AWS Steel rods £140.

AWS Jet rods need pins to caps.<br>Cylinder heads.

AWS 2 sets of patterns :<br>1 time cast. x 100 for existing customers.<br>To modify 1 set.<br>Need to provide 50 engine sets for existing customers.

AWS 2 Stages

(1) EXISTING FOR IMSA

MH Future water passages smaller. ?

AWS Water holes in blocks in the wrong place - needs slight restricting. / versus HEAD flow

AWS Heads can be modified and be suitable for IMSA.

MH To design new heads - AWS not in next 6 weeks.

AWS Ring dowels for top engine mtg.

(2) SECOND STAGE<br>Port Angles<br>Water passages - cross flow cooling ?<br>More material around bolts.

MH Different heads to engine capacity.

AWS Same heads. (combustion chamber inserts)

AWS New heads different meeting.

AWS 3 different ideas that produce the same HP. At 9000 R.P.M.

MH Valve tops modified to stop caps coming off.<br>- because of boost.

AWS Agrees ?<br>Hot spots = loss of HP - cross flow may help.

TS Angle of ports required. EXHAUST side to clear underwing

TS Need stainless steel castings to clear underwings.

Postition of Turbo :

TS Outside of underwing.

AWS On top short pipes. To test T.S. position

MH Short as possible.

MH Metric engine bolts.

TW MH redesign belt system drawn next meeting - 6 weeks.

TW MH redesign plus front of block.

TW MH plus heads plus port angles.

TW MH includes water pumps. water pump at rear.

MH Water pump design wrong - AWS agrees !NO needs to be altered pipe down

AWS Str mtr and alternator in bell housing & water pump.

AWS Timing disc in camshaft gears.

AWS Pick up for crankshaft at front.

What electronics - Zytek.

AWS Wants coils on plugs.

TW Available from Jaguar.

Turbos

AWS In America - IHI - politics can be sorted.

AWS IHI the best.<br>Garrett in the meantime.

Street Project

- MH to call Ian Brown - contact
- TW - Jim Randle.
- XJS - Street turbo to be finished.
- MH to finish project.
- Bosch want 2 cars - XJS.
- MH saloon first.
- Bosch - starts end of September.
- After Bosch finish needs to be driven day and night 50 - 60.000 Kms.
- MH wants 2nd saloon and 2 XJS'.

MH 2 saloons - turbo.<br>1 saloon - 4.2.<br>- 2 XJS.

MH Engines from TW for 4.2 x 5 off.<br>- PD to supply.

TW Turbo starts need 20.

TW Engine then built at Jaguar.<br>MH makes parts for Jaguar.

Car into production September 1989.<br>- Supply end of July 1989 - Saloon.

Bosch - 30 engine management sets by the end of April.

TW 200 plus in first year.

TW Parts for 20 saloons + 20 XJS.

Bosch - Production systems for 1991.

Saloon car back from Bosch at end of January.

TW To order March 1989 numbers following approvals.

MH 4.2 crank middle September.

JCB JaguarSport for manifolds - logo's supplied.

AWS Has 5, another 3 to come. V6

MH Needs 2nd engine. AWS to supply. V6

TW Talk to Andy Wallace.

AWS Sump drawing to MH.

TW F.3000 - MH - Zytek system.

TW 'C' - Zytek system.

TW 'C' - Bosch system, 1 set on order.

TW Schedule of meetings.<br>To allow MH to book cheap flights, 4/6 week intervals.

ROGER SILMAN

*Max Heidegger states the pin overlap, needed to convert to even firing proposed by me, is not necessary. Big-end journal spacing to produce even firing is vital.*

TW did not seem at all concerned with the increasing threat coming from Sauber using a 5-litre turbocharged V8 engine. The car that was past its best, the 962C Porsche, did not in my view select its 3 to 3.4-litre capacity flat-six engine on merit any more, it was simply that it had to choose what had already been well developed. This engine also fitted the 962 race cars concepts and design; combined with the long-term marketing philosophy of its flat-six 911 series of road cars and engines. Just as the production Mercedes V8 engine was perhaps a little larger than needed, that was all that was available to Mercedes to work with as well. With the Mercedes 2-valve head configuration, running to 6500rpm for optimum fuel economy, the larger capacity production engine produced massive torque using a maximum of 1.65 bar boost reducing the detonation risk, and would go on to prove to be the better option over the next two years.

Eventually after the work that was finally needed to upgrade the many lightweight V6 engine castings that had initially been designed for a totally different normally aspirated application, my alternative using the lower boost pressure larger capacity 3.9 to 4.2-litre V8 option would not have cost any more time and money. TW refused to consider this proposal saying Jaguar could never race with a V8 engine. Later my investigations confirmed that TW had never asked Jaguar if the V8 concept would suit their marketing policy, and by now the meetings at Browns Lane with Roger and me had stopped, and TW was the only point of contact there. In fact Jaguar had already started on designing a V8 engine to eventually replace the V12.

This change in engine philosophy had then led to initial internal discussions in 1988 that had us replacing the V12 engine with the new V6 turbo concept in the XJR-9 with suitable modifications; but TW had other plans in mind. After Tony Southgate had spent some time on a preliminary programme for the XJR-9 to update it with engine intercoolers and other revisions, Tony had presented his concepts at the first major strategy meeting at Kidlington in August 1988. TW had then simply asked Tony about producing a completely new car. The late timing of this request was typical TW strategy allowing little time to complete a programme which meant increased effort was needed with the same resources available over a shorter time period that would then reduce costs for him. This was not the way that engineers like to work, having to take shortcuts leading to the inevitable revisions and problems when first testing would begin. It was also only when that point had been reached that TW could have any direct influence over the direction development would take, and be seen to manage the fix.

Roger Silman had been made team director in 1987 and a new team manager Clive Steeper was appointed to start the 1989 year. Clive had experience in larger corporate management situations and was in the process of trying to bring some changes to the Group C structure, which was not going to be easy. Not being subject to the growth path of the TWR business as most had, he was a fresh pair of eyes but would also have difficulty with the team's allegiance to Roger. He was confident in looking first before making any change decisions that may not have been welcome. It was a difficult position to be filling.

For the first time in TWR's engine history we were having a design by committee meeting with Roger taking the notes. MH, RH and HF are the people TW has been working with in Liechtenstein. The following meeting notes give an idea of the unachievable timescales, confusion and lack of defined direction now introduced to engine programmes with the introduction of the V6 engine. My handwritten corrections show difference of opinion in what was said. These include shortening this engine by 100mm and producing new heads, F3000 engine programme, common block for Group C, IMSA and F3000, disagreement on bore size, turbocharger position by the designer to suit car lay out with no regard to primary length for engine tuning, my proposal for offset big end pins to create an even firing engine deemed not necessary. A production turbocharged version of Jaguar's straight six engine will go into production one year from the date of this meeting. In the end not one single item on this agenda with the responsibility of MH ever saw the light of day after two years!!

TW no longer knew the names of engine builders or their individual worth as was once the case. Increased TWR Group activity outside of motor racing left TW with much less time for the close contact that had built the racing team in the first place. Business expansion placing increased demands on racing budgets.

The new Jaguars, designated XJR-10 and XJR-11 with turbocharged engines, would have a total gestation period of around five months before six weeks of testing, with a completely new engine system and a commitment to use this format from as early in 1989 as possible. A decision had then been made that the IMSA programme would also go turbocharged and be introduced for 1989 as well, with TW's thoughts that using most of the 3-litre parts that came with the ARG deal would be a simple solution. Both of these turbocharged engines concepts however would be very different in capacity and concept when based on the same V6 unit. The Group C engine would be totally focused on fuel economy with no capacity constraints, but be very detonation sensitive having to use production road fuels. The IMSA engine would have a smaller fixed capacity of three litres and would be allowed high specification fuels that would reduce detonation sensitivity; but then be regulated by a pre compressor air restrictor, needing a very controlled boost curve. As it later turned out, both engines would produce similar peak power of 750bhp from two entirely different design concepts.

Approaching the start of the 1989 year the TWR team was spending all of its time on the new V6 turbo XJR-10 (IMSA) and XJR-11 (Group C) variants after introduction and build of these new cars over the winter of 88/89. It had become obvious however that the 7-litre V12 cars would have to be used in the interim until the Kidlington built 3.3-litre V6 engine to be used in the XJR-11 had reached a suitable level of competitiveness. The Liechtenstein team had been commissioned by TW to carry out initial development work on a 3.2-litre turbo V6 engine since early 1988 and it was this concept that was to be used in the race programme was TW's thinking. In the meantime, we had to produce our own 3.3-litre version to enable the programme to actually proceed; the Heidegger 3.2-litre units that were to be the basis of this programme were not available in time. They were planned to later replace the interim units we had built.

The promise of 3.2-litre V6 turbo engines from Heidegger after almost 18 months of development produced two prototypes, and this concept was to be introduced in 1990 to replace Engs first year 3.3-litre units at Kidlington. Unfortunately they turned out to be a disappointment performance wise and after two years of development and precious resources this programme was stopped. Meanwhile £20,000 per month had been sent on account to Liechtenstein over a four-year period, plus the upgrading of a new dynamometer cell there. This 3.2-litre programme would have consumed 30% of the entire Engs divisional funding available for all engine development and race support for Group C from 1987 to 1990, plus the funding needed for an additional dynamometer at Kidlington being sent to upgrade the one in Liechtenstein. By the time this collaboration with Heidegger was finally terminated at the end of 1990, with a last futile attempt at producing a Formula One specification V12 racing engine for the XJR-14, none of the road or race programmes had been fully completed or seen the light of day to return the investment.

*XJR-11 being built.*
*Note top mounting tubes bypass the V6 turbo engine directly to the two mounting points at the rear of the new extended bell housing/oil tank.*

After putting many of his development eggs in the Liechtenstein basket, and obviously feeling unhappy with an outcome that had produced many questions, TW was unable to review that situation to a satisfactory level with me by the end of 1990. This had led me to review my future at TWR. Engs was left to its own devices to rapidly procure components and produce more units for the new 3.5-litre engine we had produced in limited numbers as a backup for the following year of 1990. The V6 turbo is a story for another day, and sadly did not have the success hoped for, but took huge resources and eventually cost probably four times more than my proposed upgrade and V12 development.

With all the race programmes having to be carried out by Engs for 1989, there were many conflicting commitments other than to Group C and IMSA being proposed by TW. This showed the level of his ambition, but the problem I had was directing resources to facilitate prototype engineering or even just feasibility studies without our own internal machine shop. Engs was expected to give 100% to all these programmes, and knowing that we were short on resources even for the current programmes made positive responses to these feasibility studies very difficult.

Also at this time the Jaguar 220 concept that Jim Randle at Jaguar had produced was taken over by TWR. Plans to produce 350 of these supercars had been put in place and this endeavour would be larger than the Group C and IMSA programmes together.

There had been a considerable increase in Engs personnel by 1989. Charlie Bamber was responsible for dyno testing and trackside engineering along with Tim Cunningham for the turbo programme. Eric Crawley was workshop foreman to manage the various build needs for the two V12 programmes. Nigel Eames as head of procurement had this demanding section under his control, and new engine builders at differing levels of experience had been employed. Charlie Bamber and I covered the trackside support for both Group C and the American IMSA races with one or two engine builders on a rotational basis attending at least one Group C event each year. The attendance by engine builders at the track was part of their education on how the team worked and what was expected from their engines, and how they could better support and understand the race programme from the whole team's point of view.

MEETING WITH TOM WALKINSHAW 22ND FEBRUARY 1989

Machine shop for TWR agreed in principal. Review Nigel Eames' office plan, probably something more extensive. Increase in engineering personnel needed (Chris Middlemass indicates interest). 6 litre 1504 basic update to TW (currently at ERA reviewing EPROM) (Bill Gibson, Norman Gardner, Charles Bamber, Allan Scott). Meeting with Peter Taylor, Jaguar, agreed to establish machine shop/Jaguar links. A. Moss to attend meetings at Jaguar only with P. Davies, I. Brown, A. Scott.

Future Workload

4 valve V12 for Jaguar, 220 total 350 vehicles (400 engines?) Release date early 1990? 220/TWR concept car, what is final configuration? TWR concept car 400 vehicles per year basic modification 3/35 litre NA. Concept car top of the range twin turbo V6 horsepower TBN. Machine shop for above needs to be outlined as soon as possible. Suggestion that TW visit Zeus Pattern and Foundry, (liaison/interest).

6 Cylinder JaguarSport

Up to 2,000 vehicles per year engine not to be assembled at Radford (Gainsborough?). Progress meetings with Max Heidegger twice monthly, alternate Kidlington/ Switzerland. Meeting with Lucas (David Andrews) Wednesday 1 March. Discuss road and racing.

Holden

4 valve head for 307 V8 possible use for up market 4 seater convertible (Group A?).

TWR 3.5 litre NA Group CF1 engine. Feasibility study needed 15,000 to 18,000 rpm, valve gear (12 cylinders?).

***The note on 6-litre 1504 is the new V12 engine developed at Engs for JaguarSport to be used to replace the current 5.3-litre V12 in Jaguar production, with 1504 being the emission test the engine had to pass as well as the 400 hour full throttle endurance test being carried out at Jaguar. My suggestion that TW visit the foundry for his own interest, is shorthand for that foundry will never be able to support the quantities or timescales in his mind in the above memo.***

## New arrivals at Kidlington Engines

Steve Ridgers

Andrew Whiffen

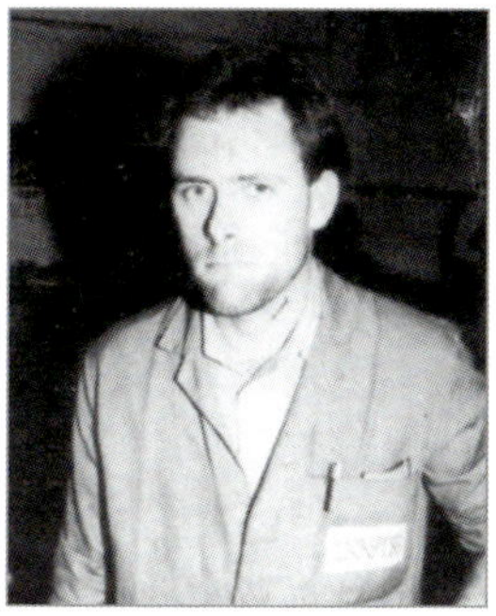
Robert Ashfield

Leonard Smith

Mark Bayley

Tim Cunningham

Richard Freestone

Peter Laye

Snow Mooney and Hugh Jenkins work on a V12 engine.

Jim Brown and Pete Tyrell

Mathew Norris, Ian Bickerton and Grant Rushton

## New appointments at the TWR Group

Richard West joined the group from a similar position at McLaren International. His role being to establish a co-ordinated and effective Press and Public Affairs Department for the Group C and IMSA racing activities, liaising between Jaguar, Silk Cut and Castrol.

Clive Steeper was appointed Team Manager – his attempts at bringing a more general view in management of the team was soon not welcomed by Roger. Another appointment was that of Alister Mitchell, formerly Jaguar Cars' International Solicitor, joining the group as Company Secretary, being responsible for all Group legal and Company Secretariat matters. Alister taught me how to write a letter that could help me out of difficult situations that arose from time to time.

*Richard West*
*Manager,*
*Press and Public Affairs*

*Clive Steeper*
*TWR Team Manager*

*Alister Mitchell*
*Company Secretary*

## Proposed race and test schedule for the following year

RACE AND PROPOSED TEST SCHEDULE FOR 1989

| | | | |
|---|---|---|---|
| 28 FEBRUARY | DONNINGTON | 289 + 189 | SHAKEDOWN + TEST |
| 5 MARCH | MIAMI RACE | 2 x IMSA V12 | RACE |
| 7-12 MARCH | JEREZ | 2 X TURBO | TESTING |
| 8 MARCH | WEST PALM BEACH | 188 | TEST |
| 16-17 MARCH | PAUL RICARD | 2 X TURBO 1 X V12 | TESTING |
| 18 MARCH | SEBRING RACE | 2 X IMSA V12 | RACE (12 HOURS) |
| 21 MARCH | ATLANTA | 2 X IMSA V12 | TEST |
| 23 MARCH | DONNINGTON | 688 | TEST |
| 31 MARCH | SILVERSTONE | 389 | TEST |
| 2 APRIL | ROAD ATLANTA RACE | 1 X TURBO 1 V12 | RACE |
| 9 APRIL | SUZUKA RACE | 2 X V12 | RACE |
| 13 APRIL | DONNINGTON | 1 X TURBO | TEST |
| 17 APRIL | ATLANTA | 389/388 | TEST |
| 19 APRIL | SILVERSTONE | 2 X TURBO | TEST |
| 23 APRIL | WEST PALM BEACH RACE | 2 X V12 1 X TURBO? | IMSA RACE |
| 2 MAY * | PEMBURY | 2 X TURBO | TEST |
| 2-4 MAY * | DIJON | 2 X TURBO | TEST |
| 16 MAY | GRATTEN | 2 X IMSA TURBO | TEST |
| 18 MAY | MID OHIO | 2 X IMSA TURBO | TEST |
| 21 MAY | DIJON RACE | 2 X TURBO | RACE |
| 29 MAY | LIME ROCK RACE | 2 X IMSA TURBO | RACE |
| 2 JUNE | DONNINGTON | 3 X V12 2 X TURBO | LE MANS SHAKEDOWN |
| 4 JUNE | MID OHIO RACE | 2 X IMSA TURBO | RACE |
| 5-11 JUNE | LE MANS | LOTS | RACE |
| 16 JUNE * | TBN | AS REQUIRED | TEST |
| 25 JUNE | JARAMA RACE | 2 X TURBO | RACE |
| 27 JUNE | WATKINS GLEN | TBN | TEST |
| 10 JULY | ELKHART LAKE | TBN | TEST |
| 16 JULY | ROAD AMERICA RACE | 2 X IMSA TURBO | RACE |
| 23 JULY | BRANDS HATCH | 2 X TURBO | RACE |
| 27 JULY | PORTLAND | TBN | TEST |
| 30 JULY | PORTLAND RACE | 2 X IMSA TURBO | RACE |
| 13 AUGUST | KANSAS RACE | 2 X IMSA TURBO | RACE |
| 20 AUGUST | NURBURGRING RACE | 2 X TURBO | RACE |
| 3 SEPTEMBER | SAN ANTONIO RACE | 2 X IMSA TURBO | RACE |
| 3 SEPTEMBER | DONNINGTON | 2 X TURBO | RACE |
| 10 SEPTEMBER | SEARS POINT RACE | 2 X IMSA TURBO | RACE |
| 17 SEPTEMBER | SPA | 2 X TURBO | RACE |
| 1 OCTOBER | COLUMBUS RACE | 2 X IMSA TURBO | RACE |
| 1 OCTOBER | USA | 2 X TURBO | RACE |
| 15 OCTOBER * | CANADA | 2 X TURBO | RACE |
| 22 OCTOBER | DEL MAR RACE | 2 X IMSA TURBO | RACE |

* = PROVISIONAL

RACE AND PROPOSED TEST SCHEDULE FOR 1989
AUGUST - NOVEMBER 1989

| | | | |
|---|---|---|---|
| 9-19 AUGUST | NURBURGRING | 1 X TURBO 1 X V12 | TEST |
| 13 AUGUST | KANSAS RACE | 1 X TURBO 1 X V12 | RACE |
| 20 AUGUST | NURBURGRING RACE | 2 X TURBO | RACE |
| 21 AUGUST* | DONINGTON | 1 X TURBO (1 X V12) | TEST |
| 29 AUGUST | DONINGTON | 1 X TURBO (1 X V12) | TEST |
| 29 AUGUST | BIG SPRING | | TEST |
| 3 SEPTEMBER | SAN ANTONIO RACE | 1 X TURBO 1 X V12 | RACE |
| 3 SEPTEMBER | DONINGTON | 2 X TURBO | RACE |
| 10 SEPTEMBER | SEARS POINT RACE | 1 X TURBO 1 X V12 | RACE |
| 17 SEPTEMBER | SPA | 2 X TURBO | RACE |
| 1 OCTOBER | TAMPA RACE | 2 X IMSA TURBO | RACE |
| 29 OCTOBER | MEXICO CITY | 2 X TURBO | RACE |
| 22 OCTOBER | DEL MAR RACE | 2 X IMSA TURBO | RACE |
| 14-15 NOVEMBER | DAYTONA | | TEST |
| 19-20 NOVEMBER | SEBRING | | TEST |
| 22 NOVEMBER | ATLANTA | | TEST |

* = PROVISIONAL
_ = CHANGES

*1989 IMSA team with V12 and V6 turbo race cars.*

**6-SPEED GEARBOX SHAKEDOWN TEST**
**SILVERSTONE SOUTHERN CIRCUIT**
**WEDNESDAY 10 JANUARY 1989**
**588 V12**

Driver: Andy Wallace
Engineer: Alastair Macqueen

* Conditions wet. Large puddles.
* Gearbox works well - no major problems.
* Gear change better (quicker and lighter) than 5-speed.
* Goodyear wets very good. They ignore puddles
* Removing 5th/6th bias spring improved change.
* Small problem with machining of bearing carrier means it is not possible to reduce spring bias against 1st/2nd plane.
* Reduction in this spring bias will improve 2nd to 3rd and 3rd to 2nd change.
* This will be available for Estoril Test.
* 80kms covered - gearbox now to be stripped and inspected prior to extended running at Estoril.
* Best time 64.75 on very wet circuit.

**ALASTAIR MACQUEEN**
10 January 1990

---

*At last the 6-speed gearbox has been introduced. However a problem with an incorrect differential specification meant it was unable to be used. These gearboxes would eventually be used in the low volume XJR-15 programme.*

JAGUAR

CHAPTER TWENTY

# The 1989 Group C and IMSA V12 programmes

**And so it was that both IMSA and Group C would start the 1989 season with a combination of V12 cars and engines that had changed little from the preceding two years, as well as new cars and turbocharged engines to different rules, with the Atlantic Ocean separating the two TWR teams. Group C had some updates to the rules with all races being 480kms in length, apart from Le Mans. To encourage participation at all rounds those entered in the series would be fined US$250,000 for failing to present a race car for scrutineering. These changes came about with the FIA taking charge of the series and owning the television rights. TWR had lost two top drivers with Eddie Cheever and Martin Brundle returning to Formula One. The Group C pairings would be Andy Wallace with John Nielsen and new recruit Patrick Tambay with Jan Lammers. The XJR programme also needed a 6-speed gearbox and this had become a reality with a unit being tested. It was especially needed at Le Mans to bridge the huge speed differentials between the slow second gear corner and the Mulsanne straight, as well as an update for the new turbocharged XJR-11. Andy Wallace had carried out this mid winter test at Silverstone.**

The opening round for 1989 was once again the Daytona 24 hour event in Florida. A three-day test session prior to the event at the banked Talladega speedway was carried out using three cars; chassis 188 (444 miles), 288 (812 miles), and 388 (304 miles). Drivers available were Davy Jones, John Nielsen, Derek Daly, Andy Wallace, Jeff Kline and Price Cobb.

## Sunbank 24 hour Daytona – February 2nd

Tony Dowe and Ian Reed had honed the 1988 Daytona winning TWR Jaguar team with attention to detail and lessons learned from the previous year, and were upbeat about a second win for the Castrol Jaguars. Engine specifications were very similar to the previous year with the addition of a new engine air intake NACA duct on each side of the engine cover. I had raised the problem of the hot air from the radiator flowing over the roof into the engine air intake reducing engine performance, and the Valparaiso team had modified an engine cover to take air from the side of the race car to avoid this. Back-to-back testing at Daytona had seen a 0.4 second reduction in lap time using this engine air entry method. It would also be the first time that the Don Devendorf run 1988 championship winning Nissan team had entered the endurance event of Daytona, in a test of the durability of its race cars that had proved almost unbeatable in sprint races the previous year. John Bristow of Castrol UK had joined the Castrol USA team for this event to carry out an extensive analysis of its products under the severe conditions encountered in this 24 hour event. Jaguar Cars UK were using Castrol and its products as original equipment suppliers, and this support came as part of Castrol's sponsorship deal, supplying special products as well as financial support.

## DAYTONA 24 HRS. 1989

**Personnel:**

Tom Walkinshaw
Roger Silman
Tony Dowe
Alan Scott

| | |
|---|---|
| Chief Mechanic | John Jackson |

**288:**

| | |
|---|---|
| Engineer | Ian Reed |
| #1 Mechanic | Howard Minckler |
| #2 Mechanic | Butch Winkle |
| #3 Mechanic | Jim Faulconer |
| Extra (For Pit Stops) | Phil Denney |
| Refueler | Frank Rafferty |
| Fuel Dead Man | Dave Girton |
| Engine Man | Charlie Bamber |
| Guy to Bring up Tires | Kenny Szymanski |
| Signaler | Larry Randlett |
| Dunlop Eng | TBN |
| Parts | Kurt Wilson |
| Gearbox | Derek Clarson |

**388:**

| | |
|---|---|
| Engineer | Dave Benbow |
| #1 Mechanic | Carl Azevedo |
| #2 Mechanic | Peter Hodgkinson |
| #3 Mechanic | Larry Zelesnik |
| Extra (For Pit Stops) | Viv Cowley |
| Refueler | Mike Barto |
| Fuel Dead Man | Tim Ellis |
| Engine Man | Don Beadle |
| Guy to Bring up Tires | Chuck Gaa |
| Signaler | Steve Ave |
| Dunlop Eng | TBN |
| Parts | Mark Freeman |
| Gearbox | Rob Gustafson |

**188:**

| | |
|---|---|
| Engineer | Alastair Macqueen |
| #1 Mechanic | Rod Benoist |
| #2 Mechanic | Jerry Pyman |
| #3 Mechanic | Chris Tuckey |
| [illegible] | [illegible] |
| Fuel Dead Man | Paul Brown |
| Engine Man | Steve Harding |
| Guy to Bring up Tires | Ian Gouldstone |
| Signaler | Alan Lewis |
| Dunlop Eng | TBN |
| Parts | Winston Bush |
| Gearbox | Tim Love |

**Fabricators:**

| | |
|---|---|
| #1 | Frank Rafferty |
| #2 | Viv Cowley |
| #3 | Chuck Gaa |

**Machinist:**

| | |
|---|---|
| #1 | Viv Cowley |

**Fuel Tower Re-Fuelers:**

Ira Chez
+ Each Dead Man Handle Person On Each Crew

**Bodywork:**

| | |
|---|---|
| #1 | Ian Gouldstone |
| #2 | Jim Kracht |

**Timing and Scoring:**

Chris Syfert
Charlie Skala
Ann Roeske

**Motorhome:**

Mike Murphy
Ann Murphy
Rosemary Ave
Lillian Lewis

**Psychotherapist & Massage:**

David Vinson
Tom Ryan

**Gearbox:**

Rob Gustafson
Derek Clarson

**To Fetch Drivers During Race:**

Dave Schuck
Karen Grady

**At Track Misc. Supplies:**

Vik Warren

**Radios:**

Craig McCann

**Tire Blankets:**

Craig McCann

**Sub Assemblies:**

Dave Girton

**Pit's Set Up:**

Vik Warren
Mark Freeman
Kurt Wilson
Mike Barto
Paul Brown
Chuck Gaa
Viv Cowley
Ian Gouldstone
John McLellan

**Spare Signaler**

Don Doyle

## *Qualifying*

With the arrival of the Electromotive Nissans there were now three evenly matched manufacturers, and close racing was expected between the Jaguar XJR-9, Nissan GTP-ZXT and Porsche 962.

Qualifying had the #83 Nissan of Geoff Brabham/ Chip Robinson on pole with a time of 1:39.18; Jaguar #60 of Nielsen/Cobb/Wallace 1:39.24; #84 Nissan Michael Roe/Arie Luyendyk 1:39.91, Brun Porsche 962C Brun/Stuck/Cheever/Larrauri 1:39.94. The #61 Jaguar of Jones/Boesel/Lammers was seventh 1:40.8 and the #66 Jaguar of Derek Daly/Patrick Tambay/Martin Donnelly 8th 1:40.8; these times proving a close fight for all. The Miller Highlife BF Goodrich Porsche 962 of Bell/Wollek/ John Andretti set a time of 1:42.94 in twelfth place.

Sixty-seven race cars would face the start at 3.30pm on Saturday from the total of sixty-nine cars that had entered this event two days before.

## *The race*

From the very start of the warm and dry conditions it was a frantic pace set by the three manufactures teams to see who would break first. This action however led to an immediate catastrophe for the Jaguar team with Derek Daly in the #66 Jaguar contacting the Roe/Luyendyk #84 Nissan on the very first lap, resulting in immediate retirement with broken suspension for that Jaguar. We were reduced to just two cars from the very start, and two race cars were never a TWR philosophy in these events. The Brabham/Robinson #83 Nissan, Klaus Ludwig/Weaver/Van der Merwe #86 Porsche and the 1988 Daytona race winning #60 Jaguar of Jones/Boesel/ Lammers ran in close company, with the Porsche being the first to drop out of this chase with reported throttle problems after three hours. The second Jaguar was soon reporting high oil temperatures and by 9pm in the cool of the evening these had crept up to 120°C engine entry oil temperature; with a corresponding 20lb drop in oil pressure to 45psi.

*The start of the Daytona 24 hour race on the banked front straight section of the track.*

The Nissan established itself in the lead from the Jaguar by late evening and this situation remained until the Jaguar suffered engine failure through lack of oil pressure around 1.30am on lap 288. We were unaware of the situation that led to this problem at the time, but the sole remaining Jaguar, also in oil temperature problems was an indicator that something in the systems was wrong. Soon after this the race was red flagged as fog had settled on the track and the race was stopped for the next four hours. The race resumed at dawn and the battle continued with Brabham's Nissan leading the Bell/Wollek/Andretti Jim Busby Porsche and Nielsen in the XJR-9 until lap 453 when the 83 Nissan suffered engine failure and both Nissans were now out, the 84 Nissan having stopped early on lap 51.

The closing stages of the race became a two-car battle between the #61 Nielsen/Wallace/Cobb Jaguar and the 962 BF Goodrich Porsche being pushed hard by its veteran drivers Bell and Wollek. The Jaguar continued to have rising oil temperatures reaching 130°C after the oil cooler, and its lower oil pressure was a concern to all. A pit stop for additional oil cooling and raising the low rear wing angle set to maintain competitive straight-line speeds on the banking had led to some handling problems on the tight infield section, and this stop started to turn the outcome against the Valparaiso team. What had actually happened was the oil cooler had become detached from its mountings and was lying on its side in the engine bay after coming in contact with a slower car. Now Cobb, who was driving on the limit in this 24 hour race, was finally caught out with his XJR-9 spinning off the track. Little damage was done and he soon regained the track but the leading Porsche was able to relax a little as it went one lap up in the lead. The last stint had Wollek in the Porsche and Lammers now transferred to the Jaguar trying to close the gap. Eight laps from the end the Porsche made a quick pit stop for a fuel only 'splash and dash' and rejoined in time to win the Sunbank Daytona 24 hour race by the closest margin in Daytona history, just 1m.26s. This would be the fiftieth IMSA event win for the Porsche 956/962 from the time of its first entry in 1984. Both leading cars had covered 621 laps at an average speed of just 91mph (148kph) reflecting the four-hour stop for the fog during the event.

The next placings were Brun/Stuck/Larrauri/Cheever Porsche 962C 19 laps behind on 602 laps; Ludwig/Weaver/Van de Merwe Porsche 962 on 600 laps, and Katayama/Yorino/Forbes-Robinson Mazda 767B Rotary on 559 laps completed. Of the nine 962/962C Porsches entered, just three were running at the end, both Nissans had failed as well as the single Group C Toyota. The Mazda 767B had started to show its potential here with fifth place.

Later inspection of the engine from #60 at Kidlington found that a different supplier had been used when the new oil-pump scavenge hoses had been made and fitted at Valparaiso. While these hoses had high burst ratings, it had been overlooked that a negative atmospheric rating was not supplied with the specifications. With the vacuum produced from the four scavenge sections the inner rubber lining over time had become detached from the hose wall and started blocking the return of oil to the tank. This had led to large amounts of oil remaining in the engine and contributed to the high oil temperatures; as well as causing the engine failure on the #60 Jaguar when the oil tank ran low with the oil staying in the engine and the pressure had then failed. It was a lesson learnt the hard way, and we weren't happy about losing the third car on the first lap of the race either.

The engine in the second placed Jaguar had survived with low oil pressure combined with high oil temperatures, and this engine was inspected by Castrol to see how their product had performed under these extreme conditions.

*Engineer Dave Benbow in conversation with drivers.*

## Castrol report on high oil temperature engine – Daytona (second place)

### INTRODUCTION

A set of bearings and camshaft lobes from Tom Walkinshaw Racing were submitted for a subjective examination to the Castrol Research Laboratories. The components were from a TWR racing engine. This was the only information supplied as the service histories of the vehicle and engine were considered confidential, except to restricted parties.

The component sets comprised of six 'big end' bearings marked 1 to 6, and main bearings identified as front, second, third and rear. The cam lobe sections comprised of end sections supplied by the original camshaft manufacturer (Lydmet, Glos.) in the form of test slices. These formed part of the engine camshaft casting batch and were probably used as test slices for quality control purposes to ensure satisfactory microstructure and hardness. The two cam lobe samples (identified as Lobes 1 and 2) were in the metallographically prepared and etched condition. Evidence of Vickers hardness surveys across the length and width of the cam lobe faces were present.

### CONCLUSIONS

1. The general appearance of the components suggest that the engine system has been run under very heavily loaded conditions.
2. The incipient failures of the big end bearings are due to gross fatigue wear, brought about by heavy cyclic loading.
3. The wear problem was not lubricant related.
4. The microstructures and hardnesses of the cam lobes appear to be satisfactory.

### RESULTS OF EXAMINATION

Visual examination of the bearings supplied can be seen in Figs. 1 to 10. Examination of the big end bearings can be seen in Fig. 1 to 6. The bearings are arranged in pairs with the con-rod side of the big end bearings always uppermost in the figures. It can be seen from the visual examination that the cap bearings from bearings set No. 1 to 6 are all in good condition with no evidence of overload, fatigue or other associated bearing wear feature. There is slight evidence of overload on bearing surfaces No. 3 and 6.

Examination of the bearings on the con-rod side of the engine are the uppermost bearings in Figs. 1 to 6. There is clear evidence of bearing fatigue shown by the 'crazed' patterns on all of the bearing surfaces and evidence of bearing overload. This form of wear is consistent with the onset of fatigue.

Examination of the main bearings can be seen in Fig. 7 and 10 and show only slight evidence of overloading.

Metallographic examination of the cam noses from Lobe 1 and 2 can be seen in Figs. 11 and 12. Both cam noses have satisfactory microstructures consistent with a good chilled white iron. Hardness testing of the cam nose 1 and 2 showed Vickers hardness results of Hv 632 and Hv 620 respectively.

### DISCUSSION

The results from component examination clearly show that the engine has been run consistently under highly loaded conditions. Evidence gathered from the visual examination of the big end bearings Fig. 1 to 6 show extensive crazed areas of the bearing surfaces on the con-rod side of the bearing. The crazed areas are the onset of fatigue wear, leading ultimately to the detachment of large particles of bearing material. The further ingress of these particles into the bearing system are likely to cause catastrophic wear of the bearing at a later stage. This form of wear is confined to the con-rod side of the bearings, and is due to the uneven loadings that occur within big end systems. The con-rod side of the bearing is subject to the thrust and impacting that occurs due to the combination of crankshaft rotation and the reciprocating motion of the piston and con-rod during the combustion cycle and therefore is subject to most severe operating conditions without the bearing system. This is confirmed by the fact that the bearings on the cap side have remained relatively untouched except for isolated areas of overloading.

The slight amount of overloading on the main bearings, shown in Figs. 7 to 10 is due to the lower loadings generally encountered in main bearings when compared to big end bearings. The major loadings in the engine tend to be absorbed by the big end bearings. This dissipation of the load results in lower loadings on the main bearings, thus less wear occurs in these bearing systems.

The lobe hardnesses and microstructures appeared to be satisfactory.

It can be seen from the results of visual examination that the major wear problem that would occur in these engine bearings is due to overload. The effectiveness of the lubricant in the system appears to be satisfactory as there is no evidence of the gross wear damage which is associated with a lubricant failure. It would appear from the evidence gathered that the engine has been run under very highly loaded conditions, likely to cause incipient failure of the big end bearings due to a gross fatigue mechanism.

**SUMMARY OF LUBRICANTS USED AND MAIN EVENTS**

Following a two day practise session on the 2nd and 3rd of February, the Jaguar team commenced the Daytona 24 Hour race with three cars numbered 60, 66 and 61.

**Table 1 : Castrol/TWR/Jaguar Daytona 24 hours Lubricants Chart**

| CAR | LUBRICANT USED | COMPONENT SYSTEM |
|---|---|---|
| 60 | Formula RS 15W/50 | Engine sump |
| | SRF | Braking/hydraulic system |
| | NEO 75W/140 | Transmission |
| | Unknown | Wheel bearing grease |
| 61 | Castrol XC27* 15W/50 | Engine sump |
| | SRF | Braking/hydraulic system |
| | NEO 75W/140 | Transmission |
| | Castrol XB 80 | Air filter oil |
| | Unknown | Wheel bearing grease |
| 66 | Formula RS 15W/50 | Engine sump |
| | SRF | Braking/hydraulic system |
| | Castrol XD71 | Transmission |
| | Unknown | Wheel bearing grease |

Table 1 provides details of the lubricants used in each of these cars. As can be seen all three cars were first filled with Castrol Formula RS 15W/50, but due to high operational temperatures were subsequently topped up with XC27, 15W/50. This oil provides provides even lower volatility, better shear stability and higher operational viscosity than the Formula RS in use. The product was developed at the request of Allan Scott, TWR, during 1988.

The Daytona race provided an opportunity to test the new transmission oil XD71 which was used in Car 66, and the new air filter oil XB80 which was introduced to the team during the practice sessions. XB80 displaced the USA PJ-1 aerosol product currently purchased by the team from local motorcycle shops prior to race events.

* Note: Car 61 started the race on Formula RS and it was topped off with Castrol XC27 from the first pit stop, approximately 1 hour into the race event.

*New Castrol product introduced at Daytona.*

## IMSA Nissan Grand Prix of Miami (3 hours) – March 5th

The two XJR-9Ds chassis # 288 and 388 were completely rebuilt after the Daytona 24 hour race and transported the length of the United States from the Valparaiso Indiana headquarters to Miami Florida for this street circuit race.

Brabham/Robinson in the Nissan ZXT set the fastest qualifying time in 1:10.496, followed by the Wollek/J. Andretti Porsche and Lammers/Jones in the XJR-9. Weaver/Ludwig in the Texaco Havoline Porsche and Cobb/Nielsen in the second Jaguar completed the top five fastest of the 25 cars that were to start the race.

The Nissan set the pace with the top five qualifiers in contention until Cobb pitted early with a puncture on his XJR-9. Lammers was stuck behind the Wollek Porsche and eventually passed, to then spin, loosing several places. Oil from a damaged cooler eventually found its way onto a rear tyre and the resulting spin made contact with barriers that was too severe to continue. Nielsen made good time to catch up to the Nissan but that was as far as he could manage till the end of the race.

This three hour race ended with Brabham/Robinson winning in the Nissan ZX-T and the Nielsen/Cobb Jaguar second after completing 131 laps; Kline/Naon Spice SE89P 130 laps; Cord/Olson Group C Toyota 128 laps and the J. Andretti/Wollek Porsche 126 laps.

*The winning Brabham/Robinson Nissan ZXT.*

Accidents terminated the Momo Porsche on lap 6, Lammers on lap 44, and the Bell/Sheldon Porsche on lap 97. The Ribbs/Fangio Toyota stopped on lap 72 with a broken timing belt.

## IMSA 12 hours of Sebring International Grand Prix of Endurance – March 18th

The twelve hours of Sebring had two XJR-9D race cars entered, with 53 cars starting this event.

The pole time of 1:55.8 was set by the Nissan ZX-T of Brabham/Robinson/Luyendyk and its sister Electromotive Engineering Nissan backed that up with 1:55.997. The two Jaguars were up next, Nielsen/Cobb 1:58s and Jones/Lammers on 1:58.82. The Busby Racing Porsche 962 of Wollek/Bell/J. Andretti 1:58.945 was fifth.

*XJR-9D rejoins the Sebring race.*

Both Nissans led the race but Luyendyk then lost a wheel and the second Nissan was out. Cobb in the XJR-9D chased the leading Nissan until it had to make an unscheduled stop to secure loose bodywork. Things were looking good with Cobb leading and Jones in third until he had an issue with a slower car and crashed. The Nissan and Jaguar traded places for the remaining hours of this twelve hour race until three laps were lost in the pits while repairs were carried out to the XJR-9D but still manage to then retrieve second place.

The final result was a win for the #83 Nissan after 330 laps, two laps behind the winners was the #61 Nielsen/Cobb Jaguar, followed in third place eight laps behind the Jaguar the Bayside Racing Porsche of Weaver/Dobson. The Momo 962 Porsche of Moretti/Sigala/Roe was a further three laps behind with the Joest Porsche a further two laps down in fifth. After a major rebuild by the Valparaiso lads of the second Jaguar taking almost two hours delayed Lammers/Jones, they finished in fourteenth place while the single Toyota was out with engine trouble on lap 149.

## IMSA (500kms) Nissan Camel Grand Prix of Road Atlanta April 2nd

If we were ever wondering about how much sympathy would come our way from the race committee and organisers in a case to return to the 6.5-litre engine capacity limit for us, we could stop any thoughts on a positive outcome with Nissan now event sponsors, its second event of the year. Just 16 cars would start this race after practice and qualifying.

> It was the All American Racers (Toms) 88C Toyota that set the fastest time here with 1:10.979. The Jaguars had then followed with 1:11.08, Cobb/Nielsen and 1:11.815, Lammers for second and fourth fastest, being split by the #83 Nissan on 1:11.186. Wollek/J. Andretti were fifth on 1:1:12.19 in the Busby Miller Porsche.

Jones had crashed the spare XJR-9 and it was too badly damaged to be repaired at the track.

A marginal call that Cobb had jumped the rolling start, disputed by the TWR team in a race sponsored by Nissan, had Cobb in for a stop and go penalty putting him to the rear of the field. Toyota, Nissan and Jaguar pushed the pace until the Toyota's engine succumbed to the pressure. It was followed shortly after with Lammers V12 having a valve clip the piston on a down shift over rev and retire, and not long after that the Wollek/J. Andretti Porsche went with engine problems as well. The Cobb/Nielsen XJR-9 was pushed to the limit on a great come back drive and was able to return to second place before its tyres began to lose grip in the hot track surface conditions and needed replacing. The XJR-9 worked itself into the lead but with tyres past their best and Brabham on fresh rubber the lead was lost just ten laps from the finish.

Once again it would be the #83 Nissan of Robinson/Brabham/Devendorf that took final honours with the Cobb/Nielsen V12 Jaguar in second place, 34 seconds

*C9 showing suspension loadings path directly into the rear bulkhead; as opposed to the transverse loadings into the gearbox suspension support beam in the XJR-9.*

behind the winners. They were followed by the Momo Porsche of Moretti/Dickens 5 laps behind the Jaguar and the Hotchkis/Adams Porsche in fourth place, six laps down. The S&L Racing Spice SE88P of Scott Schubot was winner of the Camel lights division in fifth, ten laps behind the winners.

## WSPC Suzuka 480kms (Japan) – April 9th

The first World Sports Car Championship race was in Japan and had TWR competing with V12 chassis 588 and 688. 36 cars would make the journey to this race with 34 starting in reasonably cold weather. Mercedes had won the last race of the 1988 season at Sandown Park and their C9 was improving all the time, unlike the XJR-9. The Sauber Mercedes was now a full works team with new updated 4-valve heads and factory tuned 5-litre engines with the team maintaining its driver line up of Schlesser, Mass, Baldi and Acheson.

> Qualifying produced a Toyota 89C lock out of the front row with Lees/Dumfries fastest on 1:50.635 and Ogawa/Barilla on 1:51.55; Lammers with new driver signing Tambay third on 1:53.319; ahead of Schlesser/Baldi on 1:53.474.

Mass was unwell and did not make the start leaving Acheson to complete the full distance in the second Mercedes. The two Mercedes in the historic factory colours of silver took command of the race with Acheson later being asked to let Schlesser through indicating this team's move from the very start of the season to favour one of its cars and not dilute the points. The Jaguars were uncompetitive here with the V12 cars actually seeming to have lost ground from the previous year. The team was concentrating on producing the new XJR-11 turbo and losing interest in the XJR-9.

> The final placings in this race went to Mercedes with Schlesser/Baldi winning by a six second margin from Acheson in the second C9 Mercedes; Wollek/Jelinski were third almost two minutes behind the winner; Hoshino/Suzuki fourth in the Nissan R88C one lap down and Nielsen/Wallace fifth one lap down as well.

It was all a poor start for the TWR team with the unusual situation of Lammers/Tambay running out of fuel on the last lap and being unclassified, and now struggling to match the Joest Porsche. I had started to miss some of the races as pressure to have the turbo engines ready increased.

## IMSA Pontiac Grand Prix of Palm Beach (3 Hours) – April 23rd

Once again it was Brabham fastest in qualifying followed by the Olson/Cord Toyota; Costas Los/Kline/Ricci Spice; Lammers/Jones Jaguar; J Andretti/Wollek Porsche and Cobb/Nielsen Jaguar. Twenty-one cars would start this race with the second Toyota a non-starter.

It was not to be another repeat performance however for the Brabham Nissan, out after just four laps with a blown engine. This was then followed by the Lammers/Jones Jaguar with a broken transmission on lap 22. It was a race long battle with the lead changing constantly between Porsche and Jaguar but eventually it was the Wollek/J. Andretti Miller High Life Porsche of Jim Busby racing who took this win ahead of the Cobb/Nielsen Jaguar after a problem pit stop with one of the wheel covers cost too much time, both cars completing 162 laps. The 87C Toyota of Olson/Cord finished third on 161 laps; Earl/Miller Spice 160 laps; Costas Los/Ricci/Kline Spice 158 laps. After switching to the #84 Nissan, Brabham/Robinson came home in sixth place completing 155 laps of the race.

## Dijon Group C test – May 2nd–4th

This test was was used to test some drivers which included Michel Ferté, Andrew Gilbert-Scott, Eliseo Salazar and Win Percy. The test programme carried out with the V12 XJR-9LM Jaguars was a check of systems for Le Mans and included testing of the results from our work carried out over the winter of 88/89 on the 7-litre V12 engines. This had mainly centred on new exhaust systems and changes to larger 800cc fuel injectors to allow more control over injection period and timing, along with detail work on the oil peeling tray to aid the oil scavenge system. A decision had already been made that the turbo cars were not ready for any endurance races.

In the status report (see page 261) I am complaining of the race cars inherent understeer problems that are scrubbing exit speed and causing increased fuel consumption for lap time. This comment was not appreciated but had come after many years of observing this problem and the pressure put on the drivers to not make too big a point of it. It would much later appear that the source of this problem was a torsional one centred on the bell housing.

## WSPC Coupe de Dijon 480kms (France) – May 21st

The Sauber Mercedes team were continuing to set the pace this year with Schlesser/Mass topping the times with a fastest lap of 1:07.275, followed by the Toyota of Lees and former TWR driver Dumfries in second on 1:07.675, then Baldi/Acheson C9 with 1:07.789. Fourth fastest went to the BLR Porsche of Bell/Needell on 1:08.285 ahead of the Joest Porsche of Wollek/Jelinski in fifth on 1:08.944. The two XJR-9 Jaguars had qualified seventh and ninth with 1:09.553 and 1:10.190; Lammers/Tambay being the quicker of the two. Thirty-six cars would start this race held in hot conditions that would prove to not suit the Jaguars. It appeared that the XJR-9 was slower than the year before, while others had improved.

It was the #7 Wollek/Jelinski Joest Porsche and its Goodyear tyres which took the win from Schlesser/Mass by 38 seconds ahead of its sister C9 glued to its tail for third. The Dumfries/Lees Toyota followed in fourth place one lap down and the BLR Porsche in fifth, three laps behind the winner. It had been a terrible day

## Dijon Le Mans Test Status Report

<u>DIJON TEST 2-4TH MAY 1989</u>
**ENGINE NO. 06**
**MILEAGE 788.2 MILES**

**ENGINE NO. 07**
**MILEAGE 946.4 MILES**

Engines tested at Le Mans compression ratio 12:1 new 1989 spec injector and sync position. Driver trim control changed from Suzuka (as raced in 86-87-88).

No. 5 base map - 4% to position 4 - 1½% to position 3 - 1½% to position 2 - 1½% to 1 - 4% to zero.

Note: 0 position now for pace laps only! Basically new position 4 is the same as old position 2, allowing an extra enleanment of 3% at position 1. This does away with the 'desperate' nob adjustment in the pits during a race.

Various combinations of laps were tried at 3 only, 4 only, 5 only and then 3 everywhere except the straight where 5 was selected. A move from 3 or 4, to 5 on the straight produced an increase of 200 rpm. We are looking into a switch on the steering wheel to allow full speed on the straight and very lean around the rest of the circuit, as it is very hard to pass anywhere except the straight.

Exhaust and spark plug colour is very lean 'white' on position 3 and quite driveable on position 4.

Box trim position for qualifying will be -1 and reset to -3 for the race. some poor driveability and warm up at these lean settings will be improved by specific dyno work in these areas in week 18.

4 engines will be tested by Dijon and the eprom refined in any way possible. The overun fuel cut off threshold was raised from .94 volts to .6 volts to improve engine response on overun down change.

Port throttle response, especially on the sprint car was poor when lean this was richened and will be checked out in this area before the race.

An increase in accl time of 25% did not produce any result that could be felt and was returned to the setting as used in 1988.

Side entry ducts for the intakes were tested and the telemetry showed very similar air temps (35°) and baro pressure, to the previous open top tail. Engine wise the side tail makes no difference to Group C, probably because we were running lean. Fuel temperature varied from 26°-36°, average 30°-33°.

**Conclusion:**

Car can run 6,800 rpm in all gears to the fuel, this is better than usual, and reflects the 2% improvement in fuel consumption found over the winter.

When testing to the fuel on anything less than 20 laps, fuel meter should show half a lap in hand to allow for In and Out lap i.e. 10 laps 9.5 used.

Fuel used same as laps completed, probably shows a trend to being 3-5% over.

Le Mans car tested by various drivers not used to the car, produced good fuel consumption, running 4% richer than the sprint car. Times were slower but car seemed unable to use its fuel available no matter how hard they tried.

3rd and 4th gear ratios need revaluating, 5th OK at 6,700 max.

Understeer causes big fuel/time problems, car would be very fast to the fuel (almost flat out) if understeer eliminated.

Borrowed NA system from March and rpm inaccurate because set up for V8. Good circuit visability, small blind spot, TC needs help setting up mast on top of pits roof, all the circuit should then be able to be seen.

Computer battery went flat, needing extension lead to car, ensure batteries OK in future. Need to speed up eprom changes so as not to hold up car in pits.

**4TH MAY 1989**

No. 1 car (89C06) ran without any engine problems. Car spent the day trying various set ups shared between drivers.

No. 2 car (89C07) ran without engine problems in the morning practice. Car doing 20 lap stints with 50 litre fuel, drained and refilled at each stop. Radiator blanks removed by lunch to keep engine temperatures down.

After lunch towards the end of stint driver experienced slight hesitation from engine when flat in 5th on straight, oil temp to 112°C, driver came into pits to check. Tail removed and engine checked, no problems found. Reset ECU trim to -3 pm fuel from -4), drain and refil with fuel. Clean out rubber deposits from LH oil radiator.

After 17 laps of next sting engine died when accelerating out of 3rd gear corner and did not feel as good as before. No problems experienced at start of stint. Driver returned to pits, car sent on one slow lap to observe for fuel pressure drop when engine dieing. Driver reported that pressure guage dropped to 20 (40psi) when engine hesitated. (Static pressure 74Ibs 10 bar sender.
Note: Guage needs to be changed to go with 10 bar sender.
Fuel drainage temp measured at 43°C ambiant temp 26°C oil temp at 110°C water at 85°C.

Fuel pump pack changed and 20 litres of cold fuel put in, driver sent out to check if problem still apparent. Engine now running well and strongly as earlier.

**Oil Consumption Over 3 Days**
89C06 MK 25 liners 788 miles 4 litres 197 miles/litre
89C07 MK 9 liners 946 miles 4 litres 236 miles/litre

Car no. 2 (Le Mans spec) was not running fuel cooler. Car no. 1 (Sprint spec) with fuel cooler fitted ran fuel temp of 32°C. Sprint car did not run as hot as Le Mans car. Le Mans car was running 20 lap stints against shorter 5-10 lap stints on sprint car with longer stops for set up changes, Le Mans car was using more revs on straight (200/300 rpm). The intake angle to the R.H. oil cooler was also different, the Sprint car having a 90° angle to side panel, allowing better cooling than the sloped intake (40°C) to side panel on Le Mans car.

Problems during test:- Exhaust primary cracked on Le Mans car after Tuesday this was re-welded and gave no further problems. Ensure mechanics fit pipes to head without pretension. i.e. tighten primary pipe last.

Plugs changed on Sprint car Tuesday lunchtime. Engine misfiring when exiting pit lane. (Lean port throttle dyno check - throttle system to be checked).

Note: Inside coating of jerry cans coming off - fuel filtered from cans but when fuel filter was stripped from pump pack on Le Mans car thursday - small flakes were found inside. Possibly caused by use of TFOB at prior tests.

*Analysis of this test has good fuel efficiency but still hampered by the inherent understeer of the race cars.*

for the Jaguars, in tyre trouble here as well as fuel pressure problems in the hot conditions and both had not finished the race. Wallace with a puncture had crashed and was out. Lammers/Tambay again unusually out of fuel two laps from the end. Fuel chilling was not allowed to be used in these events and the XJR-9s had been fuelled at temperatures of 27°C from the fuel towers, compared to the chilled fuel used before. This seemed to have an effect on the fuel meter but the cars were struggling with tyres and carried extra wing angle to help them. There was also a matter of the team seemingly having given up on the V12 cars reducing the enthusiasm for taking the fight to Mercedes because the V6 car was visible on the horizon. The Joest Porsche's performance was a bit of a mystery but showed that older cars could still be competitive with a concentrated effort. No fuel samples were asked for or taken.

### IMSA Lime Rock Toyota Trucks Camel Grand Prix (150 laps) – May 29th

Lime Rock was the starting point for the introduction of the new 3-litre turbocharged XJR-10 given chassis #389 to be driven by Jan Lammers, with Cobb/Nielsen would continue with the V12 #388. The non-arrival of the Heidegger 3.2-litre Group C engine had put this programme back. We were continuing the development of our own 3.3-litre V6 at Kidlington to now be used in 1989 in Group C.

Qualifying had the Olson/Fangio 88C All American Racers Toyota on pole with 48.72s and the new XJR-10 in second spot with 50.080s; third fastest was the Momo Porsche of Moretti/Jelinski 51.138s with Costas Los in the Spice SE89P on 51.460 and the second Toyota of Willy T. Ribbs in fifth with a 51.45s lap. Changeable weather had caught out many of the cars; the two Nissans would start in seventh and ninth position with the V12 Jaguar in eighth. The race would have twenty-three starters.

It was a three-way fight between Jaguar, Toyota and Nissan with the Toyota eventually retiring with engine damage and the XJR-10 in prime position before an additional stop for a splash and dash left too large a gap to overcome. It was a good first up result for the XJR-10 with Lammers finishing just eight seconds behind the eventual winner Brabham, and Cobb/Nielsen in the 6-litre XJR-9 in third in this shorter race lasting two hours and twelve minutes. Robinson was fourth in the second Nissan two laps down followed by Costas Los in his Spice three laps down. Retirements came for the Busby Porsche with a lost wheel and the HF89 Toyota with an accident and the sister 87C car with engine problems.

## IMSA Nissan Grand Prix of Ohio (500kms) – June 4th

TWR would continue to field the XJR-9 and XJR-10 strategy at Mid Ohio in a race that started twenty-two race cars. Brabham and Nissan continued to set the pole time in qualifying with 1:18.926 but Lammers/Jones next up and very close on 1:18.977. The Cord/Olson Toyota 1:19.356 while the XJR-9 was fourth with 1:19.54, followed by the Busby Porsche of Wollek/J. Andretti on 1:20.46.

Brabham/Robinson were the eventual winners in a close finish with the XJR-9 Jaguar of Nielsen/Cobb/Jones just five seconds behind them after completing 129 laps in this race lasting three hours and twelve minutes. Lammers' XJR-10 struggled with its tyres and a mid race change bought his car back into contention setting the fastest time of the race. An off-track moment by Lammers filled the radiator with debris and the inevitable overheating that followed resulted in the engine being damaged and the car was out of the race. The Moretti/Dickens Momo Porsche in third was three laps down ahead of Hessert/Morgan in the Spice SE88P a further eight laps behind the leaders. The second Eagle HF89 Toyota of Ribbs/Fangio finished nine laps down after its sister car caught fire and did not finish. Lammers' XJR-10 retired in sixteenth place after 82 laps while the Busby Porsche had transmission problems and stopping just ten laps from the finish.

**MEMO**

| From | | To |
|---|---|---|
| ALLAN SCOTT | | ALASTAIR MACQUEEN |
| Our Reference | Your Reference | 16th May 1989 |

'er the past years we have had totally inconsistent fuel specification reports for each WSCA event. We should ask the organisers for clearly defined fuel specifications 30 days before the event, this will ensure that the actual fuel delivery to the circuit can be analysed and results passed to competitors. It is important that general EEC 4 star fuel specifications are not given to cover the regulation requirements, which is what has been happening. The following is a breakdown of the maximum and minimum amounts along with the recognised methods of acquiring the data. This fuel specification is within all EEC 4 star requirements and is biased towards octane stability ~~and safer~~ fuel volatility also bearing in mind industry recognised health and safety aspects.

........................ Allan Scott

***I am seeing a generic fuel specification form being presented at race meetings, always giving the same specifications no matter what country we are competing in.***

MEETING WITH TOM WALKINSHAW - POST DIJON RACE
22ND MAY 1989 10.00 A.M.

Discussions on why fuel meter appeared to be running slower in the race than in testing. Calibration test with hot fuel and injectors to be carried out week 21. Nielson/Wallace car which crashed during the event - when fuel drained out showed similar trend however, inaccuracy approximately half that of the Lammers/Tambay car. discussions on fuel with heat, fuel to be removed from underground tanks to be kept in insulated containers but retain the underground temperature (18°C) approximately. Fuel in the tower after the race 27°C. External temperature of the tank was hot having been in the sun all day and showed quite good thermal properties to keep the fuel as low as 27°C. Rear wing adjustments by 2°. Steve Ridgers times to be analysed to show effects on fuel. Monday 19th testing on South Circuit pre-Jarama Race.

Re-building of V12 engines post Le Mans shows very tight schedule. Probable Group C races will run 1 V12 car until V6 proves reliable.

AWS
24.5.89

***Problems are beginning to appear with our normally accurate fuel meter during the race.***

**Jan Lammers analysis of the Le Mans circuit for us to gauge engine performance – the oil light comes on at 30psi**

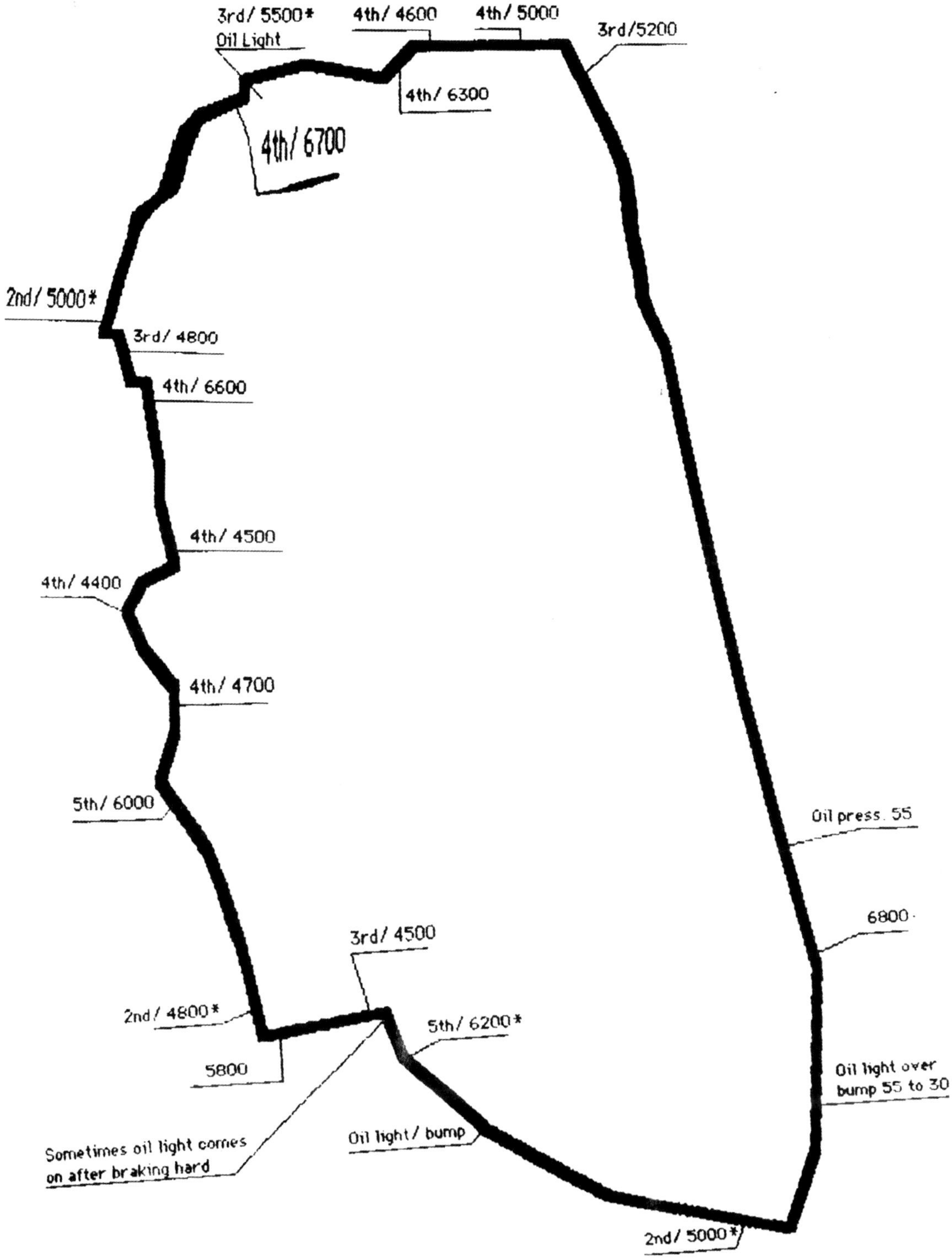

# Le Mans 24 hour – June 11th-12th

## DRIVERS INSTRUCTIONS

1. FUEL SYSTEM
2. FUEL COMPUTER
3. TYRE TEMPERATURE FUNCTIONS
4. TACHO
5. PIT SIGNALS
6. LIGHTS
7. ELECTRICAL CONSUMPTION
8. ON CIRCUIT REPAIRS
9. PIT STOPS
10. INTERRUPTION OF THE RACE
11. PACE CARS
12. FINISH
13. EXTRACTS FROM THE INTERNATIONAL CODE

1. FUEL SYSTEM :

Car Tank holds 99 Litres.
It is estimated that only 90 to 92 litres will be used in normal stint of 14 laps.
**There is no reserve system.**
If 92 litres are used, the fuel computer will read 14.3 laps, indicating that more than your allocation for 14 laps has been used, 6.57 litres per lap, instead of 6.43.

The 7 litres remaining in the tank, 92 having been used, should be enough to get the Car back to the Pits if you are forced, for some reason, to do an extra lap, but in that condition obviously some restraint should be shown!

2. FUEL COMPUTER :

Fuel Computer will set at 90 litres for 14 laps = 6.43 litres/lap.

It should be no problem to drive on, or very slightly over, this consumption.

The Computer should be re-set at each Pit Stop by the Driver getting into the Car. This is done by holding down both Red Buttons on the left of the Computer for about 3 seconds (seems like 3 minutes!) It will then flash the message "FUEL MEMORY ZERO". The lower litre count read-out on the dash should also be re-set at the same time. As this is a useful "Fuel Gauge" in the event of the Computer failing for any reason.

If the litres on Auxiliary Gauge or Computer are on, or above, 92 litres as you approach the Pits COME INTO THE PITS using the radio to warn us if the stop is unscheduled.

3. TYRE TEMPERATURE FUNCTIONS :

The temperature read-out normally is the average of the four tyre temperatures. If any lights flash, it indicates that a tyre is over a pre-set limit. At Le Mans, these will be set at 100 degrees Front and 120 degrees Rear. Pressing any individual button allows the temperature of that particular tyre to be viewed. This is valuable if the light has flashed on that tyre, and a check needs to be made as to whether this was local overheating on the exit of a corner, or if the tyre is increasing in the heat on the straight. If this is the case, the likely cause is a puncture!

To resume normal average tyre temperature read-out, touch the lit button once.

4. TACHO :

The Tacho Red light will be set to come on at 6700, which is the normal limit you will be asked to drive during the Practice and Race. This light is normally at 7000 for Sprint Races.

Rev. limiter is still set to 7050.

Tacho Amber light will appear when the engine revs are below 4000.

5. PIT SIGNALS :

Pit Signals will be shown after Mulsanne Corner at the end of the straight.

Your lap time and the number of laps into your stint (1 - 14) will be shown. The number shown on the board should correspond to the lap number on your Fuel computer the next time you PASS THE PITS.

Lap Number 14 will be accompanied by an "IN" signal, which should be acknowledged by flashing the Headlamps.

6. LIGHTS :

"Lights" switch switches on Dip Beam, Tail Lights and Ident Lights, and operates only when the ignition is on. DIP - Main/Flash switch operates Main Beam. Used as "Flash" in Day Light conditions.

MAIN BEAM - Remains on even if lights are in the off position, when "Main" switch is down. Used as normal Dip/Main in Night Conditions. Operates only when ignition is on.

It is recommended that Drivers entering the car switch both "off" to start the engine, (if they have been left on) then use as required.

7. ELECTRICAL CONSUMPTION :

If all electrical components on the car are working correctly, the only situation in which the system can be overloaded is by constant use of ALL electrical equipment. This is only likely during a wet night with prolonged use of main beam, wipers and the biggest electrical consumer, the heated front screen (HFS).

If this situation occurs, consult the "volts" gauge to judge the likely effect on the battery and if necessary, intermittent use of the main beam or HFS is recommended. Remember - the next Driver has to start the Car on the battery you leave him!

8. ON CIRCUIT REPAIRS :

If the Car stops on the Circuit, you and you alone are the only person able to affect repairs. Whilst we can advise you by radio or by sending a man to the spot, you must only use the tools carried in the Car to affect the repairs. Make sure that you stop on the INSIDE of the Circuit.

No liquids of any sort must be added to the Car outside the Pits.

Tools are carried in the Passenger Footwell Area of the Car, and contain essential items such as wire and tape to make an emergency repairs to get the Car back to the Pits.

9. **PIT STOPS** :

**Each Pit Stop you MUST switch off the engine. A normal stop will last approximately 90 seconds. During this time the Car will be refuelled, tyres changed, oil checked and topped up, screen cleaned, mirrors cleaned and all ducts and radiator cleared.**

**At certain stops the pads will be changed, at which times you are asked to keep your foot away from the brake pedal until indicated to pump the pedal by the controlling engineer.**

**It is most important that you do not start the engine or leave the Pits until indicated to do so.**

**During the stop you are asked to : -**

- **(a) Adjust mirrors if necessary.**
- **(b) Re-set both the Fuel Computer and back-up gauge.**
- **(c) Change Driver drink bottle if used.**

**You are NOT allowed to carry out any other work on the Car yourself.**

**Take care to stop in the correct position.**

10. **INTERRUPTION OF THE RACE** :

**Conditions regarding the use of pace-cars will be specified in a notification made by the Clerk of the Course during the drivers briefing. In case of interruption of the race, cars must return to the "parc ferme" the situation of which being notified by the Clerk of the Race in due time.**

11. **PACE-CARS** :

**When the order is given by the Clerk of the Course, all observers' posts will display immobile yellow flags, which will remain until the pace-car is recalled. The pace-car, with its three lights flashing, will immediately join the track regardless of where the race leader is.**

The yellow flashing lights at the starting line will be switched on, as well as the flashing yellow lights which may be situated at other points around the circuit and obligatorily at the point where, should the case arise, a second pace-car would join the track (it is normal to use 2 pace-cars).

All competing cars will line-up in single file behind the pace-car, maintaining the same speed as the pace car; all overtaking is forbidden, unless a car is signalled to do so by the pace-car. Each time the pace-car passes an Observers' Post, the yellow flag will be waved, for as long as the pace-car and the cars following it, remain in the sector between that post and the following post.

When the Clerk of the Course decides to call in the pace-car, the pace-car must effect a full lap of the circuit with the revolving lights extinguished which will be the signal for the withdrawal of the flags at the Observers' Posts as soon as the last car in the train of cars behind the pace-car has left the sector.

When the pace-car pulls off the circuit, a green flag will be waved at the Startline and the green light shown. All Observers' Posts will then show a green flag. Overtaking remains strictly forbidden until the cars pass the green flag or light. The green flag will be withdrawn after one lap.

12. <u>FINISH</u> :

The finish (checkered flag displayed) will be effective when the leading car crosses the finish line at the end of the 24th hour.

The last lap of the race is to be completed within a maximum time equal to four times the best time achieved during the official qualifying session. This time will be rounded up to the nearest unit (approximately 10 minutes).

## LE MANS PEOPLE PLAN

<u>Top Management</u>

| | |
|---|---|
| Tom Walkinshaw | Team Owner |
| Roger Silman | Team Director |
| Tony Southgate | Designer |
| Allan Scott | Engine Manager |

<u>Group C Team Drivers</u>

| | |
|---|---|
| Jan Lammers | Car 1 |
| Patrick Tambay | |
| Andrew Gilbert-Scott | |
| John Nielsen | Car 2 |
| Andy Wallace | |
| Price Cobb | |

<u>Group C Team</u>

| | | |
|---|---|---|
| Clive Steeper | Team Manager | |
| Kevin Lee | Race Manager | |
| Alastair Macqueen | Engineer | Car 1 |
| Steve Ridgers | Engineer | Car 2 |
| Tim Cunningham | Telemetry | |
| Andy Beckett | Parts & link to IMSA team | |
| Helen Shergold | Team Secretary | |
| Richard West | Press and Public Affairs | |

<u>Group C Mechanics</u>

| | |
|---|---|
| Jeff Wilson/Alva Claxton/Tim Strudwick/Martyn Bellars | Car 1 |
| Rod Benoist/Jerry Pyman/Chris Tuckey/Gary Davies | Car 2 |

| Fabricators | Race Job | Pre-race Job |
|---|---|---|
| Mark Owen | Fueller | Chief Fabricator |
| Mark Blackwell | Fueller | Fabricator |
| Roger Harding | Fireman | Fabricator |
| Mick McCrohan | Bodywork | Bodywork |

<u>Truckies</u>

| | | |
|---|---|---|
| Keith Partridge | Fueller | Chief Truckie |
| Chris Partridge | Fueller | Pit Equip + Awning 1 |
| Billy Wright | Wheels/weight tape | Pit Equip + Awning 1 |
| Rolf Steur | Wheels/weight tape | Pit Equip |
| Darren Warren | Wheels/weight tape | Wheel care |
| David Hands | Fireman | Parts |
| Patrick Rennison | Fireman | Parts/Bodywork |

<u>Group C Engine Men</u>

| | | |
|---|---|---|
| Charlie Bamber | Floating Eng Man | Floating Eng Man |
| Glen Barber | Op fuel d'man Lever 1 | Car 1 |
| Steve Harding | Op fuel d'man Lever 2 | Car 2 |
| Grant Rushton | Op fuel d'man Lever 3 | Car 3 |

| Extras | Race Job | Pre-Race Job |
|---|---|---|
| John Percy | Radio Link to Mulsanne | Pilot |
| Simon Rupp | Assistant to JPe | Pilot |
| Colin Moore | Radio Link to Mulsanne | Stickers |
| Eric Cowcill/D McGill/J English | | Timekeepers |
| D Bettison/C Haywood/N Payne | | Timekeepers |
| D Vinson/T Ryan | | Trainers |
| Dr Ian Robinson | | Doctor |
| Brian Mason | | Zytec |
| John Thompson | | ART |
| Rob Gustafson/Derek Payne | | Roni Gearboxes |
| Geoff Kingston | | Motorbike |
| A Longland/D Longland/K Quattermass | | Signaller |
| P Quattermass/C Watts/P Morley | | Signaller |
| C Foskett/M Crowley/G Britton | | Signaller |
| K Britton/I Schuler/T Scrivens | | Signaller |
| R Gunnett | | Scrutineering Driver |
| Simon Hornblow | | Tumble Dryer |

<u>Catering</u>

| | |
|---|---|
| Chris Leese | Motorhome Co-Ordinator |
| Gary Timms | Chef |
| Phil Ford | Chef |
| Val Passett | Hostess |
| Nicola Trimm | Hostess |
| Victoria Kindell | Hostess |
| Jennifer Tedder | Hostess |

<u>IMSA Team Management</u>

| | | |
|---|---|---|
| Tony Dowe | | |
| Ian Reed | Engineer | Car 3 |
| Eddie Hinckley | Engineer | Car 4 |
| Winston Bush | Parts Control | |

<u>IMSA DRIVERS</u>

| | |
|---|---|
| Davy Jones | Car 3 |
| Derek Daly | |
| Jeff Kline | |
| Alain Ferte | Car 4 |
| Michel Ferte | |
| Eliseo Salazar | |

<u>IMSA Mechanics</u>

| | |
|---|---|
| Viv Cowley/Howard Minckler/Butch Winkle/Jim Faulkner | Car 3 |
| Clive Parker/Mark Shurety/Larry Zelesnik/Carl Azevedo | Car 4 |

| IMSA Fabricator | Race Job | Pre-Race Job |
|---|---|---|
| Frank Raffety | Fueller | Fabricator |
| Jim Kracht | Bodywork | Bodywork |

<u>IMSA Engine Man</u>

| | | |
|---|---|---|
| Don Beadle | Op fuel d'man Lever 4 | Car 4 |

<u>IMSA Extras</u>

| | | |
|---|---|---|
| Craig McCann | Fireman | Electronics |
| John McCellan | Fueller | Pit Equip + awning 2 |
| Tim Ellis | Fueller | Pit Equip + awning 2 |
| Mike Barto | Wheels/weight tape | Pit Equip/Wheel Care |
| Karl Szymanski | Wheels/weight tape | Wheel Care |
| Ira Chez | Fueller | Sub-assembly/body work |

31 MAY 1989
R-LM-89.MS (people plan)

**T.W.R. SILK CUT JAGUAR RACE TEAM**
**"GUY EDWARDS PHOTOGRAPH"**
**KIDLINGTON AIRPORT**
**20 JULY 1989**

<u>PERSONNEL</u>
Tom Walkinshaw
Roger Silman / Tony Southgate
Alastair Macqueen / Allan Scott / Charlie Bamber
Clive Steeper / Kevin Lee / Helen Shergold / Andy Beckett
Richard West / Geoff Kingston / Jeff Wilson

Alva Claxton / Tim Strudwick / Martyn Bellars / Mark Shurety
Rod Benoist / Jerry Pyman / Chris Tuckey / Gary Davies
Keith Partridge / Chris Partridge / Martin Perisi
Darren Warren / Roger Harding / Mark Blackwell
Mick McCrohan / Clive Parker / David Hands / Andy Saxton
Patrick Rennison / ~~Simon Hornblow~~ / Colin Moore / Peter Dean
Richard Vetter / Daniele Montour

Glenn B / Grant R / Matt N / Nigel W / Huw J / Mark B
Andrew W / Andrew P / Roy Mc / Pete T / Jim B / Chris J
Barry H / Gavin H / Nigel W / Mark B / Len S / Steve C
Mark H / Bob A

Jan Lammers / Patrick Tambay / John Nielsen / Andy Wallace
Alain Ferte/Davy Jones

<u>CARS:</u> 688, 189, 289, 288, 287

<u>SCHEDULE</u>:

All personnel to arrive TWR 0700

**<u>ALL VEHICLES DEPART TWR AT 0715</u>**

**<u>ALL PERSONNEL TO ARRIVE AT KIDLINGTON AIRPORT AT 0725 LATEST</u>**

Our convoy of vehicles will be escorted across Airfield by fire engines at 0730 precisely

Photograph begins: 0800
Photograph Finishes: 1030 - 1300 weather dependant

<u>TRANSPORT</u>

| | |
|---|---|
| E660 AHR | JW/RH/MSh/GD/DW/MBk/MMcC/MBk/CPk/DH/ Andy S/~~Simon H~~/Pete D |
| F937 MFC | Clive/RB/JP/CT |
| E90 YUD | Alastair/CM/GWK |
| TWR 42 | Roger |
| E159 VKJ | Kevin/AB/HS/DMr |
| A639 OUD | KP |
| F131 JBM | CP/AC |
| C200 FWL | MP/MSh |
| | Engine Shop to be arranged by Lesley |
| OT | All other personnel |

## Le Mans

The workload for the TWR Group with the introduction of the V6 turbo replacement for the V12 engines in both Group C and IMSA was taking most of the available time and produced a hectic schedule for Engs. With the arrival of June, it was time to refocus on Le Mans as this was a very busy time for me. From May 24th till July 30th there were four Group C races, including Le Mans, as well as our IMSA races. With the team already at Le Mans when I arrived back from Mid Ohio in the USA on Monday it was my job to wait over on Tuesday and bring any small items that may have been left behind. Wednesday was an early morning start to Dover and the ferry crossing to Calais and then to Le Mans to catch up with proceedings before the first evening practise session. At the scrutineering sessions before the start of practice the XJR-9LM's recorded weights of close to 930kgs, while the C9 Sauber Mercedes were right on the new limit of 900kgs. Nothing could be done to rectify this.

The 1989 Le Mans cars had side air intakes for the engine, introduced at Daytona earlier in the year, and this allowed the original engine air intake to be covered over and produce a smoother airflow over the engine cover. To aid cabin ventilation the roof had an opening in that area to allow the flow through of air from the driving compartment and help keep the drivers cooler.

The TWR programme was divided into two teams with Kidlington looking after #1 and 2 and Valparaiso #3 and 4.

Wednesday practice was once again a matter of getting all drivers qualified with three laps in the day and night time without too much emphasis on fast qualifying times as the weather was changeable with some light rain falling. Schlesser had decided to drive the C9 Mercedes this year after missing 1988 over his fears on tyre safety, but with the work Michelin had carried out since then on the rear tyres he had set a fastest time of 3:16.85. TWR had also reverted to 18in rear wheels and 340/700/18 tyres from the 1988 330/700/17 tyre specification for this race. The new rear tyres were in response to the ongoing tyre developments with the prospect of introducing 18in radial ply tyres to all TWR race cars in the future, in line with Michelin and Goodyear, who it was thought had a superior product. The 17in wheels all round that had been used in 1988 were forced on the team for expediency reasons with the IMSA rules restricting wheels to the same diameter front and rear. The TWR Jaguar team's cars were numbered one to four in respect of the teams winning position the year before.

Thursday's qualifying battle was fought between the C9s and the 3.2-litre turbocharged V8 engined factory Toyota with Baldi (C9) getting the upper hand initially

*External changes for 1989 show side entry engine air intake, sealed engine cover with engine compartment cooling ducts either side.*

in 3:15.67; the Lees/Dumfries/Watson Toyota 3:15.51 and then a final effort by Schlesser to take pole with a 3:15.04. Baldi had managed to hit the magical 400kmh on the Mulsanne; but the Toyota 'T' car had its time disallowed with someone overlooking the fact that unlike Japan, test cars are not allowed to set qualifying times here, only the cars that are to be raced. The Lammers/Tambay/Gilbert-Scott Jaguar (588) was next with 3:18.35 and a top speed of 389kmh on the Mulsanne, Jones/Daly/Kline (288) 3:19.48, Stuck/Wollek in the Joest Porsche 3:19.8 and the Michel and Alain Ferté/Salazar Jaguar (287) 3:20.19. Two places further back Nielsen/Wallace/Cobb Jaguar (688) 3.20.65. The Nissan team had three R89C 3.5-litre V8 engined cars entered for British based drivers Bailey/Blundell/Donnelly qualifying twelfth in 3:24.1; their American based drivers Robinson/Brabham/Luyendyk on 3:25.38 in fifteenth; and the Japanese team of Hasemi/Hoshino/Suzuki ending up nineteenth on 3:26.9.

### Fuel Analysis

Castrol's John Bristow had taken fuel this year at my request to study the components and compare them against EU regulation road fuels as stipulated.

The Reid Vapour Pressure is one of the first to show any changes, it greatly influences the reduction in hot fuel vapourisation and reduce fuel pressure problems.

| Normal Fuel | | Le Mans Fuel |
|---|---|---|
| RVP 450–600 max | | 770 HPA |
| Density | 0.757–0.78 | 0.771 |
| Octane | 87.5–88.5 | 88.6 MON |
| | 98–99 | 99.4 RON |
| Initial Boiling Point | 26°C | 35°C |

This Le Mans fuel is special blended fuel not available from commercial outlets as Group C rules.

### *Race start*

Saturday's 4pm start in good weather conditions was watched by an estimated 230,000 spectators which some said included 50,000 British supporters, and quickly turned into a battle between Jaguar and Mercedes. The updated Jaguars looked the faster cars this time with a slight superiority not seen in previous years. Lammers however was immediately into the pits with a suspected puncture as his Zytek designed onboard tyre temperature system's indicator light had come on; a full set of tyres were changed but nothing could be found wrong with pressures in the set just removed. American Davy Jones was on a mission in car #3 lining up the two leading Mercedes on the flat in fifth gear kink on the Mulsanne and passing each on consecutive laps to take the lead. Nielsen was soon into third but Ferté's Jaguar #4 had already pitted with a similar problem to Lammers, loosing almost a lap as tyres were changed and then sent on his way. Nielsen's #2 had moved into second as the Mercedes opposition ran at a set pace with a finish in mind at this early stage. Bailey in the Nissan was on an even bigger mission, passing the Mercedes as they slipped back to fourth and fifth and he now chased the leading Jaguars. This though would all come to an end as the Nissan driver took the challenge to the Jaguars under braking at the end of the Mulsanne straight, and failing to execute the manoeuvre. It ended in hard contact with Nielsen, the second time in a 24 hour race that aggressive driving by a Nissan driver had sidelined a Jaguar. Bailey made it back to the pits but the Nissan was out of the race with suspension damage that could not be repaired, and Nielsen lost time in the pits as repairs to bodywork were made, leaving just one TWR car in a challenging position at this early stage of the race. After the first pit stops the three delayed Jaguars were #1 ninth; #4 fourteenth and #2 twentieth.

A couple of hours into the race the #63 Mercedes driven at the time by Reuter sustained underbody damage when unable to avoid parts of an exhaust system lying in the road and attempts to rectify the damage dropped this car to twentieth. One of the Toyotas was already out with accident damage. At three hours, the leading Jaguar stopped out on the track with a gearbox internal selector linkage broken. Daly carried out repairs to select a gear and return to the pits. By the time this was robustly repaired almost one hour had been lost and any chance of a win was gone. Meanwhile places changed as many of the contestants had problems; accidents had eliminated both Toyotas, and the race had yet to settle into a predictable rhythm. The Joest Porsches in the hands of Stuck/Wollek and Jelinski/Raphanel/Louis Krages aka 'John Winter' had moved into contention taking the lead after the Jaguar's gearbox problem.

The #1 and #4 Jaguars were the fastest cars on track making up ground and with these changing fortunes both had moved into top five positions only for Gilbert-Scott in the #1 Jaguar to need attention to a broken exhaust. This seemed to be an ongoing problem especially around the number five cylinder on the RH bank having failed before. The systems had been used during the year without any problems but for the first time new systems had not been made for this race, and that was actually the basic problem. By lap 82 with just 20% of the race run six of the sixteen 962 Porsches in the race were out, two from accidents, two with engine problems, one with suspension damage after a puncture and one engulfed in a huge fire.

The Joest Porches continued in the lead followed by the #61 Mercedes and then the #1 Jaguar with the Ferté brothers impressing all with their pace in fifth at quarter distance. Unknown by the team the third driver for this Jaguar, Salazar, had been in hospital just two weeks prior to the race with a collapsed lung. He had said nothing fearing he would have been dropped from the driver line up, which he certainly would have had it been known. Salazar continued his supporting drive with no apparent problems. The delayed #3 Jaguar lost its battle to make up time with no need to run to the fuel allowance as it suffered a broken valve spring from the constant over revving on the downshift as well as running flat out on the rev limiter when air born on the exit of the Dunlop 'S', recorded in the Zytek control unit's memory and confirmed as a problem by Jan Lammers, it retired on lap 85. It was then time for the Mercedes run to have its problems with Schlesser in #62 suffering faulty electrics interfering with his power delivery. He slid out of the top 20 places.

Wollek/Stuck continued in the lead into the night and had managed to produce a three-lap advantage, while their team mates were out of the race with a blown engine. After a very hard drive amazingly the #1 Jaguar had moved into second place after earlier losing almost an hour and was consistently setting lap times five seconds faster than the race leader. It became time for the leader of the race for the last six hours to have its own problems. The leading Porsche had a water leak and subsequent overheating, a fifteen-minute pit stop was required to rectify the problem; with Tambay at the wheel of the #1 Jaguar we were back in the lead. The #61 and #63 Mercedes were next, and by the time the Joest Porsche was back out it had dropped down to fourth; soon to be overtaken by a hard charging Wallace in the #2 Jaguar, all the top seven placed cars covered by three laps.

Through the later part of the night the contenders maintained their placings with a flash fire on the Joest Porsche dropping it to sixth and the leading Jaguar setting a pace that no one else could equal, and in the process taking a one and a half lap advantage on the following Mercedes. The #25 Nissan succumbed to engine problems by breakfast time after 250 laps and now all three Nissans were out. Soon after it was Michel Ferté in with a broken third gear requiring the entire back end of the Jaguar to be replaced. This was soon followed in by the fourth placed Jaguar as Nielsen was out with another broken valve spring.

Despite all the work that had gone into procuring the special steels from Sweden, Schmitthelm had been unable to totally eliminate the micro inclusions embedded in the special steel alloys purchased for their manufacture, and with the stresses involved with the .580in lift and some design limitations when using the inverted bucket cam follower design, the stresses involved had broken the outer of the two inlet valve coils. This had then allowed the valve to remain in a partially open position and after being hit numerous times by the piston, the head of the valve broke off. The valve was then punched through the head into the water jacket, producing water loss out of the exhaust pipe.

We had consistently seen only inlet valve spring breakage, and with that camshaft profile different to the exhaust I had asked Geoff Goddard (the designer at Cosworth) to reassess his design to eliminate any harmonic problems that may exist. As we would later find out this had been the source of the problem all along.

The drama was to continue with race leader Lammers now in gearbox trouble again with a very black oil liquid drained from the gearbox needing a complete rebuild of the unit. Mercedes then took the lead at Le Mans, something not seen since the factory's retirement from motor racing in the 1950s.

The race had now settled down to the survivors with Mercedes #61 and 63 leading the morning hours with a four lap lead over the Stuck/Wollek Porsche and back into an incredible fourth place for the #1 Jaguar after the demise of the Omron Porsche. The #1 Jaguar was just thirteen laps behind by midday, after a complete gearbox overhaul. It was then Alain Ferté's turn to continue the fight, setting a new lap record in his #4 Jaguar, and having no fuel consumption problems with it. The two leading Mercedes were running to a set pace and conserving their gearbox which was their perceived weakness from the high torque from the turbocharged 5-litre engine. Mercedes third car had finally found its way up to fifth. The third placed Joest Porsche was being driven at a rate to finish, it had a problem with oil seeping onto the clutch and a quick pit stop to have Coca Cola poured over the offending unit to help purge the system. The Jaguars continued to set a frantic pace; but time was running out to make up the deficit.

The change-over to Acheson in the #61 Mercedes as the race came to a close had him return to the pits after just one lap and raise the prospect of a twist in the tail of the final placings. There was a gear selection problem and a decision made to select fifth gear and just run with that, just as we had done using fourth gear the year before. After initially stalling the Mercedes made its way back into the race in second place and used the massive torque from its large engine to maintain a good pace to the end and avoid another final stop for fuel and any problem with the clutch using a fifth gear pit departure.

> And so the race finished at 4pm on Sunday with the #63 C9 Mercedes of Mass/Dickens/Reuter completing 389 laps; #61 C9 Mercedes, Baldi/Acheson/Brancatelli 384 laps; Stuck/Wollek #9 Joest 962C Porsche 382 laps; Lammers/Gilbert-Scott/Tambay Jaguar XJR-9LM 380 laps; Schlesser/Cudini/Jabouille #62 C9 Mercedes 378 laps; Ballot-Lena/Pescarolo/Ricci #8 Joest 962C Porsche 371 laps; Dieudonne/Kennedy/Hodgetts #201 Mazda 767 368 laps (IMSA class winners); Alain Ferté/Michel Ferté/Salazar #4 Jaguar XJR-9LM 368 laps.

There had been an unusually large attrition rate in this year's Le Mans with just nineteen cars listed as official finishers from the fifty-five who had started. Mercedes had managed a 100% finishing rate as well as Mazda, who along with driver Pierre Dieudonné had completed the hat trick of three consecutive wins in the IMSA class. Jaguar had a 50% finishing rate followed by Porsche with 31%, just five of the sixteen 962Cs finishing. Nissan had lost its three cars in the race between laps 5 and 250; as well as a terrible time for Toyota who had lost their three cars between laps 20 and 58 of the total 389 laps completed by the winners. Of those which did not finish, seventeen had engine failures and seven had accidents, and these accidents had all happened in the early part of the race with just 15% of the distance completed. Fires had also claimed five cars with terminal electrical faults another five. Two cars had terminal transmission failures with TWR repairing theirs.

The TWR crews were recognised by the race organisers and given the teams award for their fine efforts in rebuilding transmissions and keeping the two finishing XJR-9s in the race.

Public relations exercises abound in these situations to produce an acceptable outcome for the probable loss of victory in 1989 for Jaguar and TWR, but it was not gearbox oil seal failure on the #1 Jaguar. Castrol had obtained the oil drained from the damaged gearbox and carried out an analysis a few weeks after the event. The results had been kept very quiet and I had not been party to any of the conclusions. It was Castrol's John Bristow who some time later told me the results, and then nervously indicating that perhaps he should not have told me after he had assumed I was aware. This analysis showed incorrect oil had been used from the start of the race, in fact someone had mistakenly filled the gearbox with engine oil; and no copy of Castrol's report was made to this effect in any post race briefings or communications with Jaguar. Tony Dowe has since confirmed this. The exhaust systems were manufactured to the same specifications in the next two Le Mans races with no failures.

*After a steady pace throughout the 24 hours Mercedes took the win.*

There had however always been a shadow hanging over the team in that race of 1989. After my return from Lime Rock in the USA on the Monday I had received a late-night call at home from Roger with the shocking news that senior engine builder Steve Harding had succumbed to injuries he had received from a private car while crossing the road on the Mulsanne straight. It was then a matter of notifying the police in Witney who broke this news to his shocked parents and two sisters.

The next morning, I broke this terrible news to Engs staff at Kidlington who then returned to their work, all in a confused and subdued state of mind. The average age of the Engs staff was mid 20s and for all it was their first experience of death, and with it came disbelief, confusion, and shock.

I had then left early on the Wednesday morning driving to Dover and across to Calais by ferry arriving at Le Mans in the afternoon. The French authorities had been supportive in their investigations and TW had then made the company plane available to repatriate Steve's body back to Oxford the following week. It had been left to me to supervise these proceedings and later take the four TWR members who were witnesses through this very difficult process for us all. We had to carry out the process of identification, followed by the witnesses presented to a preliminary Coroners Court held in Dickensian like quarters in Oxford city centre; to then allow the funeral to proceed.

The day prior to Steve's funeral TW had discussed what should take place and suggested that representatives from Engs be selected to attend to keep the workshop open as we were under considerable pressure to produce engines on time; in the middle of a period that had five races covering Group C and IMSA over five weeks. All the pressures and procedures that had included the coroner's identification had combined to produce the prospect of reaching a breaking point over TW's thoughts for those involved, including myself, if not handled carefully.

As calmly as I could I told TW that was not going to happen. I then promptly left his office before I said something else that we would have both regretted. On my return to the workshop later that afternoon all were told to go home and attend the funeral the next day; the workshop would be closed for the afternoon of the funeral. Team manager Roger Silman had already left on a planned holiday.

Steve Harding was dedicated to his work, with a calmness and likeable nature that had him on the path for future leadership within the Engine Division. His loss was felt by us all for a considerable time afterward.

# STEVE HARDING

A tragic accident befell Steve Harding while out at Le Mans with the Race Team. Steve, who worked as an Engine Builder in the Engine Shop, had finished work for the day, and was struck by a passing car. It would appear that, perhaps not used to France, Steve looked the wrong way when crossing the road.

Steve was a popular member of the Engine Shop team, a man who lived for his work, and he was respected for the effort and ability he contributed to the Company. The accident saddened all of the Team and everyone rallied round to do the very best they could, in his memory.

To his parents Jack and Nancy, his sisters Ann and Ruth, his girlfriend Helen, and all his workmates, TWR extends its deepest sympathy.

Jan Lammers was a good leader of all the cars he drove for us at Le Mans and instilled in his driving partners how to best avoid any inherent weaknesses, including over rev downshifting and when the car was airborne, and he had a very good engine history at this race. He complains of excessive vibrations with different tyre changes.

## Jan Lammers Le Mans debrief ...

### *Le Mans 1989 race report*

□ Dashboard:

- 1st lap the heatspy's worked correct, but what caused the types to overheat? Did we change the temp. setting of the blankets as the race progressed?
- Later in the race when in the read the RR tyre light came on again and worked perfect, we might have saved a car there! Very important to respond immediately (2 or 3 seconds)
- Oil temp. gauge had still no light ofter commenting on it Thursdays night practise.
- Switches for lights, wipers, HFS etc where invisible in the dark.
- Brake balance gauge is a good thing to have.
- For the future a brake-pad wear warning light is needed (Problem from Sebring could be terminal at Le Mans)
- We asked to change the wiring loom, so it would be possible to reset the fuel/tyre computer with the AUX switch. It didn't happen!?
- Gearbox temp. gauge will give us more information on where the stress is increasing or decreasing.
- Radio can be improved a lot. (Smaller antenna inside the car to reduce drag?)
- Radio-plug solution from drivers helmet to car is a 1/2 job. It came undone during the race and qualifying, as it did many times before and every time again it was done in the same way, which obviously is not a sufficient solution. It locks the drivers head while driving and forces him to change from head movement to eye movement.

□ Gearbox:

- Because of the contrast between the long straight and the slow 2nd gear corners it is practically impossible to find a soothing combination that will last 36 hours (Min. target to guarantee 24 hours).
  So a different design is needed, 6 or 7 gears, electric shifting or whatever to spread the usage of one particular gear/area in the box. Accelerating out of 2nd and 3rd gear corners does most of the damage. Because of the spool in combination with inside drag.

□ Others ref. chassis reliability:

- Between the different sets of tyres there was a variation in terms of vibration and revs. The vibration just kills the cars reliability performance. (Exhaust manifolds cracking, fire extinguisher bracket break etc.)
  Lose balance weights?
- Windscreen; Top clamps holding the screen made with slots so you undo the top-bolts, slide them back and lift screen out. (Screen was cracked but not bad)

□ Brakes:

- Due to different wear pattern the brakes efficiency was variable, good one moment - spongy and inbalanced the next.
  Rears lock up when fronts wear out and the reverse. Therefore brake balance gauge is required to find a consistent pattern.

☐ Engine:
- The oil pressure drops as you go over a hill or bump in the "up" motion. For example at the exit of the Dunlop esses (T1) the rise wants to send the revs to the red light and the oil press. to the yellow light. If not taken extra care of this, the engine could easily be damaged. It forces the driver to lift before the hill at the end of the straight.
  When fast times are required this is obviously a limiting factor.
- Now and then a slight detonation at 5200
- Cuts out sometimes before Indianapolis corner on 5th and 4th downchange, and before the Dunlop esses.

☐ Dash readings:
- Straightline revs 6750/6850, with two 6900/700
- Average type temperature on the straight 71/75°
- O.P. 50\ F.P. 35\ W.T. 75\ O.T. 199 (daytime) Amps 13

☐ Pit signalling:
- The last 2 hours it was really good, before that there was more information required.

☐ Fuel economy:
- Mixture #2 was very efficient, still quick and enough power. It just takes a little longer to pickup trough the gears between 5000 and 5500 revs.

☐ Catering:
- Excellent and for 24 hours constantly very helpful!

☐ Fitness:
- Tom Ryan has become a good team member and did a very good job to serve so many drivers just on his own!
- But for those drivers who don't know exactly what to eat and drink there is very little initiative from Dave Vinson (good intentions but can be much better)
  After Patrick's hard stint DV suggested some salt tablets, which to my knowledge is one of the biggest 'noners' in sports nutrition. DV was seldom in the pits to hand the drivers drink bottle between unexpected double stints. At one stage I was handed an empty bottle by AS, who has other things to worry about.

Jan Lammers

*Jan indicates some disappointment in the level of progress with the Le Mans cars.*

## WSPC Trofeo Repsol Jarama 480kms (Portugal) – June 25th

Another hot race was the feature of Jarama with its twenty-five cars entered in practice. It was the turn of the Acheson/Baldi Mercedes to take pole with a 1:15.580 followed this time by Schlesser/Mass on 1:15.613 and a better showing from TWR that had the Lammers/Tambay Jaguar third fastest with 1:16.60, followed by Nielsen/Wallace on 1:16.717, Dumfries moved his Toyota into fifth spot on 1:15.58 and the Bailey/Blundell Nissan on 1:17.73 sixth.

Baldi took the lead in his C9 but soon ran into brake problems that led to an off-track excursion and three laps in the pits to rectify his problem. Both Jaguars were in tyre trouble in the hot track surface conditions but Lammers/Tambay managed the situation better than the Nielsen/Wallace sister car. Schlesser/Mass led the race and finally won ahead of the Lammers/Tambay XJR-9 one lap down. The next three places were all two laps down on the winner with the Brun Porsche of Pareja/Larrauri in third; a good effort by the Taylor/Thyrring Spice SE89C in fourth followed by the second Mercedes of Baldi/Acheson and the second Jaguar in sixth.

## IMSA Annual Camel Continental Watkins Glen (3 hours) – July 2nd

TWR again fielded V12 and V6 turbo engined race cars at this iconic racing circuit in upland New York State, not that far from the Canadian border. Qualifying here would be a repeat of the earlier races with Brabham and Nissan setting the fastest time with 1:35.878 and Lammers/Cobb next in the XJR-10 on 1:36.36. Fangio/Olson in the Toyota 1:36.818, Miller/Earl Spice SE89P 1:37.606 and Jones/Nielsen XJR-9 sixth on 1:38.123. Just nineteen cars would face the starter's flag.

*Jaguar's Ron Elkins in conversation with Tony Southgate.*

The XJR-10 did have the pace here and Lammers led the Brabham Nissan at the mid-distance fuel stop. Tyres were a problem but it was the puncture soon after the fuel and tyre stop at high speed that caused a crash and serious damage to the XJR-10. Once again, we did not have the answer to the winner Brabham, who had taken a fifth victory in a row. Jones had been very disappointed at not being given an XJR-10 to drive and he had proceeded to totally abuse the 6-litre V12 he did not want to continue with. The engine eventually suffering a centre main bearing failure, something we had never seen before although the oil pressure warning light would have been indicating a problem. Both Jaguars retired. With the depleted field it was the Millar/Earl MTI Vacations Spice 89P in second. A better result here for Olson/Fangio in the 87C Toyota, third on the same lap as the winners; and then the Momo Porsche of Moretti/Jelinski one lap down in fourth. They were followed by the Downing/Katz Mazda, but six laps behind the winner. Problems during this race had the second Toyota out after an accident and a blown engine for the Wollek/Andretti Porsche.

## IMSA Miller High Life Road America (Elkhart Lake 3 hours) – July 16th

Davy Jones had a point to prove as to his standing in the team and produced an amazing lap in the XJR-9 to take pole position with a 1:55.819 followed by Lammers/Cobb in the XJR-10 on 1:55.97. Robinson/Brabham were third fastest with 1:56.287, ahead of the Olson/Fangio Toyota on 1:58.759 and the Busby Porsche of Wollek/Andretti fifth in 2:01.37. With a total of 48 cars starting this race, the main problem would be avoiding the accidents having to constantly pass slower race cars.

It was good to see the Valparaiso team have two cars on the front row but it was Brabham who managed to squeeze between these two cars at the start and run in second behind Lammers for the first part of the race. Cobb managed to stay in the lead after the mid-distance driver change for the XJR-10 but failing brakes produced a need for a precautionary front pad change. He rejoined in third place behind Nielsen in the XJR-9 and moved into second place to finally get within eight seconds of the Nissan by the end of the race; producing a great race for all the Jaguar fans in the process with the Jones/Nielsen XJR-9 backing them up in third place. One lap behind these three were the #68 Busby Miller High Life Porsche and Olson/Fangio Toyota both one lap behind. The #67 Busby Porsche was driven by Bell/Bren for this race and had finished ninth, five laps behind the leaders with the #99 Toyota failing to finish with mechanical problems.

## WSPC Brands Hatch Trophy 480kms (UK) – July 23rd

Back to home shores, and Jaguar's supporting fans that along with TWR were showing concerns for the lack of performance against the Sauber Mercedes team. All the efforts this year had been on putting the finishing touches to the new XJR-11 and the XJR-9 had suffered being treated as an interim after thought. Mechanics being assigned to the XJR-9 were not motivated as the new XJR-11 was seen as the car to be with. Drivers not allocated to the new turbo programme could see it as demotion and the tide can very quickly go out with that mental division in what was normally a very united team. It was at Brands Hatch that the new XJR-11s would have their first race and although still in the early stages of development Lammers had carried out a brilliant lap to claim pole position, giving everyone something to think about with a 1:12.927. The Mercedes had been out qualified with Acheson/Baldi second fastest on 1:13.385 followed by Schlesser/Mass on 1:13.47; the Nissan of Bailey/Gilbert-Scott on 1:13.47 was fourth and the second XJR-11 driven by Jones/Ferté took fifth fastest time with a 1:13.824. Wollek/Jelinski were sixth on 1:14.79 in the fastest Porsche. What was supposed to be the last outing for a V12 XJR-9 had little support with the focus on the two new cars and Wallace/Nielsen were left to their own devices for this race with the car being engineered from outside the main race team by Tony Southgate's assistant Jeff Kingston. TW and Roger were trying to show a large step up with this new package in the process.

Fuel mileage however was still not producing the promise hoped for from a new turbo package and of course Engs were expected to fix a fundamental flaw that I had expected all along. I pointed out to Alastair Macqueen the white colour of our exhaust pipes and the grey of other competitors but kept to myself the ignition timing curve that was 5° retarded from optimum because of the 2.3 bar of boost we needed to produce the power to win from this small capacity turbo engine.

Lammers did not make a good start and fell behind the Mercedes and Toyota. Dumfries was in the Toyota with a point to prove to TWR after being dropped from the team, and Lammers passing manoeuvre resulted in the Toyota having hard contact with his side exit exhaust system closing most of it off and effecting the engine performance. Nielsen then had brake problems in the XJR-9 which took him out of the race. It was won by Baldi/Acheson with the Joest Porsche of Wollek/Jelinski just over a minute behind. The second Mercedes finished third one lap down and the Aston Martin that had two former Engs personnel now working on their V8 engines took a fine fourth place, three laps behind, followed by the Lammers/Tambay XJR-11 four laps behind the leaders. It had been an accident filled race with the casualties being the XJR-9, Nissan, Joest Porsche, and then the Toyota out of fuel six laps from the end. It was a very disappointing end to the planned demise of the V12 powered Jaguars. Inspection of the fuel system of the XJR-11 at the end of the race found that the fuel meters had been running slow by 3%, although the V12 car running the same system was accurate to 0.4%.

Some time later we would find the answer to the fuel meter problem but by then TW had committed to changing Zytek for Bosch. Jones/Ferté did not finish with ignition failure.

## IMSA G.I. Joe's Camel Grand Prix of Portland (300kms) – July 30th

The XJR-10 of Lammers/Cobb set the qualifying pace here at Portland with the #83 Nissan second ahead of the Jones/Nielsen V12 Jaguar. The HF Toyota of Ribbs/Moran had then qualified ahead of fifth fastest Nissan of Robinson. 24 cars would start the race.

The XJR-10 took the lead from the start and stayed that way for the first 52 laps with the #83 Nissan leading for just two laps of the entire race during scheduled pit stops. Lammers/Cobb took the lead again on lap 56 and remained there until the end at 94 laps, an elapsed time of 1 hour 34 minutes. Robinson finished third in the #84 Nissan and Jones/Nielsen fourth with Jones having set the fastest lap of the race, these four finishing on the same lap. The Miller/Earl Spice was next one lap down ahead of the J. Andretti/Wollek Porsche, Ribbs/Moran HF89 Toyota and the Mass/Dobson Porsche 962C all on 92 laps. It was a great first up win for the XJR-10.

*V6 turbo XJR-10*

## IMSA Camel Grand Prix of Heartland Park (Topeka 300kms) – August 13th

It was Chip Robinson who took the fastest qualifying time at Heartland Park in #84 Nissan with a 1:31.293 followed by Jones in the XJR-9 Jaguar, Brabham #83 Nissan third fastest with the Ribbs/Moran HF89 Toyota and Lammers/Cobb XJR-10 after an off-track excursion making up the fastest five. A crowd of 10,000 came to see the 19 cars start this race. Amazingly all 19 cars would be listed as finishers here, with the top five finishers all on the same lap after nearly two hours of racing.

From his lower starting place Lammers managed to work his way up to third place at the end of this race but once again it was a Nissan win with Brabham #83 and then Robinson #84 taking the winning double. Olson in the 87C Toyota fourth, followed by the XJR-9 Jaguar of Nielsen/Jones, all on 75 laps. Lammers had set the fastest lap of the race with a 1:32.3 on his last lap of the race on worn tyres in an effort to steal second place.

## IMSA Nissan Camel Grand Prix of San Antonio (2 Hours on street course) – September 3rd

Brabham continued on his qualifying way with the fastest time of 1:00.76 ahead of team mate Robinson. Davy Jones had his wish to drive the XJR-10 and with Cobb set third fastest time and the new driver pairing of Ferté/Nielsen in the Jaguar XJR-9 followed, with Ribbs in the HF89 Toyota fifth. An estimated 20,000 came to see the twenty-six cars starting this race. A second XJR-11 had been built for Jones but he had crashed this in testing at Grattan with the heavily damaged car then catching fire. This would mean the XJR-9 V12 would have to be retained until a replacement was available. Ferté had replaced Lammers who was at the UK Donington Park round of the Group C championship.

It was not to be Jaguar's day however with the Jones XJR-10 turbo suffering an early boost problem after a full course yellow, and the #60 Jaguar out after Ferté hit a wall too badly to continue. It was not to be Brabham's day either with engine failure on lap 82. The final placings were Robinson, Fangio/Olson 87C Toyota, J. Andretti Porsche; all on 94 laps.

## IMSA Lincoln- Mercury California Grand Prix (Sears Point 2 hours) – September 10th

Lammers was back in the XJR-10 and set the fastest qualifying time of 1:23.453 ahead of the Brabham and Robinson Nissans. Mass in the Texaco Havoline Porsche 962 qualified ahead of the Jones/Nielsen Jaguar, fifth of the 26 starters.

Cobb started the 300km race in the XJR-10 and led for the first 17 laps before the 83 Nissan took the lead. The hand over to Lammers continued the chase but his tyres were past their best after 20 laps and he pitted for new rubber under a full-course caution. Lammers was then the subject of a penalty, being deemed to have overtaken before the track was waved green and had to return to the pits for a stop-go penalty. The finish had a nose to tail victory for Brabham and Robinson, followed in close formation by the Jones/Nielsen XJR-9 and the Lammers/Cobb Jaguar ahead of the Fangio/Olson 87C Toyota. The first seven placings all finished on lap 75 in this race of 1 hour and 54 minutes. The four 962 Porsches competing here finished 7-8-9-10; with Mass the victor in the Porsche race.

## IMSA GTE Camel Grand Prix (Tampa Florida State Fairgrounds 380kms) – October 1st

Brabham was back in his usual place in qualifying, and then Lammers XJR-10 from the Taylor/Acheson Pontiac powered Spice SE89P and Robinson's Nissan. The Miller/Earl Chevrolet powered Spice showed these cars becoming more competitive as time went by, ahead of sixth fastest Cobb in the XJR-9.

Lammers was in hot pursuit from the start pushing to the limit and the pressure eventually took its toll with a spinning XJR-10. Lammers recovered to close down the gap to the Nissan with Brabham then making a rare mistake and in the process of spinning collected the close following Lammers. The damage was too bad to continue and Lammers' race was over. Cobb did a fine job in picking up the pieces for the Valparaiso team winning here in the XJR-9 and a fitting end to what was the close of the XJR-9's period in America. Second place went to the Miller/Earl Spice with Wollek/J. Andretti third followed by Robinson in the #84 Nissan. The Momo Porsche of Moretti/John Paul Jr. came in fifth, but five laps down on the leading four finishers. Brabham was able to finish in sixth and Lammers was eventually awarded ninth.

## IMSA Nissan Camel Grand Prix of Southern California (Del Mar Fairgrounds 2 hours) – October 22nd

This tight road circuit within a national park soon produced a problem that no one had experienced before. Not only was there a park noise limit but also an armed ranger to see it was carried out. In practice many cars were asked to reduce noise and this was impossible for us with our V6 side exit exhaust system pointing directly at the decibel meter at the end of the back straight. The problem was soon fixed with a competitor driving slightly off track and sending the meter skyward at over 200kph. The payout in IMSA for this final race had a jackpot of US$100,000 'Camel Pyramid' money coupled with the US$80,000 winner's purse. We had put together two of the latest specification V6 engines with an entirely new camshaft belt drive system as these had been marginal in their original design form. As well I had brought a special concentrated fuel additive in two whisky bottles with me for this event in my hand luggage.

For this last race of the year two XJR-10s were entered with the latest updated engines systems for Lammers and Cobb. It was the first race for this second XJR-10 and no V12s.

> The Acheson/Taylor SE 89P Spice took pole here with 1:03.414 followed by its sister car of Earl/Miller 1:03.62. Brabham Nissan ZX-T1:03.897; Cobb XJR-10 1:4.095; Ribbs Toyota Eagle 1:4.915; Robinson ZX-T Nissan 1:05.271; Lammers 1:05.405.

The battle continued between Brabham and Lammers, and Cobb not happy with the set-up with the new car. Robinson was then out with a broken driveshaft, and the pole setting Spice went as well with its Pontiac engine giving up the hard pace. Lammers finally won here ahead of Brabham's Nissan, Bob Earl drove his Spice to a fine third; Ribbs Toyota Eagle; Mass Bayside Porsche, all finishing on the same lap. Jean-Louis Ricci/Henri Pescarolo one lap down in sixth, and Cobb struggling with the new race car in seventh three laps down. All the effort had been worthwhile for the big pay day and the icing on the cake was the US$2500 'Camel smooth move' award to Lammers for his overtaking manoeuvre on Brabham.

These were good results considering the XJR-10's first year of development, and it was becoming obvious to me that with concentrated development the IMSA title could be ours to have in 1990. There was little chance in my opinion at the time of that happening in the WSPC, and IMSA was the area that our best prospects lay. It would need a change in focus and priority from Kidlington though, and that decision then suffered from internal objections from WSPC team manager Roger Silman. TW was still thinking Max Heidegger was going to produce a fix for the problems facing the WSPC programme in 1990 and was confident of winning there with his resources pushed in that direction.

## WSPC Trofeo Hermanos Rodriguez (480kms) – October 29th

The final WSPC race of the year would seal our fate and produce new Manufacturer and Driver Champions in the World Sports Prototype Championship. The last race on the WSPC calendar was the 480km race on the Hermanos Rodriguez circuit near Mexico City at an altitude of 7350ft. The V6 turbo programme had finally succumbed to the inherent lack of time and support facilities to give the cohesion needed at Engs, and we had reverted to bringing out the V12 engined Jaguars for this event. Long lead times involving surface shipping were also a factor in the decisions made for this race in Mexico. Some of us had already been across the border at Del Mar for the final race of the IMSA series the weekend before, so this would all end up a two week away from home journey to close the year. The decision we had to make of competing with the V12 cars was made all the more ironic because the altitude in Mexico would hamper the normally aspirated V12 engine much more than the forced induction opposition. Ross Brawn had joined TWR as technical director and was rapidly coming up to speed with the needs of racing to a fuel controlled formula and then assume averall command of the Group C racing programme for 1990.

It was just a matter of getting through this last race for us with the only real race being between Mercedes team mates Baldi and Schlesser; whoever won would be the world champion. It was Baldi who set the fastest time with 1:22.57 and Schlesser 1:22.665. Watson/Dumfries Toyota was on 1:24.166; Wollek/Jelinski's Joest Porsche on 1:24.393; Lammers had put in a very good lap to claim sixth fastest time of 1:25.44 among the nine turbocharged cars that had made the long haul to Mexico, and Wallace/Fete tenth 1:26. I had investigated our part throttle ignition mapping settings with reference to the barometer pressure at this circuit and took a punt with little to lose by advancing the ignition timing on the V12 engines by a further 3°, which had the pleasing reward of producing a one second reduction in lap times to the fuel. Our barometer pressure correction map for the fuel was working well and the sea level settings were being corrected automatically to the high altitude with only the fine tuning of one click on the driver's adjustment switch to produce best fuelling.

At the very start of proceedings any threat coming from one of the two Joest Porsches was over before it started with the Wollek/Jelinski 962 refusing to start and then being disqualified after a push start. Baldi had taken pole position but a determined Schlesser took the lead from the start and these two were in a race of their own with the other cars struggling to stay with their pace. The race was then placed under the pace car when Giacomelli crashed his Lancia and once again the pace car control was wrong in splitting the two Mercedes leaders and causing confusion, many cars going a lap down to the leaders by the time of the restart. After the first fuel stops Acheson and Mass took over the Mercedes driving duties until Acheson, driving hard to help team mate Baldi win the championship had tyre trouble leading to crashing his car. This left Schlesser and Mass in total control with the Brun, Joest and Richard Lloyd Porsches still putting in good lap times in the minor placings with two hours of the race left. The Jaguars ran together throughout the race and managed to pass the Bailey/Blundell Nissan towards the very end. This left Schlesser the winner of the race and 1989 World Sports Car Champion with the Brun 'Hydro Aluminium' Porsche 962 of Huysman/Larrauri in second some 36 seconds behind a cruising Schlesser; Pescarolo/Jelinski in the Joest Porsche and Needell/Bell in the BLR UK Porsche one lap down and the two Jaguars of Wallace and an unwell Lammers claiming fifth and sixth two laps down on the leader. Walter Brun was up next just managing to hold out David Leslie in the 6.3-litre Aston Martin followed by the Kremer Porsche of Reuter/Konrad.

Team manager Roger Silman had the unenviable task of going to find the man he had decided was not good enough for this series and had sacked at the end of 1986. He had to now congratulate the new World Champion; and Schlesser would eventually go on to repeat this feat again the following year. This sacking had produced the raised motivation he needed to beat TWR, Schlesser was a driver who was totally in tune with the demands of fuel consumption racing and also the most engineering minded driver I have ever worked with. We had both worked together on engine optimisation in winning the French National Championship with the Rover in 1985, and Schlesser had contributed to much of the on-track optimisation work with me in the early days of the V12 Group C engine in 1986. The German system of operation that he had then moved to with Mercedes was quite different with the drivers being told little and left to just drive, while the technicians carried out much of their work in secret in these early stages of electronic engine management. Schlesser had managed to combine and work well with the best points of both these ideals and quickly began turning around the fortunes of the Bosch managed Mercedes large capacity 5-litre V8; and that would prove to be the winning concept in this series when using standard fuels.

## Year in review

This had all been a demoralising end to a year that had broken the TWR winning ways over the period of the previous 10 years, and this was causing some confusion as to the best way forward from here. My relationship with TW was being strained with his indecision and lack of commitment to Engs, and I had seriously begun to think about my future at TWR. It was a time of confusion especially for us at Engs with TW saying the Max Heidegger engine would be used in 1990, but these 3.2 engines, after lots of talk, never quite seemed to appear. We were in the process of building a couple of V6 3.5-litre versions, still way too small an engine capacity, but with major upgrades. At best TW had a foot in both camps a position that just caused confusion, divided financing and no clear direction for me to follow. In fact, I was making myself unpopular by insisting that the 3.2-litre concepts would not work. This problem would grow with the January 1990 V6 turbo testing in Jerez having to be covered by Engs as the Heidegger 3.2 units had then failed to materialise. This had come about after some back-to-back dynamometer testing with our new prototype 3.5-litre V6 that incorporated a totally new intake system and reversed injectors and had produced considerably superior outputs in both power and fuel consumption. TW had negotiated a budget for this V6 engine development of £1,575,000.

The continuing expansion of the Engine division and the TWR Group along with the permanent relocation of TW and staff to Broadstone produced the need for added financial and organisational systems and upgrading of skills.

My end of year memo (see page 281) to TW before our progress meeting the next day shows the total confusion of all TW's engine plans. There were few answers after our meeting the next day.

Another bombshell though had arrived at the end of the 1989 year. John Bradley, our finance director whom we all respected for his patience and knowledge, and I saw as a diplomat in handling some difficult situations with TW, had decided to leave TWR. It was obvious that TW respected him as well and called him a friend during the speech he gave when finally announcing this situation to us. His departure concerned me and when I asked at his leaving party at the local Pub "What do you know that we do not know".

He smiled and replied, "Nothing."

NOTE TO ALLAN SCOTT

FROM MICHAEL BOON 4.9.89

*************************************************************

Allan,

<u>Capital Expenditure</u>

Copies of approved items have been sent to Nigel. The milling machine decision is to be taken in the overall context of a machine shop facility and has therefore been deferred for the time being.

M

Michael

cc. NE

*Engs still had no machine shop facility.*

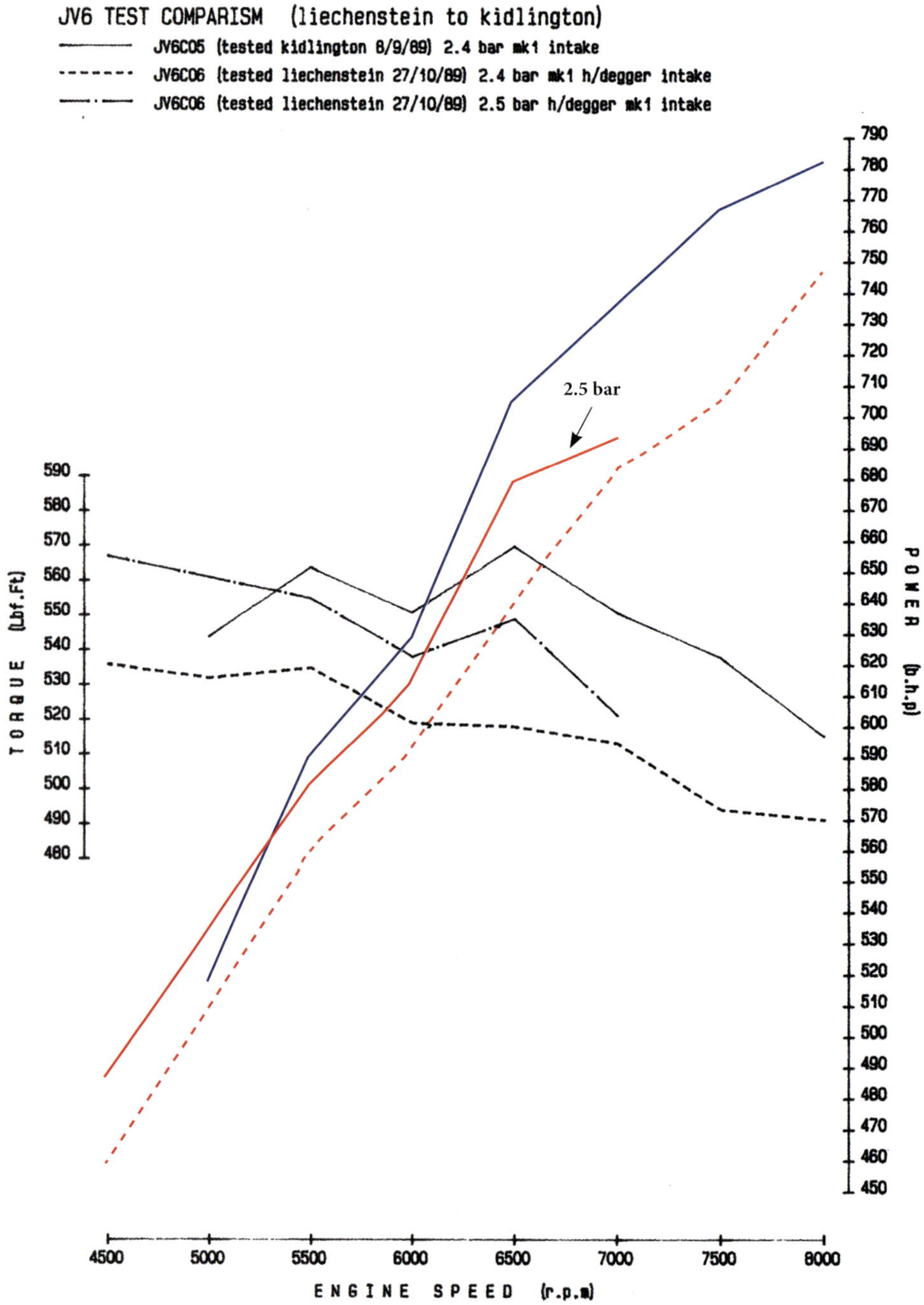


*Back-to-back testing with the Heidegger specification V6 engine (dotted red line) shows a 35bhp discrepancy at 2.4 bar boost along with poor fuel economy compared to our V6 engine (blue). It also fails to operate successfully at 2.5 bar suffering from detonation at the maximum torque area.*

MEMORANDUM

TO: TOM WALKINSHAW
FROM: ALLAN SCOTT
DATE: 5TH DECEMBER 1989
RE: TWR ENGINE DIVISION - MEETING WEDNESDAY 6TH DECEMBER

JaguarSport:

Future development and project engineer for:
N.I. 220 - production design and development - sign off procedure.
N.I. N.A. 6 cylinder/V12 two valve.
Straight six turbo.
V6 turbo.

Machine Shop:

Time scales.
Basic start up.

Nigel Eames is making up a list of Engine Division priorities and Roger King is to nominate ability from start up to cover these, allowing Nigel Eames to place orders outside as necessary.

Closed loop CAD - machine -- inspection system from Trevor Raynor has been discussed with Roger King along with the current new Engine Division inspection system. We received favourable comment from Roger King. Production of 100 V6 units in 1991 and 250 units in 1992 is to be considered whilst the current assessment of machines is taking place.

Bosch reporting system still not satisfactory. – Copy at Stuttgart (T.W.)

Gerhart Schumann to be interface with I.H.I. and build schedules and testing at M.H. - who does he report to?
Projects to be carried out at Lichtenstein.

V12 4 valve project.
Car projects.
Boat projects.

3,500 N.A. engine.
Development.
Initial build.
Rebuild.
Test programme.

SVO 2 valve V12 - 500 BHP - build team/equipment etc.

Engine future at Valporaiso.

Japanese programme.

Build centre.

Support.

Group C fuel.
Fully legal 4 star fuel from Octel now available.
Fuel specification F.I.A. nominates 87 M.O.N (mini).
ISO octane, calibration fuel for Mon motor is 100 R.O.N. 100 M.O.N.

Test Programme: Group C V6

I feel that we will not be ready for a Bosch 3,500cc V6 turbo car test till the end of January. It is important that Charlie is given time to do the Eprom correctly and see the cell systems operating properly. In 1989 the excuse of no time has resulted in tests at any cost and most of them show trends but are not accurate enough for the definition we now need at this level of development.

Capital expenditure 1990.

I05 has been found and is on its way back.
Rapid Movements coming on Friday to explain situation.

Quotes for rear building extension.

TOMMEM.AWS

*My pre-meeting brief to TW trying to establish the best way forward with the engine programmes.*

Our latest Del Mar winning V6 engine had been 'lost' in transit back to Kidlington at the end of 1989 and Rapid Movements had finally recovered it but would not tell me any details about how this had been done.

**M E M O R A N D U M**

TO: TOM WALKINSHAW
FROM: ALLAN SCOTT
CC: ROGER SILMAN, TONY DOWE
DATE: 2ND JANUARY 1990
RE: LOSS OF V6 IMSA ENGINE

The following is an explanation given to me by Mr. Moore, Managing Director or Rapid Movements.

Three engines were picked up from Daytona by a trucking firm sub-contracted by Rapid Movements.

The truck was driven to the Atlanta area where it was to pick up additional cargo to be taken to Chicago.

Whilst driving around the freighting area at Atlanta it is apparently common practice to leave the rear doors open because of the very short journeys involved between freighting areas.

Within this area there is an incline of approximately 5 to 1 and while driving up the incline at slow speed the engine fell out of the truck. The truck driver was unaware of this and did not stop. After picking up more cargo he drove to Chicago.

Two men were seen in a red pickup truck removing the engine and placing it in the rear of the pickup (Atlanta).

The same truck with the same driver proceeded to drop off cargo in the Chicago area, again with the rear doors open. The remaining 2 engines were free to fall out the rear of the truck, they did and fell onto the road (this at least appears to be the truth as the falling engines caused a minor accident and police were called to the scene).

The truck driver realised he had lost these engines, they were returned to Kidlington without further problem.

Note: At this time it was stated by Rapid Movements that the third engine had fallen out in Chicago and was now missing (in Chicago).

These events made it onto the local Chicago radio station involving an on the spot interview with the manager of the local Rapid Movements office.

Meanwhile back in Atlanta. The founder of Rapid Movements (Mr. Moore Senior) has retired to the Florida area and was called in to investigate the various versions of events.

Police were given a registration number of the utility vehicle seen departing with the engine. However, when they traced the vehicle it was not red and indeed a completely different vehicle altogether.

How did we get the engine back?

This area is slightly vague to say the least. However, what is known is that Rapids offered a sum of money via newspaper advertisements for the safe return of the engine.

It appears that the people who took the engine handed it in and collected the reward. The police have not been called as this would have involved the engine being retained as material evidence.

No charges have been brought to the people responsible.

I am working on a new design with Rapids which allows the wheels to be taken off the engine crates while they are being shipped and them refitted upon delivery at Kidlington, Valporaiso or the circuit.

My observations of the engine crates is that the two that dropped off in Chicago definately show signs of having slid along the road. The crate from the lost engine shows damage consistent with falling from a height of 3-6 feet but there is no scratching marks. i.e. the crate was *dropped* when stationery.

Allan Scott

## Chapter Twenty-One

# 1990

1990 had started with the news that the turbo engines from Liechtenstein had not performed as well as the two Kidlington units we had developed and our 3.5-litre specification would now be supplied to the Group C team. This meant that Engs had to rapidly build up an inventory of new 3.5-litre engines and put all development of the IMSA 3-litre units for 1990 on hold. With this change of plans I had not gone to Daytona because I had to concentrate on getting components from a machining industry that was still returning from the Christmas-New year shut down. TW and Roger had requested that Group C take priority over IMSA, something I could not for obvious reasons convey to TWR America at the time, and one of the reasons TW felt it best I not attend. I felt we had a good chance of success if IMSA was given priority with its 3-litre twin turbo V6 engine, feeling after the 1989 effort we had no chance of beating Sauber Mercedes in Group C. A review of the XJR-9 had been carried out by the American team in conjunction with an aerodynamic package carried out by Alastair Macqueen in the UK at Imperial College, the results built into a car designated XJR12D. For 1990 Ian Reed had produced special in-house manufactured mono block brake calipers along with a review of the suspension system and bodywork to accept the change for 1990 to Goodyear 18in radial tyres. After a long relationship Dunlop tyres would no longer be used. A testing programme had been carried out at Daytona on the 14th and 15th of November 1989, Sebring on the 19th and 20th and finally at Atlanta on the 22nd. This was a build up to the 1990 Daytona race on February 3rd and 4th using the 6-litre V12 engines to the same specifications as the year before.

left: *Daytona pit lane.* above: *Tony Dowe and Ian Reed*

APPROVED PERSONNEL

DAYTONA 24 HOUR RACE 1990

Martin Brundle
Price Cobb
Davy Jones
Jan Lammers
John Nielsen
Andy Wallace

Tom Walkinshaw
Tony Dowe
Richard West
John Szymanski
Ian Reed
Dave Benbow

John Jackson
Vik Warren
Howard Minckler
Phil Denney
Carl Azevedo
Dave Girton
Larry Zelesnik
Cooper King
Peter Hodgkinson
Mark Freeman
John McLellan
Winston Bush
Ian Gouldstone
Derek Collins
Mike Croake
Don Beadle
Steven Costello
Ira Chez
Mark Redbond
Jim Kracht
Scott Klemm
Bill Crisan
Mike Weston

Kenny Szymanski
Chris Syfert
Ann Roeske
Mike Murphy
Anne Murphy
Michael Brown

Tim Love

Steve Ave
Rosemarie Ave
Charlie Skala
Larry Randlett
Tom Ryan
Dennis Eade

Jeff Carlisi
Mark Hein

Ken Moore
Ted Moore

Ed Stevenson
Mary Elizabeth Mecom

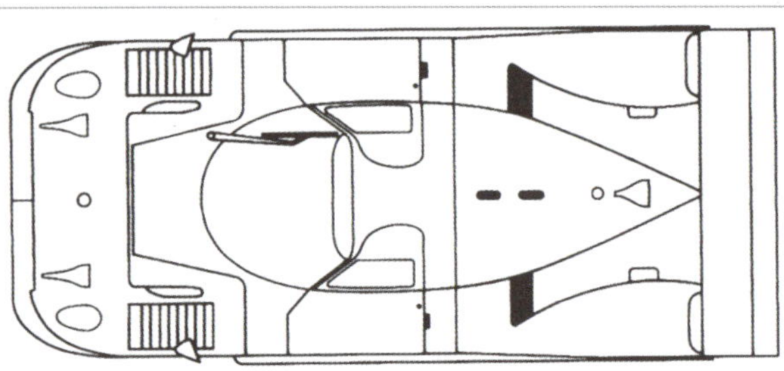

**CASTROL JAGUAR PIT CREW**

| | |
|---|---|
| CARL AZEVEDO | PHIL DENNEY |
| DAVE BENBOW | PETER HODGKINSON |
| WINSTON BUSH | COOPER KING |
| DEREK COLLINS | MARK REDBOND |
| STEVE COSTELLO | IAN REED |
| BILL CRISAN | LARRY ZELESNIK |

Once again Castrol was on hand to observe how their products were performing and the following are my archive notes from Castrol's Technical Service Engineer Charles Seymour.

Practice February 1 1990
Car 60 during practice water temperature 80°C, oil temperature 100°C. No engine running problems at this time. Early complaints of understeer in the car. Engine RPM is about 7600 down the front straight.

Oil consumption Car 61 after the first practice session, total of approximately 1 hour running time, consumption 0 liters. It has not consumed any oil since the start of this session. The exact time of Car 61, at practice, 57 minutes.

Car 61: Oil cooler temperature 230°F in inlet temperature, 220°F outlet temperature, that is 110°C inlet, 104°C outlet.

Car 60: Oil coolant temperatures inlet 110°C outlet and 104°C during first practice. That's Car 60.

Car 60: Oil consumption during first practice, 1 hour 13 minutes approximately 2 liters.

**SPECIAL NOTE:** Oil level taken after car had been sitting in pits for awhile. Oil temperature has dropped down some what.

Qualifying session Thursday 4:30 PM at this time.
Oil check Car 60, 0 oil consumption only out for 25 minutes.

Qualifying sessions Car 61; zero oil consumption. The engine on Car 61 seems to bit tighter than Car 60, perhaps it is a variable that is/can be driver affected. It has not consumed oil at any rate comparable to Car 60. That 61 has lower consumption than 60.

CAR 60 AND 61

February 2, 1990, Friday

Drivers in Car 61: Davy Jones, Jan Lammers, Andy Wallace,
Drivers in Car 60: Price Cobb, Martin Brundle and John Nielsen.

Qualifying on Friday, Davy Jones reports oil gauge, obviously oil temperature gauge not operating properly at this time. Car 60 reports oil and water temperature at 76°C approximately 10 minutes running time. Martin Brundle Car 60, oil pressure 75 lbs, oil temperature 100°C, water temperature 90°C. Experiencing some shifting problems between 3rd and 4th gears, up shifts and down shifts, this is during qualifying 1:20 p.m.

February 3, 1990, Saturday morning warmup 12:00.

During official warm-up, Jan Lammers driving Car 61 reports oil pressure running around 170 PSI. Car 61 reporting high oil pressure approximately 160 PSI. It's expected that this may be a short in the gauge and not truly reflecting oil pressure in the engine. Update to follow on oil pressure.

Morning warm-up on Saturday, February 3.

Car 60 replacement on oil pressure sending unit switch which have been reporting 150-170 PSI at all RPM has corrected the problem. The oil pressure switch is electronic and is not a mechanical gauge.

*Tony Dowe and Tom Walkinshaw discussing race strategy.*

**RACE START**

3:30PM RACE START 2/3/90.

4:25PM First pits stop, Car 60 approximately 1 liter oil added. Car 61 approximately 1/2 liter added at 4:25.

4:45PM Position update: After starting 9 and 10 on the grid, we are now running 1st and 2nd. That's position one and two.

5:15PM Car 60 pit stop. fuel, make up oil 1 liter.

5:25PM Car 61 takes half a liter. Oil temperature on Car 61 reported at 100°C, water temperature running at 90°C. No operating problems at either engines.

6:00PM Update: Car 60 position 1.; Car 61 position 2.

6:10PM Car 60 driver changed fuel, tires, Price Cobb driving. Pit stop. 1 liter oil added to Car 60.

6:20PM Pit stop for Car 61, During yellow flags, because of oil on track, takes one half liter of oil. Oil and water temperature are acceptable.

7:00PM Update. Position 1 Car 60 Jaguar. Position 2 Car 83 position 3 Car 61 Jaguar.

7:15PM Car 60 pit stop. 1 liter of oil added. Apparently, the oil light indicating the oil level in the reservoir has stopped working.

7:27PM Car 61 pit stop. 1 liter of oil added.

7:30PM Update. First place 83 Nissan at 130 laps. #60 Jaguar 130 laps. #2; position 3 Jaguar 130 laps; 17 Porsche 129 laps.

8:10PM Car 60 pit. Driver change, tires and fuel. Oil consumption for Car 60 during that stop, one liter added.

8:27PM Car 61 pit stop 1 liter of oil, fuel, tires and driver change.

9:10PM Car 60 comes for to a pit stop, brakes, brake pads, tires, fuel, driver, dip the oil tank. The oil tank is 3 - 4 liters over full. He has been added 1 liter per hour. Apparently, it doesn't use as much as has been anticipated. Next pit stop will only add 1/2 half liter.

Update on oil changes on both Cars 60 and 61: 95°C at night and 85°C water temperature. Both cars running 95°C oil temperature, 85°C water at night.

9:27PM Car 61 pit. Oil addition 1/2 liter, driver change, tires change, fuel, brake pads.

10:12PM Car 60 Price Cobbs driving. Oil temperature 100°C water temperature 95°C.

10:20PM Car 61, Reporting gear shift stiffness requesting lubrication, requesting gear shift and lubrication. It may be onset of other potential problems. Will update:

**NOTATION:** Fuel survey and racing fuel survey for John Bristow. Identify suppliers of racing fuel, octane readings, particular values, cost.

10:45PM Car 61 pit stop. Lubricate, gear shift, fuel, tires and oil 1/2 liter added. Davy Jones still driving car at this time. Car 61 also still has the radiator cleaned, water temperature a bit high, oil temperature running acceptable 100°C. Water was running at 90°C.

10:58PM Pit stop Car 60 driver changed. John Nielsen now driving. Price Cobb gets out of car. Tires, fuels, oil, radiator cleaned. Oil added 1 liter during this pit stop. Car 60 reports oil and water temperatures perfect after pit stop. 95°C oil temperature at this time.

11:20PM Car 60 reports water temp. 95°C. They were checking to make sure that all the lights were on the back of car.

11:25PM Car 61 new tail, to correct tail light problem, fuel, driver change, tires and oil - 1/2 liter oil added.

11:50PM Car 60 reports water temperature 95° - 98°C, Oil 100°C. Jan Lammers driving Car 60. Water temperature 95°C and stable.

11:55PM Car 60 pits, tires, fuel, oil - 1 liter of oil added.

12:25PM Car 61 Problems during pit stop. No air in airjack line. Approximately 1 liter was added, tires, fuel, no driver change.

12:50AM Lights are out in the pits. All power is out. Right after Car 60 pit stop. Car 60 pit stop for tires, fuel and oil makeup, approximately 1 quart added.

12:52AM All lights are back on.

1:25AM Car 61 pits. driver changed, Andy Wallace driving, tires, gas, and one liter of oil added. Minor problems with the air jack connection.

*Night time pit stop at Daytona.*

1:35AM Nissan 84 which had been in the pits for sometime has now return to the track, no obvious cause for extended pit stop.

1:45AM Car 60 reports water temperature at 98°C.

1:47AM Car 60 has shunt, nose replacement, front tires replacement just after leaving pit. Cars back out. Everything appears to be normal.

1:52AM Nissan 83 is in the pits. The tail section is off, both doors are opened and everyone is walking around quite slowing. It's very possible that #83 Nissan is out of it at this point.

1:58AM Car 60 water temperature 91°C

2:00AM Update; Car 61 position 1; Car 60 position 2, 2 laps down. Car 83 position 3, 7 laps down. It does not appear as though Car 83 will return to the track at this time.

2:25AM Car 61 pit stop: fuel, tires, oil, 3/4 liter was added.

2:45AM Car 60 pits tires, fuel, brake pads, oil. 1 liter of oil added during the stop. Driver change. The car is using about a liter an hour. The oil reservoir dip stick was checked during the driver change.

3:20AM Car 61. Driver changed, tires, fuel, oil, 1 liter of oil added, windshield and headlights cleaned.

3:45AM Car 61, Water temperature 95°C, oil temperature 100°C Normal. Davy Jones driving.

4:10AM Car 61 pit stop , tires, fuel, brake pads and oil. Oil checked. Right to the full mark - 1 liter of oil added.

4:40AM Car 60 pit stop, fuel, tires, oil. 1 liter of oil water temperature running normal and oil temperature running normal.

4:47AM Car 61 reports water temperature 90°C, oil temperature normal, 100°C.

5:05AM Car 61 pit, fuel, tires, driver, oil - 3/4 liter added of oil. Oil and water temperature reported as normal. Car 61 Jan Lammers driving. Water temperature 85°C, oil normal.

**NOTATION:** Normal on the gauge 95°C. not 100°, 95°C.

5:35AM Car 60 driver change, tires, fuel, oil - 1 liter of oil added.

5:54AM Car 60 Temperature 95°C water.

6:05AM Car 61 pit stop, tires, fuel, oil - 1/2 liter added. Temperatures normal.

6:30AM Car 60 pit stop, driver, tires, fuel, oil - 1 liter of oil added.

6:55AM Car 60 reported 95°C water, Martin Brundle driving.

7:10AM Car 61 pit stop, tires, fuel , driver change, oil - 1 liter added.

7:25AM Car 60 fuel, tires, brake pads, oil - 1 liter of oil added. Water temperature of car 60 during stop 89°C.

7:50AM Car 61 95°C water, 101°C oil.

8:05AM Car 61 pit stop, driver changed, tires, fuel 1/2 liter of oil added.

8:25AM Car 60 reporting low oil pressure and low oil light in the banking corners of track. 25 PSI indicated as the pressure reading going though the banking. Additional oil added to the sump tank to try cure the problem. Investigating potential low oil level in the system. Update to follow.

8:32AM Full Course Yellow.

Oil pressure update on Car 60, 60 PSI. There doesn't seems to be any problem at this time. During yellow, John Nielsen reported water temperature fluctuating. Potentially electrical problems, sending units for the water and oil temperature, maybe the problem, Car 60.

Yellow period continues, both cars reporting fluctuation in water temperature. Oil temperature is not indicating a problem.

8:40AM Car 60, John Nielsen reports that, water and oil temperature are at 100°C. Typical when the car slows down, temperature rises quite rapidly. At pit stop, 1 liter of oil added. The previously addition of 3 liters, may have been too much. One liter is going to be added per stop at this time. Which is now approximately at 1 hour intervals.

10:35AM Car 61 reporting high water temperature 125°C. Oil temperature normal. Car 60 has reported similar problems over the past hour without any detrimental effect. Car 61 will continue and be advise on any action.

10:50AM Price Cobb reporting fluctuating water temperature 105°C to 120°C. Oil temperature 101°C and steady.

A decision to refill the coolant system on car 60 has been made.

During numerous late race pit stops, Car 60 took 3 liters of oil, reporting fluctuating oil pressure.

Car 61 with fluctuating water temperature has received a major overall of the coolant system, performed with 5 or 6 different additions of water to the system, this was to bring the temperature down to an acceptable range. The process used preheated coolant to avoid potential block cracking, the cooling system has successfully been refilled.
One liter of oil was added, during the last pit stop to fill with fuel and continue on.

**NOTE: Coolant recovery system for Car. Typical of a normal passenger vehicle coolant recovery system.**

> **<u>Identification of over heating of cars in a 24 hours race.</u> Potential cause of the overheating may have been a result of minimal leakage during numerous stops, approximately one every hour, where a small amount of water is bleed out of the system during the stop. The accumulation over time may have accounted for the significant loss, which created the overheating situation. A coolant recovering system is suggested, potential for dual thermostats in the system; as a redundant system is highly recommended. This is common practice of Heavy Duty Diesel engines where the malfunctioning of a single thermostat could cause significant engine overheating.**

Oil temperature for Car 61 100°C, water temperature 95°C and steady.

12:40PM Car 61 Pit stop; Tires, driver, Jan Lammers is driving now. Oil 1 liter added. fuel. Water and oil temperature are okay at this time.

1:15PM Water temperature reported at Car 61 95°C to 100°C.

1:40PM Pit stop for Car 61, driver change, oil, fuel, 1 liter of oil was added during that stop. Temperature oil/water are acceptable.

3:30PM Sunday, February 4, 1990 - We won the race!!

**CASTROL/TWR/JAGUAR #61 - 1ST PLACE**
**CASTROL/TWR/JAGUAR #60 - 2ND PLACE**

My only involvement with this race was receiving a phone call from TW in the middle of the night to ask if the temperature readings the drivers were getting were real or if they were a malfunction. This is hard to diagnose having been woken in bed on the other side of the Atlantic and I suggested that Charlie Bamber was in a better position to answer that question than I was; something TW did not want to hear and insisted I make the call. With the race seemingly under control I suggested a purge of the water system with hot water from the pressurised water bottle system made for just that problem that should be sitting in the pit area. The difference between Group C pit stops and IMSA ones is that at Daytona the cars are allowed to idle during the stop and if other small repairs are needed that lengthen the pit stop, back pressure in the system builds up because of the low water pump speeds and small amounts of water are vented each time passed the pressure cap, and this seemed to be the best conclusion for the problem here (we modified the system for 1991). There was another problem somewhere however, as Tony Dowe reported to me that one of the cars had little water left on inspection after the race finish and this engine had run very hot. It appeared that a pin hole caused by a stone to the radiator was the problem.

> The final placings for Daytona 24 hour were: Jones/Lammers/Wallace, #61, Castrol XJR-12D, 761 laps; Cobb/Nielsen/Brundle, #60, Castrol XJR-12D, 757 laps; Dobson/Vandermerwe/Wollek, Texaco Havoline #86, Porsche 962, 755 laps; Hertzog/Stuck/Haywood/Groths, Alucraft, Porsche 962, 704 laps

It was a great victory for the TWR America team with Jaguar being only the second Manufacture to have won the Daytona 24 hour race twice, the other being Porsche. The winning Jaguar had set three new outright track records; a new lap record on lap 143 for Lammers 1:38.596, new average speed over the 24 hours of 112.86mph as well as the longest distance ever covered with 761 laps.

Both Jaguars had at one time led for 85% of the total race distance and the second placed Jaguar had led the field for 541 laps out of its finishing total of 757. Just five GTP cars had finished out of the eighteen that had started, Jaguar with a 100% finishing record and Porsche 962 with its nine starters a 33% finishing record, three of these with engine problems. After the race driver analysis shows the consistency in the race pace of the cars as well as the drivers. Five of the six drivers set their fastest time over the 24 hour period within 0.5 seconds of each other. The same five drivers' average lap times over their driving stints were all within 0.6 seconds of each other.

As with all winning V12 engines Castrol carried out a thorough review of how their oil had performed and these are images from the winning V12 engine.

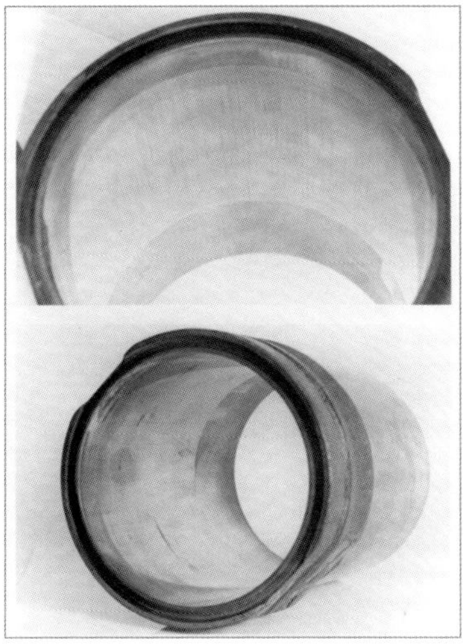

*Cast iron liner used in the winning Daytona 24 hour engine.*

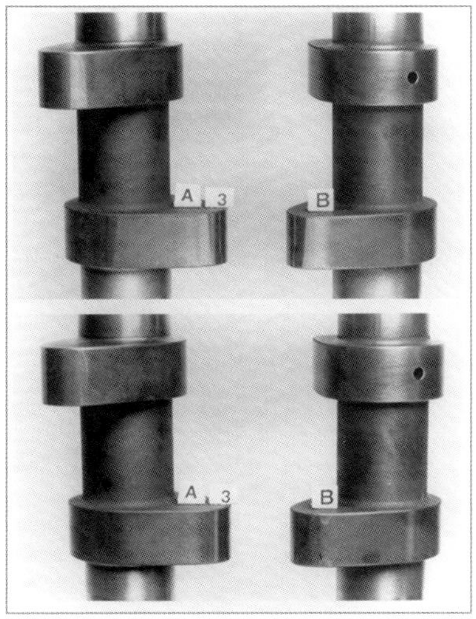

*Cast iron camshafts from the winning 24 hour engine.*

*Head gasket sealing ring patterns on the head face show this system remained intact even when subjected to excessive temperatures when running with low water levels.*

## Sebring circuit

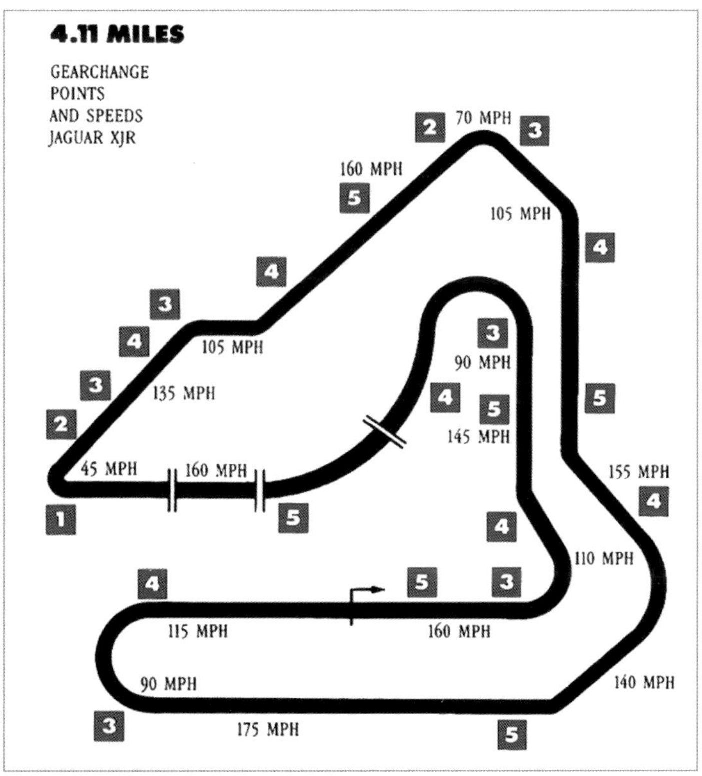

**FINAL SCHEDULE SEBRING 1990**

**Monday, March 12**

9:00 AM- 5:15 PM – Pre-Race Test, In Sessions

**Tuesday, March 13**

9:00 AM- 5:15 PM – Pre-Race Test, In Sessions
8:00 AM- 4:00 PM – In Paddock – Registration & Technical Inspection

**Wednesday, March 14**

8:00 AM- 5:00 PM – Registration & Technical Inspection
8:00 AM- 8:45 AM – Practice – Vintage
9:00 AM- 9:45 AM – Practice – Firestone Firehawk Sports & Touring
10:00 AM-11:00 AM – Practice – Camel GT
11:15 AM-12:00 N – Practice – Firestone Firehawk Grand Sports
1:00 PM- 1:45 PM – Practice – Firestone Firehawk Sports & Touring
2:00 PM- 3:00 PM – Practice – Camel GT
3:15 PM- 4:00 PM – Practice – Firestone Firehawk Grand Sports
4:15 PM- 4:45 PM – Qualifying – Firestone Firehawk Sports & Touring
5:00 PM- 5:30 PM – Qualifying – Vintage
5:45 PM- 6:30 PM – Practice – Historic

**Thursday, March 15**

8:00 AM- 3:00 PM – Registration
8:00 AM- 8:20 AM – Warmup – Vintage
8:30 AM- 9:00 AM – Qualifying – Historic
9:10 AM- 9:25 AM – Warmup – Firestone Firehawk Sports & Touring
9:35 AM-10:05 AM – Qualifying – Firestone Firehawk Grand Sports
10:15 AM-11:15 AM – Practice – Camel GT
11:35 AM- START – Vintage Race – 8 Laps
1:05 PM- 1:35 PM – Qualifying I – GTP/Lights to set Top 10
1:45 PM- 2:15 PM – Qualifying I – GTO/GTU
2:45 PM- START – FIRESTONE FIREHAWK ENDURANCE CHAMPIONSHIP 4 HOUR SPORTS/TOURING RACE
7:45 PM- 8:45 PM – Night Practice – Camel GT

**Friday, March 16**

8:00 AM- 3:00 PM – Registration
8:30 AM- 8:50 AM – Warmup – Historic
9:00 AM- 9:15 AM – Warmup – Firestone Firehawk Grand Sports
9:30 AM-10:15 AM – Final Qualifying – GTO/GTU
10:30 AM-11:15 AM – Final Qualifying – GTP/Lights
11:30 AM- START – Historic Race – 8 Laps
12:30 PM- 1:30 PM – Practice – Camel GT
2:00 PM- START – FIRESTONE FIREHAWK 4-HR GRAND SPORTS RACE

**Saturday, March 17**

8:30 AM-11:00 AM – Late Registration
8:30 AM- 8:50 AM – Warmup – Camel GT
10:00 AM- START – 12 HOURS OF SEBRING CAMEL GRAND PRIX

Schedule may be amended to accommodate local conditions

**Tom Walkinshaw Racing Ltd**

*Note to: Roger Silman* *cc. TDW*
*From: Kevin Lee*
*Date: 7 March 1990*

*******************************************************

***LE MANS CARS***

*A decision is urgently required on which cars we will run at Le Mans this year, it is defined that we will use four V12's but we need to establish which four and where they will be prepared.*

*The first two cars are easy:-*

*190 new V12 car already built in Grp C Workshop and 290 new V12 car currently in build in Grp C Workshop.*

*The second two are not as clear as there are several options:-*

*a) the IMSA team could prepare their two V12 chassis's after Sebring*

*b) the IMSA team could prepare one V12 after Sebring, return the Daytona winning car to SVO for restoration and resale, and Grp C could prepare 588 to LM spec*

*c) prepare all four cars in the Grp C workshop.*

*TWR Inc claim to have sufficient mechanical parts to support two cars at LM, therefore if the cars are prepared at Kidlington we should ship back these parts as well as the cars, in order to save money on parts expenditure.*

*With regard to personnel we only need a small number of mechanics to allow us to operate in our normal manner, four would be the ideal number. With this in mind it appears to make sense to allow IMSA to prepare one car and bring four mechanics to run it.*

*We would have sufficient staff at Kidlington to operate 4 cars, with the exception of 3 race mechanics. Therefore, using any more than 4 people from TWR Inc would be a waste of money and a waste of Kidlington resources.*

*The most sensible option appears to be to proceed as follows:-*

*190 - stays at Kidlington and continues test programme.*
*290 - finish build at Kidlington then test programme.*
*588 - full rebuild to LM Spec at Kidlington.*
*IMSA car - prepare at Valparaiso to LM Spec.*

*Kevin Lee states his concerns that the 1990 Le Mans programme needs to be finalised.*

## 12 Hours of Sebring – March 17th

The last outing for the Jaguar V12 XJR-12D in 1990 was the 12 hours of Sebring and again for this race two V12 engined cars were entered. Nissan also had two GTP-ZXT cars and #84 with Chip Robinson had set the fastest time in Qualifying with a 1:55.76. Geoff Brabham would go on to set the fastest time in this car in the race as well at 1:58.58. It was a close battle all the way with both Nissans just holding out the #61 Jaguar of Jones/Lammers/Wallace with all three cars finishing on 301 laps. The Cobb/Nielsen car #60 had dropped out earlier with engine problems and that would be it for XJR-12D for the rest of the year. The 3-litre XJR-10s would now be used in all IMSA races.

## Le Mans

It was time to turn to the 1990 Le Mans race once again but with the TWR teams focused on trying to turn the new XJR-10 V6 turbo into a winning combination, things were being left unconfirmed at Kidlington as to how many cars TWR would field here. The Daytona win had perhaps allowed some complacency but past winners simply set the bar and leave this as the example others have to overcome; and just raise their game. There were however considerable changes to the Le Mans circuit layout to now consider as speeds on the Mulsanne straight had been reduced with the introduction of two sets of chicanes placed on that part of the circuit. The aerodynamic envelop would need to move away from all the work that had previously been done; needing more downforce and less emphasis on lowest drag factor would be the obvious trend. We would however underestimate some of the effects of these new chicanes as we would later find out.

A shake down test for chassis numbers 190, 290,1090 and 990 was carried out at the Southern Loop section of the Silverstone circuit using drivers Martin Brundle, Andy Wallace, Michele Ferté and Franz Konrad on June 7th. This was followed by Alastair Macqueen and Ross Brawn carrying out a full-scale wind tunnel test of the Le Mans specification cars at the MIRA wind tunnel before departure to Dover and Le Mans.

## Castrol biography of the IMSA drivers in 1990

*Martin Brundle was born June 1st, 1957, is married to Liz and has a daughter Charlotte. Martin is 5'8" weights 147 lbs. and currently lives in Kings Lynn, England.*

*Denmark's John Nielsen was born February 7th, 1956. John, his wife Vibike and their two daughters, Sandy and Nadine line in Harrislee, West Germany.*

*Jan Lammers born on June 2nd, 1956 is single. Jan is 5'5" tall and weighs 125 lbs. Jan lives in his hometown of Zandvoort, Holland.*

left: *Davy Jones was born on June 1st, 1964. Davy is single, weights 155 lbs. and is 5'10" tall, originally from Chicago, IL. Davy now resides in Lake Tahoe, NV.*

right: *Texan Price Cobb was born December 19th, 1954. Price is married to Lisa and has two daughters Nicole and Courtney. Price weighs 170 lbs., is 5'8" tall and now lives in Evergreen, CO.*

## Driver and mileage records for IMSA V12 race cars – 1988, 1989 and 1990

### By Chassis Number

| | | |
|---|---|---|
| 188 | 13,612.6 | + Daytona 89 |
| 288 | 26,638.7 | |
| 388 | 25,048.8 | |
| 389 | 11,825.3 | |
| 489 | 557.4 | |
| 589 | 7,446.2 | |
| Total Mileage | 85,129.0 | |

### By Driver:

| | | |
|---|---|---|
| Davy Jones | 18,707.5 | |
| John Nielsen | 16,896.6 | |
| Price Cobb | 14,106.0 | |
| Jan Lammers | 13,967.7 | |
| Martin Brundle | 6,895.3 | |
| Andy Wallace | 2,617.5 | |
| Danny Sullivan | 2,265.3 | |
| Eddie Cheever | 1,812.7 | |
| Raul Boesel | 1,812.3 | |
| John Watson | 1,369.3 | |
| Johnny Dumfried | 1,089.4 | |
| Alain Ferté | 840.2 | |
| Derek Daly | 620.0 | + Daytona 89 |
| Jeff Kline | 436.8 | |
| Eliseo Salazar | 412.3 | |
| Wally Dallanbach | 320.3 | |
| Michel Ferté | 288.6 | |
| Patrick Tambay | | + Daytona 89 |
| Martin Donnelly | | + Daytona 89 |
| Scott Pruett | 144.3 | |
| Calvin Fish | 135.0 | |
| David Leslie | 132.8 | |
| Alan Berg | 111.0 | |

**Note:** As of December 18th 1990, still waiting for the driver mileages for the Chassis No. 188 for the Daytona 89 race. Had been requested from Alistair McQueen at Kindlington (the engineer of that car at that race).

## Alastair Macqueen ...

One major change was to Goodyear tyres on BBS wheels. These had been discretely tested in 1989 on a few occasions and one of the comments was that the tracks seemed to have been re-paved and much smoother on the Goodyears. Whilst the ride quality may seem unimportant on a race car, it was an indication that the tyres were supplying a constant grip level with the inevitably stiff suspension of the big V12 cars, the lap times were better than the outgoing Dunlops. I now handled the task of developing the XJR-9 to become the XJR-12 as Tony Southgate had finally left the TWR programme. The circuit of Le Mans was changed forever by the introduction of two chicanes along the Mulsanne straight. The FIA mandated that no straight should be more than 1.9kms to prevent the cars travelling at almost 400kph for prolonged periods for safety reasons and this fundamentally changed the way Le Mans cars were run. No longer were the low drag 'streamliners' the way to go. The cars would have to rely on downforce and corner speed to achieve the fastest lap time to the fuel.

In the days long before simulators, a few mathematical models and great deal of circuit experience would have to be used to create the right V12 car for the new circuit layout. It was clear that with top speeds likely to be down to around 320kph, more drag could be tolerated; but it was the lift to drag ratio (aero efficiency) that would become the dominant factor in getting the car to the fuel allowance.

With the 'streamliner' cars the drivers may not tolerate an aero split which matched the weight distribution (40-60) as this would make the cars unstable and 'pointy' at very high speed; with the 'sprint' high downforce cars this was best due to the massive grip available in medium and high speed corners. Four-day sessions in the Imperial College wind tunnel in late '89 were carried out resulting in the use of the most efficient nose (88 LM type) being paired with the 88 'sprint' underwing. A great deal of time was invested in getting the rear wing to make best use of the flows from the tail section and underwing producing a main plane running at 5° nose up but with a fairly steeply raked tail flap, all mounted quite low. More intakes were made into NACA ducts in the drive for efficiency after the success of the engine intake ducts from 1989.

Compared to the '88 winning car the Lift/Drag jumped from 2.96 to 3.92 and the front split increased from 24.1% to 38%. But would the split be right for the new Le Mans circuit? Calculations showed we should be on target for Vmax of about 330kph and that drivers could tolerate this percentage of split on other circuits, but we had to be ready at Le Mans with various 'trimming devices' depending on driver feedback. Some of the package was used successfully at Daytona (including the new wing position) but in a slightly higher overall downforce mode.

Gear ratios were agonised over. Top gear was going to be fairly simple to predict, but many of the turns at La Sarthe would become much quicker with a 60% increase in downforce. Fortunately, the big 7-litre V12 was very tolerant of lower rpm due to the huge torque, as had been demonstrated by Jan Lammers in the final 40 minutes of the '88 race.

### Wind tunnel programme on the V12 car to Le Mans '90

```
To include;
Underwings
----------
_'88 sprint type.            Driveshaft in tunnel.
_'88/89 Le mans type.        Driveshaft over tunnel
_ Proposed Le mans type;
       -Starting at max forward position.
       -Large rad into venturi angle.
       -Tunnel upto max. ht. at exit, but driveshaft over tunnel.
       -Controlled expansion area.

Tail section
------------
_'89 spec. camel tail.
       -Mods. to include square edges over wheel arches.
       -Larger '90 spec.V6 wheel covers.
       -NACA engine air intake system.

Side panels
-----------
_ NACA duct spec.

Nose
----
Starting with Le mans nose;
       -Add sprint type rad exit ramp.
       -Add '90 type wheel arch louvres.
       -Add '90 type brake ducting.
       -Blank origional brake ducts.
       -Std. splitter and bracket.

Rear wing and mounting.
----------------------
Sprint 60/40 wing.
 e mans wing.
* Position and angle respecting overall 4800 max. length.

                                  A.K.M.    9/3/90.
```

# 1990 Le Mans Car Spec (V12)

FINAL ISSUE

**A SET UP**

As per sheet included

All measurements to be taken on race tyres pressured at 26 PSI front and rear.

On set-up patch the following measurements should be checked to $^+_-$ 3mm.

Ht. of front of splitter 62mm
Ht. of rear of splitter 53mm
Tunnel exit Ht. 370mm
Ht. of top of wing return 832mm
Ht. of top of tail surface 545mm
Ht. of tunnel from 'O' line must not exceed 280mm at any point.
O/A width of car must not exceed 2000mm
O/A length of car must not exceed 4800mm
Check exhaust exit height is below 450mm
Check castor is 2$^o$ both sides.

**B AERO**

FRONT

1 Nose profile splitter
2 Solid rad under panel
3 Louvres over top of front wheels - must have inner cover plates available
4 Nose must be fitted with panel to stop radiator from being viewed in plan
5 Small rad mount plates to be fitted
6 Radiator under panel to be flush with nose box
7 Front wheel panels to be fitted
8 Nose and door shut lines to be good and flush
9 Mono floor panel to be flush and flat
10 Fill all joints where possible
11 Fill old brake duct holes
12 Fit NACA brake ducting
13 1990 Le Mans underwing to be used

REAR

1 90'LM Underwing to mono shut line must be smooth, sealed and flush
2 Any drain pipes through underwing must be cut off flush - use new pipe drain parts
3 Tail must have good shut lines to mono and side panel
4 "TP" panels to be fitted.
5 Tail to have:
- Side entry air ducting
- 2 x NACA ducts above fuel fillers
- Internal vent slot covers
- Good sealing around air box - ensure ali surround on air filter
- Top intake cover

6 Rear wing to be on 90 LM mount plates. 6$^o$ angle to be measured with car on floor at correct ride heights, from front of wing to trailing edge on top of return
7 Heli-tape leading edge of wing
8 Wheel covers to have no NACA Hole.

**C BRAKES**

1 AP 14" 48 valve, non-drilled, 4 x slots per side 9" P.C.D.
2 Fully floating bell assy
3 Bedded DS11 pads
4 AP 4-pot 14" calipers - Ali pistons - 4lbs Knock off springs. 12mm stud holes
5 Centre, caliper and face ducting only at front
6 Sprint rear brake ducts. No caliper duct
7 $^7/_8$" + $^7/_8$" master cyls
8 5" scat nose to uprights
9 Secure flexible ducting with rivets where possible
10 Castrol SRF fluid
11 12 mm Caliper studs

**D ELECTRICAL EQUIPMENT**

1 4 x 100 spot lights 7" Oscar. Set to jig
2 Headlamp covers to have rip-offs heli-taped in place
3 Illuminated trim control to be fitted
4 2 x pea lights to illuminate dash area
5 All fuel computers to have fully illuminated back lights
6 Roof marker lights
7 Number lights as per 89
8 All tail lamps to have twin festoon bulbs
9 All spare body work to be checked and working
10 Check wiper motor and linkage

10 Check wiper motor and linkage
11 Ensure dash is fully labelled and gauges have red lines
12 Check loom connections and ensure passage is safe from chaffing
13 Check battery security and terminals
14 Fuse box covers removed
15 Check mirrors for function and angle.
16 Ensure G/Box temperature gauge installed

**E FUEL SYSTEM**

1 Side pod mounted pump filter assy
2 Water pipe through side pod to be FULLY lagged
3 3 x 1.5" dia holes in side pod floor to extract air
4 Incorporate bobbins around NACA duct to allow use of scoop
5 Large fuel cooler to be fitted at angle, -6 line from return through cooler to tank
6 All cars to have fully fitted, tested and clean spare pump /filter assy
7 All cars to have tank capacity of 99 litres (Measured on fill and pump out)
8 Fuel fill to tail joint to be sealed with edging rubber.

**F OIL SYSTEM**

1 Twin oil coolers to be used. L.H. cooler full size, - 16 in and out. From main scavange out of pump to top of tank via cooler. R.H. cooler to be -12 in and out in 4th stage scavange out to top of tank return
2 1 x -16 pipe from bottom of tank into main pump inlet
3 New NACA ducts in side panels to be fitted
4 Extreme care to be taken whilst routing -12 pipes in front of engine to avoid belts and pulleys
5 Pre-fit half and full duct blanks (NACA return strips).

**G GEARBOX SPEC**

1 All boxes to be 5 speed
2 Long non-drilled 12-31 C.W.P.
3 Spool diff
4 Ratios as listed
5 Route breather to catch tank + mods as listed on G/Box meeting list.
6 -10 g/box oil cooler pipes

**H GENERAL**

1 Tool kits to be fixed in cockpits
2 Stone shielding in ali under all wheel arch panels
3 Check operation of door catches
4 Driver leg restraint to be fitted
5 Pre-fitted driver cool suit
6 Inconnel exhaust system. Check clearances
7 Ensure towing eyes are double strength and painted red
8 Ensure door catches are marked "Push/Poussez" and extinguisher and battery decals fitted
9 Check fit of radiator blanks
10 Fit removable windscreen fittings. Three screens to be trial fitted. Heli-taped leading edge - ensure paint on screens does not impair view of wing mirrors
11 Ensure water and exhaust shields are fitted to underpanel.

**I BODYWORK**

1 Nose:

As '89 except:-
- NACA entry front brake ducts
- Louvres over front wheels
- Original brake ducts blanked.

2 Side Panels:
- New NACA entry side panel
- MKII length to fit 90 V6 wheel cover
- Muds to tub to allow lead into NACA duct.

3 Tail:

Basically '89 V12 "Camel" tail with mods to allow:-
- Clearance for large dia Goodyear tyres
- Fitting for '90 V6 wheel covers
- Detailed filling around front edge to match mono.

4 Rear Wing:
- 60/40 sprint rear wing
- Set on new 90 LM mount plates
- Run approx 4$^o$ nose up
- New end plates
- 15$^o$ to 30$^o$ end flap movement
- ½" return

5 Spares to be prepared:

Ensure all bodywork fits without having to move mounting brackets

1 1 x radiator/underpanel/side plates (assembly)
2 1 x radiator only (with crossblead)
3 1 x left hand side panel
4 1 x right hand side panel
5 1 x car set wishbones
6 1 x disc/bell car set
7 1 x pair of doors
8 1 x nose
9 1 x tail
10 2 x screens
11 1 x pushrods/TCAs/car set
12 1 x pair of driveshafts (checked after run-in)
13 1 x pair of PFs
14 1 x pairs of TPs
15 1 x throttle cable assy
16 1 x fuel pump/filter assy

## 1990 Le Mans G/box Tec Spec

CW+P

- 12/31 ARROW GEARS
- HOLES SPARK ERRODED FOR LUBE

DIFF

- SPOOL

RATIOS

14 - 42
17 - 39
21 - 34
25 - 31
27 - 28

OIL SYSTEM

- STD PUMP
- MAGNET IN STRAINER ASSY
- INLINE FILTER
- -10 LINES - -10 BANJO (LONG) OUT - 10 BANJO (SHORT) IN
- NEO OIL TO BE USED
- NEW G/BOX OIL INLET AND OUTLETS
- G/BOX MACHINED FOR -10 UNION
- PLUG IN PINION SHAFT & FEED JET IN RR COVER

INSPECTION

- HUBS TO HAVE SPARK ERRODED HOLES FOR LUBE
- FINGER TO BE SOLID (NOT PART DRILLED)
- RATIOS - CRACK TESTED BY RONI
- CW+P - BLUED AND CRACK TESTED BY RONI
- SIDE PANEL SEAL RETAINING WASHERS
- FORK AND FINGER SET-UP - POLISHED RODS
- HUBS - CRACK TESTED AND POLISHED
- OIL TEMP SENDER INTO G/BOX
- LEVEL PLUG INTRODUCED
- CHECK CLUTCH SHAFT LATEST TYPE (20mm NEEDLE ROLLER, SPIGOT BRG. NO SHOULDER)
- NO FILTER GAUGE IN RR COVER

Below is a list of the engines used and spare parts to service them taken to Le Mans. This shows the attention to detail required.

*P. TYRRELL*

*ENGINE LOCATIONS*

| | *FITTED CHASSIS* | *CAR* |
|---|---|---|
| *V12 90C01* | *1090* | *3* |
| *V12 90C02* | *990* | *1* |
| *V12 90C03* | *290* | *2* |
| *V12 90C04* | *190* | *4* |
| *V12 90C05* | *SPARE NO. 2* | *-* |
| *V12 90C06* | *SPARE NO. 3* | *-* |
| *V12 90C08* | *SPARE NO. 1* | *-* |

*E.C.U. PROGRAMME LEMAN 901 7200 R.P.M.*

| | | |
|---|---|---|
| *DYNO TRIM* | *O FUEL* | *O IGNITION* |
| *CAR TRIM* | *O FUEL* | *-2° IGNITION* |
| *CAR AND TRIM TO FUEL* | *-1 FUEL* | *-2° IGNITION* |
| *DRIVER TRIM 1* | | |

*RUN AS ABOVE FOR PRACTICE*
*POSSIBLY ONE CAR RUN TO FULL*

*V12 SPARES BOX 1990*

| *PART NO.* | *DESCRIPTION* | *QTY* |
|---|---|---|
| *SECTION A* | | |
| *J12C-015-012* | *CAM FOLLOWERS* | *24* |
| *17-R0016* | *BIG END BEARINGS* | *32* |
| *17-R0007* | *MAIN BEARING VP5126* | *10* |
| *17-R0019* | *MAIN BEARING VP5128* | *4* |
| *J12C-043-001* | *ENG. MOUNTING PLATES* | *2* |
| *J12C-043-003* | *MOUNTING PLATE BUSHES* | *2* |
| *J12C-016-007* | *END FLOAT BUTTONS* | *12* |
| *J12C-024-005* | *STARTER LOWER MOUNT* | *1* |
| *18-C0021* | *184 LINK TIMING CHAIN* | *1* |
| *SECTION B* | | |
| *45-B0001* | *CLUTCH BOLTS* | *34* |
| *18-S0025* | *FRONT COVER BUNGS* | *3* |
| *17-R0021* | *SPIGOT BEARINGS* | *5* |
| *12-N0026* | *FUEL TEMP SENSOR* | *4* |
| *21-C0055* | *BANJO BOLT FOR SENDER MTG BLOCK* | *4* |
| *14-S0019* | *CAM CARRIER END BUNGS* | *8* |
| *J12C-022-003* | *SUMP FILTER* | *2* |
| *J12C-050-007* | *ALTERNATOR ADJUSTER UNIONS* | *3* |
| *21-E0061* | *OIL GALLERY WASHERS* | *30* |
| *J12C-012-016*7*8* | *THROTTLE RETURN SPRINGS* | *2* |
| *J12C-030-012* | *WASHER - SYNC. DISC* | *1* |
| *J12C-026-084* | *FLYWHEEL BOLTS* | *16* |
| *J12C-026-047* | *OIL GALLERY BUNGS* | *5* |
| *20-S0028* | *WATER RAIL GASKETS* | *24* |
| *21-S0036* | *OIL PUMP GASKETS* | *15* |
| *18-B0005* | *CAM SPROCKET BOLTS* | *8* |
| *12-N0020* | *AIR THERMISTORS* | *2* |
| *24-JOO46* | *STARTER MOTOR RAIL PINS* | *20* |
| *28-N0035* | *ROTOR ARMS* | *6* |
| *12-N0021* | *INJECTORS - BLACK* | *12* |
| *J12C-035-008*C* | *FRONT PULLEY WASHER* | *1* |
| *J12C-012-083+084* | *FUEL FILTER FITTING* | *1* |
| *30-N0008* | *ALTERNATOR TO STARTER LINK LEAD* | *2* |
| *30-N0009* | *STARTER EARTH LEAD* | *2* |
| *30-N0010* | *ALTERNATOR EARTH LEAD* | *2* |
| *35-B0002* | *FRONT PULLEY BOLT* | *1* |
| *21-S0003* | *OIL PUMP BODY 'O' RINGS* | *24* |
| *12-R0005* | *THROTTLE SLIDE BEARINGS* | *150* |

*SECTION B*

| | | |
|---|---|---|
| 23-S0034 | OIL FILTER 'O' RINGS | 2 |
| 23-S0035 | OIL FILTER 'O' RINGS | 2 |
| S0052 | -8 'O' RINGS | 22 |
| S0051 | -6 'O' RINGS | 9 |
| 21-S0004 | OIL PIPE 'O' RINGS | 8 |
| 21-S0005 | OIL PIPE 'O' RINGS | 8 |
| 12-S0012 | INJECTOR SEALS | 12 |
| 21-N0028 | 150° OIL TEMP SENDER | 1 |
| J0011 | 21-38mm HOSE CLIPS | 7 |

*SECTION C*

| | | |
|---|---|---|
| N0068 | 4 WAY SOCKETS | 3 |
| S0033 | -10 'O' RINGS | 30 |
| J12C-026-020 | EXHAUST STUDS | 24 |
| 12-S0017 | TRUMPET 'O' RINGS | 48 |
| 12-S0056 | THROTTLE TOP 'O' RINGS | 48 |
| 12-S0011 | FUEL FILTER 'O' RINGS | 5 |
| J12C-012-082 | FILTER MESH | 6 |
| 11-J0004 | INJECTOR CLIPS | 12 |
| 12-S0073 | INJECTOR 'O' RINGS | 12 |
| 12-J0002 | INJECTOR CLIPS | 24 |
| N0067 | 4 WAY SHELLS | 3 |
| 12-N0023 | THROTTLE POTENTIOMETERS | 5 |
| J12C-021-050 | OIL PUMP BRACKET | 1 |
| J12C-050-005 | ALTERNATOR MOUNTING BRACKET | 3 |
| 27-S0044 | EXHAUST GASKETS | 72 |
| 16-S0014 | COOPERS RINGS | 12 |
| J12C-012-007 | TRUMPET RETAINING RINGS | 12 |
| J12C-012-030*2 | INLET GASKETS | 12 |
| J12C-026-079 | EARTHING STUDS | 4 |
| J12C-026-048 | EARTH STUDS | 4 |
| | VALVE GRINDING PASTE | |

*SECTION D*

| | | |
|---|---|---|
| 27-N0030 | N82G SPARK PLUGS | 100 |
| | N80G SPARK PLUGS | 40 |
| J12C-021-032 | OIL PRESS SENDER MTG BLOCK | 1 |
| L0008 | 730 RTV | 1 |
| L0012 | BLUE HYLOMAR | 1 |
| N0024 | ROCAL A.S.P. PASTE | 1 |
| N0053 | MN 1604 BATTERIES | 4 |
| N0052 | MN 1500 BATTERIES | 4 |
| N0054 | MN 2400 BATTERIES | 4 |
| L0004 | STUDLOCK 270 | 1 |
| L0005 | BEARING FIT 641 | 1 |
| L0007 | LOCK 'N' SEAL | 1 |
| N0051 | MN 1400 BATTERIES | 4 |
| 21-N0027 | 0-10 BAR OIL PRESSURE SENDER | 2 |
| 12-N0039 | 0-10 BAR FUEL PRESSURE SENDER | 3 |
| | BATTERY HOLDERS | 2 |
| 27-E0064 | SPARK PLUG COPPER WASHERS | |
| L0002 | SMALL R.T.V. | 1 |
| L0021 | LOCTITE 648 | 1 |

*SECTION E*

| | | |
|---|---|---|
| 50-C0005 | ALTERNATOR BELTS | 6 |
| 21-C0004 | OIL PUMP BELTS | 6 |
| 20-C0003 | WATER PUMP BELTS | 7 |
| 17-S0015 | REAR CRANK OIL SEALS | 2 |
| J12C-030-004 | TIMING DISC | 1 |
| 18-S0026 | FRONT CRANK SEAL | 4 |
| 30-N0006 | MICRO PICK UPS | 3 |
| 12-C0007 | REGULATORS | 4 |
| 18-C0022 | CHAIN TENSIONER | 1 |
| J12C-030-001 | PICK UP BRACKET | 1 |
| J12C-035-005A | OIL PUMP PULLEY | 1 |
| | PISTON RINGS | 1 SET |
| J12C-012-068*78 | THROTTLE LINKAGE ASSEMBLY | 1 |
| 20-C0008 | 24 HOUR SPEC. WATER PUMP BELTS | 5 |

*SECTION F*

| | | |
|---|---|---|
| J12C-035-001 | CRANK PULLEY | 1 |
| J12C-035-008A | CRANK DRIVE FLANGE | 1 |
| J12C-023-002 | FILTER HOUSING | 1 |
| J12C-023-003 | LOCATING SPACER | 1 |
| J12C-023-005 | OIL FILTER | 1 |
| J12C-022-017 | 90° SUMP FITTINGS | 4 |
| J12C-024-003*1*2 | STARTER CLUTCH | 1 |
| L0017 | LARGE RTV | 1 |
| O0005 | ROCAL A.S.P. SPRAY | 1 |
| | ASSORTED VALVE TOPS | |
| | ASSORTED TY WRAPS | |

*SECTION G*

| | | |
|---|---|---|
| 28-N0005 | DISTRIBUTOR CAP BUILT WITH LEADS | 1 |
| K0004 | TANK TAPE | 1 |
| 30-N0015 | ECU | 4 |
| L0014 | GASKET EATER | 1 |
| 11-N0080 | INJECTION LOOMS | 2 |

*ALUMINIUM BOX*

| | | |
|---|---|---|
| J12C-024-003 | STARTER SHAFT & CLUTCH ASSEMBLY | 1 |
| J12C-012-023 | FUEL RAILS | 2 |
| J12C-020-011 | WATER RAILS 'A' BANK | 1 |
| J12C-020-012 | WATER RAILS 'B' BANK | 1 |
| | WATER PUMP ASSEMBLY | 1 |
| 21-Q0026 | OIL PUMP ASSEMBLY | 1 |
| 24-N0018 | STARTER MOTOR | 3 |
| | STARTER BUSHES | 2 |
| J12C-045-003 | FLYWHEEL | 1 |
| 15-C0061 | VALVE SPRINGS INNER | 12 |
| 15-C0062 | VALVE SPRINGS OUTER | 12 |
| 45-C0001 | CLUTCHES | 2 |
| 15-C0010 | VALVE COTTERS | 24 |
| | DISTRIBUTOR | 1 |
| J12C-015-020 | EXHAUST VALVES | 6 |
| J12C-015-022 | INLET VALVES | 12 |
| J12C-015-001*A | VALVE SPRING TOPS | 12 |
| J12C-015-028 | VALVE SPRING BASES | 12 |
| | DISTRIBUTOR CAP WITH H.T. LEADS | 2 |
| 30-N0017 | CD BOX | 2 |
| 27-N0030 | N82G SPARK PLUGS | 86 |
| 27-S0042 | HEAD GASKET 'A' BANK | 1 |
| 27-S0043 | HEAD GASKET 'B' BANK | 1 |
| 21-S0050 | OIL INLET HOUSING GASKETS | 3 |
| 20-S0029 | WATER PUMP GASKETS | 3 |
| 20-S0030 | WATER PUMP GASKETS | 3 |
| L0017 | LARGE RTV | 1 |
| D0001 | AIR FILTER SPRAY | 1 |
| 30-N0011 | FUEL PRESSURE SENDER LOOM | 3 |
| O0005 | ROCAL A.S.P. SPRAY | 1 |
| 50-N0001 | 80 AMP ALTERNATOR | 3 |
| O0001 | AIR FILTER SPRAY | 1 |

**RACE PLAN TO LE MANS - 1990**

Estimated Race Pace = 3'42"

Therefore Stint Time = (3.7 x 13) + (2.1) = 50.2 mins

Stints in first 12 hours = 14.34 = 186.5 laps
Maximum laps in race 186 x 2 = 372 laps
Fuel for 372 laps + warm-up
= 2550 + less 3 litres left in car 2547/373 litres = 6.82 l/lap

Total stints in race = 28

Therefore for 13 laps 6.82 x 13 = 88.76 litres
Computer set at 89 litres for 13 laps
This leaves 10 litres in car in case of an extra lap.

After 12 hours of 91 litres per 13 litres stint estimated fuel usage = 1300 litres
Therefore 1247 litres for last 12 hours
Therefore Cars must complete 13 laps with 87 litres

FIRST PIT STOPS

Two cars of the 4 (cars in positions 2 and 4 in line of pits) stop after 12 laps (11 race laps). Cars in pit positions 1 and 3 stop after 13 total laps (12 race laps).

| | | |
|---|---|---|
| Pad Stops | - | Fronts every 5 stops |
| | - | Rears every 6 stops |

PIT STOPS TO INCLUDE

| | |
|---|---|
| FUEL | : Approx 90 litres - stop time = 90 secs) |
| TYRES | : All tyres changed |
| SCREEN CLEAN | : By front wheel man |
| RAD DUCT CLEARING | : By Rt front wheel man |
| WATER PURGE | : By Rt front wheel man |
| VISUAL CHECK (Brakes, Body, etc) | : By all |
| ZERO FUEL METERS (BOTH) | : By Driver |
| DRINKS BOTTLE | : By Driver |
| OIL CHECK | : Engine Shop |
| * FRONT PADS | : Each 4 or 5 Stops |
| * REAR PADS | : Each 5 or 6 Stops |

Approximately 29 Stints therefore 28 Pit Stops
* Pad Stops to be verified after practice.

## Le Mans Personnel List and Individual Responsibilities

| Name | Race Job | Pre-Race Job |
|---|---|---|
| Tom Walkinshaw | Team Owner | Team Owner |
| Roger Silman | Race Director | Team Director |
| Ross Brawn | Technical Director | Technical Director |
| Kevin Lee | Team Manager | Team Manager |
| Tony Dowe | 3rd car manager | American Team Manager |
| Ken Page | Driver co-ordinator | Assistant Team Manager |
| Andy Beckett | Parts co-ordinator | Paddock Control |
| Helen Shergold | Administration | Administration |
| Alastair Macqueen | 1st car Engineer | Chief Race Engineer |
| Steve Farrell | 2nd car Engineer | Race Engineer |
| Dave Benbow | 3rd car Engineer | Race Engineer |
| John Piper | 4th car Engineer | Race Engineer |
| Andy Moss | Fuel Monitor | Fuel Monitor |
| Jeff Wilson | Floating Mechanic | Chief Mechanic |
| Peter Metcalf | Gearbox Mechanic | Gearbox mechanic |
| Andy McNiven | Electronics | Radio/Electronics |
| Alva Claxton | 1st Car Mech | 1st Car Snr Mech |
| Tim Strudwick | 1st car mech | 1st car mech |
| Dave Hands | 1st car mech | 1st car mech |
| Greg Baker | 1st car mech | 1st car mech |
| Rod Benoist | 2nd Car Mech | 2nd Car Snr Mech |
| Chris Tuckey | 2nd car Mech | 2nd car mech |
| Viv Cowley | 2nd car mech | 2nd car mech |
| Nigel Weeks | 2nd car mech | 2nd car mech |
| John Jackson | 3rd Car Mech | 3rd Car Mech |
| Mark Redbond | 3rd car mech | 3rd car mech |
| Peter Hodgkinson | 3rd car mech | 3rd car mech |
| Larry Zelesnik | 3rd car mech | 3rd car mech |
| Clive Parker | 4th Car Mech | 4th Car Snr Mech |
| Gary Davies | 4th car mech | 4th car mech |
| Edwin Wood | 4th car mech | 4th car mech |
| Duncan Charnell | 4th car mech | 4th car mech |
| Allan Scott | Snr Engine Manager | Engine Control |
| Charlie Bamber | Engine Manager | Engine care |
| Chris Middlemass | Telemetry | Telemetry |
| Tom Remedios | Telemetry | Telemetry |
| Alex Livadeas | Telemetry | Telemetry |
| Pete Tyrell | 1st car fuel lever | 1st Car Engine man |
| Nigel Webb | 2nd car fuel lever | 2nd car engine man |
| Grant Rushton | 3rd car fuel lever | 3rd car engine man |
| Andy Penny | 4th car fuel lever | 4th car engine man |
| Keith Partridge | 1st Car Refueller | Chief truckie |
| Mark Blackwell | 1st car Vent Man | Fabricator |
| Darren Warren | 2nd car Refueller | Parts / stickers |
| Martin Coventry | 2nd Car Refueller | Pit equip & awnings |
| Winston Bush | 3rd Car Refueller | 3rd Car Snr Mech |
| Vik Warren | 3rd Car Vent Man | Mechanic |
| Mark Owen | 4th Car Refueller | Chief Fabricator |
| Richard Ponting | 4th Car Vent Man | Spare Mechanic |
| Patrick Rennison | 1st Car Fireman | Stores / stickers |
| Roger Harding | 2nd Car Fireman | Fabricator |
| Michael Green | 3rd Car Fireman | Bodywork |
| Rob Vetter | 4th Car Fireman | Stores |
| tba truckie | 1st Car tyreman | Pit equip & Awnings |
| Andy Saxton | 2nd Car Tyreman | Wheelcare |
| Richard Dendy | 3rd Car Tyreman | Fabricator |
| Dave Jeffrey | 4th Car Tyreman | Fabricator |
| Rolf Steur | Tyre Movements | Tyre Co-ordinator |
| Simon Hornblow | Tyre Movements | Wheel care |
| Steve Baxter | Tyre movements | Wheel & Vehicle care |
| Andy Keene | Tyre movements | Wheel & vehicle care |
| Mick McCrohon | Bodywork | Bodywork |
| Dave Hanna | Biker | Stickers/ bike |
| Andy Wymer | Radio Link | Stickers / radios |
| Michael Wilson | Radio link | Clean/polish cars 1+2 |
| Steve Harvey | Radio Link | Clean/polish cars 3+4 |
| Dr I Robinson | Doctor | Doctor |
| Tom Ryan | Physio | Physio |
| Marion Campaign | Physio | Physio |
| Richard West | Press & PR | Press & PR |
| Chris Leese | Motorhome control | Motorhome control |
| Andy King | Motorhome Communication | M'home communication |
| Fiona Miller | Press & PR Assist | Press & PR Assist |
| Anthony Seyler | Overalls care/drying | Laundry/kit |
| Gary Timms | Chief Chef | Chief Chef |
| John Charlton | Chef | Chef |
| Hostess x 4 | | |

| Name | Job |
|---|---|
| John Hassan | Zytek |
| Andy Wright | Zytek |
| Rob Gustafson | Roni |
| Derek Payne | Roni |
| Alan Longland | Signallers x 13 |
| Dinah Longland | |
| Ken Quattermass | |
| Peta Quatermass | |
| George Whightman | |
| Mick Cook | |
| Tony Scrivens | |
| Karl Britton | |
| Martin Bates | |
| Peter Morley | |
| Ian Schuler | |
| Gary Britton | |
| Martin Crowley | |
| Eric Cowcill | Timekeepers x 6 |
| Terry Stevens | |
| Nick Paine | |
| Dave MacGill | |
| Lesley Dawes-Gamble | |
| Graham Lond | |
| Martin Brundle | Drivers x 12 |
| Alain Ferte | |
| David Leslie | |
| Jan Lammers | |
| Andy Wallace | |
| Franz Konrad | |
| John Nielsen | |
| Price Cobb | |
| Eliseo Salazar | |
| Davy Jones | |
| Luis Sala | |
| Michel Ferte | |

## Engine Division Race Car Check List

*CHECK LIST CAR - CHASSIS*

*Injection loom in air box and all connections.*
*Check for full throttle.*
*Check throttle pot reading.*
*Remove spark plugs and inspect.*
*Check engine loom and connections.*
*Check exhaust nuts for tightness.*
*Thoroughly check primaries for cracks.*
*Check and tighten all hose connections.*
*Inspect oil pump for leaks.*
*Remove starter shrouding and inspect.*
*Starter connections and loom for routing.*
*Check alternator connections and loo,.*
*Inspect alternator bracket.*
*Check alternator, oil pump and water pump belt tension.*
*Check all nuts and bolts for tightness.*
*Check water level and adjust if necessary.*
*Check Goodridge lines for leaks and chafing.*
*Check torque of throttle slide to head nuts.*
*Check E.C.U. settings.*
*Check fuel pressure.*
*Check coil lead tywrapped to CD box.*
*R.T.U. electrical connections to CD box.*
*Check CD box is secure.*
*Check throttle return springs.*
*Check rose joints on throttle system and lube.*
*Check RS connections, pins for security.*
*Check JagShop fixtures and fittings to engine.*

As can be seen from the specification sheet below once again the Le Mans fuel exceeded the Group C road fuel specification but we were never aware of the final specifications until race week. The sheet shows this fuel was at the very top of the density scale, an excess Benzene content that was actually illegal to use in the EU, with higher octane rating as well. This fuel was totally suited to turbocharged racing cars both aiding fuel consumption and detonation control.

**24 HEURES DU MANS**
**16 - 17 JUIN 1990**

AUTO

CARACTERISTIQUES DU SUPERCARBURANT POUR LES 24 HEURES

- Indice d'octane recherche: 99,9
- Masse volumique: 0,780
- Teneur en plomb: 0,152
- Teneur en oxygène: 1,92 %
- Teneur en azote: 0,005 %
- Teneur en benzène: 5,2 %

Le Mans always produces something new and this year it would come in the form of the Japanese assault led by Nissan who had turned up in force to win. No less than five Nissan Motorsport International race cars and two more in private hands were entered, as well as two test cars that would not be used in the race. Toyota Team Toms had two of their Lola 90C-V race cars as well as a spare car with Toyota Team Sard one race car plus a spare. Mazda Speed had four of its 787 and 767 rotary engined variants.

And so to qualifying once again and TWR were not putting much energy into this, but the Japanese teams were looking to take on the fastest Porsches as the qualifying position was very important for the people back in Japan. Turbocharged cars were here en mass with 35 eligible to start the race; and over 20 of them were Porsche 962C variants.

Pole by a large margin went to the triple Bs Nissan team of Brancatelli/Blundell/Bailey on 3.27.02 and it was only the Larrauri/Pareja/Brun Porsche 962 with a second fastest time of 3.33.06 that took total glory away from a Nissan lock out of all the top five times. After the Brun 962 Porsche came the Japanese crew of Hasemi/Hoshino/Suzuki on 3.33.17; the American team of Brabham/Robinson/Daly on 3.33.28 and European team of Acheson/Donnelly/Grouillard on 3.35.76 in

**Tom Walkinshaw Racing Ltd**
**SILK CUT JAGUAR TEAM**
**WORLD SPORTSCAR CHAMPIONSHIP**

| DATE: 23/5/90 | CIRCUIT: LE MANS | CHASSIS No: | ISSUE: (2) |
|---|---|---|---|
| ENG NO: | GBOX NO: | SET UP BY: | |

| CAMBER | TOE | RIDE HEIGHTS | CORNER WEIGHTS |
|---|---|---|---|
| -2° / -2° | 0 / 0 | 56 / 56 | |
| -1° / -1° | 3 IN / 3 IN | 86 / 86 RACE TYRES | |
| ± ⅛ DEGREE | ± 0.25 mm | ± 1.0 mm | ± 3 kg DIAGONAL SUM |

| SPRINGS FRONT | SPRINGS REAR | DAMPERS FRONT | DAMPERS REAR | PACKERS FRONT | PACKERS REAR | | |
|---|---|---|---|---|---|---|---|
| 1250 Ti | 1500 Ti | KONI BA 83 | BILSTEIN (SHORT TOP) | KONI LONG RUBBER | KONI SHORT RUBBER | CWP | 12 - 31 |
| | * 10MM PRELOAD. | R 7 | R 500 | DROOP | | 1st | 14 - 42 |
| | | B 4 | B 150 | 1/4" | GG 003 PLATES | 2nd | 17 - 39 |
| | | | | | | 3rd | 21 - 34 |
| | | | | | | 4th | 25 - 31 |
| | | | | | | 5th | 27 - 28 |
| | | | | | | 6th | / |
| | | | | | | DIFF | SPOOL |

| CASTOR | ARB | FRONT | REAR | REAR WING | | FRONT DOWNFORCE | |
|---|---|---|---|---|---|---|---|
| LEFT | TYPE | CARBON | STEEL | TYPE | SPRINT 60/40 | SPLITTER | PROFILE LE MANS |
| 2° | RATE | +25% | 8MM | POSITION | LM '90 | RAD EXIT | No |
| | POSITION | 14-15MM | F. SOFT | ANGLE | 6° O/A (15° FOR) | LOUVRES | YES |
| RIGHT | FEATURES | | | RETURN | 1/4" | BIBS | No |
| 2° | | | | FEATURES | AJUSTABLE MAIN AND FLAP | RAD VENTS | No |

| WHEELS | | CALIPERS | AP. 4-POT (ALI PISTON) | DUCTING | | FRONT MAIN | NACA |
|---|---|---|---|---|---|---|---|
| FRONT | BBS 17"x13" | DISCS | 14" 48 VANE 4X GROOVED. | REAR MAIN | SPRINT | FRONT CALIPER | OPEN |
| REAR | BBS 18x14½" | PADS | DS 11 | REAR CALIPER | No | FACE DUCT | YES |

| TYRES | |
|---|---|
| FRONT | 24.5"x17" |
| REAR | 28.5"x18" |

GENERAL FEATURES: LE MANS NOSE, NACA SIDE PANEL, 'CAMEL' TAIL - '90 V6 WHEEL COVERS.

*Le Mans race car set-up sheet.*

fifth. The Toyota of Lees/Ogawa/Sekiya was next with 3.37.13. Five Japanese based cars in the top six places making European car manufacturers nervous.

The Jaguars then qualified seventh with Jones/M. Ferté in 3.36.1; Brundle/David Leslie/A. Ferté eighth with 3.36.55; Nielsen/Cobb/Salazar ninth with 3.37 and Lammers/Franz Konrad seventeenth with 3.39.78.

The American TWR team were at Le Mans to run a single Jaguar and had over time developed some ideas of their own, after three consecutive Daytona 24 hour contests that had resulted in two wins and a second placing. There were some differences of opinion between the two teams with Kidlington Race Director Roger a little reluctant to accept what could be seen as challenges to some of the established thoughts from Kidlington. This though was all handled in a professional manner and any small inter team rivalry has its place with some productive reassessments always welcome to move forward. Tony Dowe was trying some different pieces here and with that team producing the slowest qualifying times Roger was happy with the UK specification cars and was then a little dismissive of the American team in the post qualifying meeting. Roger was a very staunch and proud supporter of all things British and was usually suspicious of other countries ways of doing things, although unusually he did like the French and France.

TWR technical director, Ross Brawn, by this time in 1990 had built up a separate team of designers to work on TWR's next project, XJR-14, and that was where his focus lay. XJR-14 had to be completed and tested ready for the completely new series in 1991. Ross had given me the impression that 24 hour events were not good career enhancing situations, and was happy to leave most of it to Roger. Clive Steeper who had been employed as team manager had resigned in May of 1990 after some of his ideas had challenged the previous decision making model, wishing to have the actual position he had been employed for, and the decision making that would go with it. Trying to break the mould he had invited himself to a board meeting which did not go down well, and he was soon gone. I had been assigned to support Tony Dowe and the American team at this event while managing each engine division person assigned to the other three cars. Roger was confident that the three Kidlington cars and their driver combinations would be the winning format and there had been an element with this small change from previous years in overall management that produced a motivating aspect for the American team, as well as myself, that he had not taken into account. Tony Dowe who worked for TWR from 1987 until 1998 as managing director of TWR USA has kindly written the following piece from his point of view on how that story unfolded; it is an interesting exercise for me to have another point of view for you all to consider. Sauber did not come to Le Mans this year as the new C11 had been developed in high downforce specification only, as well as the race this year not counting for the championship.

## Tony Dowe on Le Mans 1990 ...

During 1990 while based at TWR America in Valparaiso one of my duties was to supply a couple of cars as part of the massive TWR/Jaguar effort at Le Mans. Unfortunately, it was always made clear, never by Tom Walkinshaw of course, that the American cars were only there to support the real effort that was run from Kidlington. Obviously, this became a bit second hand and so after being the supporting act in 1988 and 1989 I gave some serious thought as to how to:

a) Win the race
b) Circumvent the restrictions placed on my U.S. team because of the supporting role we were expected to play. Let me say here that you should only undertake such an action if you are sure that you can carry it off!

To achieve anything less than the win is to open one's self up for a very long period looking for a new job! Of course, if you win, then most of your sins are forgiven. I always felt that TWR USA were a better race team for this event than the UK managed team for no other reason than by the time Le Mans came around we had done a 24 hour race (Daytona), a 12 hour race (Sebring), and a couple of sprint races. The Group C team had probably only done a couple of races and some testing with their racing season starting almost three months later than ours. We were very sharp long distance wise by 1990. We had finished first and second at the Daytona 24 hours that year, 1990, and had well prepared cars that raced each other the whole 24 hours. It was a fantastic race and result.

TWR USA also had a couple of very good engineers, Ian Reed, recently formerly head of development at Penske, and Dave Benbow recently with Prodrive. Ian and Dave were very good in their respective areas. Both were and are lateral thinkers and complemented each other very well. Ian was, as now, very good with the suspension and we were running suspension dampers, for example, that were much ahead of the ones used by the UK team. We had briefly used a pair on the rear of the Jaguar in 1989 when Davy Jones had led the race in the early stages.

The biggest problem that had to be overcome was that, along

with most of the other team cars, we were only allowed a single engine for both practice and the race. The only team car that had a qualifying engine was Martin Brundle's. As we were now running the V6 turbo cars on a regular basis in the IMSA series, we were able to take one of our V12 cars out of the mix and prepare it with a lot of love and care. We used chassis 288, which had won our first ever IMSA race in the USA back at the 1988 Daytona 24 hours. The lead mechanic Winston Bush was ex Kidlington, and he did a super job of building a car to the exact same specification as the UK cars. The week before we had to leave for Le Mans we were racing at Lime Rock Park when John Nielsen and Price Cobb won with the turbo XJR-10, exactly a year after we had débuted the first TWR Jaguar turbo. There to see the car win was the head of TWR engines, Allan Scott. Allan is now back in New Zealand enjoying his retirement and raced his own ex TWR Group A Rover and now comes over to the UK to compete in classic races in his 1995 Super Touring 323 Mazda.

After the race we had a super night at a very nice local restaurant run by an English guy called Terry with lots of drink, etc. After the meal I took Allan to one side and asked him why my car could not have a qualifying engine for Le Mans? Allan told me to use common sense, "It's just not going to happen". I then asked what would happen if we had a misfire at the end of qualifying and the problem could not be found. Allan said obviously there would be a spare engine for such an eventuality. He had been booked on a flight from Kennedy that night back to the UK. I then played the trump card. I produced an envelope from inside my jacket and told Allan that inside was a ticket for the next morning's Concorde flight to London. It was his if he found a problem with our engine after Le Mans qualifying. Allan looked around and then took the envelope and put it in his jacket pocket. The game was on! Only Ian Reed was aware of what I was planning. And he was like a kid when I told him the bait had been taken.

The now finished vanilla 288 chassis was sent to the UK for painting. We then set about putting together a care package of our IMSA goodies for fitting when we got to Le Mans. We had different roll bars front and rear, and different shock absorbers front and rear to the Kidlington specs. But the biggest item was some very special one piece (Billet) brake calipers that Ian had designed and we had built here in Atlanta. They were made to accept a much thicker brake pad than standard, Performance Friction made the pads for us. So now we could also go further without a brake pad change. We also had Rabbit (A legendary fabricator who still lives in the Georgia mountains) build us some really trick pad changing tools. The gearbox was built with a limited slip differential not a spool as used in the past. That thinking was if a driveshaft failed you could get back to the pits. We had Kenny Hill of Metalore (they now make most of the F1 world's hubs/drive shafts and axles) make us some super strong F1 type drive shafts.

One further item that would prove very useful was the use of the American radios. Every year we had gone to Le Mans the circuit length meant that the European radios supplied by a guy we called Crackly Ken usually gave up around large parts of the circuit. With the additions of the chicanes along the Mulsanne straight, Le Mans was now closer to the aero level of Daytona, making our own rear wing specification that we had used at Daytona suitable for Le Mans. We started practice with just a few bits changed, radios etc, so there was not much notice taken of what we were doing.

There was a bit more interest when the brakes went on and the roll bars were changed, but at the early morning meetings Roger's comments were mainly directed towards us in the manner of: "So what silly things have you the Americans changed now?"

Roger was more concerned with why Jan Lammers, always an independent thinker here, could not match Martin Brundle's practice times in the UK specification cars. He did not like drivers, or anyone else for that matter, to think for themselves about how the race should be run. I'm sure that Tom had some idea of what we were doing as he was a regular visitor to IMSA races and was aware of our development items, but he never said anything to me about what we were doing.

Our driver line up was very good in Big John Nielsen, Price Cobb, but Eliseo Salazar who was paying was the least experienced of all the drivers. Obviously, John and Price knew what we had fitted and were very happy because it brought the car to the same specification as they had been used to racing in IMSA. Unfortunately, after the end of practice, Allan confirmed an engine misfire in our car that had no real explanation or guaranteed fix at the post qualifying debrief; We had to change the engine. Another hurdle crossed, because if Allan had gone back on the deal then the whole plan would have probably sunk out of sight.

Friday's pre-race preparation brought to light another small problem. The gearbox dog rings (gear selector engagement ring) were being used by one of the drivers in a way that was too heavy on the gear changes. As we had lots of experience of John and Price it was obvious that Eliseo was the problem. I went and found Julian Randles, then of Spice Engineering, who Eliseo drove for sometimes in IMSA and had a discussion about his experiences with Eliseo and his use of the gearbox. Julian confirmed that Eliseo's style of gear changing was quite heavy on the dog rings. I had a long day of thinking about how to deal with this potential problem, and it was a problem because with this dog ring gearbox we were going to probably lose third and maybe fourth gear if history was any guide. I went to dinner with Tom, his lady (later wife) Martine, and a guy from Jaguar who I honestly can't remember who he was (probably Ron Elkins). During dinner I told Tom of my concerns and suggested that it might be a good strategy if I kept Eliseo out of the car for as long as possible in order to keep a seat free should one of the other favourite drivers have a problem. Tom agreed and so at our race morning briefing I told the drivers that we were going to use Big John and Price through the evening and night until Sunday morning, when Eliseo would be fresh for the remainder of the race.

## Race day

Just as we parked the car on the dummy grid, mechanic JJ found a small fuel leak from one of the fuel pump unions. Now, as it is today, there can be no work done on the car on the dummy grid. So what were we to do? One of the XJR-12LM design features was that the whole fuel system, pumps, filters etc, were mounted in the left-hand side pod on quick release clips; it would only take moments to change them. The problem was how to make the change with the whole ACO police walking up and down the grid. Fortunately, we had made some very nice mock leather pouches to protect the spare fuel pump assemblies in and while the whole team posed in front of the car with one of the features of the pre-start grid, the Hawaiian Tropic girls, JJ slid inside and changed the leaking pump assembly for a new one. Honestly, I think that in another life JJ would have made a great David Copperfield.

The race itself was quite easy (not what I remember Tony! AWS ). One of the big race advantages we had was that having run at Daytona we knew that the standard 480 compound

SATURDAY 16TH JUNE

| | |
|---|---|
| 06.30 hrs | Wake-up call by Ken Page |
| 07.00 hrs | Depart - NB: assemble in reception at 06.55 hrs |
| 07.30 hrs | Breakfast for Group B |
| 08.00 hrs | Breakfast for Group A |
| 08.00 - 09.30 hrs | ACCESS TO PIT LANE |
| 09.30 hrs | LAST CALL OF RESERVED CARS |
| 10.00 - 10.30 hrs | NON-TIMED PRACTICE |
| 11.45 hrs | TWR Drivers' briefing |
| 12.00 hrs | Lunch for Group B |
| 12.30 hrs | Lunch for Group A |
| 13.30 hrs | Complete fuel tank top-up |
| 13.30 hrs | Weather report by ACO over load-speaker |
| 13.30 hrs | Cars pushed onto track in front of pit |
| 14.10 hrs | Introduction of Drivers |
| 15.00 hrs | Fuel meters set to zero |
| 15.00 hrs | Cars pushed onto the starting grid |
| 15.10 hrs | Safety pins removed from fire extinguishers |
| 15.20 hrs | Grid completed |
| 15.30 hrs | All work stops on cars |
| 15.42 hrs | Pit Lane is about to be closed (horn sounds) |
| 15.44 hrs | Exit of pit lane is closed |
| 15.53 hrs | Formation lap begins |
| 16.00 hrs | Rolling start |
| 16.10 hrs | Snack |
| 20.00 hrs | Supper |
| 24.00 hrs | Snack |

rear Goodyear tyres would not last a double stint on the Jaguars at Le Mans. Back in February at Daytona we had run a much harder 600 compound tyre during the heat of the day. This plan had then gone wrong when we had first arrived at Le Mans to find that Goodyear Europe had no 600 compound tires available. Our tyre guy, Kenny Szymanski, had a full-time job as an American Airlines steward, who because of his seniority with that airline could chose his monthly schedule; and have a second job supporting us at all of our American races looking after our tyres. I called back to the states and had 10 sets of 600 compound tires shipped in thanks to Ken Moore of Rapid Movements.

When we started double stinting the tires and having shorter pit stops, not needing to change disc pads and returning our race car to the track with tyres that only needed half a lap to return to racing temperatures I had a very uptight meeting with Tom as to what was going on. I told Tom our strategy and then gave some of the 600 rear compound tyres to Brundle's car. It later turned out that Andy Wallace had been complaining of inconsistent tire performance. A problem then surfaced around 10pm; a car had caught fire at the Porsche curves and the ACO had put out a pace car, or safety car as it was then called. John Nielsen had been in for fuel a few of laps earlier and he had called in and told me it would take a bit of time to clean up; just like we would over in America. Good US radios at work. I called him straight into the pits to top off the fuel. I then had TW on my case about giving up track position. The UK team cars continued running slowly around under the caution flags while we topped up the race car with fuel and quickly returned to the circuit and joined the slow-moving pack. They would then have to later pit with the race back at full speed, and with the restricted refuelling flows that had to be used, loose more race distance during that time than we had. About an hour later we went into the lead after everyone else was in the pits refuelling, and this was an important move for our team. It was a lead we never gave up.

The next bit of drama was that Price was slowly dehydrating; remember these cars had no power steering, minimal ventilation and no onboard drink bottles, and over 5000 lbs. of downforce in those days. During the middle of the night we had to ask Big John to triple stint while Price recovered. Big John was a star then, still a star now. Then the Brundle car, which had been fighting a slow water leak from the engine's header tank, finally called it a day after overheating had stretched the water pump drive belt finally breaking it and not being repairable. Tom came and asked me if I thought the car would be able to last until the finish. You can imagine my reply.

TW took Eliseo off our team and told him he was not going to get in the car and he was putting Brundle in instead. You can imagine how heartbroken Eliseo was with this decision as he could see a real chance of a Le Mans win. So around 8:00 am Brundle got in the car. The only thing we now had to deal with was that 4th gear had decided it had enough and gave up around 10am with 6 hours still to go. This meant that the drivers had to change around the gate from 3rd to 5th, not a great problem, but enough to cause concern as 5th gear was selected at the end of the pit straight before heading for the Dunlop bridge, and now get some very unhappy looks from Tom.

The final drama was a couple of stops from the end, we had a scheduled brake pad change and JJ (John Jackson, our regular chief mechanic, ex Williams F1) found a couple of caliper pistons leaking as this was being done. We then had to change one of our mega expensive brake calipers. Now they were a bit tight on the locating studs, so Pete Hodge (Peter Hodgkinson, a New Zealander and now the new car build manager at Mercedes F1) took a very big hammer to our beautiful machined caliper to quickly remove it and replace it with a pre-bled new one. Job done and the total time lost six minutes but still a lap ahead of the second placed Porsche. So we finally won; it was very satisfying.

Mike Dale, then MD of Jaguar North America and a true racer had supported us all the way and gave terrific support as the laps wound down. Our car was the only chassis that had won both the 24 hour Daytona and Le Mans as far as I am aware of. After the race there was much celebrating with champagne. I remember taking Tom back to the airport and he told me I had done good, but I then had to find my way back to the Chateau where we were staying. Now that was a trip, I was so tired, and a bit the worse for champagne; I can't remember how many times I went off the road while driving Tom's personal Jaguar.

The next morning, we went back to the circuit to see the car and it was very emotional for us when we untapped the engine cover and lifted the rear deck off, we had never lifted it in the whole race. A couple of weeks later the whole team who had been at Le Mans went to New Jersey and had dinner with Mike Dale and Bob Burden, another super Jaguar person, in a small restaurant a few miles from the Jaguar headquarters; very nice.

*The author looking tired after 32 hours non-stop.*
Images: *Jaguarmagazine.com*

As mentioned before I was assigned to this car with Tony Dowe and the American team, and I will fill in a few of my own points that show how different people see the same subject. It had all started six weeks before Le Mans when Schmitthelm, our valve spring manufacturer working with some new spring material from Sweden, had then informed me that this batch of new material had been rejected because of very small internal material faults called inclusions. This was a disaster as we were already in the process of building seven engines at up to 150 hours a piece, with four needing to be fitted to cars for shake down and pre-Le Mans testing; and so the previous batch of springs had to be used for these engines.

Fast forward to the IMSA race at Lime Rock where I would normally leave before the race ended, and then drive back to New York to catch an evening flight to return to the UK. By this time a new batch of spring material had been sourced and the springs were ready to be picked up from Germany on the Monday. It has been my intention to take a plane from Heathrow to Germany, pick up some valve springs and return to Kidlington just in time to have these fitted to the last spare engine being built. This then would be the engine that we could later possibly fit to the Jaguar run by the American team. I had informed Tony of the possibility that this engine with latest spec valve springs could be built but it would be a close-run thing time wise and not available to be pre-fitted to the American run car. It was then that he came up with the plan that allowed me to stay and celebrate the XJR-10 turbo win with the team that night, and also stick to the pickup schedule in Germany- by flying Concorde. This was not a problem for me, helped by the fact that Roger had assigned me to support Tony Dowe at Le Mans and I wanted to get at least one engine with the new spring material in the race. It was no hardship for me to accept the flight offer and direct the engine Tony's way as he had always shown patience and understanding with our long-distance engine deliveries. It would then be the second time TW had very kindly paid for me to fly Concorde, although this second flight was hidden in the TWR America accounts under multiple internal team member flights, thanks to the supportive invoicing from the travel company they used.

I had then left my personal items with the team and with a completely empty carry on suitcase travelled via Concorde to Heathrow and then onto Schmitthelm in Germany, filling my small suitcase with 250 of the new material valve springs. This ended up with a questionable look as the 20kg weight stretched the handle of my small case as I tried to look inconspicuous and casually walked through the green zone with no paper work for VAT. The orchestrated engine swap was carried out although Roger was not that happy and quite rightly suspicious of the reasons put forward at the time. My main concern at Le Mans had always been the large gap between the fourth and the longer fifth gear needed for the Jaguar on the Mulsanne with fuel economy in mind, as well as the down change gaps along with missed gears and at least two places where the car was airborne, pushing the valve spring limits. At Le Mans I had suggested to Tony Dowe a 300rpm lower fifth gear ratio than that on the specification sheet to give better fifth gear response now that we were using the higher drag configuration XJR-12LM because of the chicanes built into the Mulsanne straight reducing previous top speeds. The American team then fitted this lower fifth gear ratio to the gearbox. When TW had found that we had altered the gear ratio from the approved spec he had looked up at us both sitting in the pit box a couple of hours before the start of the race, and by now knowing most of the things that were happening and perhaps feeling some pressures coming from Roger, had simply said, "You are f.....g mental". Tony Dowe held his ground and it was soon too late to change anything. This lower fifth gear would later vindicate itself when fourth gear was lost around 10am on the Sunday morning. For the next six hours the engine was taken to maximum rpm in third before shifting to fifth and the V12 engine torque helping to overcome this to produce competitive lap times, with few realising we had a problem.

The front caliper change to the USA spec was a good move on the winning XJR-12LM as the new chicanes produced the need for heavy braking and a deteriorating brake pedal over time. The cars were reported to be very demanding to drive because of the increased braking needed and Andy Wallace, already very fit, was reported as having lost 7kgs over this 24 hour event. His right leg had given up by the time of his finishing stint in the race, and with the additional throttle return spring fitted for Le Mans he was unable to hold the accelerator fully down without sliding his left leg over to use both feet on the accelerator pedal down the Mulsanne straight. The exhaust systems were to the same specifications as the year before and remained for all future endurance races; but this time they were new systems for 1990.

We were chased to the very end by the Brun Motorsport Repsol Porsche of Brun/Larrauri/Pareja only for it to suffer a blown turbocharger fifteen minutes from the end after completing 359 laps, promoting the #2 Lammers/Wallace/Konrad Jaguar four laps behind into second place and a great result for all involved. Third place was taken by the Alpha Team Porsche from Japan, driven by Britons Tiff Needell, David Sears and Anthony Reid. The Alpha team Porsche had passed the fourth placed Bell/Stuck/Jelinski Joest Porsche when it needed a new turbo wastegate fitted at lunchtime and finishing nine laps behind the winners. Masahiro Hasemi (J)/ Kazuyoshi Hoshino (J)/Toshio Suzuki (J) were in the first Nissan, 11 laps behind, and sixth place went to the Geoff Lees (GB)/Hitoshi Qgawa (J)/Masanori Sekiya (J) Toyota R32V 12 laps behind the winning #3 Jaguar.

Porsche had a high finishing rate here with 14 of the cars finishing from 18 competing at Le Mans, although a large number were driven to finish with many up to 50 laps down on the leading Jaguar. TWR had a 50% finishing record; Nissan 42%;Toyota 33% and Lancia 0%

At the end of the race TW was determined to have Roger and myself on the podium but this area at Le Mans is limited to team owners and crew. Sir John Egan was in the final week of his tenure at Jaguar after the buyout of the company by Ford America, and his Ford replacement Bill Hayden was there as well and both were now on the podium. We knew Ford's man was not that interested in motor racing and he had to be looked after and feel the excitement of the crowd, so with them allowed on the podium the security guards had stopped us; only TW allowed to go up. TW argued with the security guard for some time and then when all looked lost, as he turned away one of the two security guards did also. TW timed the shoulder charge to perfection tipping the poor man over the stairs guard rail and throwing me up the stairs before any order could be maintained. It was a great moment for us all, somehow for me more important than the first win in 1988. It proved that the first win was not a one off, and that we were the real deal and good enough to repeat it.

Was all this enough to keep new owners Ford enthusiastic for Jaguar's policy of generating sales via motor racing?

## Andy Wallace's debrief post Le Mans ...

**Chassis** : 290 (car 2)

**Gearbox** : It lasted for 24 hours ok - the only change from the start of the race was bit of grating from 3rd to 4th, this was ok if short shift at 6k into 4th. The clutch lasted well too.

**Ratios** : Ideal

**Instruments** : All fine except backlight on fuel computor went out, and display was intermitant & needed re-setting all the time.

**Radio** : Very good Wed/Thurs, a bit crackly & lower volume on race days, but ok.

**Mirrors** : Very good

**Brakes** : Early in race with blanking on front ducts, it was locking rears - without the blanking the balance was good, just locking fronts into chicanes on turn-in.
When the pads got low, there was a lot of knock-off, especially after Porsche Curves - good pedal if pumped-up.
Generally the brakes were up to the job, but the pedal effort required was far too high. If it was possible to press hard enough then the car would stop ok, but ½ way through the second of each double stint, my foot became a problem and I had difficulty keeping the throttle pedal down, let alone stopping the car at the chicanes.

**Balance Bar** : n/a

**Traction** : Generally good, although it varied between sets of tyres - my first stint set gave extremely poor traction, then in the next stint (different tyres), it was fine again all stint.

**Balance** : There were differencies in tyres, and with nose louvers blanked/open, but this is my general feeling of the balance:-

| | | | |
|---|---|---|---|
| T1 | * | turn-in | u/s 1-2 |
| | | c.o.d. | u/s 1 |
| | | exit | n to o/s ½ |
| T2 | * | turn-in | u/s 1½-2 |
| | | c.o.d. | u/s 1-2 |
| | | exit | u/s 1 to o/s ½ |
| T3 | * | turn-in | u/s 1 |
| | | mid-corner | u/s 1 |
| | | exit | u/s 1 (o/s 2 if touch kerb) |
| T4 | * | turn-in | u/s 1-2 (o/s 2 if can't stop or lock rears) |
| | | c.o.d. | n |
| | | mid-corner | u/s 1-2 |
| | | c.o.d. | n |
| | | exit | o/s ½ |
| T5 | * | turn-in | u/s 1-2 |
| | | c.o.d. | n |
| | | mid-corner | u/s 1-2 |
| | | exit | u/s 1 |
| T6 | * | turn-in | u/s 1-2 |
| | | mid-corner | u/s 1 |
| | | exit | o/s 1-3 (we try keep n) |

```
                  T7    *  turn-in      n
                           mid-corner   n
                           exit         u/s ½

                  T8    *  turn-in      u/s 2
                           mid-corner   u/s 2
                           exit         u/s 2  (o/s 2 if touch kerb)

                  T9    *  turn-in      u/s 1
                           mid-corner   u/s ½
                           exit         o/s 2-3  (we try keep n)

                  T10   *  turn-in      n
                           mid-corner   u/s 1-2

(T11 is 2xLH)     T11a  *  turn-in      u/s 1
                           mid-corner   u/s 1
                           exit         u/s 1
                  T11b  *  turn-in      u/s 2
                           mid-corner   u/s 2

                  T12   *  c.o.d.       u/s 1-2
                           mid-corner   u/s 1 to o/s 1

(off camber)      T13   *  turn-in      u/s 2
                           mid-corner   u/s 2-3
                           exit         u/s 1  (sometimes o/s 1-2)

                  T14   *  turn-in      u/s 2
                           c.o.d.       n
                           exit         n

                  T15   *  turn-in      u/s ½
                           c.o.d.       u/s ½
                           exit         o/s ½-1½
```

Bumps : Hopping from rear under braking for turn 1 over bumps, and hopping generally over bumps in first new chicane (turn 4), otherwise no problems with bumps.

Boost : n/a

Trim : 2 at start, then later 3 for rest of race.

Engine : Very good - no problems.
A small amount of det. at turn 4 in 3rd at about 3,700 but easy to avoid this.

Max Revs : 6,000 - 6,800 in gears, 6,800 on straight best before turn 4. (I went to 7k on a few occasions to overtake)

Comments : The car ran very well throughout the race with no real problems.

The tyres showed some inconsistancy, some sets were fine, others gave more u/s, and one set (my first) gave very poor traction.

The brakes were generally good, (apart from the effort required), although bad knock-off occured on worn pads.

The pit boarding and information was very good.

The radio useage/information was very good too.

The car was obviously put together very well, and everyone did a nice job in the race - many thanks.

from left: *Allan Scott (author), Price Cobb, Martin Brundle, John Nielsen, Tom Walkinshaw and Sir John Egan.*

Notice Board **Castrol Limited**

AUTOMOTIVE TECHNOLOGY
PANGBOURNE

TELEFAX (0734) 845223
PHONE : (0734) 844321

Automotive Group
Castrol Research Laboratories
Whitchurch Hill, Pangbourne,
Reading, Berkshire RG8 7QR
England

TELECOPIER MESSAGE

FROM: JOHN BRISTOW
DATE: 29/6/90.
NO. OF PAGES: 1.
TO: ALLAN SCOTT
COMPANY: TWR LTD.
REF: LEMANS. 08675 79352

PLEASE COPY TO:
COPY TO:
INTERNAL DISTRIBUTION: f ✓ 3/7

RECEIVED 27 JUN 1990

DEAR ALLAN,

LE MANS '90

PLEASE PASS MY CONGRATULATIONS TO YOUR STAFF WHO BUILT THOSE FANTASTIC ENGINES THAT BEAT NISSAN & PORSCHE & TOYOTA. ITS A PLEASURE TO BE ASSOCIATED WITH YOU & YOUR TEAM.

JOHN BRISTOW

GER GUY EDWARDS RACING INTERNATIONAL

Guy Edwards Racing International Limited
38 Tite Street, London SW3 4JA
Telephone 01-351 6925/01-351 4507 Fax 01-351 3583 Telex 9413119 GERACE

Mr. Alan Scott,
TWR Group Ltd.,
1.Station Field Road Industrial Estate,
Kidlington,
Oxford OX5 1JD

June 19th. 1990.

Dear Alan,

Very many congratulations on once again taking on the world's best and beating them - your V 12's sounded glorious right to the end , and it was a fitting result for your efforts.

Congratulations once again.

With kind regards

Yours

Guy.

*Congratulation letters sent to me from Castrol and sponsorship negotiator Guy Edwards.*

Later at the official victory dinner in the UK put on by Jaguar, TW publicly thanked members of the crew and congratulated Roger on his team management and myself for the engines. It shows the growing internal pressures that existed though as TW needed to show support for Roger who was TW's number two and main board director; with Tony Dowe and his team's efforts not being mentioned at all that evening, something Tony Dowe and his team did not deserve. Roger was not happy with the American team and the fact that we had gone our own way on a few things, and that I had appeared to prioritised them over Kidlington, but he should have known Tony Dowe and I were competitive experienced people who did what we felt would produce the best outcome. Roger would reward this situation with the American team not invited back to run a car again, and I would be sidelined to the one off 'Suntec' Japanese fund raising team the next year.

My road car was being used by the Engs crew and with the winning team flown out for PR meetings I drove Martin Brundle's JaguarSport transport back to Calais and crossed to Dover. I was in a happy mood and decided to challenge the unofficial time from Dover to Kidlington. Speeds of 145mph had me well ahead of schedule on the M40 till slowed by some traffic and a glance in the rear-view mirror saw in the distance a car I had not passed before. Soon after slowing lights flashed and it was time to talk to its driver. The simple question of who owned the car was harder to answer with a guess being a loan car from Jaguar or JaguarSport. He congratulated me on my safe driving at high speed but admitted that for the last 14 miles they had been slowly losing me. As the speed was hard to verify we settled on 106mph which sounded a good deal. Our solicitors handled the case and the reply to me is below. Interestingly he has me confused with another case, he actually drove me to court and did a fine job of painting a picture of a family man with new baby and no previous problems after holding a licence for over 20 years; and then calmly told the Magistrates that I was well rewarded for the work I did – indicating a large fine would best suit this case. All involved in this process were very understanding.

**Linnells**

SOLICITORS
12 KING EDWARD STREET
OXFORD OX1 4HX
OXFORD (0865) 248607
FAX: (0865) 728445
DX 4312 OXFORD

27th June 1990

OUR REF: PB/KM
YOUR REF:

A.W.Scott Esq.,
Engine Division Manager,
Tom Walkinshaw Racing Ltd.,
1 Station Field Industrial Est.,
Kidlington,
OXFORD.
OX5 1JD

RECEIVED
28 JUN 1990

Dear Alan,

You were of course extremely lucky that the Magistrates dealt with you by post by way of a £200.00 fine and three penalty points, with no order for costs. I admit to being pleasantly surprised. As a matter of interest to you I enclose a copy of the carbon of the letter which was sent to the Court dated 11th May.

After such a splendid win as Le Mans my conscience stops me from sending you any bill at all for this - just put it down to goodwill. I keep meaning to go to Le Mans in the vintage Bentley on the basis that they allow us to park in the secure parking area. I was asked if I would like to go on the Pirelli parade in my Austin Seven, which finished 27th in 1925. However, I thought it would be too embarassing to go down the Mulsanne straight at about 70 mph!

With best wishes.

Yours sincerely,

PETER BUTLER

***Peter Butler was a racing enthusiast and owner of a classic Le Mans race car. He decided to not charge for his services after our win.***

***We rarely think people have good sense unless they agree with us.***

– François de La Rochefoucauld

## V6 turbocharged engine – 1990

The V6 engine selected to carry on from the V12 era has its shortcomings covered in earlier chapters, based on its small engine capacity needing higher boost settings that then produced unstable combustion when using lower grade normal road fuels. Retarding of ignition timings led to reduced fuel efficiency in Group C. There was however a secondary problem with this uneven firing V6 concept which affected all engines used, IMSA included.

The uneven firing V6 turbo charged engine produced by having a six cylinder engine with 120 degree firing intervals between power strokes, when fitted to a 90 degree V8 based engine block produces the huge torsional reversals seen in the test on the opposite page. This test by Holset at Kidlington is so far off their scale that they could not produce a crankshaft damper as would have been normal practice to help control it. What was needed was a new design from that based on the 6R4 rally engine with its three common big end journals; each of these journals needing to be divided 30 degrees apart to produce six separate journals and an even firing six cylinder engine.

The uneven firing V6 engine produced two firing strokes closer together (90 degrees apart) that then produced an increased momentary torque loading. The engine then travelled through a longer dwell period during the following stroke (150 degrees). This stroke when starting its compression/ignition phase (within 30 degrees of TDC), began rapidly losing reciprocating momentum as the previous cylinder had finished it firing sequence, resulting in the beginnings of a reversal process against the crankshaft assembly's momentum. These counter rotational effects had to then be overcome by the subsequent firing of that cylinder's reduced ultimate energy potential. This uneven firing sequence was further exacerbated when applied to turbo charging and very lightweight crankshaft, flywheels and clutch assemblies with less mass and momentum. The design inherited with the 90 degree V8 based block also had its common pin crankshaft journals counter balanced using as its design concept a series of three two cylinder 90 degree V twin engines at 120 degree intervals. This would mean that the counterbalances had already passed through bottom dead centre after 120 degrees of travel and started their upwards counter rotation over the next 30 degrees, adding to the problem. These pro reversal strokes reduced maximum torque output. This was proven in our V6 engine development when it took 2.2 bar total pressure when applied to our 4 valve headed 3.5 litre Group C turbocharged engine, using the same bore and stroke as the 7 litre V12, to match the torque output of the 7 litre normally aspirated V12 engine subjected to the 1 bar of total atmospheric pressure available. Theoretically the V6 engine should have been able to match the 100% volumetric efficiency of the 7 litre V12's torque using just 2.0 bar atmospheric pressure; all things being equal.

When developing TWR's V6 turbo engine the first thing that soon happened was the constant breaking of dynamometer driveshaft universal joints at mean torque outputs lower than those constantly produced by the 7 litre V12 engines that had suffered no failures. Eventually double tube bonded rubber shafts were sourced from America and these damped out the reversal forces and allowed testing to proceed, without the spectacular driveshaft breakages we had experienced. My immediate concerns at that time were for the race cars transmissions thinking that we would be experiencing breakages there. This did not actually occur but we soon saw huge clutch plate wear, much higher than we had seen with the V12. Clutch slip at peak torque stabs had now become the damping medium, but at what cost to the racing efficiency.

Some of the precious fuel burned along with the power produced was now wasted with momentary torque stab induced clutch slip, and this then became the real Achilles heal of this uneven firing V6 turbo engine that replaced the V12.

The Jaguar 220 Supercar fitted with this V6 engine in production form was fitted with a heavy flywheel to help absorb this problem. While this is acceptable for a normal road application, these flywheels would absorb power on initial acceleration if fitted in a racing application.

Place under Holset graph. When used as a rally 6R4 engine timing belts had been reported stripped on touring stages while running constantly at 4000 rpm. The huge reversals indicated in this test show what the belt drive systems were subject to at those rpms. For the phase two development of the V6 engine I designed a set of intermediary counter rotating gears to absorb some of these driveline reversals and then have much shorter belts to drive the camshafts having greater tooth contact in the process.

While the graphs (A, B and C) opposite are diagrammatic of three production engines of the same capacity, they outline the fundamentals involved with the three engine concepts and the delivery of their power to the cars transmission system.

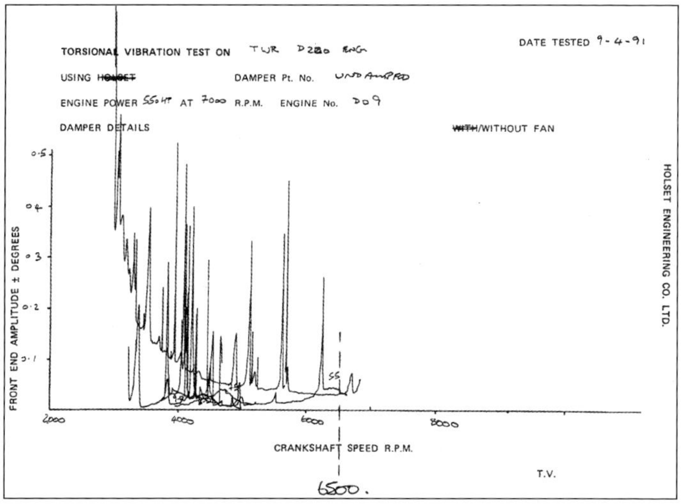


*When used as a rally 6R4 engine timing belts had been reported stripped on touring stages while running constantly at 4000 rpm.*
*The huge reversals indicated in this test show what the belt drive systems were subject to at those rpms. For the phase two development of the V6 engine I designed a set of intermediary counter rotating gears to absorb some of these driveline reversals and then have much shorter belts to drive the camshafts having greater tooth contact in the process.*

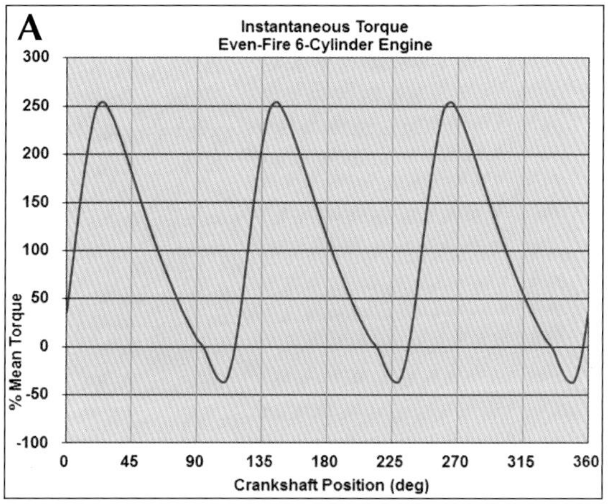


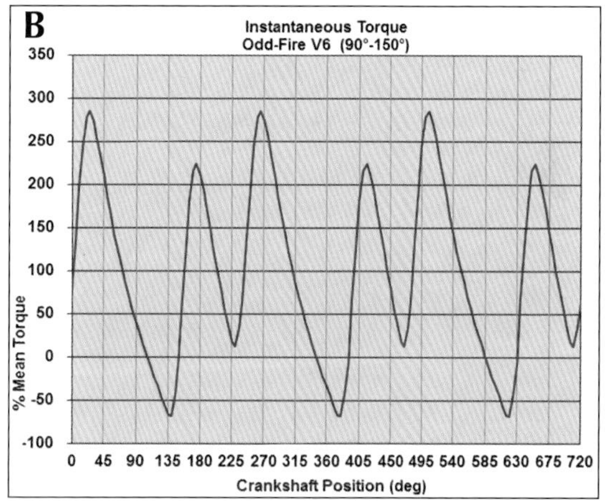


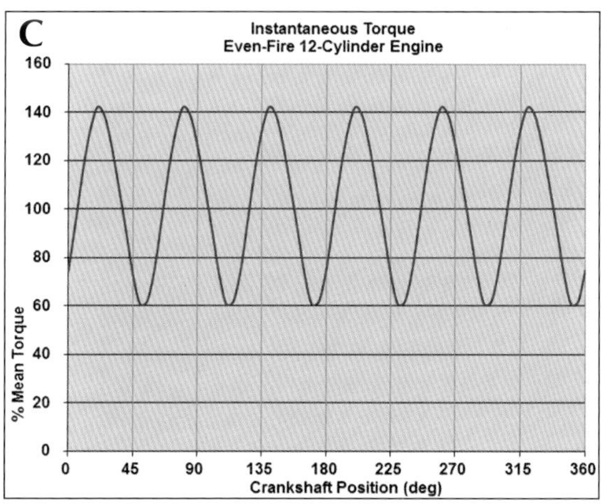


A) *This 360 degree graph shows how torque is produced in an even firing six cylinder engine. Peaking at a nominal 250, with its non productive area reaching around negative 40 below the zero line, all at 120 degree intervals. These six cylinder engines need dampers fitted to the front of the crankshaft to help remove vibrations caused by the varying torque delivery.*

B) *This 720 degree graph shows the lower peaks followed by the second power stroke just 90 degrees later and with these two power stokes working together they then produces a higher nominal torque figure around 280, then followed by the 150 degree dwell period dropping the torque output to around chart negative 65. This action then compromises the following cylinders torque reaching just 220 on the graph scale as opposed to the even firing scale for a single cylinder of 250. While this diagrammatic example suggests that these figures average out, in practise on our racing engine they do not. It is virtually impossible to produce a crankshaft damper to even out these greatly increased torque 'stabs'.*

C) *This 360 degree graph shows the constant over lapping of cylinders when using a V12 engine of the same capacity with lower peaks and lower reversals shared between 12 cylinders producing a very smooth engine. In fact our racing V12 engines did not use any crankshaft dampers.*

**Aerodynamic features of all V12 engine Jaguar race cars – 1985-1990**
*– all figures quoted in lbs at 200mph wind speed*

| Configuration of car | Downforce | Drag | L/D | % front split |
|---|---|---|---|---|
| 85 Sprint car | 4415 | 1367 | 3.23 | 29 |
| 86 Sprint car (Venturi start point moved forward) | 4705 | 1380 | 3.41 | 37 |
| 87 Sprint car | 5058 | 1417 | 3.57 | 38 |
| 87 Le Mans spec | 2244 | 814 | 2.75 | 34.4 |
| 88 Sprint car (reduced ht. tunnels, 18in rear wheels) | 5000 | 1298 | 3.85 | 38 |
| 88 Le Mans winning car (No chicanes) | 2333 | 787 | 2.96 | 24.1 |
| 89 Turbo car | 5282 | 1351 | 3.91 | 37 |
| 90 IMSA turbo car (Del Mar hign downforce spec) | 7181 | 2041 | 3.51 | 40 |
| 90 Le Man winning car (NACA ducts allround) | 3883 | 988 | 3.93 | 38 |

## Alastair Macqueen comments ...

I always knew the bell housing was the weak link in the overall stiffness of the car. Going from almost a 2M carbon tube (the tub) to the rear beam, two strong points joined by a 300mm soft mag tube (the bell housing). This showed in static twist tests and limited us to only certain spring options on the car which would work and causing the inherent understeer. It wasn't until about 10 years ago I actually saw this on the 4 post rig test when the car was 'walked' at low frequency. We placed some masking tape from the sides of the rear wing to the top of the cockpit and they sagged by almost a foot as the car twisted! Wish I'd had a bell housing cast in LM25 or similar ... we could have done so much more with the chassis!

The tub engine mounts were always pretty sound and whilst the diagonal braces stiffened the car in plan view, they were not that clever in torsion. On later cars (Bentleys) we managed to get rid of all stays from the tub, use FEA on the bell housing and its interfaces and get a hugely stiffer car.

I think what we achieved as young and relatively inexperienced engineers was mighty.

*Allan Scott and Tom Walkinshaw with trophies – Silverstone garage.*
*Martin Brundle was on hand at this track day taking journalists and others, including myself, for rides at speeds up to 190mph in the 1990 Le Mans winning race car.*

## Group C Teams Championship 1990 – V6 Turbo

| Position | Team | Chassis | Engine | Rounds | | | | | | | | | |
|---|---|---|---|---|---|---|---|---|---|---|---|---|---|
| | | | | 1 | 2 | 3 | 4 | 5 | 6 | 7 | 8 | 9 | Total |
| 1 | Team Sauber Mercedes | Sauber C9 Mercedes-Benz C11 | Mercedes-Benz M119 5.0L Turbo V8 | 9 | 9 | | 9 | 9 | 9 | 9 | 4.5 | 9 | 67.5 |
| 2 | Silk Cut Jaguar | Jaguar XJR-11 | Jaguar JV6 3.5L Turbo V6 | | 4 | 9 | 6 | 3 | 4 | | | 4 | 30 |
| 3 | Nissan Motor-sports Int. | Nissan R90CK | Nissan VRH35Z 3.5L Turbo V8 | 4 | | | 4 | 4 | 2 | 3 | 3 | 6 | 26 |
| 4 | Spice Engineering | Spice SE90 C | Ford Cosworth DFR 3.5L V8 | | 1 | 4 | 3 | 1 | | 4 | | | 13 |
| 5 | Joest Kremer Racing | Porsche 962C | Porsche 935 3.0L Turbo Flat-6 | 2 | 3 | | | | 1 | | 0.5 | 2 | 8.5 |
| 6 | Porsche Kremer Racing | Porsche 962CK6 | Porsche 935 3.0L Turbo Flat-6 | 2 | | 2 | | | | | 1.5 | | 5.5 |
| 7 | Brun Motorsport | Porsche 962C | Porsche 935 3.0L Turbo Flat-6 | 1 | | 1 | 2 | | | | | | 4 |
| 8 | Toyota Team Tom's | Toyota 90C-V | Toyota R36V 33.6L Turbo V8 | 3 | | | | | | | | | 3 |
| 9 | Richard Lloyd Racing | Porsche 962C GTi | Porsche 935 3.0L Turbo Flat-6 | | | | 1 | | | | 2 | | 3 |

## Group C Drivers Championship 1990 – V6 Turbo

| Position | Driver | Team | Rounds | | | | | | | | | Total |
|---|---|---|---|---|---|---|---|---|---|---|---|---|
| | | | 1 | 2 | 3 | 4 | 5 | 6 | 7 | 8 | 9 | |
| 1= | Jean-Louis Schlesser | Team Sauber Mercedes | 9 | 9 | | | 9 | 9 | 9 | 4.5 | | 49.5 |
| 1= | Mauro Baldi | Team Sauber Mercedes | 9 | 9 | | | 9 | 9 | 9 | 4.5 | | 49.5 |
| 3 | Jochen Mass | Team Sauber Mercedes | 6 | 6 | | 9 | 6 | 6 | 6 | | 9 | 48 |
| 4 | Andy Wallace | Silk Cut Jaguar | | 3 | 6 | 6 | 3 | 3 | | | 4 | 25 |
| 5= | Michael Schumacher | Team Sauber Mercedes | | | | | 6 | 6 | | | 9 | 21 |
| 5= | Karl Wendlinger | Team Sauber Mercedes | 6 | 6 | | 9 | | | | | | 21 |
| 7 | Jan Lammers | Silk Cut Jaguar | | 3 | 6 | 6 | 3 | 3 | | | | 21 |
| 8 | Martin Brundle | Silk Cut Jaguar | | 4 | 9 | | 2 | 4 | | | | 19 |
| 9 | Julian Bailey | Nissan Motorsports Int. | | | | 4 | 4 | | 1 | 3 | 6 | 18 |
| 10 | Mark Blundell | Nissan Motorsports Int. | | | | | 4 | 2 | 1 | 3 | 6 | 16 |
| 11 | Kenny Acheson | Nissan Motorsports Int. | | | | 4 | | | 3 | 1 | 3 | 11 |
| 12 | Alain Ferté | Silk Cut Jaguar | | 4 | | | 2 | 4 | | | | 10 |

## IMSA Teams Championship 1990 – V6 Turbo (air restrictor)

| Position | Manu-facturer | Rounds | | | | | | | | | | | | | | | Total |
|---|---|---|---|---|---|---|---|---|---|---|---|---|---|---|---|---|---|
| | | 1 | 2 | 3 | 4 | 6 | 7 | 8 | 9 | 11 | 13 | 14 | 15 | 16 | 19 | 20 | |
| 1 | Nissan | 14 | 20 | 25 | 20 | 20 | 15 | 10 | 20 | 20 | 15 | 10 | 20 | 15 | 15 | 12 | 251 |
| 2 | Jaguar | 28 | | 17 | 15 | 12 | 8 | 20 | 2 | 12 | 10 | 20 | 15 | 3 | 10 | 15 | 187 |
| 3 | Toyota | 9 | 4 | 7 | 12 | 4 | 20 | 8 | 12 | 3 | 20 | 15 | 12 | 20 | 6 | 20 | 172 |
| 4 | Porsche | 20 | 12 | 15 | 10 | 3 | 2 | 6 | 8 | 15 | 8 | 3 | 10 | 8 | 20 | 10 | 150 |
| 5 | Chevrolet | | | 8 | 3 | 10 | 12 | 15 | 10 | 1 | 2 | 12 | 4 | 2 | | | 79 |
| 6 | Pontiac | | | | 2 | 6 | | 4 | 4 | | 3 | 6 | | 1 | 2 | 3 | 31 |
| 7 | Oldsmobile | | | | | | | | | 4 | | | | 6 | | | 10 |
| 8 | Audi | | 6 | | | | | | | | | | | | | | 6 |
| 9 | Ferrari | | | | | | | | | 2 | | | | | | | 2 |

*Updated XJR-10 with dummy roof extension to allow the rear wing to be raised. Rear wing could not be above roof line.*

*1990 XJR-11*
*3.5-litre V6 turbocharged engine.*

JAGUAR

Chapter Twenty-Two

# XJR-15

**Andy Morrison and Eddie Hinckley of the TWR Special Vehicles department were given the task in early 1990 of producing a concept for a run of high performance two seater sports cars based on parts from the successful Jaguar Group C race car; but developed for road use.**

The purpose of this programme would be to use up the many spares accumulated over the years in the Jaguar sports car programmes. The TWR concept sports car would be sanctioned by Jaguar and given the XJR-15 type number, to make it an official Jaguar product as opposed to being given a TWR identity. The Jaguar XJ220 project, a high performance two-seater vehicle with its design concept by Jaguar's Jim Randle, had the first prototype built with voluntary labour by Jaguar employees known as the 'Saturday Club'.

TWR had now taken over this project and was to put the 220 concept into production using a turbocharged V6 engine. The reasoning behind developing XJ220 from a concept into a saleable manufacturing project was purely a money-making exercise, to fund TWR's proposed future move into Formula One, but there were other reasons behind the parallel concept of XJR-15.

Ford's buyout of Jaguar in 1990 had placed a large question mark over Jaguar's next long-term moves involving motor racing, and Ford were known to be very hardnosed on any partner they used in the field of motor-sport, often supplying their own finance controller. These potential problems had come to the surface as TW set his moves to retain Jaguar and take them into Formula One. Ross Brawn had been recruited at the end of 1989 to engineer the future TWR racing programmes, and Ross would oversee the 1990 XJR-11 V6 turbo programme while heading up the design team for the all new XJR-14.

The XJR-15 concept was to not only produce 30 cars for sale, but give Jaguar a marketing profile via a racing series at three selected Formula One race meetings during 1991. Another thought behind this concept was to give Fords Bill Hayden, who was not known for any enthusiasm for things motor racing, a taste of the Formula One atmosphere as a marketing tool in the automotive industry. He would be part of the series and see firsthand the style and money involved in the sport at the top level, something that would suit Jaguar's demographic.

A redundant Group C chassis was mated to the prototype Jaguar V12 engine in early 1990 and this was used as the basis to prove the concept. The project was given the initial code name R9R and leading designer Peter Stevens was tasked with producing the shape of the world's first all carbon, low volume two-seater sports car, based on the Jaguar Group C race cars chassis.

Aztec, the now TWR owned lightweight composites business situated in Gainsborough was a supplier of specialised carbon fibre race parts to the racing industry. The low volume production vehicles first envisaged with this project would have the chassis and body components made from lightweight composite materials. This programme would also be used to take Aztec onto a new phase of its business growth, in small volume production cars or limited number homologation specials for manufacturers; a direction that TW was eager to develop. This type of volume was a step up for Aztec to handle as well as a change in its culture; from small volume leading edge technology to less personally rewarding higher volume production work.

The Jaguar V12 engine would be a stressed member unit with its two lower mounting points at the forward edge of the aluminium dry sump pan and the upper mounting points from the front of the specially cast cam covers into the rear of the main tub section. Two more stay bars from the rear of the cam covers up to a position near the tub roof with two additional stay bars to run laterally from each side of the gearbox to outer points at the rear of the tub's main section would mean this engine mounting system would be the same as the race XJR cars.

The prototype engine was built at Engs using some redundant Group C V12 engine parts. To reduce production cost and power outputs, the engine capacity was reduced to 6.7 litres by boring standard Jaguar 90mm cylinder liners to 92mm and fitting Cosworth 10.5:1 forged pistons, made to our design. We were then able to use the cheaper conventional head gasket system developed in the earlier European Touring Car winning Group A XJS. Standard pre 'HE' V12 heads with larger valves were fitted, along with the larger internally recored Group A inlet manifolds. The standard Jaguar V12 63mm throttle butterflies were removed with the throttle housings then bored to take larger 70mm butterflies. A .480in lift, 74° half period camshaft at 102° phase angle, designated EA17, was used. These camshafts came from the aborted 1986 Group A XJS Australian Bathurst race programme.

With the fixed length inlet system and camshaft profile chosen set on its split centres of 102°, it was just a matter of final tuning of these components via the new tubular exhaust systems lengths and diameters. This resulted in a tuned tubular exhaust system running four sets of three 28in long 1.75in diameter primary pipes into a collector and then 23in long 2.25in diameter secondary pipes to merge into a system that would be silenced to meet environmental noise levels.

*Production carbon fibre XJR-15 chassis.*

*Rear bulkhead of the XJR-15 showing rear window*

*The Jaguar 6-litre die cast lip seal block was used as the basis for the 460bhp engine version.*

A Zytek engine management system would be based on 'Manifold pressure versus engine rpm' as opposed to the throttle angle system used in the race programmes, and would be the reprogrammable unit already in use with the JaguarSport 6-litre XJS. This prototype engine running on pump fuel at 2.5 bar fuel pressure was first tested in December 12th 1989 and produced a maximum power of 564bhp @ 6250 and 6500rpm, using a 7000rpm maximum rev limit. Maximum torque of 530lbs/ft and BMEP of 195.4lbs [13.3bar] at 4500 and 4750rpm meant that this package in a 1050kg car was going to be more than a serious threat to the Jaguar XJ220 being produced at the same time by TWR JaguarSport, with its projected production output of 520 to 540bhp.

The first prototype R9R was up and running by mid 1990 and carried out initial engineering tests in August and September of that year. After final negotiations with the Jaguar factory the programme was given their official blessing and new code name of XJR-15. Of the initial licence for 30 cars, it was decided to make the first 16 cars into racing versions with 6 speed dog type Hewland based transaxle gearboxes. These first 16 vehicles would form the basis of a proposed XJR-15 Intercontinental Challenge Series to be held in 1991. This number of cars just happened to be the number of 6-speed race gearboxes that had been made in 1989 and never used in the Group C programme. These gearboxes had been tested in the Group C V6 turbo race cars at Jerez in early 1990 but it was found that the correct crown wheel and pinion combination had not been used, making them redundant for that series. These expensive gearboxes were sitting in the stores having never been used.

The SVO team enjoyed their moment in the sun as they had produced the prototype R9R in record time, starting well after the JaguarSport XJ220 programme. TW had then tested the prototype R9R and it soon became obvious that he was concerned with just how fast the car was. A short time later it was decided to reduce the performance to below that of the JaguarSport XJ220 for obvious political

INCREASED PRODUCTION RATE FOR XJR-15

PRODUCTION OPTIONS

Requirement

1. 20 complete cars plus spares are needed for the race at Monaco on April ~~12th~~ 2nd. Rate = 3.25 per month.
2. The full 50 car sets are required for the end of Nov. Rate = 4.00 per month (Apr to Nov)

Problems at Present

1. The current production rate is 2.5 per month approx with a projected maximum rate of 2.75 per month using current practice. The limitation is primarily mould throughput.(i.e. laminating)
2. Though still in good shape, the current tooling is showing signs of degradation (normal with gel coat faced tools), and maintenance/refurb costs and the impact on the schedule due to down time might be unacceptable as the programme progresses.
3. There is no provision for repairs to the components damaged during racing (e.g. floor damage/wear)

Proposed Solutions

1. (Immediate)
Recruitment of 6 additional laminators to avoid impact on XJR-14 programme
2. (Now until April)
Introduction of full nightshift in laminating for 6 staff. This will enable the production rate to be raised to 3.25 per month.

Cost implication:- Addition of approx £500 to chassis price

3. (Jan-Apr)
Commissioning and building of new monocoque bottom, top and inner moulds and supplementary jig to achieve the following:-

Enable the repair of damaged chassis

Allow the night shift to be dropped

Allow higher rate of 4.00 per month to be met

Avoidance of effects of mould degradation.

Cost implication:- Additional tooling charge of approx £60k.

4. (Apr-Nov)
Operation of 2 sets monocoque tooling for top, inner and bottom. Deletion of full night shift.

Cost implication:- Reduction of chassis price to current level.

***Raising production levels at Aztec.***

reasons, although most of these future customers would have been happier with the V12 engines, not the V6 to be used.

I was asked to fix this problem and at the same time increase the programme's profitability by reducing the build cost. That led to the conclusion to base the new engine on the production 6-litre V12 unit assembled at Radford in Coventry to reduce both initial costs and build time. Jaguar had now begun full time production of the TWR JaguarSport 6-litre V12 engine, to my initial designs, with the first prototypes built by us at Engs. Like all the TWR Race Divisions, JaguarSport had also accumulated engines and engine parts with the various development programmes and so the first production batch of six test engines used the early rear rope seal crankshaft blocks, and basic 6-litre parts also came from this JaguarSport source. These early engines were fitted to the first cars built to allow systems to be tested and were later recycled and rebuilt into new 6-litre lip-seal blocks and refitted into the programme.

The final specification engines were based on the current V12 'HE' design head with its offset combustion chamber housing the exhaust valve and spark plug. I decided to use this production unit as a base primarily to save cost, although having to convert the engine to being a 'stressed' unit and dry sumped, would produce considerable rework as the blocks would need to be sent out for external machining.

These Jaguar V12 'HE' 6-litre engines, with emission setting and JaguarSport cold air intakes with special air cleaners and silenced exhaust systems, produced 315bhp at 5250rpm and 370lb/ft of torque at 3500rpm on the Engs test bed at Kidlington.

After TWR's win at Le Mans in June 1990 the month before, Engs started in July testing a standard

6-litre engine with dry sump pump and oil filter.

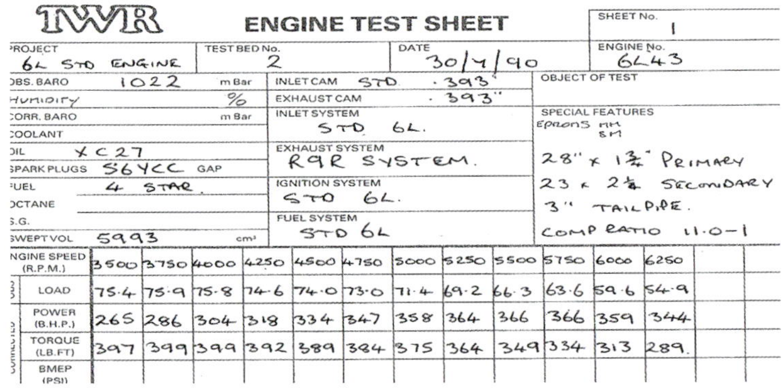

TWR ENGINE TEST SHEET

SHEET No. 1

PROJECT 6L STD ENGINE | TEST BED No. 2 | DATE 30/4/90 | ENGINE No. 6L43

OBS. BARO 1022 m Bar
HUMIDITY %
CORR. BARO m Bar
COOLANT
OIL XC27
SPARK PLUGS S6YCC GAP
FUEL 4 STAR.
OCTANE
S.G.
SWEPT VOL 5993 cm³

INLET CAM STD .393"
EXHAUST CAM .393"
INLET SYSTEM STD 6L.
EXHAUST SYSTEM R9R SYSTEM.
IGNITION SYSTEM STD 6L.
FUEL SYSTEM STD 6L

OBJECT OF TEST

SPECIAL FEATURES
EPROMS MM SM
28" x 1¾" PRIMARY
23 x 2¼ SECONDARY
3" TAILPIPE.
COMP RATIO 11.0-1

| ENGINE SPEED (R.P.M.) | 3500 | 3750 | 4000 | 4250 | 4500 | 4750 | 5000 | 5250 | 5500 | 5750 | 6000 | 6250 | | |
|---|---|---|---|---|---|---|---|---|---|---|---|---|---|---|
| LOAD | 75.4 | 75.9 | 75.8 | 74.6 | 74.0 | 73.0 | 71.4 | 69.2 | 66.3 | 63.6 | 59.6 | 54.9 | | |
| POWER (B.H.P.) | 265 | 286 | 304 | 318 | 334 | 347 | 358 | 364 | 366 | 366 | 359 | 344 | | |
| TORQUE (LB.FT) | 397 | 399 | 399 | 392 | 389 | 384 | 375 | 364 | 349 | 334 | 313 | 289. | | |
| BMEP (PSI) | | | | | | | | | | | | | | |

*Standard production 6-litre V12 engine with tuned length tubular open exhaust system added.*

6-litre V12 engine fitted with the programmable Zytek engine management, full tubular exhaust system and JaguarSport air filters. This test engine was designated 6L43. Power produced was 366bhp @5500 and 5750rpm with maximum torque of 399lbs/ft @3750 and 4000rpm, on an open unsilenced exhaust system. This test shows the results that can be obtained with resonance tuning of the exhaust system, an increase of 16% in power output and 8% in torque, with all other aspects of this engine being as standard production from Jaguar. These results were not good enough, based on minimum expenditure, and more work would be needed.

Kent Cams were keen to do production work for TWR and I selected a camshaft from their range, given the code name of No.27. The camshaft profile had to be able to be ground out of a standard chill cast unmachined Jaguar production camshaft lobe, with the need to reproduce the standard Jaguar camshaft lobe base circle to make everything work in the confined space of the standard cam carrier and cam cover. Maintaining this base circle to a close tolerance would enable the use of the standard production tappet spacer button shim range for ease of setting valve clearances. The standard Jaguar lobe centres are cast at 114° and the best we could get out of this blank set-up for the new engine was 110°, an acceptable compromise angle for both the road and race track. This profile used a 72° half period (288° total) and .425 nominal lift. Using the standard spring retainers, valves and cam followers, we then sourced high performance valve springs made to our design by Schmitthelm of Heidleburgh, Germany. This would keep the engine safe from the inevitable over revs from missed gear changes and early down shifts during the three-race Intercontinental Challenge Series to come.

The last part of the process was to send a pair of heads to Longmans in the south coast town of Christchurch who were given the task of gas flowing a pair of heads to a set budget price of £300 a pair with the prospect of 30 pairs to be reworked. Working the port throats, using three angle valve seat-cutting techniques and two angles on the valve back faces, the standard heads had improved gass flow throughout the range of 8%.

It was found at this time that the small combustion chamber of the 'HE' head was shrouding the exhaust valve which sat in the middle of the compact chamber. Careful relieving of the chamber walls in this area produced a 4% flow increase with the added benefit of reducing the compression ratio to 11.5:1, a more realistic compression ratio with the increased BMEP and allowing the use of 4-star fuels. At the designated maximum valve lift of .425in the exhaust port flowed 74% of the inlet port flow. While this lift was quite low compared to a race engine, it was 0.045in higher than the standard production 6-litre V12.

These additional modifications of replacement camshaft, gas flowed heads and tuned length tubular exhaust system added to the production 6-litre V12 Jaguar engine were the most cost-effective way to come to a suitable power level. They resulted in lifting the outputs to 460BHP at 6500rpm and maximum torque of 442lb/ft and BMEP of 182lbs [12.4bar] at 4000–4500rpm using a 11.5:1 compression ratio and increased fuel pressure from 2.5 bar to 5 bar. The increase in fuel pressure allowed the standard Jaguar 6-litre fuel injectors to be used, again for cost saving purposes, and the ability when reprogrammed to supply the additional fuel needed. This cost-effective

**RICHARD LONGMAN & CO.**

Partners: R. Longman & G. Tóth

AIRFIELD ROAD
AIRFIELD WAY INDUSTRIAL ESTATE
CHRISTCHURCH
DORSET BH23 3TG
ENGLAND U.K.
Tel: Christchurch (0202) 486569
Fax: (0202) 473398

Racing Engine Preparation
Specialist Cylinder Head Modification
Competition Engine Spares
S.U. and Weber Carburettors
Maniflow Manifolds

V12 JAGUAR          OR.NO E 9915

| INLET VALVE LIFT | STD HEAD FLOW RANGE | PERCENT FLOW | CFM | MOD HEAD | PERCENT FLOW | CFM |
|---|---|---|---|---|---|---|
| .050 | 47.6 | .505 | 24.0 | | .580 | 27.6 |
| 100 | 98.7 | .500 | 49.3 | | .540 | 53.2 |
| .150 | 98.7 | 780 | 76.9 | | .815 | 80.4 |
| 200 | 199 | .495 | 98.7 | | .520 | 103.4 |
| 250 | 199 | .595 | 118.4 | | .625 | 124.3 |
| 300 | 199 | .675 | 134.3 | | .710 | 141.2 |
| 350 | 199 | .700 | 139.3 | | .765 | 152.2 |
| 400 | 199 | .722 | 143.6 | | .800 | 159.2 |
| 450 | 199 | .730 | 145.2 | | .780 | 155.2 |
| EXHAUST VALVE LIFT | | | | MOD HEAD | | |
| .050 | 53.1 | .390 | 20.7 | | .415 | 22.0 |
| 100 | 53.1 | .710 | 37.7 | | .845 | 44.8 |
| 150 | 106 | .515 | 54.5 | | .580 | 61.4 |
| 200 | 106 | .650 | 68.9 | | .710 | 75.2 |
| 250 | 106 | .740 | 78.4 | | .805 | 85.3 |
| 300 | 106 | .792 | 83.9 | | .838 | 88.8 |
| 350 | 106 | .830 | 87.9 | | .870 | 92.2 |
| 400 | 106 | .885 | 93.8 | FOLW | .940 | 99.6 |
| 450 | 106 | .960 | 101.7 | RANGE 210 | .510 | 107.1 |

*Standard Head*          *Modified Head*

*Port Flow Rig Tests*

ENG TEST AND DATA SHEET.

| G. Modified 6 litre. | ENG NO. ~~[illegible]~~ | DATE. 4.10.1990 |
|---|---|---|
| L PRESS. 10/5 | R9R12001 | CELL TEMP. 21°C |
| L TEMP. 90°C | 100°c | HYDROM. 22 • 15 |
| ATER TEMP. 85°C | 90°c | CORR. 1.018 (+) |

| SPD. | LOAD 5 BAR Sync (2) | LOAD Sync (10) 3½ BAR | HP Sync (2) 5 BAR | Sync (10) 3½ BAR | ~~FUEL~~ 5 BAR | ~~IGN~~ 3½ BAR | ~~CO%~~ |
|---|---|---|---|---|---|---|---|
| 3500 | 76.1 | 76.5 | 271 | 273 | 14.6 | 17.0 | pulse time |
| 3750 | | | | | | | |
| 4000 | 81.8 | 80.3 | 333 | 327 | 14.3 | 17.6 | |
| 4250 | | | | | | | |
| 4500 | 82.5 | 81.4 | 378 | 373 | 15.3 | 17.3 | |
| 4750 | | | | | | | |
| 5000 | 79.1 | 78.3 | 402 | 399 | 14.8 | 17 | |
| 5250 | | | | | | | |
| 5500 | 75.1 | 74.5 | 420 | 417 | 15.0 | 16.6 | |
| 5750 | | | | | | | |
| 6000 | 74 | 73.3 | 452 | 448 | 14.5 | 17.3 | |
| 6250 | | | | | | | |
| 6500 | 69.6 | 69.3 | 460 | 459 | 14.3 | 17. | |
| 6750 | | | | | | | |
| 7000 | | | B.H.P. | B.H.P. | | | |
| 7250 | | | | | | | |
| 7500 | | | | | | | |
| 7750 | | | | | | | |

BORE / STROKE. 90mm x 78mm | COMP RATIO. 11 : 1
EXH LENGTH. | PRI. 28" x 1¾" | SEC. 23" x 2¼"
PLUGS. | CAMS. KENT 27
PORT Ø. Std | DATA SET. R9R 001
FUEL. 4 Star
VALVES. IN" Std | EXH" Std.
'MAY TYPE' Head. – Longman flowed chambers
Valve throats & Valve backs

***Note sync (2) and sync (10) are different positions in the engines cycle when the fuel starts its injection pulse and is the last part of the fine tuning for best efficiency with sync (2) and increased fuel pressure being selected.***

outcome was comfortably below the projected 520 to 540BHP of the 220's 3.5-litre V6 turbo. In a memo dated January 21st 1991, TW approved the initial build of just ten engines, leaving an uncertainty as to his intentions.

Support from the Radford assembly plant came in the form of us supplying a block selection jig needed to select engines with enough suitable material left on external mounting bosses with their new die cast blocks. Anthony Moss progressed a system whereby cylinder liners were selected for the largest piston to bore clearance possible within their production tolerances, to save build time in extra honing and reduce frictional losses from that area. These selected engines were then dismantled on arrival at Engs with parts sent out for machining or modifying. The engines were then carefully assembled by two teams of two builders each, including their conversion to a dry sump oil system. The two-man teams were given a one-week window, starting Monday morning, to complete each engine in an attempt to control production time. If the process went smoothly the engine was finished on Friday night, if not it was finished on Saturday. If there was a parts hold-up the engine builders would have words with the procurement team; and it all worked very well.

On completion the engines would be dyno tested and then delivered to TWR SVO at Broadstone, half an hour's drive away from Kidlington. The billing to TWR SVO for the development and supply for each of these first six engines was: parts and prototype machining/development, £23,056.06, administration amortisation

*XJR-15 in assembly showing the air filter housing and large exhaust silencer fitted.*

and engine build labour, £7650.00, making a cost of £30,706.06 per engine.

The next 14 engines when sanctioned by TW would be produced at a cost of £29,706.06 each. After protracted negotiations with Jaguar Browns Lane, JaguarSport's Paul Davis managed to negotiate a reduced price for the basic 6-litre engines @ £3000 per V12 unit; my initial budgets being based on a price of £6000 each. The final engines would be hand built at a cost of £26,706.06 each.

Champion spark plugs became involved as a product and technology partner and the 6-litre V12 engine was thermocouple tested to select the best suitable spark plugs for the engine. The result of this test was the need for two different heat range spark plugs.

Competition use S57C and road use Champion RS6YCC (see Champion report on page 317).

The completed car costs started at around £210,000 and as costings were reduced and efficiencies progressed from car 11 onwards these reduced to around £175,000, around half of the retail price. The lower engine specification now used compared to the initial 6.7-litre engine proposal produced an overall cost saving of £850,000, with the use of the low-cost 6-litre host engine being a very cost-effective way of reducing the cost of the overall engine programme. The XJ220 JaguarSport engine division under Roger Silman had in parallel drawn up a variable valve proposal for this V12 project, but their costings had come out at £2 million more than Engs proposals, and we were able to get this much needed contract to keep four engine builders and one procurement person fully employed for most of the year.

This was a good result considering the car was to sell for US$500,000 (£325,000.00). Added to these costs were the US$1 million and three JaguarSport XJS coupes as the prize fund for the Intercontinental Challenge Series at the three selected Formula One venues. This prize fund would not only encourage the sale of the cars that would finally be produced, but also introduce the Jaguar name to the pinnacle of motorsport with a race series in Formula One, as well as a soft introduction to this level of motor racing to Jaguar's top personnel. It was also TW introducing himself to Formula One with a higher profile than just being the new boy on the block, with the ability to manufacture thirty carbon composite sports cars and put on a show.

ISSUE: 04 XJR-15 PARTS INFORMATION NOTE DATE:14/11/1990

FROM:.A.C.Moss......... TO:.N.Eames..........

COPIES:.I.Brown........
.A.W.Scott......
.P.Davis........
.C.Wilson.......

RECEIVED 14 NOV 1990

Your ref:Memo 22/10/1990

JS8W1-----SB 6.0 LITRE ENGINES XJR-15......................

All XJR - 15 engines will be identified by the prefix "JS" etched on the block which will also mean that the block checking tool has been tried and passed.

The original requirement of 22 engines to be built at Radford starting in November has been confirmed.

The request for an extra eight engines to provide specification stabalisation causes no concern to Jaguarsport's production.

The proposed schedule is as follows:

Week 46 build and test six engines.Supply with gearboxes.
Week 47 build and test eight engines.Supply with gearboxes.
Week 48 build and test eight engines.Supply with gearboxes.
Week 49 build and test eight engines.Supply with gearboxes.

Your order R002623/S covers weeks 46 to 48.The final eight engines require additional order cover.

The recently agreed procedure with regard to gearboxes is that TWR will remove the gearboxes and Jaguarsport will supply them back to Jaguar,Radford to an agreed condition ready for refitment to Jaguarsport 6.0 litre engines.

Your ref:Memo 23/10/1990.

SPEX1138/9 CAMSHAFTS - 6.0 LITRE R-9-R.Part machined.

The drawings have been supplied to Jaguar via P.Taylor for comments and authorised issue.No reply has been received as yet.

Jaguarsport's order JS 5878/XJR - 15 covers TWR order R002624/S for twenty five pairs at a minimum rate of six pairs a month.Jaguar's internal ordering system has been overcome by using strokes and a reference number after JS 5878/XJR - 15.

Two pairs were supplied in October off this order.The two pairs due for week 44 were not delivered.Every effort will be made to recover these two and also supply two pairs due for week 46.

Your ref:Memo 26/10/1990 from AWS.

New engine specifications for the second batch of engines will involve the use of 1992 model parts.A list of the parts and their drawings that will affect the XJR-15 engines will be raised as soon as possible.

Quality build problems will be addressed during week 47.

*Progress report for basic XJR-15 engine assembly at Radford.*

As the production of the cars began TW now calmly informed the XJR-15 team that he had decided that fifty cars would be built and that we should all just increase the numbers of our respective builds accordingly. Eventually fifty-five test, race and production engines would be built by Pete Tyrell and Malcolm Howes, and Jim Brown and Mike Lonican under the direction of workshop foreman Steve Gray. Barry Pudwell was tasked with co-ordinating all the parts required to arrive in a timely fashion and not hold up the build schedule. The race-programme support for the 16 cars to be raced was under the engineering direction of Engs' very talented Mark Hemsworth, ably assisted at the race circuits by Engs' senior engine builder Nigel Webb. Additional trackside support came from Andy Penny, Steve Siddle, and Andy Whiffen.

Former Engs workshop foreman Peter Grace, who had set up on his own account also helped relieve the

**E.9106**

SUBJECT

Spark plug temperature survey of an XJR15 6.0 litre V12 engine.

PURPOSE

To determine the optimum spark plug heat ranges for this engine.

TEST DETAILS

Test Site:-
Test Cell 2, TWR Limited, Kidlington, Oxford.

Test Equipment:-
Refer to Appendices

Test Measurements:-

1) Spark plug insulator tip temperatures were recorded for engine speeds of 3500 to 6250 RPM with wide open throttle. These temperatures were recorded for three spark plug heat ranges.
2) Spark plug post ignition surveys were carried out on cylinder 6A at 6000 RPM wide open throttle. Surveys were carried out with two spark plug heat ranges.

SPARK PLUGS TESTED

BN3, BN2, S6YC,
S57C (post ignition survey only)

RECOMMENDATION

In view of the disparity of competition and road operating conditions two specifications of spark plug are recommended.

Competition: Champion S57C
Road : Champion RS6YCC

**CHAMPION SPARK PLUG — EUROPE**
**Engineering Department**

VEHICLE TWR REPORT No E.9106
ENGINE XJR15 014 SHEET No. 1
SPECIAL FEATURES DATE 14.3.91

| PLUG TYPE / TEST CONDITION & TEST No. | CYLINDER No. R.P.M. | M.P.H./K.P.H. | IGN. °BTDC | 1A | 2B | 6A | 6B | | AV. | |
|---|---|---|---|---|---|---|---|---|---|---|
| BN3 | 3500 | | | 665 | 665 | 685 | 685 | | 675 | |
| (BN509) | 4000 | | | 725 | 720 | 730 | 735 | | 728 | |
| W.O.T. | 4500 | | | 725 | 740 | 750 | 750 | | 741 | |
| | 5000 | | | 740 | 755 | 765 | 760 | | 755 | |
| | 5500 | | | 775 | 780 | 805 | 805 | | 791 | |
| | 6000 | | | 795 | 815 | 820 | 815 | | 811 | |
| | 6250 | | | 800 | 825 | 825 | 815 | | 816 | |
| | | | | | | | | | | |
| | | | | | | | | | AV. | |
| BN3 & BN2 | | | | BN3 | BN2 | BN2 | BN3 | | BN2 | |
| W.O.T. | 3500 | | | 665 | 655 | 660 | 675 | | 658 | |
| | 4000 | | | 725 | 720 | 720 | 735 | | 720 | |
| | 4500 | | | 735 | 730 | 740 | 750 | | 735 | |
| | 5000 | | | 750 | 750 | 760 | 765 | | 755 | |
| | 5500 | | | 780 | 780 | 800 | 805 | | 790 | |
| | 6000 | | | 795 | 810 | 815 | 815 | | 813 | |
| | 6250 | | | 800 | 825 | 820 | 815 | | 823 | |
| | | | | | | | | | | |
| S6YC | 3500 | | | 655 | 725 | 695 | 670 | | | |
| W.O.T. | 4000 | | | 710 | 800* | 750 | 725 | *T/C | PLUG | REPLACED |
| | 4500 | | | 725 | 720 | 765 | 735 | | 736 | |
| | 5000 | | | 750 | 745 | 795 | 765 | | 764 | |
| | 5500 | | | 780 | 775 | 830 | 805 | | 798 | |
| | 6000 | | | 800 | 810 | 855 | 820 | | 821 | |
| | 6250 | | | 795 | 815 | 850 | 815 | | 819 | |
| | | | | | | | | | | |
| S6YC | | | | | | | | | | |
| ¾ THROTTLE | 6000 | | | 785 | 800 | 850 | 810 | | 811 | |

*Champion report E9106 – Spark plug test with Champion undertaken at Engs shows plug core temperatures in degrees centigrade under wide open throttle, as well as 75% throttle conditions.*

*The SVO assembly facility at Broadstone.*

pressure on a few occasions via his engineering business Dashwood Engineering, being subcontracted to service some of the engines between races. Eddie Hinckley as chief engineer ran the test and engineering programmes assisted by Dave Fullerton, with the team mechanics being supervised by Rod Benoist. Wayne Humphreys, now Engs financial manager, controlled the spend, reporting progress to the TWR finance director.

Testing showed up the typical teething problems that these programmes have, race brake set-ups producing pad rattle, OK for racing but not for the road versions, part throttle drivability with the pressure based engine management system needed closer attention also in these early tests with the demands of the more racing orientated camshaft causing some fluctuations with the manifold pressure signals. Car interior temperatures were high and so a programme to fit air conditioning was introduced.

The triple plate sintered 7.25in AP clutch on the racing Group C flywheel gave poor takeoff and drivability and this area was re engineered with a new heavier flywheel to take the AP twin 8.5in carbon clutch. Testing had shown that with the lightweight Group C flywheel being used the rpm drop at normal gearshift speeds was such that smooth changes could not be made, with the engine speed dropping too low for the next gear engaged. The fitting of a heavier flywheel helped this problem.

The tube mountings to the rear of the cabin area from the engine and gearbox acted as amplifiers and ducted mechanical engine and gearbox noises into the cabin. Nothing much could be done about this with the design being used, so the fix was to supply a set of headphones with intercom for two people to be used while driving.

Up to car build 16, all used the 6-speed dog selector gearbox, and were destined to be the race series cars. The road cars would then be fitted with a 5-speed synchromesh version of the gearbox, and this version was tested in August/September 1990.

The testing programme continued through the winter of 90/91 moving onto refinement for the road. This later moved to high speed endurance running at the Millbrook banked oval testing facility. Andy Morrison had insisted I spend a day with the test team and we proceeded to lap the circuit at speeds up to 165mph. I really did not need familiarity with the full capabilities of the car, which I already knew were spectacular but Andy felt this would be a good experience for me with him at the wheel. At this same test was the JaguarSport XJ220 crew in their early stages of endurance testing and this process was being carried out by Andy Wallace. Andy was circulating at a slower regulated speed in the centre lane of the three lanes and there was some friendly rivalry between the two teams, with the XJR-15 being produced in half the time of the XJ220. The XJR-15 was already up to maximum speed tests and every four laps or so we would overtake Andy Wallace, and occasionally he would be on the receiving end of the international two fingered wave. Running in the top lane of the banked circuit at these speeds is an interesting experience. When you look straight ahead at the distance needed to control the car on the banking, you are looking at the bottom lane.

Standing start performance tests were carried out at Millbrook in early February resulting in:

0–60mph = 3.39 sec. 0–100mph = 9.52 sec
0-140mph = 18.33 sec.

The test programme up to the first race at the Monaco GP included:

| | |
|---|---|
| March 11/12/13 | Nogaro – tyre testing |
| March 22 | Silverstone – Customer release day. |
| April 5 | Silverstone – Promotion and tyre testing |
| April 18 | Silverstone – Final vehicle shakedowns |
| April 29 | Silverstone – Final vehicle shakedowns |
| May 1 | Silverstone – Driver familiarisation |
| May 8-12 | Monaco – GP support race. |

During these track tests some engine misfires were experienced and the problem was later traced to the poor manufacture of the sub contracted wiring looms with incorrectly crimped and sized injector terminals. These wiring looms move around under racing conditions and usually produced the problem while cornering leading to the initial thought that the problem was fuel related. These loom changes became a mission on some cars as the removal and refit time in the confined space took the mechanic five hours.

A deal had been done with BP for oil supply and so these engines were switched from the well proven Castrol XC27 we had used in all our race programmes, to BP's XF3411. The car then suffered from higher oil and water temperatures as the circuit testing moved to warmer European circuits. The racing and road needs were producing different problems to fix. Higher speeds on the open road in cool weather in earlier testing had shown the need for water thermostats to be fitted, but these thermostats had started to slow the water flow when high revs were used on racing circuits in hotter conditions.

When the race slick tyres were fitted to the XJR-15 and circuit tested, an oil surge problem surfaced causing fluctuating oil pressure, and the oil level in the dry sump tank was raised to overcome this. This raised oil level then needed a modification to the tank breather to stop small amounts of oil exiting the vent tube, the oil tank was also modified to lower the pickup tube and increase capacity by two litres, and with these changes the problem was solved.

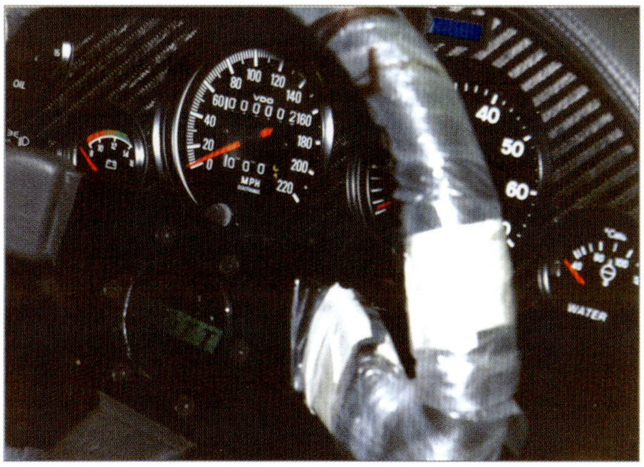


*XJR-15 instrument panel.*

## XJR-15 Test Report (France)

TEST REPORT

VENUE: NOGARO DATE: 11, 12, 13 MARCH 1991

OBJECTIVES

Two cars were prepared for the test, one in 5 speed soft set up and the other in race form. The main objectives of the test were to establish a well balanced chassis set up on race tyres, to check the suitability of the Bridgestone race tyres, to evaluate the cooling and fuel systems in higher ambient temperatures than previous and to check the operation and reliability of the 6 speed race gearbox. The 5 speed car was used to increase mileage on gearbox, clutch etc., and to check cooling systems by logging temperature data.

ACHIEVEMENTS

The chassis balance of the race car was fairly good from the start. The rear springs were stiffened to improve the change of direction. This caused some oversteer which was reduced by stiffening the front antiroll bar, the rear negative camber was increased to improve rear grip. It was noted that an increase in the front negative camber would be desirable, but this was not possible with current front top wishbone (already adjusted to maximum). Various sets of slicks were tested, a tyre endurance run of 14 laps showed no dramatic drop off in performance. We were restricted to this maximum number of consecutive laps by a slight oil surge problem, (see "Problems"). 133 laps, 300 miles were achieved over three days.

The 5 speed car ran without any major problems for three days, achieving 600 miles of hard driving (changing gear at 6000 RPM). Various data was recorded, ie., temperature, heat soak, noise levels. Surprisingly, one set of RE71 treaded tyres survived this abuse! No changes to original specification were made.

PROBLEMS

1. Oil surge was encountered on the long left hand corner behind pits as soon as slicks were fitted. This was reduced by running a higher than normal oil level, which caused oil to be blown out of the breather pipe into catch tank. As soon as the level returned to normal, surge returned. There was no surge on treaded tyres.
2. A higher than desirable water temperature was recorded (110°). Various ways of reducing this were tried, ie., removing thermostat, removing electric fans, air deflectors on intake aperture, but nothing reduced this significantly.
3. The six speed gearbox breathes rather heavily and loses oil into catch tank.
4. Some fuel vapourisation occurred when the ambient rose above 23°. This was in the form of a loss of power after left hand corners.

REMEDIES

1. A modified oil tank will be used on the race cars which lowers the oil pick-up and increases capacity by 2 litres, increased baffling and a repositioned breather.
2. My feeling is that the air intake to the radiator is too small and therefore methods of feeding extra air to the radiator are to be investigated and tested.
3. Bearing in mind the duration of the challenge events, this is not considered a serious problem. During 300 miles of running at Nogaro, it was not necessary to add oil to the gearbox.
4. A modified fuel collector pot will be used in all cars. This will enable the collector to be pressurised to 1 PSI which will assist the high pressure pick-up. (A version of this was tried at Nogaro and when fitted no further problems were encountered, although ambient temperatures were 3° lower than previously).

E Hinckley
21.3.91

cc. T Walkinshaw
A Scott

During the April 29th test at Silverstone a car driven by Tiff Needell suffered low oil pressure and the engine failed before it could be shut down. Investigation showed an oil pressure relief valve jammed open with aluminium swarf leading to the bearing failure. Further investigation found a similar problem with debris from the oil tank manufacture in another three cars as well. The cleaning process used to clear all the moulding sand from the sump castings was also not perfect, and these all had to be inspected again to remove any contamination.

The sales of the XJR-15 were made as quickly as the cars could be built and this programme took on an urgency all of its own. TWR had been haemorrhaging money in its Garage Group investments and this programme became the only additional cash flow contributor throughout the middle months of 1991 as the XJR-14 was financially supported in its successful Championship winning effort. Daily updated sales and income had to be reported by Andy Morrison and his team and this cash flow situation would finally end in rescue by Benetton at the end of the year.

With the racing series having a prize money pot of US$1 million and being support races at three famous Formula One events, the first sixteen cars with 6-speed gearboxes designed for the series had been quickly sold.

Fiona Miller was TWR's Public Relations executive and while our boss was well known for his ability to think and speak on his feet, the following Q&A notes supplied by her to TW show the level of support and attention to detail needed when TWR was communicating to the outside world. There had been some disquiet over the production of these XJR-15 V12 engined sports cars after many had committed themselves before its announcement to purchasing the XJ220. This had produced some discontent based on the presumption that owners were buying a XJ220 with a V12 engine. When it became known that it was to be a turbo charged V6, a unit that did not have the kudos of winning Le Mans, there was need for a good PR response. The XJR-15 announcement to the world was held up for good reason as it would have affected XJ220 sales and the reasoning behind this delayed announcement had to then be covered in an acceptable way for all.

*XJR-15 engine cooling with the thermostatically operated electric fans for the radiator.*

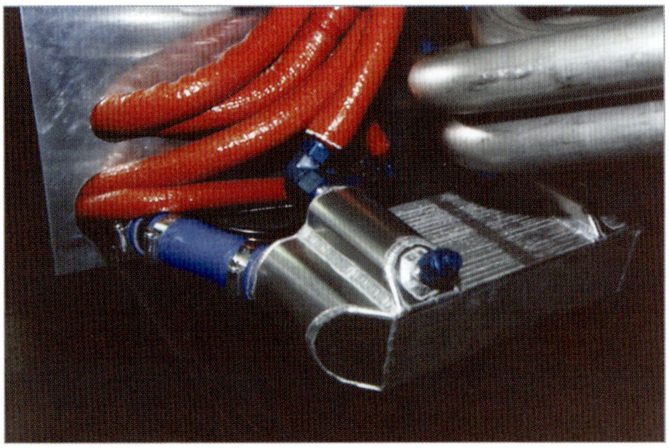

*XJR-15 water/oil inter cooler.*

## QUESTIONS AND ANSWERS – SUSCEPTIBILITIES

Q. Is Jaguar Cars involved in this new venture?
A. As a partner in JaguarSport, Jaguar Cars has been fully aware of, and is very enthusiastic about the new car and the new race series.

Q. Is the JaguarSport XJR-15 purely a race car or can it be used on as a road car?
A. The JaguarSport XJR-15 was conceived as a race car and is based on the Le Mans winning Jaguar XJR-9. It has been designed, developed and built for the race series. Unlike XJ220 it has not been conceived as a road car. The JaguarSport XJR-15 has not been type approved for road use.

Q. Do you have to commit to race in the series if you buy a car?
A. It is a condition of purchase that the car must be entered in the series.

Q. Do you have a sponsor for the series?
A. We are in negotiation with several potential sponsors and expect to make an announcement very shortly,

Q. Can individual owners seek their own individual sponsors for their entry in the series?
A. Yes – provided they adhere to the normal conditions in the regulations.

Q. Eight cars will be entered by TWR and driven by nominated drivers. Who will drive the other cars?
A. The cars can be driven by the purchaser if obviously he has the relevant licence, or he may retain the services of a driver for the series.

Q. Do you have FISA approval for the Challenge series?
A. Yes.

Q. Do you see the XJR-15 as an extension to JaguarSport's XJ220 programme?
A. No we do not. The XJ220 is a road car – the XJR-15 is a race car. The cars were designed and built for different purposes.

Q. Jaguar has consistently denied the existence of a new high performance car from JaguarSport yet now you unveil one.
A. We have consistently denied the existence of a road car from JaguarSport. The JaguarSport XJR-15 was conceived as a racing car and is being specifically built for the international challenge. Naturally we wanted to announce the new car and the new racing series at the same time. As you will appreciate it takes time to negotiate with the Sports authorities and circuit authorities to put a series like this in place. We have made the announcement as quickly as possible.

Q. You have obviously sold a majority of the cars already. How has this been possible if you have not, up to now, acknowledged the existence of the vehicle?
A. For several years TWR has been asked by drivers, team owners and private individuals about the possibility of making race cars available to private customers. Therefore we had a list of people we knew would be interested in, and more importantly able to buy a car like this. It was therefore a matter of talking to them about this project. Obviously, we wanted to be in a position to say to you today that we had a firm commitment to the series.
Incidentally the speculative stories which appeared in several magazines prompted further enquiries from seriously interested people.

Q. Have you vetted the prospective owners?
A. No. Virtually all the owners are already personally known to Tom Walkinshaw.

Q. Will the race series be televised?
A. We hope so. We are currently in negotiation with the respective authorities.

Q. Will an owner be able to race the car in any other race series?
A.

Q. How do you justify a cost of £500,000 for a car?
A. This is a very limited edition race car. It is made from extremely costly components and utilises leading edge technology. Every car is also hand built. It is fully in line with the cost of today's racing cars.

Q. Tom Walkinshaw is entering eight cars and drivers. Why is this?
A.

**QUESTIONS**

Q. Why promote a one-make race series?
Q. Why build a car that can only be used in a one-make series, doesn't this mean that the owners have paid £500,000 for a car that can only race 3 times.
Q. Why had the XJR-15 got lights and indicators?
Q. Is it not the wrong time for JaguarSport to launch a new race car with a Gulf War threatening oil supplies?
Q. What will happen to the 8 TWR owned/entered cars after the 3 race series?
Q. Is it a road going car?
Q. Have all the new owners accepted and committed their cars to the race?
Q. Will there be any 'Team' orders for TWR nominated drivers with regards to the private entries?
Q. The owners are obviously enthusiasts and investors. The car will be relatively easy to convert to road use, are you actively discouraging drivers of varying abilities from road registering these machines?
Q. Do you have any of the 8 driver places filled?

***Turnover is vanity,***
***profit sanity, cash flow reality.***

## Mike Garton produced the regulations for the XJR-15 race series

The only vehicles admitted to the 1991 JaguarSport InterContinental Challenge ('The Challenge') will be the JaguarSport XJR15 constructed specifically for the Challenge.

TR2.SAFETY.

i). The XJR15 incorporates a full roll cage structure within the monocoque which complies fully with requirements of FIA Art.253.8 and RACMSA QM.1.

ii). All vehicles are fitted with full Sabelt safety harness to FIA 8853-85 - Two shoulder straps, one abdominal strap and two crutch straps.FIA Art 253.6 and RACMSA QM.2(c)

iii).All vehicles are fitted with plumbed in Fire Extinguishers electronically operated (-----------------5kg to engine/2.5kg to cockpit) complying with FIA Art 253.7 and RACMSA QM(iv).

(iv) All vehicles are fitted with Circuit Breaker complying FIA Art 253.13.,RACMSA QM8.

(v) All vehicles are fitted with towing eyes to FIA Art 253.10.,RACMSA QG.1.1.3.

(vi) All vehicles are fitted with Rear Warning Lights -FIA Art 257.8.4.5.,RACMSA QM 5.

(vii) Drivers must wear clean CLOTHING which carries correct decals as specified in the Sporting Regulations for the Challenge throughout any event in the Challenge :-
(a)- Helmets- must carry one of the following approvals:-
Snell 90,Snell S85, Snell M85 or BSI 6658 type A.
It is recommended that all have fire resistant interiors.
(b) -Overalls-minimum 3 layer carrying FIA 1986 Homologation with fire resistant underwear,socks,boots and gloves.

TR.3 Bodywork.

(i) The only permitted bodywork is that designated by Jaguarsport for the XJR15.

(ii) Additional aerodynamic aids, splitters, etc, are forbidden.

TR.4 Engine.

(i) The 5993cc V12 sohc 24 valve power unit provided with the vehicle has specific seals affixed which may not be broken except under the supervision of JaguarSport personnel and the Challenge Eligibility Scrutineer.
(ii) Any form of modification is forbidden.

TR.5 Fuel.

(i) The only fuel permitted for the series is that specified by JaguarSport from the approved supplier.
(ii) The addition of any form of power boosting or octane boosting additives is forbidden.
(iii) All cars will start any practice or race ine the Challenge with a full tank.

TR.6 Transmission.

(i) The TWR 6speed transmission supplied with the XJR15 carries seals which may only be broken under the supervision of JaguarSport personnel and the Challenge Eligibility Scrutineer.
(ii) The 3 plate AP Racing Clutch is mandatory.
(iii) No modifications to the designated transmision are permitted.
(iv) The designated gearbox and final drive ratios will be specified by JaguarSport for each event in the Challenges.

TR7.Suspension.

(i) All the Challenge XJR 15 cars have identical suspension which will carry identifying seals.
(ii) The designated Bilstein Shock Absorbers are mandatory.
(iii) Components may only be changed by JaguarSport.
(iv) No other components may be introduced.
(v) Settings will be designated by JaguarSport.
(vi) The only permitted freedom is the adjustment for the Front Anti Roll Bar.

TR.8 Brakes.

(i) The complete system, steel discs with AP four pot calipers, fitted to the Challenge XJR 15 cars is mandatory and may not be subject to any modifications.
(ii) Only Ferodo 245 pad material is designated by JaguarSport.

TR.9 Wheels & Tyres.

(i) Only wheels supplied and designated by JaguarSport for the Challenge may be used. Front : 9.5" x 17"
Rear : 13" x 17"
(ii) Bridgestone controlled tyres will be designated by JaguarSport for each event in the Challenge.
(iii) Each competitor will be allocated eight dry (slick) tyres prior to practice. Any tyre allegedly damaged may be exchanged only by agreement of the BridgStone Technician and JaguarSport Tyres deliberately 'flat spotted' will not be included.
(iv) JaguarSport will declare the tyres for each event - Wet or Dry-. No arbitrary changes fron the designated specifications will be permitted.

TR.10. Cooling.

(i) All Challenge XJR 15 cars have identical cooling systems.
(ii) No changes to the designated specification are permitted.
(iii) Any external or internal blanking will only be permitted as designated by JaguarSport.

TR.11 Electrical.

(i) The XJR 15 is supplied with Lucas Zytek ignition system.
(ii) No components of the electrical/ignition system may be modified.

TR.12 Fuel System.

(i) The Fuel System is Zytec sequential fuel injecton with digital electronic management.
(ii) ECU's will be sealed and subject to checks throughoutthe Challenge.
(iii) The Fuel Tank is to FIA FT3 standard and all fuel lines comply with FIA Art 253.3. Maximum capacity 100 litres.
(iv) Any form of modification to the fuel system is forbidden.

TR.13. Weight.

(i) The minimum weight of the car with full fuel tank, throughout any event in the Challenge, must not be less than --------kgs. (to be advised ).

TR.14. Miscellaneous.

(i) Notwithstanding these Technical Regulations printed above,it is the competitor's responsibility to ensure he and the vehicle comply with any supplementary regulations for any event when presented at Scrutineering.
(ii) Competitors are reminded it is forbidden to modify or perform any work on designated components of the Challenge XJR 15 other than normal servicing and respecting the regulations above.

TR.15. Advertising.

(i) Advertising on any transparent surface is forbidden.
(ii) All advertising must respect the designated areas within the Sporting Regulations..

02.03.91
MEG.

## Monaco Grand Prix – May 9th–11th

The driver entry list for the first race at Monaco showed the International interest shown in this series.

JAGUAR SPORT

INTERCONTINENTAL *Challenge*

**JAGUARSPORT INTERCONTINENTAL CHALLENGE**

**MONACO - MAY 9-11, 1991**

ENTRY LIST - ALL CARS IDENTICAL JAGUARSPORT XJR-15

| Car No: | Driver: | Representing: | Entrant: |
|---|---|---|---|
| 1 | Matt Aitken (GB) | Owner/driver | JaguarSport |
| 2 | Davy Jones (USA) | The Americas | JaguarSport |
| 3 | Andy Evans (USA) | Owner/driver | JaguarSport |
| 4 | Bob Wollek (F) | Europe | JaguarSport |
| 5 | Tiff Needell (GB) | Owner's nominee | JaguarSport |
| 6 | Jim Richards (NZ) | Australasia | JaguarSport |
| 7 | Cor Euser (NL) | Owner's nominee | JaguarSport |
| 8 | Matsuaki Sunada (J) | Japan | JaguarSport |
| 9 | David Brabham (AUS) | Australasia | JaguarSport |
| 10 | Armin Hahne (D) | Owner's nominee | JaguarSport |
| 11 | Derek Warwick (GB) | Europe | JaguarSport |
| 12 | Nigel Spiro (GB) | Owner/driver | JaguarSport |
| 13 | John Nielsen (DK) | Owner's nominee | JaguarSport |
| 14 | Yohjiroh Terada (J) | Japan | JaguarSport |
| 15 | Juan Fangio II (RA) | The Americas | JaguarSport |
| 16 | Ian Flux (GB) | Owner's nominee | JaguarSport |

Reserve Driver:

David Leslie (GB)

**JAGUARSPORT INTERCONTINENTAL CHALLENGE**
BROADSTONE GRANGE, BROADSTONE HILL, Nr. CHIPPING NORTON, OXFORDSHIRE OX7 5QL.
TEL: (0608) 678763 FAX: (0608) 677297

*XJR-15 on the streets of Monaco as a Formula One support race.*

MONACO, MAY 11, 1991

**ROUND ONE, JAGUARSPORT INTERCONTINENTAL CHALLENGE**

**** WARWICK TAKES FIRST HONOURS ****

Briton Derek Warwick started Saturday's race from pole position and maintained the lead to the chequered flag in the first round of the JaguarSport Intercontinental Challenge at Monaco. He was closely followed by Australian David Brabham in second position, and American Davy Jones in third.

A huge crowd of spectators, media and Formula One personnel watched as the 16 JaguarSport XJR-15s roared away for the 16 lap race. The identically prepared cars had created enormous interest throughout the entire weekend, and all of the international line up of drivers were looking forward to a close run race.

One of the two XJR-15 owners to race their own car was Matt Aitken of the Stock Aitken and Waterman music empire. Admitting before the start of the race that he was a little out of his class compared to the professional drivers competing, Aitken nevertheless won over the crowd during the race by entertaining them with a number of spins and 'moments'. He persisted though and finished the race exhausted but happy to have fulfilled a life long dream to race at Monte Carlo.

Warwick was chased hard in the early laps by German touring car star Armin Hahne until the latter spun on some oil on the track. He struggled to find first gear but got going again some six places down the field, eventually fighting his way up again to finish in 5th place.

South American driver Juan Fangio II snaked his way through the field from 11th position on the grid to take 4th place. He said afterwards that "the race had been a lot of fun and I am very much looking forward to Silverstone in July."

Of the 16 cars to start, only one failed to finish. John Nielsen understeered his XJR-15 coming out of the swimming pool area and "ran out of road", damaging the suspension of the car.

Warwick was greeted on the rostrum by Jaguar Chairman Bill Hayden who was in Monte Carlo to watch the race. He received as first prize the keys to a JaguarSport XJR-S 6.0 litre, a trophy and champagne.

The next round in the JaguarSport Intercontinental Challenge will be following the British Grand Prix at Silverstone on Sunday, July 14th.

FINAL RESULTS - FIRST SIX:

| | | | |
|---|---|---|---|
| 1 | 11 | Derek Warwick | GBR |
| 2 | 9 | David Brabham | AUS |
| 3 | 2 | Davy Jones | USA |
| 4 | 15 | Juan Fangio II | ARG |
| 5 | 10 | Armin Hahne | GER |
| 6 | 4 | Bob Wollek | FRA |

For further information please contact Fiona Miller at TWR on 0608 678763.

# Tom Walkinshaw's post Monaco debrief held at Broadstone on May 16

RECEIVED
23 MAY 1991

MINUTES FROM SVO/XJR-15 MEETING (POST MONACO DE-BRIEF)

KIDLINGTON 10.30AM, MAY 16, 1991

Present: Tom Walkinshaw
Bill Donnelly
Andy Morrison
Eddie Hinckley
Dave Fullerton
Ken Page
Rod Benoist
Allan Scott (part)
Steve Grey (part)
Andy King
Fiona Miller

TW thanked everyone for all their efforts in making the Monaco event happen. Various areas were looked at in detail:

1) Chassis:

- Oil and water temperatures. There were overheating problems so it will be necessary to look at a new oil cooler system.
- Gear selection. All gearboxes will be looked at thoroughly before Silverstone, as will clutches.
- Loss of oil/oil mist can only be put down to overfilling. EH suggested putting a loop in the vent pipe. Only one car had an engine oil leak.
- Suspension. Race springs and dampers okay.
- All drivers felt cockpit temperature was too high, and this will be looked at before Silverstone.
- Steering racks. Cor Euser's car gave the biggest problem, although David Leslie also suffered from steering fault. EH reported that it appears to have been a machining fault, and that all racks will be taken out for inspection.
- TW suggested John Nielsen and Andy Wallace to do follow up testing work necessary before Silverstone.

2) Engine:

AS reported that there were a few small problems that will need addressing. TW thanked the engine shop for a good job in preparing all the engines.

- Misfiring. AS feels that the problem is fuel related.
- AS believes there were a few low rev counters.
- Oil pressure. The problem which occurred on the car at the Silverstone shakedown day re-occurred, so a new oil pump was fitted. Cars currently in build need to be looked at.
- Water pump. All cars will be looked at and fitted with new pumps where necessary before Silverstone.
- Oil leak. Engine inspection will be carried out.

3) Organisational:

- BP. It was felt that the French company let down the UK. They failed to bring pumps and we had to borrow hand pumps. TW warned to make sure we are self-sufficient for Silverstone.
- Bridgestone. RB reported that Peter Grelinski was not at all helpful and we had to make the running over the entire weekend. SVO to compose a letter on behalf of TW to Tony Brown, with a copy to Japan, voicing our dissatisfaction.
- Accommodation. Mechanics' accommodation was little small, due to under estimation of staff needed for the event. AK reported that there had been management problems with the VIP accommodation, but that the guests had not been aware of it.
- Transportation. One of the cars had been damaged in transit, and some of the covers had caused chafing on the paint work. SVO to claim through Toleman's insurance.
- Security. AK to write and thank them for a good job.

4) Prizes:

It was suggested that there be a grand presentation of prizes at Spa - the two cars, million dollars and trophies. This was agreed. BD to inform owners in next communication?

5) TW Overview Of Event:

While it was satisfactory in almost every area, we were far too near the line in others. We must put right the small things before Silverstone as the novelty value will have worn off and we shall be subject to a much closer scrutiny by all around us.

TW felt that the organisation was amateurish and that there had been poor communication and control and that we were forced to think on our feet too often. He accepted that a part of this may have been due to the fact that it was Monaco, a difficult circuit to work at at the best of times.

6) Silverstone:

It was agreed that two practice sessions would be necessary. Graham Lake-Grange to be contacted to arrange this. We will be working out of the support race pits and a large marquee will be erected alongside them to give us further working space.

Longines will have to run a cable from their main unit to our pits - AK to contact Serge Carnal about this.

AM confirmed that 16 cars will be the maximum for Silverstone, with the possibility to increase to 20 for Spa. FM requested to submit driver plans for next week.

BD and AK were requested to draw up a list of hospitality requirements/plans for Silverstone by next week. It was felt that plans need not be as up-market for Silverstone - perhaps a big barbecue on Sunday after the race for all to attend.

RB/KP to update job list on all cars for next week.

fm/21.5.91

MINUTES OF SVO XJR-15 MEETING

JUNE 28, 1991 AT KIDLINGTON

Present: Tom Walkinshaw
Bill Donnelly
Dave Fullerton
Wayne Humphreys
Allan Scott
Ken Page
Rod Benoist
Andy King
Fiona Miller

**1) Points Arising From Last Meeting**

There were no points arising.

**2) XJR-15 Race Programme**

RB reported that an engine problem has been discovered during a system check - a large residue of sand from the casting process in the sump. AS listed engines that had been checked and those due to be checked, and stated there would be no problems from engine 020 onwards. AS told TW that he was confident the matter was in hand.

A draft movement schedule was presented, and RB informed everyone that times for scrutineering and briefings have now been set. FM to contact drivers with these additional details.

AK said that signalling for XJR-15 race can be done from the F1 pits, and that he has requested Longines to provide two monitors in F1 pits and two in the support pits.

**3) Sales**

Andy Morrison was unavailable due to prior commitments, but KP presented the situation to date.

**4) Production**

TW expressed his dissatisfaction with XK Engineering's painting process. He suggested that in future all XK cars should be delivered in base carbon colour, for painting after delivery. KP said that they will judge from the next colour being painted by XK. TW asked for price comparisons between XK and QCR.

Otherwise production is going to schedule.

**5) Engineering**

As per DF's engineering report, the most serious problem was with gearboxes, particularly with three cars which have already been delivered to customers and are believed to be in Japan.

DF has looked at the situation fully and proposed a solution which means a mechanic going out to Japan to service the cars. AS is going in three weeks time and he and TW thought it should be possible to investigate the situation more fully then. TW warned that it may not be easy to get the customers to bring their cars to one location as they may be dispersed all over Japan.

TW asked DF to give him further details and to discuss a service base. TW also asked someone from SVO to draw up an "After Sales Service" hit list.

The handbook has now been typographically corrected, and TW asked to see it before it goes any further in the printing process.

**6) Finance**

As read in WH's report, but have not yet had Valemco money as it has not come through from Japan.

TW asked for final figures, including overspend, from Monaco. WH/AK to prepare for next week.

**7) Press and PR**

Silverstone paddock arrangements are in hand. AK informed TW that Gary Timms recommends 3 motorhomes in order to feed all the team and guests. TW feels that we should only have to provide tea for them on the practice days.

Hospitality - we have 120 places in the grandstand. There is no further news on Hartwell House at the moment, but they are trying to sell it on.

FM raised the question of replacement drivers for Spa as Jones and Fangio will not be available. She suggested Christian Fittipaldi, which was agreed, and TW suggested Salazaar as the second "Americas" driver. It was also agreed that Aguri Suzuki should be approached (if he no longer has a GP drive) for Japan. TW asked for a list to be compiled for next week's meeting.

8) Any Other Business

SVO informed TW that they intended to hold a staff barbecue after the race.

WH said that JaguarSport were intending to raise their hourly rates to cover overtime, and queried it. TW felt that this was fully justified but asked KP to discuss with Paul Davies.

AK raised the subject of livery and said that Design have mocked up a car. Polaroids were presented. There was some discussion about the timing of decals delivery, and AK will be trying to rush it through.

FM/2.7.91

*Follow up meeting to May 16th*

*Tom Walkinshaw releasing the XJR-15 at Silverstone.*

*Road testing the XJR-15 on the roads at Oxfordshire.*

## Silverstone Grand Prix – July 12th-14th

JAGUAR SPORT
INTERCONTINENTAL
Challenge

SILVERSTONE, UK SATURDAY, JULY 13, 1991

SECOND AND FINAL PRACTICE/QUALIFYING SESSION
WARWICK ON POLE FOR BRITISH XJR-15 ROUND

Briton Derek Warwick displayed all his skill and experience today to place his V12-engined XJR-15 on pole position for tomorrow's race. His time of 1m 55.50 was set early on in the dry session but as Derek said afterwards, "It wasn't actually my best lap! I feel that I did a better one straight afterwards, but just didn't manage to go any quicker."

David Brabham of Australia put car number 9 into second position, moving up from sixth place yesterday. Dutchman Cor Euser who had topped the times yesterday slipped to third position on the grid, followed by Briton Ian Flux and Frenchman Bob Wollek who made up nine places to finish up 5th on the grid. Juan Fangio was 6th.

German touring car star Armin Hahne was hampered by a misfiring engine during this afternoon's session, while Davy Jones from the USA suffered from a wrong tyre choice. However, he said afterwards, "I've got a new set for tomorrow, which I know that some of the other drivers don't, so perhaps that may give me the advantage I'm going to need."

| | | | |
|---|---|---|---|
| 1 | car 11 | Warwick (GB) | 1.55.50 |
| 2 | car 9 | Brabham (AUS) | 1.56.16 |
| 3 | car 7 | Euser (NL) | 1.56.49 |
| 4 | car 16 | Flux (GB) | 1.56.57 |
| 5 | car 6 | Wollek (F) | 1.56.74 |
| 6 | car 15 | Fangio (RA) | 1.56.75 |
| 7 | car 12 | Leslie (GB) | 1.56.95 |
| 8 | car 10 | Hahne (D) | 1.57.00 |
| 9 | car 8 | Acheson (GB) | 1.57.15 |
| 10 | car 5 | Needell (GB) | 1.57.58 |
| 11 | car 17 | Nielsen (DK) | 1.56.67 |
| 12 | car 2 | Jones (USA) | 1.58.23 |
| 13 | car 6 | Percy (GB) | 1.58.32 |
| 14 | car 1 | Aitken (GB) | 1.59.40 |
| 15 | car 3 | Evans (USA) | 2.00.73 |
| 16 | car 14 | Terada (J) | 2.01.68 |

The same driver line-up as Monaco was entered for the Silverstone GP rounds with the addition of John Nielsen making seventeen cars to start this round.

All the race cars had been insured against race damage and it was in TW's mind that a tidy sum could be made as the only supplier of the body parts, with all owners contracted to have their cars repaired by SVO at Broadstone. Owners would have to pay the excess on each accident and then insurance would pay the probably expensive repairs bill. The insurance brokers had a film crew at Silverstone and carefully filmed the race, recording each minor or major touch. Each successive contact was recorded and each successive contact triggered the excess on the policy, even if it was in the same place on the car a few laps later. Many of the race car repairs had so many multiple excess charges that it was debatable if a claim should be lodged or not.

*Non-racing XJR-15s could have custom paint colours.*

BRITISH GRAND PRIX
SILVERSTONE
12–13–14 JULY 1991

A round of the FIA FORMULA 1 WORLD CHAMPIONSHIP

Silverstone Circuits Limited · Silverstone · Towcester · Telephone 0327 857271 · Fax 0327 857663 · Telex 311164 SC BRDC G

Issued by RAC MSA Race Services

PROVISIONAL RESULTS - RACE 6
JAGUARSPORT INTERCONTINENTAL CHALLENGE
20 Laps 64.94 Miles 104.51 Kms.

| Pos | No | Cl | Driver | Car | Laps | Time | Behind | MPH | Km/H | Best | MPH | Km/H | On |
|---|---|---|---|---|---|---|---|---|---|---|---|---|---|
| 1 | 15 | | Juan FANGIO II | JaguarSport XJR-15 | 20 | 39:46.74 | | 97.95 | 157.65 | 1:57.72 | 99.29 | 159.79 | 4 |
| 2 | 4 | | Bob WOLLEK | JaguarSport XJR-15 | 20 | 39:50.05 | 0: 3.31 | 97.81 | 157.41 | 1:58.32 | 98.79 | 158.99 | 14 |
| 3 | 16 | | Ian FLUX | JaguarSport XJR-15 | 20 | 39:56.32 | 0: 9.58 | 97.55 | 157.00 | 1:57.52 | 99.46 | 160.06 | 6 |
| 4 | 12 | | David LESLIE | JaguarSport XJR-15 | 20 | 40: 5.68 | 0:18.94 | 97.18 | 156.39 | 1:58.36 | 98.75 | 158.92 | 10 |
| 5 | 10 | | Armin HAHNE | JaguarSport XJR-15 | 20 | 40:15.50 | 0:28.76 | 96.78 | 155.76 | 1:59.19 | 98.07 | 157.83 | 5 |
| 6 | 5 | | Tiff NEEDELL | JaguarSport XJR-15 | 20 | 40:19.92 | 0:33.18 | 96.60 | 155.47 | 1:58.93 | 98.28 | 158.17 | 5 |
| 7 | 3 | | Andy EVANS | JaguarSport XJR-15 | 20 | 41: 2.66 | 1:15.92 | 94.93 | 152.77 | 2: 0.37 | 97.11 | 156.28 | 15 |
| 8 | 9 | | David BRABHAM | JaguarSport XJR-15 | 20 | 41:26.94 | 1:40.20 | 94.00 | 151.28 | 1:57.41 | 99.55 | 160.21 | 4 |
| 9 | 8 | | Kenny ACHESON | JaguarSport XJR-15 | 20 | 41:42.75 | 1:56.01 | 93.41 | 150.33 | 1:59.37 | 97.92 | 157.59 | 5 |
| 10 | 14 | | Yojiro TERADA | JaguarSport XJR-15 | 20 | 41:49.83 | 2: 3.09 | 93.14 | 149.90 | 2: 3.03 | 95.01 | 152.90 | 4 |
| 11 | 2 | | Davy JONES | JaguarSport XJR-15 | 18 | 40: 2.22 | 2 Laps | 87.58 | 140.95 | 1:58.09 | 98.98 | 159.29 | 7 |
| | | | ... Not Classified ... | | | | | | | | | | |
| | 6 | | Win PERCY | JaguarSport XJR-15 | 11 | DNF | | | | 1:59.02 | 98.21 | 158.05 | 9 |
| | 7 | | Cor EUSER | JaguarSport XJR-15 | 8 | DNF | | | | 1:58.97 | 98.25 | 158.12 | 5 |
| | 1 | | Matt AITKEN | JaguarSport XJR-15 | 4 | DNF | | | | 2: 0.20 | 97.24 | 156.49 | 3 |
| | 11 | | Derek WARWICK | JaguarSport XJR-15 | 4 | DNF | | | | 1:57.54 | 99.44 | 160.03 | 4 |
| | 17 | | John NIELSEN | JaguarSport XJR-15 | 1 | DNF | | | | 2: 5.22 | 93.34 | 150.22 | 1 |
| | | | ... Fastest Laps ... | | | | | | | | | | |
| | 9 | | David BRABHAM | JaguarSport XJR-15 | | 1:57.41 | | 99.55 | 160.21 | Lap Record | | | |

*Results of the second round at Silverstone.*

## Spa-Francorchamps – August 23rd-25th

With one million dollars in prize money up for the owner of the car that won the final race of the three-race series, pressure was on the drivers of their respective cars to perform.

**TEAM PLAN**

Cars 1 - 4

| | | |
|---|---|---|
| Phil McRobert<br>Clive Parker | Engineer: | Ken Page |
| Chris Dee<br>Dave Thomas | Engines: | Pete Tyrell |

Cars 5 - 8

| | | |
|---|---|---|
| Paul Collins<br>Graeme Voller | Engineer: | Alastair MacQueen |
| Steve Allen<br>Paul Slaymaker | Engines: | Andrew Whiffen |

Cars 9 - 12

| | | |
|---|---|---|
| Alex Ayriss<br>Andy Smart | Engineer: | Eddie Hinckley |
| Roger Crook<br>Mick Wright | Engines: | Andrew Penny |

Cars 14 - 17

| | | |
|---|---|---|
| Kevin Drew<br>Mark Boughton | Engineer: | Dave Fullerton |
| Mareck Sobas<br>John May | Engines: | Nigel Webb (floating)<br>Stephen Siddle |

| | |
|---|---|
| Pit Area & Equipment<br>Fuel, Tyres, etc: | Paul Summerfield,<br>Brian Robertson |
| Electrical Maintenance: | Chris Hills |
| Wheel & Bodywork<br>Preparation & Repair: | Tim Pamphlett<br>John Hook<br>Doug Whitmore<br>Roger Tolson<br>Darren Page |

### Spa Placings

1 Armin Hahne
2 Cor Euser
3 Win Percy
4 Will Hoy
5 Bob Wollek
6 David Brabham
7 David Leslie
8 Ian Flux
9 Pierre Dieudonné
10 Jim Richards
11 Jeff Allam
12 Andy Evans
13 Tiff Needell
Derek Warwick – DNF
Thierry Tassin – DNF
John Watson – DNF

JAGUAR SPORT INTERCONTINENTAL Challenge

JAGUARSPORT INTERCONTINENTAL CHALLENGE

SPA-FRANCORCHAMPS - AUGUST 23-25, 1991

ENTRY LIST - ALL CARS IDENTICAL JAGUARSPORT XJR-15

| Car No: | Driver: |
|---|---|
| 1 | David Leslie (GB) |
| 2 | Will Hoy (GB) |
| 3 | Andy Evans (USA) |
| 4 | Bob Wollek (F) |
| 5 | Tiff Needell (GB) |
| 6 | Jim Richards (NZ) |
| 7 | Cor Euser (NL) |
| 8 | Pierre Dieudonne (B) |
| 9 | David Brabham (AUS) |
| 10 | Armin Hahne (D) |
| 11 | Derek Warwick (GB) |
| 12 | Win Percy (GB) |
| 14 | Thierry Tassin (B) |
| 15 | John Watson (GB) |
| 16 | Ian Flux (GB) |
| 17 | Jeff Allam (GB) |

25th August, 1991 Spa-Francorchamps

THE MILLION DOLLAR RACE

German driver Armin Hahne today earned his employers one million dollars by winning the final round of the three race JaguarSport Intercontinental Challenge at Spa, Belgium - earning $593 per second of the 11 lap race.

Wolfgang and Ewe Eickwinkel, the German industrialists who own Hahı :'s car, were present to witness the victory. Armin said afterwards:

"This was the most sensible race I have driven of the three. I knew I would have an edge with my new tyres so I tried to stay out of trouble for the first five laps. Derek, David and Cor all made small mistakes but for once I did not! The car was perfect and I'd like to thank the whole team for doing such a good job over the three races."

Dutchman Cor Euser finished second, followed by Win Percy in third place. Derek Warwick failed to finish the race after "running out of track and kerb" on lap 9 and spinning off at the fast corner before the Bus Stop. Hahne had already passed Euser but Warwick was not able to copy his move. Other retirements were Tassin and Watson.

The driver with the most number of points in the Intercontinental Challenge (eight drivers represented Europe, the Americas, Australasia and Japan were eligible for the Challenge) was David Brabham of Australia, and he will receive a silver trophy on behalf of his country's motor sport association.

For further information please contact Fiona Miller at the JaguarSport motorhome or in the press office.

Engs engineer, Mark Hemsworth, had managed the whole series well with an element of diplomacy needed, and recorded each car's reported problems. 'low range' was a predetermined rpm area that was selected to check some of these complaints and see who might have been a little slower onto the straight to explain a lower end of straight speed. Many drivers worked on the squeaky wheel gets the oil theory and had the Engs staff in constant demand checking engines as drivers looked for the slightest edge. Recordings of maximum rpm reached on the straight were used as excuses to have special attention and checks on particular engines after they had been compared to other drivers.

**Memorandum from Mark Hemsworth – September 2 1991 – XJR-15 Spa Practice & Race Report**

**Car 1 – David Leslie – 019**

Friday: The driver reported that the engine may have been running lean. The fuel pressure was checked and was found to be 3.5 bar. The map was correct in the ECU. The maximum engine speed for the session for 6500rpm.

Saturday: The engineer reported slight smoking from the exhaust overrun. The fuel pressure was checked and found to be 3.5 bar. The engine was borescoped and nothing abnormal was discovered. The engine underwent a leakdown test all which were normal. The spark plugs were good and were therefore refitted. Maximum speed was 6540rpm.

Sunday: The car finished in 7th places. No problems were reported and maximum speed was 6540rpm.

**Car 2 – Will Hoy – 006**

Friday: – The engineer reported a noisy starter. The clutch was checked and found to be in good condition. Several starter engagements were successfully completed without a reoccurrence of the noise. Maximum speed 6500rpm.

Saturday: The car failed to start after the practice session however this was traced to a non fully charged battery. The battery was removed and changed. The car started successfully. Maximum speed 6500rpm.

Sunday: The car finished 4th. No problems were reported and the engine log recorded 1 second in the lower speed band and a maximum speed of 6839rpm.

**Car 3 – Andy Evans – 024**

Friday: No problems reported. Maximum speed 6550rpm.

Saturday: Smoke was seen from the rear of the car. This was due to oil leaking from the gear box onto the exhaust. SVO rectified the problem. However, the driver reported that the engine seemed down on power. The fuel pressure was checked and found to be OK. The engine was leaded down, all cylinders had low leakage. The spark plugs were good. The maximum speed was 6500rpm.

Sunday: The car finished 12th. The maximum speed was 6540rpm.

**Car 4 – Bob Wollek – 004**

Friday: No problems reported. Maximum speed 6800rpm.

Saturday: No problems reported. Maximum speed 6500rpm.

Sunday: The car finished 5th. Maximum speed 6793rpm.

**Car 5 – Tiff Needell – 032**

Friday: The car crashed heavily at Eau Rouge. The engine was inspected for damage but none found. The pulleys and belts were in good condition. The air filters were cleaned. Maximum speed not recorded.

Saturday: No problems reported. Maximum speed 6500rpm.

Sunday: The car finished in 13th place. Maximum speed 6711rpm.

**Car 6 – Jim Richards – 007**

Friday: No problems reported. Maximum speed 7100rpm.

Saturday: No problems reported. Maximum speed 6500rpm.

Sunday: The car finished in 10th place. Maximum speed 6915rpm.

**Car 7 – Cor Euser – 011**

Friday: No problems reported.

Saturday: No problems reported. Maximum speed 6450rpm.

Sunday: Finished in 2nd place. Maximum speed 6506rpm.

**Car 8 – Pierre Dieudonné**

Friday: The driver reported that the alternator light flashed intermittently. A loose alternator warning connector was tightened by SVO. Maximum speed 6500rpm.

Saturday: The car failed to restart in the pits. The toshiba revealed that the water temperature and air thermistor sensors had defaulted to -99°C. The three sensors have a common earth which when found was incorrectly soldered by D. J. Harnessing. The loom was repaired and the engine ran trouble free.
The engine did not start as excess fuel was injected into the cylinder because of the default on the water temperature sensor. The driver reported the engine to be down on power between 5000–6000rpm. The fuel pressure was 3.5 bar and the leak downs were low. Maximum speed 6500rpm.

Sunday: The car finished 9th. Maximum speed 6527rpm.

**Car 9 – David Brabham – 008**

Friday: No problems reported. The engine log recorded 1 second in lower speed band and a maximum speed of 7067rpm.

Saturday: No problems reported. Maximum speed 6800rpm.

**Car 9 – David Brabham – 008** *contd*

Sunday: The car finished 6th. Maximum engine speed 6944rpm with 1 second recorded in the lower speed band.

**Car 10 – Armin Hahne – 018**

Friday: The engine would not start during a pit stop. The water temperature connector had come adrift causing the injectors to add excess fuel. Once the plug had been lockwired into place the engine did not experience any starter problems. Maximum speed 6700rpm.

Saturday: A faulty battery caused starter problems but when a fully changed battery was fitted the engine started every attempt. Maximum speed 7000rpm.

Sunday: The car was the race winner. No problems were reported and the engine log showed 2 seconds in the lower speed band and a maximum speed of 6901rpm.

**Car 11 – Derek Warwick – 012**

Friday: No problems reported. Maximum speed 6915rpm with 6 seconds recorded in the lower speed band.

Saturday: No problems reported. Maximum speed 6600rpm.

Sunday: The car retired on lap 8 having experienced a heavy contact with the barriers. Maximum speed 6644tpm.

**Car 12 – Win Percy – 013**

Friday: The driver reported that the oil light came on momentarily on the straight. The problem was thought to have been caused at the dashboard. Maximum speed 6600rpm and 2 seconds were logged in the lower speed band.

Saturday: Again the driver reported that the oil light illuminated on the straight. The oil pressure sender was changed and the problem did not re-occur. The driver reported that the engine was down on power. The fuel pressure to 3.5 bar. The leakdowns were low.
Maximum speed 6600rpm with 2 seconds recorded in the lower speed band.

Sunday: The car finished in 3rd place. No problems were reported but 5 seconds were logged in the lower speed band and the maximum speed was 6901rpm.

**Car 14 – Thierry Tassin – 015**

Friday: An additional throttle spring was fitted before the session. No problems were reported during the practice session. Maximum speed 6900rpm.

Saturday: The driver reported a rev related engine vibrations. The spark plugs were removed and the engine borescoped. No engine problems were uncovered. The throttle linkage was badly worn and was replaced and adjusted. Maximum speed 7400rpm.

Sunday: The car retired from the race on lap 3 after a collision with Win Percy. Maximum engine speed 7363rpm.

**Car 15 – John Watson – 016**

Friday: No problems reported. Maximum speed 6500rpm.

Saturday: No problems reported. Maximum speed 6497 rpm.

Sunday: The car crashed on lap 3. Maximum engine speed 6500rpm.

**Car 16 – Ian Flux – 017**

Friday: No problems reported. Maximum speed 6650rpm.

Saturday: No problems reported. Maximum speed 6800rpm.

Sunday: The car finished in 8th places. No problems were reported and the maximum engine speed 6697 rpm.

**Car 17 – Jeff Allam**

Friday: No problems reported. Maximum speed 7000rpm

Saturday: No problems reported. Maximum speed 6500rpm.

Sunday: The car finished the race in 11th place. No problems were reported. Maximum engine speed 6609rpm.

**Summary**

The corrective action taken after the Silverstone race weekend has alleviated the three main problems. The water temperature sensor connectors are now adequately shielded from the exhausts. The injector pins within the injector connectors are fully retained by the potting compound and no injection problems were encountered during the Spa weekend.

The throttle pots that are set with belville washers and RTV are maintaining the set values.

Another D. J. Harnessing loom caused a problem on Saturday but a rectification at the circuit was carried out at the Chris Hills.

The engine logs showed engine speeds of up to 7400rpm but the majority of the drivers were well behaved.

The post race engine checkover has yet to be completed.

M. A. HEMSWORTH
Engineering Assistant

**RACE ENGINE DIVISION**
**MEMORANDUM**

| | | | |
|---|---|---|---|
| TO : | ALLAN SCOTT | FROM : | CHARLIE BAMBER |
| DATE : | 18 February 1992 | cc : | |
| REF : | XJR15 7.4 | | |

| | (Corrected power : HP) | Torque FT/LB | BMEP |
|---|---|---|---|
| 3500 | 357.5 | 536.24 | 179.4 |
| 4000 | 463.8 | 608.77 | 181.06 |
| 4500 | 521.3 | 608.26 | 203.51 |
| 5000 | 595.8 | 625.62 | 209.33 |
| 5500 | 651.1 | 621.5 | 207.96 |
| 6000 | 694.5 | 607.7 | 203.3 |
| 6500 | 734.1 | 592.9 | 198.4 |
| 6700 | 731.2 | 573.02 | 191.7 |

NOTE :- Correction likely to have some error due to 3° cell temperature being outside +-10° limit.

| | Observed power |
|---|---|
| 3500 | 367.5 |
| 4000 | 476.8 |
| 4500 | 535.9 |
| 5000 | 612.5 |
| 5500 | 669.3 |
| 6000 | 714 |
| 6500 | 754.6 |
| 6700 | 751.7 |

ALSO :- Requires some full load map alteration to suit XJR15 silenced exhaust system. This will be sent to SVO with ECU.

***Power figures for the Le Mans 7.4 litre engines, fitted with air cleaners and silencing system.***

*The last five XJR-15s fitted with the 7.4-litre Le Mans engines are identified by the distinctive engine air scoop.*

## S A L E S

### X J R - 1 5 C U S T O M E R L I S T

| Chassis No. | Customer | Deposit | Type | Delivery |
|---|---|---|---|---|
| 001 | Campbell McLaren | Swop | Race | April |
| 002 | Don Salvage | Paid | Race | April |
| 003 | Roland Dane | Paid | Road | May |
| 004 | Eickwinkel | Paid | Race | April |
| 005 | Jurgen Mayer | Paid | Road | May |
| 006 | Naito | Paid | Road | July |
| 007 | Ivan Page-Ratcliffe | Paid | Road | May |
| 008 | Valemco | Paid | Road | May |
| 009 | Keith Piggott | Paid | Road | August |
| 010 | Don Salvage | Paid | Race | April |
| 011 | Safari | Paid | Road | August |
| 012 | Nigel Spiro | Paid | Race | April |
| 013 | Nigel Spiro | Paid | Road | August |
| 014 | Ivan Page-Ratcliffe | Paid | Road | August |
| 015 | Ian Donaldson | Paid | Road | September |
| 016 | Valemco | Paid | Road | June |
| 017 | Wada | Paid | Road | June |
| 018 | Valemco | Paid | Road | June |
| 019 | On Offer | | Road | October |
| 020 | Derek Warwick | ASAP | Race | April |
| 021 | Don Salvage | Paid | Road | May |
| 022 | Don Salvage | Paid | Road | May |
| 023 | For Sale | Paid | Race | April |
| 024 | Valemco | Paid | Road | July |
| 025 | Schuppan | Paid | Road | June |
| 026 | Valemco | Paid | Road | August |
| 027 | Andy Evans | Paid | Race | April |
| 028 | Valemco | Paid | Road | October |
| 029 | Don Salvage | Paid | Road | July |
| 030 | Valemco | Paid | Road | October |
| 031 | Valemco | Paid | Race | April |
| 032 | Valemco | Paid | Race | April |
| 033 | Don Salvage | Paid | Road | July |
| 034 | Matsuda (Hayashi) | Paid | Road | September |
| 035 | Valemco | Paid | Road | November |
| 036 | Valemco | Paid | Road | November |
| 037 | Matt Aitken | Swop | Race | April |
| 038 | Matsuda (Yamamoto) | Paid | Road | September |
| 039 | Rex Collection | Swop | Race | April |
| 040 | Valemco | Paid | Road | November |
| 041 | Hugh Chamberlain | Paid | Race | April |
| 042 | On Offer | | Road | November |
| 043 | Wika | Paid | Road | October |
| 044 | Schmidt | Paid | Road | September |
| 045 | Samsung | Paid | Race | April |
| 046 | Don Salvage | Paid | Road | October |
| 047 | Robin Longdon | Paid | Race | April |
| 048 | On Offer | ASAP | Race | April |
| 049 | Rex Collection | Swop | Road | September |
| 050 | Eickwinkel | Paid | Road | December |

*Charlie Bamber, Allan Scott, Tony Dowe, Don Beadle and Peter Kazmar in the Daytona pit lane. Note new lower air filter design to produce increased distance to the engine cover. New sponsor Anheuser-Busch for 1991.*

JAGUAR

Chapter Twenty-Three

# 1991 Daytona, Sebring and Le Mans

**The 1991 year was to be a defining year for the future of TWR as financial clouds were gathering, with two problems coming to a head. Firstly, Ford's buy out of Jaguar had cast question marks over any future participation in motorsport; and it was an ongoing battle for TW to keep them motivated and continue as an income producing client for TWR via JaguarSport. This involved new vehicle concepts and technology via the production 6-litre V12 engine programme. Unknown to most the much heralded and hyped TWR Group's car dealership business that had started with Mazda in 1981, and now encompassing a large number of separate vehicle franchises, was in serious trouble.**

There were major changes to the feel of the established Kidlington TWR racing organisation by now, after six years the XJR-6 to 12 variants had been progressively removed from main stream racing and priority during 1990. The future rule changes to Group C had produced the Ross Brawn managed design of the XJR-14 for TWR by late 1990. Tony Southgate had declined a full time assignment based at the Kidlington factory; he had always worked from his studio at home previously, and so chose to no longer be part of TWR's future designs. Ross Brawn had then assembled a team of new people and this had increased the design capabilities at TWR by a considerable amount. The XJR-14 was a completely new car with a much lighter weight of 750kgs and a non-production-based racing engine of 3.5 litres, the same capacity as the Formula One engines at that time. Bernie Ecclestone, Formula One leader and a maestro of the business deal had seen the growing amounts of money being put into Group C from the Jaguar, Mercedes, Porsche, Toyota, Nissan and Mazda factories, and saw the future for his Formula One series would be to have these manufacturers involved; by supplying high performance racing engines.

While the new XJR-14 team had produced a winning race car under Ross Brawn as 1991 progressed, there was a change of focus for those of us closer to the unspoken problem – creating programmes to keep the Kidlington site viable. Two programmes had already been actioned and they were the manufacture and production at Bloxham of Jaguar's concept XJ220 super car, and the TWR designed XJR-15 road and race car to be produced by TWR's Special Vehicle Operation (SVO) at its Broadstone headquarters. A third deal was being put together to run a minimal budget V6 turbo Jaguar in the Japanese endurance series, with Suntec as sponsor. The US$2,000,000 deal was to be a cash cow to cover the salaries of XJR-14 drivers and other expenses, the Japanese race car and parts support coming from the TWR museum at Broadstone!

After the non-appearance of the 3.2-litre Group C turbo charged engines from Max Heidegger in January 1990, TW had commissioned the design and build of a 12-cylinder 3.5-litre normally aspirated engine from Max to be fitted to the new XJR-14. TW's focus and enthusiasm had been transferred to Ross's new department as well as the design of this all new V12 engine. These changes had sidelined some of the original racing team members and reduced Engs racing support to mainly IMSA with the V6 turbo engine, and V12s in the 12 and 24 hour events. As the XJR-14 developed, and an endurance version of its engine became reliable in the future, the original V12 endurance race cars and engines would become obsolete, and Engs would need another programme to continue with at sometime in the near future.

Roger and chief engineer Alastair Macqueen, along with some of the racing mechanics had moved to head up the production of the new XJ220 high performance super car that was to be produced in numbers at the bespoke Bloxham facility by late 1990. This XJ220 programme was to be an important one for TWR's future, hence Roger's involvement in running the programme. The profits from this venture over the next two years were to be used to produce TWR's new Formula One team, to be headed by Ross Brawn as technical director. A green field site at the back of the Kidlington Industrial Estate had been earmarked for these new headquarters. There was now a different feeling at the original company site at Kidlington, with future aims and plans poorly, if ever, communicated, and TW based at his 800-acre estate 35 minutes away at Broadstone, with the erection of new buildings there as well.

Problems had developed during 1990 concerning the speed at which the new lightweight racing V12 engine for the XJR-14 was progressing. The three cylinder prototype was refusing to rev over 11,000rpm, and after a complete refurbishment and upgrade to their dynamometer cell in Liechtenstein this problem had persisted. I was not involved in this programme, but was becoming alarmed at the slow pace of progress and had a conversation with the engine design draftsman who had been moved from Kidlington to carry out the design work. He had decided to have a meeting with TW and Roger concerning his doubts about the abilities involved and wanted the programme to be returned to Engs at Kidlington because of the lack of answers to the many problems. TW refused his request, and shortly after the engine designer left and the programme was in in trouble; Roger confessing this to me after I had questioned him on progress a couple of weeks after their meeting.

During the time of the three cylinder tests, and what appeared to me to be increasing poor decision making, I had gone to Cosworth and presented a proposal to them for possible engine supply.

Almost one year earlier I had invited Cosworth co-founder Mike Costin to come to Kidlington with designer Geoff Goddard as TW had not met up with either of these two; I felt it was a desirable association for TW if TWR were contemplating entry into Formula One. Mike Costin showed some interest and support for our racing endeavours during our chat over lunch in the Kidlington board room. I had then approached Cosworth for possible use of the latest HB V8 Formula One engine designed by Geoff Goddard, but was then told that this engine was only available for Formula One use. The older 3.5-litre DFZ version was available and I was pushed to take that option, and although a good deal for Cosworth to sell what was now obsolete equipment, it was not a good future for XJR-14 and TWR. A request was then made to Mike Costin to present to the Cosworth board a proposal to supply TWR with the new 3.5-litre HB V8 engine. This had received his backing after I had indicated TWR's future aspirations to enter Formula One and the thought that we might as well start the engine relationship now.

This was then eventually approved by the Board and became a timely plan B with the stalling of the Liechtenstein programme; and doubts that it could actually proceed.

I presented this proposal to TW and watched as he wrote 'HB' on the large desk blotting paper he used as a daily diary. Soon after a deal was done to produce this engine with 'Jaguar' logo cam covers and fitted with the Bosch MP1.7 engine management system instead of Fords own system. This gave a level of differentiation from the original Cosworth engine so that it could be called a 'Jaguar' and worked out well for all concerned. Normally these engines are leased and remain the property of Cosworth, and Jaguar were informed of this situation. They were actually bought by TWR and then leased back to Jaguar for the same amounts paid for the original engines. This gave TWR final ownership of the engines, at no cost. (See results pages 358-360.)

While these problems were surfacing it was hard to get TW's early commitment to anything else and it was becoming obvious to a few of us that something was wrong funding-wise for the company. The XJR-14 and XJ220 programmes along with ever increasing new garages and vehicle franchises had taken on many new personnel attracted to our high profile leader with a company seen to be going places. Their needs had to be looked after to continue those feelings and motivation, soaking up not just his time but funding as well. John Bradley our approachable finance director had stunned us all when he had resigned in late 1989, and the new finance director had taken a corporate approach with little understanding of our work history and budget needs. Salaries for staff had been allocated on a company inflationary basis without individual contributions being acknowledged; he never once in his short two year tenure visited the Engine workshop or knew one member of my staff. Growing companies do need to change and plan for the future. They also need to review and give credence to the history of how the company actually became successful in the first place.

Contractual problems between TWR and long-time racing partner Jaguar were starting to emerge after the buyout by Ford. The new owner's motor racing plans were unknown to us; adding to the pressures on our boss. During one meeting at Broadstone with TW the new finance director had marched into his office and yelled out "no interest rate differentials" before turning around and disappearing back down the corridor. I asked what that meant, to be told that with most of the group's accounts at the one bank in Scotland, accounts in overdraft were charged a premium interest rate compared to the lower rate paid on accounts in credit. TW had then put two office people full time on transferring money between accounts around the clock, producing such a workload for the bank that they had finally run up the white flag. TWR was now the exception on their client list, with a common interest rate being applied to accounts overdrawn and accounts in credit at the end of the day.

Banks and the IRD have long memories.

## Sunbank Daytona (24 hour) – February 2nd-3rd

A review of the options available for the 1991 Daytona race with engine capacity versus car weights being carried out. There was always small changes made to the Jaguars year on year and for Engs it was attention to the detailed shapes of the tail section surrounding the engine air box that needed investigation, as there were some variations in manufacture in that area. It was important to seal the tail section to the engine air box to eliminate some hot air being drawn in from the engine compartment. Alastair Macqueen had previously carried out some full-scale wind tunnel test with side-entry air-ducting in an effort to eliminate the hot air coming from the front radiators entering the engine through the original air entry duct at roof level. We now needed to ensure all tail sections sealed on our engine air box.

Within this changing situation and reduced focus for things V12, Tony Dowe and I had looked at the possibilities available for the Daytona 1991 race; my engine proposals had to be worked backwards from our parts inventory after the experience with proposals to TW the year before. This meant that we could both progress a programme in a timely manner without waiting for TW's approval, which at best would be a last minute directive. We knew that if the engine costs for Daytona were virtually nothing but current overheads, TW would agree with whatever was then presented. We had parts from 1986 to build one 6.5-litre engine which would now be suitable as IMSA's weight limits had been altered to allow larger capacity engines with corresponding increases in car weights for the Daytona 24 hour race. The move to larger 6.5-litre engines suited Tony as well, as the race cars had become heavier over time with many bodywork repairs, containing heavy body filler. This move to a larger engine would save the extra costs involved in making new lightweight bodywork that would not have been approved in time to allow their manufacture anyway; a delaying tactic often used by TW rather than him having to refuse a request for any new expenditure. It would turn out however that the cars would end up having to race 40kgs over the minimum weight limit at 980kgs with the used components that were supplied from Kidlington; and reduce most of the advantage gained when using the 6.5-litre engine. The weight limits for Le Mans were to be increased to 1000kgs without any limit on engine capacity and it was felt that it would be a useful exercise to run cars at these weights to see if any problems arose over 24 hours.

Other engines and parts carried in stock were being built into 'customer' engines at this time for Andy Morrison's SVO department at Broadstone, because various Group C Jaguars were being made ready for sale. This was to raise money for ongoing projects, not necessarily race ones, and it was a matter of depleting both new and used historic stock so that items could be allocated to produce an internal profit for entities involved with SVO, rather than having inventory currently written off Engs balance sheet, remaining Eng division's asset. Time spent on these projects was chargeable but written off assets were transferred at no cost, it was a transfer of assets exercise. A 'customer' engine was then to be used as one of the Daytona spares under TW's later directive. I had requested a review of the camshaft profiles with Geoff Goddard in 1989 and some small changes had been made, but now I asked for another look to fine tune the lifting ramps. The automotive testing body MIRA would be commissioned to carry out valve spring endurance testing on original and revised camshaft profiles. We were confident that this area would be under control. (Details of work carried out in this area are seen in the 1991 Le Mans story.)

The switch to the XJR-14 programme and loss of Castrol sponsorship in IMSA had produced diminishing support from some areas of Kidlington for the American programme, with Roger Silman saying we could not afford both series, Ross Brawn was looking for total TWR financial support for the future of his Formula One aspirations, adding to moves already in place implicating a downsizing of the IMSA team. It was with these changes in focus that we started the 1991 year.

Castrol's support was greatly reduced after their three year support and brewing giant Anheuser-Busch had stepped in with support using their Bud Light brand. Just two race cars and no spare car were allocated to the 1991 Daytona event, a reflection of TW's other commitments. This two-car proposal

**RECOMMENDATIONS FOR DAYTONA 91 CARS FROM WIND TUNNEL TEST 05/11/90**

RECEIVED 13 NOV 1990

The car is assumed to run as specified in Jan '91 Daytona Test Spec:

- Sprint type nose (inc rad exit ramp)
- Long splitter
- NACA brake ducts
- IMSA '88 underwing (Lower tunnel exit to match low tail)
- '90 Le Mans car tails
- '90 Le Mans side panels
- Sprint 60/40 rear wing mounted as Daytona '90 - 15° with ¼" return.

**Main Recommendations**

1. Rear Wing could be mounted slightly forward (10 - 15mm) but more importantly with the main plane at 4° to 5° nose-up for improvement in L/D, and to match the angle of air coming off the tail. The overall downforce level can then be maintained by returning the overall wing angle to as previous (leading edge to top of return) by increasing rear flap angle.

   This could be achieved with new rear wing mount plates or bolt on additional plates.
2. Any holes cut in the top surface of the car reduces downforce. Recommend no extra holes to be cut unless there is proof positive that a decrease in under bonnet temp is achieved.
3. Radiator pressure tapping indicate that air entry area with 3" aperture nose is more than sufficient, and that the rad exit ramp is indeed a significant improvement to low pressure behind the radiator. (Should we try a pressure release by-pass hose across the rad??)
4. Take off point for driver cooling is very high pressure and ducting inside the car is important to maintain flow over driver (eg. take off point to flow air over feet).
5. A positive air box (imagine 2 x horizontal 'horrorscopes' sticking from the engine cover behind the fuel fillers) was tried extensively, and had virtually no effect on external car aero (in fact an improvement can be found by then blocking the side NACA ducts).

   This produces a significant positive pressure in the air boxes, but it must be tried on the real car to find if the air collected is warm or cool.
6. Best "low pressure" position for exhausts is where they currently exit, approx in the centre of the rear wing longitudinally.
7. Bi-plane, tri-plane and derivatives of these wings can not be made to work as well as the standard 60/40 wing on this car!

AKM 12 November 1990
Circulation
RS/ RBr/ KL/ AWS/ I Reed

***Air Box and exhaust tail pipe test. This full-size wind tunnel test was to investigate if the car's skin pressure was increased with speed to assist NACA duct entry and see any effect from surface pressure.***

would only come about if Tony Dowe's team could build the second car from all the spares that existed between Kidlington and America. This would produce another valuable car for later sale and so justify retaining the workforce and provide work for them over the period between the last race in 1990 and the Daytona race at the start of the year. Chassis #290 had then been built up at Valparaiso from mainly second hand parts supplied from Kidlington, and included a fire damaged tub and some new components made by TWR America. After a lot of hard work this produced a new race car, which was used without problems at the pre-Daytona test on the 5th–6th of January.

**AIR BOX AND EXHAUST SYSTEM FOR XJR12 1991**

**Results of Wind Tunnel tests 05/11/90**

1. The current position of exhaust pipes is in a low pressure area. The only recommended change would be that the end of the pipes should be in the centre of the complete rear wing in side view.

   Pressure at the exhaust exit is:-

   at 135 MPH - 10 MB
   180 MPH - 15 MB (or - 0.2 PSI)

   These are expressed as figures below static ambient pressure, and represent a reduction of 1 to 1.5% in static pressure.

2. Air box ears were tried on the car at a position just after and above the fuel fillers.

   Little or no effect was observed on the external aerodynamic behaviour of the car. This was believed to be because the air flow around the sides of the cockpit is inherently bad due to effect of rad exit and front wheel arch.

   If the side entry NACA Ducts for engine intake were covered, the effect was unmeasurable.

   Maximum pressure measured inside the air intake ear represents:-

   at 135 MPH + 15 MB
   at 180 MPH + 22 MB (or 2% increase).

   These were measured with some 'flow-thru' to represent engine air used.

CONCERNS

- Losses in air box max pressure to pressure at inlet trumpet will occur.
- Correct air box to be designed.
- Modifications required to tail all sections.
- Design will still rely on seal between tail and engine air box.
- Tests still to be carried out on full size car too determine temperature of air collected.
- Temperature of air is still very much more important than small pressure gains (Ref. Daytona '88 Tests).
- Should efforts be directed towards properly sealing a confirmed cold air source?

RECEIVED 15 NOV 1990

**AKM 14 November 1990**
**cc. RS/ RBr/ KL/ AWS/ GS/ CB/ MT**

***Exhaust tail pipe exit area was also tested for Engs to find the best depression behind the XJR-12 to assist exhaust scavenging.***

With everything well under control and the team feeling it was the best prepared it had ever been, the 1991 Daytona race weekend was ready to start. The usual IMSA protagonists were lined up for this event and Nissan were using their Group C Le Mans race cars with the 850kg weight limit allowed, but regulated to the slower Group C refuelling flow rates and a total allowance of 2600 litres of fuel. This was a debateable strategy, with pit stops taking up to two minutes for Group C cars, versus an IMSA car carrying 940kgs in weight and faster pit stops of 30 to 35 seconds. In their favour it was reasonable to assume that some servicing work would need to be carried out during the race and this could be done during the longer two minute refuelling pit stops without penalty for the Group C race cars, regaining some of the lost time. In all an interesting scenario to see how this would pan out; provided it could be well policed of course. Nissan took a worldwide view deciding that their Group C cars could be a better choice for the 24 hour race, and also a good test for their readiness later that year at Le Mans.

There was an added feature this year, with Dean Miller supplying special medical and hydration expertise to our drivers as well as support for TWR team members.

During the lead up to the race three of the drivers complained of headaches to differing degrees and were medicated for this, as well as some shoulder pains that probably were associated with the banking and tight infield changes of direction, with the Jaguars having no power steering. We were soon in big trouble though and well laid plans turned to disaster as John Nielsen lost control on a rain-soaked track during practice and crashed heavily into the safety barriers. Dean Miller took care of the situation after this heavy crash and subsequent move to hospital for observation.

The resulting impact was extensive, and despite hard work by the team the damage was too great and left chassis #190 irreparable in time – we would start the race with only one car and nervously await the outcome.

The #6 Joest IMSA Porsche 962 had set the fastest qualifying time for GTP cars with Wollek on 1:50.87. It was Daly in the #3 Group C Nissan showing the advantage of the lighter car with outright speed and a fastest time of 1:49.86, the next two positions going to the Nissan team as well. The #2 Jaguar with Davy Jones set fifth fastest time in the changing conditions on 1:52.07. With the IMSA GTP cars given the first starting positions the Jaguar would line up beside the Joest Porsche on the front of the 2 by 2 grids that started the forty-six car field. Varying estimates had spectators from 30,000 to 55,000 present, less than half the normal crowd at NASCAR events held here.

The race became a battle between Porsche, Nissan and the lone Jaguar with the first of the three Nissans out on lap 47. Other notable retirements were the Unser family team's Porsche 962 on lap 270 after an accident, and then the Joest Porsche on lap 360 with a damaged engine from a leaking water pump. This left the Joest team with one car still running and the Nissan team with two cars, #83 and #84. From lap 133 till lap 314 the two Nissan's and the lone Jaguar traded the leading places, and with pit stop periods crucial with the two different strategies in operation, some disputes had arisen concerning the fuel meters and fuel delivery speed of the Nissan team (this is covered in Dave Benbow's report – see page 341). The Jaguar had begun to have engine overheating problems and stopped in the pits taking on ten litres of water, and it was obvious we had a water leak from somewhere. After suffering water pump drive problems with heat expansion for a second time, the Jaguar was finally parked on lap 379 and out of the race. Lap 472 saw the demise of the second #84Nissan and the eventual battle for honours between the #7 Joest Porsche and the #83 Nissan. It was from this period of the race that the Joest Porsche took control, leading for the last 296 laps with the Nissan setting a comfortable pace in second place to win the Group C category. Davy Jones in the Jaguar set the fastest lap of the race in the IMSA class on 1:41.05 on lap 45 (a full 2.1 seconds faster than the fastest lap set by a Jaguar in 1990) and Julian Bailey the fastest lap in Group C with 1:39.76 on lap 518.

The #7 Joest Porsche 962 was the eventual winner driven by Winter/Jelinski/Pescarolo/Haywood, completing 719 laps and finishing eighteen laps ahead of the #83 Nissan of Brabham/Robinson/Daly/Earl. The Wynn's Porsche 962 of Hotchkis/Adams/Cord/Dyson was a further nine laps down – not the close contest of the previous year.

Our car's retirement was a bitter blow for the team and they felt let down by the Engine department. A combination of errors had led to the problems that surfaced, but unfortunately the Jaguar started overheating from the very start, putting pressure on the driving system of the water pump as the engine block's vertical expansion placed too much stress on the fixed drive belt and stressed the drive pulleys. It turned out that these were pattern after market belts that should have been no problem but

```
NIELSEN JOHN B              M  34 MED REC #        ED DISCHARGE INSTRUCTIONS
   0409532101  ADM: 01/31/91  040-95-32

OTHER INSTRUCTIONS

HEAD INJURY

LIMIT ACTIVITY FOR 24 HOURS

TAKE ONLY ASPIRIN OR TYLENOL FOR HEADACHE AND DISCOMFORT, UNLESS
OTHER MEDICATIONS ARE APPROVED BY A PHYSICIAN. (IF NO ALLERGIES)

CLEAR LIQUIDS FOR 12 HOURS FOLLOWED BY REDUCED AMOUNTS OF FOOD. (NO
ALCOHOLIC BEVERAGES)

SEVERE HEADACHES, CONFUSION OR WEAKNESS OF ARMS OR LEGS, OCCURRING
EVEN WEEKS OR MONTHS AFTER INJURY, SHOULD BE CHECKED BY YOUR PHYSICIAN

CONTACT YOUR PHYSICIAN OR THE EMERGENCY DEPARTMENT IF THE PATIENT
SHOWS:.
A) UNUSUAL SLEEPINESS; DIFFICULTY IN AWAKENING; CONFUSION.
B) NAUSEA AND VOMITING.
C) LOSS OF BALANCE

D) DIFFERENCE IN THE SIZE OF THE PUPILS OF THE EYES. (THE PUPIL IS
THE ROUND, DARKEST PART OF THE CENTER OF THE EYE. NORMAL PUPILS ARE
BOTH THE SAME SIZE)

PATIENTS SHOULD NOT BE LEFT ALONE FOR THE FIRST 24 HOURS. PATIENTS
SHOULD BE CHECKED FOR THE ABOVE SYMPTOMS EVERY 2 HOURS FOR THE FIRST
24 HOURS

 I HEREBY ACKNOWLEDGE RECEIPT OF INSTRUCTIONS INDICATED ABOVE.
 I UNDERSTAND  THAT I HAVE HAD EMERGENCY TREATMENT ONLY, AND
 THAT I MAY BE RELEASED BEFORE ALL MEDICAL PROBLEMS ARE KNOWN
 AND TREATED. I WILL ARRANGE FOR FOLLOW-UP CARE AS INSTRUCTED.
 I CAN RETURN TO THE ED AT ANY TIME IF I FEEL MY CONDITION IS
 NOT IMPROVED, WORSENS, OR I AM NOT ABLE TO ARRANGE FOLLOW-UP
 CARE. TO GET INFORMATION BY TELEPHONE CALL 254-4100:
  YOU WILL BE CONTACTED BY PHONE OR LETTER IF TEST RESULTS
 ARE NOT NORMAL AND REQUIRE FURTHER TREATMENT.  THIS INCLUDES
 CULTURE STUDIES THAT REQUIRE FOUR WORKING DAYS.

 A) TO TALK TO THE NURSE ABOUT YOUR CONDITION CALL 254-4000,
      EXT 3126

 B) IF YOU HAVE A QUESTION ABOUT YOUR EMERGENCY ROOM BILL,
      CALL 254-4107
```

***John Nielsen's discharge instructions from hospital.***

*The Bud Light XJR-12D at Daytona.*

were fractionally smaller and a tighter fit. The water pump used was also an early design that was sent as a used spare, and with small water loses around the five hour mark from a leaking radiator caused by a stone chip, the problem had repeated itself. I had been very reluctant to use the 'customer' spare engine that some of the team, unaware of its origins, had wanted me to change to.

right: ***New feature this year by 'Sport Health' showing a typical driver report (Derek Warwick) monitoring of driver's blood pressure, pulse rate and careful measurement of urine.***

**SPORT HEALTH**

&

TWR-JAGUAR-BUD LIGHT

RACE: Daytona DRIVER: Derek Warwick

TIME:

DATE: 2/2/- 2/3/91

SUBJECTIVE: Following first stint Derek complained of headache and mild foot and back discomfort.

OBJECTIVE TX: Medications dispensed for headache, back and feet massaged.

ASSESSMENT: Following treatment driver was reqeusted to eat a small meal then rest in preparation for the second stint.

PLAN: Continue to treat as necessary.

MEDICATION: Two Tylenol tabs given

NUTRITION: Driver while not feeling particularly hungry was encouraged to eat a lite meal prior to resting for second stint.

EXERCISE PROGRAM:

OVERALL ASSESSMENT:

ADDITIONAL COMMENTS:

| Time | BP | Pulse | Urine Output |
|---|---|---|---|
| 2:45pm | 136/78 | 66 | 160ML |
| 4:50pm | 130/75 | 72 | 300ML |
| 6:15pm | 118/76 | 64 | 600ML |
| 7:10pm | 130/82 | 70 | 100ML |

2150 North Broadway • Walnut Creek, California 94596 • 415/945-7309

TRACK DAYTONA CAR JAGUAR XJR 12

DATE 2/3 FEBUARY

DRIVER DEREK WARWICK

1) START —

2) TRACTION GOOD

3) TURN-IN, SLOW TURN IN U/S

MEDIUM O/K – GOOD

HIGH O/K – GOOD.

4) BALANCE, SLOW U/S BECAUSE DIFF

MEDIUM O/K – GOOD.

HIGH O/K – GOOD.

5) BRAKING GOOD

BALANCE BAR SETTING —

6) BARS —

—

7) SHOCKS —

—

8) BUMPS RIDES BUMPS GOOD.

9) SPRINGS —

10) TIRE LIFE, RACE GOOD.

11) TIRE LIFE, QUAL. —

12) TRACK CONDITIONS QUALIFY —

RACE FUCKING WET AND DARK.

13) FUEL FULL/EMPTY SAME FULL AND EMPTY – GOOD.

14) GEARS O/K.

15) INSTRUMENTS O/K. FUEL METER NEEDS LIGHT. FOR 12/24 HOUR RACES.

16) PITS VERY SHARP, EVERY ONE KNOWS HIS JOB

17) RADIOS VERY GOOD.

18) WHO WAS GOOD ME

19) WHAT WAS GOOD BLOW JOB FROM TONY!

20) WHAT NEEDS IMPROVING GEAR LINKAGE NOT DIRECT ENOUGH TOO MANY JOINTS.

21) COMMENTS (CHASSIS) I HAVE NO COMMENT ON CHASSIS BECAUSE CAR WAS ALL READY SET UP (VERY WELL) TEAM WORKED VERY WELL, MECHANICS GOOD, I CAN'T FAULT ANYBODY.

THE ONLY NEGATIVE POINTS ARE ENGINE IS COMPETITIVE BUT FRAGILE (VALVES ETC), ALSO I KNOW THE BUDJET IS A FACTOR, BUT A SPARE CAR MUST ALWAYS BE AVAILABLE.

*Typical driver race report – Derek Warwick*

DEPARTMENT: Stores

All endurance races put added requirements on a parts department. These requirements range from the cars being completely rebuilt with basically all new parts to being prepared for anything, no matter how major, to be repaired during the race. Like all other departments in a race team, how well it performs at a race is directly related to the work done the weeks before.

In preparing for Daytona, the biggest problem was the lack of communication between us and Kidlington. These problems ranged from incomplete parts lists on new items, used master cylinders sent without prior notification, not filling in P.O.'s completely, and sending items of different spec (again without notification). Obviously, we all got by, but the lack of communication and even a bit of apathy, when dealing with Kidlington, proved to be the largest hurdle in preparing for Daytona. A hurdle that must be dealt with expeditiously if the following season is to be run efficiently.

An area that worked well was prefitting spares. This was the single most important factor in having the spares department run smoothly at Daytona. In the future, a list of parts that must be prefitted should be compiled. Those parts, only after being prefitted, will be "at track" spares.

The inventory of prefitted and non-prefitted parts would have been tested if tub #190 would not have been damaged beyond repair. Except for one engine frame, I am confident the at track spares inventory would have had no problem in supplying what was needed not only to rebuild the car, but also build up another rear end.

During the race, the spares department (except engine department spares) was required to supply only two radiator caps, but was prepared to handle any logical problem which can occur during an endurance race.

Mike Croake

left: ***Report on parts delivery and communication with Kidlington after the 1991 race.***

**TWR GROUP OF COMPANIES**

**COMMON ABBREVIATED DIALING - KIDLINGTON SITE**

****************************************************

| | | |
|---|---|---|
| 01 | TWR Group, Broadstone | (0608) 678763 |
| 02 | - | - |
| 03 | Prophets, Solihull | 021 733 3444 |
| 04 | TWR Jaguar, Coventry | (0203) 639500 |
| 05 | Chariots, St Albans | (0727) 855266 |
| 06 | Prophets, Gerrards Cross | (0753) 889606 |
| 07 | Shires, Coventry | (0203) 407272 |
| 08 | Compak Systems, Gainsborough | (0427) 616927 |
| 09 | Holden Special Vehicles, Australia | 010 613 543 4500 |
| 10 | Nomad Travel | 081 898 4971 |
| 11 | JaguarSport, Bloxham | (0295) 252652 |
| 12 | Sheldon Bosley | (0789) 929310 |
| 13 | TWR USA | 0101 219 462 7223 |
| 14 | TWR SVO Europe | 010 352 379 559 |
| 15 | Jaguar Cars, Browns Lane | (0203) 402121 |
| 16 | Cook and Partners, Hertford | (0992) 554444 |
| 17 | Cook and Partners, Stevenage | (0438) 721877 |
| 18 | Dunning Burston | (0272) 739370 |
| 19 | Linnells Solicitors, Oxford | (0865) 248607 |
| 20 | National Westminster Bank, Oxford | (0865) 790599 |
| 21 | Silverstone Renault | (0865) 516516 |
| 22 | Royal Bank of Scotland, Edinburgh | 031 556 8555 |
| 23 | Royal Bank of Scotland, High Street, Musselburgh | 031 662 2068 |
| 24 | Royal Bank of Scotland, Bridge Street, Musselburgh | 031 665 244 |
| 25 | Stuchbery Stone | (0628) 773282 |
| 26 | Astec | (0332) 875451 |
| 27 | TWR Jaguar, Oxford | (0865) 865100 |
| 28 | Oxford Mazda | (0865) 865111 |
| 29 | Commercial Stationery | (0869) 244778 |
| 30 | TWR Racing, Broadstone | (0608) 678286 |
| 31 | Benetton Formula, Enstone | (0608) 678000 |
| 32 | Silverstone Citreon | (0865) 864000 |
| 33 | IT Helpdesk | (0608) 677177 |
| 34 | Willis Corroon | 021 200 2266 |
| 35 | Henmans | (0865) 722181 |

To obtain the required telephone number, key *73 together with the appropriate code listed above.

right: *This internally traceable dialling system shows the extent of the frequently used contacts within the TWR Group, and you can see the status of motor racing within a now very large organisation. This list includes three separate legal firms, international leasing agents and nine vehicle dealerships, but no Kidlington contacts.*

SUBJECT: Nissan Fuel Use Analysis

DEPARTMENT: Engineering

This report details the fuel usage of the Group 'C' Nissan entries Cars #83 and #84 at the 1991 Daytona 24 Hour Race. Records were also started on their Car #1, but were ceased when this car was taken "behind the wall" at the end of Race Lap 40.

Mike Garton, from England, was the IMSA appointed Group 'C' official present to ensure that Group 'C' refueling rules were enforced. (i.e. flow rate of 60 liters per minute). The regulations for this race allowed a total of 2600 liters of fuel per car, with a reduction of 2.15 liters for every lap run under full course yellow conditions, and a reduction of 1.75 liters per minute that the race is halted under red flag conditions.

Below are tables showing the fuel meter readings, fuel used, and actual flow rates of the two meters (this is based on the meter readings and the actual time the fuel probe was plugged into the car).

CAR #83

| METER READING | VENT BOTTLE CONTENTS | LAP # | NET FUEL FILLED | FILL TIME | FLOW RATE LTR/SEC | FUEL CONSUMPTION LTR/LAP |
|---|---|---|---|---|---|---|
| 91 | 2 | 29 | 89 | 97 sec | .938 | 2.966 |
| 154 | 4 | 49 | 61 | 68 sec | .926 | 3.05 |
| 215 | 3 | 71 | 62 | 71 sec | .873 | 2.818 |
| 303 | 3 | 102 | 88 | 90 sec | .977 | 2.838 |
| 393 | 2 | 134 | 91 | no taken | --- | 2.843 |
| 485 | 2 | 165 | 92 | 92 sec | 1.000 | 2.967 |
| 575 | 2 | 195 | 90 | 88 sec | 1.022 | 3.000 |
| 665 | 2 | 225 | 90 | 88 sec | 1.022 | 3.000 |
| 770 | 12 | 254 | 95 | 116 sec | 0.819 | 3.276 |
| 858 | 12 | 283 | 88 | 99 sec | 0.888 | 3.034 |
| 894 | 14 | 295 | 34 | 29 sec | 1.172 | 2.833 |

Note

As actual fill time was conducted from a distance, it is perhaps unwise to regard the times as gospel, but they will be within a ballpark region. Taking all the flow rates and averaging out will give us a reasonably accurate figure.

Average flow rate 0.876 liters/second.

CAR #84

| METER READING | VENT BOTTLE CONTENTS | LAP # | NET FUEL FILLED | FILL TIME | FLOW RATE LTR/SEC | FUEL CONSUMPTION LTR/LAP |
|---|---|---|---|---|---|---|
| 81 | 3 | 24 | 78 | 66 | 1.182 | 3.12 |
| 158 | 6 | 49 | 74 | 68 | 1.132 | 2.96 |
| ? | 3 | 85 | | 81 | | |

At this point of the race, the fuel meter was blanked out. Using the average flow rate from the first 2 stops, and the known fill time of 81 seconds, it is estimated that 94 liters was put into the car giving a meter reading of 252 liters. Prior to the next stop, the meter was reading 000(?).

After discussions with Jim Woodward of I.M.S.A., we were assured that there had been no foul play. Apparently, a mechanic had knocked the meter and caused the figures to alter. Jim Woodward informed us that the meter had been re-zeroed under the direction of Mike Garton. The correct meter reading after the third stop had been duly recorded and that number would be added to the meter total at the end of the race. A request for that number was turned down with the comment, "that's none of your business." This comment was from Jim Woodward.

As can be seen at this time, the fuel was flowing some 15% faster than permitted (averaged out over the first two stops). It was noted that Mike Garton was holding the car in the pits for some time after refueling had been completed.

| METER READING | VENT BOTTLE CONTENTS | LAP # | NET FUEL FILLED | FILL TIME | FLOW RATE LTR/SEC | FUEL CONSUMPTION LTR/LAP |
|---|---|---|---|---|---|---|
| 89 | 1 | 117 | 91 | 72 | 1.236 | 2.84 |
| 102 | 1 | 141 | 73 | No Time | | |
| 254 | 2 | 172 | 91 | 74 | 1.243 | 2.935 |
| 348 | 3 | 201 | 93 | 80 | 1.175 | 3.207 |
| 424 | 2 | 227 | 77 | 66 | 1.151 | 2.961 |
| *507 | 2 | 259 | 83 | 70 | 1.185 | 2.594 * |
| 607 | 6 | 290 | 96 | 78 | 1.282 | 3.096 |

After this time, figures were no longer recorded. Average flow rate 1.198 liters/second.

* The fuel consumption for Laps 227-259 appear unusually low when compared with the rest of the recorded figures. No explanation is immediately available.

Summary

The maximum fills that took place were 95 liters on Car #83 and 96 liters on car #84. It is reasonable to deduce that neither car was running an oversized fuel tank.

The fuel consumption does show some variation. This could be caused by variations in driving style between drivers. A separate driver log is not available. There was only one full course yellow period before Race Lap 300. That was for 7 laps, from Race Laps 50-56 inclusive.

Dave Benb[illegible]

***Analysis of how poorly the opposition Group C cars were controlled during this race is covered by both these reports.***

Tom Walkinshaw Racing Inc

SET UP SHEET

RACE

| DATE :- FEB 2/3 91 | CHASSIS NO 190/290 | CIRCUIT : DAYTONA 24 HRS | ISSUED BY : |
|---|---|---|---|
| ENGINE NO. :- V12 | GEARBOX NO : DGB | | |

| CAMBER | TOE-IN | RIDE HEIGHTS | CORNER WTS. |
|---|---|---|---|
| −2° / −1¾° ; −1¼° / −½° | OUT 2mm / 2mm ; 3 mm / 3 mm IN | 65 / 65 ; 89 SKID ; 202 BOLT | ±10 lbs ; WITH DRIVER |

| SPRINGS FRONT | SPRINGS REAR | DAMPERS FRONT | DAMPERS REAR | PACKERS FRONT | PACKERS REAR | RATIOS 10/31 | |
|---|---|---|---|---|---|---|---|
| 1400 x 7 | 1500 x 7 | 1989 CANS DT1 | 1989 CANS M2J | 0 DROOP | B PLATES | 1st | 15/40 |
| | | REBOUND −3 | REBOUND −0 | | | 2nd | ~~19/37~~ 19/36 |
| | | BUMP #6 | BUMP #1 | | | 3rd | 23/32 |
| | | | | | | 4th | 26/30 |
| | | | | | | 5th | 28/27 |

| CASTOR | | F.A.R.B | R.A.R.B | REAR WING | | FRONT D'FORCE | |
|---|---|---|---|---|---|---|---|
| LEFT | TYPE | CARBON | V12 | TYPE | V12 2 TIER | SPLITTER | LONG |
| ½° | THICKNESS | 25% | NONE | POSITION | 1991 V12 SPEC | RAD EXIT | 1990 IMSA LIP |
| RIGHT | WIDTH | – | – | ANGLE | 25° | LOUVRES | 1990 Gp C |
| ½° | POSITION | F. STIFF | DISCONNECT | RETURN | ¼" | BIBS | NONE |
| | MODS | — | — | MODS | SMALL SIDE PLATES | RAD VENTS | ALL U'TRAY CLOSED |

| WHEEL TYPE | 17" | BRAKES | ~~FAT~~ PAD CALIPERS | PERISCOPE | NO | NOTES |
|---|---|---|---|---|---|---|
| FRONT TIRES | 430 / 430 | ROTORS | ? | FRONT CENTER | YES | SPOOL G/BOX |
| REAR TIRES | 430 / 430 | PADS | ? | FRONT CALIPER | NO | IMSA TUNNELS ; 91 V12 FT SUSP'N |
| | | BELLS | — | REAR MAIN | 1990 V6 SPEC | 90 REAR SUSP'N |

*Set Up Sheet for the 1991 Daytona race.*

CHIEF ENGINEER'S 1991 POST DAYTONA RACE REPORT

The full car spec for the Daytona 24 Hours was as per the 1991 V12 kit list. The performance of the car was excellent and were it not for the engine problems, the car was capable of winning comfortably.

Points to note are as follows:

1) Handling and set-up

The cars' set up as they arrived at Daytona is as per attached set up sheet. No chassis adjustments were made all weekend.

2) Tires

The tires used were as follows:

| Compound | | Size | | Cold Press (psi) | |
|---|---|---|---|---|---|
| 430 | 430 | 25.5 | 25.5 | 22 | 22 |
| 430 | 430 | 28.5 | 28.5 | 22 | 22 |

Tire wear was excellent, it being possible to double stint at night. This was not possible with the 600/650 combination used in 1990.

There were 2 problems with the tires:

i) In the dry during the heat of the day, small blisters were encountered on the inside edge of the LH front. No driver comments were noted and the lap times were unchanged. Trimming the inside shoulder of the LH front with a 1/4" x 45 degree chamfer solved this problem.

ii) The wet tires had a tendency to blister the very center of the RH rear when they were used on a drying track. No undue pressure build up was recorded. Goodyear commented that the wet compound was too soft for this application. Goodyear have noted this for future wet races.

A point for future reference was that when the track was damp (i.e. too wet for drys and too dry for wets), the Nissans on grooved slicks were up to 8 sec/lap quicker than DJ on wets. However, when the track dried out further, DJ was 4 sec/lap quicker on slicks than the Nissans on grooved slicks.

For daytime running, the dry 430 tires were all scrubbed in. For night running, sticker tires were used.

3) Brakes

The full brake spec used was:

Front: Thick wall undrilled disks
TWR fat pad calipers
Fat carbon metallic blue pads
60% center vein cooling
40% face ducting

25% overall brake blanking was used.
Pad wear was 260 laps or 8 hours.
Paints: The green paints had gone evenly.
The orange paint had just started to go.

Rear: Thick wall undrilled disks
TWR fat pad calipers
Fat carbon metallic blue pads
100% center vein cooling

40% overall brake blanking was used.
Pad wear was 520 laps or 15 hours.
Paints: Green paints just gone evenly.
Other paints intact.

The front disks were changed as a precaution at the first water pump change. However, despite their haggard appearance, wear figures confirm that they would have completed a full race distance.

This is our best yet performance from a brake system, especially when considering that the car weighed 980 kg, considerably in excess of 1990's weight of 940 kg. There were no driver comments about excess brake effort or long pedals until after the front disks were changed!

4) Weight

On departure, Car 190 weighed 2155 pounds (977 kg) and car 290 weighted 2162 pounds (980 kg).

This is nearly 90 lbs above the IMSA weight limit for a 6.5 liter engine. A weight saving campaign had reduced the car weights by over 50 lbs but both chassis were very heavy compared with cars 288 and 388 used in 1990. Car 288 weighted 2080 lbs and Car 388 weighed 2115 lbs. This extra weight tended to completely negate any benefits from the 6.5 liter engine.

For future reference, achieving a 1000 kg weight limit at Le Mans will need virtually no ballast.

5) Engine

The performance of the 6.5 liter engine was excellent. Mapping revisions after the January test fixed the only driver complaints about the mapping.

Fuel mileage was very good. Two drivers could complete 33 lap stints and DW/DJ 32 laps, giving average mpg of 3.95.

6) Gears

Second gear was changed for the race. Race ratios were:

15/40
19/36
23/32
26/30
28/27
10/31

7) Problems

a) Water Pump

This problem put the car out of contention. This has been fully investigated so no further comments are necessary.

b) Water Leak

Car 290 experienced a small, persistent water leak after about 5 hours. Extensive investigation has shown that this came from the area of the front water radiator. There were no leaks in the pipes, Wiggins couplings or engine bay.

The CB method of adding water using the dump churn and driver was excellent. Front water radiators are very susceptible to stone damage and so thought must be given to overcoming this problem.

c) Zytek Telemetry

This performed well. However, DW nearly ran out of fuel yet the telemetry showed that only 112 liters were consumed out of a possible total of 117. The car fuel system has been checked and no defects found. Are telemetry drop-outs responsible for this?

d) Water Ingress

In the heavy rain of the first 5 hours of the race, a large quantity of water got into the cockpit and engine bay. Pre-drilled water exit holes and the sealing of the LMS door all helped, but if the race was wet for longer, this could have been a problem.

e) Socks

The "socks" in the water radiator inlets successfully collected large amounts of debris and were easily cleared out in pit stops. The only problem was that in the wet behind a pace car, the airflow velocity through them was not high enough to blow all the water out of the matrix, resulting in high water temperatures. As soon as the track went green, the increased air speed blew the water out and the engine water temperature fell.

f) Steering Wheel

The Nardo wheel gave no problems and allowed faster driver changes.

I C Reed.
Ian Reed

***Ian Reed's debrief report on the 1991 Daytona race. Overheated engines vertical expansion sheared the water pump fixed drive system after water had leaked from a small hole in the radiator. This area was susceptible to damage from stones.***

## Sebring 12 hours – March 16th

Two XJR-12Ds were entered for Sebring but after an accident in practice this endurance race effort was reduced to just the one car. Jones/Boesel/Nielsen would drive the sole Jaguar with Acheson missing out on the drive. Geoff Brabham/Gary Brabham/Daly took pole position1:49.761, followed by the Joest Porsche of Wollek/Schneider/Sigala on 1:50.275; Robinson/Earl/Bailey were at 1:50.682 in the second of the NPT-90 Nissans. Fangio/Ribb's Eagle HF-90 Toyota on 1:52.604 were followed by Jones/Boesel/Nielsen's XJR12 at 1:53.505.

Sebring is a day out for the locals with the crowd estimated at 80,000 spectators watching the Joest Porsche set the early pace. This was not to last, and by the three-hour mark the #83 NPT-90 Group C Nissan had settled into the lead. The race progressed with the usual for Sebring pace car periods with the circuit's bumps and large speed differentials causing accidents. Both Nissans circulated at the front but the #83 finally took the lead to finish this 12 hour race after 298 laps. Wollek/Schneider/Sigala had produced a good race in their Porsche to finish one lap down on the winning Nissans, supported by their sister car of Jelinski/Pescarolo/Winter on 295 laps. The XJR-12 finish fifth on 284 laps after struggling to find a good set up over the bumps here. TWR's American team was entering survival mode with cut-backs from Kidlington and the loss of the badly damaged car putting the team under pressure knowing that a new replacement would not be available, with all the support given to the successful Ross Brawn managed XJR-14 contesting the World Sportscar Championship for 3.5-litre race engines.

## Valve springs

Planning for Le Mans had started earlier than usual with Ross Brawn now controlling the technical direction of any updates needed, TW was impressed by his handling of the XJR-14 programme and with the promise of a future in Formula One Ross would be the best to push against the usual procrastination coming from TW. The engine updates for Le Mans 1991 were based on three fronts; valve springs and camshaft profiles, exhaust system and air supply.

Geoff Goddard was asked again to rework the original EA15/16 profiles with my brief to smooth out the lifting ramp profiles in the hope of removing any possible contributions to a resonance problem, assisted by a reduction in lift of 0.010in on the inlet profile. Spring breakages and a couple of valve seat failures were associated with the inlet valve train. Geoff Goddard had revised the profile design to help eliminate their part of the problem with new camshaft profiles EA24/25; Schmitthelm also contributed with changes to the inner valve spring design (EA24 inlet).

The valve spring testing process was started with my letter to Derek Charters at the British automotive industries MIRA research institute on the February 28th 1991. Working with non-racing mentalities and open-ended research institutions can produce good expertise; but also comes with open ended time management. Tom Chatterley then assumed control of this exercise and a suitable testing rig was produced and time table agreed for testing. In a memo dated April 11th 1991 this would take place from April 19th to the 31st. Mark Hemsworth would oversee this testing programme.

By June 13th I was able to send a report to TW, Roger and Ross with the latest results. A valve spring had broken running at the constant speed of 7000rpm equivalent (camshaft speed 3500). This was caused by a small piece, about 4mm long from the last coil end where it is ground flat, to becoming jammed in the system. These thin end pieces of spring had always been removed before being fitted to the engines.

*Brabham/Brabham/Daly Sebring winning Nissan NPT-90*

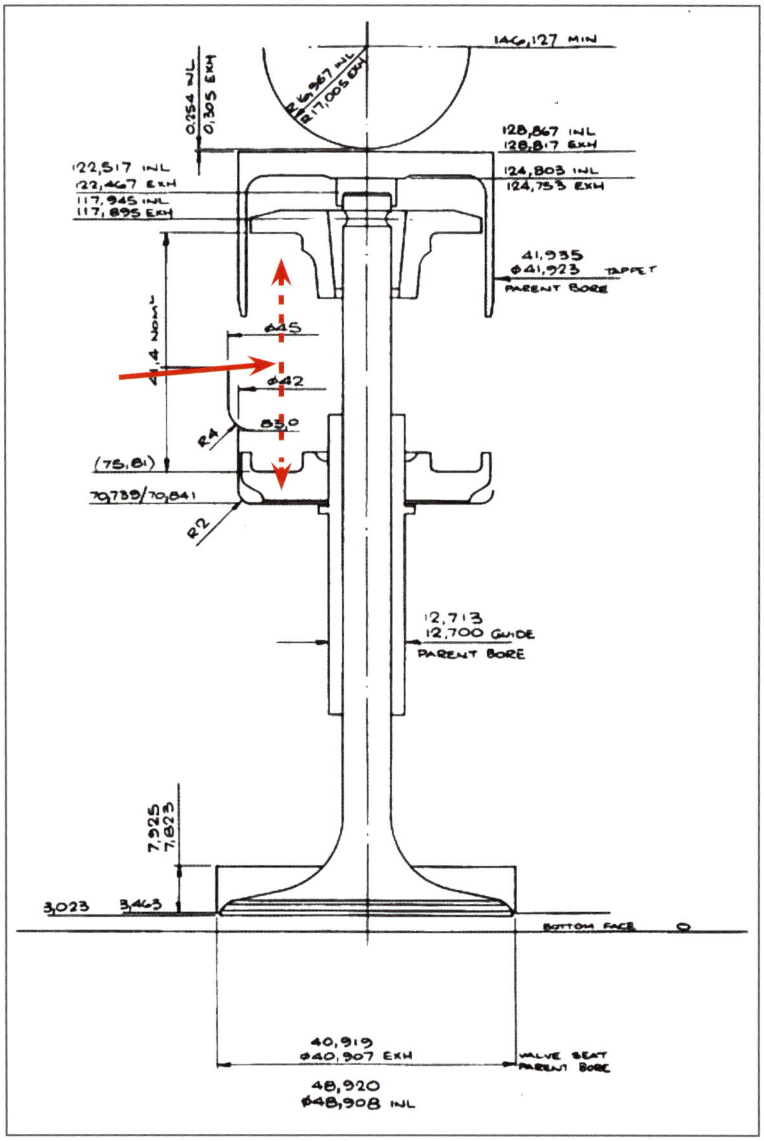


*This is an actual size diagram of the exhaust valve assembly and shows the space that the spring design has to fit within the follower, spring seat and spring top (red arrows).*

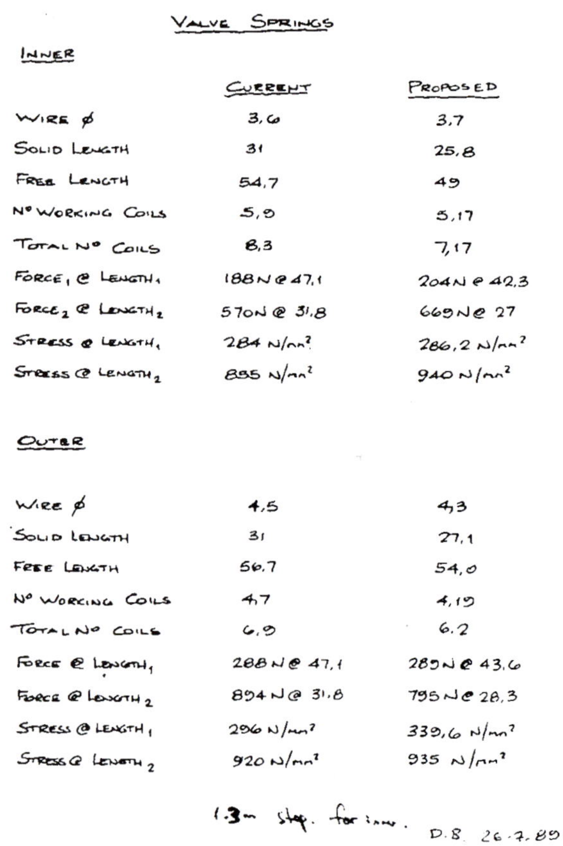

VALVE SPRINGS

INNER

| | CURRENT | PROPOSED |
|---|---|---|
| WIRE ø | 3,6 | 3,7 |
| SOLID LENGTH | 31 | 25,8 |
| FREE LENGTH | 54,7 | 49 |
| N° WORKING COILS | 5,9 | 5,17 |
| TOTAL N° COILS | 8,3 | 7,17 |
| FORCE₁ @ LENGTH₁ | 188 N @ 47,1 | 204 N @ 42,3 |
| FORCE₂ @ LENGTH₂ | 570 N @ 31,8 | 669 N @ 27 |
| STRESS @ LENGTH₁ | 284 N/mm² | 286,2 N/mm² |
| STRESS @ LENGTH₂ | 885 N/mm² | 940 N/mm² |

OUTER

| | CURRENT | PROPOSED |
|---|---|---|
| WIRE ø | 4,5 | 4,3 |
| SOLID LENGTH | 31 | 27,1 |
| FREE LENGTH | 56,7 | 54,0 |
| N° WORKING COILS | 4,7 | 4,19 |
| TOTAL N° COILS | 6,9 | 6,2 |
| FORCE @ LENGTH₁ | 288 N @ 47,1 | 289 N @ 43,6 |
| FORCE @ LENGTH₂ | 894 N @ 31,8 | 795 N @ 28,3 |
| STRESS @ LENGTH₁ | 296 N/mm² | 339,6 N/mm² |
| STRESS @ LENGTH₂ | 920 N/mm² | 935 N/mm² |

1.3mm step. for inner. D.S. 26-7-89

*Schmitthelm's new valve spring specification.*

TABLE 1

Results of Resonance Searches on Valve Spring/Cam Profile Combinations

Using Magnetically Triggered Strobe System

| Test No | Components | | | Camshaft Speed, rpm | | | | | | | | | | | | | | |
|---|---|---|---|---|---|---|---|---|---|---|---|---|---|---|---|---|---|---|
| | Valve Type | Spring Type | Cam Profile | 1000 | 1500 | 2000 | 2500 | 3000 | 3100 | 3200 | 3300 | 3400 | 3500 | 3600 | 3700 | 3800 | 3900 | 4000 |
| 1 | Exhaust | Old | Old | ✓ | ✓ | ✓ | ✓ | ✓ | ✓ | ✓ | ✓ | ✓ | ✓ | ✓ | ✓ | ✓ | ✓ | ✓ |
| 2 | Exhaust | New | New | ✓ | ✓ | ✓ | ✓ | x | x | x | x | x | x | x | x | x | x | x |
| 3 | Exhaust | New | Old | ✓ | ✓ | ✓ | ✓ | ✓ | ✓ | ✓ | ✓ | ✓ | ✓ | ✓ | x | x | x | x |
| 4 | Exhaust | New | New | ✓ | ✓ | ✓ | ✓ | ✓ | ✓ | ✓ | ✓ | ✓ | ✓ | ✓ | ✓ | ✓ | ✓ | ✓ |
| 5 | Inlet | New | Old | ✓ | ✓ | ✓ | ✓ | ✓ | x | x | x | x | x | x | x | x | x | x |
| 6 | Inlet | New | New | ✓ | ✓ | ✓ | ✓ | ✓ | ✓ | ✓ | ✓ | ✓ | ✓ | ✓ | ✓ | ✓ | ✓ | ✓ |
| 7 | Inlet | Old | Old | ✓ | ✓ | ✓ | ✓ | x | x | x | x | x | x | x | x | x | x | x |
| 8 | Inlet | Old | New | ✓ | ✓ | ✓ | ✓ | ✓ | ✓ | ✓ | ✓ | ✓ | x | x | x | x | x | x |

Note: ✓ = pass, no resonance condition detected
x = fail, resonance detected

*Camshaft speed is half engine speed. This test with old and new camshaft profiles and valve springs shows the cause of the inlet valve spring breakages is from the inlet cam profile causing resonances. The revised camshaft profile fixes this problem.*

The final test results show that the basic problem was with the Cosworth EA15 profile used on the inlet valves where we had seen previous breakages. The *revised* profile with the *original specification* valve springs did not produce resonance problems till 7000rpm, where as the *original* specification camshaft profile and valve spring had resonance problems above 6000rpm, a main area of operation for us. These tests showed that the original problem lay with resonance problems associated with the inlet camshaft profile which was where we had seen the spring breakages more than with the valve springs themselves. The final four page report was received on October 11th, two months after Le Mans.

RACE ENGINE DIVISION
MEMORANDUM

| | | |
|---|---|---|
| TO | : | N. EAMES |
| FROM | : | A.W. SCOTT |
| CC | : | M. BOON |
| DATE | : | 30 August 1991 |
| REFERENCE | : | VALVE SPRING TEST - MIRA |

Tom Chatterley will invoice us for the Le Mans valve spring tests at their base cost with no profit margin, therefore we should pay their invoice when it is received of £5702.00

Our initial order cover was for a maximum of £4350 however a lot of time was spent on the project and in view of their possible future use, and that we were under budget on the Le Mans programme, we should pay their invoice.

***TWR Accounts disputed the invoice for the additional time MIRA spent on the valve spring test. This amounted to £1352.00, but money well spent.***

MIRA The Motor Industry Research Association

The Motor Industry Research Association
Watling Street, Nuneaton,
Warwickshire CV10 0TU, England
Telephone: (0203) 348541
Telex: 311277
Fax: (0203) 343772

Our Ref TCC/LR/K310053
9 October 1991

RECEIVED 11 OCT 1991

Mr A W Scott
TWR Group Limited
Race Engine Division
1 Station Field Industrial Estate
Kidlington
Oxford OX5 1JD

Dear Alan

Please find attached a resumé of the work that we carried out for you on various combinations of valve springs and cam profiles for your V12 Le Mans Race Engine.

You will recall that our original attempt to assess where any resonance conditions occurred made use of a Laser Interferometer system that MIRA had developed to measure such resonances in vehicle body structures. Whilst this system is extremely useful for the measurements for which it was developed we found that it did not work well when it rastered over a valve head which was opening and closing at a high frequency. We considered that the excessive movement of the component (compared to a vibrating body panel for example) was the cause of the inconclusive results that we obtained.

Never-the-less, we repeated the same series of measurements using a Xenon strobe light which was triggered from the camshaft by a magnetic pick-up arrangement. This system worked well and although we had to assess when a resonance condition occurred subjectively (a minimum of two viewers were used, sometimes three), it was quite obvious when such resonance conditions occurred. These results can be found in Table 1.

Table 2 gives the results of the durability tests that we ran in your specified order. As you will see, we obtained several failures, most of which were attributed to a small piece of the chamfered tail-end of the outer spring breaking off; this then caused further damage as it moved around the spring area. We now know that it would have been prudent to have ground this tail-end away altogether as you did for the engine in order to prevent early failure of this part of the spring causing damage (and thus premature failures) to the rest of the system.

The tests we ran at 3500 rpm were clearly too severe for any of the component combinations. However, the tests that we ran where we altered the camshaft speed every 6 hours were both less severe, and thus perhaps more realistic to the race condition, produced passes for the combination of components that were ultimately used in the engine in the 1991 Le Mans race.

Despite all our mutual efforts the rig work was inconclusive but we certainly learnt a great deal about high speed race engine cams, cam-followers and springs and their associated problems which we had not been involved with previously.

Our invoice to cover all the test work that we carried out for you will be sent to you under separate cover. As you will remember from our recent fax and telephone conversation, the value of this invoice is greater than your order limit. This was mainly caused by the fact that we carried out more durability tests (whether successful or not) that your order cover allowed for.

If you have any further test work in mind, where you consider that we may be of assistance to you, please do not hesitate in contacting us again.

Yours sincerely

Tom Chatterley

T C Chatterley
Section Head
Power Train Components

*The International Centre for Automotive Research and Development*

*A Company Limited by Guarantee Registered in England No. 402570 Registered Office Watling Street, Nuneaton, Warwickshire, CV10 0TU*

The next tests for Le Mans were for optimisation of the exhaust system and included differing lengths for the 1.75in primary exhaust pipes as well as testing of 2.25in and 2.125in secondary diameters and lengths. As well, the original slip fit system for ease of fitment to the race cars had the collectors welded to seal them against any leakage effect on the resonance pulses in further dynamometer tests. The optimised lengths from a 1990 7-litre V12 specifications were the base line for these tests. Primary length variation from 19in to 28in were tested, as well as 0.125in diameter changes for the secondary pipes, but produced smaller amounts of power improvement than was expected. The largest changes were from using the smaller diameter for the secondary pipes. The choice of welded or slip-fit joints had no effect on the outcome, so the slip-fits remained (see page 348).

Alastair Macqueen had previously undertaken full-size wind tunnel testing at MIRA to see if we could use the XJR-9's aerodynamics to increase the pressure differential between intake and exhaust to enhance engine breathing (see page 336). The central position below the rear wing created a negative pressure of 10 to 15 millibars (0.2psi) and this was where the exhaust tailpipe would exit. The main in car problem however was with the engine cover which came down and touched the rear of the engine's air cleaner system, which consisted of a wire cage supporting three different-density foam layers wrapped around it. This directed us to carry out engine tests on the dynamometer with a redundant engine cover from an XJR-12LM attached, in the hope of finding increased *in car* power and efficiency.

The engine cover actually touched the rear of the foam filter over the back cylinders in Tony Southgate's design, and it was now time to work within that shape as this would not be changed to suit the V12 engine. A base line was set as we would normally test the engine, with the unrestricted air filter, and then the rear bodywork mounted to the engine as the exact in car situation. This test showed an immediate power loss between 6000 to 7000rpm of 17 to 18bhp, a 2.5% power loss from 771bhp to 754bhp using the IMSA spec 6.5-litre engine and the engine cover bodywork that we had used throughout the V12 programme. Various tests using side feed holes to introduce air around the sides of the trumpets and then three 2.375in holes in the bodywork of the engine cover produced no improvements. When the engine cover was raised 50mm higher than as fitted in the car, the power loss was eliminated at 6000rpm and halved above that range.

The fix was to test a revised air filter system with attention to detail around the edges of the trumpets and see how close the foam filter could be placed above the trumpets before any loss of power occurred. These tests showed that using a newly profiled and lower supporting cage, the foam filter could be within 12 to 15mm of the large trumpet opening without any effect on power output. The important thing was that the air had to come into the rear cylinders from the top, between the engine cover and the foam filter, which it was unable to do before because it touched in that area. The final fix was to make two new trumpets for the two rear cylinders 25mm shorter. This gave us a 35mm air gap between filter and engine cover when fitted to the race car. This final in-car arrangement produced a loss of only 6bhp across the 6000 to 7000rpm range, an in-car improvement of 2%. Pipercross, our original air filter suppliers, made bespoke reproductions for us.

We had suffered a piston failure at the Sebring 12 hour race in 1990 while running with very lean settings to avoid an extra fuel stop and gain some time with a race car that was also running very high water and oil temperatures. Piston specifications were revised to give a crown thickness increase of 0.5mm. Long distance races were subject to all the competitors' small oil leaks and over time these gathered dust, rubber and track grime in the radiator core, leading to overheating. John McLaughlin produced the 'shark's tooth' radiator filter design for 1991 to help alleviate this problem. My memo regarding meeting with Cosworth's Jeff Roper can be seen on page 348.

## LE MANS 91 EXHAUST REPORT

| | 4000 | 4500 | 5000 | 5500 | 6000 | 6500 | 7000 | 7250 |
|---|---|---|---|---|---|---|---|---|
| 1990 V12 GROUP C. 2 1/4" SECONDARY, 22P, 23S, ONE PIECE | | | | | | | | |
| SPEED | 4000 | 4500 | 5000 | 5500 | 6000 | 6500 | 7000 | 7250 |
| POWER | 475. | 534. | 611. | 638. | 670. | 753. | 773. | 751. |
| P 1 3/4" 22, S 2 1/4" 23 SEALED PIPES — POWER | 537. | 617. | 672. | 732. | 763. | 739. | 762. | |
| P 1 3/4" 28, S 2 1/4" 23 — POWER | | 532. | 616. | 671. | 721. | 758. | 760. | |
| P 1 3/4" 22, S 2 1/8" 17 — POWER | 513. | 539. | 627. | 673. | 731. | 761. | 761. | 755. |
| P 1 3/4" 19, S 2 1/8" 23 — POWER | | 538. | 618. | 671. | 731. | 760. | 761. | 753. |
| P 1 3/4" 19, S 2 1/8" 23 — POWER | | 538. | 618. | 671. | 731. | 760. | 761. | 753. |
| P 1 3/4" 28, S 2 1/8" 23 — POWER | 495. | 533. | 619. | 675. | 730. | 758. | 760. | 750. |
| P 1 3/4" 22, S 2 1/8" 23 — POWER | 508. | 539. | 616. | 673. | 729. | 761. | 762. | |
| P 1 3/4" 22, S 2" 23 — POWER | 507. | 532. | 613. | 666. | 729. | 761. | 761. | 749. |
| P 1 3/4" 28, S 2" 23 — POWER | | 519. | 620. | 671. | 731. | 760. | 760. | |

*Exhaust resonance testing on the V12 7.4-litre engine.*

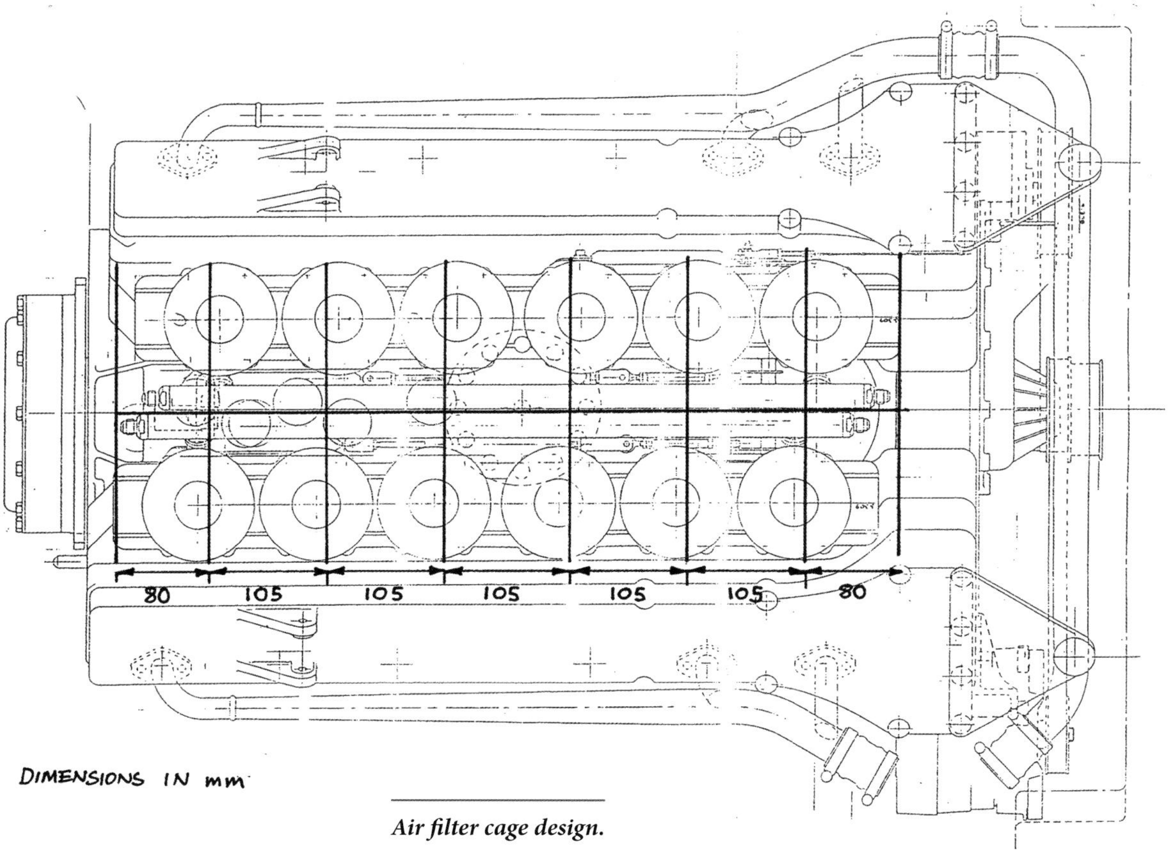


*Air filter cage design.*

M E M O R A N D U M

TO : N. EAMES
S. GRAY
C. BAMBER

FROM : A.W. SCOTT

DATE : 21 March 1991

REFERENCE : MY MEETING WITH JEFF ROPER @ COSWORTH TODAY

Initial inspection by Jeff Roper suggests chronic piston overheat caused by combination of excessive water temperatures and lean mixtures. I feel we have been on borderline for some time without realising it eg. sample piston from 2nd placed car at Le Mans 1990 has hairline fatigue crack. Please ensure all V12 rebuilds utilising used pistons are crack tested at every build.

S. Gray to nominate exact number of hours and maximum RPM to Jeff Roper on the engine that had piston failure at Sebring. I have already nominated Sebring practice water temperatures at 95°C. Future modifications to water systems and radiator will reduce our operating temperatures at Le Mans and at this time I feel happy with the mechanical structure of our piston.

*Jeff Roper of Cosworth introduced an increase in crown thickness of 0.5mm to help this problem.*

1991 XJR12 LE MANS CAR
BASIC CHANGES RECOMMENDED FROM 1990 SPEC

1. Adoption of 7.3 litre engine as proposed by AWS (see performance comparisons).

2. Change in aerodynamic spec to create more down force.
Figures of average 940 KG 7 litre car raced in 1990:-

| Downforce | Drag | L/D | Split |
|---|---|---|---|
| 3884 | 1070 | 3.630 | 41% |
| Proposed for 1991:- | | | |
| 4444 | 1157 | 3.841 | 40% |
| These represent changes of :- | | | |
| +15% | +8% | +6% | -1% |

Downforce
The proposed downforce level will allow the car to overcome the 60 KG WT. penalty at in cornering any speed over 100mph.

Drag
The proposed drag level will allow the car a very similar top speed as last year, with the 7.3 litre engine despite WT. penalty.
Changes in car to produce this are:-
(a) Rear wing mount plates (scheme drawn).
(b) Full size splitter (known part).
(c) Radiator exit ramp (to be moulded).

3. Weight Increase
Cars to be ballasted to 1003 KG:-
- 12 KG lead beneath gearbox
- 35 KG complete ali. under skin
- Remainder as lead ballast in pass seat area.

This will produce a C of G height reduction in the car of 18 mm, which will put the C of G 8mm lower than the turbo car! This should produce as real advantage in the V12 car.

4. Detailed changes as 1991 car spec sheet and 1991 car set up sheet.

5. Air box and exhaust systems. See wind tunnel test sheets for discussion.

*Basic race car changes recommended by Alastair Macqueen for Le Mans.*

**STRAIGHT LINE PERFORMANCE COMPARISONS V12 LE MANS CAR FOR 1991**

The times represent the time taken to cover the speed range 160 to 340 KPH (100 to 211 MPH) typical of the sprint between chicanes at Le Mans.

All models run with aero drag typical of 1990 Le Mans.

No account of cornering times is taken.

Ballast mounted low could largely offset weight handicap in cornering.

| ENGINE TYPE | WT + (75kg DRIVER + 50kg FUEL) | REVS AT GEAR CHANGE | FUEL TYPE | RATIOS | (SEC's) TIMES 160 TO 340 kph |
|---|---|---|---|---|---|
| 7 LITRE '90 | 930 kg | 7000 | 4* | As '90 | 16.96 |
| 7 LITRE '90 | 1000 kg | 7100 | 4* | As '90 | 18.08 |
| 7 LITRE '90 | 1000 kg | 6800 | 4* | As '90 | 18.69 |
| 7.3 LITRE STD | 1000 kg | 7000 | 4* | As '90 | 16.09 |
| 7.3 LITRE STD | 1000 kg | 6800 | 4* | As '90 | 16.38 |
| 7.3 LITRE STD | 1000 kg | 6600 | 4* | As '90 | 16.74 |
| 7.3 LITRE BEST | 1000 kg | 7000 | 4* | As '90 | 15.52 |
| 7.3 LITRE BEST | 1000 kg | 6700 | 4* | As '90 | 15.98 |
| 6.5 LITRE | 930 kg | 7000 | 4* | As '90 | 19.96 |
| 6.5 LITRE | 900 kg | 7000 | 4* | As '90 | 19.25 |
| 6.5 LITRE | 900 kg | 7000 | 4* | Shorter 3rd,4th 5th | 18.40 |
| 6.5 LITRE | 930 kg | 7000 | 10% TFOB | Shorter 3rd,4th 5th | 19.12 |

NOTE:- 7.3 Litre 'STD' is figures supplied by AWS, and what he expects on first run.

7.3 litre "Best" is power increased by 1.5% and is an expected best.

**CAR WTS AT LE MANS 1990 (DRY)**

| | | | |
|---|---|---|---|
| 1 | 990 | - 931 KGS * | CARS WERE FOR THE FIRST TIME AT LE MANS |
| 2 | 290 | - 938 KG | WEIGHED IN THE PIT ROAD INC. FUEL. |
| 3 | 1090 | - 958 KG | LIGHTEST WT. RECORDED BEING 948 INC FUEL. |
| 4 | 190 | - 941 KG | |

***To maintain the V12 engine in its best efficiency rpm window I proposed an increase in capacity of 7.3 to 7.4 litres to maintain the acceleration ability of the Le Mans cars with as little increase in fuel consumption as possible. We eventually settled on 7.4 litres for 1991.***

## Le Mans – June 1991

The major change for 1991 involved a cross over period between the original Group C race cars and the new lighter maximum capacity 3.5-litre cars introduced in 1991. Rule changes had been made to make the earlier Group C race cars obsolete as quickly as possible, and push competitors and manufacturers to the new series specifications by raising the original Group C minimum weight limit to 1000kgs. Alastair Macqueen had carried out initial wind tunnel work in late 1990 when this change had been notified and a solution was put forward to best comply with the new problem of increased weight. The solution was higher downforce to maintain corner speed lost by the added weight. This chassis solution to the new ruling meant the actual problem in this fuel regulated formula

**MINUTES OF LE MANS MEETING**

**Tuesday 12.03.91**

Present: RS/ RBr/ AKM/ AWS/ CB/ KL/ GS/ SF/ DR
cc.: Attendees/ JMc/ HS

| | Action |
|---|---|
| - AWS can supply 6 - 7.3 ltr engine and 4 - 7.0 ltr engines. Not all will be able to be rebuilt after running. | |
| - Expect 60 bhp more for 4% more fuel @ 68/ 6900 rpm. | |
| - GS predicts more power if we would improve entry conditions into airbox duct and utilise dynamic pressure. Recent rig testing suggests this area is quite poor. SF to decide practical restrictions versus gain. | SF |
| - Engine Shop work on air filter and trumpet area can be adopted - 15 hp gain from 1990 on this alone. | SF |
| - Need to confirm number of people required for telemetry work. 1½ people per car. AWS says 5 systems available. | HS |
| - DO can supply drawing capacity in 2 weeks. Need some now? | RBr |
| - Noses - NACA ducts, 4 headlights, louvres and tyre clearance. IMSA will have drawings for tyre clearance & o' centre clips. | SF/ DR |
| - Compile DO list. | SF |
| - Confirm with I Reed (TWR Inc) re difference list and ensure he knows what we are ordering so he can offer objections/ suggestions. | SF/ DR |
| - Technical spec of TWR Kidlington cars to be issued. | SF |
| - Build schedule to be compiled for Thursday. RBr/ RS/ KL/ AWS/ SF to discuss then. | SF |
| - Need to mod car here for IMSA front suspension to test. | SF |
| - Get parts list & drawings for all IMSA front suspension items. Assy drawings etc... | SF/ DR |
| - Can IMSA send kit of f. susp. parts in engines returned during Sebring weekend? | SF/ DR |
| - Long lead items - Ratios, gearboxes, driveshafts, screens, exhausts, radiators. | |
| - Is TWR Inc happy with parts they have now to prep. 1/2 cars for Le Mans? Need to flag up problems now. | SF/ DR |
| - Order some Unicarden shafts to cover Superboot order. Only 6 pairs of S/Boots to arrive in May - not enough. Xtrac could make shafts? | KL |
| - Issue Le Mans car test schedule. | SF |
| - Garretson to manufacture radiators? CB wants airflow test results today. | SF |
| - Order current cores to cover Garretson order. | KL |
| - KL + SF to go to Astec today to discuss LM requirements. | |
| - Could we get current water system rig tested by Cosworth? | SF/ RBr /AL |
| - Wheels - will we have enough? Stock take required (Kidlington + Valpo). | SF/ DR |
| - Exhausts ordered. Ensure we use good second hand systems in testing. New units to be fitted to cars for qualifying and race. | SF |
| - SF is devoted to engineering of Le Mans project. Not chasing parts or admin. KL to discuss this aspect with RS. | |
| - Will have 3 "Team" cars & one Jap car for sure (3 in Kid, one in Valpo). 1 or 2 more Jap cars possible! One of which to be prepared in Valpo. | |
| - Next meeting late next week - arrange as convenient. | HS |

was simply handed over to us at Engs to compensate for the increased chassis weight and the higher drag factor triggered by its greater downforce; Without engine developments we were heading into an acceleration and fuel consumption problem.

After initial discussions surrounding the number of race cars and TWR America's involvement to get the 1991 Le Mans programme underway, the first real meeting was held on March 12th. Steve Farrell had taken over the main engineering tasks as Alastair Macqueen was now spending the majority of his time on the XJ220 project.

TW did not attend or have input into any of the proceedings as he had bigger problems to attend to with the Garage Group haemorrhaging millions of pounds.

A first test with the race car ballasted to 1000kgs was carried out at Donington; a circuit that had always been hard on the Jaguar's braking system. This test included caliper seals and different pad materials.

## Donington test – March 20th

Tony Dowe with his reduced workforce at TWR America had now informed Kidlington that he was unable to build the one or two cars hoped for; he could supply personnel only. This meant we only ordered parts for three cars (Four V12 cars were eventually raced at Le Mans).

Le Mans engines were now being built with the main bottle-neck for us the machining of new head castings. Many of our cylinder heads had been in the system for three to four years of use and some had been subjected to overheating. Without any in-house machine shop we were subject to suppliers' own timetables, but Nigel Eames was progressing well with these tasks. The new Pankl connecting rods had

**RACE ENGINE DIVISION**

**MEMORANDUM**

TO : S. FARRELL
J. McLOUGHLIN

FROM : A.W. SCOTT

CC : R. BRAWN
A. MacQUEEN
T.D.WALKINSHAW

DATE : 3 June 1991

REFERENCE : LE MANS 1991

1. I am concerned that to date we do not have an approved in car fuel meter readout for Le Mans.

2. Gear Ratios for Le Mans

   The additional torque of the 1991 engine will allow a similar level of performance using 300 RPM less than 1990. Bearing in mind the additional 60 odd kilos to carry for 1991 and its effect on fuel consumption, I feel our starting point should be to aim for a maximum RPM of 65/6600 on the straight and probably raising 3rd and 4th gears as well eg. entry to the Porsche curves could be taken in 5th (J. Neilson) but the second corner could not be. Raising of 4th gear should be looked at to save fuel. Larger RPM drops (ie. 6500 - 5000/5250 RPM) can be tolerated with the new engine (depending on additional drag this year).

3. Engine has been mapped for best torque and maximum leanness on position 3 of the dash control.

   Trim Positions

   5 +5%
   4 +2%
   3 Max lean/best torque
   2 -1½%
   1 -3%
   0 -5% (pace car only)

   I envisage using position 3 for the race and any changes in leanness will depend directly on the ability to keep the water temperature at 80/85°C. We have seen thermal cracking of pistons on the Sebring engines running 3% lean from best torque and water temperatures in the mid 90's (this is almost a guaranteed piston failure mode for 24 hours).

   The twin socks fitted to the radiator at Sebring seemed to raise water temperatures by 6°C. We could probably run these after 10.00pm until 8.00am and first remove one and the other as temperatures rise. This reduces direct exposed time to around 12/14 hours.

4. Oil Temperature

   Whilst efficiencies have been found running oil temperatures of 110-115°C Le Mans is a 24 hour event and pistons and bearings will benefit from a gallery in temperature of 95-100°C.

TWR **ENGINE TEST SHEET**

| PROJECT | TEST BED No. | DATE | ENGINE No. |
|---|---|---|---|
| V12 LM. | 2 | 4/6/91 | V1291C17. |

| | | | |
|---|---|---|---|
| OBS. BARO | 1016 mBar | INLET CAM | EA25 |
| HUMIDITY | % | EXHAUST CAM | EA24 |
| CORR. BARO | mBar | INLET SYSTEM | 40mm GPC. |
| COOLANT | WATER | | |
| OIL | XC27 | EXHAUST SYSTEM | ONE PIECE. |
| SPARK PLUGS | 82G GAP | | |
| FUEL | 4* | IGNITION SYSTEM | CD |
| OCTANE | | | |
| S.G. | | FUEL SYSTEM | DYNO 5BAR. |
| SWEPT VOL | 7.4. cm³ | | |

OBJECT OF TEST: POWER TEST.

SPECIAL FEATURES: EPROMS MM SM

| | | | | | | | | |
|---|---|---|---|---|---|---|---|---|
| ENGINE SPEED (R.P.M.) | | 4000 | 4500 | 5000 | 5500 | 6000 | 6500 | 7000 |
| OBS | LOAD | 114.3 | 120.3 | 123.5 | 122.8 | 121.7 | 116.9 | 106.9 |
| CORRECTED | POWER (B.H.P.) | 462 | 518 | 597 | 655 | 713 | 750 | 740 |
| CORRECTED | TORQUE (LB.FT) | 606 | 638 | 655 | 651 | 646 | 620 | |
| CORRECTED | BMEP (PSI) | | | | | | | |

top right: ***The Zytek fuel meter was not part of the 1991 Le Mans specification and the additional weight and drag that year would demand engines run at very lean settings.***

right: ***Typical dyno test on full lean race setting 13.8:1 air/fuel ratio on the 7.4-litre V12.***

not been made to drawing and produced a problem with side thrusting when the engines were inspected after the in-car tests, and it was too late to rectify the situation with new ones. We came up with a mod in the workshop to bias additional oil to that area and the problem was resolved. New engines were fitted to cars for the test programmes at Silverstone on April 25th and May 8th and then Pembrey on the 14th and 15th. The new engines were then removed and checked over at Engs ready to be fitted for the Le Mans race.

Garretson in America had come up with a new radiator design and new oil tanks had also been fitted and these were tested at Paul Ricard in the south of France on the May 24th and 25th. This circuit was chosen for its stable weather conditions and long straight. Final checking and running in of gearboxes was complete by David Leslie and Andy Wallace at Silverstone on June 6th before the final announcement of drivers and cars was made.

**Tom Walkinshaw Racing Ltd**

**1, Station Field Industrial Estate, Kidlington, Oxford OX5 1JD**

JAGUAR ENTRIES ANNOUNCED FOR 1991

LE MANS 24 HOUR RACE

Six Jaguars are entered for the 1991 Le Mans classic and, to comply with FISA regulations, two of these entries will be the car currently raced in the Sportscar World Championship, the 3.5 litre normally aspirated XJR-14. The other four cars will be the V-12 powered endurance racers, based on the cars which won the race in 1988 and 1990.

The driver entries are as follows:

First car: XJR-14
Derek Warwick (GB)
Andy Wallace (GB)

Second car: XJR-14
Teo Fabi (I)
Kenny Acheson (GB)

Third car: XJR-12
Derek Warwick (GB)
Bob Wollek (F)

Fourth car: XJR-12
John Nielsen (DK)
Teo Fabi (I)

Fifth car: XJR-12
Davy Jones (USA)
Raul Boesel (BR)
Michel Ferte (F)

Sixth car: XJR-12
David Leslie (GB)
Mauro Martini (I)
Jeff Krosnoff (USA)

For further information please contact Colin Cook in Public Affairs on 0203 402121 or Fiona Miller at TWR on 0608 678763.

**Telephone: (08675) 71555 Telex: 837649 Fax: (0865) 841855**
**Company registered in England No: 1290423**

*Car and drivers entered for 1991 Le Mans.*

Jan Lammers was missing from the driver line up with Roger not happy with some of his post 1989/1990 Le Mans comments. Of the final twelve drivers entered in the four XJR-12LM race cars, six drivers had never raced these cars before.

The engines supplied to the 1991 team used the original 7-litre bore size of 94mm with the longer stroke crankshaft of 88.5mm fitted with shorter connecting rods to produce 7.4 litres. Six engines had been converted to this specification and given the numbers V1291C11; V1291C12; V1291C13; V1291C14; V1291C17 and V1291C18. The seventh engine would be used as a last spare option and was a 7-litre unit V1290C03.

The final decision on race cars to be entered at Le Mans was a mixture of old and new, with two of the new XJR-14s entered to cover contractual obligations in the Group C WSPC series. The aim of the XJR-14s was purely to take pole position and produce exposure for Jaguar, their Cosworth HB V8 racing engines were not suitable for 24 hour events. The four XJR-12LM V12 engined race cars would be split into a main group of three in Silk Cut livery, and the fourth a privately funded deal entered for Suntec. Suntec was a Japanese based education and university complex and a deal had been made at the start of the year between TWR and company principal Mrs Yamazaki to race a V6 turbo Jaguar in the Japanese endurance series, as well as compete at Le Mans in a V12. This US$2 million deal had been struck to help fund the XJR-14 programme, it was seen as a means to an end by TW with virtually zero budgets allocated and all components for the venture sourced from the Broadstone museum cars. Dave Benbow had engineered it, with assistance from myself. Long trips back and forth to Japan were a diversion I did not need, but it was all about ensuring money came in, with TWR in increasing financial problems.

Italy's Mauro Martini and American Jeff Krosnoff were the Suntec Jaguar Japanese sports car series drivers who also raced F3000 in Japan, but they would be racing at Le Mans for the first time. They would be joined by Britain's David Leslie in the fourth Jaguar XJR12, with limited preparation, managed by the Kidlington based crew who had supported the Japanese series. Dave Benbow would be the supervising engineer with me in a supporting role and liaison to the Japanese client. Roger did not want a repeat of the independent direction Tony Dowe and I had produced the year before.

From a quarter that had in the past been largely ignored, there had however been a situation developing that had largely gone unnoticed. Mazda had been a competitor at Le Mans over many years, including twice being supported by TWR in 1980/81. Mazda had never been seen as a threat with their reliance on traditional Japanese drivers in at least one of its cars and smaller budget sub contract support from the Alan Docking organisation for the Le Mans event. There had now been some major changes to strengthen their organisation and a line-up of top drivers, along with updates from designer Nigel Stroud to his original 757 design; producing the current four rotor 787B for 1991. There was also a political situation that would be in their favour as well that we were not aware of at the time, but team manager Ohashi had played some cards well as we would later find out.

Some things do change from tradition and it was the new pit complex that had people's attention with much upgraded facilities and pit areas, to welcome back all the teams once again. It was onto the normal Wednesday and Thursday qualifying for drivers in both the day and night times, starting in changing wet conditions, with some drivers new to the TWR Jaguars as well as the circuit all adding to the mix. The XJR-14 that Derek Warwick and

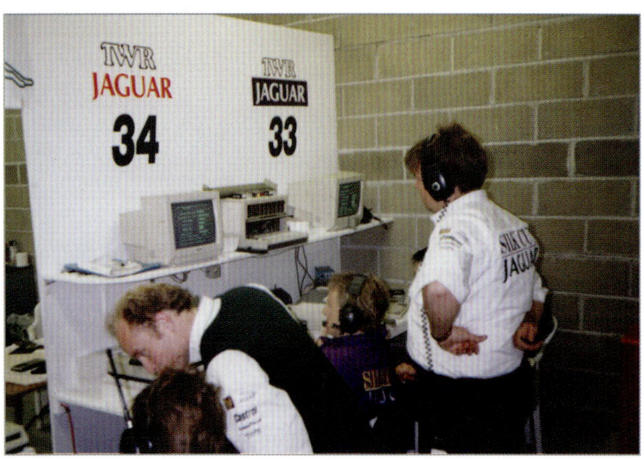


*Kevin Lee and Charlie Bamber monitor progress of the Jaguar racing cars during 1991.*

Teo Fabi were campaigning this year was a very different type of race car to the XJR-12; with its race craft focused on all out speed without fuel consumption concerns. It was Andy Wallace in the absence of the experienced but more expensive Jan Lammers this year that helped bring some sense to the driving techniques needed here. After going over the circuit map with Derek Warwick he removed seven downshift gear changes allowing a higher gear to be used in those areas, and with the corresponding number of up shifts eliminated, the lap time to fuel used improved, as well as the reduced wear on the gear selector dog rings.

For some this race was seen as a sideline to the real XJR-14 focused attack in its first year of the new 3.5-litre World championship. The XJR-12s were seen as passed their best times, and the Le Mans race something to be endured. It had from the start been decided that Cosworth's HB engined XJR-14 was not going to be used here, with its many new team members focused on these revised regulations being a stepping stone to a future in Formula One, a totally TWR focused philosophy. Few now had been involved in the early days of communications with Jaguar and Jaguar's philosophy; Le Mans first and World Championship second.

The Formula One theme had reached a point where TW had finalised a deal with Benetton to be its engineering director and he had moved his office to Enstone earlier in the year. To say we felt abandoned was an understatement. After pressure from senior managers he later returned to Broadstone.

With the older Group C2 cars running within the new 3.5-litre series, the first ten of the 3.5-litre cars would line up at the front irrespective of their qualifying times. These consisted of slower Spice-Cosworth's and Peugeot's new and fast 905 that was not that far speed-wise behind the XJR-14. Former TWR driver Schlesser was out to once again prove a point to his former TWR team and in the XJR-14 versus Sauber Mercedes C11 battle during the drier circuit conditions on the Thursday the final result was Schlesser the fastest Mercedes driver, which also included a young Michael Schumacher, with 3:31.27, and Wallace 3:31.9. The #34 Jaguar had averted disaster with some great car control from Bob Wollek having his first outing in the XJR-12LM when his right hand rear tyre had blown out on a high-speed part of the track. He had managed to keep it under control and return to the pits where damaged underbody and tail section parts were replaced before it could return to the track. The TWR team had concentrated on race set-up and driver familiarisation, with half of the drivers having never raced a V12 Jaguar before, and many new to the Le Mans circuit as well; but it was still a disappointing range of results with eleventh for Jones/Boesel/M. Ferté; eighteenth. Warwick/Nielsen/Wallace; twenty-first. Fabi/Wollek/Acheson and twenty-second Leslie/Martini/Krosnoff.

One of the three Mazda 787Bs now employing recognised top line drivers Herbert/Gachot/Weidler, had qualified immediately behind the fastest Jaguar. It was only now that we found out that team manager Ohashi had played his hand by leveraging the fact that he had been the only Japanese manufacturer to register for the whole 1991 series, and his commitment to racing at Le Mans. Nissan and Toyota had withdrawn as Japan began to face the effects of a recession, leaving the Le Mans organisers with a reduced spectacle. Europeans wanted the Japanese to compete, mainly because they seemed to have little chance of winning, and that would help to neutralise what was seen by European car manufactures as the threat coming from Japan in the car markets of the world. Ohashi had argued on safety aspects that their car could not race to the heavier class weight penalty of 880kgs for this race and a sympathetic hearing at the Sarthe had allowed their cars to race at the 830kgs they claimed their car was designed for. This was 170kgs lighter than the Jaguars that had to be ballasted up to 1000kgs – in a fuel consumption dominated race! This was never challenged by TW or Roger.

## The Race

Patchy rain during the Saturday had mostly gone by the 4pm start with just the problem of sorting out positions over the first few laps with the slower C2 Spice-Cosworth's starting ahead of the faster endurance cars. From the start the Jaguars could not cover the fast pace and it was left to the Peugeot 905 to circulate for French honours while the Mercedes and Porsche 962s set the pace. It had always been a rule I followed that we should not go more than three percent over the fuel allowance as it was then proportionally slower to regain these amounts, but TW and Roger had difficulty in accepting the situation early in the race and asked the cars to speed

*Pit stop for the second placed #35 Jaguar.*

up and stay in touch using many drivers not used to the fuel consumption formula. The first major retirement was the Peugeot 905 with its 3.5-litre engine broken and with its sister car having electrical problems, the first effort for a manufacturer in the new 3.5-litre series was over in the first one and a half hours. Of the Jaguars, #34 seemed to be struggling with its set-up and suffered a spin, and then it was the #36 Suntec car with Martini suffering from a fuel pump electrical failure and loosing forty-five minutes out on the track, before temporary repairs had him back in the pits. Later Martini had an off which damaged the front suspension and after a long time with repairs this car would be just going through the motions for the rest of the race.

Leading up to the six hour mark the C11 Mercedes were well in control with the #33 Jaguar working its way up to third at one stage before Warwick had a spin into the gravel and lost over a lap getting going again. The Mazda's were covering the top ten places and appeared to be on the fuel allowance.

By quarter distance it was the C11s of Schlesser/Mass/A. Ferté on 92 laps; Palmer/Dickens/Thiim 91 laps and Schumacher/Wendlinger/Kreutzpointner on lap 90 as were Weidler/Herbert/Gachot (Mazda); Winter/Schneider/Pescarolo (Porsche 962); Jones/Boesel/M. Ferté #35 (XJR-12LM); Stuck/Bell/Jelinski (Porsche 962); Fabi/Acheson/Wollek #34 XJR-12LM; Warwick/Wallace/Nielsen #33 (XJR-12LM); Kennedy/Sala/Johansson (Mazda).

This situation more or less continued as the race progressed towards the halfway mark with just the Joest Porsche of Bell/Stuck starting to struggle to keep up with the pace. During this period a young Michael Schumacher, fighting back after team mate Wendlinger's accident had delayed their car, produced the fastest lap of the race with 3:35.50. The first setback to the leading Mercedes three car train happened eight hours into the race with track debris damaging one of the C11's underbody producing instability in the high-speed corners. Nine laps were lost as repairs were made before the Palmer/Dickens/Thiim car returned to the track. This had raised some concerns for the other two Mercedes and with the aerodynamic problems that has been experienced by the team in previous years and Schlesser's reluctance to drive these cars here, both of the leading C11s were carefully inspected at the next pit stop losing some time and eating into their advantage. Meanwhile the three Jaguars continued to circulate getting a handle on the driving needs for a fuel based race slowly coming under control for those drivers not used to it. Warwick stopped out on track around 2.30am with loss of fuel pressure and after advice over his radio he managed to find a connector problem and return to the pits, losing thirteen minutes. All through this period the #35 Jaguar and the #55 Mazda ran in close formation and it was obvious by now Mazda did not have a fuel problem.

Half distance had the #1 Mercedes on 184 laps; #31 Mercedes 183 laps;#55 Mazda 181 laps; #35 Jaguar 181 laps; #34 Jaguar 180 laps; #57 Porsche 179 laps; #58 Porsche 179 laps; #18 Mazda 179 laps; #33 Jaguar 177 laps and #49 Porsche 176 laps.

One hour later this pattern changed with the second placed Mercedes of the junior team pitting with gearbox problems, stuck in fourth gear. Two attempts were made before a solution was found, but nine laps had been lost in the process and they were out of contention dropping to ninth. Soon after the (Konrad) Joest #57 Porsche retired after suffering overheating problems and finally a broken transmission. As dawn appeared the #33 Jaguar was once again in trouble with Wallace off the track and loosing three laps in the process and then Acheson was in with the #34 to have a new nose fitted with the remains of a rabbit removed in the process. Dawn also bought a slowing of the lead Mercedes as its engine began to overheat with a failing head gasket and the Mazda–Jaguar battle looked to be in a position to move to the front although still three laps behind. The backup for Mercedes evaporated around 7.15am with the #32 finally stopping with engine vibration problems and final failure. The out of contention Suntec Jaguar had been off the track again and had a new rear wing fitted. This had been set at a lower angle with reduced downforce, soon catching Jeff Krosnoff out, and this car was off the track for about the fourth time and soon after this the LH front chassis had cried enough with a major failure of a bonding repair on the carbon tub completely fractured and the car was retired.

The #55 Mazda was starting to get the better of the Jaguar and continued to catch the slowing Mercedes at the rate of five seconds a lap. By 75% distance the leading Mercedes was still three laps ahead of the Formula One young guns in the Mazda, with the #35 Jaguar one lap behind them. The #34 Jaguar followed a further lap behind and comfortably ahead of the Mercedes junior team by two laps. After its off-circuit problem the #33 Jaguar was up next nine laps behind the leaders with the Kennedy/Sala/Johansson Mazda close behind. Stuck/Bell/Jelinski were the highest surviving Porsche drivers but now fourteen laps behind the leader, the next Porsche being eighteen laps down.

Just before midday the junior team's Mercedes had a lengthy stop to rectify overheating and had its water pump belt replaced, allowing the two Jaguars to settle into third and fourth places. One hour later the whole race changed for good with the leading Mercedes slowing and returning to the pits. Much activity ensued as its three laps and ten minute advantage evaporated, with pressure filling of the water system and ominous clouds of blue exhaust smoke on the restart. The engine had lost too much water and cooked the internals, and Mercedes were now left with just the junior team holding fifth position, five laps behind the leading Mazda and the final position it would finish in. Jaguar now held second, third and fourth running without problems, but could not gain on the leader with their 170kg disadvantage; and that was the way it would stay till the 4.00pm finish. Herbert finished the last two hour stint for Mazda and was dehydrated and completely exhausted when the car finished the race with a lead of two laps over the Jaguar. It took so long for him to recover that he missed the victory accolades he so deserved on the emotional rostrum ceremony.

*TW congratulating Takayoshi Ohashi, the Mazda team manager.*

TW was the first to congratulate and take the photo opportunity with Mazda's emotional Ohashi and TW seemed happier with this result than you would expect. I was disappointed with the early decisions on pace that had hampered the race to fuel, as well as the second placed Jaguar having three laps of fuel, 21 litres, still left in the tank at the end of the race after losing by two laps. TW had become anti Zytek since they had turned down his buyout proposals a couple of years before, and this had permeated through the team to include the removal of the V12's lap/fuel meter that had previously been used so successfully to help train the drivers to get the best results on track. Our first win with this system in 1988 had allowed just seven litres left in the tank at the end of the race. All in all though it was about carrying the extra 170kgs, an additional 20% in weight to the Mazda, for 24 hours to the same fuel allowance, and that was an impossible task. Had it been an even playing field we would have exited the seven years of the XJR-V12 programmes with the best result ever, a 1-2-3 at Le Mans; and that was a large disappointment for me. The race though had served its purpose as well as it possibly could under the circumstances, and handed the XJR-14 programme a good points total with its opposition scoring next to nothing. TWR Jaguar's Fabi was now the Championship leader on 47 points; Mass/Schlesser 37; Wendlinger/Schumacher 33 and Warwick 30.

TW was never one to miss an opportunity and with Mazda's win that company would be staying in motor-sport for some time to come, and he was already no doubt keeping his options open with his early congratulations to Ohashi and Ford's non-committal to Jaguar in motor-sport. There were growing problems at Jaguar with its Ford parents seeming lack of interest in progressing to Formula One on hold ups over the approval of the new budget asked by TW of £14,288,000. The likelihood of the XJR-14 winning the 1991 Championship triggering a deal for Ross Brawn to move into Formula One with TWR was already on his mind; finance being the only problem. Perhaps Mazda would like to purchase the rights to the XJR-14 and fit their own engine sometime in the future?

Mazda had completed a finishing record of 100%, Jaguar 75% and Mercedes 33%. Of the eleven 962 Porsches entered three finished, the leading Stuck/Bell/Jelinski car in seventh and thirteen laps behind the second placed Jaguar. Engs had been able to have many new parts produced, mainly new head castings , and used up the last of existing new parts stock to produce a good confidence level in six of the engines built for Le Mans in 1991.

Engineer John McLaughlin had devised the 'sharks tooth' concept of removable metal filters in front of the radiator. These had collected the fine track debris successfully and helped to eliminate the engine overheating problems that occurred in these 24 hour events. As these filter elements became clogged they were removed on the Sunday morning to leave the radiator core exposed for just eight hours. I was hopeful with this better equipment that we would be able to service additional 24 hour races at little cost in the future; but unfortunately this was not to be the case. Towards the end of the year the last of the fifty XJR-15 road cars were becoming difficult to sell and five of these 'special' cars were fitted with the Le Mans 7.4-litre engines and these proven 24 hour engines were lost to any future programme.

**LE MANS 1991 - PROBLEMS LIST**

- Pit signal boards not good, especially at night. Review. Discuss with drivers what they think would be better.
- Not enough radios available. Need to do radio plan with scanners + talkies specified.
- Some Willans buckles came loose again - why? They were modified to Sabelt spec?!
- Rear tyres foul tail.
- Exhaust tail pipes foul tail.
- Better Engine Shop/ Engineer communications required. Procedure for <u>all</u> changes to go thru' Engineer.
- Drivers with no Le Mans V12 experience struggled initially on fuel economy.
- Cars off the pace, difficult to drive to fuel, slow on straight.
- Fuel allowed to get too far away? Had to drive too slowly at finish?
- Need engine oil & G'Box oil temp on telemetry as well as auto trigger.
- Radio performance generally good, although some worse than others.
- Throttles slow to return; extra return springs help but make throttle effort too much.
- Means to stop wheel covers rubbing tyres?
- Rad gauze very good.
- Brakes (effort, bite & temps) OK once balance set to drivers preference (estimate 600 - 510).
- Nose fit:- Some mono's not drilled with jig. Splitter fouling on rad underpanel. Tight fit to side of mono.
- Car 36 front suspension failure? Weakness around IMSA mods?
- Car 36 drive failure? Input shaft - fault in manufacture? Change circlip groove detail.
- Car 34 exhaust primary failure?
- Rear brake ducts could be 40% smaller.
- Rear air jack bottom cap came loose on some cars. Spec lockwire in build sheet.

*Pit stop for the Japanese backed Suntec Jaguar at Le Mans.*

- Mirrors. Some drivers' happy, other not. Good electric mirrors would be ultimate. Is best compromise for larger manual mirrors (like car 35).
- Only car 36 had a full header tank. In other cars water levels were less than ¼ full both sides. Review this system for next race.
- Front towing eyes to be stronger still?
- Car 36 fuel pump switch failure? Item sent to manufacturer.
- Car 33 loose fuel pump connector.
- Cars a little too heavy (going by FISA scales). Could afford to be (say) 10.15kg lighter. Need means to reduce floor's weight & add some tuning ballast in nose box. Floor slightly thinner?
- Review wiring re: 'IGN' switch. Couldn't start engine without it. Should be able to eliminate lights etc. with it.
- Rad underpanel drwg updated to provide rad gauze inserts.
- Splitter brkt broke on one car. Better way?
- Still some variations on splitter height to ride height. More diligent setting up on rad plates.
- A little front bump steer. Why & best way of eliminating?
- Car 34 had offset steering rack. Why?
- Driveshafts still rub a little to hard on underwing. Can we get more clearance?
- Need nicer (& legal) underwing extensions. Up-issue to longer tunnels that are less than 280mm off 'o' line (4mm floor makes it worse. (This could possibly help drive shaft clearance).
- Fuel policy incorrect (in retrospect).
- Required to write a complete indepth strategy for next years race/ test program asap.
- We should adopt Inc's computer program to assist in controlling and recording each cars progress during the race.
- Do we need so many people to run a race?

Ford were an American based company and focused on costs with the V12 engine in Jaguar production cars costing much more than its known V8 technology. TWR had extensive business programmes with Jaguar including JaguarSport, and Ford had a policy of no joint ventures, and little or no interest in motorsport.

They wanted to phase out the V12 engine in production and therefore saw no reason to support Jaguar's point of difference. This was causing contractual problems for TW and negotiations with Ford had started to reach a stalemate with progress payments. TW's demands were being challenged by people with no remote interest in motor racing.

The business case of doing a Porsche and proving engineering excellence in endurance racing was a possibility for Jaguar, but that was not the direction TW and Ross Brawn wanted Jaguar to go in.

In September of 1991 TW had taken a view of where Ford may want to go in the future; as opposed to a Jaguar focus. A proposal with backing from Jackie Stewart was presented to Vickers, who were owners of the Cosworth automotive engineering group. To strengthen Benetton's Formula One hand TW had asked Cosworth to supply just the one team he was acting for, Benetton. This was to remove McLaren who were using the same HB V8 based engine.

With America and CART single seater formula in mind, a viable programme for the American IMSA team to move up to was now his thought process. Eliminating the engine supply to the second Formula One team, and placing the resources to develop a suitable engine for the top tier CART series, to be funded by Ford, was proposed as a better alternative for Cosworth. TWR would then have a factory suppported engine programme to continue in America, while TW gained first hand knowledge from the resources of Benetton, as its engineering director. Ross Brawn would be switched to that team for 1992, gaining experience for TWR's future Formula One team.

***TWR would return to the winner's circle once again with the Ross Brawn managed XJR-14 powered by the Cosworth 3.5 litre Formula One (phase 2) engine. This engine was rebranded with 'Jaguar' on the camshaft covers and fitted with the Bosch MP1.7 engine management system.***

## Teams Championship 1991 – 3.5-litre HB V8 XJR-14

| Position | Team | Chassis | Engine | Rounds | | | | | | | | |
|---|---|---|---|---|---|---|---|---|---|---|---|---|
| | | | | 1 | 2 | 3 | 4 | 5 | 6 | 7 | 8 | Total |
| 1 | Silk Cut Jaguar | Jaguar XJR-14<br>Jaguar XJR-12 | Cosworth HB<br>35L V8<br>Jaguar 7.4L V12 | | 20 | 20 | 15 | 20 | 12 | 6 | 15 | 108 |
| 2 | Peugeot Falbot Sport | Peugeot SA35<br>3.5L V10<br>Peugeot 905<br>Ego 1B | Peugeot SA35<br>3.5L V10<br>Peugeot SA35<br>3.5L V10 | 20 | 3 | 6 | | | 20 | 20 | 10 | 79 |
| 3 | Team Sauber Mercedes | Mercedes C291<br>Mercedes C11 | Mercedes M291<br>3.5L Flat-12<br>Mercedes M119<br>5.0L Turbo V8 | 15 | 12 | 15 | 8 | | | | 20 | 70 |
| 4 | Euro Racing | Spice SE90 C | Ford Cosworth<br>DFR 3.5L V8 | 10 | 10 | 8 | | | 10 | 10 | 6 | 54 |
| 5 | Mazdaspeed | Mazda 787<br>Mazda | Mazda R26B<br>2.6L 4-Rotor | | 4 | | | 8 | 4 | 2 | | 47 |
| 6 | Porsche Kremer Racing | Porsche<br>962CK6 | Porsche<br>Type-935 3.2L<br>Turbo Flat-6 | 12 | 8 | 3 | 2 | 12 | 6 | | | 43 |
| 7 | Courage Compétition | Porsche 962C<br>Porsche 962 GTi<br>Cougar C26 S | Porsche<br>Type-935 3.2L<br>Turbo Flat-6<br>Porsche<br>Type-935 3.2L<br>Turbo Flat-6<br>Porsche<br>Type-935 3.2L<br>Turbo Flat-6 | 8 | 2 | 2 | | 6 | 2 | 4 | 4 | 28 |
| 8 | Team Salamin Primagaz | Porsche 962C | Porsche<br>Type-935 3.2L<br>Turbo Flat-6 | 2 | | | | 10 | 1 | 12 | | 25 |
| 9 | Repsol Brun Motorsport | Porsche 962C<br>Brun C91 | Porsche<br>Type-935 3.2L<br>Turbo Flat-6<br>Judd EV 3.5L V8 | 4 | 6 | 4 | 1 | 4 | | 3 | | 22 |

## Drivers Championship 1991

| Position | Driver | Team | Rounds | | | | | | | | Total |
|---|---|---|---|---|---|---|---|---|---|---|---|
| | | | 1 | 2 | 3 | 4 | 5 | 6 | 7 | 8 | |
| 1 | Teo Fabi | Silk Cut Jaguar | | 15 | 20 | 12 | 15 | 12 | | 12 | 86 |
| 2 | Derek Warwick | Silk Cut Jaguar | | 20 | | 10 | 20 | 8 | 6 | 15 | 79 |
| 3= | Philippe Alliot | Peugeot Talbot Sport | 20 | 3 | 6 | | | 15 | 15 | 10 | 69 |
| 3= | Mauro Baldi | Peugeot Talbot Sport | 20 | 3 | 6 | | | 15 | 15 | 10 | 69 |
| 5 | Cor Euser | Euro Racing | 10 | 10 | 8 | | | 10 | 10 | 6 | 54 |
| 6 | Charles Zwolsman | Euro Racing | 10 | 10 | | | | 10 | 10 | 6 | 46 |
| 7 | Jochen Mass | Team Sauber Mercedes | 15 | 12 | 10 | | | | | 8 | 45 |
| 7= | Jean Louis-Schlesser | Team Sauber Mercedes | 15 | 12 | 10 | | | | | 8 | 45 |
| 9= | Michael Schumacher | Team Sauber Mercedes | | | 15 | 8 | | | | 20 | 43 |
| 9= | Karl Wendlinger | Team Sauber Mercedes | | | 15 | 8 | | | | 20 | 43 |
| 11 | Manuel Reuter | Porsche Kremer Racing | 12 | 8 | 3 | 2 | 12 | 6 | | | 43 |
| 12 | Harri Toivonen | Porsche Kremer Racing | 12 | 8 | 3 | | 12 | 6 | | | 41 |
| 13= | Keke Rosberg | Peugeot Talbot Sport | | | | | | 20 | 20 | | 40 |
| 13= | Yannick Dalmas | Peugeot Talbot Sport | | | | | | 20 | 20 | | 40 |
| 15 | Maurizio Sandro Sala | Mazdaspeed | 6 | 4 | | 6 | 8 | 4 | | 3 | 31 |
| 16= | Johnny Herbert | Mazdaspeed | | | | 20 | | | | | 20 |
| 16= | Volker Weidler | Mazdaspeed | | | | 20 | | | | | 20 |
| 18 | David Brabham | Silk Cut Jaguar | | | | | | | 6 | 12 | 18 |
| 19 | David Kennedy | Mazdaspeed | 6 | | | | 8 | | | 2 | 16 |
| 20 | Jésus Pareja | Repsol Brun Motorsport | 4 | | 4 | 1 | 4 | | 3 | | 16 |
| 21= | Davy Jones | Silk Cut Jaguar | | | | 15 | | | | | 15 |
| 21= | Raul Boesel | Silk Cut Jaguar | | | | 15 | | | | | 15 |
| 23 | Bernd Schneider | Konrad Motorsport/ Team Salamin Primagaz | | | | | | | 12 | | 12 |
| 24= | Kenny Acheson | Silk Cut Jaguar | | | | 12 | | | | | 12 |
| 24= | Bob Wollek | Silk Cut Jaguar | | | | 12 | | | | | 12 |
| 24= | Martin Brundle | Silk Cut Jaguar | | | 12 | | | | | | 12 |

*The Ross Brawn developed and managed XJR-14 – winner of the 1991 Group C Series.*

## IMSA Drivers Championship 1991

| Position | Driver | Team | Total |
|---|---|---|---|
| 1 | Geoff Brabham | Nissan Performance Technology | 175 |
| 2 | Chip Robinson | Nissan Performance Technology | 170 |
| 3 | Davy Jones | Bud Light Jaguar Racing | 158 |
| 4 | Wayne Taylor | MTI Racing | 117 |
| 5 | Juan Manuel Fangio II | All American Racers | 107 |
| 6 | Raul Boesel | Bud Light Jaguar Racing | 72 |
| 7 | Tom Kendall | Jim Miller Racing/MTI Racing | 69 |
| 8 | Brian Bonner | Tom Milner Racing | 54 |
| 9 | Bernd Schneider | Joest Racing | 49 |
| 10 | Derek Daly | Nissan Performance Technology | 48 |
| 11 | Henri Pescarolo | Joest Racing | 44 |
| 12 | Frank Jelinski | Joest Racing | 43 |
| 13 | Rocky Moran | All American Racers | 41 |
| 14 | Jim Adams | Dyson Racing/Hotchkis Racing | 40 |
| 15 | James Weaver | Dyson Racing/John Shapiro Racing | 36 |
| 16 | Chris Cord | Dyson Racing/Hotchkis Racing | 32 |
| 17 | Scott Sharp | Tom Milner Racing | 30 |
| 18= | Giampiero Moretti | Momo-Gebhardt Racing | 29 |
| 18= | Jeff Purner | Tim Milner Racing | 29 |
| 20 | Bob Earl | Nissan Performance Technology | 28 |

CHAPTER TWENTY-FOUR

# Daytona 1992

**1991 had been a successful year for TWR once again and the Ross Brawn managed XJR-14 programme with drivers Derek Warwick/Teo Fabi dominating Mercedes to eventually win the Sports Car World Championship; making it a total of three World championship wins for Jaguar with TWR. Although we were not aware of it at the time it would also be the last time the V12 powered Jaguars would compete at Le Mans with this final departure producing second, third and fourth in 1991. While this was a great achievement for that team there were continuing growing problems and challenges at the Kidlington base, and the TWR Group as a whole. Various programmes had kept Engs busy in the meantime but with the completion of the machining and build facility to manufacture the 3.5-litre V6 turbocharged engines for the XJ220 road car, half of Engs staff had been relocated to that department as work began to dry up for us with the cessation of programmes for the V6 turbo racing engines and prospects of limited V12 endurance racing ahead. There were now some ongoing disputes with Jaguar (Ford) and that long relationship was looking increasingly like not having the contract renewed causing TW to have to take a view on where his motor racing future lay, and what little expenditure could be put to complying with the existing contract. The TWR Group car franchise business was separate and at arm's length from Kidlington but we had already heard of problems from that area in 1991.**

It was then that Ford's men Bill Hayden and Bill Brooks said that the Group C contract would not be resigned. With no replacement programmes in the pipe line, it was an inevitability that a situation that was new to TWR had to be faced up to. It was a hard and difficult situation for TW to have to finally admit to himself that the rampant development of his business over the last 10 years was now facing problems and cuts were needed. TWR was intertwined on many levels with Jaguar, not just racing, with JaguarSport and XJ220, as well as working on a replacement design for the XJS. The XJS make over under Ian Callum would then morph into a deal with Aston Martin and eventually became the DB7; the XJ-14 cars would later be sold in a deal to Mazda and become the base for their Sports Car programme. Later TWR's 50% holding in JaguarSport would be sold to Ford making a considerable profit (JaguarSport was the second most profitable division in Ford's empire at the time of sale, after an engine production plant in Portugal). These situations show TW's considerable ability in big picture financial deals.

Although senior managers had been aware of the cash flow problems of 1991 the true extent of the salvage operation that was needed was generally unknown, with the extent of the problems kept from employees. It was impossible for TW to admit defeat, but it had become clear later in 1991 that some simple cutting back may not provide the answers. TW was the consummate deal maker and had come down to my office in late 1991 to tell me he had bought 25% of the Benetton Formula One team, with Ross Brawn and a few TWR employees to be placed at their factory in the future. This meant the end of the Jaguar's XJR-14 programme – after just one year. TW had set up an office at the Benetton team as engineering director at the end of 1991; and we had to travel there for our meetings, something he was showing increasing disinterest in. We felt abandoned and frustrated with this move. The Benetton receptionist had then asked me to stop parking in the visitor's car park by the front door and park some distance away in the workers car park; but that was something that was not going to happen in mid-winter.

What had actually happened though was that Benetton had signed a deal with TW on November 9th 1991 to buy 50% of the TWR Group in exchange for much needed funding, and TW being placed as Benetton engineering director with a performance related deal that eventually included the signing of Michael Schumacher and a World Championship. This set of circumstances would switch the focus for TW to now having an equal business partner for the first time, a business savvy Flavio Briatore making demands on behalf of the Benetton family, over the next five years. This arrangement would finally be unwound in 1996 with Benetton making a reported tripling of their investment.

In a tense meeting at Broadstone at the start of the 1992 new year I was given a set of figures to stick with and no guidance on total programme aims, numbers of cars etc, or the full extent of TW's intentions or association with Benetton. His 'divide and rule philosophy' meant it was difficult to have meaningful discussions on this situation with other divisional managers. It was now a matter of working backwards from these fixed numbers and cutting procurement, Engs would have to perform, but carry all the risks of the decisions made within the spend cap, with no programme performance aims.

On my drive back to Kidlington after this meeting I at least had the satisfaction of knowing I had made the hard but correct decision almost two years earlier to put in place a strategy to leave TWR; something that I hoped would ensure Engs ability to continue to function as a standalone entity, with sound management from Charlie Bamber and Nigel Eames.

This changing situation at TWR was one consideration and my family's future was another. My wife Karen had brought up two children in the UK without any family support and this had been hard with a husband who was away for considerable amounts of time. She had settled into village life and schools over time, but moving to another position in motorsport would mean starting all over again in another part of the country for her if we were to commit to long term staying in the UK. I was happy in my work in motorsport and accepted the challenges as part of life, but there were also best financial decisions to consider and these would prove to be the correct course for us to follow. The buoyant house market from 1983 when we had first purchased our home with help from TW had produced a 250% increase in value by late 1989. Karen and our two children had been on holiday in New Zealand and she had phoned in the January of 1990, after the Jerez V6 turbo test, to say she had seen a large inner-city property. We had also previously been looking at buying a 250 acre farm property with large house in the South Island of New Zealand with its possible use as a tourism venture.

With TW avoiding the implications from the Liechtenstein experiment and its failure to produce a workable engine, I had then agreed we buy this inner city property. This New Zealand property could be bought for one-third of the cost of a similar UK property mainly because of exchange rates at the time, and was within five to ten minutes walking distance to private schools whose fees were also one-third of those in the UK. We completed the purchase in early 1990 and soon after sold our Oxfordshire home. Our eldest daughter Martina would start the New Zealand high school first year at the beginning of 1995; and so the end of 1994 would be my exit plan; not conveyed at the time of course. Things had also come to a head at Liechtenstein by late 1991 and TW had cancelled all programmes there and then stopped the association with Heidegger altogether.

A review of divisional head count was now asked for in 1992 and this challenged many long term TWR managers as well. From a peak number of thirty-eight in 1990, Engs had now been reduced to fifteen after the transfer of skilled engine builders to the XJ220 programme, and this was up again for review when I was asked to put forward a staff reduction proposal at the start of 1992. I could see no future for me in making this highly skilled team any smaller as it would mean we would not be able to handle any future new programmes for another manufacturer. After our successful liaisons with Mazda, Rover and Jaguar I conveyed that assumption to TW. When asked to submit names for redundancy I had put my name forward and nothing more was said; Engs was the only TWR racing department that did not have any redundancies. TWR America had also reduced its head count starting in 1991 and we had all lost some confidence over the future with these negotiations.

*TWR IMSA factory workshop.*

## Rolex 24 at Daytona – February 2nd-3rd

With these mixed messages circulating Andy Wallace had moved to Toyota and in his debut with team mates Juan Fangio jnr/Kenny Acheson set the fastest qualifying time of 1:35.86 for the Dan Gurney run American Eagle operation. Davy Jones had set second fastest time with a 1:36.26 in the XJR-16, a new specification twin rear-wing XJR-10 based turbo V6 car that had not been to Daytona before. This effort was as much about PR for Budweiser and getting a choice of pit position for the next race which was important on the Miami street circuit, as part of race strategy.

They were followed by Hasemi/Hoshino/Suzuki #23 Nissan 1:36.47; Stuck/Jelinski/Pescarolo/Moretti #30 Joest/Momo 962 Porsche 1:36.89, and the #83 Nissan of Brabham/Robinson/Earl/Luyendyk in 1:37.6. The #2 XJR-12D TWR/Bud Lite Jaguar to be driven here by David Brabham/Scott Pruet/Scott Goodyear as well as Jones qualified in eleventh on 1:39.894, just 0.4 seconds faster than the time set in 1990 with the 6-litre engine, but Brabham was baulked twice on his best lap. Daytona once again would have a sole V12 car for the 1992 race after withdrawing the updated XJR-16 V6 turbo race car as a backup programme; although this had never been seen as a proposition for the 24 hour event anyway.

Once again, the dual regulations of IMSA and Group C were allowed and once again the rules had been tweaked with some lobbying pressure from teams' interests. IMSA still with 3-litre turbo engines governed by an air restrictor, 120 litre fuel tank and unrestricted fuel flow; and in our case a 6.5-litre normally aspirated engine with a minimum weight limit of 940kgs. The Group C regulations of engine capacity freedom, a 100 litre fuel tank that would need additional fuel flow regulated stops during the race, along with the allocation of 2600 litres of fuel, had been countered by the 90kg lighter 850kg weight limit in 1991. Some problems in administrating these regulated pit stops had occurred last year and now the simple answer for this was to just allow unregulated fuel flow – and freedom of fuel amounts for the race, as IMSA rules. Not only did this move the goal posts a long way in the Japanese manufactures favour, Nissan mainly, but what was missed was that the approved circuit fuel that had to be used was 112 research-octane, not the 98 that Group C had been governed by. This aspect added hugely to the reliability of the larger 3.5-litre turbo engine of the Group C Nissan and was their weapon of choice instead of their IMSA Championship winning ZXT. The only downside for Nissan was that Group C cars were now not eligible for IMSA Championship points as they had been last year, and as in 1991 they could not start on the front row of the grid. Nissan covered their option here with a show of force with both NISMO and NOVA fielding Group C race cars and NPTI using Group C based cars with down sized 3-litre engines and entered in GTP to allow them to gain points in the IMSA Championship. The Nissan groups also used Goodyear and Bridgestone tyres, some were the original Lola chassis and some of these modified, as well as new replica cars built in Japan that used carbon brakes. TWR America had planned to use carbon brakes here on the XJR-12D but after testing had decided to stay with the proven option of the previous year. Just three 962 GTP Porsches would start the race to emphasise the changes occurring at Daytona and the Sports Car world, as well as the fact that the base design of this car had started 10 years before.

## Report by TWR America's John Szymanski

### MORAL VICTORY FOR BUD LIGHT JAGUAR

DAYTONA BEACH, Florida – The Bud Light Jaguar team finished second overall and first in class at the 30th Annual Rolex 24 Hours at Daytona. A constant challenge to the winning Nismo Nissan R91 CP, Bud Light Jaguar XJR-12 D drivers Davy Jones, Scott Pruett, David Brabham and Scott Goodyear, fought gallantly to overcome the Nissan Group C type car.

The second Bud Light Jaguar entry, the twin turbocharged XJR-16, was withdrawn from competition following an internal engine problem during the morning warm-up. The team took this decision to completely focus their efforts on the Jaguar V-12 powered XJR-12 D.

Davy Jones started the race with a 'double stint' and quickly moved up to run in the top three during the early stages of the twice round the clock race. Davy commented on his performance following his first outings in the car, "We are running a conservative pace and we need to stick to it. Our plan is to run a very disciplined race and be around tomorrow so we can race for the win."

Battling with first the NPTI Nissan and then the Nismo Nissan, the Bud Light Jaguar team provided the only constant threat to Nissan for the victory. Three separate incidents set back the team's carefully sculpted plan for victory. The first, an unfortunate trip into the pit lane guard rail for Jaguar SWC regular David Brabham, which cost the team over three minutes while repairs were made to the nose and right front suspension. This dropped the team down to seventh place, five laps behind the leader. Now into the rythym of the race, Jones, Brabham, Pruett and Goodyear clawed their way back up to third. Unfortunately, during the night, Scott Pruett reported that the XJR-12 D had lost the use of third gear. Following a driver change, David Brabham called into the pits with irregular sounds eminating from the gearbox. The Bud Light Jaguar crew quickly changed the entire gear 'cluster' and had David back into the fray, but had lost 24 minutes in the pits, putting themselves back into fourth place, 18 laps in arrears.

Running laps in the same range as the leaders, the team clawed their way back to third only to be delayed again by a front brake problem. Only seven minutes were lost but once again, the team had to fight their way up the leader board. They moved into second early Sunday morning. At one point the team were 19 laps down on the lead Nismo Nissan, but as mid day approached, the team slowly chipped away at the gap and closed to only nine laps behind.

Davy Jones commented on the race, "The Nismo Nissan team have had a faultless race and we have had our share of problems, which cost us valuable time." During the closing stages, Jones played a waiting game with the leader as they had been experiencing some high engine running temperatures. With the expiration of Geoff Brabham and Chip Robinson, and most of the regular IMSA team encountering problems, the team realised they were in a position to garner the first place points for finishing first in the 'Camel GT' class. Decreasing the gap down to just nine laps showed the determination that has become their trademark in the World's classic endurance races.

Team Manager, Tony Dowe gave the team a directive prior to the race that said, "First we want to finish, then we want to finish well, and of course, we want to win," commented Dowe. The plan worked to perfection as the winning car ran to the 'Group C' rules and was not eligible for Camel GT points, thus giving Jones and company the IMSA points lead going into the next IMSA Camel GT round at Miami, February 23rd.

The race results were:

1. Hasemi/Hoshino/Suzuki – Nissan Gp. C
2. Jones/Pruett/Brabham/Goodyear – Jaguar GTP
3. Haywood/Elgh/Ratzenberger/Brayton – Porsche GTP
4. Moran/PJ Jones/Dismore – Toyota
5. Johnstone/Marvin/Vasser/Cameron – Acura Spice Camel Light
6. Evana/Velez/Bender/Dobson – Buick Kudz Camel Light
7. Greer/Bacon/Uria/Mees – Mazda RX7 GTU
8. Weidler/Martini/Krosnoff – Nissan Gp. C
9. Dallenbach/Schroeder/Gordon – Mustang GTS
10. Brassfield/Robinson/Kline/Gentilozzi – Oldsmobile GTS

Note: GTO have become GTS

The problems encountered during the race by TWR had taken the pressure off the NISMO team and when you can run your race at a safe pace you are in complete control, just watching the gap which at one stage was a lead of eighteen laps. Although the Jaguar had reduced this to nine laps by the end of the race the Nissan team could do the sums and run to a suitable pace. The Schuppan Porsche was rewarded after long time efforts in this race with third, four laps behind the Jaguar and the 2.1-litre Eagle-Toyota Mk3 was rewarded with fourth a further ten laps behind and twenty-three laps down on the leader.

## Contact 12 hours of Sebring (Camel) – March 21st

Just one XJR-12 was sent to Sebring for sponsor Bud Light to be driven by Davy Jones and David Brabham.

> The Toyota powered 2140cc twin turbocharged Eagle Mk3 of Fangio/Wallace 1:48.004 took the pole time followed by its sister car of Jones/Moran 1:49.449. Larrauri/Sigala/Moretti 1:50.335, Gary Brabham/Luyendyk 1:51.751 Jones/David Brabham 1:52.95.

The Toyota team had set the pace in qualifying and continued with its best showing to date with pace and reliability producing a win for the #99 car co driven by former TWR driver Wallace. After a poor qualifying result the Nissans once again set fast times to challenge for the win but the # 83 car ended its challenge with a problem wheel to finish second. Joest once again showed its consistency in the changing conditions to stay ahead of the XJR12D, it coming one place better than last year in fourth.

> Finishing order was: #99 Fangio/Wallace – 360 laps; Brabham/Daly/Gary Brabham – 355 laps; Larrauri/Sigala/Moretti – 345 laps; Jones/David Brabham 338 laps.

Some confusion remained as to whether we would return to Le Mans in 1992 and here are some of the thoughts around that time. The memo to TW below says it is already too late to source many new parts and most item will be well used.

Alternative race programmes were consistently being investigated at TWR.

With the 7.4-litre V12 engines assigned to the XJR-15 project and others to be refurbished for Group C race cars for sale, Le Mans has now officially finished for the V12 programme. The proposals for future programmes continued. My visits to Cosworth to assess the switch to a YB 4 cylinder engine for the BTCC Mondeo, and Ford at Dearborn USA to assess their new 4.7-litre V8 engine for possible use in Aston Martin and a racing project in IMSA. These motivated by the association with Jaguar's owner Ford.

*The Sebring 12 hour winning Toyota Eagle.*

Development of the first engines for the Australian V8 series was ongoing to then be relocated to Melbourne and run from there. After I had completed the in-house design of an all new 4-valve head for the V12 with patterns completed in 1991, this project had been left with TWR's new 220 machine shop to be machined. It was treated as a non priority item as the 220 engine programme took precedence. These 4-valve heads would finally be finished by 1993 and we had fitted a 6.4-litre engine to a V12 XJR-S saloon. When TW drove it as a 490bhp road going car he had actually phoned me at home to say how impressed he was with it. It was all too late now to insert them into the Le Mans /Daytona programmes.

**XJR-S 6.4L 48 VALVE V12 SUMMARY**

**Vehicle Details**

XJR-S fitted with:

- 6.4L 48 valve V12 engine
- Modified Getrag 290 5 speed gearbox
- AP Racing twin plate clutch
- 18" × 9" front wheels, 18" × 10" rear wheels fitted with 285/55 × 18" Bridgestone RE71 tyres
- Enhanced suspension
- Non Catalyst exhaust system with fabricated manifold

**Engine Performance**

Test bed figures, using a simulated vehicle exhaust system running on 98 super unleaded (corrected to SAE standards):

Max power 489.4bhp at 6010rpm
Max torque 490.0 lbft at 4486rpm

**Vehicle Performance**

Tested two up with full fuel tank, test weight 1920kg. Test conditions 20°C, 997 mb pressure, 7mph windspeed, 86% humidity.

| | | | *3rd* | *4th* | *5th* |
|---|---|---|---|---|---|
| 0–60 | 4.6 | 50–70 | 2.5 | 4.1 | 6.0 |
| 0–100 | 10.5 | 30–50 | 2.9 | 4.0 | 5.6 |
| 0–150 | 28.7 | 30–120 | - | 18.0 | 28.0 |

Estimated top speed 175mph at 6300rpm.

I. M. Harrop
Projects Co-Ordinator

*HB Cosworth 'Jaguar' 3.5 V8 and the new Engs designed 4 valves per cylinder 6.4-litre V12 engine, for road use. This 6.4 litre V12 was fitted to a Jaguar XJR-S saloon, and the performance tests are shown above.*

# Typical Build Data Sheet of the V12 engine

| | | | |
|---|---|---|---|
| ENGINE NUMBER | V1292I001 | BUILD TEAM | PT & AP |
| DATE | 2/12/92 | START DATE | 3/12/92 |
| BUILD NUMBER | 1343 | FINISH DATE | |
| BLOCK | V1292I001 (1282 M) | | |
| CRANKSHAFT | NO.70 84mm STROKE NEW | | |
| CONROD 1A | ASB (1282 M) | CONROD 1B | ASB (1282 M) |
| CONROD 2A | ASB (1282 M) | CONROD 2B | ASB (1282 M) |
| CONROD 3A | ASB (1282 M) | CONROD 3B | ASB (1282 M) |
| CONROD 4A | ASB (1282 M) | CONROD 4B | ASB (1282 M) |
| CONROD 5A | ASB (1282 M) | CONROD 5B | ASB (1282 M) |
| CONROD 6A | ASB (1282 M) | CONROD 6B | ASB (1282 M) |
| LINER 1A | ASB (1282 M) | LINER 1B | ASB (1282 M) |
| LINER 2A | ASB (1282 M) | LINER 2B | ASB (1282 M) |
| LINER 3A | ASB (1282 M) | LINER 3B | NEW |
| LINER 4A | ASB (1282 M) | LINER 4B | ASB (1282 M) |
| LINER 5A | ASB (1282 M) | LINER 5B | ASB (1282 M) |
| LINER 6A | ASB (1282 M) | LINER 6B | ASB (1282 M) |
| PISTONS | NEW PA1174 (0.010") | | |
| TOP RING | BEARING STEEL NEW | GAP | 0.015" – 0.018" |
| SECOND RING | NEW | GAP | 0.016" – 0.018" |
| OIL CONTROL | NEW | GAP | |
| GUDGEON PINS | USED GOOD | | |
| BIG END BEARINGS | NEW | | |
| MAIN BEARINGS | NEW | | |
| PISTON WEIGHT | | | |
| CONROD WEIGHT | | | |
| CYLINDER HEAD A | ASB (1282 M) | CYLINDER HEAD B | ASB (1282 M) |
| CAM CARRIER A | ASB (1282 M) | CAM CARRIER B | ASB (1282 M) |
| CAMSHAFT A | EA24/25 | CAMSHAFT B | EA24/25 |
| VALVE INLET | ASB (1282 M) | VALVE INLET | ASB (1282 M) |
| VALVE EXHAUST | ASB (1282 M) | VALVE EXHAUST | ASB (1282 M) |
| FOLLOWERS | ASB (1282 M) | FOLLOWERS | ASB (1282 M) |
| VALVE SPRING | NEW 38mm | VALVE SPRING | NEW 38mm |
| VALVE GUIDES | ASB (1282 M) | VALVE GUIDES | ASB (1282 M) |
| TOPS/BASES | ASB (1282 M) | TOPS/BASES | ASB (1282 M) |
| HEAD THICKNESS | | HEAD THICKNESS | |
| CHAMBER VOL | 0.125" THICK | CHAMBER VOL | 0.125" THICK |
| TAPPET CLRNCE | 0.011",0.013" | TAPPET CLRNCE | 0.011",0.013" |
| OFF COIL BIND | 0.030 OFF COIL | OFF COIL BIND | 0.030 OFF COIL |
| SPRING TYPE | SCHMITTHELM | SPRING TYPE | SCHMITTHELM |
| CAM TIMING | 100 DEGREES PISTON TO VALVE 0.060" AT 8 DEG | | |
| PISTON SKIRT | 3.6965" | | |
| PISTON TO BORE | 0.005–0.0055,0.0055–0.006 | | |

| MAIN CAP No. | 1 | 2 | 3 | 4 | 5 | 6 | 7 |
|---|---|---|---|---|---|---|---|
| CRANK JOURNAL DIA | 3.000 | 3.000 | 3.000 | 3.000 | 3.000 | 3.000 | 3.000 |
| CRANK JOURNAL DIA | 3.000 | 3.000 | 3.000 | 3.000 | 3.000 | 3.000 | 3.000 |
| BOWERS GAUGE 1 | 3.0032 | 3.0035 | 3.0035 | 3.0043 | 3.0033 | 3.0036 | 3.0041 |
| BOWERS GAUGE 2 | 3.0037 | 3.0033 | 3.0036 | 3.0039 | 3.0032 | 3.0037 | 3.0037 |
| MIN CLEARANCE | 0.0027 | 0.0027 | 0.003 | 0.0037 | 0.0025 | 0.003 | 0.0035 |
| MAX CLEARANCE | | | | | | | |

| CYLINDER No. | | 1 | 2 | 3 | 4 | 5 | 6 |
|---|---|---|---|---|---|---|---|
| CRANK PIN DIAMETER | A | 2.0994 | 2.0992 | 2.0994 | 2.0993 | 2.0993 | 2.0992 |
| | B | | | | | | |
| CRANK PIN DIAMETER | A | 2.0996 | 2.0993 | 2.0995 | 2.0995 | 2.0995 | 2.0995 |
| | B | | | | | | |
| BOWERS GAUGE 1 | A | 2.1015 | 2.1017 | 2.1016 | 2.1018 | 2.1015 | 2.1016 |
| | B | 2.1017 | 2.1013 | 2.1017 | 2.1016 | 2.1013 | 2.1016 |
| BOWERS GAUGE 2 | A | 2.102 | 2.102 | 2.1014 | 2.1022 | 2.1018 | 2.102 |
| | B | 2.102 | 2.1017 | 2.1021 | 2.1019 | 2.1017 | 2.102 |
| MIN BEARING CLEARANCE | A | 0.0019 | 0.0023 | 0.0018 | 0.002 | 0.002 | 0.0021 |
| | B | | | | | | |
| MAX BEARING CLEARANCE | A | | | | | | |
| | B | | | | | | |
| BEARING CRUSH | A | 0.008 | 0.008 | 0.008 | 0.008 | 0.008 | 0.008 |
| | B | 0.008 | 0.008 | 0.009 | 0.009 | 0.009 | 0.009 |


| CYLINDER No. | | 1 | 2 | 3 | 4 | 5 | 6 |
|---|---|---|---|---|---|---|---|
| CRANK PIN DIAMETER | A | 2.0994 | 2.0992 | 2.0994 | 2.0993 | 2.0993 | 2.0992 |
| | B | | | | | | |
| CRANK PIN DIAMETER | A | 2.0996 | 2.0993 | 2.0995 | 2.0995 | 2.0995 | 2.0995 |
| | B | | | | | | |
| BOWERS GAUGE 1 | A | 2.1015 | 2.1017 | 2.1016 | 2.1018 | 2.1015 | 2.1016 |
| | B | 2.1017 | 2.1013 | 2.1017 | 2.1016 | 2.1013 | 2.1016 |
| BOWERS GAUGE 2 | A | 2.102 | 2.102 | 2.1014 | 2.1022 | 2.1018 | 2.102 |
| | B | 2.102 | 2.1017 | 2.1021 | 2.1019 | 2.1017 | 2.102 |
| MIN BEARING CLEARANCE | A | 0.0019 | 0.0023 | 0.0018 | 0.002 | 0.002 | 0.0021 |
| | B | | | | | | |
| MAX BEARING CLEARANCE | A | | | | | | |
| | B | | | | | | |
| BEARING CRUSH | A | 0.008 | 0.008 | 0.008 | 0.008 | 0.008 | 0.008 |
| | B | 0.008 | 0.008 | 0.009 | 0.009 | 0.009 | 0.009 |


| VALVE | SPRING | + SETTING OFF COIL BIND + LIFT – TAPPET CLEARANCE | DTI AND SPACER | SPRING SHIM | TAPPET SHIM |
|---|---|---|---|---|---|
| EX 1A | 0.992 | 0.597 | 1.614 | 0.025 | |
| IN 1A | 0.995 | 0.62 | 1.625 | 0.01 | |
| EX 2A | 0.99 | 0.597 | 1.617 | 0.03 | |
| IN 2A | 0.988 | 0.62 | 1.618 | 0.01 | |
| EX 3A | 0.978 | 0.597 | 1.615 | 0.04 | |
| IN 3A | 0.978 | 0.62 | 1.628 | 0.03 | |
| IN 4A | 0.976 | 0.62 | 1.605 | 0.009 | |
| EX 4A | 0.977 | 0.597 | 1.604 | 0.03 | |
| IN 5A | 0.985 | 0.62 | 1.615 | 0.01 | |
| EX 5A | 0.979 | 0.597 | 1.615 | 0.039 | |
| IN 6A | 0.979 | 0.62 | 1.619 | 0.02 | |
| EX 6A | 0.99 | 0.597 | 1.597 | 0.01 | |
| EX 1B | 0.982 | 0.597 | 1.624 | 0.045 | |
| IN 1B | 0.984 | 0.62 | 1.634 | 0.03 | |
| EX 2B | 0.979 | 0.597 | 1.626 | 0.05 | |
| IN 2B | 0.985 | 0.62 | 1.625 | 0.02 | |
| EX 3B | 0.984 | 0.597 | 1.631 | 0.05 | |
| IN 3B | 0.981 | 0.62 | 1.631 | 0.03 | |
| IN 4B | 0.99 | 0.62 | 1.63 | 0.02 | |
| EX 4B | 0.991 | 0.597 | 1.628 | 0.04 | |
| IN 5B | 0.981 | 0.62 | 1.631 | 0.03 | |
| EX 5B | 0.984 | 0.597 | 1.621 | 0.04 | |
| IN 6B | 0.979 | 0.62 | 1.628 | 0.029 | |
| EX 6B | 0.984 | 0.597 | 1.615 | 0.034 | |

| | | |
|---|---|---|
| INJECTOR SPECIFICATION | | |
| PORT DIAMETER | 40 38 TAPER | |
| STACK DIAMETER | 40mm | |
| AIR FILTER TYPE | NEW PIPERCROSS | |
| TRUMPET TYPE | SHORT NEW | |
| THROTTLE POTENTIOMETER | CHECKED BLACK | |
| THROTTLE RETURN SPRINGS | 2 LIGHT, 1 HEAVY | |
| FUEL PRESSURE REGULATOR | NEW | |
| SPARK PLUGS | N82G | |
| PLUG GAP | 0.020" | |
| SYNC POSITION | 2 DEG ATDCVO NEW SPEC | |
| ROTOR ARM POSITION | 40 DEG TO 8 DEG | |
| TRIGGER DISC ADVANCE | MAX | MIN |
| ALTERNATOR | NEW | |
| ALTERNATOR BRACKETS | NEW | |
| STARTER | NEW | |
| STARTER BRACKETS | NEW | |
| STARTER BENDIX | NEW | |
| OIL PUMP | USED | |
| BELTS | NEW | |
| AIR FILTER | NEW | |
| CAGE | NEW | |
| FUEL RAILS | NEW | |
| WATER RAILS | NEW | |
| CLUTCH | NEW 24HR | |
| FLYWHEEL | NEW | |
| DISTRIBUTOR ASSEMBLY | USED | |
| CRANK INSPECTION SHEET | SUPPLIED | |
| INSPECTION LABELS | | |
| POWER TEST DATA | | |

V1292I001 was originally built new for Daytona 1992.
The engine was used for the test only (1282 miles)
The engine has new valve springs and PA1174 pistons

# Status Report after meeting with TW

MINUTES

- No Le Mans
- Proceed with turbo V12 presentation (top priority to secure this contract)
- Division dyno systems to be re-appraised
  Meeting needed TDW, AWS, GC-W
- Other V12 engine configurations to assist XJR15 sales
- What Range Rover 4.7 litre engine sales?
- One Ford 2 litre British Touring Car Series 1993
  TWR/Cosworth commercial considerations to be finalised
- F3000 - exclusive use of the new Cosworth unit. RED to rebuild units
- Group C - possibility of JaguarSport 220/Aston Martin for 1994
  Engine development programme to be advised
- Need for high performance derivatives of Ford's Granada range.
  Need for high performance multi-cylinder engine for future mid engined production car.
- Holden - behind schedule. Further de-rating of V8 engines because of the move to 2 litre units greatly lessens the need for the current engine specifications. Current engines in build use best US technology (looks very good). Dummy engine to Australia to assist installation.
- JaguarSport AJ6 - efficiency tests. 4 litre unit currently being installed in vehicle for assessment after Engs modifications.
  New base unit supplied for efficiency test and re-head with new 4 valve unit currently produces a maximum of 198 BHP after 10 hours dyno running.
- V12 4 Valve 6.4 litre - two engines built.
  Development programme after AJ6
- Engs general policy discussion
  Engine builders sent to 220 project in 1992 on loan only. To be returned as Engs workload increases.

---

*Dated June 4th 1992*

Minutes of the meeting were as follows :-

HOLDEN

Need to pay Pierce Engineering account
Owe approximately $90,000 total
Payment of $45,000 will ensure continuation of parts for 4th and 5th engines

R9R V6 N/A

The purpose of this exercise is to see what engine noise can be insulated from the car and its performance (handling, etc) using these rubber mountings.

The N/A engine should be based on a 220 unit because of the known engine noise from this unit. The 220 syncro gearbox should be quieter than the race unit and the feasibility of fitting this to the rear of the R9R is to be investigated.

FORD ALLOY V8

The all alloy 4.6 litre Ford V8 was discussed for suitability for IMSA racing and Aston Martin road car.

It was agreed if a meeting could be put together that AWS and GCW should visit Detroit and assess the suitability of the unit.

---

*Dated August 14th 1992*

JAGUAR

## Chapter Twenty-Five

# 1993

**The lead up to the Daytona race had begun in late 1992, with TWR Kidlington engineer John McLaughlin running the UK end in collaboration with TWR America. With the prospect of racing in America now reduced to selected races only, with the lack of funding available, Tony Dowe and Ian Reed were engaged in proposals to update the XJR-12 to continue a competitive life at Le Mans and Daytona until 1995; to keep their team in continued employment. An extensive five page proposal had been sent to TW from Tony Dowe and copied to me on November 12th 1992 which outlined a case for TWR America to run the long distance races including Le Mans, with what was proposed to be the XJR-16. Since 1991 we had the new 4-valve head designed and castings made to support the long distance races of Daytona, Sebring and Le Mans if that was a programme Jaguar and TW wished to continue with.**

Point (4) of this document states:

> "Quite simply, parts do not know where they are being built, but the current personnel and systems at Valpo are the very best at taking the maximum from every situation, and with our well demonstrated build quality it will ensure the best possible result".

TW however was side tracked while these proposals were being put forward as his top priority at that time had been trying to rescue TWR's loss making Garage Group. TW was also in the process of facing his peers in the motor racing establishment who had become hostile to, and very much against, a non notified merger agreement between the TWR Garage Group and Silverstone Circuits. TW had background support for this merger from Bernie Ecclestone who had a vested interest in bringing the Silverstone Circuit's owners, the British Racing Drivers Club (BRDC) out of their historical view of automatic rights in hosting Formula One races. More money was needed from Silverstone Circuits to retain the hosting rights in the future, and so a move into the commercial world had been put forward by TW, now Chairman of Silverstone Circuit, as a means to produce these additional funds.

TW's position as chairman of the Silverstone racing circuit and the putting together of the £5.3 million buyout deal for his troubled car retail business was seen by most members of the BRDC, owners of the Silverstone complex, as an abuse of position and unwelcome influence over current board members. The TWR Garage Group had amassed losses of £2.2 million in 1990 and £1.4 million in 1991, and was much of the reason why we had such a difficult boss to deal with as the racing budgets were trimmed. The buyout of the TWR Garage Group by Silverstone Circuits had gone through in late 1992 and no doubt was being influenced by TWR partner Benetton as well; to produce profits and dispose of assets to raise cash and remove a drain on funds. Many of the Garage's staff had chosen to work for Tom Walkinshaw as much as their respective positions in the various franchises, and now were in the process of feeling abandoned.

During 1992 considerable psychological pressures had emerged for the workforce as well at Kidlington. As we pushed through with proposals for future programmes we were getting little or no comment back from TW creating concerns about their future employment. This was coupled with the personal problem for individuals now facing a large reduction in, or complete loss of their main asset; their home. The overheated housing market of the late 1980s had collapsed, and most young men were in the middle of the worst housing asset reversal on record. I had sold our home before the main reversal had happened and reinvested in New Zealand and was renting at this time; but virtually all the Engs staff members were now facing a problem that had become uppermost in their minds – with no solution in sight. This situation and possible effect on moral of the workforce was the last thing that TW would want to hear as another problem. Across the other side of the Atlantic there was no housing problem to pressure the workforce.

Tony Dowe's proposals in his five page document to TW, continues with this point in mind.

> "A further point not to be underestimated is that the Valpo work force has not experienced any financial hardships such as is happening in the UK, with the obvious advantage of not being overly concerned with the non work related pressures; hence increased build quality."

Tony was always good at selling TWR America and the fact he was so frank with his thoughts to TW showed the level of openness and rapport he felt existed between them. This report would not have been well received by many at Kidlington if it had been distributed, but was copied me only being seen as more neutral at Kidlington, with direct involvement via the supply of engines. It also shows the increased efforts managers were taking at this time to retain their respective teams and influence within racing.

After discussion documents had been worked through, John McLaughlin at Kidlington had then compiled a work list to produce a working programme for 1993 that would suit both Daytona and Le Mans. It was felt that both Group C and IMSA regulation cars should compete at the 1993 Daytona race and this would help justify and set in place the move to return to Le Mans with upgraded V12 race cars. Many of the upgrade thoughts were coming out of the now finished Ross Brawn managed XJR-14 programme, and centred on weight reduction as well.

The engines available at this time are listed below and the capacity versus weight limits put forward for the TWR America team to decide on the best compromise weight to race at. TW had been very impressed with the road going 4-valve 6.4 litre V12 but would not support the introduction of an upgraded V12 engine to allow a future in endurance racing. With the new IMSA rules however the XJR-12 would remain competitive as Group C cars if the weight could be reduced.

**ENGINES AND EVENTS**

Jaguar V12: Daytona

6.5 litre as raced in 1992

1 engine suitable for 24 hour event.
1 engine update pistons for 24 hour event.
1 engine suitable practice only.

7 litre as raced Le Mans 1990

1 engine suitable for 24 hour event.
The 6.5 litre piston update can be converted to 7 litre engine suitable for 24 hour event.

6.5 IMSA able to race at:

1900 lbs (860 kgs) with GpC tunnels
1950 lbs (886 kgs) with IMSA tunnels

Car raced at Daytona 1992 at 2250 lbs 1022 kgs

A 7 litre GpC 1990 regulation car may run at Daytona at 909 kgs with Daytona silencing.

A 6 litre 4 valve V12 can run at 1850 lbs (841 kgs).

Power to weight at 900 kgs

| | | | |
|---|---|---|---|
| Max 7200 | 6.5 litre | .79 HP/kg | .63 lb/ft/kg |
| Max 7200 | 7 litre | .827 HP/kg | .705 lb/ft/kg |
| Max 7800 | 6 litre 4v | .8 HP/kg | .6 lb/ft/kg |

Air Box for Daytona with "EARS"

*Air box for Daytona with 'EARS'*
*No new items for the V12 engine; with revised engineering depending on our parts inventory and secondhand stock.*

# John McLaughlin's Work List
# Development of the XJR-12 for Daytona and Le Mans

DEVELOPMENT OF THE XJR12 FOR DAYTONA AND LE MANS

The work to develop the V12 has been agreed for some time amongst TWR USA and Kidlington Engineers.

This has been well documented and includes the updates that are proposed for the test on 9 and 10 January 1993 in America! This test is in preparation for the 1993 Daytona 24-hour race and part of an overall package for Le Mans.

Daytona

It is proposed that three cars are prepared (2 x race, 1 x spare), one of these cars will be prepared in Kidlington to the proposed spec, and two cars identical to the Kidlington car will be prepared at Valparaiso. One of Valparaiso cars will be the test and spare race car. The Kidlington car will be the development car and will then be prepared as a race car.

Intended Updates

1. Carbon brakes requiring ventilated uprights.
2. Revised brake ducts to suit above.
3. Two-tier rear wing with revised body to suit. (Layout as Mark Thomas XJR12-bodied XJR11 wind tunnel results.)
4. Nose - version to be decided (small or large rad entry) with brake duct and sharks teeth to suit.
5. Air Box - if we can find a more efficient entry we should aim to revise the design. If no reason to change is found apart from weight saving then we must look at a light weight version of the existing side entry.
6. A revision of all body work construction to reduce weight without making it less robust. - Rear wheel arch.
7. A revision of all mechanical parts of the car to reduce weight without affecting reliability.

The intention of these modifications are three-fold:

a. to enable the car to better its previous races lap times by at least two seconds;
b. to improve fuel economy;
c. To speed up pit stops by reducing the number and the time taken for pad and disc changes.

Le Mans

The development programme at Kidlington will carry on with input from the American January test and the Daytona 24-hour race.

To carry out this programme the Kidlington prepared car will be returned here asap from Daytona, will be serviced and prepared as a test car for track and comparative dyno testing to check the effect of the proposed air restriction on performance, fuel consumption, engine temperatures (could require less cooling?) reliability etc.

Other work required should include:

a. improvements from our experiences at Daytona;
b. development intended to be but not carried out for Daytona;
c. aero development to cater for the special low drag requirements of Le Mans.

## Work List – *continued*

To manufacture one set of uprights to take as hand luggage for the USA test on January we will require: 3/4/5

| | | Working Days from today |
|---|---|---|
| - | the Billets | 8 days |
| - | centre machining drawings | 10 days |
| - | wire erode drawings | 13 days |
| - | detail parts drawings | 15 days |
| - | fabrication drawings | 17 days |
| - | final machining drawings | 27 days |
| - | the parts should be complete in | 32 working days |

NOTE: although a working day week to us is assumed 7 days for our own staff, we cannot guarantee that our contractors would work more than 5-day weeks.

Useful Information

| | |
|---|---|
| Working days to Christmas | 31 |
| Total days to Christmas | 43 |
| Working days to 8 January | 42 |
| Total days to 8 January | 58 |
| (at and including 11.11.92) | |

Brake ducts would be manufactured out of carbon similar to the XJR14. Because of the shortage of time we may have to test using flexible hose brake ducts!

Summary

The aero work appears to be fairly easily completed without the air box change.

The air box intake is probably placed in a reasonable position now. To install bunny ears would cause all kinds of installation problems.

The uprights are not a big problem, but the detail work in axles, disc bells, brake ducts etc would require some extra (possible temporary) design staff.

To achieve good air flow over the brakes we should use 'Speedline-type' wheels. The upright assemblies have been designed around uprated XJR14 wheels.

The weight of a complete XJR12 car (the one in unit 17A) is 40kg with oil and water but without fuel, radio or mirrors.

Weight saving estimates:

| | |
|---|---|
| carbon brakes | 15kg |
| lighter bodywork | 16kg |
| lighter underwing | 5kg |
| plastic windscreen | 4kg |

Other savings including:

| | |
|---|---|
| carbon fire bottle | ? |

Main differences between IMSA and Le Mans cars are that IMSA cars have brass rad, thicker brake discs, cool suit and ice chest, TWR-designed brake calipers, modified rear bodywork with wet lay up louvres to cool tail pipes, IMSA underwing and brackets, revised fuel system with fuel cooler, uprated front suspension, aluminium rear uprights (Le Mans are magnesium).

JOHN McLOUGHLIN
11.11.92

***Below is Tony Dowe's proposal to allow the Jaguar programme to continue with major modifications. But will Ford continue with this programme as well as the unknown influence by 50% shareholder Benetton?***

## PROPOSAL FOR 1993 AND BEYOND FOR THE LE MANS 24 HOURS RACE AND OTHER ENDURANCE EVENTS

ASSUMPTIONS

The ground rules for this race call for three (3) cars.

The cars are to be V12 XJR-12LM with "suitable" updates.

The engine capacity to be agreed with A.W.S. following rule publication and assessment of restrictor sizes.

The aero package to be updated.

The mechanical package requires updating.

The availability of a 6-speed gearbox needs assessment.

A front mounted water radiator to be retained whilst the existing tub is used.

Consideration should be given to changing both track, front and rear and wheelbase.

The utilization of a "modern" engine management system must be thoroughly investigated, both for the engine and the chassis installation benefits.

OBJECTIVE

To build an updated V12 car using proven mechanical and aerodynamic information for 1993 and beyond.

To reduce the weight increments that have taken place since 1986 as a "whole" reliable package to enable continued competitive V12 racing until, at least, 1995 season.

To improve chassis performance to take advantage of better radial tires now available from Goodyear (existing suspension geometry is still as designed for Dunlop crossply tires).

FUTURE DEVELOPMENT

The use of carbon/carbon braking system perhaps incorporating ABS, given the wide variety of drivers that we expect to use!

Traction control: While we feel that the 1991 Le Mans car suffered from less than adequate shock absorber development and control hence excessive wheel spin from the 7.4 liter engines, a traction control system would be advantageous.

QUESTION

Are we ready for a fully active V12 in 1994?

PRACTICAL CONSIDERATIONS

The design and building of these cars, or indeed any cars, should not be restricted to geographical location. Indeed we should seek to utilize all resources within the Group.

It is quite clear, and I believe practical, to build these cars in the U.S. There are a number of advantages to this situation.

1) All design work must be complete and therefore costing will be extremely accurate. There will be no opportunity for the engineering staff <u>not</u> to produce an integrated design by using the excuse that "I will finish it off as the build progresses!", or, "The fabbies or mechanics will do that."
2) The necessity to produce complete parts lists to enable P.O.s etc. must ensure that the accountability trail is complete.

3) The current system of building cars at Valpo is extremely precise and to duplicate in the U.K. would be both time consuming and expensive.
4) Quite simply, parts don't know where they are being built, but the current personnel and systems at Valpo are the very best at taking the maximum from every situation and with our well demonstrated build quality it will ensure the best possible result.

   A further point not to be underestimated is that the Valpo work force has not experienced any economic hardships such as is happening in the U.K. with the obvious advantage of not being overly concerned with non-work related pressures hence increased built quality.
5) I think we should build three cars in the USA. The first car as soon as possible following Daytona, tested at Road America with any development parts that are available for at least 2 three-day tests. This particular car should then be stripped and prepared prior to shipment to the U.K. The other 2 race cars would then be prepared to this specification. This should ensure that no one has any problem being involved with any car prepared in this manner. This should mean we can operate with existing staffing levels and smooth integration of resources at all levels.

SPECIFICATION

Overview

It would be wrong to approach this redesign on a "piecemeal" basis.

For example, we should retain a spool both for reliability and weight, but the current front track, geometry and aero package means that we are always fighting understeer. A wider front track with corresponding increase in nose width would eliminate the "add on" Silman bibs and reduce the understeer characteristics of the current car with spool.

While we are doing this we should look very hard at using the XJR-14 tyre torsion bar assemblies as part of the front end package.

The introduction of restrictors plus the now standard chicanes at Le Mans must mean we use a 6-speed gearbox as we will potentially be on "the nozzle" a lot of the time.

Ian Reed would like to increase the wheelbase to more normal N/A car dimensions, but he would like to put the increased length between the engine and gearbox to put more weight on the front wheels.

We can then put the oil tank in the bell housing. At this point there is now very little stopping us using all of the XJR-14 rear tyre suspension with suitable strengthening mods and hence using the basic XJR-14 tunnels, wings, etc. etc.

We should not use the XJR-14 gearbox configuration as reliability is still paramount and the ability to replace gears during a race remains very important (as at Daytona 1992).

A further advantage of a six speed box would be that the drop between ratios is much closer than we currently enjoy with corresponding extended "dog ring" life (a common 5-speed gearbox fault as we have found at both Le Mans and Daytona).

The longer bell housing will confer an aero advantage similar to the XJR-14 engine cover.

There is absolutely no sound engineering reason not to reduce the cross section of the cockpit and use an XJR-14 type cockpit assembly, with all the advantages this brings.

Carbon/carbon brakes with XJR-14 levels of brake ducting must produce less time in the pits changing pads, better driver efficiency with less pedal effort, substantial weight savings and increased performance. A win, win situation with cost the only downside for individual components, but expended over a 24 hour race is not a lot different to carbon metallic/steel components.

LOGISTICS

I think we should seriously investigate costings for shipping our current IMSA transporter to UK/France with all of our existing pit equipment, etc. etc. etc.

There is no doubt that the IMSA approach to pit stop efficiency has paid off in previews of 24 hour races and this should continue.

The practical aspect of this would be that following Daytona we would overhaul wheel guns, air jack probes, etc. etc. and would not be in the situation of using unfamiliar equipment. I recall this was an advantage in 1990 and see nothing to have changed since them. This approach is not new as Nissan also did this in 1990 and various other teams have adopted this situation successfully in previous years.

It just means we have to be organised ahead of time.

I would like to layout the pit and garage in the same way as we do at IMSA races. Has anyone ever measured up the Le Mans garages including door access etc., to enable flow charts for mechanic efficiency, motorhome and truck access, driver accommodations, etc. to correctly take place?

There should be no difference between car preparation and pit and team preparation.

PRE-RACE TESTING

As it not possible to test at Le Mans the following criteria has been used to source a suitable alternative.

1) Long straights with heavy braking.
2) High load corners.
3) Long total lap.
4) Rough in braking areas.
5) Similar ambient to mid-June at Le Mans.
6) Cost effective (not to be ignored).

Road America (Erkhart Lake) meets all of our requirements including a 195mph back straight with a kink and heavy braking as per mulsane, and a 4 mile lap and 3 heavy braking areas.

SHAKE DOWN

Silverstone prior to despatch to Le Mans, all cars.

RADIOS

Previous experience has demonstrated that the U.S. radios have enjoyed measurably better performance and good consistency. The only failing being one of range, and it would be proposed to locate a repeater station somewhere between the pit area and the mulsane hairpin to cover the complete track. With the Erkhart Lake distances involved, we would be able to satisfy testing prior to departure. It should also be noted that we have been working on a very high-powered radio assembly that exceeds FIA regulations but is instantly switchable to low power when anything locks in on it, and this should not be dismissed.

The problem with these proposals was that both Roger Silman and Ross Brawn were absent from any input because they did not support this direction. Ford could support a Cosworth engine programme in Formula One along with the American CART and Indianapolis races. As a secondary consideration, fifty percent owner Benetton would have a view, something we would never be made aware of.

Another problem was Ford's reluctance to finance a V12 engine programme as that 'point of difference' was contrary to their marketing strategy. This fact was being used by Ford to renegotiate terms, something we were not made aware of at the time. With the Joint 220 Supercar project using a Jaguar sanctioned turbo V6 engine, that concept had to be tolerated by Ford as its efforts continued to extract itself from TWR.

The post 1991 Group C budget proposal of £14,288,000 had not been signed off by Ford and TW was looking for even more money with Formula One in mind.

*New chassis 193 had its first shake down test with driver David Brabham on January 15th 1993 and although it was hampered by wet weather conditions it was a good test and bought all the little niggling problems to light that are associated with a new car, built at the last minute.*

## John McLaughlin – Test Report and Problems List

XJR12 CHASSIS 193
DAYTONA SHAKEDOWN TEST
SILVERSTONE SOUTH CIRCUIT
FRIDAY 15 JANUARY 1993

TEST REPORT

The weather conditions were terrible with high winds and driving rain.

The car was set-up similar to the best set up for this circuit during testing prior to 1991 Le Mans.

David Brabham completed just 9 laps in the morning session. JMc decided that if the rain kept away, the wind would dry the circuit; therefore team had an early lunch and resumed testing at 13.00hrs. Unfortunately, there was a very heavy rain storm at 11.30hrs which meant that when testing resumed, the circuit was very wet. There was no rain in the afternoon, therefore the lap times recorded reflect the improving track conditions rather than any set-up changes.

Nose bibs were fitted to balance the improved rear downforce.

| | |
|---|---|
| Weather: | wet & windy |
| Temp: | 11°C |
| Rad: | blanked 70% |
| Oil Cooler: | blanked .75" fence |
| Brakes: | blanked 80% front & rear |
| Fuel in: | 40 litres |

10.23hrs: David Brabham driving. Starts on wets 24PSI cold installation lap all OK. Car feels very unstable, probably due to the high wind.

10.32hrs: 9 laps - fastest = 1 min 29.26 sec
Throttle sticking - spring pressure too low.

| Brakes cold | 167 | ↑ | 210 |
|---|---|---|---|
| | 225 | | 228 |

Increasing front brake blanking from 100mm open to 80mm.

Testing stopped due to rain.

13.06hrs: John Nielsen driving. No changes apart from increasing throttle return spring pressure. 5 laps, fastest = 1,23.06

Track still very wet but drying quickly, very slippery on new patches of track. Temps: water = 80, Oil = 110. Car feels too pointy, there is no hint of understeer at all.

13.27hrs: Rear brakes too cool, moving balance 2 turns to the rear.

Front splitter scraping, raising front ride height. 1 turn on push-rods. 2 laps - no time.
Front splitter still scraping.

13.36hrs: Removed nose bibs to reduce front downforce.
4 laps, fastest = 1m 17.43s.
Fast corners neutral, turn in slow, some understeer in slow corners.
Stone damage to bodywork behind rear tyres.
Front brakes too hot.
Still scraping the centre of the splitter.

14.07 hrs: Reduced front brake blanking.
Front ride height up ½ turn on push rods.
Softer (blue) front anti-roll bar. 4 laps, fastest = 1m 15.86s.
Better in slow speed corners. Has some mid to exit understeer, in mid-speed corners the car feels better balanced.

14.33hrs Front bump from 0 to 4 no other changes.
5 laps, fastest = 1m 14.75s. Mechanical balance feels very good.
Some aerodynamic understeer but not bad. Brakes a little hot.

14.50hrs: David Brabham driving.
Front brake blanking opened to 140mm, rear opened 15mm more.
New wets (left rear wearing). Centre support fitted to splitter.
5 laps, fastest = 1m 17.71 secs.
Turn in slow, then oversteer, mid-corner understeer going to exit oversteer. Feels unpredictable probably new tyres.

15.00hrs: Tyre pressures to 28PSI, no other changes.
6 laps, fastest = 1m 15.59s.
Mid corner understeer then power oversteer on exit.
Balance feels quite good.

The circuit is too dry now for wets, the resurfaced parts have not dried and are too slippery to risk slicks.

Temps: Water = 100°C, Oil = 103°C, Amb = 11°C.

JOHN McLOUGHLIN

*The evolution twin rear wing XJR-12 Advanced. This update had not been wind tunnel tested.*

XJR12 CHASSIS 193
DAYTONA SHAKEDOWN TEST
SILVERSTONE SOUTH CIRCUIT
FRIDAY 15 JANUARY 1993

**PROBLEMS LIST**

| | | Date Req'd | Responsible |
|---|---|---|---|
| 1. | Require correct wheel bearing spacers asap. | 19.01.93 | PF |
| 2. | Axle bolt washers do not fit through axle. | modified | D.O. |
| 3. | Front upright/top wishbone retaining nut inaccessible. | 19.01.93 | D.O. |
| 4. | Front brake duct/upright retaining ring fouls top upright fabrication. | no further action | |
| 5. | FARB link locknut difficult to tighten. | | |
| 6. | New carbon rad under tray too wide also requires titanium leading edge to avoid stone damage. | 21.01.93 | MO |
| 7. | Rear wing/damper cross beam carbon support panel difficult to fit, also wrong profile. | Le Mans | D.O. |
| 8. | Brake pedal reinforcing structure required redesigning. | Le Mans | D.O./PF |
| 9. | Front roll bar tight in housings also top housing/damper mount bobbins out of line. | Le Mans | D.O./JW |
| 10. | Too much paint on body panels will probably add an extra 5-6kg on car weight. | Le Mans | PF |
| 11. | Gearbox/oil cooler lines too long. | no further action | |
| 12. | Inner cv under wing access hatches too small. | 21.01.93 | NB |
| 13. | Rear towing eye (none) ? | use XJR14 | PF |
| 14. | Quick change system required for screens in front of rear wheel. | 21.01.93 | D.O./PF |
| 15. | Rear body/mono bullets shortened to 15mm to enable body to be fitted. | 21.01.93 | D.O./PF |
| 16. | No sharks teeth blanks at the test. | 21.01.93 | MO |
| 17. | Require Simpson seat belt buckle. | Daytona | IR |
| 18. | Rear wheels difficult to remove because of lack of wheel arch clearance. | Le Mans | D.O. |
| 19. | Body clearance to rear brake ducts marginal, requires careful additional trimming. | Daytona | JW |
| 20. | Rad undertray to splitter definitely requires a central support. | 19.01.93 | D.O./MO |
| 21. | Caliper temperatures high when using excessive brake blanking. | | |
| 22. | Rear jack lifts too high, requires shorter foot. | 19.01.93 | PF |
| 23. | Garetson water radiator weights 20 kg full of water, the one used on the Group 'C car in Europe weighs 10kgs. | | |
| 24. | Tacho flickering. | 19.01.93 | JW |
| 25. | The joint between the centre and outside parts of the nose splitter has the joggle the wrong way making it difficult to fit the nose. | Le Mans | MT |
| 26. | No steering wheel spacers at the test. | 19.01.93 | D.O./PF |
| 27. | Selection of steering wheels need pre-fitting. John Nielsen requested a smaller diameter one. | 19.01.93 | JW |
| 28. | Oil cooler and radiator blanks required. | 19.01.93 | PF/MO |
| 29. | Master switch pull cable requires fitting. | 19.01.93 | JW |
| 30. | Bracket to stop oil line running on the drive shaft required. | 19.01.93 | DO/JW |
| 31. | Drivers cooling duct requires fitting. | 19.01.93 | JW |
| 32. | Door windows require rear edge packing out. | 19.01.93 | JW |
| 33. | Fuel fillers require seal to bodywork. | 19.01.93 | JW |
| 34. | Fit passenger seat. | 19.01.93 | JW |
| 35. | Air box requires rubber seal. | 19.01.93 | JW |
| 36. | Mirrors not fitted at test, require fitting to all noses. | 19.01.93 | JW |
| 37. | Tail hits rain light. | 19.01.93 | D.O./JW |
| 38. | Front towing eye requires moving or re-locating to enable the sharks teeth to be replaced quickly. | 19.01.93 | D.O./JW |
| 39. | Use hose clamp to retain gearbox oil filter to replace tie wrap. | 19.01.93 | JW |
| 40. | Nose box appears to be low on the RH side at the test. | 19.01.93 | JW |
| 41. | Lower push-rod rod end fouls upright. | | |

JOHN McLOUGHLIN

## 1993 DAYTONA BUDGET

| | Retail £000's |
|---|---|
| 2 engines 6.5 litre | 50 |
| 1 rebuild after January's test | 15 |
| Support and freight | 5 |
| Telemetry update | ? |
| TOTAL COST | 70 |

## 1993 SEBRING BUDGET

| | Retail £000's |
|---|---|
| 2 rebuilds - new heads | 40 |
| Support and freight | 2 |
| TOTAL COST | 42 |

*Final agreed budgets to support IMSA in 1993.*
*Engs was now full time subcontracted to Cosworth, rebuilding the HB V8 Formula One engines.*

# Personnel for Daytona 1993
# Job during race

**Management:** T. D. Walkinshaw and T. Dowe

**Drivers:** D. Jones, J. Andretti, S. Goodyear, S. Pruitt, D. Brabham and J. Nielsen

**Engineering:**
Chief Engineer & O/all Engineering Responsibilities: I. Reed
Engineering Car #2: I. Reed
Engineering Car #3: D. Benbow
Engines O/all: Allan Scott
Engines Car #2: Charlie Bamber
Engines Car #3: Don Beadle

**Tires:**
O/all: Mark Redbond
Car #2: Mark Redbond
Car #3: Mark Stevens
Assisting: John McLennan and Dan Enslen
Fetch Drivers During Race: D. Schuck

**Pit Coordinators**: John Jackson and Steve Costello

**Team Physical Maintenance (Drivers and Crew):** Dean Miller and Sean Eden

**Fuel Dead Man Handle:**
Car #2: M. Croake
Car #3: J. Kracht

**Fuel:** B. Wright, J. Kracht and M. Freeman
Refilling Fuel Towers & Nitrogen Bottles
Car #2 Refueler: (B. Wright)
Car #3 Refueler: (J. McLellan)
Assisted by: J. Kracht and M. Freeman

**Bodywork:** D. Burroughs, S. Schiewer (Aerodyne) and J. Kracht

**Spares:** M. Croake

**Gearbox:** W. Bush and G. Mulkey

**Signallers**: S. Ave, D. Doyle and P. Spano

**Timing & Scoring:** C. Syfert, A. Kalian and P. Luderitz

**Operations & Pit Set-up – Overall**: V. Warren
B. Wright, M. Stephens, M. Redbond, M. Weston, J. McLellan, K. Bova and D. Enslen

**Sub Assembly:** S. Costello, G. Mulkey and J. Jackson

**Radios & Electronics:** M. Weston

**Fabrication:** K. Bova and J. McLellan

**Fireman:** W. Bush and C. Lovely

**Motorhome:** M. Murphy, A. Murphy and R. Ave

**Press & PA:** J. Crawford (Jaguar Cars) and M. Cook (Jaguar Cars)

# Race Report – Daytona 1993

**1230pm Saturday – End of Pre-race Warm Up**

| | |
|---|---|
| 99 Toyota | 138.78 |
| 3 Jaguar | 141.43 |
| 2 Jaguar | 141.47 |
| 32 Jaguar | 142.1 |
| Porsche | 142.48 |
| Nissan | 144.26 |
| Porsche | 144.7 |
| Porsche | 145.07 |
| Porsche | 145.02 |
| Nissan | 149.31 |

**1345pm Saturday – 24 minutes of Daytona, Competitors from the Past:** 4 GD 40s, Alfas, Group 44 V12 Jaguar, BMWs, Mustangs, Corvettes, AC Cobras, Cortina, Ferrari, March V8

**1500pm Saturday 30 January 1993 – Start of the Daytona 24 hours:** Cars No. 2, 3 and 32 start.

**1530pm:** No. 32 Jaguar elects to stop. Out of race.

**1545pm:** Car Number 3 in the Pits after trailing some smoke. Oil pressure low. Oil levels low.
Car to the back of the pits to have the oil leak checked
Car 32 rejoins the race.

**1600pm:** Toyota 99; Toyota 98; Jaguar (1 lap down)

**1630pm:** No. 2 Pit

**1650pm:** First Yellow
Toyotas 1st and 2nd; Porsche 3rd; MOMO 4th;
2 V12 Jaguars, 5th; Jaguars (1 lap behind Toyota)
Race pace generally slower than anticipated
Toyotas 2.42/5; Jaguars 2.44/48

**1700pm:** Rear crankshaft seal replaced on car 3
Gearbox replaced

**1745pm:** Jaguar Car Number 3 has been retired. Sump scavenge problem caused oil seal leak

**1905pm:** Toyota 1st; Jaguar Number 2 (1 lap down); Number 7 3rd (same lap); Porsche 4th (3 laps down)
At this stage, showing the 99 Toyota 6 laps down with a second gearbox problem.
Wynn's Porsche in 6th place (8 laps down)
7th position, the GDS Oldsmobile car (9 laps down)
Jaguar car Number 32, the new prototype twin rear wing car is having problems with handling and is now at the back of the pits to be thoroughly checked over. This car is showing to be in 18th place.

**1915pm:** Toyota number 99 (2 laps down) in eighth place goes back into the race. The first four cars all travelling approximately 2:44/2:46s in time. Although the fastest laps have been 2:41.42s.

**1925pm:** Pace car is on the track – unknown reason

**2015pm:** 99 Toyota has lost another 7 laps so it's in 12th place with a total of 17 laps lost. It is circulating at the moment quite quickly so it looks like whatever problem they had is fixed.
The positions are: 98 Toyota, 7 Porsche (29 seconds behind), 2 Jaguar, GDS Nissan (9 laps down), Porsche (10 laps down) GDS Mustang (7 laps down), GDS Nissan (down 12) Accura Camel Lite (13 laps down).
Weather is cool, no wind.

**2045pm:** Jaguar Number 2 Pits

**2045pm:** Changing Disk Pads. Jaguar Number 2 pitting under the yellow. Checking Disk Pads

**2130pm:** The fuel pump pack is being changed along with the tyres. We have a fluctuating fuel pressure problem on the banking.
Fuel pressure now OK.

**2215pm:** Number 2 Jaguar Pits for routine stop.
The car positions are: 98 Toyota, 2 Jaguar (1 lap down), 6 Joest Porsche (7 laps down), GDS Nissan (14 laps down), 99 Toyota (15 laps down), 1 GDS Nissan (15 laps down), 11 Mustang (16 laps down).
The MOMO Nissan at 2345 after a slow stop by the leading Toyota to fit a new nose.
Car Number 2 V12 Jaguar takes the lead and is now one lap in front.

**1245am Sunday morning:** 98 Toyota is in the lead. Jaguar 2 same lap (7 seconds down). A gap of 13 laps between the third place car 99 Toyota. 17 laps down is the GDS Mustang. 21 laps down is the GDS Nissan. 22 laps down is the second GDS Nissan Number 1.
During the last Pit stop, a half inch Guerney flap in the oil inlet to raise the oil temperatures. Currently running at 100 degrees.

**0130am:** Jaguar Number 2 in the Pits checking the rear disk pads, re-fueling, changing the ECU part throttle from 1.5 to 3. Retained our lead during the Pit Stop. Toyota Number 98 second on the same lap. Toyota 99 third in laps down, GDS Mustang 20 laps down, second GDS Mustang Number 15, 25 laps down in 6th place, the GDS Nissan, 27 laps down. 7th place the MOMO Nissan minus thirty laps, 8th place GDS Nissan minus 32, 9th the Porsche, 45 laps down and the GDS Mustang 48 laps down.
Pace car has just come out at 1.33. One lap after we've been in and re-fueled.

**0150am:** Re-start on the Yellow, Toyota and V12 side by side on the same lap.

**0215am Sunday morning:** Toyota 10 seconds ahead of Jaguar.

**0220am:** After the Toyota Pit Stop, Jaguar Number 2 now leads by 54 seconds.

Official places after 10 hours: Davy Jones, Jaguar; P. J. Jones, Toyota; Fangio, Toyota; Tom Candle, Ford; Steve Millen, Nissan; Geoff Brabham, Nissan; Mark Martin, Ford; Maretti, Nissan; Innes Ace, GDP Porsche; Frank Jelenski, Mazda.

**0320am Sunday morning:** After Pit Stops, 98 Toyota leads. 2 Jaguar, 2nd (one lap down); 99 Toyota, 3rd (11 laps down).

**0720am Sunday morning:** Toyota 99, previously in 3rd place, is out with suspected engine damage.
Toyota 98 that was leading had some problems and went off the track and has dropped back leaving the Number 2 Jaguar in the lead by 5 laps.
The Toyota pits at 7.30.
Coming in for fuel, tyres not changed.

**0940am:** Second place car, Toyota number 98 in the Pits bleeding the brakes.
Jaguar has gone past for the second time.
The carbon disks are being measured but are staying on, Jaguar passes for the third time, nose back on the Toyota.

**0942am:** The Toyota leaves the Pits.

**0945am:** Jaguar Number 2, 7 laps ahead of Toyota 98 in second place.

**1030am:** Jaguar Number 2 in the lead under the Pace Car, 12 laps ahead of Toyota 98.
Car Number 98 in second, 12 laps behind with a broken gearbox. The complete rear suspension and gearbox has to be changed. It is still in the pits.
The car that is on the circuit in second position is the MOMO Nissan although it is 34 laps down from the Jaguar and 23 laps behind the Toyota.
The gear linkage problem in the Number 2 Jaguar was repaired by the driver Scott Pruett a new selector rod fitted, minor adjustments were needed in the Pits afterwards. The car is now circulating happily, oil pressure is OK. At this stage we do not intend to change the oil, the rev limit has been set at 68.

**1038am:** Pace Car lights off. Ready to re-start.

**1140am:** Car stops in Pits with a broken valve spring. (Later found to be a valve seat insert failure.)

---

*Success has many fathers –*
*but failure is an orphan.*

*Two XJR-12Ds and the XJR-12D Advanced twin wing line up at Daytona.*

## Rolex 24 hour at Daytona

It was time to return to the Daytona Speedway on January 27th in readiness for the 3pm race start on the 30th. It soon became obvious that it was not just TWR and Jaguar facing funding issues as the large numbers of Nissan's that had competed in earlier Le Mans and Daytona races had not turned up this year; with a reversal in the Japanese economy. Just the singleton Momo 3-litre NPT Nissan had arrived. Toyota though was in a better position with their American based Eagle 2.1-litre turbo, and they went about a serious challenge setting the two fastest times in qualifying.

These were the P. J. Jones/Moran/Dismore team with 1:33.87 and Fangio II/Wallace/Acheson on 1:34.66. Joest's Porsche 962 with Robinson/Haywood/Pescarolo/ Sullivan was next on 1:36.19; Momo Nissan of Moretti/ Bell/Sigala/John Paul Jnr 1:36.42 and the second Joest Porsche 962 on 1:37.14. The three Jaguars entered this year then followed with chassis 190 #2 driven by Goodyear/Pruet/Jones on 1:38.51; chassis 588 #3 driven by Nielsen/ Andretti/David Brabham on 1:39.41; and the new twin wing XJR-16 chassis 196 #32 with 1:41.19. John Nielsen though had reported strange handling with this car on the banking that seemed to defy any remedy.

We would find out later that a valve seat insert had fallen out of the #2 car just over three hours from the end with its lead at the time of 20 laps and this had damaged the engine. Recycling of well used items had been a factor in this result with some of these heads into their fifth long distance race. The #3 Jaguar had a crankshaft-bung come loose and this had scraped the side of the aluminium block sending slivers of the material onto the scavenge filters and blocking them in the process. The oil could not be removed from the engine and this caused the rear seal to fail, eventually running out of oil. There was no excuse for this and no real reason found but half of our experienced V12 builders were in another unit building Jaguar 220 V6 units.

No cars were entered for the Sebring 12 hour.

*Jeff Wilson, Viv Cowley, Alva Claxton and John McLaughlin*

JAGUAR

## Chapter Twenty-Six

# Conclusion of the V12 programme

**And so the Jaguar V12 programme would end, but not the way it could have at Daytona. In retrospect taking too long to discover the source of the valve spring resonance problem in the long distance races was one negative feature in an otherwise very good engine supporting package for the series, with its fuel economy from advanced electronics surprising most engineers at the time. The much talked about engine size and weight though produced a secondary problem for its self with this being used as the reason the Jaguar would be disadvantaged from the very start, these internal thoughts coming from the top down. This removed the pressure to focus on the fundamental fuel sapping inherent understeer via the less rigid magnesium bell housing attached to a rigid engine and carbon chassis. As Martin Brundle has alluded to in his foreword, the engine's weight contribution was not always the cause of any handling problems. The new turbo Jaguars with their much more expensive and lighter engines and even longer bell housing, now filled with hot oil, could not improve on the lap to fuel times of the V12 cars at Silverstone.**

Engs staff count had now been greatly reduced with redeployment to the 220 programme with a core for racing programmes retained. Special racing versions of the 220 turbocharged V6 engines were developed by Engs and these cars were raced at the 24 hours of Le Mans in 1993. It produced a class win for the 220 and tenth overall, but later lost an appeal against the organisers over the use of catalytic converters. I had made special large capacity catalysts as this had become a discussion point at the earlier Le Mans test but TW had refused to fit them for the race.

Early in 1993 I attended a meeting at Benetton Formula's factory in Enstone to progress the supply of Cosworth HB engines to the Minardi Formula One team. These were engines that had been used in the XJR-14 programme in 1991 and it was an indication of the respect that Cosworth had for Engs at Kidlington, emphasising the skill level available at Engs for any future racing projects that TWR could undertake. Two original members currently work on the Mercedes Formula One engine programme (2017).

A progress meeting was held with Dick Scammell at Cosworth to discuss the upgrading of these engines to the latest valve spring specifications before a contract was signed. Cosworth would supply all the parts and we would be paid £12,500 for each rebuild and full test at our Kidlington facility, Minardi would be billed £25,000 for this work. This was a valuable contract keeping good people well employed.

As 1993 progressed, TWR SVO's Andy Morrison had been looking at a 2-litre British Touring car programme, firstly with the Mondeo as a Ford deal, and then later we both flew to Sweden to investigate a possibility with Volvo. They had been working on a project themselves and had

## ENGINE TEST – FORMULA ONE ENGINE COMPARISON

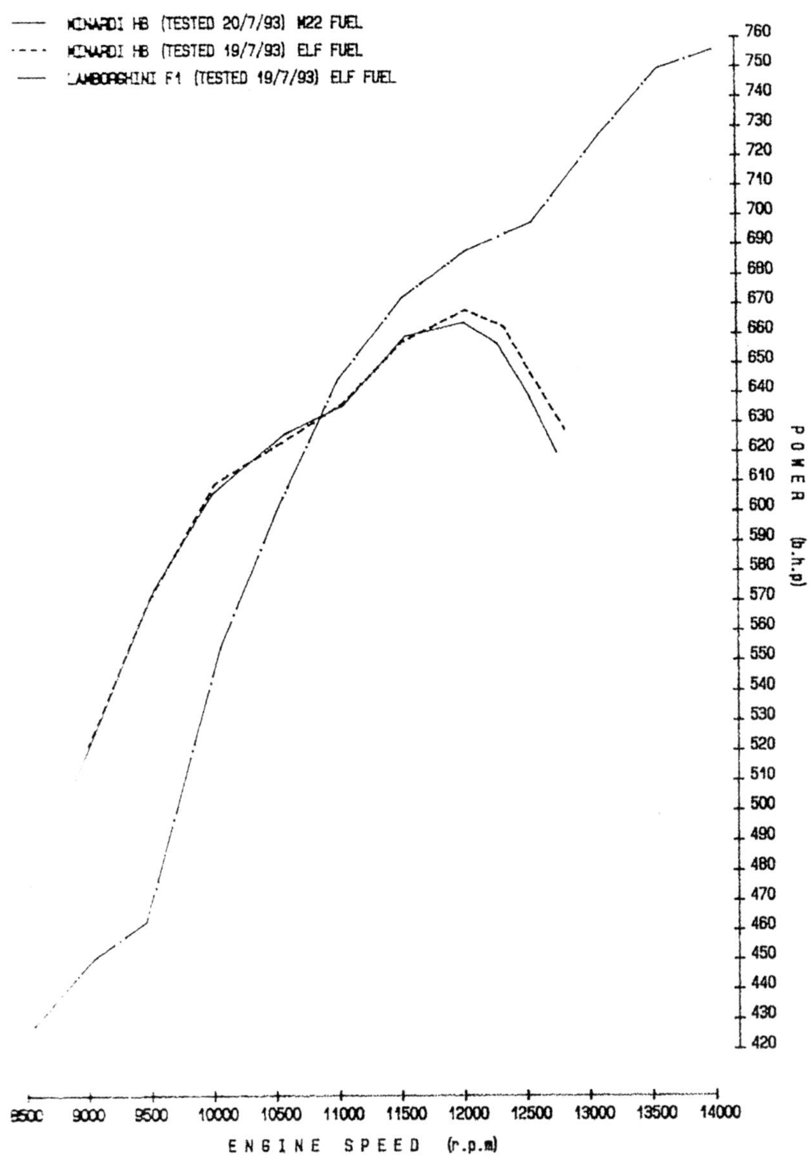


*The Lamborghini V12 shown here has superior horsepower to the valve spring HB V8, but a reduction in power below 10,500rpm.*

*The evolution air spring HB produced peak power 1000rpm higher with an additional 50bhp.*

### Lamborghini V12

Another V12 engine programme was investigated with Lamborghini in 1993 for possible use in the Benetton Formula One team. Lamborghini was in financial trouble and Tom Walkinshaw was trying to do a rescue deal for the company itself. Engs were tasked with fitting this test of that V12 engine around the rebuilding contract with Cosworth of their HB V8 3.5-litre lower specification valve spring engine. This was carried out in secret during one weekend with continuous shifts over a 48 hour period to produce all the systems involved in mounting and testing the engine. The latest version of the HB V8 engine (not shown here) when fitted with the air valve system produced an increase of approximately 30 to 50 bhp with an increase in upper limits of 1000 rpm.

finished an engine development exercise producing 260 bhp at 8500 rpm. We were given £60,000 to develop their five cylinder 2-litre engine over a 12 week period with the results to be given before Christmas shut down, and depending on this a contract for 1994 would be given. The day before Christmas we were able to demonstrate a 300 bhp at 9000 rpm engine, it would need a lot more work to produce better mid-range power but Volvo were impressed and a three year contract negotiated. This would become Engs full focus for 1994.

As 1994 drew to a close plans for my departure continued to be put in place with Charlie Bamber and Nigel Eames increasing their rolls in managing engineer and technical procurement respectively. I had given three months notice in August and later departed 15 years to the day after my arrival at Kidlington. A black tie evening was kindly put on by TW at Lords of the Manor near Stow and I was presented with an inscribed gold Ebel watch, but not the V12 show engine I had asked for. This would take pride of place in his office.

TWR
RACE ENGINES

TWR Racing
Race Engines Division
Station Field Industrial Estate
Kidlington, Oxford OX5 1JD

Telephone (0865) 842220
Facsimile (0865) 841901

Mr Dick Scammell
Cosworth Engineering
St James Mill Road
Northampton
NN5 5JJ

22 March 1993

Dear Dick

Firstly, thank you for the help from yourself and your staff in getting us through our first four builds. I believe we are now on top of the situation and look forward to successful races with Minardi.

My concerns at this time are the parts supply situation, build book and the effect the 1993 rules on race practice may have on engine mileage and our cashflow.

We understand your shortage problems and have accepted that this cannot be improved until the end of March. I must also point out that should this problem continue, we will be unable to build the engines in the required time. The trips to and from Northampton for parts to keep the builds going, would amount to considerable expense in time and vehicle costs as you can well imagine and would have to be reclaimed from Cosworth as additional costs.

The shorter practice periods will limit mileage bringing with it attempts to use one engine per car per event. Therefore, it is important to all concerned that the 550 km life is kept at all times.

The invoicing situation also needs addressing as we are on proforma invoice with Cosworth and I assume the same applies to our invoices to Cosworth for the HB rebuilds.

I enclose our current concern report and hope we can address these problems as soon as possible. May I suggest a meeting in Week 13?

Yours sincerely

ALLAN SCOTT

***Initial progress and cash flow situations to be concluded with Cosworth.***

*Black tie evening at Lords of the Manor.*

TWR
GROUP

TWR Group Limited
1 Station Field Industrial Estate
Kidlington, Oxford OX5 1JD

Telephone (0865) 842220
Facsimile (0865) 841855

**For immediate release** **10 October 1994**

**TWR RACE ENGINES MANAGER LEAVES FOR NEW ZEALAND**

General Manager of TWR Race Engines, Allan Scott, is returning to his homeland in New Zealand on 10th November for family reasons.

TWR's Race Engine division has played a key role in TWR's successes since the many national Touring Car Championship wins, with Mazda and Rover in the early 1980s.

Allan's department is perhaps most well known for turning Jaguar's V12 production engine into arguably the most efficient race engine of modern times. The superb V12 unit won two World Sportscar Championships and the unprecedented 24 hour double of Le Mans and Daytona; incredibly a feat achieved in both 1988 and 1990. Most recently, TWR Race Engines have rebuilt Ford's F1 Hbs, uniquely on behalf of Cosworth, and of course are responsible for the 5 cylinder unit in the Volvo Touring Car programme.

TWR Chairman Tom Walkinshaw said: "Allan has been with TWR for 15 years, and we share many fond memories. Allan has made a significant personal contribution to TWR's many championship successes in Touring Cars, the Sportscar World Championship and IMSA, and to the formation of a reputable and talented department."

Allan will continue independently in motor sport in the Asia Pacific area from his base in Christchurch, New Zealand.

For further information please contact Karen Roberts at TWR Racing, Broadstone Grange, Broadstone Hill, Nr Chipping Norton OX7 5QL (Tel: 0608 678763, Fax: 0608 677698).

236 Papanui Road
Christchurch
New Zealand
Tel: (64 3) 3559731
Fax: (64 3) 3559742

JAGUAR

# Epilogue

Many people have asked me …

*"What it was like to work for Tom Walkinshaw?"*

It certainly was a roller coaster ride with many highs, lows and twists along the way.

TW thrived on achieving success, highly driven and possessing a huge ambition and determination to win at any cost. His business acumen and ability to think on his feet challenged the best, along with his vision to see years ahead to a point where he wanted his many businesses to be. This permeated down the ranks to the newest team member feeling part of his success in the early days with workshop visits and greetings of "hello team" creating a strong spirit and loyalty. He raised staff confidence to levels that would have been unattainable without his motivation; for many of us this meant often putting TWR before family.

The racing business expanded rapidly with TW showing a need to appear more financially successful than other team owners. As the TWR racing brand became increasingly well established it became evident that TW wished to be recognised as more than just a successful racing driver and businessman, it seemed his legacy aspiration was to be considered a leading motor racing engineer. His team philosophy was safety in numbers on the track to counter reliability, and a racing business that had to make a profit. I witnessed TW's introduction to Dan Gurney and saw his genuine respect for that man who with the "Gurney Flap" had left a very public legacy in motor racing circles. The TWR Group concept then took precedence over the original racing team focus and his departure from Kidlington to an 800 acre estate at Broadstone produced a physical and mental separation from the team members that I doubt he fully realised as he expected little to change.

His venture into Formula One became a bridge too far, and along with other ventures his focus became business survival, rather than the racing team. It was a sad end to his ambitions when Arrows and then TWR were forced into liquidation. This diverse group of UK based companies was closed in 2002 with no buyers for any of its entities, with just the one exception; the Race Engine Division. This all had a profound effect on him personally leading, many believe, to the ill health he suffered and cancer that finally took his life in 2010.

We all miss him.

**Tom Walkinshaw**

I wrote to Tom Walkinshaw out of the blue when I was 19 years old in 1979 and asked him to give me a chance to drive one of his BMWs at an upcoming race at my local track Snetterton in the UK. So, he did, and I had a spectacular race against some star names. I won the next race at Donington Park and 'overnight' my name was on the international racing scene.

I often wonder what I would be doing now if I hadn't written that letter because I would go on to drive for Tom until 1997, and we remained friends until his premature and sad death due to cancer in 2010. We won a lot of international races together with his mighty TWR team.

I loved driving for Tom, and having him on the pit wall. He was a racer who could think on his feet under pressure. He had total faith in me, and the feeling was mutual. I was able to deliver world class performances in his cars at a level I did not quite reach in anybody else's cars.

He could be fearsome, difficult to please and a hard task master, but he was a leader of people. We raced as team mates and against each other in his formidable Jaguar XJSs, and there is no doubt he was a fast and aggressive racing driver.

He stood down from driving when it came to the Group C cars, and even declined a ride around Silverstone GP circuit with me in a Le Mans Jaguar one day. He couldn't have been scared, and so I think he just didn't want to have to accept how spectacularly good we were in those incredibly fast cars, otherwise he knows we would have asked for more money.

Tom pushed all the rules to breaking point, and sometimes beyond. He read the rules twice, once to see what they said, and a second time to fathom a way around some of them. But let's be clear, none of the successful racing mavericks like him, dead or alive, are saints.

Tom took me with him to F1 and the Benetton team in 1992 where I had my most successful season in F1. I always felt that the pressure, politics and finances of F1 was the undoing of the real Tom and I lost touch to some extent with him for a while.

Tom was like a second father to me, we did our best for each other with great success, and I miss him and his blunt advice.

*Copies of internal documents.*
*No responsibility is taken for any omissions, errors or consequences that may arise from the vehicles identified in the following lists.*

## V12 CHASSIS NUMBERS AND HISTORY

- 2 -

**V 1 2 C H A S S I S N U M B E R C H A N G E S**

From 1985 to 1990. A total of 15 new cars were constructed

1. 185
2. 285
3. 385
4. 186
5. 286
6. 386
7. 187
8. 287
9. 387
10. 288
11. 488
12. 588
13. 688
14. 190
15. 290

During 1988

386 became 188

387 became 388

During 1990

288 became 790

388 became 890

588 became 990

890 became 1090

= Total 21 chassis numbers

- 4 -

From 1985 to 1990

A total of 18 monoques have been constructed for the Programme.
15 are already identified, see page 2.

1. The original monoque on Chassis No. 286 was replaced due to the Win Percy accident at Le Man during 1987. The car was rebuilt and sold to Mr Waterman.

2. During 1988

Chassis No. 386 became 188, ironically chassis no. 188 was sold to Mr Lippmann. The new monoque for chassis no. 386 is in stock. (Awaiting sale).

During 1988

Chassis No. 387 became chassis no. 388. The new monoque for chassis 387 was rebuilt and sold to Mr Schuster.
Chassis 388 raced successfully in the I.M.S.A. series.
During 1990 it changed chassis no. to 890 for the Daytona and Sebring races, and for the Le Man race it has changed again to chassis no. 1090!

- 5 -

To complete the rebuild Programme, based on the total to date of 21 chassis numbers with history, TWR will have to construct a further four monoques.

For Chassis Numbers

288 or 790
388 or 890
588 or 990
890 or 1090

This would give TWR the opportunity to produce from 15 race cars a total of 21 chassis numbers.

- 6 -

V12 CARS RETAINED BY THE TWR COLLECTION

1. Chassis No. 185 - 1st car built
2. Chassis No. 287 - 1987 W.S.P.C. Championship Winning Car
3. Chassis No. 288 - 1988 I.M.S.A. Daytona 24 Hour Winning Car
4. Chassis No. 588 - 1988 W.S.P.C. Championship Winning Car
5. Chassis No. 790 - 1990 I.M.S.A. Daytona 24 Hour Winning Car
6. CHASSIS NO. 1090 - 1990 LE MAN 24 HOURS WINNING CAR.

At the time of compiling this Report, the 1990 Le Man 24 Hour Race is yet to be run. Dependent upon results, i.e., winning, TWR could add one more V12 car to its Collection.

## V12 CHASSIS NUMBERS AND HISTORY

**Chassis #185** Built May/June 1985. First run Brundle July 2, Snetterton.

| Date | Venue | No. | Drivers | Grid | Result |
|---|---|---|---|---|---|
| 03.08.85 | Mosport Canada | #51 | Brundle/Thackwell | 3 | DNF – wheel bearing |
| 01.09.85 | Spa Francorchamps | #51 | Brundle/Thackwell | 8 | 5th |
| 22.09.85 | Brands Hatch | #51 | Jones/Schlesser | 5 | DNF – Engine |
| 06.10.85 | Fuji Japan | #51 | Nielsen/Thackwell | 19 | DNS – Rain |
| 09.12.85 | Shah Alam, Malaysia | #51 | Lammers/Nielsen/Thackwell | 4 | 2nd |

**Tested**

03-06.02.86 Esteril, Portugal. Restored, kept by TWR.

**Chassis #285** Built May/June 1985. First run August 1, 1985 Mosport, Canada. Heyer/Schlesser drove.

| Date | Venue | No. | Drivers | Grid | Result |
|---|---|---|---|---|---|
| 03.08.85 | Mosport Canada | #52 | Brundle/Thackwell/ Schlesser | 5 | 3rd |
| 01.09.85 | Spa Francorchamps | #52 | Heyer/Schlesser | 11 | DNF – Handling/accident |
| 22.09.85 | Brands Hatch | #52 | Heyer/Lammers | 6 | DNF – Engine |
| 06.10.85 | Fuji, Japan | #52 | Heyer/Soper | 20 | DNS – Rain |
| 09.12.85 | Shah Alam, Malaysia | #52 | Brancatelli/Lammers | 5 | DNF – Puncture |

**Tested**

03-06.02.86 Esteril, Portugal. Not raced again.

**Chassis #385** Built January 1986. First run March 3, 1986, Snetterton. Derek Warwick. 1985 monocoque built to '86 specs.

| Date | Venue | No. | Drivers | Grid | Result |
|---|---|---|---|---|---|
| 02.04.86 | Monza | #53T | T-Car | | |
| 05.05.86 | Silverstone | #53T | T-Car | | |
| 31.05.86 | Le Mans | #53 | Brancatelli/Hahne/Percy | 14 | DNF – Driveshaft |

*Only race was Le Mans '86. Privately owned in Le Mans specs.*

**V12 1986**

**Chassis #186** Built February 1986 First run March 17, 1986 Silverstone by Cheever.

| Date | Venue | No. | Drivers | Grid | Result |
|---|---|---|---|---|---|
| 20.04.86 | Monza | #52 | Brancatelli/Schlesser | 9 | DNF – Fuel surge |
| 05.05.86 | Silverstone | #52 | Brancatelli/Schlesser | 5 | 7th |
| 31.05.86 | Le Mans | #52 | Haywood/Heyer/Redman | 7 | DNF – Fuel pump |
| 29.06.86 | Norisring, Germany | #52 | Warwick | 6 | 3rd |
| 20.07.86 | Brands Hatch | #52 | Warwick/Schlesser | (To T-car #53) | |
| 03.08.86 | Jerez, Spain | #53 | Brancatelli/Schlesser | 2 | DNF – Driveshaft |
| 24.08.86 | Nurburgring | #53 | Brancatelli/Lammers/Warwick | 9 | DNF – Broken oil pipe |
| 14.09.86 | Spa | #51T | Cheever/Lammers/Schlesser/Warwick | T Car | |
| 21.09.86 | Norisring | #51 | Cheever | 3 | 1st – non champs |

*October '86 upgraded to Le Mans specs. Tested in Winter as XJR8-LM.*

| Date | Venue | No. | Drivers | Grid | Result |
|---|---|---|---|---|---|
| 10.05.87 | Silverstone | #6 | Brundle/Nielsen | 10 | DNF – Timing chain tensioner |
| 13.06.87 | Le Mans | #6 | Brundle/Hahne/Nielsen | 4 | DNF – Valve spring |

*Winter 1987 rebuilt to XJR9-LM. Tested Paul Richard 16-19 February 1988.*

| Date | Venue | No. | Drivers | Grid | Result |
|---|---|---|---|---|---|
| 11.06.88 | Le Mans | #2 | Cogan/Daly/Perkins | 11 | 4th |

*After Le Mans restored as raced at Le Mans, owned by Jaguar Netherland.*

**Chassis #286** First run March 1986, Donington, Cheever.

| Date | Venue | No. | Drivers | Grid | Result |
|---|---|---|---|---|---|
| 20.04.86 | Monza | #51 | Cheever/Warwick | 6 | DNF – Driveshaft |
| 05.05.86 | Silverstone | #51 | Cheever/Warwick | 3 | 1st |
| 31.05.86 | Le Mans | #51 | Cheever/Warwick/Schlesser | 5 | DNF – Suspension |
| 29.06.86 | Norisring | #51 | Cheever | 4 | 2nd |
| 20.07.86 | Brands Hatch | #51 | Cheever/Brancatelli | 2 | 6th |
| 03.08.86 | Jerez | #51 | Brundle/Cheever | 3 | DNF – Driveshaft |
| 24.08.86 | Nurburgring | #51 | Cheever/Heyer/Schlesser | 3 | DNF – Driveshaft |
| 14.09.86 | Spa | #51 | Cheever/Schlesser | 4 | 5th |
| 05.10.86 | Fuji | #51 | Cheever/Warwick | 13 | 3rd |

*Winter 1987 Converted to XJR-8LM. Tested Donington April 1987.*

| Date | Venue | No. | Drivers | Grid | Result |
|---|---|---|---|---|---|
| 14.06.87 | Le Mans | #5 | Lammers/Percy/Watson | 5 | DNF – Crashed |

*Severely damaged. Rebuilt as '86 Sprint car minus gullwing doors.*

**Chassis #386 XJR-6** Tested June 23, Silverstone, Win Percy.

| | | | | Grid | |
|---|---|---|---|---|---|
| 29.06.86 | Norisring | #53 | Schlesser | 8 | 17th – Jammed accl. pedal |
| 20.07.86 | Brands Hatch | #53 | Schlesser/Warwick | 3 | 4th |
| 03.08.86 | Jerez | #52 | Lammers/Warwick | 4 | 3rd |
| 24.08.86 | Nurburgring | #52 | Lammers/Warwick | Warwick crashed in practice. | |
| 14.09.86 | Spa | #52 | Lammers/Warwick | 5 | 2nd |
| 05.10.86 | Fuji | #52 | Brancatelli/Lammers/Schlesser | 17 | 17th – Front hub |
| 23.03.87 | Jarama | 4T | T-car | | |
| 29.03.87 | Jerez | 4T | T-car | | |
| 12.04.87 | Monza | 4T | T-car | | |
| 10.05.87 | Silverstone | 4T | T-car | | |

*Converted to show car. – Rebuilt as XJR-12LM. Le Mans 1991. Spring 1991.*
*Became #991.– Tested May 24 1991, Silverstone.*

| | | | | | |
|---|---|---|---|---|---|
| 22.06.91 | Le Mans | #34 | Acheson/Fabi/Wollek | 27 | 3rd |

**Chassis #187 XJR-8** January 1987 build, first test February 6, 1987, Donington, John Watson. One of two new sprint cars.

| | | | | Grid | |
|---|---|---|---|---|---|
| 22.03.87 | Jarama | #5 | Lammers/Watson | 2 | 1st |
| 29.03.87 | Jerez | #5 | Lammers/Watson | 2 | DNF – Driveshaft |
| 12.04.87 | Monza | #5 | Lammers/Watson | 4 | 1st |
| 10.05.87 | Silverstone | #5 | Lammers/Watson | 5 | 2nd |
| 28.06.87 | Norisring | #5 | Lammers/Watson | 7 | DNF – Transmission |
| 26.07.87 | Brands Hatch | #5 | Lammers/Watson | 1 | 3rd |
| 30.08.87 | Nurburgring | #5 | Lammers/Watson | 4 | DNF – Cam follower broken |
| 19.09.87 | Spa | #5 | Lammers/Watson | 3 | 2nd |
| 27.09.87 | Fuji | #5 | Lammers/Watson | 5 | 1st |

*1988 Upgraded to XJR-9*

| | | | | | |
|---|---|---|---|---|---|
| 06.03.88 | Jerez | #3 | Nielsen/Watson/Wallace | 4 | 2nd |
| 13.03.88 | Jarama | #3 | Nielsen/Watson | 4 | 3rd |
| 10.04.88 | Monza | 1T | T-car | | |
| 08.05.88 | Silverstone | #2 | Dumfries/Lammers<br>T-car replace 488 | 6 | 6th – Out of fuel |
| 10.07.88 | Brno | | T-car | | |
| 24.07.88 | Brands Hatch | (4 valve engine) | Jones/Watson | 8 | DNF – Distributor rotor |

*In private ownership.*

**Chassis #287** Built February 1987. Tested March 2, Silverstone. Sprint car for Cheever and Boesel. Drivers 1987 World Championship.

| | | | | Grid | |
|---|---|---|---|---|---|
| 22.03.87 | Jarama | #4 | Boesel/Cheever | 1 | 3rd |
| 29.03.87 | Jerez | #4 | Boesel/Cheever | 4 | 1st |
| 12.04.87 | Monza | #4 | Boesel/Cheever | 5 | DNF – Spin off circuit |
| 10.05.87 | Silverstone | #4 | Boesel/Cheever | 4 | 1st |
| 28.06.87 | Norisring | #4 | Boesel/Cheever | 4 | 4th |
| 26.07.87 | Brands Hatch | #4 | Boesel/Nielsen | 2 | 1st |
| 30.08.87 | Nurburgring | #4 | Boesel/Cheever | 2 | 1st |
| 13.09.87 | Spa | #4 | Cheever/Nielsen | 4 | 4th |
| 27.09.87 | Fuji | #4 | Boesel/Dumfries | 10 | 2nd |

*1988/1989 Upgraded to XJR-9*

| | | | | | |
|---|---|---|---|---|---|
| 11.06.88 | Le Mans | #3 | Boesel/Pescarelo/Watson | 12 | DNF – Transmission |
| 25.08.88 | Donington – Radial tyre testing. | | | | |
| 04.09.88 | Nurburgring | 1T | T-car | | |
| 18.09.88 | Spa | 1T | T-car | | |
| 10.06.89 | Le Mans – XJR9-LM | #4 | Ferté/Ferté/Salazar | 6 | 8th |
| 23.07.89 | Brands Hatch | 1T | T-car | | |
| 29.10.89 | Mexico | | Wallace/Alain Ferté | 10 | 5th |

**Chassis #387 XJR-9** Built 1987.

| | | | Grid | |
|---|---|---|---|---|
| 13.06.87 | Le Mans | Boesel/Cheever | 3 | 5th |
| 28.06.87 | Norisring – Test Car | | | Not raced |
| 05.07.87 | Hockenheim | Boesel | 7 | 4th |
| 26.07.87 | Brands Hatch – Test Car | | | Not raced |

**Chassis #387 XJR-9** – *continued*

| Date | Venue | No. | Drivers | Grid | Result |
|---|---|---|---|---|---|
| 30.08.87 | Nurburgring – Test car | | | | Not raced |
| 19.09.87 | Spa | | Brundle/Dumfries/Boesel | 6 | 1st |

*The car was re-built and retired from competition use.*

**Chassis #118 – to USA** Built July-August 1987. First run August 20, 1987, Silverstone, Lammers. Then to first IMSA Spec. XJR9.

| Date | Venue | No. | Drivers | Grid | Result |
|---|---|---|---|---|---|
| 30.01.88 | Daytona XJR9D | #66 | Cheever/Dumfries/Watson | 4 | 3rd |
| 28.02.88 | Miami | #66 | Boesel/Cheever | 14 | DNF – Oil pump |
| 19.03.88 | Sebring | #60T | Boesel/Jones | T-car | |
| 10.04.88 | Road Atlanta | #61T | Wallace/Watson | T-car | |
| 24.04.88 | West Palm Beach | #61T | Jones | T-car | |
| *To UK for Le Mans – in Silk Cut Livery.* | | | | | |
| 11.06.88 | XJR9-LM | #21 | Cobb/Jones/Sullivan | 9 | 16th |
| *Back to USA.* | | | | | |
| 17.07.88 | Road America | #66 | Jones/Nielsen | T-car | |
| 31.07.88 | Portland | #66 | Brundle | T-car | |
| 14.08.88 | Sears Point | #66 | Lammers | T-car | |
| 14.09.88 | San Antonio | #60 | Jones/Watson | Grid 7 | 2nd |
| 02.10.88 | Columbus | #60 | Jones/Lammers/Nielsen | Grid 5 | 10th – Accident |
| 23.10.88 | Del Mar | #61 | Jones/Lammers | Grid 1 | 1st |
| 04.02.89 | Daytona – XJR-9D | #66 | Daly/Donnelly/Tambay | Grid 8 | DNF – Accident |
| 06.03.89 | Miami | #66 | Jones | T-car | |
| 18.03.89 | Sebring | #66 | | T-car | |
| 02.04.89 | Road Atlanta | #66 | Jones | Badly damaged week before. Returned to UK. | |

*Restored and sold by TWR.*

**Chassis #288 XJR-9** Built September 1987. Tested October 15, 1987 Donington, Watson.

| Date | Venue | No. | Drivers | Grid | Result |
|---|---|---|---|---|---|
| 30.01.88 | Daytona | #60 | Boesel/Brundle/ Lammers/Nielsen | 6 | 1st |
| 28.02.88 | Miami | #60 | Brundle/Nielsen | 3 | 2nd |
| 19.03.88 | Sebring XJR-9D | #60 | Boesel/Brundle/Nielsen | 3 | DNF – Cracke piston |
| 10.04.88 | Road Atlanta | #60 | Nielsen/Watson | 1 | 2nd |
| 24.04.88 | West Palm Beach | #60 | Brundle/Nielsen | 4 | DNF – Transmission |
| 30.05.88 | Lime Rock | #60 | Brundle/Nielsen | 1 | 2nd |
| 05.06.88 | Mid Ohio | #60 | Brundle/Nielsen | 6 | 2nd |
| 03.07.88 | Watkins Glen | #60 | Brundle/Nielsen | 5 | DNF – Chassis wiring loom |
| 17.07.88 | Road America | #60 | Brundle/Nielsen | 2 | 4th |
| 31.07.88 | Portland | #60 | Brundle/Nielsen | 6 | 3rd |
| 14.08.88 | Sears Point | #60 | Brundle/Nielsen | 2 | 2nd |
| 04.09.88 | San Antonio | #66 | Nielsen/Wallace | 3 | DNF – Brakes |
| 12.10.88 | Columbus | #66 | Brundle/Nielsen | 4 | DNF – Accident |
| 23.10.88 | Del Mar | #60 | Nielsen | Crashed in qualifying – sent to UK. | |
| 14.02.89 | Daytona XJR-9D | #60 | Boesel/Jones/Lammers | 2 | DNF – Oil temp/pressure/ bearings |
| 05.03.89 | Miami | #60 | Jones/Lammers | 3 | DNF – Accident |
| 18.03.89 | Sebring | #60 | Jones/Lammers | 4 | 14th |
| 02.04.89 | Road Atlanta | #60 | Jones/Lammers | 4 | DNF – Valve/piston contact |
| 24.04.89 | West Palm Beach | #60 | Jones/Lammers | 4 | DNF – Transmission |
| *To UK for Le Mans – into Silk Cut Livery.* | | | | | |
| 10.06.89 | Le Mans – XJR-9LM | #3 | Daly/Jones/Kline | 4 | DNF – Valve spring |

**Chassis #790 XJR-9**

*Back to US for IMSA. (#790)*

| Date | Venue | No. | Drivers | Grid | Result |
|---|---|---|---|---|---|
| 30.08.89 | Heartland Park | #66T | Michel Ferté/Jones | T-car | |
| 03.09.89 | San Antonio | #66T | Practice Only | | |
| 10.09.89 | Sears Point | #60 | Jones/Nielsen | 5 | 3rd |
| 01.10.89 | Tampa | #60 | Cobb | 6 | 1st |
| *Upgraded to XJR-12D.* | | | | | |
| 04.02.90 | Daytona | #60 | Cobb/Brundle/Nielsen | 9 | 2nd |
| 17.03.90 | Sebring | #60 | Cobb/Nielsen | 4 | DNF – Engine/electrical/ wiring |

**Chassis #388 – to USA**

| Date | Event | No. | Drivers | Grid | Result |
|---|---|---|---|---|---|
| 30.01.88 | Daytona XJR-9D | #61 | Jones/Lammers/Sullivan | 2 | DNF – Oil pump |
| 28.02.88 | Miami | #61 | Jones/Lammers | 7 | 6th |
| 19.03.88 | Sebring XJR-9D | #61 | Jones/Lammers/Nielsen/Sullivan | 5 | 7th |
| 10.04.88 | Road Atlanta | #61 | Jones/Wallace | 3 | 4th |
| 24.04.88 | West Palm Beach | #61 | Jones/Lammers | 2 | 2nd |
| 30.05.88 | Lime Rock | #61 | Jones/Lammers | 6 | 3rd |
| 05.06.88 | Mid Ohio | #61 | Jones/Lammers | 4 | 3rd |
| 03.07.88 | Watkins Glen | #61 | Jones/Lammers | 6 | DNF – Accident |
| 17.07.88 | Road America | #61 | Jones/Lammers | 4 | 5th |
| 31.07.88 | Portland | #61 | Jones/Lammers | 5 | 4th |
| 14.08.88 | Sears Point | #61 | Jones/Lammers | 3 | 3rd |
| 04.09.88 | San Antonio | #61 | Jones/Watson | | Jones crashed in practice, and returned to UK for repairs. |

*Not raced again in 1988.*

| Date | Event | No. | Drivers | Grid | Result |
|---|---|---|---|---|---|
| 04.02.89 | Dayton XJR-9D | #61 | Cobb/Lammers/Nielsen/Wallace | 7 | 2nd |
| 05.03.89 | Miami | #61 | Cobb/Nielsen | 5 | 2nd |
| 18.03.89 | Sebring XJR-9D | #61 | Cobb/Nielsen | 3 | 2nd |
| 02.04.89 | Road Atlanta | #61 | Cobb/Nielsen | 2 | 2nd |
| 23.04.89 | West Palm Beach | #61 | Cobb/Nielsen | 6 | 2nd |
| 29.05.89 | Lime Rock | #61 | Cobb/Nielsen | 8 | 3rd |
| 04.06.89 | Mid Ohio | #61 | Cobb/Jones/Nielsen | 4 | 2nd |
| 02.07.89 | Watkins Glen | #61 | Jones/Nielsen | 6 | DNF – Centre main bearing |
| 16.07.89 | Road America | #61 | Jones/Nielsen | 1 | 3rd |
| 30.07.89 | Portland | #61 | Jones/Nielsen | 3 | 4th |
| 13.08.89 | Heartland Park | #60 | Jones/Nielsen | 2 | 5th |
| 03.09.89 | San Antonio | #60 | Michel Ferté/Nielsen | | DNF – Crashed, badly damaged and sent back to UK. |

**Chassis #890**

*Upgraded to XJR-12D.*

| Date | Event | No. | Drivers | Grid | Result |
|---|---|---|---|---|---|
| 03.02.90 | Daytona | #61 | Jones/Lammers/Wallace | 10 | 1st |
| 17.03.90 | Sebring | #61 | Jones/Lammers/Wallace | 11 | 3rd |

**Chassis #1090**

*Given new chassis #1090*

| Date | Event | No. | Drivers | Grid | Result |
|---|---|---|---|---|---|
| 16.06.90 | Le Mans | #3 | Brundle/Cobb/Nielsen (Salazar never drove) | 9 | 1st Le Mans win |

**Chassis #488 XJR-8**

| Date | Event | Drivers | Grid | Result |
|---|---|---|---|---|
| 06.03.88 | Jerez | Dumfries/Lammers | 2 | DNF – Transmission |
| 13.03.88 | Jarama | Dumfries/Lammers | 2 | DNF – Spin off circuit |
| 10.04.88 | Monza | Dumfries/Lammers | 5 | DNF – Spin off circuit |
| 08.05.88 | Silverstone | Dumfries/Lammers | | Not used after practice |
| 11.06.88 | Le Mans | Dumfries/Lammers | 6 | 1st Le Mans win |

*Returned to Jaguar Daimler Heritage as part of the TWR/Jaguar contract*

**Chassis #588 XJR-9** Built January 1988

| Date | Event | No. | Drivers | Grid | Result |
|---|---|---|---|---|---|
| 06.03.88 | Jerez | #1 | Brundle/Cheever | 3 | DNF – Transmission |
| 13.03.88 | Jarama | #1 | Brundle/Cheever | 3 | 1st |
| 10.04.88 | Monza | #1 | Brundle/Cheever | 4 | 1st |
| 08.05.88 | Silverstone | #1 | Brundle/Nielsen | 2 | 1st |
| 11.06.88 | Le Mans (LM) | #1 | Brundle/Nielsen | 4 | DNF – Faulty head casting |
| 10.07.88 | Brno | #1 | Brundle/Nielsen | 3 | 2nd |
| 24.07.88 | Brands Hatch | #1 | Brundle/Nielsen/Wallace | 6 | 1st |
| 04.09.88 | Nurburgring | #1 | Brundle/Cheever | 4 | 2nd |
| 18.09.88 | Spa | #1 | Brundle/Cheever | 5 | DNF – Handling/fuel pickup |
| 09.10.88 | Fuji | #1 | Brundle/Cheever | 7 | 1st |
| 20.11.88 | Sandown | #1 | Brundle/Cheever | 4 | 3rd |

**Chassis #588 XJR-9** – *continued*

| | | | | | |
|---|---|---|---|---|---|
| 09.04.89 | Suzuka | #1 | Lammers/Tambay | 3 | DNF – Fuel |
| 21.05.89 | Dijon | #1 | Lammers/Tambay | 7 | DNF – Fuel |
| 10.06.89 | Le Mans (LM) | #1 | Lammers/Gilbert-Scott/Tambay | 3 | 4th |
| 25.06.89 | Jarama | #1 | Lammers/Tambay | 3 | 2nd |
| 20.08.89 | Nurburgring | #1T | Nielsen | T car only | |
| 29.1089 | Mexico City | #1 | Lammers/Tambay | 5 | 6th |

**Converted to Chassis #990**

| | | | | | |
|---|---|---|---|---|---|
| 16.06.90 | Le Mans (LM) | #1 | Brundle/Alain Ferté/Leslie | 8 | DNF – Water pump |
| 22.06.91 | Le Mans (LM) | #35 | Boesel/Michel Ferté/Jones | 18 | 2nd |
| 30.01.93 | Daytona (D) | #3 | John Andretti/Brabham/Nielsen | 7 | DNF – Blocked oil scavenger filter |

**Chassis #688 XJR-9** Post Le Mans 1988 to replace chassis #488 returned to Jaguar.

| | | | | | |
|---|---|---|---|---|---|
| 10.07.88 | Brno | #2 | Dumfries/Lammers | 5 | 3rd |
| 24.07.88 | Brands Hatch | #2 | Dumfries/Lammers | 4 | DNF – Dashboard Electrics |
| 04.09.88 | Nurburgring | #2 | Dumfries/Lammers | 4 | 8th |
| 10.09.88 | Spa | #2 | Brundle/Dumfries/Lammers | 2 | 2nd |
| 09.10.88 | Fuji | #2 | Dumfries/Lammers | 6 | DNF – Accident |
| 20.11.88 | Sandown | #2 | Dumfries/Lammers | 3 | 4th |
| 09.04.89 | Suzuka | #2 | Nielsen/Wallace | 12 | 5th |
| 12.05.89 | Dijon | #2 | Nielsen/Wallace | 9 | DNF – Tyre/spin |
| 10.06.89 | Le Mans (LM) | #2 | Cobb/Wallace/Nielsen | 8 | DNF – Valve spring |
| 25.06.89 | Jarama | #2 | Nielsen/Wallace | 4 | 6th |
| 23.07.89 | Brands Hatch | #2 | Nielsen/Wallace | 11 | DNF – Accident |

*Retired after accident to TWR Collection.*

**Chassis #190 XJR-12** First run Silverstone by Wallace – to USA.

| | | | | **Grid** | |
|---|---|---|---|---|---|
| 16.06.90 | Le Mans (LM) | #4 | Michel Ferté/Jones/Perez-Sala/Salazar | 7 | DNF – Over rev/piston/valve |
| 02.02.91 | Daytona (D) | #3 | Acheson/Cheever/Nielsen | | DNS – Crashed in practice |
| 16.03.91 | Sebring (D) | #3 | Boesel/Jones/Nielsen | 5 | 5th |
| 30.01.93 | Daytona (D) | #2 | Goodyear/Jones/Privett | 6 | DNF – Valve insert Classified 10th |

*TWR Collection.*

**Chassis #290 XJR12** Built January 1990 – to USA.

| | | | | **Grid** | |
|---|---|---|---|---|---|
| 16.06.90 | Le Mans (LM) | #2 | Konrad/Lammers/Wallace | 17 | 2nd |
| 02.02.91 | Daytona (D) | #2 | Boesel/Jones/Privett/Warwick | 2 | DNF – Overheating/ water pump |
| 16.03.91 | Sebring | #2 | | | Jones crashed in practice. DNS |
| 22.06.91 | Le Mans (Suntec) | #36 | Knosnoff/Leslie/Martini | 28 | DNF – Gearbox/Chassis/ Suspension failure |

**Chassis #891 XJR12** First tested May 1991. Built for Le Mans.

| | | | | **Grid** | |
|---|---|---|---|---|---|
| 22.06.91 | Le Mans (LM) | #33 | Nielsen/Wallace/Warwick | 24 | 4th |
| 01.02.92 | Daytona (D) (D) | #2 | Brabham/Goodyear/Jones/Privett | 7 | 2nd (1st GTP) |
| 21.03.92 | Sebring | #2 | Brabham/Jones | 10 | 4th |

**Chassis #193 (was #790)** Built late 1992. First run January 15, 1993 Siverstone – Brabham/Nielsen
Built for Le Mans – not raced.

| | | | | **Grid** | |
|---|---|---|---|---|---|
| 30.01.93 | Daytona (Advanced) | #32 | John Andretti/Brabham/Jones/Nielsen | 8 | DNF – Handling |

*See John McLaughlin specification pages 371-377.*

JAGUAR

# Index

*Figures in italics denotes image*

**Drivers**

**Motor Racing Circuits**